50 YEARS

lonely planet

OF TRAVEL

FLORIDA

Amy Bizzarri, David Gibb, Jennifer Edwards, Adam Karlin, Regis St Louis, Terry Ward

CONTENTS

Plan Your Trip

The Guide

Surfing, Jacksonville (p317)

Key West (p156)

Robbie's Marina, Islamorada (p144)

St Petersburg (p348)

Toolkit

Storybook

SEAN PAVONE/SHUTTERSTOCK ©

Fort Lauderdale (p170)

FLORIDA

THE JOURNEY BEGINS HERE

It's a little clichéd, but Florida always hits me hardest on the coast. The sun sets and the salt licks onto my skin – perfect. Not that I need saltier skin, because I've probably already been swimming, at least enough to work up an appetite. On that note, if I've got a grouper sandwich or some *mojo* pork and rice in front of me – well, that's just gravy. Which coast? There's a lot to pick from, but any sand works for me. If I'm on Sanibel I've got shells under my feet; in the Keys I can hear people laughing at a fishing bar; in the Panhandle there are white dunes like lunar mountains; in Miami the music drips off the city like slow nectar. But I'm focused on smelling the waters, because at the end of the day it's the ocean (or the Gulf) that gets me in the heart.

Adam Karlin

@adamwalkonfine

Adam is a journalist, writer and teacher who has contributed to dozens of Lonely Planet guidebooks in Asia, Africa and the Americas.

My favorite experience is the sort of full Miami day that leaves me absolutely gasping: a big breakfast, swimming, galleries, a Caribbean dinner, a night out in neon.

WHO GOES WHERE

Our writers and experts choose the places which, for them, define Florida.

FROM LEFT TO RIGHT: JIM SCHWABEL/SHUTTERSTOCK ©, DOMINIC GENTILCORE PHD/SHUTTERSTOCK ©, LUNAMARINA/SHUTTERSTOCK ©

'Just follow me,' Garl, my barefooted guide, said as he marched into knee-deep water. We soon entered the cypress dome, full of fiery bromeliads and wispy epiphytes. No one who set foot beneath this magical canopy would ever make the mistake of calling the **Everglades** a swamp.

Regis St Louis

@regis.stlouis

Regis writes about travel and culture, and he has contributed to over 100 Lonely Planet titles.

Cocoa Beach can be very touristy, but the further south you go, the lonelier the sands get. It's mostly a local crowd down around 13th St South, where the dunes are particularly beautiful. Sunrise walks here are spectacular, alone with the surf glowing golden and sandpipers dashing in and out of the tide.

Terry Ward

@TerryWardWriter

Terry is a Tampa-based travel writer who loves scuba diving and camping.

Henderson Beach State Park is just 2 miles from downtown Destin, but once you get into the Gulf, it's like you're in pre-population-boom Florida. You can spot dolphins, sea turtles and sometimes jellyfish in the crystal clear water. But it's the sense of apartness that makes this place so special.

Jennifer M Edwards

@fitjenned

Jennifer M Edwards is an editor, author and former daily newspaper journalist.

LEFT: DELRAY BEACH PHOTOG © RIGHT: JAMES KIRKIKIS/SHUTTERSTOCK ©

Cap's Place at Lighthouse Point transcends time, to an era of rum running, illegal gambling and decadent speakeasies. History oozes from its crumbling wooden walls. If they could only speak! Scores of dignitaries, celebrities, presidents and athletes have passed through, so the stories would surely be endless. As I feast on some of the best crab cakes I've ever had, and toss back a shot, I can almost feel Hemingway's ghost sitting beside me.

David Gibb

@HappyWanderlusters

David is a journalist, author and travel writer.

Even as a grown-up, riding the monorail at **Walt Disney World** as it rounds the Seven Seas Lagoon and reveals Cinderella's Castle in the distance still makes my heart swell with joy. The ecofriendly Walt Disney World Monorail System, which launched in 1971, encapsulates Walt Disney's vision for a brighter, greener future. Today, it's one of the most heavily used monorail systems in the world, with over 150,000 daily riders.

Amy Bizzarri

@amybizzarri

Amy is a freelance writer and public school teacher.

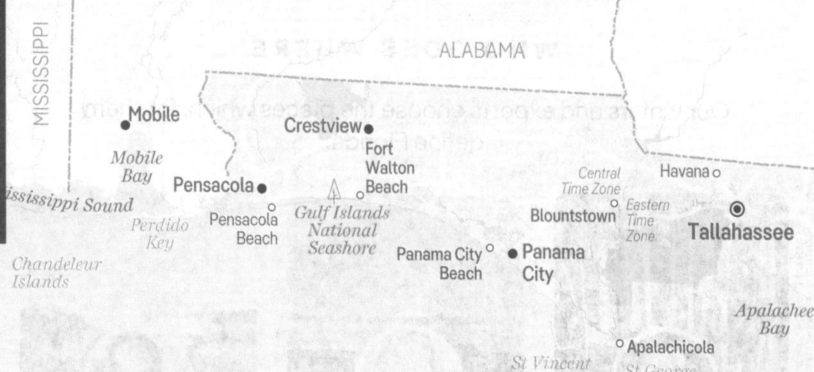

Orlando
Where theme parks reinvent imagination daily (p204)

Tampa
Dine in an industrial space turned food hall (p338)

Miami
Museums and galleries galore (p50)

Gulf of Mexico

Everglades National Park
Spot gators and birds in a wet wilderness (p112)

Key West
Lose your inhibitions (and clothes!) at Fantasy Fest (p156)

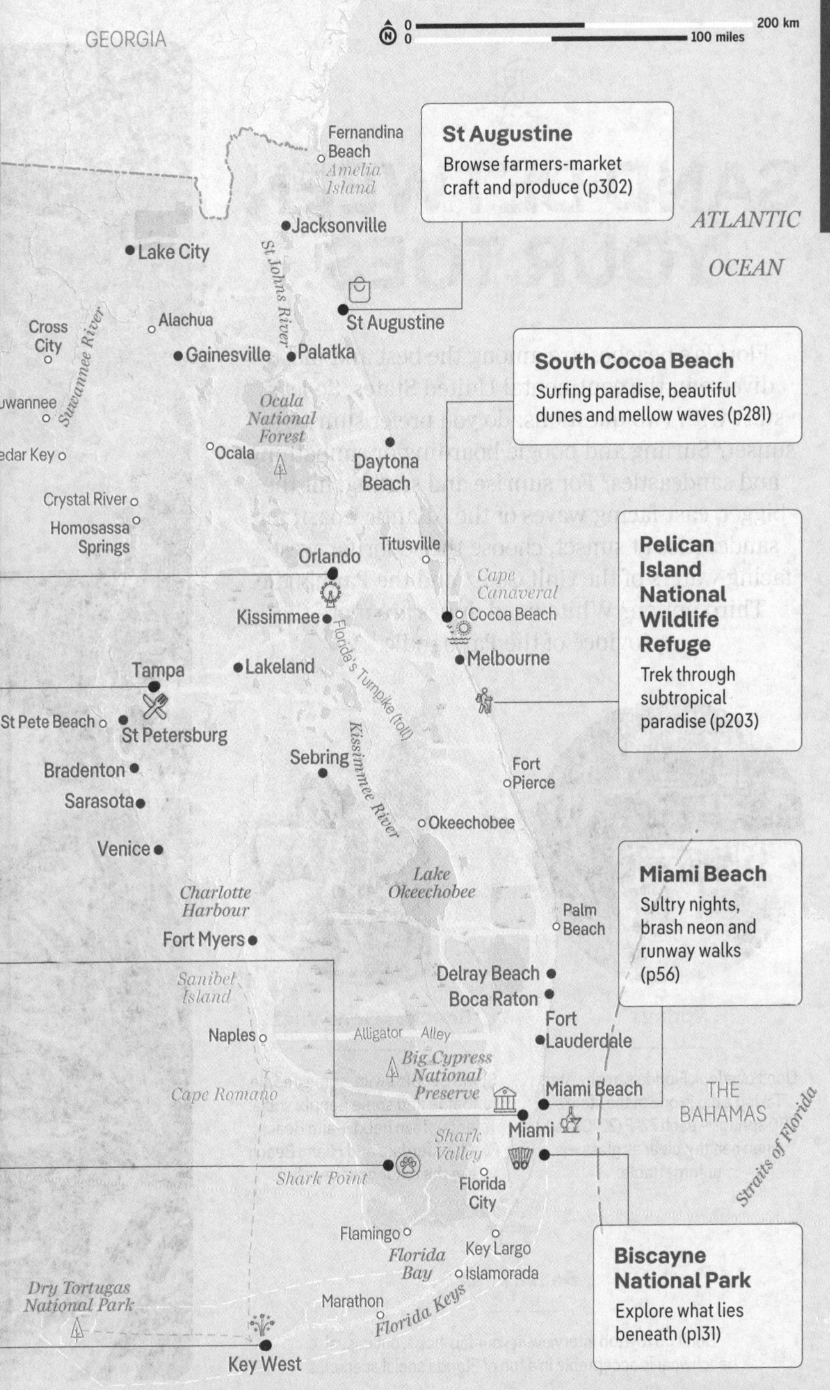
GEORGIA
0 200 km
0 100 miles
ATLANTIC OCEAN
Fernandina Beach
Amelia Island
St Augustine
Browse farmers-market craft and produce (p302)
Jacksonville
Lake City
St Johns River
St Augustine
Alachua
Cross City
Suwannee River
Gainesville
Palatka
South Cocoa Beach
Surfing paradise, beautiful dunes and mellow waves (p281)
uwannee
Ocala National Forest
edar Key
Ocala
Daytona Beach
Crystal River
Homosassa Springs
Pelican Island National Wildlife Refuge
Trek through subtropical paradise (p203)
Orlando
Titusville
Cape Canaveral
Kissimmee
Cocoa Beach
Florida's Turnpike (toll)
Melbourne
Tampa
Lakeland
St Pete Beach
St Petersburg
Kissimmee River
Sebring
Bradenton
Fort Pierce
Sarasota
Okeechobee
Venice
Miami Beach
Sultry nights, brash neon and runway walks (p56)
Lake Okeechobee
Charlotte Harbour
Palm Beach
Fort Myers
Delray Beach
Sanibel Island
Boca Raton
Fort Lauderdale
Naples
Alligator Alley
Big Cypress National Preserve
Cape Romano
Miami Beach
THE BAHAMAS
Miami
Straits of Florida
Shark Valley
Shark Point
Florida City
Flamingo
Key Largo
Biscayne National Park
Explore what lies beneath (p131)
Florida Bay
Islamorada
Dry Tortugas National Park
Marathon
Florida Keys
Key West

SAND BETWEEN YOUR TOES

Florida's beaches are among the best and most diverse in the continental United States. So let's start with two questions: do you prefer sunrise or sunset? Surfing and boogie boarding or sunbathing and sandcastles? For sunrise and surfing, hit the bigger, east-facing waves of the Atlantic Coast; for sandcastles at sunset, choose the soporific, west-facing waters of the Gulf Coast and the Panhandle. Third option? White-sand dunes are more the province of the Panhandle.

Springs

Don't overlook Florida's freshwater. Taking a dip in one of the state's 700 springs – each 72°F (22°C) and, when healthy, clear as glass – is unforgettable.

Beaches Gone Viral

Some people swim, some people sunbathe and some people social (media). Take heed: Palm Beach, Fort Lauderdale and Miami Beach are the influencer beaches.

Beachwear

Don't go to a job interview in your flip-flops, but casual beachwear is acceptable in a ton of Florida social scenarios.

Calusa Beach, Bahia Honda State Park (p149)

BEST BEACH EXPERIENCES

Not every Miami beach is a fashion show; head to beautiful, laid-back **Crandon Park** 1 and enjoy great views of the Magic City skyline. (p102)

Explore **South Cocoa Beach**, 2 which has some of the most beautiful dunes on Florida's east coast and mellow waves. (p282)

The glistening hot sands of **Hollywood Beach** 3 beckon to those strolling its pedestrian-friendly promenade, the Broadwalk, where beach bars, patios and buskers compete to be the star attraction. (p180)

The Panhandle contains some of Florida's finest sand, including the pristine dunes of **Henderson Beach State Park** 4 – easily accessible, a drifter's dream. (p390)

Out in the Keys, you'll find beautiful isolation, rare birds and the ruins of a railroad at **Bahia Honda State Park**, 5 which cups the arms of Big Pine Key. (p149)

ONE STATE, MANY WORLDS

Florida is a world that creates worlds. Down here the artificial environment is authentic – you can be whatever you want to be in destinations like Walt Disney World®, Universal Orlando Resort and LEGOLAND. Yes, there's crass commercialism, but there are rainbow sparks of imagination that set the minds of children alight in a thousand inspiring ways. People come to Florida to be whatever they want to be, and the theme park is the ultimate expression of that impulse.

Line Up

Don't like lines? Various iterations of fast passes exist at most Florida theme parks now, and the line experience itself is becoming its own attraction.

Themed Lodging

To stay at a park resort or away from it? The former option is always easier and, inevitably, a heck of a lot more expensive.

Family or Thrills?

You don't have to pick! These days, you can easily find seat-of-your-pants rides and family-friendly fun in most parks.

Universal Studios (p247)

BEST THEME PARK EXPERIENCES

Learn why **Walt Disney World®** ❶ is the benchmark other theme parks are measured against, a world of worlds that constantly strives for reinvention. (p210)

Lose yourself in the ride experience at **Universal Orlando Resort**, ❷ then immerse yourself in imagined realms like The Wizarding World of Harry Potter. (p247)

Disney's Animal Kingdom ❸ is more than a wildlife park – it's where Disney innovation meets the natural world and accentuates it. (p232)

LEGOLAND ❹ is the ideal park for those who want a slightly more laid-back theme park that still offers the chance to (literally!) build new worlds. (p266)

Kennedy Space Center Visitor Complex ❺ has theme park–like rides taking you into the darkest, wildest corners of the solar system. (p277)

A TOUR FOR TASTEBUDS

Florida's culinary scene is an enticing mix of ingredients: Gulf and Atlantic seafood, the best citrus fruits in the US, recipes from America's Deep South and Latin America, and some extremely talented chefs. Together, they give Florida serious culinary cred. Throw in quirky outliers, such as gator tail and fried snake, and there's so much to look forward to. At higher-end places, especially in big cities like Miami, you need to book seats in advance.

Alligator

Alligator tastes like a cross between fish and pork. It's healthier than chicken, with as much protein but half the fat, fewer calories and less cholesterol.

Cuban Cuisine

Cuban food is itself a mix of Caribbean, African and Latin American influences, and in Tampa and Miami it's a staple of everyday life and tables.

Frog's Legs

Good frog's legs taste, honestly, like chicken, but with a fishy texture. Those who know say the 'best' come from the Everglades.

Poblano pesto shrimp, Fat Snook (p282)

BEST EATING EXPERIENCES

Head to **Enriqueta's** ❶ in Wynwood, Miami, for the pure joy of Cuban coffee and *chisme* (gossip) first thing in the morning. (p89)

Once a streetcar repair garage, now **Armature Works** ❷ is Tampa's destination food hall, showcasing Mexican street food, creative Floridian fare and fresh baked goods. (p340)

Sip sunshine with the Dole Whip, vanilla ice cream with a pineapple swirl, at **Aloha Isle** ❸ near the Enchanted Tiki Room in the Magic Kingdom. (p221)

Check out the **Fat Snook** ❹ in Cocoa Beach – it's a much beloved local favorite for Caribbean-inspired seafood in a stylish setting. (p282)

Maybe you've had Wagyu steak, but have you prepared it? You can at Fort Lauderdale's **Casa Sensei**, ❺ where table grills and madcap indulgence are the norm. (p173)

FRATERNIZE WITH FAUNA

Florida's natural world is one in which charismatic wildlife species roam against a backdrop of an extraordinary patchwork of landscapes. It's the panthers and black bears, alligators and manatees who are the headline acts. Plus, the Everglades is a fragile and precious ecosystem, one of the most important wilderness areas in the Lower 48.

The Land

Florida is many things, but elevated it is not. In this pancake-flat state, the interplay of freshwater and saltwater defines the presence of fauna.

The Panhandle

Peninsular Florida isn't the only ecological game here. The Panhandle's Apalachicola River basin is a Garden of Eden, in which ice-age plants survive in lost ravines.

The Climate

What really sets Florida apart, in terms of its ecology, is that it occupies a subtropical transition zone between northern temperate and southern tropical climates.

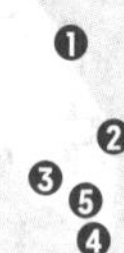

BEST WILDLIFE-WATCHING EXPERIENCES

Roll along Merritt Island National Wildlife Refuge's **Black Point Wildlife Drive** 1 to spot gators, manatees, wading birds and more. (p280)

Join the manatees at **Manatee Lagoon** 2 in West Palm Beach, which attracts hordes of manatees, nurse sharks, stingrays and other marine life. (p187)

Explore the **Corkscrew Swamp Sanctuary** 3 – a glorious nature reserve filled with gators, wood storks and Florida panthers. (p375)

Don't miss gators, birds, manatees and crocs at **Everglades National Park**, 4 one of North America's best wildlife spots, and mere minutes from Miami. (p112)

Have a soggy stomp through **Big Cypress National Preserve**, 5 home to a slew of alligators, as well as birds and other wildlife. (p115)

Ocean Drive, Miami Beach (p60)

NIGHT MOVES

Long, sultry nights, outdoor patios that benefit from year-round good weather, views of the ocean, an incredibly diverse population that ranges from immigrant enclaves to military-base towns, and a general sense of hedonism all inform Florida's nightlife scene. We'll see you at the club...or the patio...or the college bar...well, there are a lot of options.

Last Call

Across the state of Florida, last call is set at 2am, but individual communities are allowed to set the rules for their own closing times.

Drinks, Alfresco

Year-round warm weather and/or views of the water means that there is a glut of outdoor patio areas and straight-up patio bars inundating the state.

BEST NIGHTLIFE EXPERIENCES

Sip a fine cocktail amid an even finer crowd of pretty people at **Broken Shaker** ❶ in Miami Beach. (p66)

Like craft cocktails? Like steampunk? Then you'll love the **Edison** ❷ in Disney Springs, a kind of old-school-meets-sci-fi power plant bar. (p246)

Do shots at the **Green Parrot**, ❸ one of the most distinctive bars in Key West. (p160)

In Fort Lauderdale, the 'gays and grays' hit up art galleries, restaurants and bars in LGBTIQ+ hub **Wilton Manors.** ❹ (p177)

Tampa's party people pack into **Ybor City**, ❺ a district where you can't walk for tripping over a bar or a cigar lounge. (p342)

MAKE A SPLASH

Naturalist Marjory Stoneman Douglas once said Florida is like a spoon of freshwater resting delicately in a bowl of saltwater – a spongy brick of limestone hugged by the Atlantic Ocean and the Gulf of Mexico. These two bodies of water are both playground and backdrop to a thousand adventures awaiting those willing to get a little wet. Be it surfing, diving, snorkeling or kayaking, there is no lack of waterborne activities for Sunshine State explorers.

LEFT TO RIGHT: FRANCISCO BLANCO/SHUTTERSTOCK ©, MARIDAV/SHUTTERSTOCK ©, F PHOTOGRAPHY R/SHUTTERSTOCK ©

Paddling

The winter 'dry' season is best for kayaking. Evaporation and receding waterlines force wildlife into highly visible concentrations amid the state's waterways and pools.

Fishing

Fishing in Florida, especially saltwater angling, is among the best the US offers. For variety and abundance, few places in the world can compete.

Snorkeling

Be it offshore by its reefs, or within its crystal-clear springs, the Sunshine State is unmatched for snorkeling in the Lower 48.

Sebastian Inlet (p283)

BEST WATER EXPERIENCES

Go underwater at **Biscayne National Park**, ❶ where it's all about undersea exploration and marine life, manatees and bird rookeries. (p131))

Try to catch a wave along the surf-centric Space Coast, from **Cocoa Beach** ❷ south to the famed break at Sebastian Inlet. (p282)

Plunge into crystal-clear shallow waters at Blue Heron Bridge at **Phil Foster Park** ❸ in West Palm Beach, which teems with divers and snorkelers. (p187)

Get wet at **John Pennekamp Coral Reef State Park**, ❹ the first dedicated underwater park in the country, adjacent to its own Keys coral reef. (p141)

Dive a 900ft-long aircraft carrier, the *Oriskany*, deliberately sunk in 2006 off the coast of **Pensacola**. ❺ (p387)

FLORIDA FESTIVITIES

Florida does not lack festivals. Year-round sunny weather gives people an excuse to be outside and in a celebratory frame of mind. Florida's ethnic diversity is another reason the calendar is full: people are serious about commemorating their heritage. Plus, this is a state with an economy that is unapologetically built on tourism, so every town and region is always angling to shape and host events that attract more and more visitors.

LEFT TO RIGHT: YES I SHOOT MODELS/SHUTTERSTOCK ©, RAWPIXEL.COM/SHUTTERSTOCK ©, CHUCK WAGNER/SHUTTERSTOCK ©

Fall & Winter

Florida's winter is the 'dry' season. In northern Florida, cool temps make this off-season. In southern Florida, a busy time of events and parties kicks off.

Spring

Come spring, beaches start to fill with spring breakers, while towns try to either attract partiers or mollify their worst tendencies with cultural events.

Summer

High season for Florida's theme parks. Muggy weather drives off some tourists, who are lured back by food festivals and the like.

Fantasy Fest, Key West (p163)

BEST FESTIVAL EXPERIENCES

Let your inner freak flag fly high and proud at the October bacchanalia that is **Fantasy Fest** ❶ in Key West. (p163)

Tiny Apalachicola's population swells during the **Florida Seafood Festival**, ❷ when the bounty of the waters is showcased in a ridiculously charming town. (p402)

Come spring, the world blooms, and Disney World – specifically Epcot – comes alive with Disney-themed topiaries at the **International Flower & Garden Festival**. ❸ (p239)

Witness the pure creative energy and chaos that is **Art Basel** ❹ in Miami in December, one of the biggest international art shows in the world. (p90)

Join over 200 talented artisans who blanket the street in October at the **Las Olas Annual Art Fair** ❺ in Fort Lauderdale. (p177)

FIND IT, LOVE IT, BUY IT

Florida is unapologetically into selling you stuff, from five-digit works of original art in a Miami art gallery, to handmade jewelry at a Winter Park crafts fair, to lots of terrible T-shirts. This is the second-most-visited state in the USA, and it would be silly not to grab a souvenir while you're here.

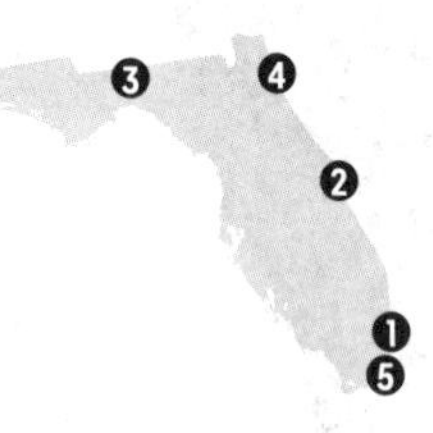

Malls

We know good execution of a genre when we see it, and few states do malls, especially outdoor open-air shopping centers, like Florida does.

Boutiques

A state with this much creativity and diversity is bound to have some little independent shops and boutiques, most evident in cities like Miami and Tampa.

Galleries

A piece of original art or craft is a one-of-a-kind gift, and every tourism area is rife with galleries and markets.

BEST SHOPPING EXPERIENCES

Visit the unashamedly ritzy **Palm Court** ❶ shopping center in Miami's Design District, which is part mall and part art installation. (p86)

Peruse **Historic Cocoa Village,** ❷ a haven for vintage shops, boutiques and galleries stuffed into a few, tree-lined blocks. (p283)

Tallahassee's **Railroad Square Art District** ❸ is a fun fair of food trucks, artsy curios and crafts, and good times. (p406)

The St Augustine Amphitheatre (the Amp) hosts a **farmers market** ❹ that's all independent vendors, live music and Anastasia Island sea breezes. (p308)

Find the read, beach or otherwise, of your dreams at **Books & Books,** ❺ a fantastic independent book retailer. (p92)

WONDER & WANDER

You think Florida doesn't have an intellectual side? Think again. The confluence of immigrants and domestic seekers of a better life has stirred a cultural and cerebral pot that constantly pushes human expression and knowledge. These gifts are showcased in state museums, which are a welcome respite from the more commercialized edges of Florida travel.

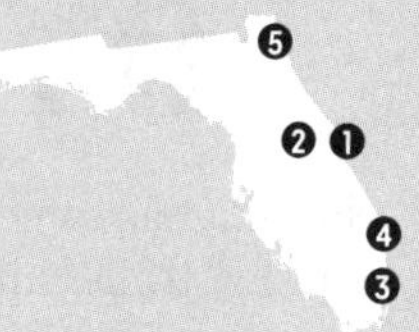

LEFT TO RIGHT: EGROY/SHUTTERSTOCK ©, THOMAS BARRAT/SHUTTERSTOCK ©

Art Museums

Every Florida town worth its salt boasts an art museum; Miami's are obviously the most famous, but you'll find gems in Jacksonville and Pensacola.

Nature & Science Museums

We'll say it again: this state has a truly unique blend of environments, and there's a glut of museums that dissect this natural backdrop.

History Museums

From specialist museums on diving to museums covering Florida before European settlement and everything that has followed, Florida's got you covered.

BEST MUSEUM EXPERIENCES

Head to the **Wizard of Oz Museum,** ❶ a surprising newcomer in Cape Canaveral, home to more than 2000 artifacts from the books and film. (p288)

Explore Orlando's African American history and culture at the **Wells' Built Museum,** ❷ a hidden gem of a museum housed in the former Wells' Hotel. (p260)

Lose yourself in the light-filled galleries overlooking Biscayne Bay at the **Pérez Art Museum** ❸ in Miami, itself an architectural wonder. (p71)

Dig into Palm Beach's **Flagler Museum,** ❹ testament to one man's love for his wife, for whom the tycoon built this grandiose mansion. (p191)

Gorgeous gardens and a riverfront location underline the thousands of paintings and sculptures housed at Jacksonville's excellent **Cummer Museum of Art.** ❺ (p318)

FLORIDA BY FOOT

Florida has some exceptional hiking. The state's hiking trails can be challenging because of the weather and, in the Everglades, trail conditions when you stray from the boardwalk. South Florida swamps tend to favor 1- to 2-mile boardwalk trails; these are excellent and almost always wheelchair accessible. But they can only take you so far. In the Everglades, you can also embark on 'wet walks,' which are wading trips deep into the blackwater heart of the swamps.

LEFT TO RIGHT: EWY MEDIA/SHUTTERSTOCK ©, JAROMIR CHALABALA/SHUTTERSTOCK ©, SIMON DANNHAUER/SHUTTERSTOCK ©

Florida National Scenic Trail

The Florida National Scenic Trail runs north from Big Cypress National Preserve, through the Ocala National Forest and then west to the Gulf Islands National Seashore.

Supplies

Mosquitoes are an unavoidable reality. Sunscreen is a must when hiking in Florida, and a good bug repellent (and insect-proof clothes) comes a close second.

Hydrate

Florida hikers never have to worry about elevation gain, but the weather makes up for it. Hike in the dry season.

Mahogany Hammock Trail, Everglades National Park (p124)

BEST HIKING EXPERIENCES

The Florida National Scenic Trail runs throughout the state, including a memorable knee-deep 'wet walk' through the swamps of **Big Cypress National Preserve**. ❶ (p115)

Explore the National Wild and Scenic Rivers–designated Wekiwa River at **Wekiwa Springs State Park**, ❷ which is far off the tourist radar. (p268)

Hobe Mountain Observation Tower at **Jonathan Dickinson State Park** ❸ is the highest point in the state (86ft), and it's lovely: a sand dune where wonderful views abound. (p193)

Stride some boardwalks through classic Everglades scenery at **Anhinga Trail**; ❹ this may be an easy boardwalk 'hike,' but it doesn't lack for alligators. (p122)

Lose yourself in true Florida wilderness at the **Pelican Island National Wildlife Refuge**, ❺ 5445 acres of pristine salt marsh and mangroves. (p203)

REGIONS & CITIES

Find the places that tick all your boxes.

The Panhandle

EXPLORE BEACH, OCEAN AND SPRING WILDERNESSES

The northernmost part of Florida is its most culturally Southern region, a land of wild spaces, wind-blown sand dunes, stick-to-your-rib restaurants and military, alongside the sugary sands of Destin and old oyster-harvesting villages like Apalachicola.

p376

Northeast Florida

OLD FLORIDA AND NEW EXPERIENCES

St Augustine has been around for almost 400 years, and has the charming historical core to prove it. Jacksonville, on the other hand, is a blend of barbecue, dive bars and surf culture, while Amelia Island weaves genteel charm into a Southern landscape dripping with rural coastal beauty.

p296

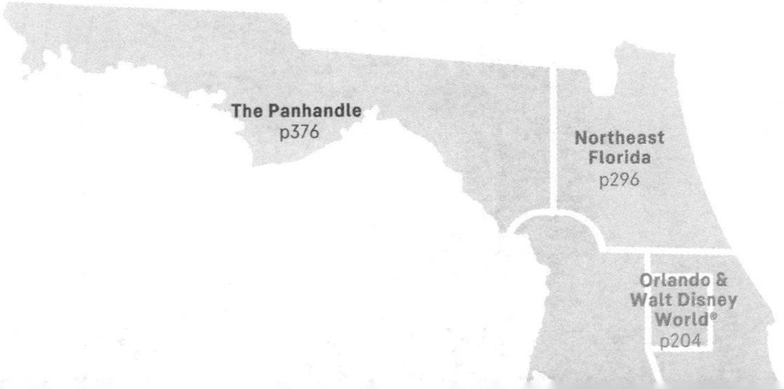

The Panhandle
p376
Northeast Florida
p296
Orlando & Walt Disney World®
p204

Orlando & Walt Disney World®

FROM SWAMP TO THEME-PARK CAPITAL OF THE WORLD

The theme-park experience dominates Greater Orlando, and truly, the folks at Disney, Universal and other parks have perfected simulated environments. But the fun isn't all artificial. Orlando is an international hub, with a thriving LGBTIQ+ scene and an enthusiastic arts community.

p204

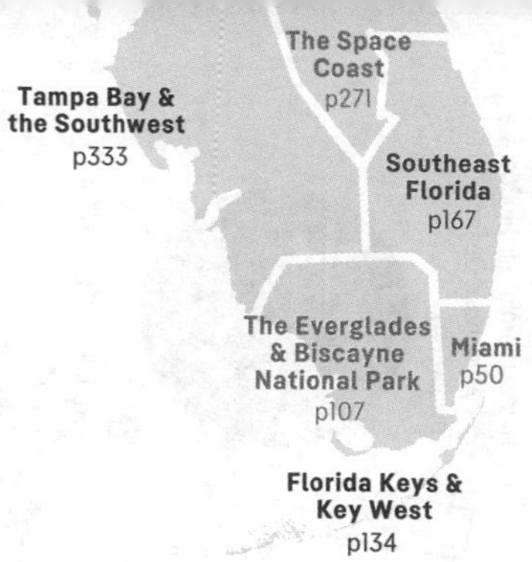

Tampa Bay & the Southwest p333
The Space Coast p271
Southeast Florida p167
The Everglades & Biscayne National Park p107
Miami p50
Florida Keys & Key West p134

Tampa Bay & the Southwest

ISLANDS, OUTDOOR ACTIVITIES AND CITY LIFE

The Gulf of Mexico is a calmer body of water than the Atlantic Ocean, but the Gulf Coast isn't sedate. Wild nights beckon in Tampa, while Sarasota and St Petersburg boast family-friendly beaches and arts institutions, and idyllic islands dangle just offshore.

p333

The Everglades & Biscayne National Park

WETLAND ADVENTURES, WILDLIFE AND ISLANDS

The Everglades are a natural space amid seemingly endless urban sprawl, an ecological escape that can appear deceivingly gentle at first blush. Yet this waterlogged wilderness hides raw, primeval beauty: alligators and countless species of birds and fish, tied together by flooded prairies and misty swamp.

p107

Florida Keys & Key West

ISLANDS AT THE END OF IMAGINATION

The Florida Keys float in a teal penumbra of bars, beaches and fishing camps. Each of the islands has its own idiosyncrasies, but nowhere is as unique and creative as Key West, the colorful terminus of the Keys rainbow.

p134

The Space Coast

ROCKETS, SURF AND WILD NATURE

So named for the presence of NASA at Cape Canaveral, the Space Coast is also notable for possessing the longest stretches of unspoiled Atlantic coastline in the state, along with surf stops, kayaking opportunities and a glut of family-friendly beach towns.

p271

Miami

LATIN AMERICA AND THE CARIBBEAN COLLIDE

No city but Miami can so thoroughly embody the diversity and energy of Latin America and the Caribbean, while wrapping said soul in a package of glamour, neon, tropical weather, beaches and sunsets. Past the flash are small neighborhoods where deep community ties bind enclaves from around the world.

p50

Southeast Florida

BEACHES, TREASURES AND NATURAL WONDERS

If Miami is a part of Florida and apart from it, cities like Fort Lauderdale are where the state asserts its anything-goes identity via yachts, outdoor malls and gigantic mansions. But you'll also find world-class art museums, great dining and the state's best surf.

p167

ITINERARIES

Iconic South Florida

Allow: 10 days

Distance: 205 miles

For sheer South Florida box-ticking, you can't do better than taking in Miami, the Everglades and the Florida Keys, with three ecosystems to pick from – urban, flooded and archipelagic. To get here, start along the Atlantic Coast and soak in the sunshine that the state is (nick)named for.

Riverwalk, Fort Lauderdale (p173)

1 JUPITER 2 DAYS

The 'Treasure Coast' is known for unspoiled nature rather than condos and cosmopolitans. Stop first in **Jupiter** (p193, pictured); among its pretty parks, don't miss the seaside geyser at Blowing Rocks Preserve. Catch a nice glimpse of the Loxahatchee River from the top of the Jupiter Inlet Lighthouse, or strap on climbing gear and ascend the Highest – Point – In Florida! at Hobe Mountain Observation Tower (86ft).

2 THE PALM BEACHES 1 DAY

In the quintessentially ritzy **Palm Beach** (p191), ogle the uberwealthy gliding from mansion to Bentley to beach; stop by the Flagler Museum to understand how this all got started; and each day decamp to **West Palm Beach** (p185), the hipper, more happening sister city.

3 FORT LAUDERDALE 1 DAY

Preen along the promenade amid skating goddesses and be-thonged gay men; ride a romantic gondola in the canals; enjoy fine art and gourmet cuisine: **Fort Lauderdale** (p170) is a suite of pleasures, which the Gold Coast specializes in. If you want to change it up, try the local museum of art for an excellent cultural escape or rent a bicycle for a breezy canalside pedal.

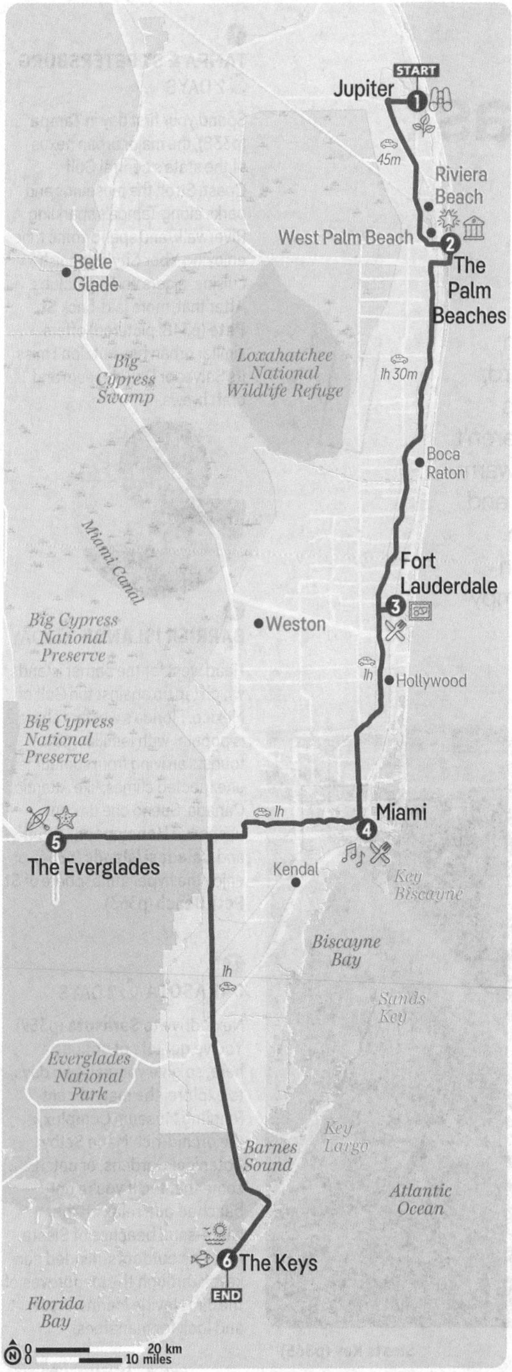

START
Jupiter
45m
Riviera Beach
West Palm Beach
The Palm Beaches
Belle Glade
Big Cypress Swamp
Loxahatchee National Wildlife Refuge
1h 30m
Boca Raton
Miami Canal
Fort Lauderdale
Weston
Big Cypress National Preserve
1h
Hollywood
Big Cypress National Preserve
1h
Miami
The Everglades
Kendal
Key Biscayne
Biscayne Bay
1h
Sands Key
Everglades National Park
Key Largo
Barnes Sound
Atlantic Ocean
The Keys
END
Florida Bay
0 20 km
0 10 miles

4

MIAMI 3 DAYS

Spend three solid days exploring **Miami** (p50) and **Miami Beach** (p56). Florida's most exciting city offers everything from South Beach's pastel art deco hotels and hedonistic beach culture to Cuban sandwiches, Jewish delis, Haitian botanicas and modern art. Plus Latin hip-hop and mojitos. And punk shows and graffiti art in a Wynwood warehouse. Or the neon night of the skyline after dark... The list is endless.

5

THE EVERGLADES 1 DAY

Take a day to visit the sunning alligators of **Everglades National Park** (p112; pictured). En route, Homestead has prime roadside attractions (Coral Castle and Robert Is Here, to name just two). The Everglades' Flamingo Marina offers opportunities to kayak among the mangroves or spy manatees in the harbor, while the boardwalk at the Royal Palm Visitor Center gets you face-to-face with some gators.

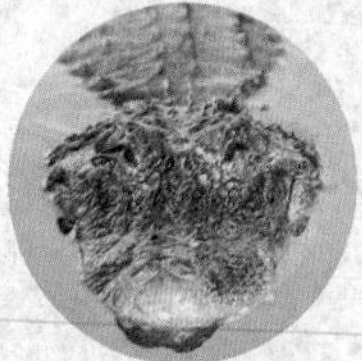

6

THE KEYS 2 DAYS

Spend two days (or more) in the **Florida Keys** (p140). Stop first in Key Largo for key lime pie, conch fritters and jaw-dropping coral reefs. Enjoy tarpon fishing in Islamorada and beach napping at Bahia Honda State Park, then – finally – hit Key West to ogle the craziness of Mallory Sq and raise a cocktail as the tangerine sun drops into an endless ocean.

STEVEN HODEL/SHUTTERSTOCK ©

ITINERARIES

Gulf Coast Swing

Allow: 8–9 days

Distance: 245 miles

Though less famous than Florida's eastern seaboard, the Gulf Coast still has its admirers – the beaches aren't as built up, soporifically warm waters lap at white sand and the sun sets over the sea. Plus it's easy to mix urban sophistication with swampy adventures.

SUNCOAST AERIALS/SHUTTERSTOCK ©

Siesta Key (p365)

1 TAMPA & ST PETERSBURG 2 DAYS

Spend your first day in **Tampa** (p338), the major urban nexus of the state's central Gulf Coast. Stroll the museums and parks along Tampa's sparkling Riverwalk, and spend some time enjoying Ybor City's Spanish cuisine, cigars and nightclubs. After that, more laid-back **St Pete** (p348; pictured) offers similar urban fun, but don't miss its Salvador Dalí Museum and craft brews.

2 BARRIER ISLANDS 1 DAY

Head west for the barrier islands, which lap up against the Gulf of Mexico. Florida's western shore is popular with families, plus tourists arriving from sometimes unexpected climes, like Atlantic Canada. Spend one day on unspoiled **Honeymoon** (p354) and **Caladesi Islands** (p354), or enjoy the hyper atmosphere of **St Pete Beach** (p353).

3 SARASOTA 2 DAYS

Next, drive to **Sarasota** (p359). You've got lots of options here, so give yourself two days to explore: the magnificent Ringling Museum Complex, the orchid-rich Marie Selby Botanical Gardens, or catch some theater. If you're not beached out, relax on the white-sand beaches of Siesta Key. The outdoors-minded can kayak through the mangroves of the Jim Neville Marine Preserve and look for manatees.

CATERINA TASSARA/SHUTTERSTOCK ©

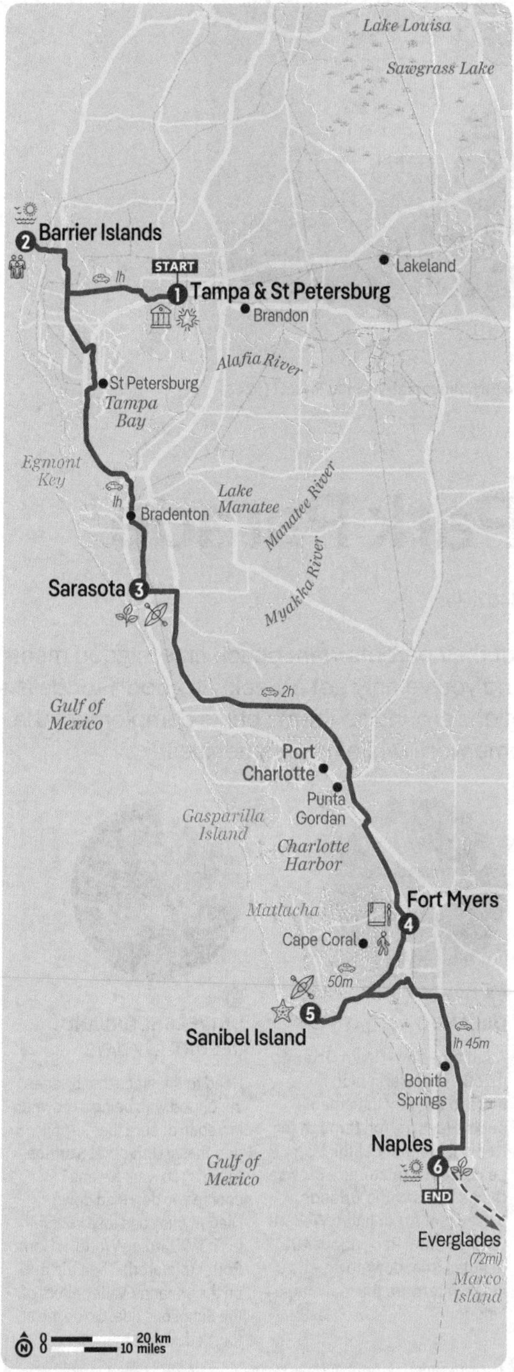

Lake Louisa
Sawgrass Lake
2 Barrier Islands
START
1 Tampa & St Petersburg
Lakeland
Brandon
1h
Alafia River
St Petersburg
Tampa Bay
Egmont Key
1h
Bradenton
Lake Manatee
Manatee River
Myakka River
3 Sarasota
2h
Gulf of Mexico
Port Charlotte
Punta Gordan
Gasparilla Island
Charlotte Harbor
Matlacha
Fort Myers 4
Cape Coral
50m
5 Sanibel Island
1h 45m
Bonita Springs
Naples 6
END
Gulf of Mexico
Everglades (72mi)
Marco Island
0 20 km
0 10 miles

4

FORT MYERS 1 DAY

Skip down to **Fort Myers** (p369) for some more regional exploring. This is still the Gulf Coast, but the attitude here is a little different: less ritzy than Sarasota, less in-your-face than Tampa (well, depending on the time of year). Take a stroll through its historic downtown River District to browse for art and gifts, then visit Thomas Edison's former Florida home and science lab.

5

SANIBEL ISLAND 1 DAY

Save some time for **Sanibel Island** (p371). World-famous for its shelling, it's also a bike-friendly island with great eats and wildlife-filled bays ripe for kayaking. There's a more nature-friendly approach to travel here, best exemplified by a slow drive through the lush jungles of the JN 'Ding' Darling National Wildlife Refuge – itself something of a birder's paradise.

6

NAPLES 1 DAY

End your trip in **Naples** (p372, pictured), the quintessential Gulf Coast beach town: upscale, artistic and welcoming to all ages, with perhaps Florida's most pristine city beach and one of the state's finest botanical gardens.

***Detour:** It's easy to fit in a day trip to the **Everglades** (p112). Zip along the Tamiami Trail to Shark Valley, and take a tram tour or bike ride among the sawgrass plains and alligators.*

6 hours

UNIVERSAL ORLANDO RESORT ©

Volcano Bay, Universal Orlando Resort (p248)

ITINERARIES

Theme Park Parade

Allow: 8–9 days **Distance:** 140 miles

The kids want Disney, but their parents want beach time, a good meal and some culture. Oh, and you've only got a week. All good! Florida is a big state, and the attractions around its theme parks complement the world of fantasy with some worthwhile travel amenities.

1

DISNEY WORLD 2 DAYS

The mouse abides, people. Budget at least two days (if not more!) to get the most out of **Walt Disney World®** (p210; pictured). There are so many attractions it's hard to pick just a few, but pick we shall: don't miss Avatar Flight of Passage or Star Wars: Rise of the Resistance. And for you nostalgia buffs: it's a small world.

2

ORLANDO 1 DAY

Adult time now! Hit up **Orlando** (p260). There is, in fact, far more to this city than theme parks. Have a stroll through the tropical greenery of the Harry P Leu Gardens (pictured). Browse the galleries of the Orlando Museum of Art or hit up Wekiwa Springs State Park, about 40 minutes from downtown – its clear waters are the real magic kingdom.

3

UNIVERSAL ORLANDO RESORT 2 DAYS

Head to the place that bridges childhood with being a grownup in a span of pure theme-park goodness: **Universal Studios** (p255). You want a wand? Of course you do. Head down Diagon Alley and lose yourself in The Wizarding World of Harry Potter (pictured). Then trip out on the uncanny-valley allure of the Simpsons ride. Go on, be a (big) kid.

JEROME LABOUYRIE/SHUTTERSTOCK ©, JILLIAN CAIN PHOTOGRAPHY/SHUTTERSTOCK ©, UNIVERSAL ORLANDO RESORT ©

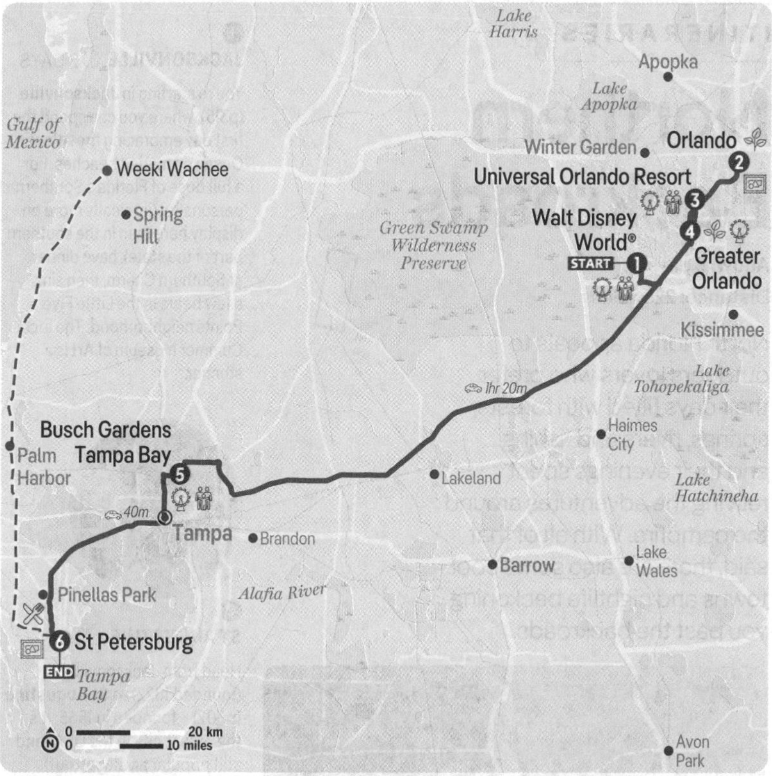

Lake Harris
Apopka
Lake Apopka
Gulf of Mexico
Winter Garden
Orlando
Universal Orlando Resort
Weeki Wachee
Spring Hill
Green Swamp Wilderness Preserve
Walt Disney World®
START
Greater Orlando
Kissimmee
Lake Tohopekaliga
1hr 20m
Haimes City
Busch Gardens Tampa Bay
Palm Harbor
Lakeland
Lake Hatchineha
40m
Tampa
Brandon
Lake Wales
Barrow
Pinellas Park
Alafia River
St Petersburg
END
Tampa Bay
0 20 km
0 10 miles
Avon Park

4 GREATER ORLANDO ⏱1 DAY

Head back to **Orlando** (p260) and visit another one of those sites that does it for kids and their adults: WonderWorks, a cross between a science fair and an amusement park. Now drive south to Bok Tower Gardens Bird Sanctuary (pictured), where the natural beauty of central Florida is set off by gorgeous gardens, classical music concerts and a 205ft stone bell tower.

5 BUSCH GARDENS TAMPA BAY ⏱1 DAY

We heard you like theme parks, so we put some theme parks on your theme parks. In this case: **Busch Gardens** (p345; pictured), which blends some very fine roller coasters with an affected, Floridian take on an African safari experience. Feel your stomach pleasantly leap into your skull on the impossibly steep Iron Gwazi.

6 ST PETERSBURG ⏱1 DAY

Can great art connect parents with their children in the same way a roller coaster can? Head to **St Petersburg**'s (p348) Salvador Dalí Museum (pictured) to find out. There are more museums to explore out here, and the restaurant scene is top-notch.

***Detour:** You can also squeeze in a day trip north for the mermaid shows at **Weeki Wachee** (p344) and the manatees of **Homosassa Springs** (p345). Everybody's happy!*
⏱4–5 hours

ITINERARIES

Northern Backroads

Allow: 8 days
Distance: 225 miles

North Florida appeals to outdoors lovers who prefer their days filled with forests, springs, rivers and fishing... and their evenings spent reliving the adventures around the campfire. With all of that said, there are also some cool towns and nightlife beckoning you past the backroads.

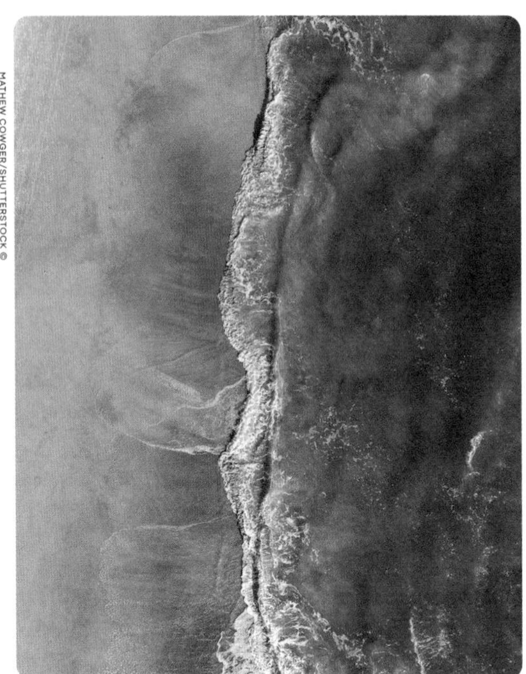

MATHEW COWGER/SHUTTERSTOCK ©

Anastasia Island (p307)

❶

JACKSONVILLE ⏱ 2 DAYS

You're starting in **Jacksonville** (p315), where you can spend the first day embracing the Atlantic Ocean on myriad beaches. For a full dose of Florida's Southern personality (ironically more on display here than in the southern part of the state), have dinner at Southern Charm, then sink a few beers in the Little Five Points neighborhood. The local Cummer Museum of Art is a stunner.

❷

ST AUGUSTINE ⏱ 1 DAY

Head from Jacksonville (founded 1822) to **St Augustine** (p302) – founded in 1565, it's the oldest city in the USA (and still popular as all get-out). Stroll down St George St (pictured), the main drag of the town's historical district, gawk at the Cathedral Basilica of St Augustine, then lounge in the Plaza de la Constitución.

❸

ANASTASIA ISLAND ⏱ 1 DAY

Just across from St Augustine is lovely **Anastasia Island** (p307), where visitors will find some 1600 acres of buttery dunes and Atlantic coastline that will grab your heart in its salty fingers and never let go. There's lots to do: sail, hit a playground with the kids or swim (be careful of the tides), but there's something to be said for getting here and doing absolutely nothing.

SEAN PAVONE/SHUTTERSTOCK ©

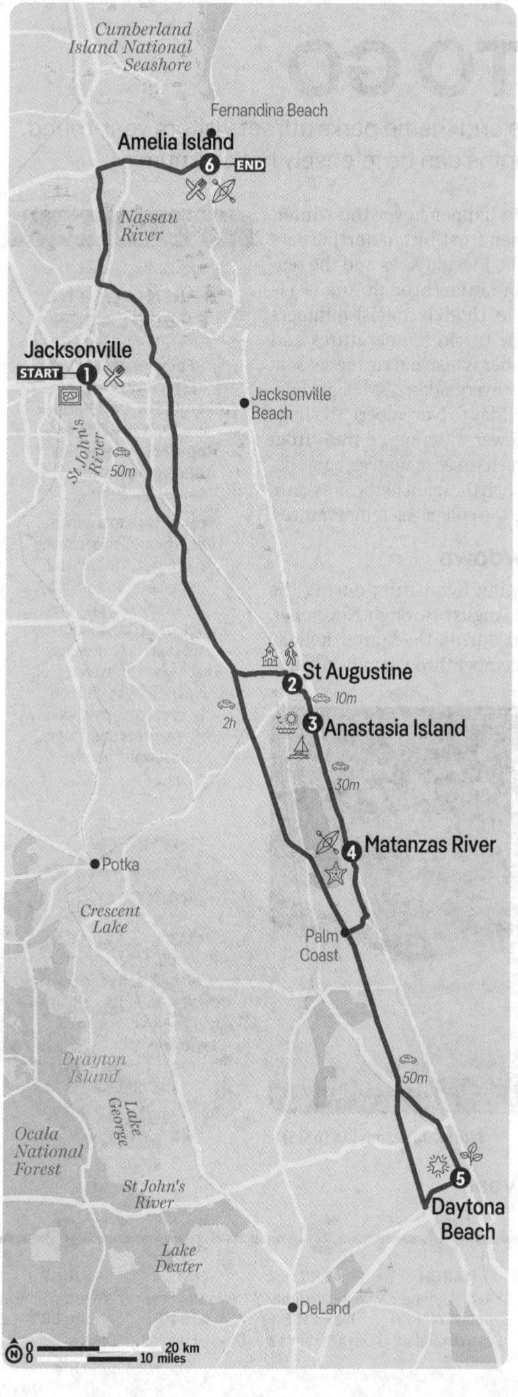

Cumberland Island National Seashore
Fernandina Beach
Amelia Island
6 END
Nassau River
Jacksonville
START 1
Jacksonville Beach
St John's River
50m
St Augustine
2
10m
3 Anastasia Island
2h
30m
4 Matanzas River
Potka
Crescent Lake
Palm Coast
50m
Drayton Island
Lake George
Ocala National Forest
St John's River
5
Daytona Beach
Lake Dexter
DeLand
20 km
10 miles

4

MATANZAS RIVER 1 DAY

As (over)developed as the Floridian coast can feel, there are swathes of the old, soft beauty of North Florida waiting by the highway. The **River to Sea Preserve** (p312), which encompasses some 90 acres fed by the Matanzas River, is one such spot. Kayak or stand-up paddleboard through the calm waters, pushing through marine hammock woodlands while keeping an eye out for birds and dancing fish.

5

DAYTONA BEACH 1 DAY

Daytona Beach (p327) is what happens when you marry the North Florida coast with a Nascar rally and sprinkle in a boardwalk laced with neon. It's an in-your-face kinda destination, where you can catch a race at the Daytona Speedway (pictured), take the kids to the arcades at the Daytona Lagoon or just wander through one of the 15 coastal parks that wind through the area.

6

AMELIA ISLAND 2 DAYS

Nothing personal, but after all those beaches, arcades and scenic rivers, it's clean-up time. Drive back past Jacksonville and spend a final day or so on **Amelia Island** (p323), which straddles the line between country-club vibes and rural Florida island escape. Spoil yourself with a Victorian B&B and some gourmet seafood or hit the outdoors again with a paddle around the barrier islands.

WHEN TO GO

Florida's beaches, cities and theme parks attract visitors year-round, though the summer months can be intensely hot and humid.

High season in South Florida happens over the winter, from December to March, when frost-bitten northerners flood the beaches of Miami, the Florida Keys and the seaside south of Tampa. Summer (June through August) is high season on the Panhandle, though tourist numbers are lower elsewhere given the torrid temperatures and high humidity. June to November is also hurricane season.

For outdoor adventures in the Everglades, it's wet and buggy during the warmer months (May to November). You'll see more wildlife and encounter fewer waterlogged trails from December to March. If you're keen to see manatees, come between December and March, when the giant herbivores gather in natural springs to escape the colder sea temperatures.

Accommodations Lowdown

You can save money on lodging by visiting during the months of February and late August through November. Prices are especially elevated during the winter holiday season, running from mid-December through mid-January.

I LIVE HERE

SPRING IN THE EVERGLADES

Founder of Garl's Coastal Kayaking in the Everglades, Garl Harrold is a trusted guide for top media companies, including National Geographic.

I came down to southern Florida from Michigan many years ago, fell in love with the place and never left. It's amazing to visit the Everglades in the springtime, especially in April or May. That's when the water level is at its lowest, and you can spot so much wildlife in the cypress domes and freshwater ponds.

Storm, Jacksonville (p315)

RAINY DAYS

One of America's rainiest states, Florida receives around 54in of rainfall each year. Showers are a year-round possibility, although Florida receives its biggest share of precipitation in the warmer months, from May to October.

Weather through the year

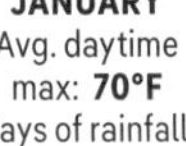

JANUARY	FEBRUARY	MARCH	APRIL	MAY	JUNE
Avg. daytime max: **70°F**	Avg. daytime max: **71°F**	Avg. daytime max: **74°F**	Avg. daytime max: **79°F**	Avg. daytime max: **84°F**	Avg. daytime max: **88°F**
Days of rainfall: **7**	Days of rainfall: **7**	Days of rainfall: **8**	Days of rainfall: **7**	Days of rainfall: **9**	Days of rainfall: **15**

OCEAN VS GULF

Florida's Gulf side has warmer water temperatures in the summer and cooler temperatures in the winter than its Atlantic side. Swimming off Marco Island in February means entering chilly 69°F (21°C) waters compared to Miami with its more tolerable 76°F (24°C) water temperatures.

Big Festivals & Events

Over a century old, the **Florida State Fair** in Tampa is classic Americana: two weeks of livestock shows, greasy food, amped-up music and old-fashioned carnival rides. **February**

The **Okeechobee Music & Arts Festival** held in Sunshine Grove sees more than 100 performers playing at six different stages. The four-day event also has art installations, yoga classes, food vendors, a lakeside beach and camping. **March**

During **Mickey's Not-So-Scary Halloween Party** (p209), Disney World ups the excitement with spooky entertainment, trick-or-treating and special fireworks displays. It happens on select evenings over three months. **August to October**

One of the biggest contemporary-art shows in North America, **Art Basel** (p90) showcases unique works from over 280 art galleries, representing some 40 different countries. **December**

Local & Quirky Festivals

Over two weekends, **Fort Myers** (p336) celebrates inventor Thomas Edison with a block party, concerts, crafts, a science fair and whimsical competitions like 'break the bed' races. The highlight is a creative nighttime parade. **February**

On Perdido Key locals are famous for tossing dead fish over the Florida–Alabama state line during the **Interstate Mullet Toss**. Distance beats style, but some have lots of style. **April**

Key West hosts **Fantasy Fest** (p139), a 10-day costumed extravaganza. Pool parties and a parade feature scantily clad (body painted) revelers. The more family-friendly, Bahamian-style Goombay Festival happens the first weekend. **October**

The 1891 Tampa Bay Hotel (now a museum) celebrates the holiday season with the **Victorian Christmas Stroll** (p342). See themed displays, hear holiday music and enjoy winter snacks. **December**

I LIVE HERE

SUMMER ESCAPES

Terry Ward is a Tampa-based travel writer *@TerryWardWriter.*

Once the summer heat is firmly upon us, central Florida's incredible springs beckon me inland from the coast. The captivatingly turquoise waters stay a consistent 72°F (22°C) year-round. Spots like Ichetucknee Springs State Park are epic for tubing with friends. Ginnie Springs begs you to paddle a kayak between dips. And I love Rainbow Springs State Park for snorkeling through what I can only describe as a mermaid's dreamscape.

Ginnie Springs near Jacksonville (p315)

SUNSHINE

Don't tell anyone, but Florida just barely scrapes into the top-10 list of America's sunniest states. Nevertheless, the Sunshine State averages over 230 days of clear skies each year. Fort Myers tops the charts with around 270 days of annual sunshine.

JULY	AUGUST	SEPTEMBER	OCTOBER	NOVEMBER	DECEMBER
Avg. daytime max: **90°F**	Avg. daytime max: **89°F**	Avg. daytime max: **87°F**	Avg. daytime max: **83°F**	Avg. daytime max: **77°F**	Avg. daytime max: **73°F**
Days of rainfall: **18**	Days of rainfall: **18**	Days of rainfall: **16**	Days of rainfall: **9**	Days of rainfall: **6**	Days of rainfall: **7**

FORESTPATH/SHUTTERSTOCK ©

GET PREPARED FOR FLORIDA

Useful things to load in your bag, your ears and your brain.

Clothes

Hot-weather fabrics: Even in winter, daytime highs can reach the low 80s. You'll want to bring lightweight, breathable fabrics to stay cool and feel less sweaty.

Layers: In the evenings things can cool off, and even in the summer, it's wise to pack a light jacket for breezy walks by the ocean.

Rain gear: Precipitation is a year-round possibility, although the biggest storms happen during the summer. Bring a lightweight rain jacket or an umbrella.

Hats: A wide-brimmed hat is wise, whether it be for hiking or a classier Panama-style hat for dressier attire. Baseball hats are also popular, but you'll need to slather extra sunscreen on the back of your neck.

Footwear: Water shoes are handy for slogs along saturated trails and in the Everglades. Bring sandals or flip-flops for the beach and walking shoes for urban wanders and hikes.

Manners

Most Floridians are quite cordial and will happily share insights into their local attractions, restaurants and drinking spots.

Locals tend to avoid topics like politics and instead talk sport. With nearly a dozen pro teams, plus college powerhouses, there's always something afoot.

In small towns and less-busy areas (such as state-park trails), **it's common to say hello** to people you see.

READ

Swamplandia! (Karen Russell; 2011) Comic, thought-provoking tale about the struggles of an alligator-wrestling Everglades family.

The Everglades: River of Grass (Marjory Stoneman Douglas; 1947) Landmark book that changed perceptions of Florida's wetlands.

Florida (Lauren Groff; 2018) Surreal and beautifully written short stories from one of the state's best literary fiction writers.

Squeeze Me (Carl Hiaasen; 2020) The latest from Florida's most prolific humorist is a biting satire about the political scene.

Words

Conch (konk) Originally used to describe Bahamian immigrants with European ancestry. These days it refers to a native of Key West – as well as the tasty sea snail usually served deep fried.

Cracker A name given to early pioneer settlers who worked as farmers and cowhands. Some still use it today as a sign of a multi-generational connection to the Florida countryside.

Gladesmen Rough-and-ready characters who enjoy fishing, hunting and camping in the Everglades.

Hammock Not the thing you swing in, but rather an area of higher ground that contains hardwoods like oaks, hickory trees and palms.

Intracoastal Waterway A series of canals, bays, inlets, rivers and channels that provide sheltered travel by boat along both the Gulf and Atlantic Coasts.

Key From the Spanish *'cayo,'* a small island made of ancient remnants of coral reefs. 'The Keys' refers to the 1700-island archipelago in Florida's far south.

Old Florida The vintage Florida of yesteryear, which may include state parks, ungentrified towns or traditional seaside communities.

Panhandle Part of northwest Florida that stretches across some 250 miles between the Alabama border and Apalachee Bay.

Snowbird A person who comes to live in Florida part-time during the winter months in order to escape the cold weather up north.

Y'all Short for 'you all,' which is commonly used to address a group of people.

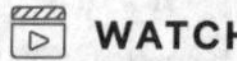

WATCH

Adaptation (Spike Jonze; 2002) Award-winning film inspired by Susan Orlean's non-fiction book *The Orchid Thief.*

Moonlight (Barry Jenkins; 2016) Coming-of-age story grappling with sexuality and self-discovery.

The Florida Project (Sean Baker; 2017) Powerful film about childhood innocence and overlooked communities.

Key Largo (John Huston; 1948) The classic Bacall-Bogart film noir features fugitives, double crossing and an ominous hurricane.

Dolphin Tale (Charles Martin Smith; 2011) A family favorite about a wounded dolphin given new life by a prosthetic tail.

LISTEN

Danger High Voltage (Betty Wright; 1972) Evocative grooves from Miami's trailblazing queen of soul.

Songs You Know by Heart (Jimmy Buffett; 1985) Compilation of Buffett's greatest hits including 'Margaritaville' and 'Cheeseburger in Paradise.'

Signs (Tedeschi Trucks Band; 2019) Led by a husband-wife duo, this Jacksonville-based band blends blues, jazz and southern rock.

The Miami Guide (Miami Mike; 2022) South Florida podcast that touches on urban art, wildlife, development and sustainability.

KRISTI BLOKHIN/SHUTTERSTOCK ©

Road sign, Walt Disney World® (p210)

TRIP PLANNER

FLORIDA'S THEME PARKS

Every year Walt Disney World®, Universal Orlando Resort and LEGOLAND draw millions of visitors to Orlando, the theme-park capital of the world. There's also Busch Gardens near Tampa and a handful of other lesser-known parks. Here's the bottom line on what's what and how to tackle them.

The Big Four

WALT DISNEY WORLD®

The so-called 'Happiest Place on Earth,' **Walt Disney World®** (p210) encompasses 42 sq miles and includes four completely separate and distinct theme parks, each with rides and shows for all ages, from toddlers to adults looking for a chance to feel like a kid again: **Magic Kingdom** (p217), **Disney's Hollywood Studios** (p226), **Disney's Animal Kingdom** (p232) and **Epcot** (p237). There are also two water parks (Typhoon Lagoon and Blizzard Beach), more than 32 resorts, 200 restaurants and two shopping and nightlife districts (Disney Springs and Disney's BoardWalk), as well as four golf courses, two miniature-golf courses and lagoons with water sports. All are connected by a system of free buses, boats and monorails.

UNIVERSAL ORLANDO RESORT

Universal Orlando Resort (p247) is a colorful and walkable complex, with two star-studded theme parks – **Islands of Adventure** (p250) and **Universal Studios** (p255) – and one water park (**Volcano Bay**; p248), plus eight first-rate resorts and **CityWalk** (p249), a carnival-like restaurant and nightlife district. All are connected by garden paths and a boat shuttle. Fans of Mario and Luigi can step into the game at the resort's brand-new land, Super Nintendo World, where visitors can race in an augmented-reality Mario Kart ride, dine at a Toad-inspired restaurant and meet Mario, Luigi and Princess Peach as they stroll their immersive land.

WHEN TO GO

Slow Times & Peak Periods The slowest times are mid-January through February, September through mid-October, the first half of May, and between Thanksgiving weekend and mid-December.

Crowds and prices soar during US school vacations, including summer (June through August), spring break (March to mid-April), Thanksgiving weekend, and between Christmas and New Year. If possible, avoid these high seasons. Smaller holiday weekends can also bring on peak crowds, especially for President's Day (February), Memorial Day (May) and Veterans Day (November).

Special Events & Ticket Planning Some events worth planning for are the Epcot International Food & Wine Festival (mid-July to mid-November), Mickey's Very Merry Christmas Party (November to December) and Universal Orlando's Halloween Horror Nights (September/October).

At Disney and Universal, per-day theme-park admission costs plummet the more days you buy; visit park websites for details on current specials, accommodations packages and dining plans. You do not need admission to enter the resort complexes themselves, only the theme and water parks. There are all kinds of entertainment and activities options beyond the theme-park gates (especially at Walt Disney World).

LEGOLAND

Build your dream at **LEGOLAND** (p266), where LEGO sets come alive in full-size fun. Smaller in scale than the other big Florida theme parks, LEGOLAND has a calmer vibe and smaller crowds, making it a good pick for families with little ones. Steps away, **Peppa Pig Theme Park** (p266) immerses tiny tots in the colorful world of Peppa and her friends.

BUSCH GARDENS

A throwback to the days when theme parks meant roller coasters, **Busch Gardens** (p345) is for those who like their rides fast and scary. Divided into 10 different African-themed zones, Busch Gardens also puts animal encounters front and center (more than 2700 animals call this theme park home), and has various shows and musical entertainment.

Cheetah Hunt rollercoaster, Busch Gardens (p345)

ESSENTIAL STRATEGIES

In Advance

- Download theme-park apps to purchase park tickets, plan itineraries and reserve entertainment and dining options. On the ground, visitors can see the latest wait times, access maps and order food and drink on the My Disney Experience and Official Universal Orlando Resort apps.
- At many parks, tickets cost less if bought in advance. You'll also spend less time waiting in lines. Use online calendars to peruse prices over several months.
- Buy multiple day-admission tickets and be flexible. It's exhausting tackling the parks at 110% day after day. You'll enjoy yourself more if you allow room for downtime by the pool or elsewhere.
- Reserve Disney dining up to 180 days in advance. Select a few don't-miss eating experiences (take location into account).

Once There

- Arrive early, before park gates open, march straight to popular rides before the lines get long, and consider leaving by lunch, when crowds are at their worst. This won't work every day, but a few efficient mornings make a real difference.
- Pack snacks. Items as simple as peanut-butter sandwiches and an apple stuffed in your bag will save time, money and stress.
- Factor in travel time. When planning each day, carefully consider travel to and within the parks. At Disney especially, transportation logistics can waste hours and leave you drained.

PETER ACKER/SHUTTERSTOCK ©

Grouper sandwich

THE FOOD SCENE

Florida provides a countless array of temptations, from bountiful fruit markets to fresh-off-the-boat seafood.

Florida's culinary scene is one enticing mix of ingredients: Gulf and Atlantic seafood, the best citrus and tropical fruits in the US, recipes from America's Deep South and Latin America, and a diverse mix of talented and innovative chefs.

Given the narrow width of the peninsula, you're never more than 80 miles from a coastline. Not surprisingly, fresh catch of the day, along with crustaceans of every shape and size, play starring roles on menus across the state. For Floridians out for a meal, this can mean indulging in blackened grouper sandwiches at a rustic dockside eatery, or it might entail sitting down to a multicourse oceanic feast at one of the state's many award-winning dining rooms.

Seafood aside, there are countless ways to eat well in Florida, from assembling a picnic at a market to munching on flavors from around the globe at a burgeoning food hall. There's just as much variety when it comes to drinking, including tropical fruit smoothies, energizing Cuban-style coffee and myriad craft beers.

Bounty of the Sea

Grouper is far and away the most popular fish. Grouper sandwiches are to Florida what the cheesesteak is to Philadelphia or pizza to Manhattan – a defining, iconic dish and the standard by which many places are measured. Hunting the perfect grilled or fried grouper sandwich is an obsessive Floridian quest – the issue of fried versus grilled has been known to provoke fights – as is finding the creamiest bowl of chowder.

Other popular fish include snapper (with dozens of varieties), mahimahi (which is sometimes labeled as dolphin, to the consternation of many a tourist) and catfish.

Florida really shines when it comes to crustaceans: try pink shrimp and rock shrimp, and don't miss soft-shell blue crab – Florida is well known for its blue-crab hatcheries, making them available fresh year-round. Locals boil their crabs, as is common across the American South, but plenty of Northeastern transplants means crabs are also steamed. Why not try both?

Winter (October to April) is the season for Florida spiny lobster and stone crab (out of season both will be frozen). Florida lobster is all tail, without the large claws of its Maine cousin, and stone crab is heavenly sweet, served steamed with butter or the ubiquitous mustard sauce. Usually, only the stone-crab claw is served.

Fruits & Vegetables

Today, most restaurants with upscale or gourmet pretensions promote the local sources of their produce. Florida has worked long and hard to become an agricultural powerhouse, and it's famous for its citrus fruits. The state is the nation's largest producer of oranges, grapefruits, tangerines and limes, not to mention mangoes and sugarcane. Bananas, strawberries, coconuts, avocados (once called 'alligator pears'), and the gamut of tropical fruits and vegetables are also here. The major agricultural region is around Lake Okeechobee, with field upon field and grove upon grove as far as the eye can see.

Cuban & Latin American Cuisine

Cuban food is itself a mix of Caribbean, African and Latin American influences, and in Tampa and Miami it's a staple of everyday life. Sidle up to a *loncheria* (snack bar) and order a *sándwich Cubano* or 'Cuban sandwich': a grilled baguette stuffed with ham, roast pork, cheese, mustard and pickles.

Integral to many Cuban dishes are *mojo* (a garlicky vinaigrette, sprinkled on sandwiches), *adobo* (a meat marinade of garlic, salt, cumin, oregano and sour orange juice) and *sofrito* (a stew-starter mix of garlic, onion and chili peppers); this is basically meat-and-starch cuisine, with an emphasis on huge portions. Main-course meats are typically accompanied by rice, beans and fried plantains.

With its large number of Central and Latin American immigrants, the Miami area is a culinary hot pot. Seek out Haitian *griot* (marinated fried pork), Jamaican jerk chicken, Brazilian barbecue, Central American *gallo pinto* (red beans and rice) and Nicaraguan *tres leches* ('three milks' cake).

In the morning, try a Cuban coffee, also known as *café Cubano* or *cortadito*. This hot shot of liquid gold is essentially sweetened espresso, while *café con leche* is just *café au lait* with a different accent: equal parts coffee and hot milk.

MARIDAV/SHUTTERSTOCK ©

Sándwich Cubano

CLAYTON HARRISON/SHUTTERSTOCK ©

Oysters

BEST FOOD & DRINK FESTIVALS

Visit Lauderdale Food & Wine Festival (p176) Beat the winter doldrums in January with poolside barbecue battles, cooking demonstrations and cocktail competitions.

Isle of Eight Flags Shrimp Festival (p326) In May, Fernandina Beach celebrates its favorite crustacean with food stalls, arts and crafts, live music and a parade.

Marathon Seafood Festival (p138) This two-day March festival features fresh-off-the-boat seafood, plus music and rides.

Florida Seafood Festival (p402) Apalachicola is the place to be in November for oyster eating, a parade and a 3.1-mile run.

Orlando Whiskey Festival (p208) Get your fill of single malt whiskeys, food and cigars in March.

Lions Seafood Festival (p300) In March St Augustine holds a seafood feast alongside kids' rides and a craft fair.

Another Cuban treat is *guarapo* or fresh-squeezed sugarcane juice. Cuban snack bars serve the greenish liquid straight or poured over crushed ice, and it's essential to an authentic mojito. It also sometimes finds its way into *batidos*, a milky, refreshing Latin American fruit smoothie.

Southern Cooking

The further north you travel in Florida, the more Southern the cooking gets. This is the sort of cuisine that makes up in fat what it may lack in refinement. 'Meat and three' is Southern restaurant lingo for a main meat – like fried chicken, catfish, barbecued ribs, chicken-fried steak or even chitlins (hog's intestines) – and three sides: perhaps some combination of hush puppies (small deep-fried maize cakes), cheese grits (a sort of cornmeal polenta), cornbread, coleslaw, mashed potatoes, black-eyed peas, fried green tomatoes, collard greens or buttery corn. End with pecan pie, and that's living. Po' boys are Southern hoagies (long rolls filled with meat or seafood – fried nuggets of goodness).

Barbecue in the American South is all about the smoke. In fact, open flames are anathema to true American barbecue, which refers to a slow cooking process that involves smoke, smoke, more smoke, spices (sometimes), vinegar (maybe) and another dash of smoke.

Cracker cooking is Florida's rough-and-tumble variation on Southern cuisine, but with more reptiles and amphibians. And you'll find a good deal of Cajun and Creole as well, which mix in spicy gumbos and bisques from Louisiana's nearby swamps.

These days, Southern food isn't confined to North Florida. Fancy variations on the theme – haute Southern, if you will – are all the rage from Jacksonville to Key West.

Floribbean Cuisine

'Floribbean' cooking refers to Florida's tantalizing gourmet mélange of just-caught seafood, tropical fruits and eye-watering peppers, all dressed up with some combination of Nicaraguan, Salvadoran, Caribbean, Haitian, Cajun, Cuban and even Southern influences. Some call it 'fusion,' 'Nuevo Latino,' 'New World,' 'nouvelle Floridian' or 'palm-tree cuisine,' and it can refer to anything from a ceviche of lime, conch, sweet peppers and Scotch bonnets to grilled grouper with mango, *adobo* and fried plantains.

LIBATIONS

As elsewhere in the US, craft cocktails are all the rage in Florida, though you'll also find plenty of places devoted to simple classics popularized by the likes of Ernest Hemingway and Jimmy Buffett.

The **mojito** may belong to the world now, but we still think some of the best ones to be had are mixed in Miami, where the herbaceous-yet-sweet collision of mint, sugar and rum just tastes better (ideally sipped while watching the sun set over the skyline or beach).

The **Cuba libre** – basically rum, cola and lime – is another Cuban invention that became a brand name due to its popularity in the Southern United States. Trivia fact: the cocktail may have been the first mixed drink to incorporate cola. While it was named during the Cuban independence struggle of the early 20th century, the name took on another meaning for the state's Cuban diaspora during the Castro years.

The **rum runner** was actually invented in the state of Florida, supposedly at the Holiday Isle Tiki Bar in Islamorada in the Florida Keys. As these sagas so often go, a bartender was told to find a marketable way of ridding the bar of some excess inventory. Rum, grenadine, brandy and banana liqueur were mixed together, and a sugary legend was born.

As for Hemingway, he favored **piña coladas**, lots of them. Jimmy Buffett memorialized the margarita – now every beach bar along the peninsula claims to make the 'best.'

Margaritas, Ocean Drive, Miami (p60)

Local Specialties

Local favorites vary from region to region, though you're never far from a seafood feast.

Seafood

Peel-and-eat shrimp A decidedly old-school Florida treat, served boiled and pink in their shells; there's always cocktail sauce nearby.
Conch fritters Popular in the Keys, this giant sea snail is battered and fried; a great late-afternoon snack.
Stone crabs Only one claw is taken from a stone crab – the rest is tossed back into the sea (the claw regrows in 12 to 18 months; crabs plucked again are called 'retreads').

Sweet Treats

Key lime pie A custard of key lime juice, sweetened condensed milk and egg yolks in a cracker crust, topped with meringue.

Dare to Try

Boiled peanuts In rural North Florida, green or immature peanuts are boiled until mushy, and sometimes spiced up with Cajun or other seasonings.
Alligator tail Alligator tastes like a cross between fish and pork. It's healthier than chicken, with as much protein but half the fat, fewer calories and less cholesterol.

Alligator tail

Cracker cooking This being Florida, they don't stop at gators. Cracker cooking also celebrates smoked eel and fried snake.
Frogs legs Those who know say the 'best' legs come from the Everglades; imported ones are smaller and less flavorsome.
Swamp cabbage Heart of palm, or 'swamp cabbage,' has a delicate, sweet crunch. Try it if you can find it served fresh.

MEALS OF A LIFETIME

Fat Snook (p282) A seafood-centric restaurant in Cocoa Beach with a small, beautifully executed menu and heavenly desserts.

Casa Sensei (p175) Latin America crashes into Asia in the boldly imaginative dishes served at this elegant spot in Fort Lauderdale.

Enriqueta's (p89) Old-school spot in Miami serving outstanding daily specials like oxtail stew and seafood paella.

Blue Heaven (p161) Tuck into spiny lobster followed by key lime pie in a delightful backyard setting in Key West.

Sandbar (p366) Watch the sunset over the beach while eating the fresh catch of the day at this classic on Anna Maria Island.

THE YEAR IN FOOD

SPRING

Farmers markets are overflowing from spring up until the summer heat arrives. Blueberries, cantaloupe, grapefruit and oranges are all part of the largesse. Further north, seek out field peas, a Southern favorite and traditional delicacy.

SUMMER

Indulge in the hot summer season's countless tropical temptations, including mangoes, papaya, passion fruit, lychees and dragon fruit. Fishing is also at its best, with outstanding fresh catches of the day on restaurant menus.

FALL

Forget pumpkins and apple cider. In Florida fall is the season of zucchini, kale, eggplants and artisan lettuces. In mid-October stone-crab season arrives, with Floridians feasting on the delectable crustacean until about mid-May.

WINTER

The sweet Key West pink shrimp is available from November through June. It's strawberry season in the south; places like Knaus Berry Farm near the Everglades offer pick-your-own strawberries from late December to early April.

FINE ART PHOTOS/SHUTTERSTOCK ©

Sea turtle, Florida Keys (p140)

THE OUTDOORS

The only state that borders both the Atlantic and Gulf coasts, Florida is an adventurer's playground with world-class aquatic activities, as well as hiking and cycling.

Florida has been a top destination for outdoor lovers for over a century. Hundreds of miles of sandy beaches, wildlife-rich wetlands and verdant subtropical forests form the backdrop to days of adventures. Fronting two major bodies of water, Florida has stellar kayaking, snorkeling, fishing and surfing options. On land, you can take to scenic paths on foot and by bike, or plot a multiday trek on the 1500-mile Florida National Scenic Trail. There are plenty of less common adventures, too, from caving to skydiving.

Snorkeling & Diving

Florida has the continent's largest coral-reef system. The two best spots are John Pennekamp Coral Reef State Park in Key Largo and Biscayne National Park south of Miami, at the tip of the Florida mainland. Biscayne is actually the only national park in the US park service system to exist primarily under the waves – 95% of it is underwater. Further along the Keys, you won't be disappointed at Bahia Honda State Park or Key West.

Wreck diving in Florida is equally epic, and some are even accessible to snorkelers. So many Spanish galleons sank off the Emerald Coast, near Panama City Beach, that it's dubbed the 'Wreck Capital of the South.' Biscayne National Park also has an impressive maritime heritage trail below the waves.

Named for its sea turtles, the Dry Tortugas are well worth the effort to reach them, as their pristine waters offer fine snorkeling.

Alternative Adventures

HORSEBACK RIDING
Lazy H Ranch leads scenic trail rides along lake and forest in **Kissimmee Run** (p268).

DUSK PADDLING
Paddle **Indian River Lagoon** (p279) at dusk to glimpse sea grass lit by a bioluminescent glow.

SLOUGH SLOGGING
Immerse yourself in the **Everglades** (p123) on a guided walk into a cypress dome.

FAMILY ADVENTURES

Learn about the resident dolphins off **Marco Island** (p119) on a naturalist-focused boat tour.

Sign up for surfing lessons with a local outfitter on **Cocoa Beach** (p282), a great spot for beginners with its sandy bottom and a variety of waves.

See marine life glide below your feet on a glass-bottom-boat tour or get closer while snorkeling in **John Pennekamp Coral Reef State Park** (p141).

Spot wildlife along boardwalks off Main Park Rd in the Everglades, then take a boat excursion at **Flamingo** (p125).

Kayak a crystal-clear river then catch a mermaid show in the undersea theater at **Weeki Wachee Springs** (p344).

Go for a scenic bike ride along the 18.5-mile Timpoochee Trail that winds past pretty scenery in the **Panhandle** (p396).

Kayaking & Canoeing

Canoeing and kayaking are two brilliant ways to explore this watery state. The 207-mile Suwannee River is quintessential Florida. A muddy ribbon ideal for multiday trips, decorated with 60 clear blue springs, it meanders from Georgia's Okefenokee Swamp to the Gulf of Mexico.

Other unforgettable rivers include: Loxahatchee River in the Jonathan Dickinson State Park; Orlando's Wekiwa River in the Wekiwa Springs State Park; and the Tampa region's placid Hillsborough River.

The Everglades National Park has both saltwater and freshwater paddles, including memorable forays through mangrove tunnels in Nine Mile Pond. The nearby Ten Thousand Islands offer more wilderness adventures.

Other great spots for a paddle include Miami's Bill Baggs Cape Florida State Park, Little Talbot Island, Econfina Creek, and the Indian River Lagoon near Vero Beach.

BEST SPOTS

For the best outdoor spots and routes, see the map on p46.

FRANCISCO BLANCO/SHUTTERSTOCK ©

Kayaking, Nine Mile Pond (p125)

Hiking

The state's hiking trails can be challenging because of the weather and, in the Everglades, trail conditions when you stray from the boardwalk.

South Florida swamps tend to favor 1-mile boardwalk trails; these are excellent and almost always wheelchair accessible. But they can only take you so far. In the Everglades, you can also embark on 'wet walks,' which are wading trips deep into the blackwater heart of the swamps.

The Florida National Scenic Trail runs north from the swamps of Big Cypress National Preserve, around Lake Okeechobee, through the Ocala National Forest and then west to the Gulf Islands National Seashore near Pensacola.

Other prime areas for hiking include the pine flatwoods and cypress stands of Jonathan Dickinson State Park and the maritime hammock of Weedon Island Preserve.

SKY DIVING
Feel the rush as you leap from a plane at **World Skydiving Center** (p322).

ART DIVING
Check out the undersea artwork on a scuba dive at **Underwater Museum of Art** (p396).

ZIPLINING
Take a treetop walk, then glide over the canopy on ziplines at **Jungle Island** (p75).

GHOSTBUSTING
Look for signs of the supernatural on a nighttime ghost walk in **St Augustine** (p307).

National Parks

1. Everglades National Park (p112)
2. Dry Tortugas National Park (p157)
3. Biscayne National Park (p131)
4. Gulf Islands National Seashore (p388)
5. Castillo de San Marcos National Monument (p305)
6. Fort Matanzas National Monument (p305)
7. Canaveral National Seashore (p279)
8. Big Cypress National Preserve (p115)

Hiking

1. Everglades National Park (p114)
2. Jonathan Dickinson State Park (p193)
3. Hillsborough River State Park (p346)
4. Big Cypress National Preserve (p115)
5. Pelican Island National Wildlife Refuge (p203)
6. Corkscrew Swamp Sanctuary (p375)
7. Wekiwa Springs State Park (p268)

Snorkeling/Diving

1. John Pennekamp Coral Reef State Park (p141)
2. Biscayne National Park (p133)
3. Florida Panhandle Shipwreck Trail (p386)
4. Dry Tortugas National Park (p157)
5. Looe Key (p155)
6. Lauderdale-by-the Sea (p183)
7. Robbie's Marina (p144)

ACTION AREAS

Where to find Florida's best outdoor activities.

Surfing

1. Cocoa Beach (p282)
2. Jacksonville (p317)
3. Jupiter (p194)
4. St Augustine Beach (p306)
5. Jetty Park (p287)
6. Satellite Beach (p293)

Kayaking/Canoeing

1. Everglades National Park (p125)
2. Ten Thousand Islands (p118)
3. Biscayne National Park (p132)
4. Indian River (p200)
5. Weeki Wachee Springs State Park (p344)
6. Crystal River National Wildlife Refuge (p346)
7. Turtle Beach (p365)

GEORGIA
0 200 km
0 100 miles
Fernandina Beach
Amelia Island
Jacksonville
Lake City
St Johns River
St Augustine
Alachua
Cross City
Suwannee River
Gainesville
Palatka
Suwannee
Ocala National Forest
Ocala
Cedar Key
Daytona Beach
Crystal River
Homosassa Springs
Orlando
Titusville
Kissimmee
Cocoa Beach
Florida's Turnpike (toll)
Tampa
Lakeland
Melbourne
St Pete Beach
St Petersburg
Kissimmee River
Bradenton
Sebring
Fort Pierce
Sarasota
ATLANTIC OCEAN
Okeechobee
Venice
Lake Okeechobee
Charlotte Harbour
Palm Beach
Fort Myers
Sanibel Island
Delray Beach
Boca Raton
THE BAHAMAS
Naples
Alligator Alley
Big Cypress National Preserve
Fort Lauderdale
Miami Beach
Miami
Everglades National Park
Biscayne National Park
Florida City
Straits of Florida
Flamingo
Key Largo
Florida Bay
Islamorada
Dry Tortugas National Park
Marathon
Key West
Florida Keys

FLORIDA

THE GUIDE

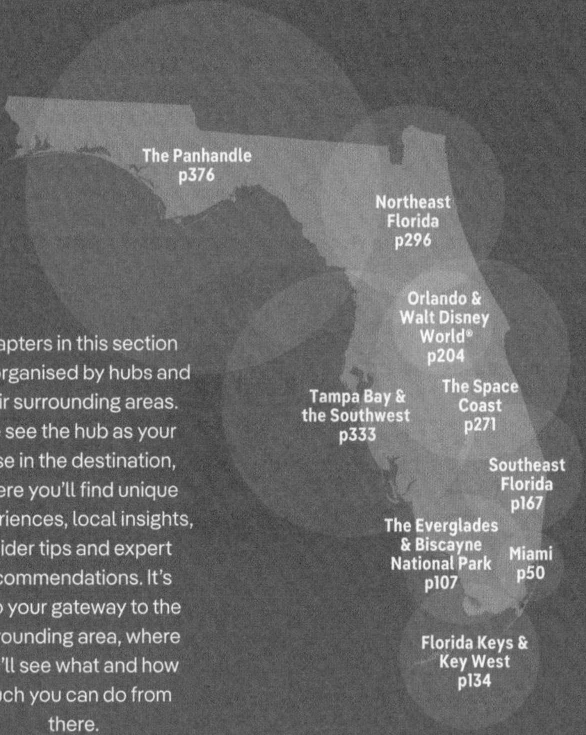

Chapters in this section are organised by hubs and their surrounding areas. We see the hub as your base in the destination, where you'll find unique experiences, local insights, insider tips and expert recommendations. It's also your gateway to the surrounding area, where you'll see what and how much you can do from there.

Cape Florida Lighthouse (p104)

MIAMI

LATIN AMERICA AND THE CARIBBEAN COLLIDE

Miami defines South Florida but stands apart from it, encompassing demographic enclaves from across the world, lashed together by the arts, creativity and sensory overload.

Miami straddles the Caribbean, North America and Latin America like nowhere else, and showcases its diversity via a constant display of hedonism and a deep appreciation of beautiful things (and people!). Art deco architecture and graffiti murals are the backdrop, Cuban coffee is the fuel, and reggaetón and clacking dominoes are the soundtrack to a city tinged by pink sunsets on a silver skyline and humid air whispering off Biscayne Bay.

Creativity is one of the great hallmarks of this city. From art and design to global cuisine, Miami remains ever on the search for bold new ideas. You'll find inventive chefs blending Eastern, Western, Southern American and South American cooking styles next to open-air galleries where museum-quality artwork covers once-derelict warehouses. The one constant in Miami is its uncanny ability to astonish.

Few American cities are as blessed as Miami when it comes to natural beauty. White sandy beaches are lapped by teal waters – perfect for sunrise strolls along peaceful stretches of Mid-Beach or scenic paddles in search of manatees off Virginia Key. You can look for colorful bird species while walking the trails of Oleta River State Park, or go to any of the tropical gardens across the city. With year-round sunshine, and a love for celebration, the open air is also where Miami's biggest parties unfold – whether at massive music and dance festivals or the neighborhood fiestas that pack Miami's calendar.

Even if there was no sand, Miami would still entice. The gorgeous 1930s hotels lining Ocean Dr are part of the world's greatest collection of art deco buildings. Tropical motifs, whimsical nautical elements and those iconic pastel shades create a cinematic backdrop for exploring the streets of Miami Beach.

When evening takes hold and the brilliant colors of a South Florida sunset fill the sky, that's when the best part of the day begins for Miami's party people. By moonlight, all the magic of the city unfolds, but while there's plenty of bling on display, Miami has something for all, from backyard bars full of indie rockers to hidden dens of debauchery concealed behind neon-lit taco stands.

THE MAIN AREAS

MIAMI BEACH
Sun, sand, clubs and deco delights. p56

DOWNTOWN & BRICKELL
Museums, a monorail and glittering skylines. p68

LITTLE HAVANA
Murals, bars, shops and cafes. p78

DMITRY TKACHENKO PHOTO/SHUTTERSTOCK ©

Right: Bay watch tower, South Beach (p60); above: Ocean Drive (p60)

Find Your Way

Miami and Miami Beach are two separate cities, connected by a series of causeways. Otherwise, Greater Miami sprawls north and south, connected by highways and, inevitably, lots of traffic. The waterways and major highways that run through Miami are often the boundaries and borders of its neighborhoods.

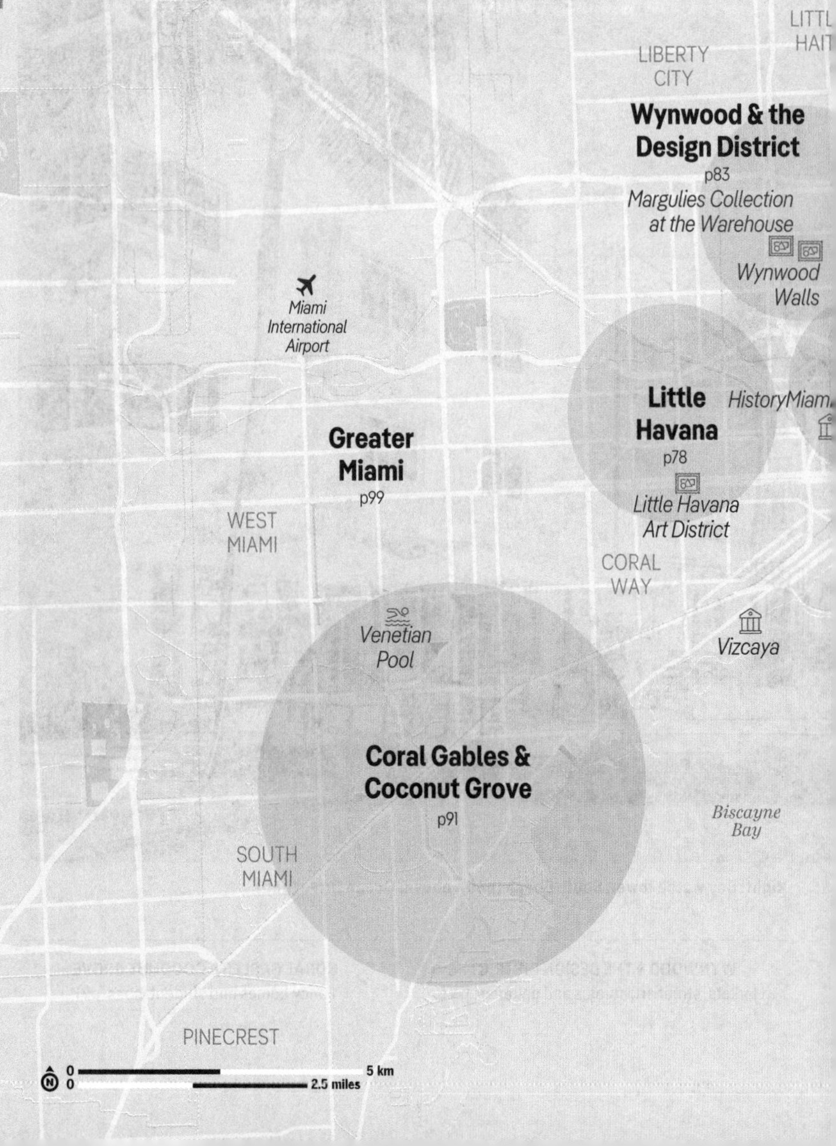

ATLANTIC OCEAN

NORMANDY SHORES

NORTH BEACH

UPPER EAST SIDE

NORTH BAY VILLAGE

Miami Beach
p56

Patricia & Phillip Frost Museum of Science

Pérez Art Museum Miami

Miami Children's Museum

South Beach

Freedom Tower

Art Deco Historic District

Bayfront Park

Downtown & Brickell
p68

Fisher Island

VIRGINIA KEY

Crandon Park

KEY BISCAYNE

Bill Baggs Cape Florida State Park

FROM THE AIRPORT

You can access the usual ride apps from Miami International Airport at 10 locations on Arrivals Level 1. Otherwise, metered taxis are available at the ground level, outside baggage claim. Fares are metered – it's around $35 to $50 to Miami Beach and $25 to Downtown.

CAR & MOTORCYCLE

The most important highway is I-95, which ends at US Hwy 1 south of Downtown. If you're crossing town from around 7am to 9am or 3pm to 6pm, allow at least an extra hour (really) of travel time, especially if going to Miami Beach.

BICYCLE

Citi Bike is a bike-share program where you can borrow a bike from scores of kiosks spread around Miami and Miami Beach. Miami is flat, but traffic can be horrendous. A variety of scooters are available to rent via third-party apps throughout Greater Miami.

BUS

Miami's local bus system is called Metrobus. It can get you to most places, but it won't get you there quickly. Each bus route has a different schedule, and routes generally run from about 5am to 11pm, though some are 24 hours.

Plan Your Days

Start your day with a *cafecito* (strong, sweet Cuban espresso) and a *pastelito* (puff pastry) – the coffee alone ought to keep you awake and exploring for the next 48 hours!

LAZYLLAMA/SHUTTERSTOCK ©

Beachfront cycling, Ocean Drive (p60)

Day 1

- Start with a morning stroll along South Beach, then stop in the **Art Deco Museum** (p61) for an overview of this iconic architectural district. Wander Ocean Dr and see these deco beauties in person, or go on a guided tour with the **Miami Design Preservation League** (p61). For more deco insight, visit the **Wolfsonian-FIU** (p56).

- Have lunch at the **11th Street Diner** (p62), then take a stroll along Lincoln Rd, a pedestrian boulevard packed with shops, restaurants, models, people gawking at models etc.

- For dinner, head to **Stubborn Seed** (p65) for New American cuisine, before admiring the Spanish architecture along **Española Way** (p58). Finish with drinks at **Sweet Liberty** (p65).

You'll Also Want to...

In Miami, you have all South Florida at your fingertips – the Magic City is the beating urban heart of this wet, wild region.

CATCH A FESTIVAL

They seriously kick off at least once a month, and range from **Jewish film showcases** to massive neighborhood **street parties**.

GO BACK TO SCHOOL

The **University of Miami** (p91) campus is a mix of traditional 'Great Lawn' college campus and Coral Gables tropical style.

APPRECIATE THE ARTS

The **Museum of Contemporary Art North Miami** (p104) is notable for its fine exhibits and thoughtful curation.

YES MARKET MEDIA/SHUTTERSTOCK ©, YES MARKET MEDIA/SHUTTERSTOCK ©, JEAN BAPTISTE LACROIX/GETTY IMAGES ©

Day 2

- Start the day with espresso at **Enriqueta's** (p89) on the edge of Wynwood. Check out the murals at **Wynwood Walls** (p85) and explore the **Margulies Collection at the Warehouse** (p85). Head to the **Museum of Graffiti** (p84) to contextualize the street art.

- Spend the afternoon exploring **Pérez Art Museum Miami** (p71), which has some of the city's best contemporary art. Afterwards, head to **Bayfront Park** (p71), check out the **Noguchi sculptures** (p85) and join locals for a picnic by the sea.

- Head back up to Wynwood for dinner at Asian food hall **1 800 Lucky** (p89), then down some drinks at the **Sylvester** (p88) or **Wynwood Marketplace** (p86).

Day 3

- Spend the morning wandering the European gardens and art- and antique-filled interiors of **Vizcaya** (p93). Next, go over to Coconut Grove for shopping. **Barnacle Historic State Park** (p91) has attractive views.

- Now head to Little Havana, stopping for lunch at **Xixon** (p82) – you can't go wrong. Check out the domino action in **Máximo Gómez Park** (p79). Stop for a fresh-squeezed pick-me-up juice at **Los Pinareños Frutería** (p82).

- Have a contemporary Cuban dinner at **Doce Provisions** (p82), then catch some live music at **Cafe La Trova** (p81), where you can hear Latin jazz, flamenco, Cuban son and other musical styles.

EXPLORE THE OUTDOORS
Head to the **ROAM Oleta River Outdoor Center** (p65), rent a kayak or paddleboard, and explore some jungly waterways.

HIT THE BEACH
Well, of course you were gonna do this, but few tourists make it to **Crandon Park** (p102), out on Key Biscayne.

GO BIG IN LITTLE HAITI
The **Sounds of Little Haiti** (p101) brings Haitian bands to crowds every third Friday evening.

RUN TO THE RUBELL
It's a little off the radar even for locals, but the **Rubell Museum** (p74) is a gem of an arts institution.

MIAMI BEACH

SUN, SAND AND SHOWING OFF

When outsiders imagine 'Miami,' they're often thinking of the separate city of Miami Beach, specifically the neighborhood of South Beach. 'SoBe' ticks a lot of South Florida boxes – sparkling beach, beautiful art deco architecture, top-end boutiques, and buzzing bars and restaurants. Still, there's more to this district than velvet ropes and high-priced lodging. You'll find some great down-to-earth bars, good eating and cool museums, all set against a backdrop of relentlessly attractive pastel deco architecture.

The typical South Beach experience is anything but. Early risers can run on the beach, breakfast at a vegan spot, do yoga in the afternoon, followed by a healthy meal and a concert at the New World Center. Night owls can start with coffee and Bloody Marys at noon, laze on the beach, shop on Lincoln Rd, dine in Sunset Harbour, then hit the late-night lounges, rooftop bars and dance clubs.

TOP TIP

South Beach caters to a lot of tastes. It can be both chaotic and hedonistic (Ocean Dr around 9th St) and local and sedate (SoFi – or the blocks south of 5th St). All that said, 'sedate' is a relative term, and you can burn the candle at both ends anywhere out here.

JAMES KIRKIKIS/SHUTTERSTOCK ©

The Carlyle, Art Deco Historic District

The Art Deco Historic District

TIMELESS TROPICAL DESIGN

The world-famous art deco district of Miami Beach is pure exuberance: an architecture of bold lines, whimsical tropical motifs and a color palette that evokes all the beauty of the palm glades and flowering prairies that once carpeted South Florida. Among the 800 deco buildings listed on the National Register of Historic Buildings, each design is different and strolling among these restored beauties from a bygone era is utterly enthralling. Classic art deco structures are positioned beautifully between 11th and 14th Sts – each bursting with individuality.

Wolfsonian-FIU

INTERIOR ART AS MUSEUM MARVEL

Visit this excellent design museum early in your stay to put the aesthetics of Miami Beach into context. It's one thing to see how wealth, leisure and the pursuit of beauty manifest, but it's another to understand the roots and shadings of local movements. By chronicling the interior evolution of everyday life, focusing on the time period encompassed by the late 19th century to the end of WWII, the Wolfsonian reveals how these trends manifested architecturally in SoBe's exterior deco. It's worth nothing the Wolfsonian has its own memorable architectural features, such as Gothic-futurist angles and a lion-head-studded grand elevator.

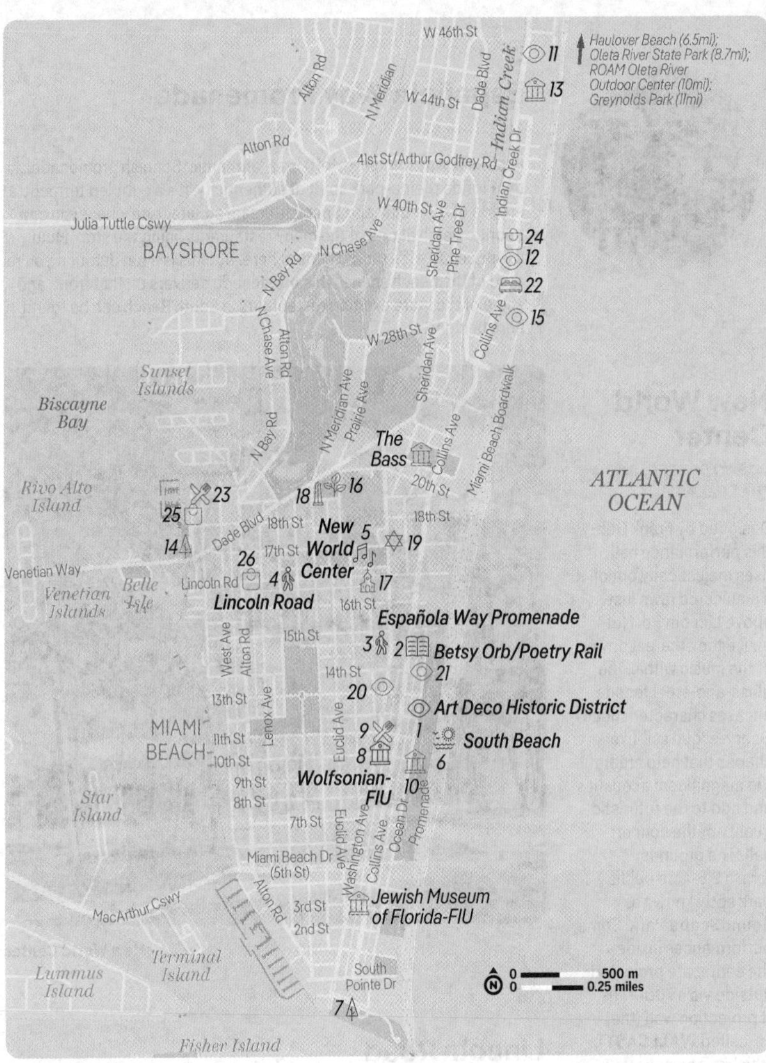

HIGHLIGHTS
1 Art Deco Historic District
2 Betsy Orb/Poetry Rail
3 Española Way Promenade
4 Lincoln Road
5 New World Center
6 South Beach
7 South Pointe Park
8 Wolfsonian-FIU

SIGHTS
9 11th Street Diner
10 Art Deco Museum
see 1 Cardozo
see 1 Carlyle
11 Eden Roc
12 Faena Forum
13 Fontainebleau
see 1 Leslie Hotel
14 Maurice Gibb Memorial Park
15 Miami Beach Boardwalk
16 Miami Beach Botanical Garden
17 Miami Beach Community Church
18 Miami Beach Holocaust Memorial
19 Temple Emanu-El
20 US Post Office
21 Winter Haven Hotel

SLEEPING
22 Faena Hotel

DRINKING
23 True Loaf

SHOPPING
24 Faena Bazaar
25 Sunset Clothing Co
26 Taschen

Española Way Promenade

AN ANDULICIAN AMBLE (SORTA)

Española Way (pictured, left) is an 'authentic' Spanish promenade...in the Florida theme-park spirit of authenticity. It's a cobbled terracotta arcade of rose-pink and Spanish-cream architecture where you can people-watch at one of the many restaurants lining the strip. Mind the price tag – it's tourist central here. But this is a fun detour if you're tired of the beach scene. This promenade delivers on that front, and some of the more exciting restaurants in South Beach can be found here besides.

New World Center

OCEAN BREEZE, SHOWS THAT PLEASE

Designed by Frank Gehry, this performance hall rises majestically out of a manicured lawn just above Lincoln Rd. Not unlike the ethereal power of the music within, the glass-and-steel facade encases characteristically Gehry-esque sail-like shapes that help create the magnificent acoustics and add to the futuristic quality of the concert hall. The grounds form a 2.5-acre public park aptly known as **SoundScape Park**. Some performances inside the center are projected outside via a 7000-sq-ft projection wall (the so-called **WALLCAST**), which might make you feel like you're in the classiest open-air theater on the planet. Reserve ahead for a 45-minute guided tour.

New World Center

Lincoln Road

SHOP, STRUT, REPEAT

Lincoln Road Mall, an outdoor pedestrian thoroughfare between Alton Rd and Washington Ave in South Beach, is all about seeing and being seen; there are times when Lincoln feels less like a road and more like a runway. Carl Fisher, the father of Miami Beach, envisioned the road as a Fifth Ave of the South. Morris Lapidus, one of the founders of the loopy, neo-baroque Miami Beach style, designed much of the mall, including shady overhangs, waterfall structures and traffic barriers that look like the marbles a giant might play with. The west side of the road is anchored by 1111 Lincoln Rd, a geometric pastiche of sharp angles, winding corridors and incongruous corners, like something Pythagoras would dream up after a long night out.

South Pointe Park

FAMILY FRIENDLY, EPIC VIEWS

The very southern tip of Miami Beach has been converted into a lovely park, replete with manicured grass for lounging, a popular pier, warm scrubbed-stone walkways, as well as a tiny water park for the kids. It also has a restaurant and refreshment stand for all the folks – families are strongly represented – who want to enjoy the great weather and teal ocean views minus the South Beach strutting. The vistas here are pretty wonderful; follow a 20ft-wide promenade and see Fisher Island and Miami's skyline.

South Pointe Park

The Betsy Orb/Poetry Rail

LIT LOVERS LOOK UP

Two excellent examples of public art grace Española Way where it runs by the ever-stylish Betsy Hotel. **The Orb** (pictured, left) is just that: a sort of giant white beach ball-ish sculpture squashed into an alley between Ocean Dr and Collins Ave. Check with the hotel to see when video and/or photography exhibitions get projected onto the Orb's surface. Steps away is the **Poetry Rail**, a metal wall etched with the words of 12 poets, including Adrian Castro, Richard Blanco and Gerald Stern, paying tribute to Miami's multicultural population and unique geography. The Betsy itself frequently hosts readings and provides residencies to visiting writers and poets.

Jewish Museum of Florida-FIU

REUBENS Y ROPA VIEJA

Housed in a 1936 Orthodox synagogue that served Miami's first congregation, this small museum chronicles the outsized contribution Jews have made to the state of Florida, especially that slice of the Sunshine State where the museum is located. After all, it could be said that while Cubans made Miami, Jews made Miami Beach, both physically and culturally, from the first deco-hotel developers to the preservationists of the late 20th century who fought hard for those earlier aesthetics. And yet, there were times when Jews were barred from the American Riviera they carved out of the sand, and this museum tells that story, along with some amusing anecdotes (like seashell Purim dresses). There are also walking tours that take in famous local Jewish landmarks.

Ocean Drive

EPIC NEON NIGHTS

Ocean Dr is the great cruising strip of Miami – an endless parade of classic cars, celebrities pretending to be tourists, tourists who want to play celebrity, beautiful people, ugly people, people people and the best ribbon of art deco preservation on the beach. Some of the classic buildings you'll find out here include the **Carlyle** (1250 Ocean Dr), where *The Birdcage* was filmed; the next-door **Cardozo**, one of the first hotels saved by the **Miami Design Preservation League**; and the **Colony** (736 Ocean Dr), the first hotel in Miami, and perhaps America, to incorporate its sign (a zig-zaggy neon wonder) into its overall design.

Ocean Drive

The Bass

ART, AT AN ANGLE

The best art museum in Miami Beach (pictured, left) has a playfully futuristic facade, a crisp interplay of lines and a bright, white-walled space – like an Orthodox church on a space-age Greek isle. All designed, by the way, in 1930 by Russell Pancoast (grandson of John A Collins, who lent his name to Collins Ave, Miami Beach's main strip). The collection isn't shabby either: art from around the world is represented, and there is a focus on cutting-edge contemporary pieces. This is, after all, the city that gave the Western Hemisphere the contemporary-arts festival that is Art Basel, and the interior of the Bass is mainly filled with pieces that are in the Basel wheelhouse. All that said, it's hard to predict what you'll find here; the galleries showcase temporary exhibitions, so two spaced-out visits are seldom the same.

The museum forms one point of the **Collins Park Cultural Center** triangle, which also includes the three-story **Miami City Ballet** and the lovingly inviting **Miami Beach Regional Library**, which is what the Bass was before it became an art museum.

South Beach

THE SUN, THE SAND, THE LEGEND

When most people think of Miami Beach, they envision South Beach (SoBe), a label that applies to both the beach itself and the neighborhood that adjoins it. The latter includes clubs, bars, restaurants and a distinctive veneer of art deco architecture. The beach is a sweep of golden sands, dotted with colorful deco-style lifeguard stations and countless souls uploading panoramic shots to their social-media platforms. The shore gets crowded in high season (December to March) and most weekends. You can escape the masses by avoiding the densest parts of the beach (5th to 15th Sts) – heading south of 5th St, to the area known as SoFi, is a good means of eluding the crowds.

BYYALET/SHUTTERSTOCK ©

Art Deco Museum

MORE IN MIAMI BEACH

An Art Deco Amble

HISTORY AND HOTELS

Start at the **Art Deco Museum**, at the corner of Ocean Dr and 10th St (named Barbara Capitman Way here, after the Miami Design Preservation League's founder). Step in for an exhibit on art deco style, then head out and north along Ocean Dr, between 12th and 14th Sts, where you'll see three examples of deco hotels: the **Leslie**, a boxy shape with eyebrows (cantilevered sunshades) wrapped around the side of the building; the **Carlyle**, boasting modernistic styling; and the graceful **Cardozo**, built by Henry Hohauser, owned by Gloria Estefan and featuring sleek, rounded edges.

At 14th St take a peek inside the **Winter Haven Hotel** to see its fabulous terrazzo floors, made of stone chips set in mortar that's polished when dry. Turn left and head down 14th St to Washington Ave and the **US Post Office**, at 13th St. It's a curvy block of white deco in the stripped classical style. Step

WHICH BEACH?

Maps refer to the area above South Beach as Miami Beach, but locals use the jargon Mid-Beach (around the 40th streets) and North Beach (70th St and above). Communities like Surfside, Bal Harbour and Sunny Isles are further north and can be included in spirit. Indian Creek waterway separates the luxury hotels and high-rise condos from the residential districts in the west. Keep in mind that the separate city of North Miami Beach (as opposed to the region of Northern Miami Beach) is not, technically, on the mainland. Confused? So are most residents.

WHERE TO SLEEP IN MIAMI BEACH

Aqua Hotel
Crisp rooms embrace marine-like hues, with wood floors and a few touches of artwork. **$**

Cavalier South Beach
The exterior plays with tropical and marine themes. Inside are exposed-brick walls, plus marble bathrooms. **$$**

Hotel Shelley
This deco beauty has a lively lobby-lounge and affordably stylish (if slightly small) rooms. **$$**

I LIVE HERE: WHERE TO SOAK UP SOUTH BEACH

Neysa King is the author of two poetry chapbooks and co-founder and executive director of Miami Poetry Club. Follow her *@neysaking* and *@miamipoetryclub*.

South Pointe Park at Sunset
Every day at the southernmost tip of Miami Beach is a block party with music, yoga, and dancing. Bring a blanket and a bottle of wine and watch the skies change.

La Playa
A convenience store and food counter where they cook up fried fish, plantains and empanadas with good tunes playing loud over the PA.

Stubborn Seed
Recklessly welcoming to locals and visitors wanting to experience exquisite food and cocktails south of Fifth St (make sure you get their house negroni).

Miami Beach Holocaust Memorial

inside to admire the wall mural, domed ceiling and marble stamp tables. Eat at the **11th Street Diner**, a gleaming aluminum Pullman car that was imported in 1992 from Wilkes-Barre, PA. After your meal, walk half a block east from there to the imposing **Wolfsonian-FIU**, an excellent design museum, formerly the Washington Storage Company. Wealthy snowbirds of the '30s stashed their pricey belongings here before heading back up north.

Grim History: Miami Beach Holocaust Memorial

SOMBER SPACE FOR GRIEF, REFLECTION

Even for a Holocaust piece, this memorial is particularly powerful. With more than 100 sculptures, its centerpiece is the **Sculpture of Love and Anguish**, an enormous, oxidized bronze arm that bears an Auschwitz tattoo number – chosen because it was never issued at the camp. Terrified camp prisoners scale the sides of the arm, trying to pass their loved ones, including children, to safety only to see

WHERE TO SLEEP IN MIAMI BEACH

Royal Palm
Even the fish tank feels deco at South Beach's most striking example of the building-as-cruise-liner theme. **$$$**

Delano
Rooms are almost painfully white: all long, smooth lines, reflective surfaces and modern, luxurious amenities. **$$$**

Setai
The stunning interior mixes elements of Southeast Asian temple architecture and contemporary luxury. **$$$**

them later massacred, while below lie figures of all ages in various poses of suffering.

Around the perimeter of the memorial are dozens of panels, which detail the grim history that led to the worst genocide of the 20th century; the intent is to show the Holocaust did not simply happen, but was the end product of millennia of structural oppression and state-sponsored hatred. This is followed by names of many – but obviously nowhere near all, or even a fraction of all – who perished. The light from a Star of David is blotted by the racist label of Jude (the German word for 'Jew'), representative of the yellow star that Jews in ghettos were forced to wear. It's impossible to spend time here and not be moved.

OOLITE ARTS

Once known as ArtCenter/South Florida South Beach, this exhibition space includes dozens of artists' studios, many of which are open to the public. Oolite also offers a slate of sought-after residencies, which are reserved for artists who do not have major exposure, making this is a good place to spot up-and-coming talent. Monthly rotating exhibitions keep the presentation fresh and pretty avant-garde. Along with the art you can view, there is a printshop on hand, open by appointment (email printshop@oolitearts.org), and the facility hosts virtual and in-person arts classes.

Beaches Past South Beach

BEACH, PLEASE

South Beach is the section of sand most people think of when they hear the words 'Miami Beach,' but there's far more coast to saunter along out here. Unless otherwise noted, the numbered streets here all extend off Collins Ave (A1A), which runs north and south parallel to the beach itself.

Mid-Beach encompasses the beaches from 23rd to 63rd Sts. It's not like the crowds out here stop preening and showing off – this is still model/influencer territory – but at least *some* of those influencers are past the 'post TikToks of my night at the club' phase and are moving into the 'boost reels of my growing family' end of the algorithm pool. The Mid-Beach area is attached to a lot of the area's big luxury hotels, such as the Fontainebleau and Faena. On the bay side of the beach is North Bay Rd, where you can see (well, glimpse over the walls) some of the area's largest mansions. This area includes the official **Miami Beach Boardwalk** (21st to 46th Sts), where Orthodox Jews often mix with the social-media mavens.

North Beach extends from 63rd St to 87th Tce, and the beaches here are smaller and more family friendly, although this is also where you'll find **Haulover Beach** (4.5 miles north of 71st St); the northern section of this beach park is clothing optional and has been popular with naturists since the 1990s.

Churches, Temples & Gardens

GET DIVINE ON THE BEACH

Not a ton of people would put 'Miami Beach' and 'quiet, worshipful reflection' in the same trip itinerary, let alone sentence, but guess what? There are some cool worship spaces out here.

WHERE TO EAT IN MIAMI BEACH

Taquiza
The tacos at this Mexican takeout stand have acquired a stellar reputation among Miami's street-food lovers. **$**

Pubbelly
A mix of Asian and Latin flavors, Pubbelly serves hip fusion takes on small plates. **$$**

Big Pink
Looks like a '50s sock hop and South Beach club, and does American comfort food with whimsy. **$$**

KEEPING IT KOSHER IN MIAMI BEACH

The center of gravity for American Jews is New York or Los Angeles, but you should also visit Miami Beach, specifically the area around Arthur Godfrey Rd (41st St) and Harding Ave between 91st and 96th Sts in Surfside. There's a unique cross-section of Jews here, from Northeast transplants to immigrants from former Soviet states, to native-born 'Jewbans' (descendants of Jews and Cubans).

Just as the Jewish population have shaped Miami Beach, so has the beach shaped them: you can eat *lox y arroz con moros* (salmon with rice and beans), and while the Orthodox men don yarmulkes and the women headscarves, many people have nice tans and flashy SUVs.

In rather sharp and refreshing contrast to the ubermodern structures muscling their way into the art deco design of South Beach, the **Miami Beach Community Church** puts one in mind of an old Spanish mission – elegantly understated in an area where overstatement is the general philosophy. Built in 1921, this is the oldest church sanctuary in Miami Beach, and it has a history of progressive politics, including ordaining African American men, women and recognizing same-sex marriage. Sunday worship services are at 10:30am.

A quarter mile away is the smooth dome and sleek, almost aerodynamic profile of **Temple Emanu-El**, established in 1938. The design may seem deco-esque, but it's more influenced by Byzantine and Moorish influences – although elements of deco fit that rubric too. Shabbat services are on Friday at 6pm and on Saturday at 10am.

If you need a spiritual moment absent a house of worship, head to the **Miami Beach Botanical Garden**. This lush but little-known 2.6 acres of plantings is operated by the Miami Beach Garden Conservancy, and is a veritable green haven amid the urban jungle – an oasis of palm trees, flowering hibiscus trees and glassy ponds.

Faena Fun

ARCHITECTURAL DREAMS ON MIAMI BEACH

The area of Mid-Beach from 32nd St to 36th St, known as the **Faena District** (named for an Argentine businessman and developer), is Miami Beach's answer to Wynwood on the mainland – a design-focused district where urban character grows out of the intersection of the arts and attached commercial retail. The area is anchored by the **Faena Forum**, an architectural dream that hosts performances, exhibitions, lectures and other events in a circular Rem Koolhaas–designed building.

Nearby is **Faena Hotel**, characterized by heavy use of animal-print fabrics, coral and seashell decorative touches. Each room has butler service, because this is Miami, damn it. Finally, high-end shoppers should check out **Faena Bazaar**: four floors of expensive homewares and furniture for the visitors who happen to have lots of space in their carry-on luggage.

Get Outdoors Already

NAVIGATING NORTH BEACH

If you're looking to get outdoors in that sweet Miami tropical weather, the northern stretches of Miami Beach have you covered.

WHERE TO EAT IN MIAMI BEACH

Lilikoi
Head to this laid-back, indoor-outdoor spot for healthy, mostly organic and veg-friendly dishes. **$$**

Macchialina
This buzzing, rustic-chic Italian trattoria has all the right ingredients for a terrific night out. **$$**

Chotto Matte
Peruvian-Japanese cuisine is served in a relentlessly impressive roofless space that encloses a tropical garden. **$$$**

DANIEL KORZENIEWSKI/SHUTTERSTOCK ©

Oleta River State Park

With a playground, green fields, an intact hardwood hammock, mangrove forest and views of the Oleta River, 249-acre **Greynolds Park** is a nice spot to cop some fresh air and let the kids run around.

The big outdoor outfitter around here can be found at **Oleta River State Park**. The park itself is a treat; Tequesta people were boating the Oleta River estuary as early as 500 BCE, so you're following a long tradition if you canoe or kayak in this park. At almost 1000 acres, it's the largest urban park in the state and one of the best places in Miami to escape the maddening crowds. Boat out to the local mangrove island, watch the eagles fly by or just chill on the pretension-free beach.

How to access the aforementioned mangroves and inlets? On-site **ROAM Oleta River Outdoor Center** offers both guided and self-directed adventures. If you're into the latter, the center rents out kayaks, canoes, stand-up paddleboards and mountain bikes for exploring this stretch of North Biscayne Bay.

BEST BARS OF SOUTH BEACH

Mac's Club Deuce
The oldest bar in Miami Beach, the Deuce is a seedy neighborhood dive par excellence.

Kill Your Idol
This lovable hipster spot has graffiti and shelves full of retro bric-a-brac covering the walls.

Sweet Liberty
Friendly bartenders whip up excellent cocktails amid flickering candles and a long wooden bar.

Bay Club
A great Sunset Harbour neighborhood bar with low lighting, antique wallpaper and old chandeliers.

FOR OUTDOORS LOVERS

Cross the Rickenbacker Causeway and lose yourself on the tiny island of Key Biscayne, especially **Crandon Park** (p102), where there are plenty of pathways through mangroves and nice beaches besides.

Puerto Sagua
This beloved Cuban diner has been slinging *ropa vieja* (in huge portions!) since 1962. $

Paul
Gourmet sandwiches and light pastries make for a refreshing Lincoln Rd lunch stop. $

Stubborn Seed
Won a Michelin star and a James Beard award for its adventurous haute American cuisine – book it. $$$

WORLD EROTIC ART MUSEUM (WEAM)

WEAM has a staggering collection of erotica, including sexually charged pieces by Rembrandt and Picasso, ancient sex manuals, X-rated Chinese porcelain art, explicit pre-Columbian sculptures, the stylized genitals used as a murder weapon in *A Clockwork Orange*, and an elaborate four-poster (four-phallus rather) Kama Sutra bed, with carvings depicting 138 ways to get intimate. Much of the content has been thoughtfully curated and interpreted by the Kinsey Institute, a research center dedicated to human sexuality.

The museum dates back to 2005, when Naomi Wilzig turned her personal collection of erotica into a South Beach mainstay. WEAM is located in the **Wilzig Museum Building**, which also houses a small museum for photographer George Daniell.

Fontainebleau

You can also sign up for daily paddling tours, yoga classes on stand-up paddleboards and other activities. The park is off 163rd St NE/FL 826 in Sunny Isles, about 8 miles north of North Miami Beach.

Bayfront Bounce

SOUTH BEACH'S QUIET(ISH) CORNER

Away from Ocean Dr, palm-lined promenades and a bayfront shopping enclave draw a mix of local residents and savvy travelers who are less into flash, clubs and couture, and more attracted to indie stores, galleries, outdoor cafes and bakeries, which all give this neighborhood plenty of character.

Start the day with fresh pastries at **True Loaf**. This well-regarded bakery is a breadbox-sized space where you can pick up heavenly croissants, tarts and *kouign amman* (Breton-style butter cake).

Just around the block, **Sunset Clothing Co** is a great little fashion boutique for stylish gear that won't cost a fortune (though it isn't cheap either). You'll find well-made shirts, soft cotton T-shirts, lace-up canvas shoes, nicely fitting denim

WHERE TO DRINK IN MIAMI BEACH

Abbey Brewery
The oldest brewpub in South Beach is friendly and packed with folks listening to throwback hits.

Broken Shaker
This well-equipped bar produces expert cocktails, which are mostly consumed in the beautiful, softly lit garden.

Twist
There's never a dull moment at this two-story gay club, which boasts seven different bars.

(including vintage Levi's), warm sweaters (not that you need them here) and other casual gear.

Maurice Gibb Memorial Park is a five-minute walk away. This small palm-fringed green space overlooking the water has a playground, benches and grassy areas. It's a favorite destination for dog walkers, runners, and families with kids. Against a backdrop of bobbing sailboats and the Venetian Causeway, it's worth stopping by to admire the view.

Finally, jaunt to **Taschen**, on Lincoln Rd, where an inviting well-stocked collection of art, photography, design and coffee-table books will make your home look that much smarter on your next Zoom meeting.

BEST PLACES TO SLEEP IN MIAMI BEACH

1 Hotel
Simply one of the top hotels in the USA, balancing both luxurious and ecofriendly features. $$$

Betsy Hotel
A historic gem with two wings set in either tropical Colonial style or art deco. $$$

Surfcomber
Rooms have elegant lines, in keeping with art deco aesthetics, while bursts of color keep things contemporary. $$

Millionaire's Row Revealed

BIG BRASH BUILDINGS

As you proceed north on Collins Ave, leaving the deco of South Beach for the high-rises of Mid-Beach, the condos and apartment buildings grow in grandeur and embellishment until you enter an area nicknamed Millionaire's Row. One of the brightest jewels in this crown is the **Fontainebleau**. If you've never been here in person, you may have visited cinematically – this was the setting for the classic final showdown in Brian de Palma's *Scarface*.

Well, sort of. This iconic 1954 leviathan is a brainchild of the great Miami Beach architect Morris Lapidus, but it has undergone many renovations; in some ways, it is utterly different from its original form. Then again, it undoubtedly retains a sense of overblown glamour.

The same can be said of the **Eden Roc**, the second groundbreaking resort from Morris Lapidus, a five-minute walk from the Fontainebleau. The Eden Roc has also undergone renovations, but better retains the architectural aesthetic known as MiMo (Miami Modern); while some of Lapidus' style has been eclipsed, the building is still an iconic piece of Miami Beach architecture and an exemplar of the brash beauty of Millionaire's Row. Speaking of brash, historical sidenote: this was the hangout for the 1960s Rat Pack – Sammy Davis Jr, Dean Martin, Frank Sinatra and crew.

FOR MUSEUM LOVERS

Design and aesthetics are the heart of the urban Miami Beach experience. If you want to explore the history of these movements, and see some beautiful arts and crafts, head to the **Wolfsonian-FIU** (p56).

Pool Bar at the Sagamore
Head to the back pool and sip a beer (or a nice cocktail) in the shadows.

Bodega
This popular taco stand also offers a bit of old-school glam in a sprawling drinking den.

Bob's Your Uncle
Classic cocktails, good beer, spacious seating, old games, friendly service and the chillest vibe in Miami Beach.

DOWNTOWN & BRICKELL

GLITTER AND GLASS

Downtown Miami, the city's financial and banking center, is split between old indoor shopping arcades and new condos and luxury hotels. At night, these towers are illuminated in hot pinks and cool blues, and the effect is magical. You don't need a car here – free public transport can whisk you around, and parts of Downtown (like Bayfront Park and the riverside) are well worth exploring on foot.

Construction here is a near constant, but there are still creative pockets of iconoclastic identity, and one of the city's best museums to boot. You could easily spend a few days taking in local attractions before catching a show at a performing-arts venue. You could also sample the rooftop bars, plush nightclubs and creative eateries that have sprung up to cater to waves of well-heeled condo-dwellers.

TOP TIP

Downtown Miami has leaned into the hot-pink and electric-blue aesthetics of the 1980s, and those colors, often evident in Brickell high-rises, are magic highlighted against the night sky. You can see them best driving the A1A causeway – itself swathed in neon palettes – between Downtown and Miami Beach.

FELIX MIZIOZNIKOV/SHUTTERSTOCK ©

Patricia & Philip Frost Museum of Science

Patricia & Phillip Frost Museum of Science

KID-FRIENDLY STEM-TRAVAGANZA

This Downtown museum spreads across 250,000 sq ft that includes a three-level aquarium, a 250-seat state-of-the-art planetarium, and two distinct wings that delve into the wonders of science and nature. Exhibitions range from weather phenomena to creepy crawlies, feathered dinosaurs and vital microbe displays, while Florida's fascinating Everglades and rich coral reefs play starring roles. It's as family friendly as Miami museums get, but not as explicitly aimed at younger kids as, say, the children's museum on the MacArthur Causeway.

Miami-Dade Arena

HOME OF THE HEAT

Resembling a massive spaceship that perpetually hovers at the edge of Biscayne Bay, this arena has been the home of the city's NBA franchise, the Miami Heat, since 2000. Throughout the year the venue hosts concerts, Broadway performances and the like. It's as much an anchor of the Miami skyline as any condo cluster – at night, the arena gets the full floodlight and neon treatment, and ends up looking like a UFO from the planet of the nightclubs.

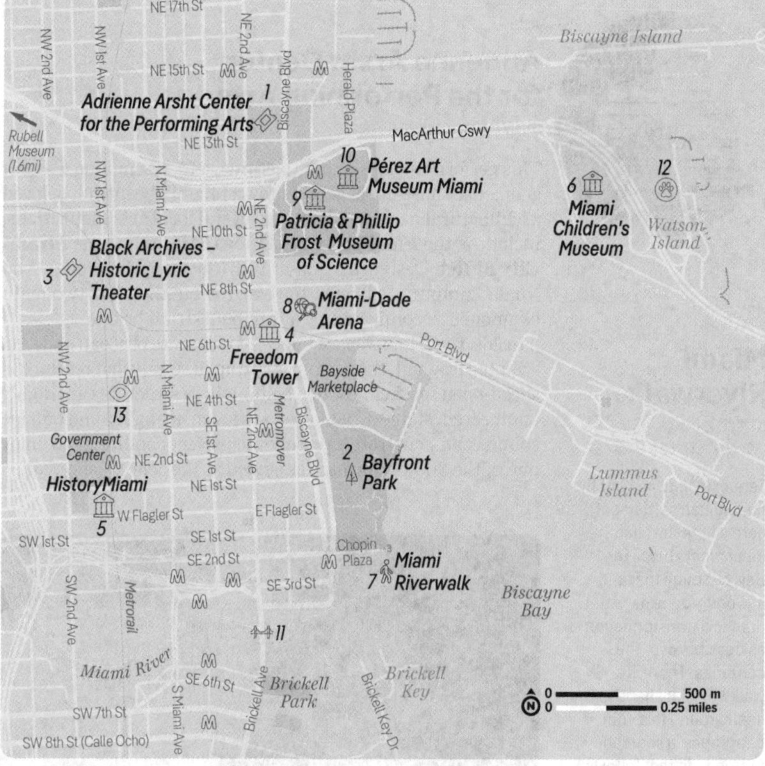

HIGHLIGHTS
1 Adrienne Arsht Center for the Performing Arts
2 Bayfront Park
3 Black Archives – Historic Lyric Theater
4 Freedom Tower
5 HistoryMiami
6 Miami Children's Museum
7 Miami Riverwalk
8 Miami-Dade Arena
9 Patricia & Phillip Frost Museum of Science
10 Pérez Art Museum Miami

SIGHTS
11 Brickell Avenue Bridge
12 Jungle Island
see 4 Miami Museum of Art & Design (MOAD)
13 MiamiCentral

Black Archives – Historic Lyric Theater

OVERTOWN'S OWN VENUE

Duke Ellington and Ella Fitzgerald once walked across the stage of the Lyric, a major stop on the 'Chitlin' Circuit' – the black live-entertainment trail of pre-integration USA. As years passed, both the theater and the neighborhood it served, Overtown, fell into disuse, and residential flight led to the area taking on an abandoned, forlorn atmosphere. Then the **Black Archives History & Research Foundation of South Florida** took over the building (pictured, left), even as the surrounding neighborhood changed again, into a substrata of local gentrification. Today the theater hosts shows, while the Archives hosts exhibitions exploring African American heritage, both in Miami and beyond.

Adrienne Arsht Center for the Performing Arts

PERFORMING ARTS HEART

This performing-arts center (pictured, left), resembling a sort of geometric short stack, is Downtown Miami's beautiful, beloved architectural baby, and home to several local arts institutions, including the **Florida Grand Opera Miami** and the **Miami City Ballet**. Designed by César Pelli (the man who brought you Kuala Lumpur's Petronas Towers), the building has two main components, connected by a thin pedestrian bridge.

Inside, you'll find a space informed by a sense of ocean and land sculpted by wind; the balconies rise up in spirals that resemble a sliced-open seashell. Hidden behind these structures are highly engineered, state-of-the-art acoustics ensuring that no outside sounds can penetrate, creating the perfect conditions to enjoy one of the 300 performances staged at the center each year.

Miami Riverwalk

STROLL INTO DOWNTOWN'S PAST

Tequesta Indians built the first human settlement here where the Miami River meets Biscayne Bay, although the land has undergone as drastic a transformation as possible over the centuries. There is a walkway that shapes itself around this vital geography, a shoreline promenade that follows along the northern edge of the river as it bisects Downtown, leading past high-rise condos and battered warehouses, with a few small tugboats pulling along the glassy surface. Fisherfolk float in with their daily catch, while fancy yachts make their way in and out of the bay. At night, you can see the Brickell skyline's lights, but close up and in person.

TOP: MIAZYOU/SHUTTERSTOCK © BOTTOM: GABRIELE MALTINI/SHUTTERSTOCK ©

Pérez Art Museum Miami

Pérez Art Museum Miami

CREATIVITY BY THE COAST

One of Miami's most impressive spaces, designed by Swiss architects Herzog & de Meuron, this museum integrates foliage, glass, concrete and wood – a melding of tropical vitality and fresh modernism that fits perfectly in Miami. Pérez Art Museum Miami (PAMM) stages some of the best contemporary exhibitions in the city, with established artists and impressive newcomers. The permanent collection rotates through unique pieces every few months – drawing from a treasure trove of work spanning the last 80 years.

The temporary shows and retrospectives bring major crowds (past exhibitions have included the works of artist Ai Weiwei and kinetic artist Julio Le Parc). The outdoor space has hanging gardens that took an entire two months to install.

If you need a little breather amid all this contemporary culture, PAMM has a first-rate cafe, or you can simply hang out in the grassy park, or lounge on a deck chair enjoying the views over the water.

This art institution inaugurated **Museum Park**, a patch of land that oversees the broad blue swath of Biscayne Bay.

Bayfront Park

DOWNTOWN'S BEATING GREEN HEART

Few American parks can claim to front such a lovely stretch of turquoise as Biscayne Bay, but Miamians are lucky like that. Notable features of Bayfront Park (pictured, below) are two performance venues: the **FPL Solar Amphitheater**, which boasts excellent views over the bay and is a good spot for live-music shows, and the smaller 200-seat (lawn seating can accommodate 800 more) **Tina Hills Pavilion**, which hosts free springtime performances.

Look north for the **JFK Torch of Friendship**, and a fountain recognizing the accomplishments of US congressman Claude Pepper. A bunch of activities kick off here on almost any day of the year. One dsay you'll see a flying trapeze class; another day folks will be lined up to salute the sun during yoga classes. This spot is consistently full of kids taking advantage of local playgrounds, friends enjoying a picnic with some of the city's best views, and tourists who have decided they might as well linger here after visiting a local museum.

TOP: TVERDOKHLIB/SHUTTERSTOCK © BELOW: FELIX MIZIOZNIKOV/SHUTTERSTOCK ©

Freedom Tower

Freedom Tower

ARCHITECTURAL AND IMMIGRATION ICON

The richly ornamented Freedom Tower is one of two surviving towers modeled after the Giralda bell tower in Spain's Cathedral of Seville. As the 'Ellis Island of the South,' it served as an immigration processing center for almost half a million Cuban refugees in the 1960s. Placed on the National Register of Historic Places in 1979, the tower also houses the **Miami Museum of Art & Design (MOAD)**, which features exhibits ranging from contemporary sculpture to historical photography. The tower and MOAD were scheduled to reopen to the public in 2023.

Miami Children's Museum

IMAGINATION UNLEASHED

This museum (pictured, right), located on the MacArthur Causeway between South Beach and Downtown Miami, is like an uber-playhouse, with areas for kids to practice all sorts of adult activities – banking and food shopping, caring for pets or being a firefighter. Other imaginative areas let kids make music, go on undersea adventures, make wall sketches, explore little castles made of colored glass or simply play on outdoor playgrounds. It's arguably one of the most dedicated 'kid' sites in the city, but it does a decent job of keeping the adults engaged, too.

HistoryMiami

UNFOLDING THE FLORIDA STORY

South Florida – a land of escaped enslaved people, guerrilla Native Americans, gangsters, pirates, tourists and alligators – has a special history, and it takes a special place to capture that narrative. This museum, located in the **Miami-Dade Cultural Center**, does just that, weaving together the stories of the region's successive population waves, from Native Americans to Nicaraguans.

Interactive exhibits show life among the Seminoles and early Florida industries like sponge diving. Other areas touch on the history of Jewish and African American communities in South Beach; Cuban refugees, complete with a rustic homemade boat, that managed to survive the Florida crossing; and cultural expression in public spaces (highlighting traditions such as street art, parades, protests and even vehicle customizing).

JEAN'S WORLD/SHUTTERSTOCK ©

The Metromover

MORE IN DOWNTOWN & BRICKELL

Metromover Groovin'

A FREE, ELEVATED DOWNTOWN TOUR

What's that train whirring overhead throughout some of Miami's densest built-up real estate? The answer is the Metromover, an elevated, electric monorail that was meant to provide mass transit and alleviate the traffic woes of Downtown and Brickell. The Metromover did not succeed in doing this, as anyone who has driven in South Florida can attest. But it is a beloved, complete rail line that moves thousands of people a month through Downtown – for free! It also happens to be a pretty cool way of seeing central Miami from a height, which is a nice thing, given the urban geography out here is basically skyscraper canyons (and again: it's free!).

The Metromover opened in 1986, and it has that particular so-modern-it-looks-dated appearance of public works from that period. There are three different lines that span 4.4 miles

ALL OVER THE UNDERLINE

The Metromover isn't the only elevated rail line in these parts. Miami's **Metrorail** connects Downtown to residential neighborhoods, including Coral Gables and Coconut Grove. But it's what's beneath the Metrorail that we're focusing on here: the well-titled **Underline**, a planned 10-mile linear park that will run underneath much of the Metrorail's tracks. The park is set to be complete by 2025, but the portion that runs through Brickell is already present. You'll find yoga classes there, because Miami law requires all public spaces to host yoga classes (kidding – sort of), an outdoor gym, a meditation garden and, of course, a walking and biking path.

WHERE TO EAT IN DOWNTOWN MIAMI

Niu Kitchen
Stylish living-room-sized restaurant serving delectable, often sharable Catalan cuisine alongside a killer wine list. **$$**

Verde
Inside the Pérez Art Museum, this is a local favorite for its tasty market-fresh dishes and great setting. **$$**

River Oyster Bar
A few paces from the Miami River, this buzzing little spot whips up excellent plates of seafood. **$$**

BRICKELL CITY CENTRE

There are malls, and then there are *malls*, and Brickell City Centre is the latter. This massive billion-dollar complex spreads across three city blocks, encompassing glittering residential towers, modernist office blocks and a soaring five-star hotel (called EAST, Miami).

There's much to entice both Miami residents and visitors to the center, with restaurants, bars, a cinema and loads of high-end retailers (Ted Baker, All Saints, Kendra Scott). You'll find shops scattered across both sides of S Miami Ave between 7th and 8th Sts, including a massive Saks Fifth Ave. There is a three-story Italian food emporium, with restaurants, cafes, a bakery, an enoteca and a culinary school.

MIAZYOU/SHUTTERSTOCK ©

Jungle Island

connecting major Downtown locations such as Bayfront Park, the Pérez Art Museum and the Adrienne Arsht Center, among others. The mover is a particularly good way of seeing the full architectural span and beauty of **Freedom Tower**, and there is talk of expanding it north into Wynwood. Trains run from 5am to midnight, roughly every three minutes (more frequently during rush hour).

Next Big Thing at Rubell Museum

ALLAPATAH ART OUTPOST

Don and Mera Rubell started collecting art from the beginning of their marriage in 1964 and, over the decades, earned an enviable reputation for identifying the Next Big Things. Since then, the Rubell family's private art collection has helped make Miami synonymous with the contemporary-art scene, and their Wynwood museum helped set the stage for that neighborhood's gentrification.

In 2019, the family museum relocated to **Allapattah**, a neighborhood just northwest of Downtown Miami and below

WHERE TO EAT IN DOWNTOWN MIAMI

Pollo & Jaras
Peruvian spot serves up outstanding barbecued chicken (and chicken crackling – ie deep-fried skin – oh yes!). **$$**

Bonding
Multiple Asian cuisines, including Thai, Japanese and Korean, come together into an excellent whole at Bonding. **$$**

Soya & Pomodoro
Feels like a bohemian Italian retreat, where you can dine on fresh pasta under vintage posters. **$$**

Wynwood, which had by then entered a sort of supercharged era of gentrification. The new Rubell Museum – six industrial buildings since converted into a frosty, yet inviting museum space – was redesigned by Selldorf Architects into one of the largest private contemporary-art institutions in North America.

The institution consists of some 53,000 sq ft of soaring exhibition space divided into 40 galleries. Artists on display include Kehinde Wiley, Jeff Koons, Cindy Sherman and Cady Noland. While many art museums of this size may be sustained by temporary exhibitions, at the Rubell the split is roughly 65% long-term holdings and 35% special (ie temporary) shows.

The Rubell is noted for presenting work with thematic consistency and exhaustive context; curators here are very good at their jobs, and proud of the art they're presenting to the public.

The Unmissable Angles of MiamiCentral

BIG BOLD BRIGHTLINE BASE

This train station has been converted into a mixed-use complex that stretches (and stretches; seriously, it's like the station never ends) across six city blocks. Within the station space you'll find a food hall and shopping arcades, plus offices and apartments. Architecturally, it's like the space age has landed in South Florida; MiamiCentral is an unmissable jumble of odd angles, enormous windows and twisted steel, designed by Skidmore, Owings & Merrill, the firm responsible for Dubai's Burj Khalifa. The station serves as the Miami home of the Brightline trains, which connect the Magic City to Fort Lauderdale and West Palm Beach.

Jungle Island Escapes

ZIPLINES AND CAPYBARAS, WHY NOT?

Packed with tropical birds, alligators, orangutans, chimps, lemurs and a Noah's ark of other animals, Jungle Island is a good bit of smelly fun. It's one of those places kids (justifiably) beg to go, so just give up and prepare for some bright-feathered, bird-poop-scented enjoyment in this artificial, self-contained jungle. Also on offer: rope bridges among the trees, a flight-generating wind tunnel, an escape room and Adventure Bay – an area with rock-climbing walls and kid-friendly bungee jumping. Do all of these activities cost a fair amount extra? You better believe it.

BEST HOTELS IN DOWNTOWN MIAMI

EAST Miami
Past the design-focused, contemporary aesthetic, you'll find four pools, a rooftop bar, and spacious, attractive rooms and suites. $$$

YVE Miami
A simple but trendy choice. Offers proximity to Downtown's pulsing neon heart at a competitive rate. $

Mandarin Oriental Miami
A world within a world located on Brickell Key, with swanky restaurants, a private spa and skyline views. $$$

Guild Downtown
If you want privacy to complement the Miami skyline, consider these apartments. $$

CVI.CHE 105
Beautifully presented ceviches go down nicely with a round of specialty Peruvian cocktails. **$$**

Manna Life Food
This airy, stylish eatery wows diners with its plant-based menu loaded with superfoods. **$$**

Garcia's Seafood Grille & Fish Market
Come to this riverside spot for freshly caught fish and pleasant views of the Miami River. **$$$**

BEST BARS IN DOWNTOWN MIAMI

Baby Jane
Small but sexy, Baby Jane is a Brickell outpost filled with tropical accents and lotsa neon.

Blackbird Ordinary
Has great cocktails and a vibe that strikes a balance between laid-back and Miami hedonism.

Mama Tried
This dark bar has a speakeasy feel, giant metallic light fixtures and a retro-chic aesthetic.

Lost Boy
Vintage Cuban furniture, exposed brick and old wood come together in this enormous pub.

OMAR GHRAYEB/SHUTTERSTOCK ©

Brickell

Gawk at Glass Towers in Brickell

NEON NIGHTS AND CROWDED CONDOS

Concrete and neon and the dense space where those two elements blend characterize much of Downtown Miami, and the association is only amplified in Brickell, perhaps the ritziest neighborhood in Miami (which is saying something). Located just south of Downtown, Brickell has a reputation as the financial heart of South Florida (and a fair chunk of the southern US). That identity remains, but it's been glittered over by a glut of restaurants, bars and nightclubs. Walk around here in the evenings, and you'll see a crowd that's arguably as sexy, beautiful and well-off as any gaggle of models you can spot around South Beach.

The Miami River forms the northern border of Brickell, spanned by the lovely Brickell Ave Bridge, which sits between SE 4th St and SE 5th St. At the edge of the bridge is a bronze statue of a Tequesta (Native American) warrior aiming his arrow at the sky; the bridge itself is accented with reliefs that honor Miamians like Everglades conservationist Julia Tuttle. Walking here is the best way to see the sculptures, and will also allow you to avoid one of the most confusing traffic patterns in Miami.

Brickell Key is an island that is technically part of Brickell proper. It looks more like a floating porcupine, with glass towers for quills, than an island. To live the life of Miami glitterati, come here, pretend you belong and head into a patrician hangout like the **Mandarin Oriental Miami** hotel, where the lobby and intimate lounges afford sweeping views of Biscayne Bay.

FOR NEON LOVERS

Exploring Downtown Miami is like swimming through a neon ocean, but there are more bright city lights. Cross the bay and go to **Ocean Drive** (p60) on Miami Beach, where the neon becomes a spilled rainbow by the sand.

WHERE TO DRINK IN DOWNTOWN MIAMI

Esotico
It's all leafy plants, green murals, excellent tiki drinks and hot neon at this jungly bar.

Elleven
Go-go dancers, aerialists and racy (striptease-esque) performances get down amid a state-of-the-art sound system.

Sugar
Verdant oasis of a rooftop bar, with a spacious open-air deck full of plants and trees.

A DOWNTOWN STROLL

Downtown Miami is constantly reinventing itself via construction and early adoption of whatever the world thinks is cool. If you want to have your finger on the pulse of what's on trend, this walk will lead you past the shiniest corners inhabited by Miami's relentlessly cool kids. Airy, stylish **1 Manna Life Food** has wowed diners with its plant-based menu, which offers superfood ingredients like red quinoa, baked tofu, roasted veggies, coconut brown rice and raw falafel. It's also a good spot for fresh juices, coffees and matcha cappuccinos. Head from here to **2 Supply & Advise**, where menswear enthusiasts can head if they're looking to get looked at. There's a ton of handsome clothing, which is housed in a historic building that dates to the 1920s. Now stroll through **3 Bayfront Park**, and head to the **4 Miami Riverwalk**; walk from the south end of Bayfront and follow it under bridges and along the waterline until it ends just west of the SW 2nd Ave Bridge. Crossing the Miami River, the lovely **5 Brickell Avenue Bridge**, between SE 4th St and SE 5th St, was made wider and higher some years back, affording even better views of the Downtown skyline. Note the 17ft bronze statue by Cuban-born sculptor Manuel Carbonell of a Tequesta Indian warrior and his family, which sits atop the towering Pillar of History column.

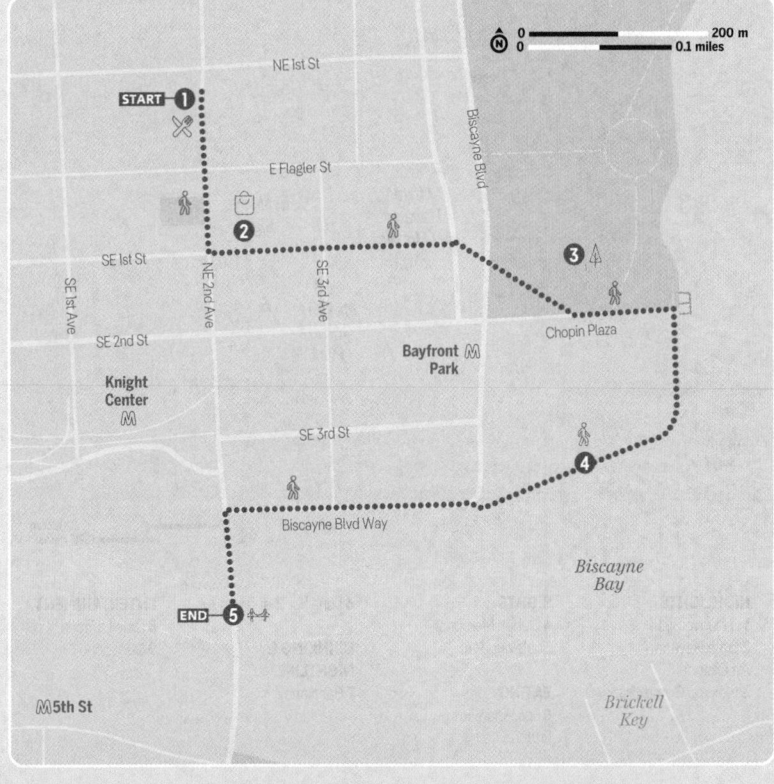

LITTLE HAVANA

CALLE OCHO CALLING

The Cuba-ness of Little Havana is slightly exaggerated for visitors, though it's still an atmospheric area to explore, with the clack of dominoes, the scent of wafting cigars and the sound of salsa spilling into the street. Keep an eye out for murals; older art often references the Cuban revolution, while newer pieces contain contemporary references to hip-hop and the Miami Heat.

Little Havana's main thoroughfare, Calle Ocho (SW 8th St), is the heart of the neighborhood, which is most vibrant during the day (preferably on a weekend), when you can see wise-cracking old timers chattering over fast-moving games of dominoes in Máximo Gómez Park and ponder modern art at the galleries. Cap the day with souvenir and cigar shopping, pausing for strong coffee along the way. Come back for dinner (there's great Cuban fare, and much more besides), then catch live bands at a salsa club or craft cocktail joint.

TOP TIP

Exploring Little Havana isn't about ticking off sights. Rather, it's soaking up atmosphere, spending time at lunch counters and taking in everything. Be on the lookout for the Cuban Walk of Fame, a series of sidewalk stars emblazoned with the names of Cuban celebrities that runs up and down much of 8th St.

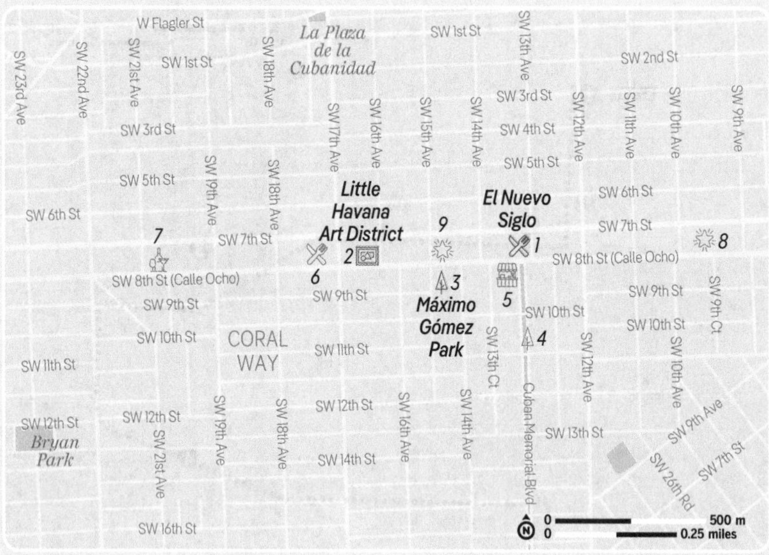

HIGHLIGHTS
1 El Nuevo Siglo
2 Little Havana Art District
3 Máximo Gómez Park

SIGHTS
4 Cuban Memorial Boulevard Park

EATING
5 Los Pinareños Frutería
6 Lung Yai Thai Tapas

DRINKING & NIGHTLIFE
7 Bar Nancy

ENTERTAINMENT
8 Cafe La Trova
9 Cubaocho

Máximo Gómez Park

DOMINOES AND SPANISH TRASH TALK

Perhaps Little Havana's most evocative reminder of Cuba is Máximo Gómez Park ('Domino Park'), where the sound of elderly men trash-talking over games of dominoes is harmonized with the quick clack-clack of slapping tiles – though photo-taking tourists do give an odd spin to the experience. That said, the players don't seem to mind people watching them – if anything, they feed off the crowd's energy. The heavy cigar smell and a sunrise-bright mural of the 1994 Summit of the Americas add to the atmosphere.

Domino game at Máximo Gómez Park

El Nuevo Siglo

A GROCERY STORE (AND MORE)

Any immigrant, or child of immigrants, knows that the heart of the community is generally not to be found in statues or cultural centers. Instead, it's in the stores and restaurants that contain a literal taste of the old country. To this end, join the crowds of locals who come to El Nuevo Siglo supermarket and rock up at the shiny black countertop for delicious cooking at excellent prices, plus an unfussy ambience. Everything is good: nibble on roast meats, fried yucca, tangy Cuban sandwiches, grilled snapper with rice, beans and plantains, and other daily specials.

Little Havana Art District

STREETS COME ALIVE

The slice of Little Havana between SW 15th and 17th Aves is, for visitors, probably the most vibrant and tourist-focused section of the neighborhood. Here you'll find a ton of colorful murals, as well as galleries, many within a block of the **Futurama Building**, a shared creative workspace located at 1637 SW 8th St, and **Ball & Chain** (pictured, above), a music venue and restaurant that fuses memories of Old Havana with the melting-pot vibe of Little Havana. The celebrations of **Viernes Culturales** (cultural Fridays) center on the arts district – on the third Friday of the month you'll find a main stage here, and galleries stay open until 11pm. The party is a fantastic introduction to Spanish-speaking Miami, and generally starts at noon.

VA A VERSAILLES

Few Little Havana sights make the stomach rumble as much as **Versailles**' green and white sign. The self-proclaimed 'most famous Cuban restaurant in the world' (and, to be fair, that boast is hard to argue with) has been around since 1971. Generations of Cuban Americans, along with Miami's Latin political elite, rub elbows here in this dining room, over plates of black beans, *ropa vieja, croquetas* (croquettes) and countless cups of sweet, strong Cuban coffee. The mainstays are all here, but you can also find more involved, regional cuisine from the island, up to and including a seafood paella, shredded dry beef (unlike the sauce-y *ropa vieja*), and grilled liver steak.

Eternal Torch of Brigade 2506

MORE IN LITTLE HAVANA

Cuban Memorial Boulevard Park

SACRED SHRINE, LIVING HISTORY

This boulevard is a testament to the enormous cultural significance of an island that thousands of Miamians have never set foot on, yet remains, in a vital way, a place they consider integral to their identity.

Taken on its own, it's a skinny public space occupying the median of SW 13th Ave, taking up four blocks of real estate. There are statues and memorials popping up every few feet, and it takes some cultural or historical context to appreciate many of them.

The **Eternal Torch of Brigade 2506** is dedicated to those soldiers who gave their lives in the 1961 Bay of Pigs Invasion of Cuba. Anti-communism is also given a nod in a bronze statue of **Nestor 'Tony' Izquierdo**, a Bay of Pigs veteran who went on to fight for Nicaragua's right-wing Somoza regime.

WHERE TO SHOP IN LITTLE HAVANA

Havana Collection
Has a full and most striking collection of the classic traditional *guayaberas* (Cuban dress shirts).

Guantanamera
This place sells high-quality hand-rolled cigars, strong Cuban coffee, and bonus, has a bar and rocking chairs.

La Isla
This hip Little neighborhood outpost showcases a thorough sampling of Cuban-inspired pop art and gifts.

Other monuments include a bust of **Antonio Maceo Grajales**, a hero of the Cuban War of Independence, and the **Plaza de Los Periodistas Cubanos**, dedicated to Cuban journalists critical of the Castro regime.

In the middle of the block connecting SW 10th St and Calle Ocho (SW 8th St) is a striking **Ceiba tree**, which is important to practitioners of Santería, an Afro-Cuban religion that blends traditional West African beliefs with Roman Catholicism in a manner similar to (but distinct from) *vodou* (voodoo). You may spot votive candles and offerings of rum or tobacco.

LOOKING UP TO THE TOWER

Think all the best South Florida deco is in South Beach? Come to the **Tower Theater**, located right on Calle Ocho, and think again. This renovated 1926 landmark has a proud deco facade and a handsomely renovated interior. In its heyday it was the center of Little Havana social life and, via the films it showed, served as a bridge between immigrant society and American pop culture. Today, it frequently shows independent and Spanish-language films (sometimes both). The theater also hosts varied art exhibitions in the lobby. It's also just a lovely neighborhood anchor, a landmark and point of reference that generations have grown up with and fought to preserve and protect.

Making Music in Little Havana

SONGS OF A DIASPORA

Music is at the heart of the Cuban diaspora, and several businesses in Little Havana make a point of tapping into the island's soul via songs.

The jewel of the Little Havana Art District, **Cubaocho** is renowned for its concerts, with excellent bands from across the Spanish-speaking world. It's also a community center, art gallery and research outpost for all things Cuban. The interior resembles an old Havana cigar bar, yet the walls are decked out in artwork that references both the classical past of Cuban art and its avant-garde future.

With its wood accents, immaculately dressed bartenders and faded Havana-esque walls, **Cafe La Trova** really nails the 'Old Cuba' concept (how you feel about said concept is, of course, another question). Regular live shows featuring classic Cuban dance music accompanied by a crowd decked out in their best dresses and *guayaberas* is insanely fun; if the scene here doesn't get you dancing, we're not sure what will.

But music in Little Havana doesn't always have to evoke the old island, and locals don't always need a conga accompaniment to shake their tail feathers. At craft-cocktail-centric **Bar Nancy**, millennial and Gen Z Cuban Americans (among others) dance to hard rock, punk, Southern blues, Latin trap, chiptune and whatever the heck else catches their fancy.

Comer, beber y ser feliz

EAT, DRINK AND BE MERRY

You can do that all over Miami, but you can make a trip around the Spanish-speaking world doing it in Little Havana. We do mean the world, too – Cuban cuisine is only a small slice of Little Havana's pan-Latin palate. There are menus from

WHERE TO EAT AROUND THE WORLD IN LITTLE HAVANA

Lung Yai Thai Tapas
Shareable Thai small plates make for spicy snacks that go perfectly with the Calle Ocho street scene. **$$**

San Pocho
For a quick journey to Colombia, head here for hearty, meat-heavy dishes that fill you up for a week. **$**

Yambo
Nicaraguan *carne asada* (grilled beef), sweet plantains, and piles of rice and beans – and it's open late. **$**

BEST RESTAURANTS IN LITTLE HAVANA

Doce Provisions
Creative Caribbean meets American fare – think fried chicken with sweet plantain waffle – plus local microbrews. $$

El Carajo
An incredible Spanish tapas restaurant/wine cellar tucked into the back of a gas station! $$

La Camaronera Seafood Joint and Fish Market
Come for the *pan con minuta* (fish sandwich), stay for everything else at this excellent market. $

Taqueria Viva Mexico
From a takeout window, smiling ladies dole out some of the best tacos in town. $

JUAN LLAURO/SHUTTERSTOCK ©

Cuban dish *picadillo*

all over *el Sud,* from Ecuador to El Salvador and Mexico to Mendoza, Argentina. And while locals say you have to go further afield than Calle Ocho for the best *comida latino* (Latin food), you'll rarely go wrong when you stroll into ethnic eateries in this part of town.

You don't even need to stick to the Western Hemisphere. Take a little gem of a restaurant like **Lung Yai Thai Tapas** – at places like this, you realize the whole concept of sharing lots of little snack-ish plates on a humid afternoon is not exclusive to the Spanish-speaking world (by the way, the chicken wings here will blow your mind).

All that said, nothing says refreshment on a sultry Miami afternoon like a cool glass of fresh juice (or *batidos* – milkshakes) from **Los Pinareños Frutería**, a fruit and veggie stand beloved by generations of Miamians. Sip a *guarapa* (sugar-cane extract) *batido* while roosters cluck and folks gossip and argue in Cuban-accented Spanish; this is as Miami as it gets, short of being in a Pitbull song.

WHERE TO EAT AROUND THE WORLD IN LITTLE HAVANA

Xixon
Modern Spanish tapas joint with excellent *bacalao* (cod) fritters, sizzling shrimp and baby eel. **$$**

El Cristo
Down-to-earth El Cristo has options from all over the Spanish-speaking world – fish the standout. **$$**

Azucar
One of Little Havana's oldest ice-cream parlors serves sweet treats like *abuela* used to make. **$**

WYNWOOD & THE DESIGN DISTRICT

AN ADULT ARTS THEME PARK

Whatever is on trend in the world is emulated, if not started, on the streets of Wynwood, in the shadow of public art and Instagrammable food halls. The Design District is a high-end shopping area, where the line between neighborhood and mall is tough to draw.

Wynwood used to be a working-class, Spanish-speaking area before rapid-onset gentrification roared in. The area is busy by day, but truly comes alive at night, when the creative set mingle in candlelit brewpubs and backyard music joints. The Design District has a more refined feel. Its main shopping strip is filled with lovely, if stratospherically priced, objects. You could easily explore it in one day – hitting the shops and galleries during daylight hours, then sticking around (or returning) for dining and nightlife in the evening.

TOP TIP

Wynwood covers a large area, with attractions spread across many blocks. However, you'll find the densest concentration of sights on or near NW 2nd Ave. A handy approach is to head north from 23rd St to about 29th St, dipping in and out of intersecting streets along the way.

Institute of Contemporary Art

Institute of Contemporary Art

CUTTING-EDGE CREATIONS

A solid contemporary-arts museum in the Design District, the ICA hosts a good range of contemporary exhibitions alongside its permanent collections. The building, designed in 2017 by Aranguren & Gallegos architects, is especially beautiful, with sharp geometric lines and large windows overlooking the garden. The metallic gray facade is both industrial and elegant. When you're here, keep an eye out for geometric designs, odd angles and other aesthetic elements. Note that the museum recommends booking your visit in advance.

Bakehouse Art Complex

ARTS – INDOORS AND OUTDOORS

One of Wynwood's most pivotal art destinations (which is saying something), the Bakehouse has been an arts incubator since well before the creation of the Wynwood Walls. The space – it used to be a bakery, hence the name – is managed as a non-profit, which frees it from some of the more blatant commercialism in this area; all visits to the Bakehouse are free. Today the Bakehouse galleries accommodate some 60 studios, as well as a spread of murals that open to the public 24/7. Check the website (bacfl.org) to learn about upcoming talks and other events.

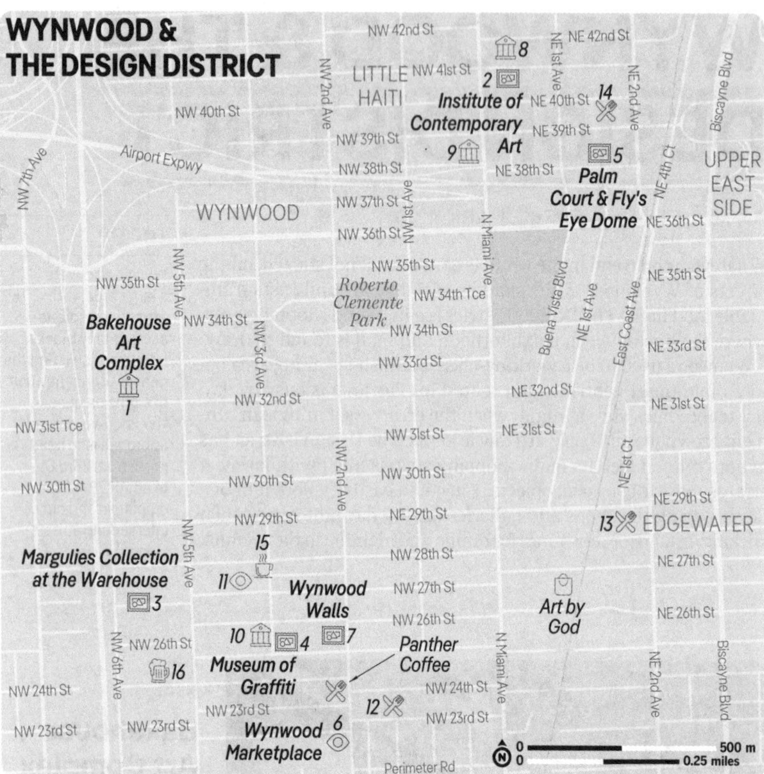

HIGHLIGHTS
1 Bakehouse Art Complex
2 Institute of Contemporary Art
3 Margulies Collection at the Warehouse
4 Museum of Graffiti
5 Palm Court & Fly's Eye Dome
6 Wynwood Marketplace
7 Wynwood Walls

SIGHTS
8 De La Cruz Collection
9 Locust Projects
10 Walt Grace Vintage
11 Wynwood Building

EATING
12 1 800 Lucky
13 Enriqueta's
14 Michael's Genuine

DRINKING & NIGHTLIFE
15 Miam Cafe
16 Wynwood Brewing Company

Museum of Graffiti

GRAFITTI RE-IMAGINED

The Museum of Graffiti (pictured, left) gives visitors a quick dive into the history of this particular art form, which is so obviously and brilliantly in evidence on the urban blocks of surrounding Wynwood. As museums go, it's a bit small, but the people behind it are passionate: there are kids' art classes on Sundays, photos from graffiti's earliest days, temporary exhibitions from graffiti masters and beginners' graffiti workshops – it's like taking a watercolor painting class, but instead of paints and outdoor tableaus, there are spray cans and concrete walls. The gift shop alone is a must for anyone who likes graffiti or pop art.

TIM CLARK/ALAMY STOCK PHOTO ©

Wynwood Walls

MOMENTOUS MURALS

One of the most photographed locations in Miami (if social media hashtags are anything to go by), Wynwood Walls is a collection of murals and paintings laid out over an open courtyard that bowls people over with its sheer exuberant colors and commanding presence. What's on offer tends to change with the coming and going of major arts events, such as Art Basel, but it's always eye-catching, interesting stuff, and the energy that congregates around the Walls is buzzy and exciting.

Depending on your worldview, the Walls are either a triumph of Wynwood's unwritten mission of bringing street-generated contemporary art to the masses...or a triumph of the commercial forces that have taken the creative energy of the street and repackaged it for conspicuous consumption. Are we thinking too hard about it? Maybe, but that's the point of art, right? In any case, if you want to take a little piece of the Walls home, make sure to pop into the on-site shop.

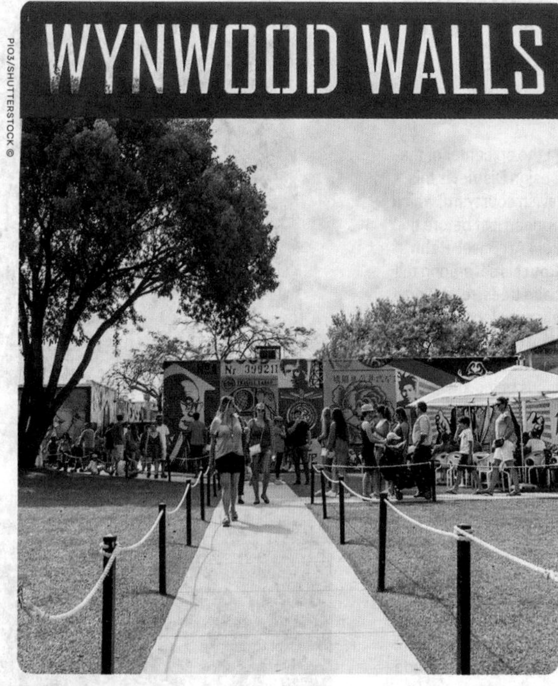

PIO3/SHUTTERSTOCK ©

Wynwood Walls

Margulies Collection at the Warehouse

ENORMOUS ART ARENA

Encompassing 50,000 sq ft, this vast not-for-profit exhibition space houses one of the largest art collections in Wynwood – Martin Margulies' 4000-piece collection includes **sculptures** by Isamu Noguchi and Olafur Eliasson (among many others), plus sound installations and room-sized works. Thought-provoking installations are the focus at the Warehouse, as is an effort to carefully curate and feature works by leading contemporary artists. With that said, the space doesn't limit itself to 21st-century creators, as evidenced in exhibits by artists like Dorothea Lange and Walker Evans. While this is a non-profit space, there is a $10 admission, but we'd recommend contacting the Collection and joining a $25 tour – these excursions are notable as they're often led by the institution's lead collectors or curators.

Palm Court & Fly's Eye Dome

RETAIL AND DESIGN, UNITE

At the epicenter of the Design District is this lavish courtyard, which opened just before the 2014 Art Basel. **Palm Court** is set among tall palm trees, reflecting mirrors along the sides, two floors of swanky retailers (the commercial focus being, obviously, homewares, decor, furniture and the like) and one particularly eye-catching sculpture sitting at the center of everything: the **Fly's Eye Dome**.

Designed by Buckminster Fuller, this geodesic dome appears to float in a small reflecting pool surrounded by slender, gently swaying palm trees, themselves often decorated with temporary art exhibitions. The 24ft-tall sculpture was dubbed an 'autonomous dwelling machine' by Fuller when he conceived it back in 1965; now it's a backdrop to high-end shopping, and a covered entry/exit point connecting the below-ground parking lot with Palm Court.

There are some fantastic vantage points for photographers both inside and outside the dome – the light is particularly fine at night, when fairy lights, floodlights and the reflection of the stores in the mirrored glass makes for a particularly arresting backdrop.

Wynwood Marketplace

Wynwood Marketplace

BIZARRE BAZAAR

An enormous open-air marketplace takes over several blocks of Wynwood real estate on weekend evenings, and plays host to artisan shops, food trucks, a performance stage, live music and art exhibitions. The Marketplace is more or less a weekly carnival, and given Miami's consistently good weather, it's a pleasant one to stroll. Indeed, on a popular night it can feel like the whole city is here, and given the confluence of general green-lit hedonism, it's not hard to see why folks show up. With their kids, by the way; while booze is sold at the Marketplace, the vibe is family friendly.

FELIX MIZIOZNIKOV/SHUTTERSTOCK ©

Bacardi Building

LOCAL LANDMARKS: THE BACARDI BUILDING

The former Miami headquarters of Bacardi, located at 2100 Biscayne Blvd, is a masterpiece of tropical architecture, and holds a spot on the National Register of Historic Places. The main event is a beautifully decorated jewel-box-like building built in 1973 that seems to hover over the ground from a central pillar supporting the entire structure. One-inch-thick pieces of hammered glass cover the exterior in a wild Mesoamerican-style pattern modeled after a mosaic designed by German artist Johannes M Dietz.

Also on-site is the older 1963 building, a tower covered with blue-and-white handmade tiles – some 28,000, in fact – in a striking ceramic pattern designed by Brazilian artist Francisco Brennand.

MORE IN WYNWOOD & THE DESIGN DISTRICT

Art & High Design

BEAUTY, UNBOUND

The Design District is compact, but it overflows with galleries, high-end designer boutiques and places to eat. You'll also find some lovely contemporary architecture throughout, along with intriguing outdoor installations that bring the art out of the gallery and into the public sphere. The main drags are along NW 39th and 40th Sts.

Locust Projects has become a major name for emerging artists in the contemporary gallery scene. Run by artists as a non-profit collective since 1998, Locust Projcts has exhibited work by more than 250 local, national and international artists over the years. The gallery often hosts site-specific installations by artists and is willing to take a few more risks than more commercial venues.

WHERE TO EAT IN WYNWOOD & THE DESIGN DISTRICT

Buena Vista Deli
Come in the morning for bakery temptations, and later in the day for thick slices of quiche. **$**

SuViche
Serves a blend of Peruvian dishes (including half-a-dozen varieties of ceviche), plus sushi. **$**

Beaker & Gray
Join the crowds downing cocktails and indulging in a menu of globally inspired pub grub. **$$**

BEST BARS IN WYNWOOD & THE DESIGN DISTRICT

Sylvester
Mixes neighborhood vibe with contemporary art and lots of beautiful people, especially on weekends.

Gramps
Friendly and unpretentious spot for live music, DJs, the occasional dueling-synthesizers show or bingo.

Coyo Taco
A secret bar hidden behind a taco stand? Sign us up, especially when DJs spin Afro-Cuban funk.

R House
Great food and cocktails, but best known for an immensely popular drag brunch (reserve *way* in advance).

BKUEEE77/SHUTTERSTOCK ©

Coffee at Panther Coffee

Next, stroll by **Palm Court**, which more or less anchors the district, and head to the **Institute of Contemporary Art**, which is deeply in touch with the area's aesthetic: the bleeding edge of arts innovation, or at least the edge embraced by the contemporary-art-criticism scene.

Need to refuel? Double back just a little ways and pop into **Michael's Genuine**. This long-running upscale tavern combines excellent service with a well-executed menu of wood-fired dishes, bountiful salads and raw-bar temptations.

Finally, make your way to 41st St and the **De La Cruz Collection**, a 30,000-sq-ft gallery with a treasure trove of contemporary works scattered across three floors, which you can roam freely.

Wynwood Eats: Old & New School

TASTE BUDS, WE GOT YOU

Creativity is one of the hallmarks of the culinary scene in Wynwood. You'll find innovative takes on American comfort

WHERE TO EAT IN WYNWOOD & THE DESIGN DISTRICT

Michael's Genuine
This tavern turned temple to New American cuisine serves up locally sourced comfort food and buzzing crowds. $$$

Salty Donut
Lines stretch for these artfully designed creations featuring seasonal ingredients like guava and cheese. $

1800 Lucky
Miami's take on an Asian hawker market, with tons of street food and Wynwood neon to boot. $

food, Japanese fusion fare cooked over open flames, imaginatively topped tacos, healthy vegan fare, single-origin coffee, paradigm-shifting doughnuts and much, much more.

A perfect example, as well as more evidence of Wynwood becoming a sort of adult playground for cosmopolitan world wanderers: **1800 Lucky**. This sprawling eatery tries to recreate an Asian food hall in the midst of South Florida. The atmosphere is excellent: red lanterns, booming lounge and hip-hop, a slick bar, beautiful people. The food is pretty good too, ranging from sashimi bowls to Thai-style chicken wings to Chinese pork-belly buns. The food hall more or less becomes an outdoor bar as the night wears on, and is as popular as the most packed Miami club.

Where did people eat before successive waves of gentrification washed away old Wynwood? One institution stands out, and it drips with character: **Enriqueta's**, an outpost of old Miami in the heart of that city's (arguably) flashiest neighborhood. At this roadhouse diner, local Spanish speakers, as opposed to international installation artists, rule the roost. Head here for truly excellent coffee, *pan con bistec* (steak sandwiches), *croquetas,* Cuban sandwiches, daily specials such as *picadillo* (spiced ground beef) and *lechón asado* (roast pork), and lots of good-natured Spanish trash-talking among regulars.

Art, Culture, Coffee, Beer

WHAT MORE DO YOU NEED?

Wynwood is Miami's unofficial capital of art and all things avant-garde. Its mural-lined streets are one giant canvas – albeit one that's ever changing – and the gallery scene is unrivaled.

Start off at the sprawling **Art by God**, full of matter from the natural world. Triceratops horns, taxidermy of all shapes and sizes and even prehistoric human skulls fill the shelves of this cabinet of curiosity. After perusing dinosaur bones to your heart's content, consider putting some espresso-laced fuel in your tank with a visit to **Panther Coffee**, a beloved local roaster that is fast becoming internationally known for its quality caffeine.

From here, walk up NW 2nd Ave, then turn left onto 26th St and head to NW 3rd Ave. In this area you'll be strolling past some truly staggering mural 'galleries.' At the corner of NW 27th St is the zebra-striped **Wynwood Building**, which functions as a creative office and retail space. You'll also find **Miam Cafe**, another fine coffee spot.

WYNWOOD ARTS WALK(S)

One of the best ways to take in the Miami art scene is to join in the **Wynwood Art Walk Block Party**, held on the second Saturday of every month. Many galleries around Wynwood host special events and art openings, with ever-flowing drinks (not always free), live music, food trucks and special markets.

Another way to see the neighborhood is the similarly named **Wynwood Art Walk** (wynwoodartwalk.com). This 'walk' is actually a 90-minute guided tour to some of the best gallery shows of the day, plus a look at some interesting street art around the 'hood. It also offers other tours like a golf-cart trip around the area's best graffiti.

FOR ART LOVERS

Wynwood gets the attention as the city's official arts enclave, but visual treats and creativity extend far beyond this 'hood. The **Rubell Museum** (p74) is one of the largest private art collections on the continent, and well worth a visit.

Mandolin
It's all Mediterranean whites and blues at this Greek restaurant, serving grilled bass, lamb kabobs and more. **$$$**

Amara at Paraiso
This waterfront restaurant trots out New American/Latin American hybrid cuisine in a regal setting. **$$$**

Lemoni Cafe
Easygoing cafe with French toast, paninis, pancakes and lots of pleasant alfresco seating. **$**

From here you can turn right down 27th St. Two blocks on, you'll reach the Margulies Collection at the Warehouse (p85). Although you'll have to pay admission, it's well worth it, as this vast gallery houses an incredible collection of contemporary art. It's a quick walk from here to the **Wynwood Brewing Company**, one of the pioneers of the Miami microbrewery scene.

Walt Grace Vintage

FERRARIS AND FENDERS

There are a hundred galleries in Wynwood, but Walt Grace Vintage is the only one showcasing two specific products: classic cars and classic guitars. If you're into either one, or both, of these things, come in and gawk at the immaculately polished Gibsons, Fenders, Porsches and Jaguars. To the gallery's credit, they're not just showing off shiny toys; there's a genuine respect and admiration for that specific crossroads where engineering, artistry and sheer, indefinable cool are created. If you've got a few thousand dollars (or a few hundred thousand, if cars are your thing) burning a hole in your pocket, you can take a gallery piece home and (possibly) stave off an impending midlife crisis.

Embrace Art Basel

SEE AND BE SEEN

Art Basel is one of the biggest international art shows in the world, and one of the most Miami things to ever take place in Miami. It's all there: selfie sticks, people preening, conspicuous consumption (often blended with a dash of either activism or intellectualism), and parties that only stop long enough to upload the next viral snapshot. Even if you're not a billionaire collector, there's plenty to enjoy at this festival, with open-air art installations around town, special exhibitions at many Miami galleries and outdoor film screenings, among other goings-on. While a lot of the action is in Miami Beach, Wynwood is a huge Basel center of gravity, hosting a mural festival and temporary venues for drinking, eating and general hedonism.

BEST RESTAURANTS IN WYNWOOD

Dasher & Crank
Quite literally churns out ice cream, ranging from passion fruit sorbet to (of course) mojito. $

Kush
Gourmet burgers plus craft brews is the simple but winning formula at this lively eatery. $$

Zak the Baker
This Miami bakery deserves the hype, delivering some-off-the-charts fresh baked breads, croissants and pastries. $

La Latina
Popular with both Midtown locals and transplants who dig into *arepas*, pulled pork and Venezuelan favorites. $

WHERE TO DRINK IN WYNWOOD & THE DESIGN DISTRICT

Wynwood Brewing Company
The first craft brewery in Wynwood still produces the best beer, served in a spacious taproom.

Dirty Rabbit
Colorful cocktails, edgy if cute art and live music attracts all the cool kids.

Dante's HiFi
Have an excellent cocktail in a laid-back lounge that doubles as a vinyl listening room.

CORAL GABLES & COCONUT GROVE

PASTEL PALACES UNDER THE BANYANS

Coral Gables, filled with a pastel rainbow of mansions, feels a world removed from the rest of Miami. Here you'll find pretty banyan-lined streets and a walkable village-like center. Much of the Gables is defined by unique urban planning and aesthetics, reminiscent of an old Mediterranean village-town. Boutiques, cafes and upscale eateries are scattered along (and near) the so-called Miracle Mile.

Coconut Grove was once a hippie colony, but these days its demographic is mall-going Miamians and college students. It's a compact place with intriguing shops and cafes. It's particularly appealing in the evenings, when residents fill the outdoor tables of its bars and restaurants. The Grove backs onto the water, so you're never far from the salt-and-skyline breezes that make Miami so magical.

TOP TIP

Want to soak up some local life? The **Coral Gables Farmers Market**, held on Saturday mornings (around 8am to 2pm) in front of City Hall (405 Biltmore Way), is the spot to load up on seasonal fruits, fresh breads and other goodies. You can also rub elbows with locals at **GableStage**, which anchors a vibrant local theater scene.

JOHNNY MICHAEL/SHUTTERSTOCK ©

Barnacle Historic State Park

Barnacle Historic State Park

HISTORIC HIDEAWAY

In the center of Coconut Grove village is the residence of pioneer Ralph Munroe, Miami's first honorable snowbird. The house, which was built in 1891, is open for guided tours (every 90 minutes between 10am and 2:30pm, Sunday to Wednesday). The 5-acre park it's located in is a shady oasis for strolling and a great spot to let the kids run off some energy. The Barnacle hosts frequent events, from sailing regattas to yoga classes to moonlight concerts, usually featuring jazz or classical music. As outdoor venues for this sort of chilled-out music go, the place is just a chef's kiss.

Lowe Art Museum

ART ON CAMPUS

The **University of Miami** has a lovely campus to stroll around: it exhibits the area's Mediterranean-chic design sense, and is home to a few destination gems, including the Lowe. The university's resident art museum, the Lowe has a solid collection of modern works, a permanent collection of Renaissance and baroque paintings, Western sculpture from the 18th to 20th centuries, and archweological artifacts, art, and crafts from Asia, Africa, the South Pacific and pre-Columbian America.

CORAL GABLES & COCONUT GROVE

HIGHLIGHTS		SIGHTS	ENTERTAINMENT
1 Barnacle Historic State Park	**4** Lowe Art Museum	**7** Biltmore Hotel	**10** GableStage
2 Books & Books	**5** Plymouth Congregational Church	**8** Merrick House	
3 Kampong	**6** Venetian Pool	**9** Peacock Park	

Books & Books

AND BOOKS, AND BOOKS...

The most recognizable indie bookstore in South Florida has branches across town, but the Coral Gables store is its flagship and a special sort of place. Think of the images that spring to mind when you imagine a wonderful old library, then place that temple of literature in the tropics and wash it with golden Miami sunshine. We're not the only ones taken with Books & Books; it feels like every writer who ever visited Florida trots across the store's stage or stops into the excellent in-house cafe and restaurant, fronted by a Mediterranean-redolent patio. Books & Books was founded by Mitchell Kaplan, a teacher-turned-founder of Miami Book Fair International, an event that has no small presence at this store.

Ermita de la Caridad

CHURCH BY THE BAY

The Catholic diocese purchased some bayfront land from Deering's Villa Vizcaya estate and built a shrine here for its displaced Cuban parishioners. Symbolizing a beacon, it faces the homeland, 290 miles due south, a lighthouse for those Miamians who long for a land they may never have visited. This isn't the only way this church – full title: Santuario Nacional de Nuestra Señora de la Caridad – engages with Cuba. A mural depicts the island's history and a Spanish-language presence is the norm for the congregation. Outside the church is a grassy stretch of waterfront that makes a fine spot for a picnic.

Ermita da la Caridad

Vizcaya

MAGIC CITY, MAGIC MANSION

Back in 1916, industrialist James Deering started a Miami tradition of making a ton of money and building ridiculously grandiose digs. He employed 1000 people (then 10% of the local population) and stuffed his home, Vizcaya, with Renaissance furniture, tapestries, paintings and decorative arts.

The mansion is a classic of Miami's Mediterranean Revival style. The largest room is the informal living room, sometimes dubbed 'the Renaissance Hall' for its works dating from the 14th to the 17th centuries. The music room is intriguing for its beautiful wall canvases, which come from northern Italy, while the banquet hall with its regal furnishings evokes the grandeur of European imperial dining rooms.

On the south side of the house stretch a series of gardens modeled on the formal Italian gardens of the 17th and 18th centuries, which form a counterpoint to the wild mangroves beyond. Sculptures, fountains and vine-draped surfaces give an antiquarian look to the grounds, and an elevated terrace (the Garden Mound) provides a fine vantage point over the greenery.

Matheson Hammock Park

GABLES GREEN DREAM

The first park in Dade County, and thus the oldest park in Miami, Matheson (pictured, left) is a green dream: 630 acres of hungry raccoons, fragrant lawns, banyan trees, palms, dense mangrove swamps, a marina with a sailing school and (pretty rare) alligator-spotting, all located just south of Coral Gables. Besides the trees and the landscaping, keep an eye out for a human-made atoll pool, which rises and falls with the tide of nearby Biscayne Bay and is a popular swimming hole for local families.

Plymouth Congregational Church

MISSION-STYLE MIAMI

This 1917 coral church is one of the most striking houses of worship in Miami, from its solid masonry to a hand-carved door from a Pyrenees monastery, which looks like it should be kicked in by Antonio Banderas carrying a guitar case full of explosives and with Salma Hayek on his arm. Which is all to say: even in a city blessed with many fine Spanish Mission-style churches, architecturally this is a particularly fine example. The church opens rarely, though all (and we mean 'all' – this is an LGBTIQ+ friendly congregation) are welcome at the organ- and choir-led 10am Sunday service.

The Kampong

The Kampong

TROPICAL PLANT PARTY

David Fairchild, the Indiana Jones of the botanical world and founder of Fairchild Tropical Garden, would rest at the Kampong (Malay/Indonesian for 'village') in between journeys during which he sought beautiful and profitable plant life. As a pioneer of tropical botany, Fairchild was no slouch when it came to his own tropical backyard. Today the Kampong and its lush gardens are listed on the National Register of Historic Places, while the fecund grounds serve as a classroom for the National Tropical Botanical Garden. Self-guided tours (allow at least an hour) are available by appointment, as are $25 one-hour guided tours. Keep an eye out for the peanut butter fruit (a real thing!), the ylang-ylang flower and jackfruits (the trees and the actual fruit).

Venetian Pool

PRETTIEST POOL IN MIAMI

There are pools and then there are pools, and this is one of the few that is listed on the National Register of Historic Places. We need to emphasize what a palatial, over-the-top swimming experience this is: a wonderland of rock caves, cascading waterfalls, a palm-fringed island and Venetian-style moorings. If Miami – and, particularly, Mediterranean Coral Gables – could morph itself into a swimming space, this would be it. Take a swim and follow in the footsteps of stars like Esther Williams and Johnny 'Tarzan' Weissmuller.

Back in 1923, rock was quarried for the completion of Coral Gables, leaving an ugly gash, a sort of nasty scar to balance out the 'City Beautiful.' Of course, if you're the sort of urban planner who is going to develop a place you nickname the City Beautiful, you're not going to let a pit like that remain, and cleverly, it was laden with mosaic and tiles, and filled up with water. Back in the day, actual gondolas plied the water, and every now and then the pool would get drained so the Miami Symphony Orchestra could perform and take advantage of the natural acoustics.

The orchestra doesn't perform anymore and the gondolas are gone, but the Venetian Pool still looks like a Roman emperor's aquatic playground (there's even a 12ft grotto). The water ranges in depth from 4ft to a bit over 8ft, although there's a 2ft kiddie area too.

Venetian Pool

CORAL GABLES CITY HALL

It's a little funny to think of the often tedious grind of city council business being conducted in this grand building, which opened in 1928 and, architecturally, suggests romance and power, as opposed to parking ordinances. That's the idea, though: the Corinthian colonnade, stucco exterior and central clock tower are all meant to evoke the grace of Iberian-Mediterranean design. Check out Denman Fink's **Four Seasons** ceiling painting in the tower, as well as his framed, untitled painting of the underwater world on the 2nd-floor landing.

GATES TO THE CITY BEAUTIFUL

Designer George Merrick planned a series of elaborate entry gates to Coral Gables, but a real-estate bust meant that many projects went unfinished. It's a shame, as the gorgeous Gables deserves over-the-top entrances. On the other hand, the unfinished nature of the project adds a timeless atmosphere, or maybe speaks to humanity's hubris? Whatever, they look cool.

Among the completed gates worth seeing – many of which resemble (and are named for) the entrance pavilions to grand Andalucian estates – are the **Country Club Prado**, the **Alhambra Entrance**, the **Granada Entrance** and the **Coral Way Entrance**. Also notable is the **Alhambra Watertower**, where Greenway Ct and Ferdinand St meet Alhambra Circle, which resembles a Moorish lighthouse.

Fairchild Tropical Garden

MORE IN CORAL GABLES & COCONUT GROVE

Botanical Legacy: Fairchild Tropical Garden

BLOOMING BOTANICAL RAINBOW

The Fairchild is one of America's great tropical botanical gardens. A butterfly grove, a tropical-plant conservatory and gentle vistas of marsh and keys habitats, plus frequent art installations from artists such as Roy Lichtenstein, all contribute to the beauty of this peaceful, 83-acre garden.

The garden was founded in 1936 by businessman and tropical-plant aficionado Robert Montgomery, and named for explorer and scientist David Fairchild, who played a pivotal role in the garden's creation. He donated many of the plants, including the large African baobab growing by the gatehouse. He also

WHERE TO DRINK IN CORAL GABLES & COCONUT GROVE

Seven Seas
Genuine neighborhood dive, decorated like a nautical theme park and filled with all walks of life.

Titanic
All-American-type brewpub that turns into a popular University of Miami watering hole on a nightly basis.

Taurus
Cool mix of wood paneling, smoky-leather chairs, about 100 beers to choose from and a convivial vibe.

went on official plant-collecting expeditions for the garden, sailing a Chinese junk around the Indonesian archipelago just before the outbreak of WWII.

At **Wings of the Tropics**, hundreds of butterflies flutter freely through the air, the sheen of their wings glinting in the light. One behind-the-scenes highlight is the **Vollmer Metamorphosis Lab**, where visitors can watch in real time as butterflies emerge from chrysalises. The butterflies are then released into the Wings of the Tropics exhibit several times a day.

Amid the lushly lined pathways of the **Tropical Plant Conservatory** and the **Rare Plant House** is a glass sculpture with colorful tendrils unfurling skyward like flickering flames. Created by American artist Dale Chihuly, the **End of Day Tower** sits in a small pond, with African cichlids swimming about the base of the sculpture.

Beauty at the Biltmore

JAZZ AGE GRANDE DAME

In the most opulent neighborhood of one of the showiest cities in the world, the **Biltmore Hotel** has a classic beauty that seems impervious to the passage of years.

This elaborate hotel spreads across 150 acres that encompass pretty tropical grounds, tennis courts, a massive swimming pool and a restored 18-hole golf course. Inside, there's even more afoot, and indeed, you could spend a few days occupied by the many activities on offer. One example: local theater company **GableStage** puts on thought-provoking contemporary works, staged at one end of the Biltmore, in an intimate setting where there's not a bad seat in the house.

Design-wise, there's nothing subtle about the soaring central tower, which was modeled after the 12th-century Giralda tower in Seville, Spain. The showy grandeur continues inside, starting with the colonnaded lobby with its hand-painted ceiling, antique chandeliers and Corinthian columns, and continues to the lushly landscaped courtyard set around a central fountain. Back in the day, gondolas transported celebrity guests like Judy Garland and the Vanderbilts around because, of course, there was a private canal system out the back. Though the waterways are gone, the lavish pool remains.

Are there ghosts? The mobster Thomas 'Fatty' Walsh was gunned down by another gangster on the 13th floor, and some say his spirit still roams the hallways.

FINDING EVA MUNROE'S GRAVE

Completed in 1963, the photogenic **Coconut Grove Library** has limestone walls and a steep roof paying homage to the original 1901 library that stood here. Inside, there's a small, well-curated reference section on South Florida.

Tucked into a small gated area nearby, you'll find the humble headstone of Eva Munroe. Eva, who died in Miami in 1882, lies in the oldest American grave in Miami-Dade County (a sad addendum: local African American settlers died before Eva, but their deaths were never officially recorded). Eva's husband Ralph entered a depression, which he tried to alleviate by building the **Barnacle**, now one of the oldest homes in the area.

IF YOU LIKE BIG HISTORIC HOUSES...

You can't do better than the **Vizcaya** (p93), the enormously opulent, dream-fashioned-into-a-residence mansion. It's the giant house against which all other giant houses in the area are measured.

WHERE TO EAT IN CORAL GABLES & COCONUT GROVE

Coral Bagels
They are bagels, and they are cheap, and they are so very, very good. **$**

PLANTA Queen
This bright, beautiful queen is a vegan dream, serving plant-based Asian-inspired fare. **$$**

Matsrui
Miami boasts many trendy sushi spots, but this strip-mall hideaway serves the real deal. **$$**

WHY I LOVE CORAL GABLES & COCONUT GROVE

Adam Karlin, writer

OK, maybe Wynwood is more bohemian, South Beach more famous and Little Havana more international. But Coral Gables and Coconut Grove include all these elements. This may not be the most artsy/famous/international part of Miami, but by containing all of the above, these two neighborhoods sure manage to be interesting. And, let's be honest: they're beautiful, unique, spacious, special. After a great Italian, Argentine, Thai or vegan meal, you feel the sun and the breeze off Biscayne settle on your skin, while sipping a Cuban coffee on Ponce or Grand Ave, and the world sort of whispers, if only for a moment, 'Yeah. Life can be this good.'

Modest Merrick House

GABLES GENESIS

It's fun to imagine this simple homestead, with its hints of Med-style, as the core of what would eventually become the residential seed from which the gaudy Gables grew. When George Merrick's father purchased this plot, site unseen, for $1100, it was all dirt, rock and guavas. The modest family residence looks as it did in 1925, outfitted with family photos, furniture and artwork. Free guided tours are offered most weekends on the hour from 1pm to 3pm, but because the house is used for private engagements, you should call ahead (305-774-0155) to make sure it's open before you visit.

Take in the Views at Peacock Park

BAY VIEWS AND FAMILY FUN

Extending down to the edge of the waterfront, Peacock Park serves as the great open backyard of Coconut Grove. Young families stop by the playground and join the action on the ball fields, and power-walkers take in the view while striding along the bayfront. In fact, the boardwalk 'trail' that runs by the bay offers some of the cleanest, most peaceful views of Biscayne Bay on the mainland side. What's in a name? You'd think gaudy birds roamed the grounds, but no. This 9-acre plot of land was once the site of the Bayview Inn, owned by Charles and Isabella Peacock. The Peacocks employed black Bahamanian workers, who formed the core of the oldest black community in Miami.

FOR PARK LOVERS

Bayfront Park (p71) in Downtown Miami may not have the foliage and tree cover you'll find in the Gables and the Grove, but it does have great views and central access to some of the best sights of the city.

WHERE TO EAT IN CORAL GABLES & COCONUT GROVE

Caffe Abbracci
This fine Italian outpost offers delicious pasta and red wine at a sidewalk table. Perfection. **$$$**

LoKal
There are beers, there are craft burgers, there are good times on tap at LoKal. **$**

Threefold
Strong espresso, pillowy eggs Benedict and fresh salmon salad set this cafe apart from the rest. **$$**

GREATER MIAMI

MORE MAGIC IN THE MAGIC CITY

Little Haiti and the Upper East Side are at the northern edge of mainland Miami. Little Haiti is the largest Haitian community in North America, and while it feels as Caribbean as the rest of Miami, it is also undeniably distinct: the *kreyòl* language dominates, as do Haitian businesses and community institutions. Further east, the Upper East Side is best known for the so-called MiMo on Bibo, which stands for Miami Modern on Biscayne Blvd – encompassing a spread of photogenic buildings running from 50th St to 77th St.

Key Biscayne and neighboring Virginia Key are easy getaways from Downtown Miami, boasting magnificent beaches, lush nature trails in state parks and aquatic adventures aplenty. The sights are spread along the two islands, with one of the biggest highlights – the Bill Baggs Cape Florida State Park – anchoring the south end of Key Biscayne. You'll need a car or a bicycle to get around here.

TOP TIP

You can purchase an outstanding spread at **Marky's Gourmet**, which has fine cheese, breads, wines, deli items and uncommon fare from across Europe. Afterwards, head over to **Morningside Park** and assemble your smorgasbord of smoked herring, dark bread and sausage slices for a perfect picnic.

MORE IN GREATER MIAMI

Upper East Side Surprises

ARCHITECTURE, ART AND URBAN OASES

Northeast of Wynwood, the Upper East Side is stuffed with creative shops, art studios and cafes, many of which have opened in the past few years. There are plenty of pleasant surprises here, from mid-20th-century architecture to cutting-edge arts collectives.

An icon in the MiMo (Miami Modern) district, the **Vagabond Hotel** is a 1953 motel and restaurant where Frank Sinatra and other Rat Packers used to hang out. Today it's been reborn as a boutique hotel, and has lost none of its allure. It also has a great bar.

A few blocks away, **Miami Ironside** is a pleasant hub of creativity where you'll find art and design studios, showrooms and galleries as well as a few eating and drinking spaces. It's a lushly landscaped property, with some intriguing public art.

BOTANICAS

You might notice a few storefronts with 'botanica' signs in Little Haiti. They specialize in the Afro-Caribbean belief system of *vodou*. Forget stereotypes about pins and dolls. *Vodou* recognizes supernatural forces in everyday objects. Notice the statues of what look like people; these represent *loa* (pronounced lwa), spirits that form a pantheon below God. Drop a coin into a *loa* offering bowl before you leave.

WHERE TO DRINK IN GREATER MIAMI

Anderson
Great neighborhood bar with a dim interior sprinkled with red couches, animal-print fabrics and neon wallpaper.

Boteco
Come here on Friday evening to see the biggest Brazilian expat reunion in Miami. Cariocas, unite!

Vagabond Pool Bar
Tucked behind the Vagabond Hotel, this sultry, atmospheric bar serves up perfectly mixed cocktails.

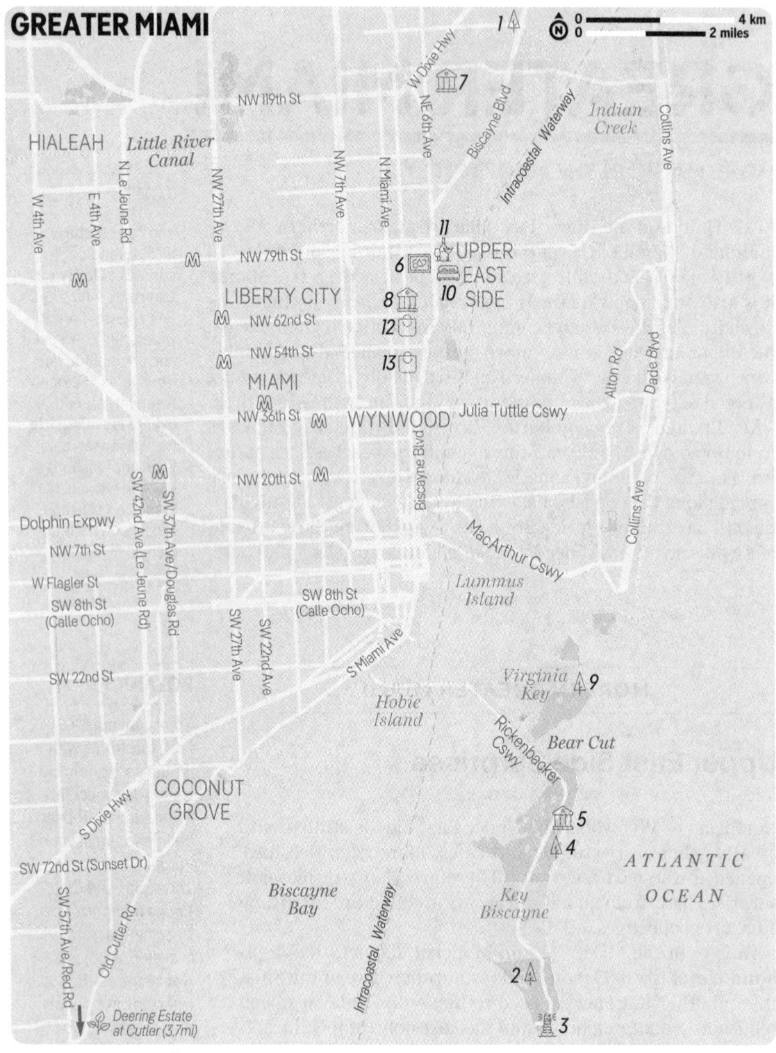

SIGHTS
1 Arch Creek Park
2 Bill Baggs Cape Florida State Park
3 Cape Florida Lighthouse
4 Crandon Park
see 12 Little Haiti Cultural Center
5 Marjory Stoneman Douglas Biscayne Nature Center
6 Miami Ironside
7 Museum of Contemporary Art North Miami
8 Pan American Art Projects
9 Virginia Key Beach North Point Park

SLEEPING
see 10 Hotel New Yorker
10 Vagabond Hotel

DRINKING & NIGHTLIFE
11 Anderson

SHOPPING
12 Caribbean Marketplace
see 12 Libreri Mapou
see 12 Sweat Records
13 Upper Buena Vista

Thirsty? The **Anderson** is a great bar with a dimly lit interior sprinkled with red couches, animal-print fabrics, wild wallpaper and lots of 1980s affectations. Head to the back patio for a tropical-themed setting where you can dip your toes in the sand (absent an actual oceanfront).

The **Hotel New Yorker**, with its frosty white walls and vintage neon, looks MiMo enough to star in a Tarantino movie. Speaking of which, the patio bar is a perfect spot for people-watching a fascinating cross-section of Miami creative types.

Exploring Little Haiti

MUSIC AND MACHE

Little Haiti has been a major nexus of the Haitian diaspora since the late 1970s. Within the neighborhood, the **Little Haiti Cultural Center** serves as both a cornerstone and an access point for outsiders. It hosts an art gallery with thought-provoking exhibitions from Haitian painters, sculptors and multimedia artists. You can also find dance classes, drama productions and a Caribbean-themed market during special events. The building itself is a confection of bold tropical colors, steep A-framed roofs and lacy decorative elements. Next door is the **Caribbean Marketplace**, also known as *Mache Ayisyen,* a 9000-sq-ft venue that replicates the Iron Market in Port Au Prince, Haiti's capital.

Little Haiti is a sprawling neighborhood where street crime is a concern. If you're looking to visit the neighborhood, it's easy enough to start at the Cultural Center, and probably the best time to visit that space is during the Sounds of Little Haiti, a music- and food-filled fête held on the third Friday of every month from 6pm to 10pm. The celebration is rife with music, Caribbean food and kids' activities.

Another can't miss in the neighborhood is **Pan American Art Projects**. Formerly located in Wynwood, PAAP made the move up to Little Haiti in 2016 – a growing trend as gallerists were priced out of the neighborhood they helped popularize. Inside the space, you'll find excellent contemporary work by emerging and established artists from across the Western Hemisphere.

Sweat, Books & Banyans

BOOKS, BOUTIQUES, BUENA VISTA

A few businesses, some at the edge of Little Haiti, and one in the heart of the neighborhood, speak to the roots of the neighborhood, and the rapidly changing cityscape of the Upper East Side.

BEST RESTAURANTS IN LITTLE HAITI & THE UPPER EAST SIDE

Boia De
Ridiculously tasty contemporary Italian fare cooked and served by a punk-rock crew. $$

Blue Collar
American comfort food done to perfection in a classic 1960s coffee-house interior. $$$

Chef Creole
Delicious Caribbean food; head here for stewed conch, fried pork and oxtail. $

Phuc Yea
A little Latin, a little Cajun, a lot Vietnamese and always delicious. $$$

Jimmy's East Side Diner
A classic greasy spoon that's excellent for big breakfasts, or burgers and such later in the day. $

FOR CULTURE LOVERS

If you're into the ethnic enclaves of Miami, make sure to head to **Viernes Culturales** (p79; cultural Fridays), the big street party that kicks off in Little Havana on every third Friday of the month.

WHERE TO DRINK IN GREATER MIAMI

Jada Coles
Dark and cozy, this is one of Miami's best dive bars, on the edge of posh Coral Gables.

Kaiju
Speakeasy-style bar with Japanese pop-culture themes in the Citadel food hall.

Miami Kava & Coffee
Sip on kava (a root drink) and kratom teas, allegedly all-natural stress-relief potions.

PICNIC PROVISIONS

Hungering to eat alfresco? Picnic lovers rejoice, and stop by **Legion Park** for a bustling local farmers market that, for now, strikes a balance between representing neighborhood old-timers and fresh-faced newcomers. It's got all the produce (especially tropical fruits), cheese and breads you'd need for a good picnic, and as with most markets of this ilk, it's a nice place to wander and soak up the community vibe.

Alternatively, you could do as the local Eastern Europeans do and go to **Marky's Gourmet**, a Miami institution going strong since 1983. In-the-know foodies from afar flock here to load up on Russian gourmet cheeses, olives, European-style sausages, wines, cakes, teas, jams, chocolates, caviar and much more.

Sweat Records might feel like a new kid on the block, but it's been in Little Haiti for well over a decade. This is almost a stereotypical indie record store – there's funky art and graffiti on the walls, tattooed staff arguing over LPs and EPs you've never heard of, and a general air of vigorous musical knowledge married to iconoclastic hipness. It's great.

Libreri Mapou is arguably the center of literary life in the Little Haiti neighborhood. This bookstore specializes in English, French and Creole titles and periodicals, and features thousands of great titles and live events. The owner, Jan Mapou, is a writer and political thinker of some distinction.

As for the newer gentrification game, it's hard to get fancier, or more beautiful, than **Upper Buena Vista**. We've never thought we could describe a mall as being 'banyan-chic,' yet that is the vibe here: enormous trees shade a series of outdoor shopping kiosks linked by pleasant breezeways. The retailers are all local boutique-level vendors, mainly selling clothes, home goods and jewelry.

Come Out to Key Biscayne

BEAUTIFUL JEWEL OF THE BAY

Floating like a glittering residential jewel in the bay it is named for, Key Biscayne and neighboring Virginia Key are a quick and easy getaway from Downtown Miami. Once you pass some scenic causeways you'll feel like you've left Miami for a floating suburb with magnificent beaches, lush nature trails in state parks and aquatic adventures aplenty. The stunning skyline views of Miami alone are worth the trip out.

Virginia Key Beach North Point Park is an attractive green space with several small, pleasing beaches and some short nature trails. Pretty waterfront views aside, the big reason for coming is to hire kayaks or paddleboards at **Virginia Key Outdoor Center** (vkoc.net).

Marjory Stoneman Douglas Biscayne Nature Center is a child-friendly space and a great all-ages introduction to South Florida's unique ecosystems, with hands-on exhibits as well as small aquariums full of local marine life. You can also stroll a nature trail through coastal hammock (hardwood forest) or enjoy the beach in front.

Finally, head to 1200-acre **Crandon Park**, a serene clump of dense coastal hammock, mangrove swamps and a 2-mile-long beach, which is clean and often uncluttered, and faces a lovely sweep of teal goodness. In a city well-known for its beaches, this is one of the best.

WHERE TO EAT IN GREATER MIAMI

Lots of Lox
Bustling, old-school deli that serves a mean chopped liver on rye. **$$**

Kebo
Spanish outpost on Key Biscayne serving excellent grilled prawns and Galician octopus. **$$$**

MsCheezious
One of Miami's best-loved food trucks whips up original, delicious grilled-cheese sandwiches. **$**

753CRISTIANPHOTO/SHUTTERSTOCK ©

Key Biscayne

A Taste of the Keys at Bill Baggs

KINDA LIKE THE KEYS

If you don't make it to the Florida Keys, **Bill Baggs Cape Florida State Park** is the next best way to get a taste of their unique island ecosystems. The 494-acre space is a tangled clot of tropical fauna and dark mangroves – look for the 'snorkel' roots that provide air for half-submerged mangrove trees – all interconnected by sandy trails and wooden boardwalks, and surrounded by miles of pale ocean.

A concession shack rents out kayaks, bikes, in-line skates, beach chairs and umbrellas. Head to the western side of the park for some excellent shore fishing. Or if that's not your thing, head there for hiking, cycling or skating – there are trails running throughout this side of the island, including some concrete paths. A mile-and-a-quarter of Atlantic-side beach here is also open to swimming, but bear in mind that there are no lifeguards on duty, so you swim at your own risk.

HISTORIC VIRGINIA KEY PARK

A short drive (or bike ride) from Downtown Miami, the Historic Virginia Key Park is great for a dose of nature, with a small but pretty beachfront and playgrounds for the kids (plus a carousel). Sometimes there are concerts, ecology-minded family picnics and other events. Coming from Downtown Miami, this is the second park entrance on the left (past the entrance to the Virginia Key Beach North Point Park).

In the dark days of segregation, this beachfront, initially accessible only by boat, was a segregated beach for African Americans, Cubans, Haitians and many others from Latin America. It wasn't until the early 1960s that the city's beaches were finally desegregated.

FOR BEACH LOVERS

It's not all models and glam in Miami Beach. **South Pointe Park** (p59), for example, is a great example of a stretch of South Beach where you can let your hair down or visit with kids without feeling self-conscious.

Gold Hog
The place in Key Biscayne to grab picnic fare before hitting the beach or state parks. **$**

Andiamo
Excellent thin-crust pizzas from a brick oven at a converted industrial space on Biscayne Blvd. **$$**

Boater's Grill
Waterfront restaurant has a menu packed with South Florida maritime goodness on Key Biscayne. **$$**

SEEING STILTSVILLE

Head to the southern shore of Bill Baggs Cape Florida State Park and you'll see, in the distance, seven houses standing on pilings in Biscayne Bay. The buildings, known as Stiltsville, have been around since the early 1930s, ever since 'Crawfish Eddie Walker' built a shack on the waves. The 'village' was, at times, a gambling den, smuggling haven and bikini club.

At its peak in 1960, there were 27 'homes' here. Predictably, hurricanes and erosion took their toll. No one lives in Stiltsville today, but it's possible to take a boat tour out here with the Biscayne National Park Institute (biscaynenational parkinstitute.org) and see the remaining buildings up close.

LUCKY-PHOTOGRAPHER/SHUTTERSTOCK ©

Cape Florida Lighthouse

At the state recreation area's southernmost tip, the 1845 brick **Cape Florida Lighthouse** is the oldest structure in Florida (it replaced another lighthouse that was severely damaged in 1836 during the Second Seminole War). As lighthouses go, this one has been through a lot, from sabotage by Confederate soldiers in the Civil War to getting bought by James Deering, the same heir who designed Vizcaya. Free tours run at 10am and 1pm Thursday to Monday.

Contemporary Art in the North

ART OFF-THE-BEATEN-TRACK

The **Museum of Contemporary Art North Miami** has long been a reason to head up north (like, way north Miami: NE 125th St). The galleries feature excellent rotating exhibitions of contemporary art by local, national and international artists, usually themed along socially engaged lines of interest.

WHERE TO EAT IN GREATER MIAMI

Legion Park Farmers Market
Besides having fresh produce, this is an excellent spot to soak up the vibe in the Upper East Side. **$**

Novocento
Buenos Aires–style bistro on Key Biscayne serving up gnocchi pasta and some fine steak. **$$$**

BarMeli69
Swinging, friendly Mediterranean cafe with a huge wine selection, lots of tapas and live music. **$$**

There is a 'pay what you wish' gallery policy during **Jazz@ MOCA** from 7pm to 10pm on the last Friday of every month, when live outdoor jazz concerts are held.

Nature in a Small Package

GREEN PARKING SPACES AND MUSEUMS

Compact, cute **Arch Creek Park**, located near the Oleta River, encompasses a cozy habitat of tropical hardwood species that surrounds a pretty, natural limestone bridge. Naturalists can lead you on kid-friendly ecotours of the area, which include a lovely butterfly garden, or visitors can peruse a small but well-stocked museum of Native American and pioneer artifacts.

Awash at Deering Estate at Cutler

ADVENTURE WITH DEERING

The Deering Estate at Cutler is sort of 'Vizcaya lite,' which makes sense as it was built by Charles, brother of James Deering (of Vizcaya mansion fame). The 150-acre grounds are awash with tropical growth, and a slew of activities are generally on offer, including moonlight kayak trips into the surrounding mangroves and tours of the surrounding nature preserve.

Also on the estate is the **Cutler Burial Mound**, one of the few surviving prehistoric mounds in the region. The mound has been repeatedly excavated as far back as the 1860s, although some of the bones removed from the mound have since been reburied. It is thought that the mound is the burial site of 12 to 18 Native Americans. It's accessible via a boardwalk.

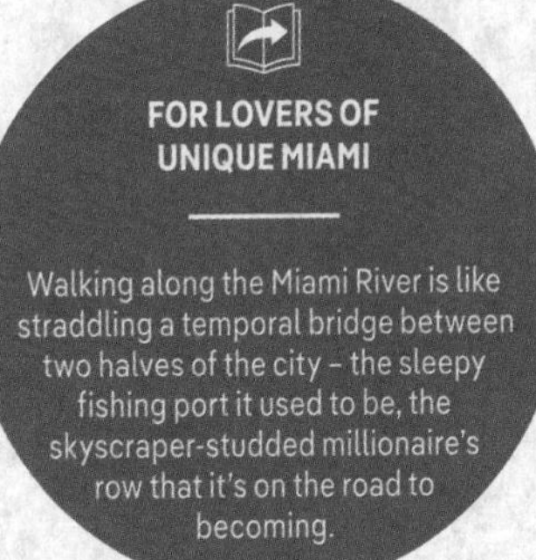

BEST PLACES TO EAT IN GREATER MIAMI

Islas Canarias
We won't say 'best Cuban food in Miami,' but this restaurant is certainly a contender. $

Kush by Stephen
Damn if the pastrami isn't a religious experience at the oldest deli in Miami. $

Fritanga Montelimar
This beloved spot serves up huge portions of Nicaraguan favorites (grilled pork, chicken stew etc). $

Steve's Pizza
Multi-branch but local-oriented outfit serving thin-crust pie, handmade with care and good ingredients. $

Chayhana Oasis
A gorgeous Silk Road–esque outpost for Uzbek cuisine like pilaf and steamed lamb dumplings. $$

WHERE TO SLEEP IN GREATER MIAMI

Landon Hotel
Cheerful, hip option with cool, clean lines offset by bright, bouncy colors. **$$$**

Silver Sands
Old Florida–style independent resort delivers a warm, homey vibe, plus a nice pool. **$$**

Vagabond
A step back in time to 1950s modernism splashed with 21st-century luxury amenities. **$$**

GALYNA ANDRUSHKO/SHUTTERSTOCK ©

Above: Cypress trees, Everglades; right: Great blue heron, Big Cypress National Reserve (p115)

THE EVERGLADES & BISCAYNE NATIONAL PARK

WETLAND ADVENTURES, WILDLIFE AND ISLANDS

One of the world's biological treasures, the Everglades teems with unique plant and animal life. Nearby, Biscayne National Park encompasses reefs, wrecks and islands.

There is no wilderness in the world quite like the Everglades. Called the 'River of Grass' by Native American inhabitants, it's not just a wetland, lake, river or grassland – it's all of these, twisted into a series of soft horizons, long vistas and sunsets stretching across your entire field of vision, animated by an extraordinary cast of wild creatures.

The park's quiet majesty is evident in the sight of an anhinga opening glistening wings to the sun after a mid-morning feed, or in the slow, rhythmic flap of a great blue heron gliding over the mirror-like surface of a saturated prairie. Or the primeval silence of a cypress dome, broken only by a sapsucker's hopeful tapping or the prehistoric roar of an alligator. Out on Florida Bay, the marsh gives way to a seemingly endless expanse of shallow seabed, with manatees bubbling up to the surface and aquatic birds nesting by the thousands on mangrove-backed mudflats.

The third-largest national park in the continental US continues to face threats from encroaching development, invasive species and agriculture. The importance of this ecological treasure, however, is no longer in doubt thanks to tireless preservation efforts by visionary conservationists like Marjory Stoneman Douglas.

Nearby is Biscayne National Park, best known for its coral reefs and wreck dives, history-themed boat trips and kayaking excursions amid islands fringed with mangroves.

THE MAIN AREAS

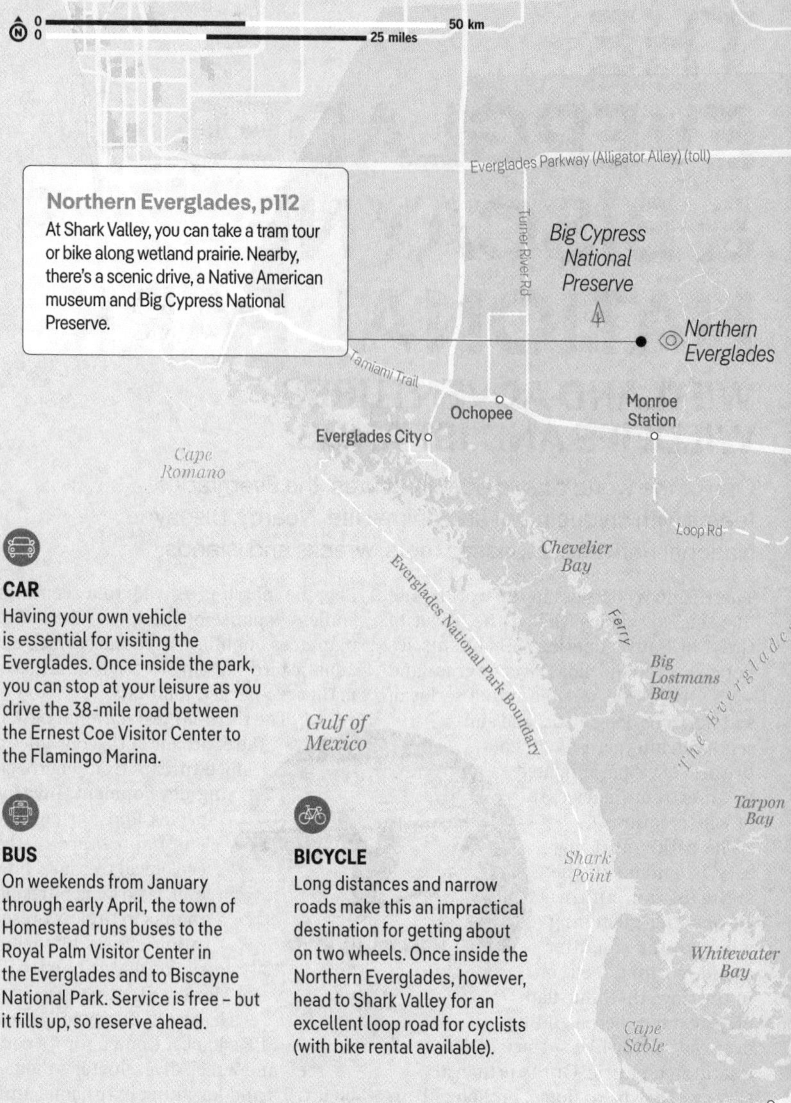

Northern Everglades, p112

At Shark Valley, you can take a tram tour or bike along wetland prairie. Nearby, there's a scenic drive, a Native American museum and Big Cypress National Preserve.

CAR

Having your own vehicle is essential for visiting the Everglades. Once inside the park, you can stop at your leisure as you drive the 38-mile road between the Ernest Coe Visitor Center to the Flamingo Marina.

BUS

On weekends from January through early April, the town of Homestead runs buses to the Royal Palm Visitor Center in the Everglades and to Biscayne National Park. Service is free – but it fills up, so reserve ahead.

BICYCLE

Long distances and narrow roads make this an impractical destination for getting about on two wheels. Once inside the Northern Everglades, however, head to Shark Valley for an excellent loop road for cyclists (with bike rental available).

Find Your Way

The Everglades anchors Florida's lower end. Visit the northern Everglades for a cycling tour; to the south, see wildlife from short trails. East of the Everglades, Biscayne National Park protects an island-dotted marine reserve.

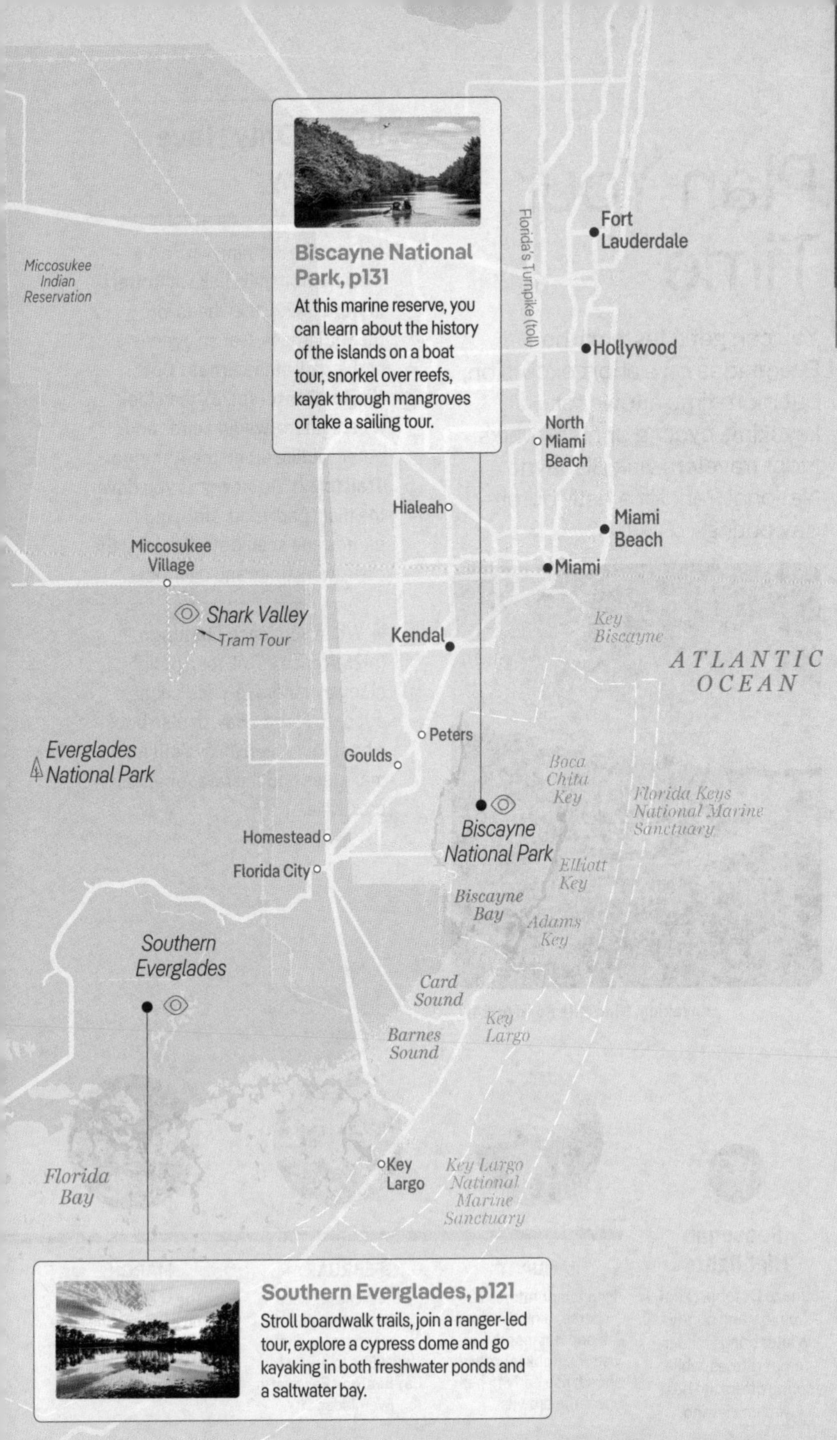

Biscayne National Park, p131

At this marine reserve, you can learn about the history of the islands on a boat tour, snorkel over reefs, kayak through mangroves or take a sailing tour.

Miccosukee Indian Reservation

Florida's Turnpike (toll)

Fort Lauderdale

Hollywood

North Miami Beach

Hialeah

Miami Beach

Miccosukee Village

Miami

Shark Valley

Tram Tour

Kendal

Key Biscayne

ATLANTIC OCEAN

Peters

Goulds

Everglades National Park

Boca Chita Key

Florida Keys National Marine Sanctuary

Biscayne National Park

Homestead

Florida City

Elliott Key

Biscayne Bay

Adams Key

Southern Everglades

Card Sound

Key Largo

Barnes Sound

Florida Bay

Key Largo

Key Largo National Marine Sanctuary

Southern Everglades, p121

Stroll boardwalk trails, join a ranger-led tour, explore a cypress dome and go kayaking in both freshwater ponds and a saltwater bay.

Plan Your Time

You can get a taste of the Everglades on a short excursion, but more time allows for kayaking, cycling or night walks. Most travelers visit Biscayne National Park for a half- or full-day outing.

FRANCESCO BLANCO/SHUTTERSTOCK ©

Kayaking, Nine Mile Pond (p124)

If You Only Have One Day

- Start the morning with a tropical-fruit milkshake at **Robert Is Here** (p129), then head into the wilderness. Get an overview of the park at the **Ernest Coe Visitor Center** (p123), then look for alligators, wading birds and other wildlife along the **Anhinga Trail** (p122). Go slowly as you drive the main park road, stopping for photos and scenic strolls along the boardwalk trails and overlooks.

- When you reach **Flamingo** (p125), rent a kayak for a paddle along a mangrove-lined canal or out onto Florida Bay, or else book a boat tour. Keep an eye out for manatees and the rare American crocodile.

Seasonal Highlights

June to October is hot, humid – and buggy. Winter brings milder temperatures, while spring offers the best wildlife viewing.

JANUARY

Mild temperatures and sparse rainfall mean a popular month for visitors. Book tours well ahead; rise early to beat the crowds.

FEBRUARY

The pleasant, near-perfect weather continues – a fine backdrop to the three-day **Seafood Festival** in Everglades City.

MARCH

The scent of fresh fruit lingers in the air as visitors load up on goodies at local farm stands.

MARIDAV/SHUTTERSTOCK ©, IRINA WILHAUK/SHUTTERSTOCK ©, PELOW MEDIA/SHUTTERSTOCK ©

A Weekend Visit

- After a day in the Everglades, drive east to **Biscayne National Park** (p131). At the **Dante Fascell Visitor Center** (p132), learn about the park's different ecosystems, its wildlife and human history before taking a park excursion (reserved in advance).

- After some adventure? Book a paddle and snorkel trip, where you'll get a fish-eye's view of the bay's coral reefs (or, weather permitting, one of its shipwrecks). You can also spy marine and avian life while gliding along the edge of a mangrove forest on a stand-up paddleboard. At trip's end, head back into the Everglades for a nighttime stroll along the **Anhinga Trail** (p122).

Three Days or More to Spare

- On day three, head to **Shark Valley** (p114) and rent a bike for a spin on the 15-mile loop road, a great place to see alligators, birds, turtles and snakes. Don't miss the views from the observation tower. Afterwards, learn about indigenous traditions at the **Miccosukee Village** (p115), an open-air museum. Further along Hwy 41 is a **scenic drive** (p115) on a forest-lined loop road, with stops for hikes and wildlife photos along the way.

- For a different perspective on the region, head to **Everglades City** (p118), gateway to the **Ten Thousand Islands** (p118) and a watery wilderness famed for its dolphins and birdlife.

APRIL
Temperatures are rising but the water levels are low, making it a great time to see wildlife in the cypress domes.

JUNE
Soaring temperatures and mosquito swarms keep many visitors away. It's also the start of hurricane season (through November).

JULY
It's a great time for aquatic activity in the mirror-like waters of **Biscayne National Park** and the **Ten Thousand Islands**.

DECEMBER
Migrating avian species, including yellow-throated warblers, draw bird-watchers. Homestead hosts fun holiday events, like **Las Posadas** (p129).

NORTHERN EVERGLADES

It's hard to believe that Florida's largest city abuts its greatest wilderness reserve. Less than an hour's drive west of Miami's Little Havana district, the signs of civilization quickly evaporate against the vast expanse of wetland prairie. The ramrod-straight, two-lane Tamiami Trail highway forms the northern boundary of the national park and its principal attraction, Shark Valley.

In 1946, a project to dig two exploratory wells in the area was abandoned, and the Everglades became a national park the following year. But long before oil workers came on the scene, Native Americans thrived in this seemingly inhospitable region. The Miccosukee tribe still has a visible presence and operates an open-air museum, various airboat tours and a fuel station. Keep motoring west on the Tamiami and you can visit the Big Cypress National Preserve, as well as curious roadside attractions like the Skunk Ape Research Headquarters and the Clyde Butcher Gallery.

TOP TIP

If you have limited time you can see a lot in just one day, starting out at Shark Valley and ending up at Big Cypress. Dining options are very limited, so pick up snacks and picnic fare before coming to the area.

Cycling, Everglades

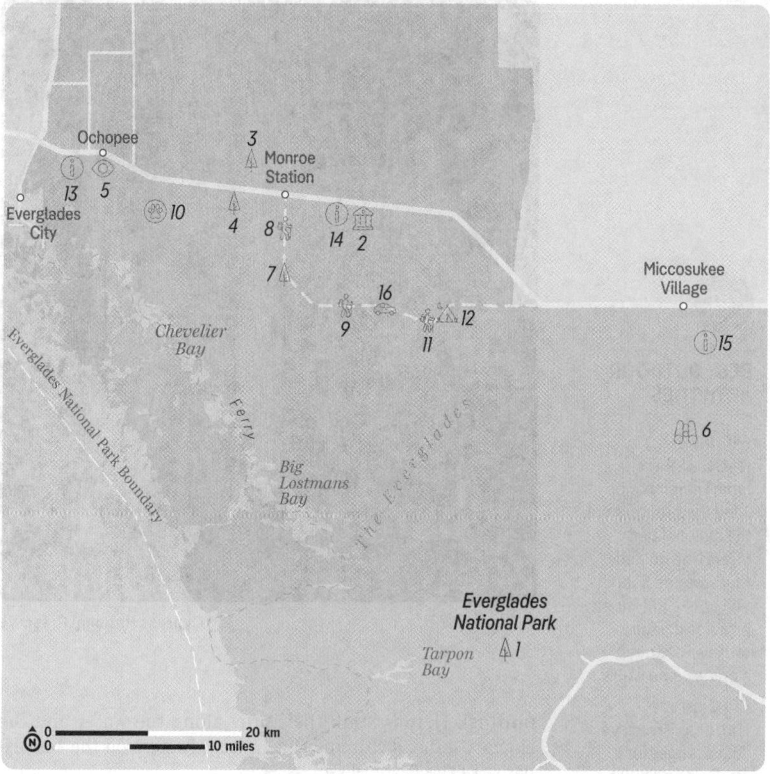

Ochopee
Everglades City
Monroe Station
Miccosukee Village
Chevelier Bay
Everglades National Park Boundary
Ferry
Big Lostmans Bay
The Everglades
Everglades National Park
Tarpon Bay
0 20 km
0 10 miles

HIGHLIGHTS
1 Everglades National Park

SIGHTS
22 Big Cypress Gallery
3 Big Cypress National Preserve
4 Kirby Storter Roadside Park
5 Ochopee Post Office
6 Shark Valley Observation Tower
7 Sweetwater Strand

ACTIVITIES, COURSES & TOURS
8 Gator Hook Trailhead
9 Roberts Trail
10 Skunk Ape Research Headquarters
11 Tree Snail Hammock Trail

SLEEPING
12 Mitchell Landing Campground

INFORMATION
13 Nathaniel P Reed Visitor Center
14 Oasis Visitor Center
15 Shark Valley Visitor Center

TRANSPORT
16 Loop Road Scenic Drive

Cycling the Primordial Wilderness

A WILDLIFE-FILLED LOOP TRAIL

The major destination for many visitors to the Everglades is named not for its marine life, but rather its location at the headwaters of the little-known Shark River, which drains into the Gulf of Mexico. The big draw is the 15-mile paved **loop trail** that takes you into Shark River Slough. You'll pass small creeks, tropical forest and 'borrow pits' (human-made holes that are now basking spots for gators, turtles and

MIAMI PROVISIONS

On your way from Miami, grab takeaway lunch from a Latin spot in **Little Havana** (p78), which is less than an hour's drive from Shark Valley. Cuban sandwiches, taco bowls or burritos will give you the fuel you need after a morning in the park.

Big Cypress National Preserve

MIA2YOU/SHUTTERSTOCK ©

BEST OUTDOOR ACTIVITIES

Everglades National Park
From December or January through April, the national park offers free guided tours around Shark Valley, like full-moon bike rides, nature walks and 'slough slogs' swamp walks.

Big Cypress National Preserve
Join a ranger for a stroll along Kirby Storter Boardwalk, take a swamp walk or go canoeing (free watercraft provided).

Everglades Adventure Tours
From Skunk Ape Research Headquarters, EAT offers excellent private tours, including kayak trips, night safaris and old-fashioned pole-boat excursions.

birdlife). Herons stalk their prey along the water and the clouds overhead shimmer like mirror images on the vast expanse of the River of Grass.

Closed to cars, the pancake-flat trail is perfect for bicycles. The halfway point is the spiraling 45ft **Shark Valley Observation Tower**, a brutalist concrete structure with dramatic 360-degree views over the landscape.

If you don't feel like exerting yourself, the most popular and painless way to immerse yourself in the Everglades is via the two-hour **tram tour** that runs along Shark Valley's entire loop trail. If you only have time for one Everglades activity, this should be it – the guides are informative and witty, and you may get to see gators sunning themselves on the road.

You can reserve bikes or tram tours in advance (advisable in the winter) through **Shark Valley Tram Tours** (at the visitor center). Plan to go early in the day, both to beat the heat and to maximize your chance of seeing wildlife.

WHERE TO STAY ON THE TAMIAMI TRAIL

Trail Lakes Campground
Pitch a tent, stay in a cabin with air-con or sleep in a traditional Seminole *chickee*. **$$**

Explore Big Cypress
Well-equipped bungalows behind Clyde Butcher's gallery offer enchanting views from screened-in porches. **$$$**

Monument Lake Campground
Enjoy rosy sunsets over the water at this small, NPS-run campground. **$**

Roadside Adventures

CULTURE, ART AND MYTHICAL CREATURES

Hwy 41, better known as the **Tamiami Trail**, marks the northern boundary of Everglades National Park. Along this fast-moving, two-lane road are vast flooded forests, pine woods, swamp-buggy tours and roadside food shacks.

Despite the inhospitable terrain, the native Miccosukee have deep roots in the Everglades. Just west of the turnoff to Shark Valley, the **Miccosukee Village** is a great place to learn about their culture. At *chickees* (wooden platforms above the waterline) are demonstrations on cooking, beading, patchwork and other craft; photos, film clips and life-sized dioramas feature in the museum. The highlight is the alligator demonstration, where a brave soul gets up close and personal with one of these fearsome reptiles while describing some of its surprising features (they continually regrow teeth!).

A 20-minute drive west, the **Big Cypress Gallery** showcases the work of Clyde Butcher, an American photographer in the great tradition of Ansel Adams. His large-format B&W images elevate the swamps to a higher level.

Some 15 miles further is another key roadside attraction: the **Skunk Ape Research Headquarters** is dedicated to tracking down southeastern USA's version of Bigfoot, the eponymous Skunk Ape, a large gorilla-human hybrid (who supposedly stinks to high heaven). You might not spot a Skunk Ape, but you can see a zoo with colorful birds and reptiles, like Goldie, a 24ft reticulated python.

Just before the turnoff to Everglades City, you'll find America's smallest **post office** at **Ochopee**. It's housed in a former toolshed set against big park skies, where a friendly postal worker poses patiently for snapshots.

Wetland Scenic Drive

GATORS, BIRDS AND CYPRESS SWAMPS

Stretching across nearly 1140 sq miles, **Big Cypress National Preserve** plays a vital role in the health of its better-known neighbor to the south, the Everglades: rains that flood the Preserve's prairies and wetlands get slowly filtered down through the Everglades. One of the best ways to get a taste of the primeval scenery of Big Cypress is to take the 24-mile **Loop Road scenic drive** (aka County Rd 94), just off the Tamiami Trail. Around 4 miles west of the Oasis Visitor Center, look for the brown sign that says, 'Monroe Station/ Loop Road,' off to your left. This marks the beginning of the scenic drive, which will quickly take you into a landscape of

WILDERNESS GATEWAYS

Nathaniel P Reed Visitor Center
Peruse exhibits on plant and animal life, and watch a short film about Big Cypress preserve. A viewing platform faces a canal that sometimes draws manatees.

Kirby Storter Roadside Park
This short (1 mile round-trip), elevated boardwalk leads to a lovely overlook where you can often see a variety of birdlife (like ibis and red-shouldered hawks) amid tall cypresses and strangler figs – plus, of course, alligators.

Oasis Visitor Center
About 20 miles west of Shark Valley, Oasis has a platform overlooking a small, water-filled ditch, a great spot to see alligators, particularly in the dry season (December to May).

WHERE TO SPOT WILDLIFE ON THE TAMIAMI TRAIL

American alligator
The famed predators bask on the road or lurk in culverts or near the Sweetwater Strand.

Great egret
These graceful, white, long-legged wading birds can be seen patiently fishing just off the road.

Florida gar
Long, narrow, olive-brown fish with small fins that can grow over 2ft long.

sawgrass prairie. Keep your eyes peeled for hawks and other raptors perched on dead trees overlooking the open terrain.

Around mile 2.2, you'll reach a small picnic area and the **Gator Hook Trailhead**. For immersion in the swampland, there's no better place. The out-and-back trail (5 miles round trip) initially follows an elevated logging tram road, though you'll soon be ankle- or thigh-deep in water, depending on the season (it's driest in the spring) as you trudge past cypress trees with views over the prairie. Use a walking stick to avoid tripping on roots and other invisible hazards.

Back behind the wheel, cypress strands dot the sides of the road, with memorable views around mile 5, the so-called **Sweetwater Strand**. Out of slightly deeper water, towering cypresses stand covered with ferns, bromeliads and Spanish moss. Look for alligators and fish in the water and songbirds in the trees.

Near mile 10, you'll pass the blue-blazed **Roberts Trail**, an 8.2-mile (one-way) trail that goes up to the Oasis Visitor Center on the Tamiami Trail. From there, you can keep going along the **Florida National Scenic Trail**, a meandering, 1500-mile route that travels the length of the state. Be prepared to walk through knee-deep water if hiking the Big Cypress section.

Mile 15.6 offers the chance to take another walk. The short **Tree Snail Hammock Trail** winds through hardwood hammock, a jungle-like environment of broadleaf trees, like gumbo limbo, that grow on higher (and drier) sections of the wetlands. Look for endemic Liguus tree snails clinging tightly to tree trunks.

A few miles east of there, you'll pass through the remains of **Pinecrest**, an abandoned town that once had a population of 400 during its peak in the 1930s. According to legend, the gangster Al Capone ran a hotel and brothel here. Nearby, you can extend your stay in Big Cypress by pitching a tent at **Mitchell Landing**, a primitive campground with sites scattered along a dirt road.

The last few miles of the road pass through a Miccosukee community, with private homes sheltering among the dense greenery. At journey's end (which is not technically a loop), you'll intersect at a different point along the Tamiami Trail, from where you can continue back to your starting point 20 miles to the west.

GUARDIAN OF THE GLADES

One of Florida's most beloved iconoclasts, Marjory Stoneman Douglas fought tirelessly to save the Everglades decades before conservation was a popular topic. In 1947, she published her beautifully written classic, *The Everglades: River of Grass*. A commercial success, the book helped shift public perception of the wetlands from 'infernal swamp' to 'national treasure.'

For years afterwards she continued writing and speaking about the threats posed by development and agriculture, and in 1970 (at the age of 79) Douglas formed the Friends of the Everglades, a non-profit that continues to play a pivotal role in garnering political and financial support for the area's restoration.

WHERE TO SPOT WILDLIFE ON THE TAMIAMI TRAIL

Red-cockaded woodpecker
Rare, robin-sized bird with barred, black-and-white horizontal stripes. Nests only in living pine trees.

Pig frog
Green-brownish amphibians with a breeding call (heard April to August) reminiscent of a pig grunting!

Florida panther
You're unlikely to encounter this 6ft-long endangered brown cat, but look for footprints and scat.

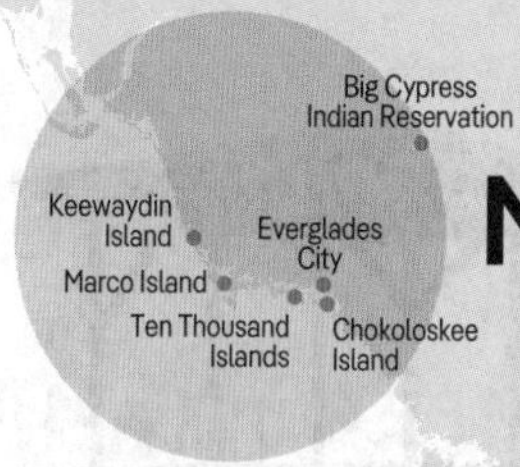

Beyond the Northern Everglades

Outside the national park, you'll find an island-dotted nature reserve, a Seminole heritage museum and some fascinating dolphin encounters.

The eastern edge of the Everglades intersects the estuarine mangrove forests of the Ten Thousand Islands, a large wilderness reserve that sets the stage for aquatic adventures both large and small, from multiday canoe-camping trips to short boat rides through the tangled maze of tree-covered islands.

While mostly uninhabited, there are a few developed islands here, including Chokoloskee (population 350), once a remote frontier settlement reachable only by boat. Native tribes occupied the area for over 1500 years, leaving behind great mounds of shells later used as house foundations by 19th-century settlers.

To the northwest, Marco Island is the chain's largest barrier island, and a major holiday destination for boaters and beachgoers.

TOP TIP

Plan accommodations carefully and well in advance – it's sparse in Everglades City and can be quite pricey on Marco Island.

Chokoloskee, Ten Thousand Islands

EXPLORING LOCAL HISTORY

Museum of the Everglades
Explores the region's latter-day human habitation, from white settlers in the 1800s to the boom days of the 1920s, and the area's devastating storms (including Hurricane Donna in 1960).

Smallwood Store
This rustic building on Chokoloskee Island dates back to 1906, when it served as trading post, post office and general store. Wooden shelves are lined with antiques and old artifacts, along with descriptions of events and characters from the frontier days.

Marco Island Historical Museum
On Marco Island, you can see a replica indigenous Calusa village and fascinating archaeological relics, including the 500- to 1500-year-old Key Marco Cat, a small, exquisitely crafted hardwood carving of a feline.

MATT A CLAIBORNE/SHUTTERSTOCK ©

Kayaker approaching a *chickee*, Wilderness Waterway

Island-studded Wilderness

BOATING AND WILDLIFE-WATCHING

On the western edge of the Everglades, the River of Grass transitions into a series of mostly uninhabited islands and mangrove islets that are teeming with life. Pods of bottlenose dolphins glide through the waters, with ospreys and bald eagles soaring overhead; loggerhead turtles nest on sandy islands while great blue herons, alligators and even the rare American crocodile stealthily stalk their prey just offshore.

Stretching from the southern edge of Marco Island down to Flamingo, the **Ten Thousand Islands** set the stage for both big adventures and short day trips. Competent navigators (with up-to-date NOAA charts) can paddle or motorboat their way along the **Wilderness Waterway**, a 99-mile path with *chickees* available for camping along the way.

The small waterfront town of **Everglades City** is the key gateway to the islands. The National Park Service (NPS) runs the **Gulf Coast Visitor Center**, which doles out essential information on exploring the region. From the center, **Everglades Florida Adventures** runs 90-minute tours aboard a 45ft catamaran, taking you through Chokoloskee Bay, Indian

WHERE TO EAT IN EVERGLADES CITY

Camellia Street Grill
Munch on fresh-off-the-boat seafood on the waterfront deck of this Everglades City classic. **$$**

HavAnnA Cafe
Enjoy Latin-fusion Cuban sandwiches or blackened grouper on a colorful patio. On Chokoloskee Island. **$$**

Island Cafe
Get morning pancakes at this comfort-food diner, then shrimp tacos and fried gator later on. **$**

Key Pass and various mangrove islets in the Everglades. You can also rent out your own kayaks and canoes, for a few hours or up to 10 days of island-hopping explorations.

For guided excursions, book a private tour with **Everglades Adventures Kayak & Eco Tours**, which runs multiday itineraries, camping under starry skies at islands along the way. The same outfit also offers shorter (two- and three-hour) paddling tours.

Native Traditions & Ancestral Landscapes

EPICENTER OF SEMINOLE CULTURE

It's a long drive north of the Everglades – nearly two hours from Shark Valley – but it's well worth the effort to visit one of Florida's most important Native American museums. Set on the Big Cypress Indian Reservation, **Ah-Tah-Thi-Ki** lives up to its name, which in the Seminole language means 'a place to learn; a place to remember.'

Start off your visit here with the 17-minute film *We Seminoles,* which touches on the tribe's history, myths and traditions, then explore the galleries of the museum, with its displays of clothing, basketry, jewelry and impressive 30ft dugout canoes that were once poled through the wetlands. Dioramas with life-sized figures depict various scenes out of traditional Seminole life, from the formal meeting of a soon-to-be-married couple at the bride's mother's house to the colorfully attired celebrants taking part in the Catfish Dance – a key component of the sacred Green Corn Ceremony held each year.

Nature plays a starring role at Ah-Tah-Thi-Ki: behind the museum is a 1-mile boardwalk trail that loops through a lush cypress dome. Signs along the way point out plant and animal species that are vital not only to the Seminoles (like marsh pennywort, a traditional treatment for asthma and other lung ailments) but for the entire Everglades ecosystem. Other stops along the boardwalk pass beside ceremonial grounds and the dwellings and workshops of a recreated traditional Seminole village.

Dolphin-watching off Marco Island

DEEPER INSIGHT INTO MARINE MAMMALS

Some 65 miles west of Shark Valley, Marco Island is the departure point for one of the best boat tours in Florida. Ever since 2006, **Dolphin Explorer** has operated a long-term scientific study of the behavior and movements of southwestern Florida's

FAKAHATCHEE STRAND STATE PRESERVE

Besides having a fantastic name, the Fakahatchee houses a 100-sq-mile estuarine wetland seemingly from the beginning of time. Several trails run through this wild wonderland, where panthers stalk their prey amid the dark waters. While it's unlikely you'll spot the elusive cats, you'll see blooming orchids, birdlife and reptiles (ranging from tiny skinks to oversized alligators).

For a quick visit, walk the 0.5-mile **Big Cypress Bend Boardwal**k, located off the Tamiami Trail. With more time, take the rugged, unpaved Janes Scenic Dr (off SR 29) and then hike along one of the old logging trails, like stunning **East Main Tram**, which runs 2 miles north to an old cabin (then gets progressively overgrown from there).

TRAILS NEAR ALLIGATOR ALLEY (I-75)

Florida Trail Ochopee
Escape the crowds on this 15-mile loop along part of the Florida National Scenic Trail.

Panther Trail
Hunt feline prints along a 1.3-mile trail in Florida Panther National Wildlife Refuge (off SR 29).

Sabal Palm Hiking Trail
Hear woodpeckers hammering while walking amid the cypresses in the Picayune Strand State Forest.

I LIVE HERE: DOLPHIN TALES

Dolphin Explorer's master naturalist **Bob McConville** has the inside scoop on several aquatic residents of Marco Bay.

One of our most famous dolphins out here is Skipper, who survived a shark bite. We saved her life getting some fishing line off of her tail when she was one year old; she'd just had her first calf. Skipper's mom Halfway is the most important dolphin in these waters: she's had seven calves. So if that gene gets passed on, Skipper could be responsible for seven, eight, nine – even 10 offspring.

You might also see Clover, a dolphin nicknamed 'Satan' by local fishers since he likes to steal the catch right off of their lines!

SUNFLOWERMOMMA/SHUTTERSTOCK ©

Tigertail Beach, Marco Island

bottlenose dolphins. Using photo ID of dorsal fins, you'll have the opportunity to get involved in spotting, counting and confirming individual sightings – data which is then shared with the Mote Marine Laboratory in Sarasota and other marine-life organizations around the globe.

As the catamaran disembarks, visitors can page through a photo album depicting dorsal fins of the 130 or so cetacean residents. The naturalist on board points out bite marks and tears that will help you tell the difference between dolphins Wyatt, Dolly and Fireball, and fill you in on various dolphins' life stories: which bulls (males) like to hang out together (Capri and Hatchet, for instance), how they sometimes work together in feeding and defense against sharks, and who has recently given birth. Dolphins recognize the boat and may come up and slap the water with their tails, indicating they want to ride in the boat's wake. Sometimes whole pods will gather to pay a visit, even leaping through the wash behind the boat.

If you spot a dolphin not already catalogued (eg newly born offspring), everyone on board gets to name it. The tour ends with a stop for some shelling at remote and beautiful **Keewaydin**, the largest unbridged barrier island in South Florida.

Excursions last three hours and depart from Rose Marina.

COASTAL DREAMING

Marco Island has picturesque coastline (particularly around Tigertail Beach), but if you're hungry for more action on the waterfront, head to **Naples** (p372), which has some stunning beaches just a half-hour drive to the north.

WHERE TO EAT ON MARCO ISLAND

Dolphin Tiki Bar
Watch boats bobbing lazily in the harbor over fresh seafood platters and happy-hour drinks. **$$**

Lee Be Fish
Mahimahi tacos or grouper sandwiches make a fine prelude to key lime pie at this casual spot. **$**

Oyster Society
Don't miss this buzzing place for its raw bar, sushi plates and grilled seafood and lamb. **$$$**

SOUTHERN EVERGLADES

The wilderness comes into sharp focus in the southern Everglades. At the entrance to the national park, you leave behind the ordered lines of roads and farm fields and enter a realm of freshwater prairies, pinelands and hardwood hammocks, along with six other distinct ecosystems, from biologically diverse cypress domes and grassy marshes dotted with mangrove islands to the shallow Florida Bay, home to manatees and other marine life.

The cycles of nature dominate here, with seasonal levels of precipitation bringing dramatic changes to the landscape. During the wet season (May through November), heavy rainfall causes an explosion of plant and animal life, as fish, frogs, snails and crawfish reproduce in the marshland. In December, water levels begin receding from sawgrass habitats, and by spring, fish and other sea creatures are concentrated in the few remaining water holes – easy pickings for birds, reptiles and other animals.

TOP TIP

The only transport to the park is the free seasonal bus that goes from Homestead to the Royal Palm Visitor Center, running weekends only from January through early April.

Pine Glades Lake (p123)

SOUTHERN EVERGLADES

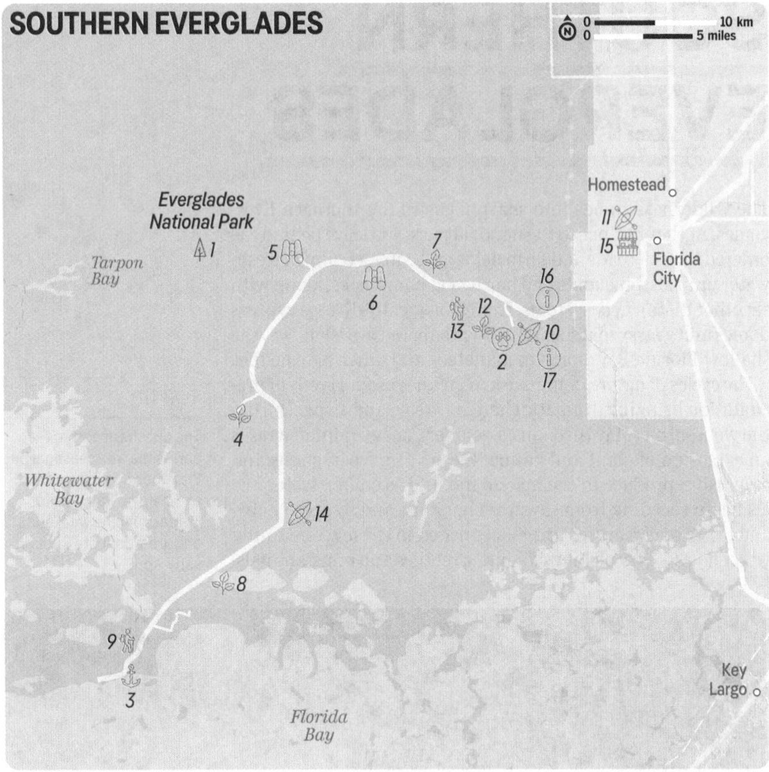

0 10 km
0 5 miles

Everglades National Park
Tarpon Bay
Whitewater Bay
Florida Bay
Homestead
Florida City
Key Largo

HIGHLIGHTS
1 Everglades National Park

SIGHTS
2 Anhinga Trail
3 Flamingo
4 Mahogany Hammock Trail
5 Pa-hay-okee Overlook
6 Pine Glades Lake
7 Pinelands Trail
8 West Lake Trail

ACTIVITIES, COURSES & TOURS
9 Christian Point Trail
10 Everglades National Park Institute
11 Garl's Coastal Kayaking
12 Gumbo Limbo Trail
13 Long Pine Key
14 Nine Mile Pond

EATING
15 Robert Is Here

INFORMATION
16 Ernest Coe Visitor Center
17 Royal Palm Visitor Center

Trails of Royal Palm

SPOTTING ALLIGATORS, ANHINGAS AND HERONS

Around 2 miles past the park entrance station, take the turn-off to Royal Palm Visitor Center. Here you'll find one of the best places to see a variety of Everglades creatures. You'll get

EVERGLADES ECOSYSTEMS

Hardwood hammocks
Shady island forests on slightly higher land nurture tropical mahogany, live oak and gumbo limbo.

Cypresses
Long-lived cypress trees thrive in flooded forests, often growing in a 'dome' shape.

Mangroves
Growing where fresh and salt water mix, they provide key habitats for fish and wading birds.

a close-up view of wildlife on the short (0.8-mile) **Anhinga Trail**, a mostly boardwalk path that winds through a verdant sawgrass marsh. Anhinga spear their prey and various wading birds stalk haughtily through the reeds. In the tea-colored waters below, Florida gar and mosquito fish swim beneath heart-shaped, lily-like spatterdock, while turtles poke their heads above the surface before descending once again. At various overlooks you can sometimes see dozens of alligators basking in the sun.

Come back at night (be sure to bring a flashlight) for a view of the gators swimming along the waterways – sometimes right beside you. The park offers periodic ranger-led walks along the boardwalk after dark, though the park stays open 24 hours so you can also do it yourself. Seeing the glittering eyes of alligators prowling the waterways is an unforgettable experience.

Nearby, the **Gumbo Limbo Trail** (0.4 mile) takes you through a quite different environment from the open slough. Here the path goes through tropical hardwood hammock, which feels like dense jungle amid the strangler figs, ferns and the gumbo limbo trees, easily identified by their red, peeling bark. Move quietly to increase your chances of spotting birds, including great blue herons, cormorants, egrets and warblers. You'll also pass a small pond, yet another favorite refuge for gators.

An Everglades Traverse

HIKING, CANOEING AND WILDLIFE

The 38-mile drive between the park entrance and end-of-the-road Flamingo takes only an hour to drive, but you could spend many days doing activities – hiking, night walks, canoeing, slough slogs – in this biologically diverse stretch of the national park.

First, stop at the **Ernest Coe Visitor Center**, where exhibits detail the Everglades' unique ecosystems and resident wildlife. An 18-minute film captures the area's beauty and complexity, along with the many threats to its survival. In back, a deck overlooks a small pond, where you might spy alligators.

At **Long Pine Key**, you can walk or mountain bike along the 6-mile Long Pine Key Trail, which runs through a pine rockland habitat. The level hike through slash pines might seem featureless at first, but there's a wide variety of birds and you may even see animal tracks (including bears and panthers). Enjoy scenic views over **Pine Glades Lake** near the end of the walk (also accessible off the main road).

Just up the road, the 0.5-mile **Pinelands Trail** loops through a pine island with some of the greatest variety of plant species in the park – and one of North America's most endangered pine communities. As you pass both tropical plants and cacti,

BEST FREE PARK RANGER ACTIVITIES

Slough slog
Wilderness immersion on a fascinating guided walk (wade) through watery terrain into a cypress dome.

Starlight walk
Evening stroll along the Anhinga Trail looking for gators and other creatures. Bring a flashlight.

Canoe the wilderness
Three-hour paddle through some of the Everglades' most sublime scenery.

Early bird walk
Join a morning hike to observe some of the Everglades' feathered species.

Glades glimpse
Learn about the wonders of the Everglades at a daily talk given at a visitor center.

Pineland
Rare Everglades habitats of slash pine forest, saw palmetto and some 200 different tropical plants.

Freshwater sloughs
Marshy, slow-moving rivers that channel water through the Everglades and remain flooded year-round.

Coastal lowlands
Between mudflats and dry land, coastal prairies have salt-tolerant, desert-like plants that experience periodic flooding.

SIMON DANNHAUER/SHUTTERSTOCK ©

WILDLIFE-WATCHING

One of the not-to-be-missed highlights off the main park road is the **Anhinga Trail** (p122) in the Royal Palm area. You can also go on ranger talks and even night walks here.

Mahogany Hammock Trail

WHY I LOVE THE EVERGLADES

Regis St Louis, writer

I remember the first time I came here years ago and feeling like I'd stumbled onto the set of a nature film. I was awestruck by the sight of prehistoric-looking alligators juxtaposed with elegant wading birds staring motionless at the sun-sparkling water as the grunt of some great beast erupted from the cypress woods – a pig frog, it turned out. Kayaking on Florida Bay has also made me appreciate this incredible wilderness. On my last trip there, I saw an endangered saw fish, enjoyed close encounters with a curious manatee and witnessed a fiery sunset over the water.

keep an eye out for tree snails clinging to branches and the smooth bark of species like the Jamaican dogwood.

As the road begins its southward descent, the **Pa-hay-okee Overlook** lies off to the right. *Pa-hay-okee* means 'river of grass' in Seminole, and this observation platform off a short boardwalk trail yields a sweeping panorama over the low, freshwater expanse – a magical place to be at sunset.

Around 10 miles further is another wooden path on the **Mahogany Hammock Trail**. The dense undergrowth feels almost Amazonian, with vines criss-crossing the boardwalk and air plants sprouting amid thick branches of tropical hardwoods and the distinctive hooting of barred owls occasionally piercing the air. A handful of towering, old-growth mahogany trees steal the show, including one of the oldest in the US. If starting the path in a counterclockwise direction, look for it on the left, about 131yd along.

A handful of canoe trails lie up the road. At **Nine Mile Pond**, you can paddle amid sawgrass prairies and mangroves, spying wading birds and a fair number of alligators. Despite the name, the marked route here is around 5 miles, though you can also take a shorter 3.5-mile loop. If you don't have your own canoe, rent one at the Flamingo Marina or book a tour on a guided three-hour canoe trip offered by the **Everglades National Park Institute**.

On the **West Lake Trail**, you'll get a closer look at life between land and sea on a 0.5-mile boardwalk trail through a

WHERE TO PICNIC IN THE PARK

West Lake
Open-sided pavilion with nicely shaded tables overlooking the lake.

Long Pine Key
Picnic tables scattered beneath pine trees offer views across a small pond.

Flamingo
Look for manatees and American crocodiles while picnicking near the marina.

mangrove forest that runs to an open deck overlooking the lake. Keep an eye out for the three local species: red, black and white mangroves.

Just before reaching Flamingo, squeeze in a final hike on the **Christian Point Trail**, a 1.6-mile one-way route that passes through diverse terrain, including buttonwood forest, coastal prairie and out to the edge of Snake Bight, a bay within larger Florida Bay.

Immerse Yourself in the Glades

FULL-DAY WALKING AND KAYAKING ADVENTURES

A full-day guided trip provides an immersive experience in three unique ecosystems of the Everglades. The most reputable outfitter – and the only one offering multi-experience excursions over a single day – is **Garl's Coastal Kayaking**, at Robert Is Here Fruit Stand in Homestead.

After gearing up (which may include mosquito suits in summer), you'll head into the park. From the main road, you'll join your guide on a walk into the wilderness. The water may be ankle- or knee-deep (depending on the season) as you squish through sawgrass en route to the famous tree islands known as **cypress domes**. It feels like entering another world, with towering cypresses covered in air plants and the silence broken only by the sound of birdsong. You may also spot alligators, snakes and other wildlife, with guides providing helpful insight about Everglades flora and fauna.

Further along, you'll stop for a paddle at **Nine Mile Pond**, where you can look for more alligators and crocs while paddling across mirror-like lakes and through narrow channels thickly lined with mangroves. Herons and egrets stalk the waterline while great flocks of ibis nest in the trees.

Finally, you'll kayak out along **Florida Bay**. The birding is even better here, with flocks numbering in the hundreds or even thousands, depending on the season: you may see bald eagles, roseate spoonbills or even flamingos. Manatees occasionally pop up from below the surface.

Weather permitting, your guide may lead you to the **Anhinga Trail** for an evening stroll along the boardwalk, with the chance to see nighthawks and other creatures by lamplight.

Waterways of Flamingo

KAYAKING AND BOAT TOURS

Anchoring the southern end of the national park, **Flamingo** is home to a small visitor center, a campground and a new lodge and restaurant. The main reason to come, however, is

I LIVE HERE: EVERGLADES SEASONS

Garl Harrold, who has guided film crews for National Geographic, sheds light on seasonal shifts in the Everglades.

They say the Everglades has two seasons – wet and dry – but I disagree. It's more like 11 or 12 seasons. So many things change here: what plants and animals are doing at different times of year, the water levels and which birds come and go.

Summer is one of my favorite seasons. That's when there are very few visitors and the wildlife-watching is so good. It's buggier and hotter, but it rains every day, which cools things off. The storms make such beautiful sunsets and the best rainbows.

ESSENTIAL SUPPLIES FOR OUTDOOR ACTIVITIES

Optics
Polarizing sunglasses let you see creatures in the water; binoculars give close-up views of birds.

Proper Clothing
Wear pants; light-colored, long-sleeved shirts (dark shades attract mosquitoes); water shoes (not flip-flops or Crocs).

Food & Drink
Bring lunch and ample water for the day. Limited snacks are available at the Flamingo Marina.

COASTAL HIKING

If the rest of the park hasn't satisfied your appetite for hiking, head to the **Coastal Prairie Trail**. Unlike the boardwalk paths, this 12-mile (out and back) route is more of a rugged adventure – be prepared for mud and even a short wade to reach a shell-covered beach at the end, where you can even pitch a tent (back-country permit required). Along the way, keep an eye out for osprey and wading birds as you make your way through buttonwood forest and the thick foliage of the coastal prairie. Find the trailhead near the western end of the C loop of the Flamingo campground.

FRANCISCO BLANCO/SHUTTERSTOCK ©

Flamingo Marina

the **Flamingo Marina**, where you can head off on a paddling or boating adventure.

Flamingo Adventures runs two different boat tours throughout the day. The 90-minute back-country excursion takes you up through the mangrove-lined Buttonwood Canal, along Tarpon Creek and into the mouth of islet-dotted Whitewater Bay. Naturalist guides shed insight into the southern Everglades ecosystems, while pointing out great blue herons, snowy egrets, roseate spoonbills and many other animals you'll likely see. For less of a jungle-like journey, opt for the Florida Bay tour, which glides out past countless keys in the shallow bay, offering the chance to see osprey, sea turtles and dolphins.

You can also go on a DIY paddling adventure, with kayaks available for hire from the marina. Paddling along Buttonwood Canal, you can see a wide range of wildlife, and with luck manatees in the water and alligators basking along the banks. It's about 3 miles to paddle up to Coot Bay. Allow yourself three or more hours to make the return trip, including time to stop and admire the scenery.

Before or after an excursion, stop a while for some quiet time by the docks. You can sometimes see manatees here, as well as alligators and the rare American crocodile – this is one of the few places on earth where the two reptile species coexist.

WHERE TO STAY IN THE EVERGLADES

Long Pine Key Campground
Well-located, with 108 tent and RV sites amid spindly pine trees. Book through Flamingo Adventures. **$**

Flamingo Campground
At the end of the road, with tent and RV sites, glamping-style eco-tents and houseboats. **$**

Flamingo Lodge
Opening in 2023, this restaurant and lodge has guest rooms with views over Florida Bay. **$$$**

Homestead
Florida City

Beyond the Southern Everglades

Experience the overlooked attractions outside the park, including tropical fruit fare, a 20th-century 'castle' and a peaceful Buddhist temple.

Homestead and neighboring Florida City (2 miles south) make great bases for forays into Everglades National Park, but have little obvious appeal upon arrival – they're closer in spirit to Miami than the River of Grass. Part of ever-expanding South Miami subdivisions, this bustling corridor can feel like an endless strip of big-box shopping centers, car dealerships and gas stations.

But look beneath the veneer and there's much more than meets the eye: strange curiosities like a 'castle' built single-handedly by a lovestruck immigrant; a magnificent Buddhist temple that looks like it's been airlifted in from Thailand; a winery showcasing Florida's finest produce (hint: not grapes); and one of the best farm stands in America.

TOP TIP

Homestead's almost-quaint main street runs along Krome Ave near the Historic Town Hall. September to April sees occasional concerts and food fests.

Fruit & Spice Park (p129)

MADHU KONERU/SHUTTERSTOCK ©

Coral Castle

EVERGLADES OUTPOST

The Everglades Outpost houses, feeds and cares for previously abused or neglected wild animals who have been seized from illegal traders or simply donated by people who could not care for them. Residents here include a lemur, wolves, a black bear, a zebra, cobras, alligators and a majestic tiger. Visit on weekends to see the crocs in action. You can also book a private behind-the-scenes tour, seeing a day in the life of a volunteer.

Fantastical Carving in Stone

A CASTLE-LIKE MASTERPIECE

'You will be seeing unusual accomplishment,' reads the inscription on a rough-hewn quarried wall. That's an understatement. There is no greater temple to one man's obsessive genius than the **Coral Castle**, a monumental work of art sitting just north of Homestead, about a 30-minute drive from the Everglades park entrance.

The story goes that Edward Leedskalnin, born in Latvia, was jilted by the love of his life one day before his wedding. Heartbroken, he immigrated to the US and eventually found his way to a then-sparsely populated corner of southern Florida, where he began his life's work: a massive, castle-like installation dedicated to unrequited love, which he would spend the next 28 years building.

This rock-walled compound includes a 'throne room'; a clever sundial that tells both the time and the month; a stone stockade intended as a 'time-out' area for the children he would

WHERE TO STAY IN HOMESTEAD

Hoosville Hostel
Good-value dorms and private rooms with shared bathrooms, plus a leafy backyard with gazebo. $

Hotel Redland
Vintage rooms with grandmotherly charm set in a 1904 building. Decent restaurant and bar below. $$

Fairway Inn Florida City
Budget hotel with comfy rooms and a palm-fringed swimming pool, set along the busy highway. $

never have; a telescope (of sorts) trained precisely on Polaris; and a revolving, 9-ton boulder gate that was once easily opened with just one finger.

Even more incredibly, all this was built by one diminutive man – Edward was just 5ft tall and weighed 100lb – working alone, without heavy machinery. He accomplished it all using pulleys, hand tools and other improvised devices, and often worked at night by lantern-light to protect his privacy.

Enthusiastic guides point out some of the impressive details hidden within his works, like the Florida-shaped table (with its perfectly positioned Lake Okeechobee), or the machine part he crafted into a primitive sort of crockpot.

Fruit of the Gods

FARM STANDS, WINERIES AND ORCHARDS

Farm fields, palm plantations and nurseries are woven into the landscape outside of Homestead. You could happily spend an afternoon taking in some of the exotic wonders flourishing in this verdant corner of southern Florida, starting at one the finest fruit stands in the country: **Robert Is Here**. More than a farmer's stand, Robert's is an institution. This is Old Florida at its best, in love with the Glades and the agriculture that surrounds it. You'll find loads of eye-catching, Florida-grown fruits you won't get elsewhere – including black sapote, carambola (star fruit), dragon fruit, sapodilla, guanabana (soursop), mamey sapote, tamarind, jackfruit, lychee, mangoes and passion fruit. The juices, coconut water and smoothies are fantastic, and the shop also stocks plenty of homemade preserves, honey and sauces. Out back, you can visit their animal farm to see chickens, ducks, goats, tortoises, pigs and emus.

Around 7 miles north of Robert's, the **Fruit & Spice Park** is a lush, 37-acre garden where you can experience the tropics in all its fecundity. The park makes for a peaceful wander past various species – in total around 500 different types of fruits, spices and nuts. Unfortunately, you can't pick the fruit, but you can eat anything that falls to the ground: go early for the best gathering! Get an overview of the offerings on a twice-daily narrated tram tour (11am and 1:30pm) that's free with admission. Or pay a little extra for the Tasting Tour (3pm) and indulge in some of the seasonal delicacies. You can also bring your own picnic.

In winter, from about mid-December to early March, you can pick your own strawberries (as well as tomatoes) at **Knaus Berry Farm**, a famed producer that's been around since the 1950s. Knaus also runs a bakery and snack counter that

LITTLE MEXICO

For more than two generations, Mexicans and Mexican-Americans have been an integral part of the community in the South Miami-Homestead-Florida City area. Initially working as farm laborers, nowadays many participate in a wide range of industries and hold leadership roles on the city council.

You'll also find one of South Florida's most colorful Christmas traditions here: **Las Posadas** ('the Inns') features nightly processions from December 16 through Christmas Eve. Accompanied by a donkey, children dressed as Mary, Joseph, angels and shepherds parade through the streets singing traditional carols, like 'Burrito de Belén' ('Little Donkey of Bethlehem'). Capping the night is a fiesta with food, live music and piñatas.

WHERE TO EAT IN HOMESTEAD

Yardie Spice
Lovingly made Jamaican and Haitian dishes, from classics like curry goat to vegan jerked tofu. **$$**

La Patrona
Pick up guava turnovers and other Latin-style pastries and baked goods before hitting the trail. **$**

Casita Tejas
Friendly, unfussy eatery with the best Tex-Mex in town. Big menu, plus great combo platters. **$**

IMAGEMD/SHUTTERSTOCK ©

Wat Buddharangsi

WAT BUDDHARANGSI

Tucked amid the green fields and palm-fringed lanes northeast of Homestead, the steep golden roofs of Wat Buddharangsi emerge like something out of a fairy tale. Statues adorn the bougainvillea-lined walkways, and two carved lions guard the main entrance. Inside, an elegant, gold-leaf-covered Buddha presides over the peaceful chamber. Built in 1998, this Buddhist temple was the culmination of two decades of effort by the Thai community to build a suitable gathering place. Visitors are welcome to Wat Buddharangsi, which periodically hosts guided English-language meditation sessions.

draws hungry admirers from as far away as Miami. There are heavenly cinnamon rolls, guava pies, fruit-laden cheesecakes and many other temptations. You can also refresh yourself over frothy milkshakes or ice cream. The whole place closes down in the warmer months, so don't bother visiting from mid-April through October; it's also closed on Sundays year-round. Cash only.

Schnebly Redland's Winery transforms the region's tropical produce into surprisingly good sweet wines. Given the climate, you won't find malbec, pinot noir or zinfandel: wines here are made of mango, passion fruit, lychee, guava, avocado and coconut. Tucked along a quiet farm road west of Homestead, Schnebly has the distinction of being the southernmost winery in America. Come any time for a tasting that includes five different wines, or visit on weekends for a tour of the estate (though there are no fruits grown on-site) and some insight into wine-making. There's also a restaurant overlooking a lushly landscaped waterfall out back, as well as a brewery.

WHERE TO FIND NIGHTLIFE IN HOMESTEAD

Miami Brewing Company
First-rate craft brews, pub grub and occasional live music. Behind Schnebly Redland's Winery.

City Hall Bistro & Martini Bar
Easygoing spot for swilling tropical cocktails and dining on mahimahi sandwiches or rack of lamb.

Exit One Taproom
Inviting indoor and outdoor spaces, with rotating food trucks and regional and global craft brews.

BISCAYNE NATIONAL PARK

Miami

Biscayne National Park

Just to the east of the Everglades – and right on Miami's southern doorstep – is Biscayne National Park, 95% of which is made up of the waters of Biscayne Bay and the Atlantic Ocean. A portion of the world's third-largest reef sits here just off the coast, along with mangrove forests and the northernmost Florida Keys. This is some of the best reef viewing and snorkeling you'll find in the USA (outside Hawaii and nearby Key Largo).

The human presence in the park spans more than 10,000 years, from nomadic prehistoric tribes to folly-fueled developers in the 20th century. Littering the reefs are dozens of shipwrecks, some dating back to the 18th century. Although the keys that are part of the national park are today uninhabited, you can learn about the history of former 19th-century homesteaders and Gatsby-esque industrialists here on a visit to the islands.

TOP TIP

The gateway to the park, the Dante Fascell Visitor Center (on the mainland) has exhibitions on ecology, marine life and human settlement. A 20-minute film gives a fine overview of Biscayne's four ecosystems, while the gallery features nature- and wildlife-themed pieces by artists working in a variety of media.

Biscayne National Park

OTHER ADVENTURES IN BISCAYNE NP

Kayak the Mangroves
A naturalist-led kayaking trip (1½ hours), with time to explore the shoreline on your own.

Sail, Paddle, Snorkel & Island Visit
Full-day experience on a 42ft sailboat that lets you do it all (six passengers maximum).

Snorkel & Paddle Eco-Adventure
Combine two of the park's best activities: paddling amid mangroves and snorkeling over coral reefs.

Adventures Above & Below the Water

BOAT TRIPS, PADDLING AND SNORKELING

Most travelers come for a day's adventure in the national park, which could entail kayaking, snorkeling or island exploring. **Biscayne National Park Institute**, which operates out of **Dante Fascell Visitor Center**, runs a variety of excursions, all of which are best reserved before you visit the park. Wherever you visit in Biscayne, you're likely to see plenty of seabirds, from cormorants perched on mooring posts and flocks of brown pelicans flying in formation to steely-eyed osprey gliding just above the water. Pods of bottlenose dolphins zip across the horizon, while crabs and lizards scuttle amid the roots of red mangroves along the water's edge.

The **Heritage of Biscayne cruise** takes you out across the bay and past Adams, Elliott and Boca Chita keys. Once aboard this half-day tour, guides bring the islands' past to life relating the stories of some of the people who've lived here over the years. There was Israel Jones, an African American man who settled on **Porgy Key** in the 1850s and transformed it into one of South Florida's most prosperous key lime and pineapple farms. His descendants were instrumental in helping to

WHERE TO EAT NEAR BISCAYNE NP

Black Point Ocean Grill
Outstanding seafood and breezy waterside views, plus a resident crocodile often spotted in the lagoon. $$

El Puerto de Vallarta Mexican Seafood
Tasty ceviches, fish tacos, seafood platters and margaritas in a colorful setting. $$

La Playa Grill
Munch on conch fritters and fried snapper while taking in the seaviews over Bayfront Park. $$

preserve the islands for future generations (instead of taking a hefty payout from developers).

The industrialist Mark Honeywell, on the other hand, left his mark on **Boca Chita Key**. After founding his eponymous thermostat and home heating company, he bought Boca Chita as a holiday retreat, building an ornamental lighthouse and a chapel and polishing up some old Spanish cannons that would be fired to welcome guests to the lavish parties he loved to host. The cruise typically stops at Boca Chita, where you can admire the views from atop the lighthouse, walk a short nature trail amid the mangroves and enjoy some downtime on the island's tiny beach.

For a closer look at the park's natural beauty, you can sign up for one of several **paddling tours**. Hidden between Totten Key and Old Rhodes Key, **Jones Lagoon** has calm, clear waters fringed by mangrove trees. After a 30-minute motorboat ride from the mainland, you'll hop onto a stand-up paddleboard (which allows better perspectives for viewing marine life than a kayak) and look for great blue herons, great egrets and roseate spoonbills as you glide silently along. In the aquamarine waters below, you might spy sea turtles, baby sharks, rays, upside-down jellyfish or sea stars.

Snorkeling trips offer you immersion in Biscayne's most biologically diverse ecosystem. On a half-day trip, you'll visit two different sites, exploring coral reefs, a shipwreck or a bayside setting amid the mangroves, where you can see soft coral and sea sponges. Scuba-certified divers can sign on for a six-hour trip (two dives). There's also the option to explore half a dozen sunken ships contained within the park on an excursion to the **Maritime Heritage Trail**. Three of the vessels are suited for scuba divers, but the others – particularly the *Mandalay*, a lovely, two-masted schooner that sank in 1966 – can be accessed by snorkelers.

SPITE HIGHWAY

On Elliott Key, you can hike the longest trail in the national park, a wooded stretch known as the Spite Highway. In the 1960s, developers had grand designs on this coastline, envisioning hotels, roads and even a small airport that would be part of the new city of 'Islandia.' Conservationists, however, managed to convince the public that this region was worth preserving.

Having lost the public-relations battle, developers brought bulldozers to Elliott Key and blazed a six-lane, 7-mile-long swath down the middle of the island in hopes of spoiling the area's preservation. Their wanton destruction failed, however, and President Lyndon B Johnson signed the bill creating Biscayne National Monument in 1968.

EXCURSIONS FROM MIAMI

Biscayne National Park Institute (biscaynenationalparkinstitute.org) also runs boat trips from Coconut Grove in Miami. Excursions from here include snorkeling and kayaking trips, island visits and historical tours of the Stiltsville houses.

GETTING AROUND

If you don't have a car, time your visit for a weekend sometime from January to early April, when Homestead runs a free bus to the Dante Fascell Visitor Center (reservations recommended).

FLORIDA KEYS & KEY WEST

ISLANDS AT THE END OF IMAGINATION

Bridges and causeways span teal gaps and dozens of islands where folks of all stripes work hard at being laid-back.

Curving beneath Southern Florida are the Florida Keys: a 113-mile-long archipelago of mangrove and sandbar islands, teal waters and magnificent sunsets. A memorable journey down the Overseas Hwy takes you from the bustle of Key Largo to Key West, passing arts-loving villages, old-fashioned roadside eateries and stretches of verdant hardwood forest, crossing some 42 bridges along the way (including one that stretches 7 miles across open waters).

Paddling across mirror-like coves and joining the free-spirited party people in Key West is just a sample of the great Florida Keys experience. You can also take in the unusual plant and animal life and explore the fascinating history still visible on these shores – from abandoned railroad trestles built in the early 20th century to grand homes and museums filled with treasures (much of which was discovered by the region's once-thriving salvaging industry).

'Salvaging,' by the way, means harvesting shipwrecks, which speaks to a sort of pirate-y roguishness that has long characterized Keys identity. In short, this is a place that sets its own sunbaked rules. Key West, in particular, has always been a place where people buck trends. A large society of artists and craftspeople congregated here at the end of the Great Depression, and that community has grown into one of the most renowned and best organized gay-friendly cities in the country.

THE MAIN AREAS

T-ANDERSON PHOTOGRAPHY/SHUTTERSTOCK ©

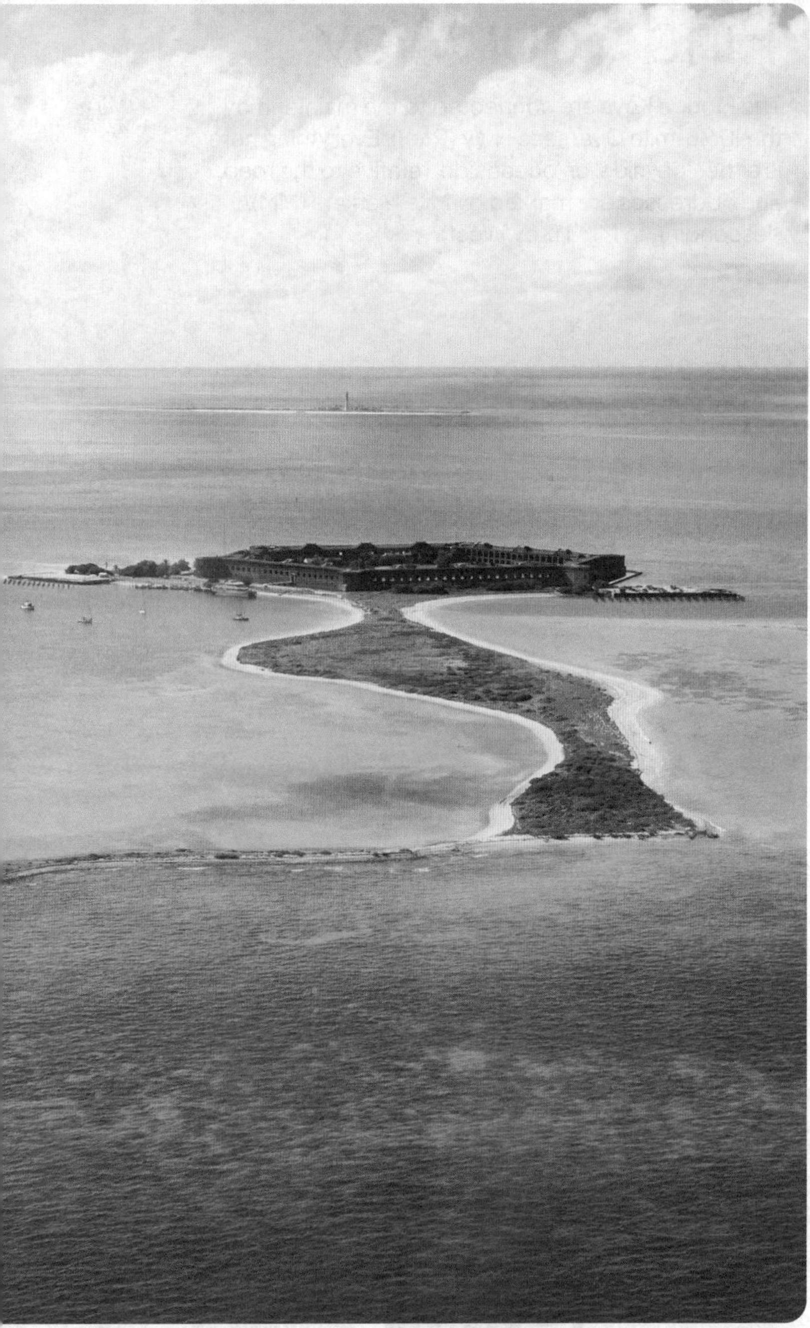

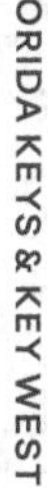

Left: Seven Mile Bridge (p154); above: Dry Tortugas National Park (p157)

Find Your Way

The Florida Keys are connected to the mainland by the 106.5-mile Overseas Hwy (Rte 1). Everything here is either 'bayside' or 'oceanside' relative to the road, and addresses are marked by Mile Markers (MM), descending to MM 1 (Key West).

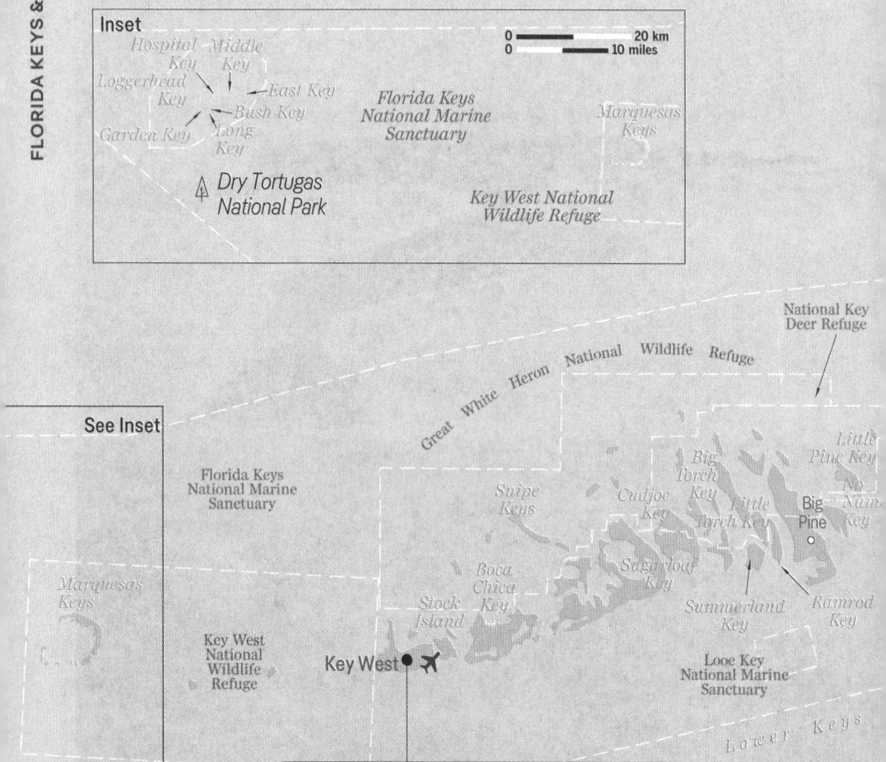

Gulf of Mexico
Inset
0 20 km
0 10 miles
Hospital Key
Middle Key
Loggerhead Key
East Key
Bush Key
Garden Key
Long Key
Dry Tortugas National Park
Florida Keys National Marine Sanctuary
Marquesas Keys
Key West National Wildlife Refuge
National Key Deer Refuge
Great White Heron National Wildlife Refuge
See Inset
Florida Keys National Marine Sanctuary
Little Pine Key
Big Torch Key
Snipe Keys
Cudjoe Key
Little Torch Key
Big Pine
No Name Key
Sugarloaf Key
Boca Chica Key
Stock Island
Summerland Key
Ramrod Key
Marquesas Keys
Key West National Wildlife Refuge
Key West
Looe Key National Marine Sanctuary
Lower Keys

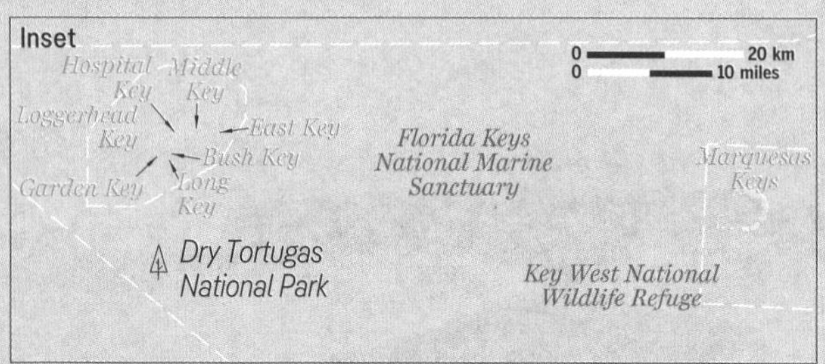

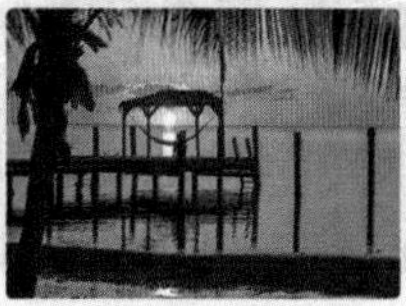

Key West, p156
An iconic destination all its own, this beautiful town mixes tropical Caribbean architecture with an anything-goes attitude and a cast of eccentric residents.

CAR

Driving is the easiest means of getting between the Keys. On a good day, motoring along the Overseas Hwy is the US road trip in tropical perfection. On a bad day, you end up sitting in gridlock for hours.

BUS

Key West Transit operates the Lower Keys Shuttle, which runs between Key West and Marathon 10 times daily. It's mainly used by commuters, but can connect you to Key West in a pinch. Greyhound also runs to key West.

BICYCLE

The flat elevation and ocean breezes that are the backdrop of the Keys are perfect for cycling, and the Florida Keys Overseas Heritage Trail gives gorgeous vantage points along the way. Around 90 miles (out of 106 miles) of this multiuse trail are complete.

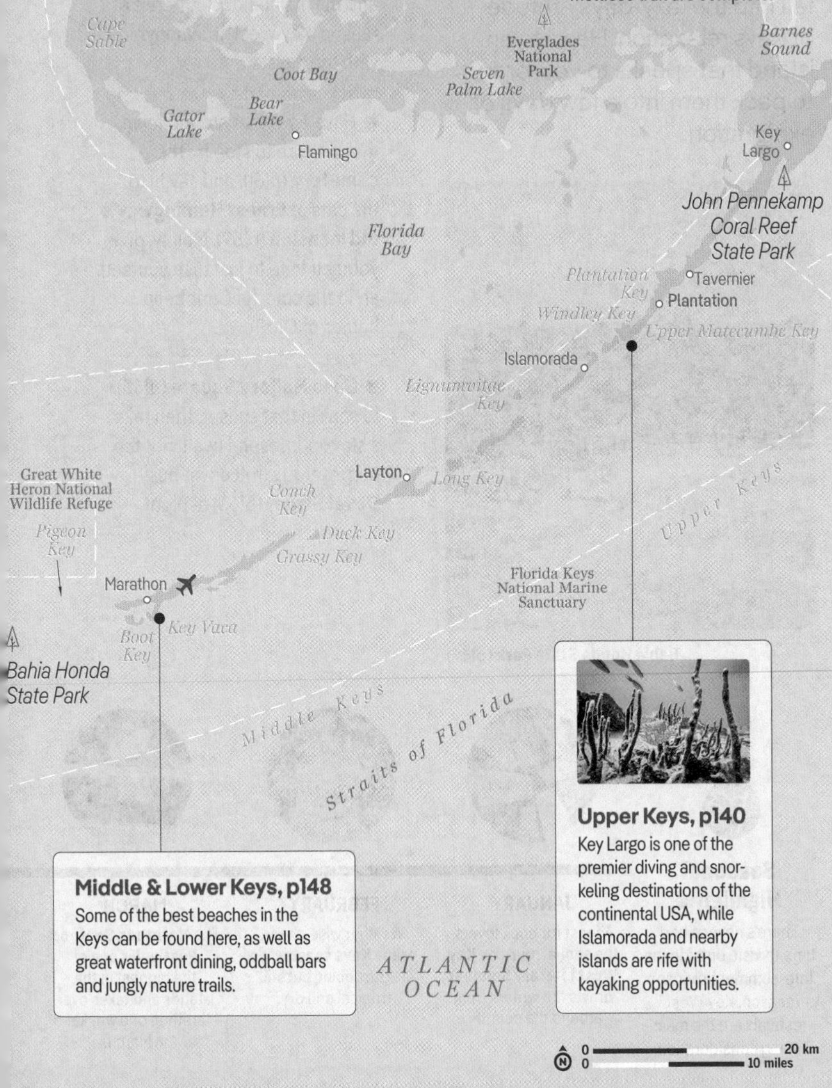

Upper Keys, p140

Key Largo is one of the premier diving and snorkeling destinations of the continental USA, while Islamorada and nearby islands are rife with kayaking opportunities.

Middle & Lower Keys, p148

Some of the best beaches in the Keys can be found here, as well as great waterfront dining, oddball bars and jungly nature trails.

Plan Your Time

It's easy (and appropriate!) to fall into the lazy-days attitude of Keys relaxation. Head to an island that speaks to you, or try to pack them into a few days of exploration.

SIMON DANNHAUER/SHUTTERSTOCK ©

Bahia Honda State Park (p149)

If You Only Do One Thing

- Head straight to **Key West** (p156), at the end of the Overseas Hwy. We know, there are a lot of wonderful islands between here and the mainland, but there's a reason 'Key West' is synonymous with the Keys.

- Have a wander around town, making sure to stop by the **cemetery** (p161), and say hi to the cats at **Ernest Hemingway's old mansion** (p159). Mainly, give yourself time to just lose yourself amid the colorful Caribbean homes of Old Town.

- Go to **Mallory Square** (p163) to soak in that sunset, then take a slow, purposeful (well, not too purposeful) stroll down busy **Duval Street** (p163) at night.

Seasonal Highlights

There's never a bad time to visit, outside the late-summer hurricane season. Key West festivals are the main timing consideration.

JANUARY

A feast for book lovers, the annual four-day **Key West Literary Seminar** draws top writers from around the country.

FEBRUARY

Weather wise, this is **prime Keys season**: it's a little cooler, but still tropical and dry.

MARCH

The **Marathon Seafood Festival** is one of the biggest in the islands and takes over Marathon one weekend in March.

BILLION PHOTOS/SHUTTERSTOCK ©, STOCKDONKEY/SHUTTERSTOCK ©, CHUCK WAGNER/SHUTTERSTOCK ©

Three Days to Travel Around

● We're not done in Key West just yet. Book a trip out to **Dry Tortugas National Park** (p157) and have a snorkel around the historic fort there, then head to the **Florida Keys Eco-Discovery Center** (p165) to get a grounding in the natural habitat of the islands, which you should begin exploring in earnest.

● Get in a car and drive toward the mainland, making sure to stop at **Bahia Honda State Park** (p149) for – you guessed it – some beach time. Head to **No Name Key** (p152), have a pizza and a beer at the **No Name Pub** (p152), and gawk at some tiny Key deer.

If You Have More Time

● You'll be driving (and driving) again, this time over the Seven-Mile Bridge that connects Big Pine Key to the island of **Marathon** (p154), the center island of the Keys. On Marathon, head into the jungle at **Crane Point Hammock** (p151) and lose yourself amid the coastal views and tropical trees.

● Now go to Islamorada and book a kayaking excursion at **Robbie's Marina** (p144) – from this raucous marina, you can paddle out to eerie islands like **Indian Key** (p144). Wade into the water at **Anne's Beach** (p147), then head to Key Largo and get under the water with a snorkeling or diving trip at **John Pennekamp Coral Reef State Park** (p141).

APRIL
The **Conch Republic Independence Celebration** celebrates the need for even more eccentric autonomy with a drag-queen footrace (among other events).

MAY
The rainy season begins (and lasts through summer), but anglers, take note: this is prime time for **sportfishing**.

SEPTEMBER
Head to Key West for **Womenfest**, one of the largest lesbian celebrations in the country.

OCTOBER
Key West's **Fantasy Fest** (p163) is 10 days of burlesque parties, parades, street fairs, concerts and loads of costumed events.

UPPER KEYS

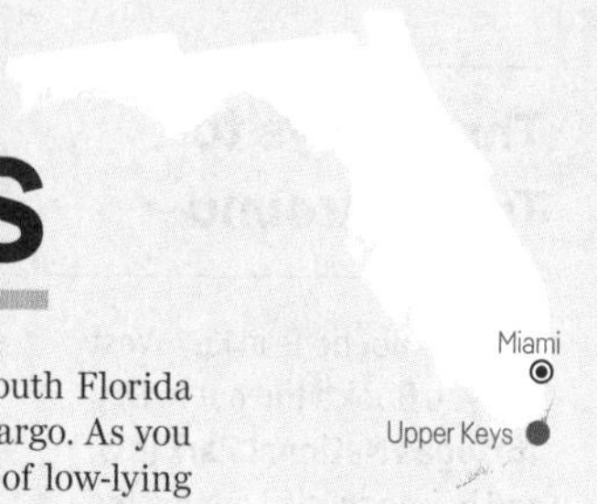

The blanket of mangrove forest that forms the South Florida coastline spreads like a woody morass into Key Largo. As you drive onto the islands, they resemble a long line of low-lying hammock and strip development. But head down a side road and duck into this warm little bar or that converted Keys plantation house, and the island idiosyncrasies become more pronounced.

Keep heading south and the mangroves give way to wider stretches of road and ocean, until you're in Islamorada (is-luh-murr-ah-da) and the water is suddenly everywhere. Also known as 'The Village of Islands,' Islamorada resembles nothing so much as a beautiful string of pearls, or rather, five keys – Plantation, Upper and Lower Matecumbe, Windley and Teatable – which shimmer as one of the prettiest stretches of the islands. The scrubby mangrove is replaced by unbroken horizons of ocean and sky, one perfect shade of blue mirroring the other.

TOP TIP

If you want to avoid traffic on US 1 south of Florida City, you can try the less trafficked FL 997 and Card Sound Rd to FL 905 (toll $1), which passes Alabama Jack's, a famous bar and restaurant popular with fishers, drinkers and people who like to fish and drink.

Islamorada

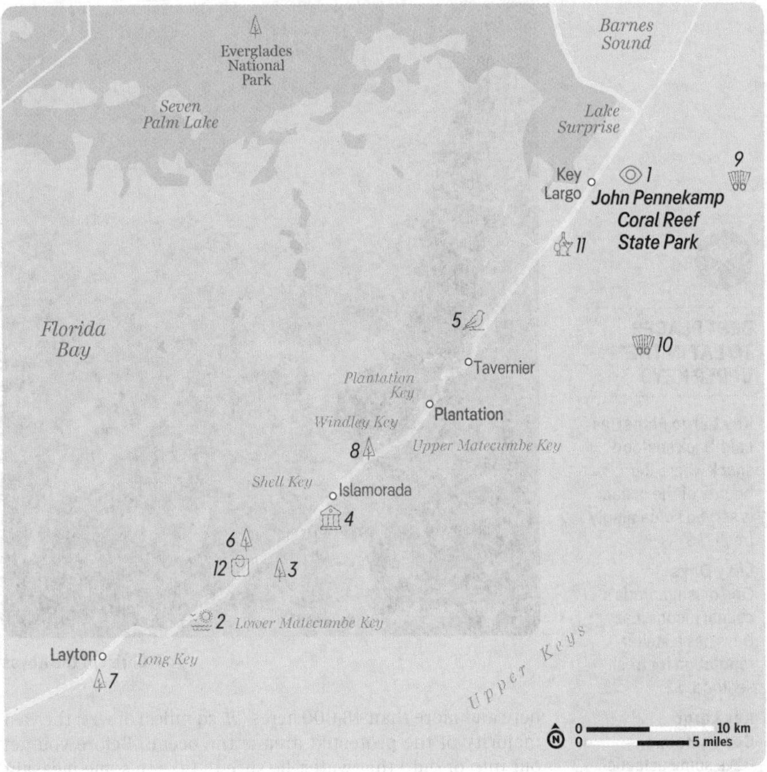

HIGHLIGHTS
1 John Pennekamp Coral Reef State Park

EATING
2 Anne's Beach
3 Indian Key Historic
4 Keys History & Discovery Center
5 Laura Quinn Wild Bird Sanctuary
6 Lignumvitae Key
7 Long Key State Recreation Area
8 Windley Key Fossil Reef Geological State Park

ACTIVITIES, COURSES & TOURS
9 Christ of the Abyss
10 Molasses Reef

DRINKING & NIGHTLIFE
11 Keys Meads

SHOPPING
12 Robbie's Marina

Exploring John Pennekamp Coral Reef State Park

DIP YOUR WHOLE BODY IN

John Pennekamp has the singular distinction of being the first underwater park in the USA. There's 170 acres of dry parkland

WHERE TO SLEEP IN THE UPPER KEYS

Baker's Cay Resort
Hilton property with clean, designer rooms outfitted in blues and greens with balconies overlooking the water. **$$**

Sunset Inn
This former motel has earned a new following for its bright, spacious rooms and appealing amenities. **$$**

Jules Undersea Lodge
Once a research station, this module has been converted into a delightfully cheesy, underwater (!) Keys motel. **$$$**

IMAGE SOURCE TRADING LTD/SHUTTERSTOCK ©

Christ of the Abyss

here and more than 48,000 acres (75 sq miles) of wet: the vast majority of the protected area is the ocean. Before you get out into or onto that water, be sure to take in some pleasant beaches and stroll along the nature trails.

The park features three **trails**, all of which are short, flat and more educational than a physical huff. The **Mangrove Trail** is a good boardwalk introduction to this ecologically awesome species (the trees, often submerged in water, breathe via long roots that act as snorkels). At a whopping 0.6 miles long, the **Grove Trail** is the longest, and per the name, wends through tropical fruit groves that occasionally attract butterflies. If you're curious about the trees of the Keys, have a jaunt around the **Wild Tamarind Trail**, where many of the hardwoods are labeled.

Stick around for nightly campfire programs. The **visitor center** is well run and informative, and has a small saltwater aquarium and nature films that give a glimpse of what's under those waters. To really get beneath the surface, you should take a 2½-hour glass-bottom boat tour. You'll be brought out in

BEST PLACES TO EAT IN THE UPPER KEYS

Key Largo Fisheries
Laid-back seafood shack where the bounty of the ocean is served screamingly fresh. $$

Lazy Days
One of Islamorada's culinary icons, Lazy Days has a stellar reputation for fresh seafood. $$

Key Largo Conch House
Have some eclectic modern island cuisine in a gorgeous, wedding-cake kinda historical home. $$

Fish House
Delivers on its title – great fish, bought from local fishers, prepared as you like it. $$

Square Grouper
Creative salads, jasmine rice bowls and, of course, brilliant seafood. $$$

WHERE TO SLEEP IN THE UPPER KEYS

Largo Resort
This resort sits on pristine waterfront. Design leans toward Zen-like minimalism, with greenery all around you. **$$$**

La Siesta Resort
This pretty option consists of renovated suites and apartments that let in generous amounts of light. **$$$**

Lime Tree Bay Resort
Hammocks and lawn chairs are front-row seats for spectacular sunsets at this 2.5-acre waterfront hideaway. **$$$**

a 38ft catamaran to **Molasses Reef**, where you'll see see filigreed flaps of soft coral, technicolor schools of fish, dangerous-looking barracuda and perhaps massive, yet graceful, sea turtles.

The park's most famous attraction is the coral-fringed **Christ of the Abyss**, an 8.5ft, 4000lb bronze sculpture of Jesus – a copy of a similar sculpture off the Portofino Peninsula in northern Italy. On calm days, the park offers snorkeling trips to the statue, which is 6 miles offshore. You can also arrange diving excursions, which are obviously a big draw, or paddle through several miles of 'blue' trails among the mangroves.

HISTORY OF DIVING MUSEUM

You can't miss the diving museum – it's the building with the enormous mural of whale sharks on the side. This journey 'under the sea' covers 4000 years, with fascinating pieces like the 1797 Klingert's copper kettle diving machine, a whimsical room devoted to Jules Verne's Captain Nemo, massive deep-diving suits and an exquisite display of diving helmets from around the world. These imaginative galleries reflect the charming quirks of the Keys.

Museum staff can provide information on diving in a vintage Mark V diving suit (the ones with the bulbous onion-heads connected to surface pumps). The space also stages free lectures on diving entitled 'Immerse Yourself' at 7pm on the third Wednesday of every month.

Take a Peck at the Laura Quinn Wild Bird Sanctuary

FIND FINE-FEATHERED FRIENDS

The Florida Keys aren't just popular with tourists. The islands – like much of outdoors South Florida – serve as a waypoint for migrating birds; acre for acre, the archipelago is a birding paradise. But many birds sustain injuries over the course of their transit, and that's where this sanctuary steps up. The 7-acre space serves as a protected refuge for a wide variety of injured birds. A boardwalk leads through various enclosures where you can learn a bit about some of the permanent residents – those unable to be released back in the wild. The species here include masked boobies, great horned owls, green herons, brown pelicans, double-crested cormorants and others. The same organization also runs a bird hospital just south along the main highway. They're the ones to contact if you see injured birds – or have any other bird emergencies – during your travels.

If you want to see some birds up close, contact **Garl's Coastal Kayaking** (garlscoastalkayaking.com). Although it specializes in Everglades excursions, its saltwater paddle trip will get you out on the teal waters of Florida Bay, which is like Miami Beach for avian species.

Delving into the Keys History & Discovery Center

LEARN ABOUT THESE ICONIC ISLANDS

The Florida Keys are deceptively pleasant to the contemporary visitor, but it's worth remembering these islands were once dubbed Los Martires (The Martyrs) because Ponce de León thought they looked like refugees. For a long time life here was hard, a struggle for folks trying to fish or salvage shipwrecks.

Explore this fascinating history at the well-appointed **Keys History & Discovery Center**, located in Islamorada, which

WHERE TO EAT IN THE UPPER KEYS

Lorelei
Sunsets and excellent seafood abound at this open-sided restaurant overlooking Florida Bay. **$$**

Mrs Mac's Kitchen
This downhome diner, serving jalapeño bacon and Caribbean crab cakes, packs in the locals (and some calories). **$**

Midway Cafe
This homey cafe is a safe bet for excellent coffee and good sandwiches, wraps, salads and omelets. **$**

delves into the people and major events that have shaped the archipelago's past. The context the center provides isn't just historical, but extends to flora and fauna. For example, the 1st floor takes in coral reefs (with several aquariums boasting live coral as well as elegant angelfish, butterfly fish and otherworldly lionfish), Native American peoples and Spanish treasure fleets (and the salvagers and pirates who thrived off them).

Trails follow the old layout of the city streets, or you can walk among ruins and paddle around, spotting rays and dolphins in utter isolation in a canoe or kayak. Inside the center itself, come face to face with the stories of the homesteaders, fisherfolk, botanists, hermits and artists who settled here over the years. Upstairs, a comfy theater screens a number of worthwhile films that capture the incredible challenges of building Henry Flagler's Oversea Railway (completed in 1912) and survivors' accounts of the horrific 1935 Labor Day Hurricane.

There's also a handsome **scale model** of Indian Key, named the first seat of Dade County back in 1836. Four years later the inhabitants of the island were killed or scattered by a Native American attack during the Second Seminole War. You have to kayak out to Indian Key, and there's not much left at the historic site – just the foundation, some cisterns and a jungly tangle. Arriving by boat or kayak is the only way to visit, which adds to the allure.

THE ORIGINAL RUM RUNNER

The rum runner is the signature cocktail of the Florida Keys. It's more or less a tropical garden in a glass, made up of pineapple juice, orange juice, banana juice, grenadine and, yeah, rum. Lots of rum. Sometimes topped with Bacardi 151. *Jeez.*

Anyways, the drink was invented at the Holiday Isle Tiki Bar in Islamorada, supposedly as a means of getting rid of excess rum before a shipment of liquor arrived. Plan achieved! The Holiday Isle is now the Postcard Inn Resort, but the Tiki Bar is still there – a lovely establishment where you can feel the sand squish beneath your toes, which is about as much physical activity as we can recommend after two rum runners.

Dive into Robbie's Marina

GIANT FISH AND KAYAK TRAILS

The scruffy jewel of Islamorada, Robbie's Marina covers all the bases – it's a local flea market, tacky tourist shop, sea pen for tarpons (massive fish), waterfront restaurant and jumping-off point for fishing expeditions, all wrapped into one driftwood-laced compound. Boat rental and tours are also available.

When you park, you'll first be confronted with the market portion of Robbie's, which showcases crafts and art from around the islands and is a good spot for a piece of unique memorabilia. If folks aren't perusing paintings, they might be knocking back beers while checking out the waterfront view. If this all feels like it's a bit of sensory overload, you can quickly escape the bustle by hiring a kayak for a peaceful paddle through nearby mangroves, hammocks and lagoons. In fact, this is the major launching point for paddlers who are looking to get out to Indian Key and Lignumvitae Key, both only accessible by boat, and both state parks.

Now lonely and eerie, **Indian Key** was once a thriving town, complete with a warehouse, docks, streets, a hotel and about

WHERE TO EAT IN THE UPPER KEYS

Bad Boy Burrito
Whips up superb fish tacos and its namesake burritos – with quality ingredients and all the fixings. $

Harriette's
Sweet, breadbox-sized eatery is famed far and wide for its utterly addictive key lime muffins. $

Shipwreck's Bar & Grill
Sit over the water, while noshing on fish sandwiches, shrimp, burgers and conch fritters. $$

FELIX MIZIOZNIKOV/SHUTTERSTOCK ©

Indian Key

BEST PLACES TO SLEEP IN THE UPPER KEYS

Casa Morrada
Contemporary chic comes to Islamorada with a keystone standing circle, freshwater pool and bar worthy of *Wallpaper* magazine. $$$

Kona Kai Resort
This Key Largo hideaway is a botanical garden that integrates a hotel onto its grounds. $$$

Ragged Edge Resort
A popular Islamorada apartment complex with quiet units, friendly hosts and a happily comatose vibe. $$$

Bay Harbor Lodge
This lush 2.5-acre Key Largo property has its own private beach and a temperature-controlled pool. $$$

40 to 50 permanent residents – this was actually the first seat of Dade County, now dominated by metro Miami, which is just a wee bit larger on the population scale. **Lignumvitae Key** is a 280-acre island of virgin tropical forest ringed by alluring waters. The official attraction is the 1919 **Matheson House**, with its windmill and cistern; the real draw is a nice sense of shipwrecked isolation. Strangler figs, mastic, gumbo-limbo, poisonwood and lignum vitae trees form a dark canopy that feels more South Pacific than South Florida.

Back at Robbie's, you can also book a snorkeling trip and bob amid coral reefs. If you don't want to get out on the water, you can feed the freakishly large tarpons from the dock ($4 per bucket, $2.25 to watch). 'Watch,' in this case, isn't just looking at the fish, but the shocked reactions of tourists when a fish the size of a large dog comes snapping out of the water.

FOR TROPICAL HIKE LOVERS

Crane Point Hammock (p151), on the island of Marathon, is a wonderful place to walk around and soak up (and, if it has rained, sink into) the natural jungle-and-mangrove environment of the Keys.

WHERE TO DRINK IN THE UPPER KEYS

Sundowners
The name gives it away, but yeah, the sunsets at this Key Largo bar/restaurant are legendary.

Florida Keys Brewing Company
Innovative beers with a hint of the tropics (including flavor notes like hibiscus and key lime).

Morada Bay
Holds monthly full-moon parties that attract the entire party-people population of the Keys, starting around 9pm.

KEY LIME PIE

The iconic Keys dessert has featured on *The Great British Bake-Off* and is Florida's state pie. The crisp of the graham cracker crust is balanced by sweet cream, further opened up by the citric acidity of the lime. Do you have to use Key limes? The tiny fruits, tart and sweet, are tough to find outside the Keys, and that special lime variant, 'whatever is at the store,' usually turns out fine. Arguably, the more important ingredient is sweetened condensed milk, which provided sweetness and creaminess sans spoiling in pre-refrigeration Florida.

If you're in the Keys during the first weekend of July, make sure to pop into the Key Lime Festival – pie, cocktails and margaritas abound.

STEVE HEAP/SHUTTERSTOCK ©

Anne's Beach

Soaking up Windley Key & Anne's Beach

A LITERAL KEYS CROSS-SECTION

Islamorada is a stand-out town as far as the Keys go, inasmuch as it offers up one of the most serene beaches in the Keys, and lets visitors see what lies beneath said beaches.

To get his railroad built across the islands, Henry Flagler had to quarry out some sizable chunks of the Keys. The best evidence of those efforts can be found at a former quarry-turned-state park: **Windley Key Fossil Reef Geological State Park** (usually just called Windley Key). The island, now managed by the state, has leftover quarry machinery scattered along an 8ft former quarry wall, with fossilized evidence of brain, star and finger coral embedded in the rock. The wall offers a cool (and rare) public peek at the coral that forms the substrate of the Keys – the cake layers of fossilized shells used to be known as Key Largo limestone, or keystone.

WHERE TO DRINK IN THE UPPER KEYS

Cruisin' Tiki's Key Largo
Technically a sunset cruise that must be booked in advance, where the 'boat' is a floating Tiki Bar. Because Florida!

Alabama Jack's
Zonked-out fishers, exiles from the mainland and Harley heads swill beers on a mangrove bay.

Hog Heaven
This well-worn saloon deserves pride of place for its excellent al fresco back porch imbibing area.

There are also various short trails through tropical hardwood hammock that make for a pleasant glimpse into the Keys' wilder side – plenty of birds abound in the tropical hammocks. Borrow a free trail guide from the visitor center.

Head south for about 11 miles past Windley to get your toes wet. Named after local environmentalist Anne Eaton, **Anne's Beach** is one of the finest seascapes in these parts. The small ribbon of sand opens onto a sky-bright stretch of tidal flats and a green tunnel of hammock and wetland. A short (quarter-mile) boardwalk leads through the mangroves with lookouts and picnic tables along the way. There are two parking lots you can use to access Anne's Beach, each about a quarter mile away from each other, at Mile Marker 73.

UNDERSTANDING THE TEQUESTA

The area's earliest known inhabitants were the Tequesta (Tekesta) people, who left behind 24 holes, inscribed in bedrock and arranged in the shape of a perfect circle, in Downtown Miami – at 2000 years old, the oldest structure of its kind on the US East Coast.

The Tequesta were mostly wiped out by Spanish first contact, which brought violence and disease. Survivors likely melted into the Miccosukee and Seminole nations. There is evidence of shell middens left behind by the Tequesta in Key Largo and the Upper Keys. Their lives seem to have been relatively peaceful, even comfortable; the shallow waters of Biscayne Bay provided a ceaseless flow of shellfish, sharks, turtle eggs and other readily available calories.

A Short Stop at Long Key State Recreation Area

WATERFRONT VIEWS AND CAMPING

The 965-acre Long Key State Recreation Area takes up much of Long Key. It's about 30 minutes south of Islamorada, and comprises a tropical clump of gumbo-limbo, crabwood and poisonwood trees; a picnic area fronting a long, lovely sweep of teal water; and lots of wading birds in the mangroves. Two short nature trails head through distinct plant communities. The park also has a 1.5-mile canoe trail through a saltwater tidal lagoon and rents out ocean-going kayaks.

If you want to stay here, make reservations this minute: it's tough to get one of the 60 sites at the campground. They're all waterfront, making this the cheapest (and probably most unspoiled) ocean view – short of squatting on a resort – you're likely to find in Florida.

Sweet Sipping Keys Meads

HONEY WINE ON ISLAND TIME

For something completely different, stop in for a tasting at this artisanal, family-run mead producer. Yes, mead, the fabled honey drink of the gods, also has a producer in the Upper Keys. Owner Jeff Kesling has an encyclopedic knowledge of all things mead-related, and has created many unique varieties of his award-winning libation, all made from locally sourced honey. Who needs rum, anyways?

During a tasting, you can try up to 12 different meads (small pours since the alcohol content ranges from 7% to 14%), with a regularly changing lineup, including jackfruit, Jamaican cherry and orange blossom.

GETTING AROUND

The Keys system of addresses – Mile Markers (MM) attached to the Overseas Hwy – begins here in the Upper Keys. Parking isn't that hard to find if you're driving. If you're not, you'll find the bicycle infrastructure is OK – Islamorada is one of the nicest areas in the islands for cycling. Greyhound buses stop here on the route between Miami and Key West.

MIDDLE & LOWER KEYS

On this stretch of the Keys, the bodies of water get wider, and the bridges get more impressive. This is where you'll find the famous Seven Mile Bridge, one of the world's longest causeways and a natural divider between the Middle and Lower Keys. As you drive the Overseas Hwy, you'll cross specks like Conch Key and Duck Key; green, quiet Grassy Key; as well as Key Vaca, where Marathon, the second-largest town and most Keysy community in the archipelago, is located.

The people of the Lower Keys are usually either winter escapees or native 'Conchs' – some local families have been Keys castaways for generations. The islands are at their most isolated and rural before opening onto (relatively) cosmopolitan, heterogeneous and free-spirited Key West. People aside, the big draw in the Lower Keys is nature. You'll find the loveliest state park in the Keys here, and one of its rarest species.

TOP TIP

The National Key Deer Refuge takes up over 8000 acres of Big Pine Key and No Name Key. The speed limit within the refuge drops to 35mph, which is strictly enforced for the safety of the animals (and lands unsuspecting drivers with speeding tickets).

Bahia Honda State Park

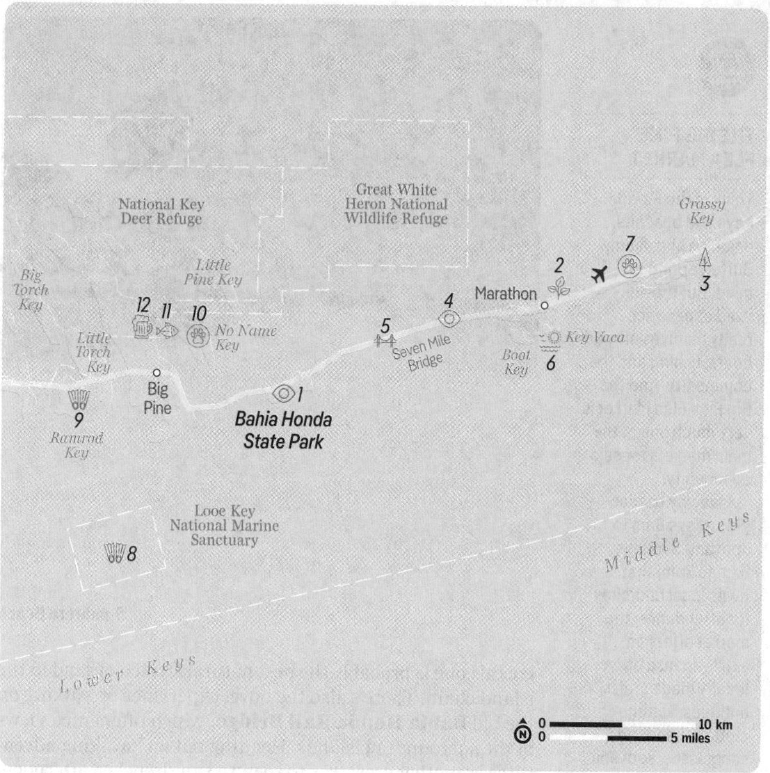

National Key Deer Refuge
Great White Heron National Wildlife Refuge
Grassy Key
Big Torch Key
Little Pine Key
Little Torch Key
No Name Key
Marathon
Key Vaca
Boot Key
Seven Mile Bridge
Big Pine
Bahia Honda State Park
Ramrod Key
Looe Key National Marine Sanctuary
Middle Keys
Lower Keys
0 10 km
0 5 miles

HIGHLIGHTS
1 Bahia Honda State Park

SIGHTS
2 Crane Point Hammock
3 Curry Hammock State Park
4 Pigeon Key National Historic District
5 Seven Mile Bridge
6 Sombrero Beach

ACTIVITIES, COURSES & TOURS
7 Florida Keys Aquarium Encounters
8 Looe Key
9 Looe Key Dive Center
10 No Name Key
11 Old Wooden Bridge Guest Cottages & Marina

DRINKING & NIGHTLIFE
12 No Name Pub

Sit in the Sand at Bahia Honda State Park

BRIDGES AND BEACHES

With its long, often seaweed-strewn white-sand beach (named **Sandspur Beach** by locals), this park is the big attraction in the Lower Keys. Because the Keys are mangrove islands, they tend to possess mangrove coasts, but as Keys beaches

WHERE TO SLEEP IN THE MIDDLE & LOWER KEYS

Bahia Honda State Park Campground
Wake to the sky as your ceiling and the ocean as your shower (and – ouch! – sand flies). **$**

Old Wooden Bridge Resort & Marina
A marina with sparsely furnished cottages on land, plus small but charming Floating Cabins. **$$**

Parmer's Resort
Takes up Little Torch Key and fills it with inviting rooms that overlook local waterways. **$$**

THE BIG PINE FLEA MARKET

Think of the Florida Keys and beaches, daiquiris and Jimmy Buffett spring to mind. But the daily lived experience really revolves around boats, fishing and the community. And the Big Pine Flea Market is very much one of the main markets for said community.

A weekly bazaar (Saturdays 8am to 3pm and Sundays 8am to 2pm) that rivals local churches for attendance, the market offers an extravaganza of locally made crafts, antiques, vintage clothes, handbags, sunglasses, souvenir T-shirts and beach towels, wood carvings, wind chimes and hand tools – plus all the secondhand gear you might need for a fishing trip. Food vendors abound, so stock up if you're planning a picnic.

SIMON DANNHAUER/SHUTTERSTOCK ©

Sombrero Beach

go, this one is probably the best natural stretch of sand in the island chain. There's also the novel experience of walking on the old **Bahia Honda Rail Bridge**, which offers nice views of the surrounding islands. Heading out on kayaking adventures is another great way to spend a sun-drenched afternoon.

You can also check out some **nature trails** and a **science center**, where helpful park employees can help you identify stone crabs, fireworms, horseshoe crabs and comb jellies. You can also snorkel near the shore, although you're not likely to see much beyond some sand and someone else's feet. But the park does offer **boat trips** out to a reef, where there's a lot more sea life to spot.

So what's the deal with the rail bridge? Down in the Keys, you'll notice everything is named for Henry Flagler, the industrialist who (literally) paved the way for South Florida's mass settlement. This rail bridge was originally part of the Overseas Railway, which connected the Keys to the mainland, and was largely destroyed by a hurricane in 1935, only to eventually be replaced by the Overseas Hwy in 1938.

Every wild space in the Keys is good for bird-watching, but Bahia Honda is superlatively so. The park blends all genres of

WHERE TO SLEEP IN THE MIDDLE & LOWER KEYS

Sea Dell Motel
This is a Keys classic: bright, low-slung rooms with a pastel color scheme and floral bedspreads. **$$**

Seascape Resort
The understated luxury of this B&B manifests in its rooms, which feature minimalist, sleek decor. **$$$**

Deer Run on the Atlantic
A state-certified green lodge and pet-friendly B&B isolated on a lovely stretch of Long Beach Dr. **$$$**

avian wildlife, from raptors (hawks) to wading birds (great blue herons and snowy egrets, to name a few) to shore birds (sanderlings and plovers, among others). Come summer, the vulnerable white-crowned pigeon likes to nest in local poisonwood trees.

Jungle Jaunt in Crane Point Hammock

THE KEYS, AU NATURALE

The environment of the Florida Keys is utterly unique, and as you might guess, often under threat from overdevelopment; Key West, for example, is almost completely built up. It's hard to find examples of pristine pre-construction ecosystems in the islands, but they exist – like at this 63-acre reserve in Marathon, which encompasses dense tropical hammock (groves), solution holes (karst pits formed when the water table and sea level were lower), mangroves, a butterfly meadow and a lovely stretch of coastline. A looping 1.5-mile trail with various boardwalk detours transports you quickly onto the wild side.

Highlights along the way include the restored **Adderley House** (built by Bahamian immigrants in 1903), the jungle-like palm hammock (which only grows between Mile Markers 47 and 60), and a wild bird center (where injured birds are nursed back to health). Start off with a short film that gives an overview of the park, and have a look at the natural history museum (dugout canoes, pirate exhibitions, a simulated coral reef). It's a great spot for kids.

Just across the Overseas Hwy, down Sombrero Beach Rd, is (imagine that) **Sombrero Beach**, one of the few white-sand, mangrove-free beaches in the Keys. It's a good spot to lounge on the sand or swim, has full accessibility for wheelchairs, and there's also a small playground. Turtles (mainly loggerheads) like to nest here from April through October, and during those months, human activity is limited in the areas that a turtle has laid eggs.

BEST RESTAURANTS IN THE MIDDLE & LOWER KEYS

Keys Fisheries
Pricey, but worth it for fine fresh seafood (especially that lobster reuben) and better waterfront views. $$

Burdine's Waterfront
Much-loved haunt where you can sit around the thatch-roof bar or at a picnic table. $$

Good Food Conspiracy
Great sandwiches and fresh-juice bar on-site, a nice counter to the usual Keys fried food. $

Kiki's Sandbar
Join locals for drinks with a view, plus excellent seafood and, often enough, live music. $$$

Feel the Wind at Curry Hammock State Park

QUIET ESCAPE FOR OUTDOOR ADVENTURE

The largest swatch of undeveloped land between Key Largo and the Lower Keys is Curry Hammock, a state park located on Little Crawl Key (no, really) that is as popular with peregrine falcons, the fastest birds in the world, as it is with human visitors. This is a spot for getting on the water, and the pretty coastal scenery

FOR MARKET LOVERS

In Key West, there's no shortage of galleries, shops and souvenir stands. Many of them are concentrated on **Duval Street** (p163), where you can browse for the painting, T-shirt or tatty gift of your dreams.

WHERE TO EAT IN THE MIDDLE & LOWER KEYS

Mangrove Mama's
This groovy roadside eatery serves globally inspired seafood best enjoyed on the backyard patio. **$$**

Coco's Kitchen
Excellent-value diner that serves a good mix of American standards and Cuban fare. **$**

Wooden Spoon
Down-at-the-heels diner ambience and great breakfasts, from fluffy pancakes to airy biscuits and sausage gravy. **$**

makes for some solid paddling if you're on a kayak or stand-up paddleboard (both of these craft can be rented at the park).

On windy days, kiteboarders rule the scene, and watching them do their gravity-defying thing is time well spent. You can also hike a 1.5-mile trail amid preserved tropical hardwood and mangrove habitats. The trailhead is 1 mile past the park's main entrance on the bayside (heading toward Marathon); look for the parking area on the right.

If you wanna camp here, book now. The 28 sites are beloved by dozens of visitors, who come back here year after year.

KEY DEER

What would make Bambi cuter? Mini Bambi. Introducing the Key deer, an endangered subspecies of whitetail that prances about primarily on Big Pine and No Name Keys. If you head down the side roads of Big Pine Key, there's a decent chance you'll spot some. Once mainland dwellers, the deer were stranded on the Keys during the formation of the islands. Successive generations grew smaller and had single births, not large litters, to adapt to the archipelago's scarcer food supply. While you won't see thundering herds of dwarfish deer, you will see them if you're persistent and patient. In fact, they're so common you should pay attention to the reduced speed limits.

Deer Watching on No Name Key

WHERE THE KEYS HAVE NO NAME

Perhaps the best-named island in the archipelago, No Name gets few visitors, as it's basically a quiet, empty island but for a few homes. It's one of the most reliable spots for Key deer watching. From Overseas Hwy, take Wilder Rd to Watson Blvd. Cross Bogie Bridge and you'll be on No Name.

So, what's here? Well, not a ton...but doesn't it feel cool to visit a literal no name island? Past that novelty, there are several barely signed trails here, including one off to the right about 0.8 miles after crossing Bogie Bridge. It leads through mangrove forest and out to the waterfront, passing an old rock quarry with abandoned machinery along the way.

And there's pizza! Good pizza. The **No Name Pub** is one of those off-the-track places that everyone seems to know about. Despite the isolated location, folks come from all over to this divey spot to add their dollar bills to the walls, drink locally brewed beer, enjoy some classic rock playing overhead, and feast on pizzas, burgers and pub grub.

Take in the kooky ambience from a bar stool or head out back to a shaded yard full of picnic tables. Note: full disclosure, No Name Pub is (gasp) not on No Name Key, but rather on Big Pine, just over the causeway. Also out this way – again, on Big Pine, just before the bridge to No Name – is the **Old Wooden Bridge Guest Cottages & Marina**, a bare-bones outfit with guest homes that leads fishing trips around the Lower Keys.

FOR UNDERSEA EXPLORERS

The **Florida Keys Eco-Discovery Center** (p165), located on Key West, is where you want to head if you're into interactive exhibits and learning about the marine wildlife and ecosystems of the islands.

Enter the World of Florida Keys Aquarium Encounters

MARINE LIFE LESSONS

If you passed the Upper Keys without seeing what lurked beneath the waves, don't worry: this

WHERE TO EAT IN THE MIDDLE & LOWER KEYS

Sunset Grille
Huge, festive spot with an extensive menu of seafood and grilled meat dishes, plus great views. $$

Baby's Coffee
This very cool coffee counter has an on-site bean-roasting plant and is famed for its open-faced bagel sandwiches. $

Stuffed Pig
A locals' favorite for breakfast serving excellent omelets and fresh seafood along with killer Bloody Marys. $

DANIELE NOVATI/SHUTTERSTOCK ©

Turtle Hospital

Marathon destination has you covered. Taking in the small, interactive aquarium starts with a free guided tour of local marine ecosystems. But you don't need to relegate yourself to lectured instruction; there are also more immersive experiences, where you snorkel in the coral-reef aquarium or the lagoon, which is filled with tropical fish.

Some of the ecosystems you will encounter include a mangrove-lined basin full of tarpon, a tidal-pool tank with queen conch and horseshoe crabs, and a 200,000-gallon coral-reef tank with moray eels, grouper and several different shark species. You can also observe mesmerizing lionfish, a pig-nosed turtle, juvenile alligators and various fish species from the Everglades, plus snowy egrets and little blue herons that come by for a visit.

Slightly more controversial are the 'touch tanks' and 'stingray encounters', where you can handle shallow-water marine species and touch stingrays (the barbs have been trimmed). Please note that the stress of human interaction can be detrimental to the well-being of aquatic creatures.

TURTLE HOSPITAL

There's an odd glut of wildlife-oriented destinations in Marathon. About 4 miles down the road from Florida Keys Aquarium Encounters is Marathon's famous Turtle Hospital. Be it a victim of disease, boat-propeller strike, flipper entanglement with fishing lines or any other danger, an injured sea turtle in the Keys will hopefully end up in this motel-cum-sanctuary. It's sad to see the injured and sick ones, but heartening to see them so well looked after. Ninety-minute tours are educational, fun and offered every 30 minutes from 9am to 4pm. Reservations are highly recommended.

Note that there are about a dozen permanent resident turtles here, too injured or traumatized to be returned to the wild.

WHERE TO DRINK IN THE MIDDLE & LOWER KEYS

My New Joint
This spacious Cudjoe Key lounge has artfully made cocktails, excellent brews and platters of oysters.

SS Wreck Galley & Galley Grill
On Grassy Key, this is a classic, where fisherfolk knock back brews and feast on wings.

Island Fish Company
Friendly staff pour strong cocktails on a Marathon-based, sea-breeze-kissed tiki bar overlooking Florida Bay.

FOR ANIMAL LOVERS WITH KIDS

Just before you hit Key West, you may want to take a brief detour to the **Sheriff's Animal Farm** on Stock Island. Operated by local law enforcement working in partnership with a local farmer, this is a home for Monroe County animals that have been abandoned or given up. It's a nice (and free) place to take the kids, although note that the farm is only open to the public on the second and fourth Sunday of each month, from 1pm to 3pm. There are miniature horses, pot-bellied pigs, kinkajous, sloths, birds, snakes, alpacas, an ostrich, lemurs and some massive tortoises.

Seven Mile Bridge

Cross Seven Mile Bridge & Explore Pigeon Key

BIG BRIDGE, LITTLE ISLAND

Marathon connects to the Lower Keys (specifically, tiny Little Duck Key) via the Seven Mile Bridge. If you want to be accurate (or insufferable), feel free to point out that the bridge is actually only 6.765 miles long. Simply crossing the bridge is a cool, only-in-the-Keys endeavor – it's rare to find infrastructure that makes you feel like you've fallen off the face of the Earth. While you're crossing, note that there's a parallel bridge. This is the imaginatively named **Old Seven Mile Bridge**, which crosses the little island of Pigeon Key and is only accessible to pedestrians and cyclists (and a small tourist train).

For years this speck of land, located 2 miles west of Marathon, housed the rail and maintenance workers who built the infrastructure that connected the Keys. Today you can tour the structures of the **Pigeon Key National Historic District** or relax on the beach and do some snorkeling. Buy tickets from the visitor center at Mile 47.5 on the main highway, or book a tour at pigeonkey.net.

You can either take a short train ride out to Pigeon Key, or walk or bike out here via the old bridge. If you

FOR BRIDGE LOVERS

One of the nicest things about driving in the Florida Keys is the sheer mass of bridges over blue waters. To this end, **Islamorada** (p140; literally 'village of islands') is full of bridges and causeways.

WHERE TO DRINK IN THE MIDDLE & LOWER KEYS

Brass Monkey
This Marathon dive is where local off-duty service industry types go to release all their tensions.

Coconuts
This Big Pine bar has local characters, pool tables and a drive-thru window.

JJ's Dog House & Sports Bar
Has live music several times a week, games on TV and plenty of cold beer.

go with the latter option, note the bridge is only open from 9am to 5pm. Keep hydrated; that Caribbean sun will be beating down on you.

Just before Seven Mile Bridge, on the Gulf side of the highway, is the **Marathon City Marina**, better known as Boot Key Harbor. This is one of the better maintained working waterfronts in the Keys, a place where you can watch pelicans fight over the guts left behind by local fishers. Come during Christmas to see a 'parade' of boats decked out with Christmas lights.

Seek (Marine) Sanctuary on Looe Key

THIS PLACE IS A DIVE

Looe (pronounced 'loo') Key, located 5 nautical miles off Big Pine, isn't a key at all but a U-shaped reef, part of the **Florida Keys National Marine Sanctuary**. This is an area of some 2800 sq nautical miles of 'land' managed by the National Oceanic & Atmospheric Administration. The reef here can only be visited through a specially arranged charter-boat trip, best organized through any Keys diving outfit, the most natural one being the **Looe Key Dive Center**. Located in a resort of the same name on Ramrod Key, this center runs day trips for divers and snorkelers out to the reef in the mornings and afternoons.

Looe Key itself is named for an English frigate, the HMS *Looe*, that ran aground on the reef in 1744 during the War of Jenkins' Ear, a name that could only have been invented in the 18th century. Apparently unfazed by losing their ship, the crew of the *Looe* proceeded to board smaller boats and capture a nearby Spanish sloop, before setting fire to their own irreparably damaged vessel.

The remains of the original *Looe* and her cargo form part of the marine sanctuary, but they're not the only sunken ships in this part of the islands. The Looe Key reef contains the 210ft *Adolphus Busch,* used in the 1957 film *Fire Down Below* and then sunk (110ft deep) in these waters in 1998.

The waters around the reef are generally shallow, which is why this is a good location for both snorkelers and beginner divers. With all that said, there is a deeper section of the reef where there's a steep drop (about 100ft at one point) that will appeal to advanced divers. All skill levels may spot species like barracuda, jacks and parrotfish, among others.

THE BLUE HOLE

Located on Big Pine Key, along Key Deer Blvd off Mile Marker 30.5, the **Blue Hole** is a little pond (and former quarry) that is now the largest freshwater body in the Keys. That's not saying much, but the hole is a pretty dollop of blue (well, algal green) surrounded by a small path and information signs. The water is home to turtles, fish, wading birds and the odd alligator – don't feed them, as it makes the animals way too comfortable around humans! You can't swim here, nor would you want to (ahem, alligators). A quarter-mile further along the same road is **Watson's Nature Trail** (less than 1 mile long) and **Watson's Hammock**, a small Keys forest habitat.

GETTING AROUND

Greyhound buses stop in Marathon and Big Pine on the Miami–Key West run, while Keys West Transit connects Marathon and the Lower Keys to Key West (many waiters, bartenders and even nurses and teachers in Key West actually live out here).

Marathon has good public parking, as the Keys go. The cycling here can be lovely, especially if you find back roads on Big Pine or head out to Old Seven Mile Bridge, but you'll also want to beware of areas with very narrow shoulders.

KEY WEST

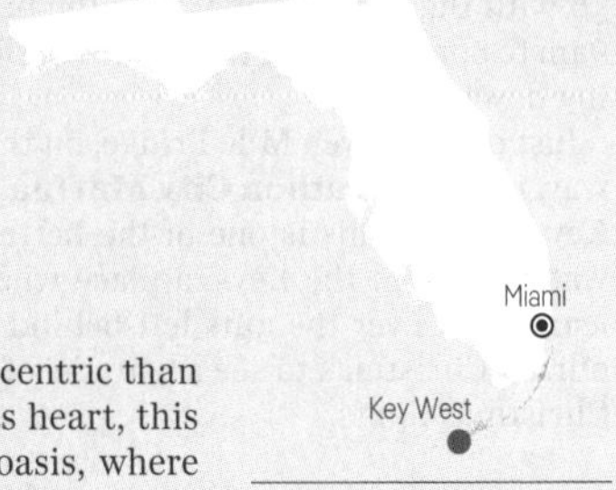

Key West is the far frontier: edgier and more eccentric than the other Keys, and also more captivating. At its heart, this 7-sq-mile island feels like a beautiful tropical oasis, where the moonflowers bloom at night and the classical Caribbean homes are so sad and romantic it's hard not to sigh at them.

While Key West has obvious allure, it's not without its contradictions. On one side of the road, there are literary festivals, Caribbean villas, tropical dining rooms and expensive art galleries. On the other, you may see an S&M fetishist parade, frat boys passing out on the sidewalk and grizzly bars filled with bearded burnouts. With all that in mind, it's easy to find your groove in this setting, no matter where your interests lie.

As in other parts of the Keys, nature plays a starring role here, with some breathtaking sunsets – cause for nightly celebration down on Mallory Sq.

TOP TIP

Key West effectively is split into two sides – the eastern half, which has shopping plazas, gas stations, cheaper high-density lodging, marinas and other modern 'stuff'; and Old Town, which has the historical buildings, sit-down restaurants and nightlife, and almost everything else of tourist interest.

GAGLIARDIPHOTOGRAPHY/SHUTTERSTOCK ©

Waterfront, Key West

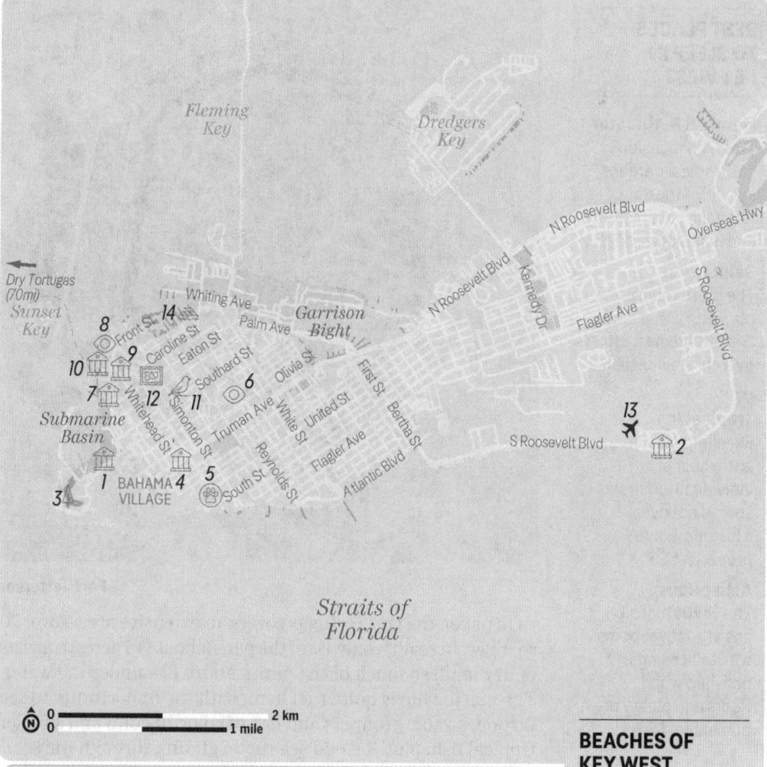

SIGHTS
1 Florida Keys Eco-Discovery Center
2 Fort East Martello Museum
3 Fort Zachary Taylor State Park
4 Hemingway's House
5 Key West Butterfly & Nature Conservatory
6 Key West Cemetery
7 Little White House
8 Mallory Square
9 Mel Fisher Maritime Museum
10 Museum of Art & History at the Custom House
11 Nancy Forrester's Secret Garden
12 Studios of Key West

TRANSPORT
13 Key West Seaplane Adventures
14 Yankee Freedom Dry Tortugas Ferry

Get Wet at Dry Tortugas National Park

HISTORY AND TURQUOISE WATERS

After all those keys, connected by that convenient road, the nicest islands in the archipelago require a little extra effort. Welcome to the **Dry Tortugas**, one of the National Park Service's least accessible parks, reached only by boat or seaplane.

Is the trip out here worth the work? Two-word answer: hell, yes! The park rewards you for your persistence with amazing snorkeling amid coral reefs full of marine life. You'll also get to tour a beautifully preserved 19th-century **brick fort**, one of the largest such fortifications in the USA despite its location 70 miles off the coast of Key West.

BEACHES OF KEY WEST

Spoiler alert: Key West is *not* about beachgoing. In fact, for true sun 'n' surf, locals go to Bahia Honda in Big Pine. Still, the three city beaches on the southern side of the island are lovely. Tiny **South Beach** is at the end of Simonton St. **Higgs Beach**, at the end of Reynolds St, has barbecue grills, picnic tables and a pier. **Smathers Beach**, further east, is longer, though not easily accessible on foot. The best local beach is at **Fort Zachary Taylor**; it's worth the admission to enjoy the relative calm.

BEST PLACES TO SLEEP IN KEY WEST

Mermaid & Alligator
This 1904 mansion has tropical gardens set with a trickling fountain, plunge pool and hammocks. $$$

Saint Hotel
The plush rooms play with 'Saint' and 'Sinner' themes, offset by a chic minimalist lobby. $$$

Tropical Inn
Excellent service and a host of individualized rooms spread out over a historic-home property. $$$

Artist House
This 1890s mansion has attractive rooms with tall ceilings, polished wood floors and plenty of originality. $$$

Fort Jefferson

On paper, the Dry Tortugas covers an extensive area – over 70 sq miles. In reality, only 1% of the park (about 143 acres) consists of dry land, so much of the park's allure lies under the water. The marine life is quite rich here, with the opportunity to see tarpon, sizable groupers and lots of colorful coral and smaller tropical fish, plus the odd sea turtle gliding through the sea.

Explorer Ponce de León named this seven-island chain Las Tortugas (The Turtles) for the sea turtles spotted in its waters. Thirsty mariners who passed through and found no water later affixed 'dry' to the name. In subsequent years, the US Navy set an outpost here as a strategic position into the Gulf of Mexico. But by the American Civil War, **Fort Jefferson**, the main structure on the islands, had become a prison for Union deserters and at least four other people, among them Dr Samuel Mudd, who had been arrested for complicity in the assassination of Abraham Lincoln. Hence a new nickname: Devil's Island.

The name was prophetic: in 1867 a yellow fever outbreak killed 38 people, and after an 1873 hurricane the fort was abandoned. It reopened in 1886 as a quarantine

FOR WILDLIFE LOVERS

There's an odd surplus of wildlife sanctuaries in the Keys; in Key Largo, the **Laura Quinn Wild Bird Sanctuary** (p143) is one of the nicest, housing all kinds of injured, migrating feathered friends.

WHERE TO SLEEP IN KEY WEST

Ridley House
This getaway has wraparound porches, leafy grounds, a secluded swimming pool and spacious, airy rooms. **$$$**

Avalon Bed & Breakfast
Restored Victorian house blends attentive service with stately old ceiling fans and tropical lounge-room rugs. **$$**

Seascape Tropical Inn
Uniquely designed rooms with floral comforters and art; some have French doors opening onto private terraces. **$$$**

station for smallpox and cholera victims, was declared a national monument in 1935 by President Franklin D Roosevelt, and was upped to national park status in 1992 by George Bush Sr.

If you have your own boat, the Dry Tortugas are covered under National Ocean Survey chart No 11438. Otherwise, the **Yankee Freedom** operates a fast ferry between Garden Key and the Historic Seaport (at the northern end of Margaret St). Reservations are essential if you want to book the 2½-hour crossing. Continental breakfast, a lunch buffet, snorkeling gear, a 45-minute tour of the fort and a park admission fee are all included.

Key West Seaplane Adventures can take up to 10 passengers (flight time 40 minutes each way). The half-day tour is four hours, allowing 2½ hours on the island. Again, reserve at least a week in advance.

Dodge the Cats at Hemingway's House

LITERARY PAPA PILGRIMAGE

Key West's most famous resident, Ernest Hemingway, lived in this gorgeous French Colonial house from 1931 to 1940. Papa moved here with his second wife, Pauline Pfeiffer, *Vogue* fashion editor and (former) friend of his first wife (he left the house when he ran off with his third wife). *The Short Happy Life of Francis Macomber* and *The Green Hills of Africa* were produced here, as well as many cats - maybe? The cats could have been owned by a neighbor, but either way, their descendants run the grounds these days. About half of them are polydactyl (six-toed).

The home would be worth a visit even if one of the iconic novelists of the 20th century hadn't lived here. It was built in 1851 by famed salvager Asa Tift and looks like a tropical wedding cake. Note the **pool**, which apparently cost twice the purchasing price of the house itself. Pfeiffer had it built while Hemingway was reporting. He threw a penny down and told her to take his last cent; she later had the coin embedded in the concrete adjacent to the pool (after Hemingway started enjoying it, along with a habit of swimming in the buff - hence, the high brick walls).

Admission includes a guided tour. You're also free to poke around the house and grounds on your own.

Make for the Museum of Art & History at the Custom House

WRECKERS AND RUM-RUNNERS

This excellent museum, set in a grand 1891 red-brick building that once served as the island's Custom House, covers the history of the southernmost city in the continental USA and fourth-oldest city in Florida. There's a while lot of history to

SOUTHERNMOST POINT: BUOYS OF SUMMER

We should at least mention the most-photographed spot on the island... and explain why it disappoints. We're talking about the big barrel-like marker that lets tourists know they've made it all the way to Mile Marker 0, the end of the road, the one and only (drumroll): Southernmost Point in the Continental USA. Except this is a lie! First, this red-and-black buoy isn't the southernmost point in the USA (that's in the off-limits naval base around the corner). Second, it's... Look, it's a let-down, is all we are saying. A low-key boring buoy often swarmed with little kids. There's just not a lot to the famed (and falsely placed) Southernmost Point.

Gardens Hotel
This boutique, environmentally friendly property lives up to its name with extravagant greenery surrounding lavish rooms. **$$$**

Lighthouse Hotel
Warm hardwood floors are set off by the right amount of tropical breeziness and cool colors. **$$$**

Curry Mansion Inn
Southern colonnades and a New England–style widow's walk enclose bright Floridian rooms with canopied beds. **$$$**

BEST PLACES TO DRINK IN KEY WEST

Green Parrot
Oldest bar on an island of bars, this rogues' cantina is an essential Keys experience.

La Te Da
Locals gather for mellow vibes, good beer, high-quality drag acts and all kinds of cabaret.

Captain Tony's Saloon
This pleasant dive, grizzled but friendly, was the original Sloppy Joe's that Hemingway drank in.

Virgilio's
A dark, candlelit lounge where you can chill to jazz and get down with some salsa.

pick from down here, but here are some highlights covered in the museum: the archival footage from the building of the ambitious Overseas Hwy (and the hurricane that killed 400 people), a model of the ill-fated USS *Maine* (sunk during the Spanish-American War), exhibitions on the role of the navy (once the largest employer in Key West) and the 'wreckers' of Key West, who scavenged sunken treasure ships (and also among the largest sources of employment down here). In addition, there's info on rum-running to Havana during the Prohibition days and some excellent folk art: seek out Mario Sanchez' art naïf paintings of Key West from the 1960s and '70s.

Go Big at the Little White House

TRUMAN'S RETREAT

This sprawling 1890s mansion (a former naval officer's residence) is where President Harry S Truman used to vacation when he wasn't molding post-WWII geopolitics. In fact, the first time the president came down here was in 1946, when a doctor told him that he needed a warm weather break. Truman arrived in Key West in November, and after one visit, he vowed to make a point of returning every year.

Plenty of visiting dignitaries and big wigs visited the Little White House, where Truman would treat them to (what else?) fishing trips on the water. In March 1948, the president convened the Joint Chiefs of Staff (the heads of the American military) at the Little White House, where they drafted the Key West Agreement, a policy paper that had a huge bearing on the organization and function of the armed forces.

The Little White House is a beautifully preserved space, one of the finest slices of architecture on the island, and open only for guided tours, although you are welcome to visit one small gallery with photographs and historical displays (and a short video) on the ground floor. Plenty of Truman's possessions are scattered about, but the real draw is each of the guides, who are intensely knowledgeable, quirky and helpful.

Find Flying Rainbows at the Key West Butterfly & Nature Conservatory

RAINBOWS ON GOSSAMER WINGS

This huge domed conservatory lets you stroll through a lush, enchanting garden of flowering plants, tiny waterfalls, colorful birds (including flamingos) and up to 1800 fluttering butterflies comprising some 50 species – all live imports from around the globe. The shimmery blue morpho butterflies winging past are

WHERE TO EAT IN KEY WEST

BO's Fish Wagon
Looks like a maritime wreck, serves fantastic seafood: conch fritters, soft-shell crab sandwiches and fish tacos. **$$**

The Cafe
This (mostly) vegetarian spot is a sunny luncheonette that morphs into a buzzing restaurant at night. **$$**

Mo's Restaurant
Haitian home cooking that will stick to your ribs and put a smile on your face. **$$**

Key West Cemetery

particularly captivating, although you could say this of any of the iridescent residents, all tiny, flapping miracles. Don't miss the small viewing area, where butterflies emerge from their chrysalises (most frequently in the morning). A tiny exhibition center has intriguing videos and displays describing the life cycle, anatomy and migratory patterns of these wondrous creatures.

There are birds here too! 'Butterfly-friendly' birds that won't make a meal of the other conservatory residents, and represent a palette of feathers as rainbow bright as the butterflies.

Get Lively in Key West Cemetery

DEAD CENTER OF TOWN

A darkly alluring Gothic labyrinth beckons at the center of this pastel town. Built in 1847, the Key West Cemetery crowns Solares Hill, the highest point on the island (with a vertigo-inducing elevation of approximately 16ft). Some of the oldest families in the Keys rest in peace – and close proximity – here. See, this is an island, and not a very big one at that. With space at a premium, mausoleums stand practically shoulder to shoulder. Island quirkiness penetrates the gloom: seashells and macramé adorn headstones with inscriptions like, 'I told you I was sick.'

THE CONCH REPUBLIC: ONE HUMAN FAMILY

A Conch (pronounced 'conk') is someone born and raised in the Keys. You will see the flag of the Conch Republic everywhere in the islands.

In 1982, US customs agents erected a roadblock at Key Largo to catch drug smugglers. As traffic jams mounted, tourists disappeared. Subsequently, a bunch of Conchs formed the Conch Republic and made three declarations: secede from the USA; declare war on the USA and surrender; and request $1 million in foreign aid.

Today the Conch Republic is largely a marketing gimmick, but that doesn't detract from its official motto: 'One Human Family.' An emphasis on tolerance and mutual respect has accelerated acceptance of peoples of all backgrounds, sexual orientations and religions.

Blue Heaven
Customers, along with free-ranging fowl, flock to dine on Caribbean fare in a ramshackle tropical garden. **$$$**

Nine One Five
Modern and elegant space, which serves a creative, changing New American menu with global accents. **$$$**

Little Pear
Sink into a cerulean-blue banquette and let the evening unfold while indulging in Asian-inspired dishes. **$$$**

WHY I LOVE KEY WEST

Adam Karlin, writer

How can you not? Think of it: the rainbow-colored homes, the obsession with individual weirdness *and* community spirit; the whiff of a Cuban cigar; rum soaking your lips, cracked from the salt breeze; the sunset and the smell of fresh fish and mangoes; the moonlight, slotting through the palm fronds, resting on a colonial house that was so pastel pretty by day, and reeks of ghosts by night.

It's not any one of these things. It's all of them, somehow finding each other here, an island at the end of everything.

ERIKA CRISTINA MANNO/SHUTTERSTOCK ©

Mallory Square

Haunts & History at Fort East Martello Museum & Gardens

FOLK ART AND MURDER DOLLS

This old fortress was built to resemble an old Italian Martello-style coastal watchtower, a design that quickly became obsolete with the advent of the explosive shell. Now the fort serves a new purpose: preserving the past. There's historical memorabilia exploring Key West's role in the Civil War, its wrecking and cigar-industry heyday, plus the folk art of Mario Sanchez, self-taught son of a cigar roller, and 'junk' sculptor Stanley Papio, a Canadian-turned-Conch who turned scrap metal into things of chaotic, anarchic beauty.

Perhaps the most haunted thing in Key West is kept here: 'Robert the Doll,' a child's toy from the 19th century who reportedly causes much misfortune to those who question his powers (get the backstory on robertthedoll.org). Indeed, the doll looks like it's about to step out of a Stephen King novel and devour your soul, so that's fun.

FOR HISTORY LOVERS

If you want to dive into – well, paddle around – the history of the Keys, head to **Indian Key** (p144) in the Upper Keys, once a town, now an island of ghosts and mangroves.

WHERE TO EAT IN KEY WEST

Pierogi Market Place
Seasonal workers from Central and Eastern Europe (and locals) come for pierogies, dumplings, blinis and more. **$**

Duetto Pizza & Gelato
This little pizza and gelato stand is a good-value stop for a quick slice or scoop. **$**

Croissants de France
Stop by for eggs Benedict, cinnamon brioche French toast or lovely pastries, plus delicious baguette sandwiches. **$$**

Street Performance at Mallory Square

SUNSET, SQUARED

Take all the energies, subcultures and oddities of Keys life and focus them into one torchlit, family-friendly (but playfully edgy), sunset-enriched street party. The result of all these raucous forces is **Mallory Square**: a cinematic, if tourist-clogged, show that starts in the hours leading up to dusk, the sinking sun a signal to bring on the madness. The waterfront location is magnificent, and food vendors often congregate here. Watch a dog walk a tightrope, a man swallow fire, and British acrobats tumble and sass each other. The showmanship and camaraderie of the performers is matched by the energies of the crowds and the dying fires of the day. Then – lucky you – you'll find yourself positioned right at the top of Duval St, ready to begin the Duval Crawl. **Duval Street** is the main drag in Old Town Key West, a Key West conglomeration of neon and historic buildings. Its upper reaches in particular are packed with bars and restaurants, while the southern end has more galleries and gift shops – although it certainly doesn't lack for bars and restaurants either.

Go Wild at Fantasy Fest

GLITTER, GLAM AND DEBAUCHERY ABOUND

Akin to New Orleans' riotous Mardi Gras revelry, Fantasy Fest is 10 days of burlesque parties, parades, street fairs, concerts and loads of costumed events held in late October. Bars and inns get competitive about decorating their properties, and everyone gets decked out in the most outrageous costumes they can cobble together (or get mostly naked with daring body paint – and as a side note, while public nudity is illegal in Key West, women can get away with painted breasts in Fantasy Fest's designated 'Fantasy Zone').

As wild as Fantasy Fest gets, there is meaning to the madness, up to and including: a pride-esque celebration of LGBTIQ+ culture, and a public affirmation of the Key West ideal of 'One Human Family,' a space where all are accepted as long as they accept everyone else. Of course, Fantasy Fest isn't all about positive messaging – this is the biggest tourist event of the year in Key West. If you're visiting at this time, prepare to pay high rates for hotels, and make sure to reserve lodging and dining options well in advance.

BEST PLACES TO EAT IN KEY WEST

Santiago's Bodega
This beloved tapas bar has an easygoing front porch and an elegant interior filled with whimsical artwork. $$

Banana Cafe
Sun-drenched spot serving up creatively topped eggs, fluffy omelets and delicious sandwiches. $

Cafe Sole
South French cuisine using South Florida ingredients, served in a cozy yet airy space. $$$

5 Brothers Grocery & Sandwich Shop
Loyal locals come for first-rate Cuban coffee, guava pastries, bacon-and-egg rolls and sandwiches. $

FOR SUNSET LOVERS

Bahia Honda State Park (p149), further up in the Lower Keys (sorry, was that confusing?), is a wonderful spot to feel the sand between your toes as the sun dips into the ocean.

WHERE TO DRINK IN KEY WEST

Burgundy Bar
This convivial bar deserves special mention for its Bloody Marys – among the best you'll find anywhere.

Lagerheads
This beach bar has umbrella-shaded chairs and a small swimming area where you can cool off.

Viv
This French-run bar is tiny but utterly charming, with velvety wines by the glass or bottle.

THE TENNESSEE WILLIAMS MUSEUM

Tennessee Williams, author of plays like *The Glass Menagerie*, *Cat on a Hot Tin Roof* and *A Streetcar Named Desire*, lived in Key West for over 30 years. Although he actually lived a mile away (at 1431 Duncan St), this small museum outlines his contributions to the literary world.

On display are photos, manuscripts, typewriters, newspaper articles and such. Williams partially lived in Key West because it embraced the gay community; he often wrote on issues facing those individuals long before such topics were commonly broached in literary circles, and his own homosexuality was an open secret.

Discover Nancy Forrester's Secret Garden

BIRD IS THE WORD

Nancy, an environmental artist and fixture of the Keys community, invites you into her backyard oasis where a veritable flock of chatty rescued parrots and macaws await visitors. She gives an overview of these marvelously intelligent and rare birds ('Parrot 101' as she calls it) daily. This **secret garden** is a great place for kids, who often leave inspired by the hands-on interactions; family-friendly activities down here can feel same-samey, but this experience is utterly unique. Musicians are welcome to bring their instruments to play in the yard. The birds love it – particularly flutes!

Peruse the Studios of Key West

ART OF THE ISLANDS

This nonprofit showcases about a dozen artists' studios in a three-story space, and hosts some of the best art openings in Key West, as well as open-studio showcases, on a regular basis – check tskw.org for details. Besides its public visual-arts displays, it also hosts readings, literary and visual workshops, art auctions, painting 'boot camps,' concerts, lectures and community discussion groups. The Studios also host a popular residency program, which helps explain the constantly rotating presence of creative talent on the island. Don't miss **Hugh's Views**, a rooftop deck that offers a fine perspective over town, which is open to the public on Tuesday evenings from 5pm to 7pm.

Learn Local History at the Mel Fisher Maritime Museum

HISTORY BY THE SEA

For a fascinating glimpse into Key West's complicated history, through the lens of the waves, pay a visit to this popular museum near the waterfront. It's best known for its collection of gold coins, rare jewels and other treasures scavenged from Spanish galleons by Mel Fisher and crew. But with that said, the more thought-provoking material would be the exhibition devoted to the slave trade, with artifacts from the wreck of the *Henrietta Marie,* a merchant slave ship that sank in 1700, which throws a light on how central chattel slavery was in an often romanticized

FOR LITERARY LOVERS

One of Tennessee Williams' literary contemporaries, Ernest Hemingway, also made his home in Key West, and his giant former **home** (p159) – now overrun with six-toed cats – is also a major tourism draw.

WHERE TO DRINK IN KEY WEST

Aqua
Hosts some fantastic drag shows and attracts people of all ages and sexual orientations.

Bourbon Street Pub
Great DJs, drag shows and striking male dancers keep the party going at this New Orleans-themed bar.

Vinos on Duval
Pours a good selection of wines from around the globe in a cozy setting.

'Old Florida.' The museum is located within a turn-of-the-20th-century neoclassical building that once served as a local storehouse for the US Navy.

Environmental Immersion at the Florida Keys Eco-Discovery Center

KEY TO THE NATURAL KEYS

This much beloved nature center and science museum has traditionally been one of the best places in the Keys to learn about the extraordinary marine environments of South Florida, which makes sense, given this is the flagship museum for the Florida Keys National Marine Sanctuary. After a significant renovation and upgrade, the center is expected to be an even better all-round destination for learning about local ecosystems. The emphasis will be on the interactive and virtual experiences – visitors will be able to 'dive' into simulated reefs, 'paddle' through created mangrove coasts, and undertake similar activities.

Find Beaches & History at Fort Zachary Taylor Historic State Park

SOUTHERNMOST STATE PARK

'America's Southernmost State Park' is home to an impressive fort, built in the mid-1800s, that played roles in the Civil War and in the Spanish-American War. The beach here is the best one Key West has to offer. This isn't really saying much, but there is white sand to lounge on (even if it is rocky in parts), water deep enough to swim in and tropical fish under the waves. It's also a fine spot for sunset viewing. Learn more about the fort on free guided tours offered at 11am.

The fort was a crucial naval base for the Union in Confederate waters during the Civil War, and served as a vital line of defense against blockade runners. During the third weekend of each month, re-enactors put on historical interpretation shows for visitors.

BAHAMA VILLAGE

Bahama Village was the old Bahamian district of the island, and in days past had a colorful Caribbean feel about it. Today many areas have been swallowed into a pseudo-Duval St periphery. If you want a taste of the old rhythms of Bahamanian Village life, visit during **Goombay Festival**, which occurs around the time of Fantasy Fest, typically over the third weekend of October. Goombay is a more family-friendly party, although the music still gets loud. Have some fried conch fritters and wash them down with a Switcha (a tangy, carbonated limeade, and the national drink of the Bahamas) or a Goombay Smash (a cocktail that does what the name promises).

FOR BEACH LOVERS

Fort Zachary Taylor may have the best beach in Key West, but it's not the only beach. There are several other **local beaches** (p157) on which you can get sand between your toes.

GETTING AROUND

The best way to get around is by bicycle – you can rent beach cruisers from just about any Duval St area hotel. For transportation within the Duval St area, the free Duval Loop shuttle (carfreekeywest.com/duval-loop) runs from 8am to 10pm.

Other options include Key West Transit, with color-coded buses running about every 15 minutes.

Parking can be tricky in town. There's a free parking lot on Fort St off Truman Ave.

Above: Fort Lauderdale (p170); right: Treasure Coast (p202)

SOUTHEAST FLORIDA

BEACHES, TREASURES AND NATURAL WONDERS

Explore some of the wealthiest communities in the US along the aptly named Gold Coast, then discover your own riches along Florida's adventure-inspiring Treasure Coast.

Beyond the grand allure of Southeast Florida's many white sand beaches and whispering palms, worshipped by countless surfers, divers and sun lovers, radiates all manner of arts and culture, culinary delights and hedonistic pursuits. It feels fresh and natural, yet wild and truly decadent at the same time. Wealth is flaunted without shame here.

The region celebrates its rich, yet sometimes lurid, history with plenty of museums and historical sites, proudly displaying its evolution from a tropical outpost to a vacationer's hub. And it continues to evolve. Fort Lauderdale is now widely celebrated as the LGBTIQ+ capital of Florida.

Sunseekers needn't stray beyond Fort Lauderdale's famous white wall and promenade or Hollywood Beach's Broadwalk, where hot sand seems to stretch forever. The adventurous might consider diving or snorkeling the crystal-clear waters below Blue Heron Bridge in West Palm Beach or chartering a boat to fish off the coast of Sebastian. Hike the area's countless parks, botanical gardens and nature centers, or study the region's flora and fauna at the Environmental Learning Center in Vero Beach. If your palms get itchy, head for a flashy casino or rent a metal detector and scour the beaches of the Treasure Coast for hidden bounty – it's famous for a reason!

From laid-back solitude to all-night carousing, there's lots to explore here, all within a few hours' drive. Let's get started.

FLORIDASTOCK/SHUTTERSTOCK ©

THE MAIN AREAS

FORT LAUDERDALE
Beaches, fine dining and barhopping. **p170**

WEST PALM BEACH
Luxury shopping, diving and family fun. **p185**

VERO BEACH
Treasure hunting, deep-sea fishing, nature walks. **p197**

Find Your Way

Follow Hollywood's packed and lively Gold Coast beaches north along the Atlantic seaboard to Sebastian's quieter Treasure Coast shores. Each stop along this sun-soaked, 144-mile route has a unique blend of sights, colorful history and charm.

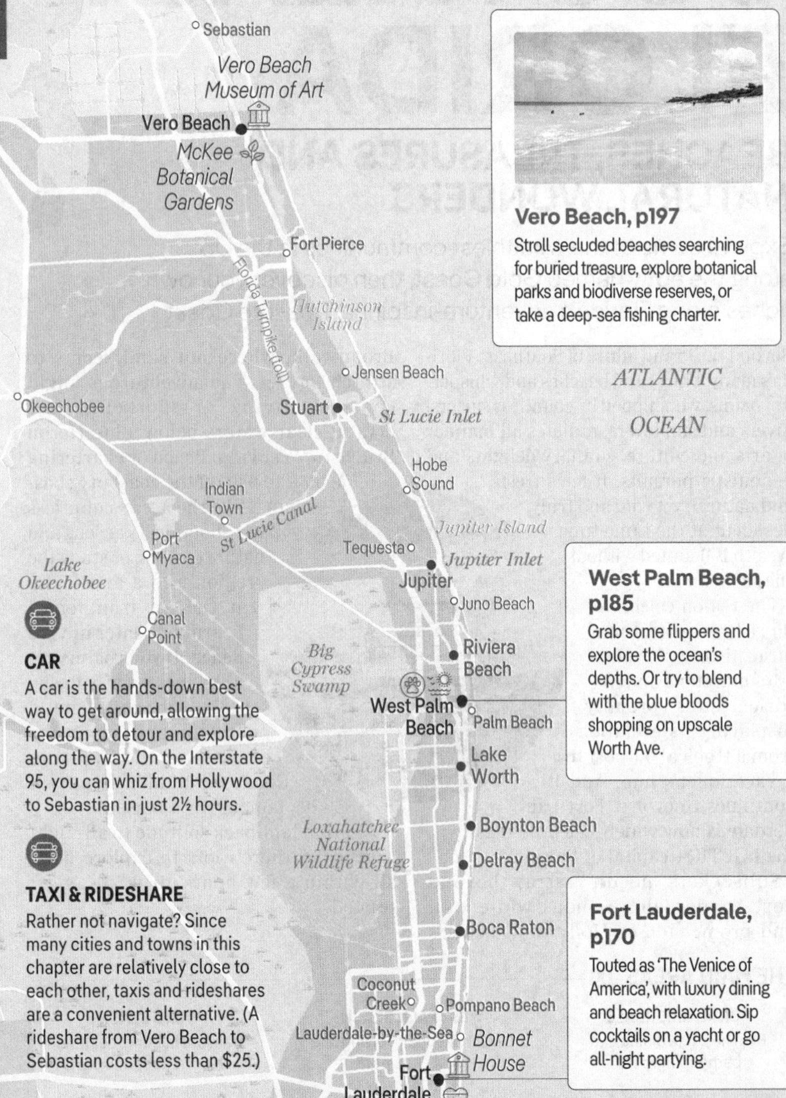

SERGEY AND MARINA PYATAEV/SHUTTERSTOCK ©

Vero Beach, p197

Stroll secluded beaches searching for buried treasure, explore botanical parks and biodiverse reserves, or take a deep-sea fishing charter.

West Palm Beach, p185

Grab some flippers and explore the ocean's depths. Or try to blend with the blue bloods shopping on upscale Worth Ave.

Fort Lauderdale, p170

Touted as 'The Venice of America', with luxury dining and beach relaxation. Sip cocktails on a yacht or go all-night partying.

CAR

A car is the hands-down best way to get around, allowing the freedom to detour and explore along the way. On the Interstate 95, you can whiz from Hollywood to Sebastian in just 2½ hours.

TAXI & RIDESHARE

Rather not navigate? Since many cities and towns in this chapter are relatively close to each other, taxis and rideshares are a convenient alternative. (A rideshare from Vero Beach to Sebastian costs less than $25.)

KAMIRA/SHUTTERSTOCK ©

Plan Your Time

Coming to bask on the beach? Party all night long? Explore natural wonders? Dive for hidden treasures? Depending on what you're wanting to do, timing, and proper planning, is paramount.

Pressed for Time

- Basing yourself in **Fort Lauderdale** (p170, pictured), hit the beaches for some fun in the sun. Sip cocktails along Las Olas Blvd, then stroll **Riverwalk** (p173), where you can hop on a water taxi. Enjoy a narrated cruise to **Hollywood Beach** (p180) and take a bike ride down its famous **Broadwalk** (p180). Grab a coffee and explore downtown's scenic **ArtsPark at Young Circle** (p181).

A Week to Explore

- After the previous itinerary, head to the **Treasure Coast** (p202) and **Palm Beach** (p192). Tour the **Flagler Museum** (p191), bike the **Palm Beach Lake Trail** (p193) and visit the **Jupiter Inlet Lighthouse** (p194). Take a pontoon down the Loxahatchee River at **Jonathan Dickinson State Park** (p193). Marvel at **Mel Fisher's Treasure Museum** (p202).

Seasonal Highlights

SPRING

Enjoy dry, warm, **sunny days** with cool breezes in the evenings. Off-season rates begin in May but avoid March break at all costs. Bring bug spray!

SUMMER

Hot, humid, and rainy. Calm, clear ocean waters make for **splendid diving**. Enjoy smaller crowds and off-season rates. Hurricane risk peaks in August/September.

FALL

The heat is slightly more tolerable. Rainy season ends in October, hurricane season in mid-November. Great time to see **sea turtles nesting** on the beach.

WINTER

Snowbirds arrive to stay warm. So do **manatees**. The air is dry and temps are a bit cooler, so it's an ideal time to venture inland.

FORT LAUDERDALE

Fort Lauderdale
Miami

After the release of *Where the Boys Are* in 1960, Fort Lauderdale shone as a beacon for sex-crazed, beer-guzzling spring breakers. Students flocked like birds for the next quarter century, packing mediocre motels along the waterfront. Bars welcomed underage kids, and drunkenness, lewdness and even death became commonplace. Residents eventually yanked their welcome mats.

Fast forward 35 years. Sure, spring breakers still come, but not in the same invasive numbers. Fort Lauderdale has instead reinvented itself as a refuge for more mature, subdued vacationers – appealing to boaters, sun worshippers, retirees and families.

With 300 miles of inland waterways and over 50,000 yachts, Lauderdale has earned the titles, 'The Venice of America' and 'The Yachting Capital of the World.' Dining and drinking establishments are chic and luxury hotels now line the A1A beach highway. Lauderdale's new, clean face attracts visitors of all ages.

TOP TIP

Avoid unnecessary driving and parking fees by prioritizing what's most important to you when selecting accommodations. If the beach is supreme, many hotels lining the A1A are an easy walk away. But if you'd rather be close to restaurants, nightlife and downtown shopping, choose a hotel near Las Olas Blvd instead.

NAPA/SHUTTERSTOCK ©

Waterfront, Fort Lauderdale

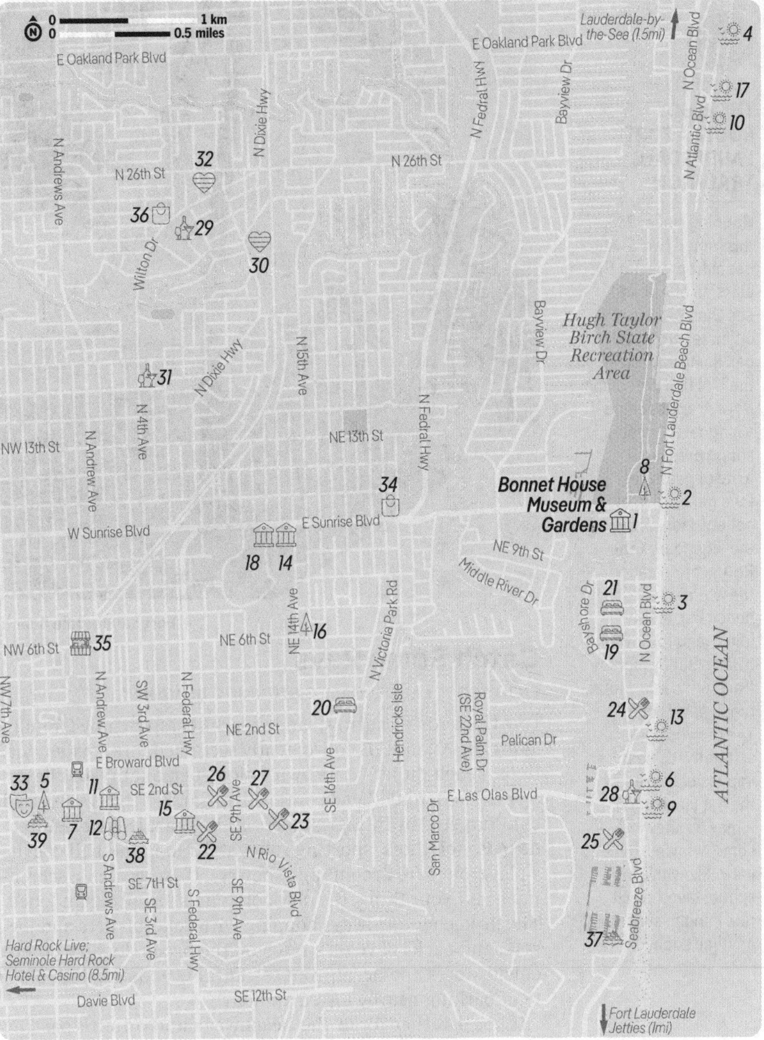

HIGHLIGHTS
1 Bonnet House

SIGHTS
2 Canine Beach
3 Central Beach
4 Earl Lifshey Ocean Park Beach
5 Esplanade Park
6 Fort Lauderdale Beach & Promenade
7 History Fort Lauderdale
8 Hugh Taylor Birch State Park
9 Las Olas Beach
10 Loggerhead Park Beach
11 NSU Art Museum
12 Riverwalk
13 Sebastian Street Beach
14 Stonewall National Museum & Archives
15 Stranahan House
16 Victoria Park
17 Vista Park Beach
18 World AIDS Museum

SLEEPING
19 Grand Resort & Spa
20 Pineapple Point
21 Royal Palms

EATING
22 Boathouse at the Riverside
23 Casa Sensei
24 Casablanca Cafe
25 Coconuts
26 El Camino
27 YaMas! Tavern

DRINKING & NIGHTLIFE
28 Elbo Room
29 Georgie's Alibi
30 Pride Center
31 Ramrod
32 The Manor

ENTERTAINMENT
33 Broward Center

SHOPPING
34 Out of the Closet
35 Sistrunk Marketplace & Brewery
36 To the Moon

TRANSPORT
37 Jungle Queen Riverboat
38 Riverwalk Water Trolley
39 Water Taxi Stop

THE ELBO ROOM: A FORT LAUDERDALE TRADITION

Hopping since 1938, this famed two-level beachfront bar (at the junction of A1A and Las Olas Blvd) is the ultimate throwback bar. Immortalized in the 1961 film *Where the Boys Are*, it became a magnet for annual spring breakers, a rite of passage for a generation of college kids. Today, the legendary **Elbo Room**, often called the world's best beach bar, feels lonely and forgotten by day. But by night it transforms into a loud, brash party zone. The crowds pack so tightly it's near impossible to reach the bar (cash only). It may be showing some wrinkles, but it's unlikely this old-school favorite will ride into the sunset anytime soon.

SEAN PAVONE/SHUTTERSTOCK ©

Fort Lauderdale Beach

Catch Some Rays

ENJOY FORT LAUDERDALE'S STUNNING BEACHES

Fort Lauderdale's narrow, sandy beachline, stretching for miles along the Atlantic, is conveniently sectioned into smaller portions – each radiating its own unique personality and flavor.

Fort Lauderdale Beach is the city's largest. It's swank and chic, targeted by Instagrammers. At its heart is **Fort Lauderdale Beach Park**, sporting volleyball and basketball courts, a playground, restrooms and showers. If exercising in scorching heat's your thing, the outdoor gym is usually abandoned. The promenade's always hopping with rollerbladers and joggers, and packs of yogis stretch on the beach. Luxury hotels, chichi stores and oceanfront restaurants abound, with plenty of parking nearby for $6 an hour.

If you'd rather forgo the beachwear and admire passing cruise ships, freightliners and fishing boats instead, head a bit south to the **Fort Lauderdale Jetties**. This hidden stretch (look for fishers on the rocky shoreline) is next to Port Everglades cruise docks. Best to park at Fort Lauderdale Beach and walk down; metered parking is limited.

CHEAP EATS ALONG LAS OLAS BLVD

Luigi's Pizza
Delicious coal-oven pizzas, half-priced wine, cheap beer, $4 food plates during happy hour (3pm to 6pm). **$**

Coyo Taco
It's 50% off on Taco Tuesdays! Try the incredible smoky cauliflower tacos. **$**

Wild Sea
Overnight oats (with fresh berries) for breakfast ($4), $10 lunch specials and $5 happy hour drinks. **$**

Las Olas Beach is a small enclave at the terminus of busy Las Olas Blvd. With easy access to bars, tacky souvenir shops and burger shops, it's usually hectic – and noisier than other spots along the stretch. Look for the **Elbo Room** across the road, a salty, 85-year-old bar made famous in 1960's *Where the Boys Are.* It's standing room only on weekends, when live bands rock the tiny stage.

Sebastian Street Beach is popular with the LGBTIQ+ crowd – although everyone's welcomed here. Kick back and relax with a good book – but bring an umbrella or a hat since there's not much shade. Oddly, there are showers but no bathrooms. Parking can be tough – try the garage on Cortez St. If you get thirsty, cross the street to **Casablanca Cafe**, to enjoy happy-hour boozing (weekdays 4pm to 7pm) on its breezy patio.

Ready to party? Then head to **Central Beach**. This section attracts guests from surrounding luxury hotels, all clamoring for lounges. Nearby pizza shops and beer counters encourage a somewhat rowdy energy at times.

The best-kept secret among beachgoers is **Hugh Taylor Birch State Park**. It's tucked between the ocean and intracoastal waters and, for the $6 entrance fee, you can park all day. A pedestrian tunnel leads under the A1A to the beach.

If you've got a dog, head for Canine Beach, located off A1A near Sunrise Blvd. It's the only place they're welcome.

Head north for secluded beach hideaways popular with locals. **Loggerhead Park Beach** offers privacy and great sunrise photo ops. Embrace serenity at **Vista Park Beach**, hidden among an oceanfront residential community. With a shallow reef close to shore, it's popular with divers and great for spotting sea turtles. **Earl Lifshey Ocean Park Beach**, at East Oakland Blvd, offers a hidden reprieve, with plenty of cheap parking.

Cruise the Waterfront

ENJOY THE INTRACOASTAL WATERWAY

The Atlantic might steal most of the attention, but Fort Lauderdale's got over 300 miles of *inland* waterways too, including the Intracoastal and New River.

Incredible views await along the Riverwalk, a footpath spanning both banks of New River. Park at the Riverside Hotel Garage off SE 4th St and indulge in some well-priced cocktails on the waterfront patio at **The Boathouse at the Riverside** restaurant before starting out. Enjoy the snazzy sailboats and million-dollar yachts drifting by.

Along the path are historical homes, luxurious condos and art sculptures. Take a couple of hours to enjoy the circular

CELEBRATE ON A GONDOLA OR FLOATING TIKI BAR

Birthday? Anniversary? Popping the big question and can't afford tickets to Italy? In the 'Venice of America,' options abound.

Las Olas Gondola, the only authentic Venetian gondola in Florida, offers 75-minute romantic rides, accompanied by soft music and cocktails (BYOB), through Fort Lauderdale's scenic canals and waterways. Starting at $100.

Or jump aboard a modernized electric gondola at **Riverfront Gondola Tours** (90-minute tours, $229, up to six people). Partnering with their neighbor, **Casa Sensei**, dinner cruise options are available.

Love tiki bars? Love cruising? Combine both with a **Cruisin' Tikis** tour while floating past the homes of Florida's rich and famous. No bathrooms, so drink accordingly ($325, up to six people, BYOB to serve onboard).

Boathouse at The Riverside
Tucked behind the Riverside Hotel, this waterfront delight offers fresh seafood at great prices. **$$**

Argentino Las Olas
Sangria for $3, mix-and-match empanadas (15 options: three for $12). Try spinach, cheese and ricotta. **$**

Ann's Florist & Coffee Bar
Buy flowers with lunch. Unique, floral-inspired drinks at the back bar. Delish snack items too. **$$**

route, but if you succumb to the heat just hop aboard the **Riverwalk Water Trolley**. It makes eight stops – and it's free! Bicycle and segway rentals are also available, but narrow paths and sharp turns present a challenge when it's crowded.

If you're feeling lazy, **Jungle Queen Riverboat** offers 90-minute, fully narrated cruises for $29.95, showcasing homes of the rich and famous ('Millionaire's Row'). Or, if you'd rather something more intimate, Captain Danny at **Floridian Coastal Charters** will take you (and three of your friends) on his Mako 221 for a private, two-hour, fully personalized Waterway Discovery Tour for $350.

The **Water Taxi** provides lighthearted, narrated cruises for $35 per day ($20 after 5pm), with 10 stops around town. Hop on and off randomly between 10am and 10pm daily.

I LIVE HERE: GREAT LOCAL HANGOUTS

Captain Danny Grant, owner of Floridian Coastal Charters, shares his favorite local spots to eat and drink.

Boardroom Bar
An awesome saloon in the north entertainment district, serving strong drinks in a surf-skate-hot-rod-inspired setting. Free vintage car shows every Saturday night.

Bohemian Latin Grill
A friendly couple serves up the tastiest Latin food in town. They'll even deliver to your bar stool next door (at the Boardroom Bar).

Southport Raw Bar
Locals love grabbing fresh oysters and a pitcher at this casual waterfront restaurant. Tasty seafood.

Café Seville
Every menu item's a winner – featuring Spanish cuisine. Start with *gambas ajillo* and *ensalada maite,* followed by a meat dish. Great wine list. Reservations recommended.

Embrace Local History

MUSEUMS AND GARDENS

To learn about Fort Lauderdale's progression from wartime fort to booming metropolis, head to **History Fort Lauderdale**, downtown by the Riverwalk. Here, surrounded by vast modern structures, are three buildings seemingly lost in time: the **New River Inn** (1905) houses the History Museum, next to the 1907 Pioneer House and 1899 Schoolhouse Museum. Artifacts and displays also celebrate contributions and influences of Native Americans and African Americans. Allow one to two hours for the highly entertaining tour.

A short walk away is **Stranahan House**, Fort Lauderdale's oldest surviving structure. Built as a trading post in 1901, Frank Stranahan (heralded as the city's founder) converted it to a residence for his family five years later. It has also been a post office and a city hall. (Stranahan later committed suicide by throwing himself into the adjacent New River, following the Wall Street Crash of 1929.)

Bonnet House Museum & Gardens is a whimsical, plantation-style oceanfront homestead on 35 acres of subtropical gardens, featuring one of America's most esteemed orchid collections. Buildings were designed by professional artist, and self-taught architect, Frederic Bartlett, in the early 1920s. Frederic's second wife, Evelyn, deeded the property to an historical trust prior to her death in 1997 to secure it against greedy developers. Thanks to her, you can enjoy **nature trails** that wind through five distinct ecosystems on the area's last bastion of undeveloped shore land. (Watch for spider monkeys in the treetop canopies.)

GREAT PLACES TO STAY IN FORT LAUDERDALE

Kimpton Shorebreak
Comfortable, spacious rooms, scenic rooftop bar and pool, cozy dining, and close to the beach. **$$$**

Riverside Hotel
Historical splendor paired with modern amenities. Conveniently located on Las Olas, right by the Riverwalk. **$$$**

La Quinta Inn by Wyndham Fort Lauderdale NE
Basic tidy rooms, swimming pool, free breakfast. Near the beach. Free airport shuttle. **$$**

TASFOTONL/SHUTTERSTOCK ©

Bonnet House Museum & Gardens

White Linens to Greasy Grills

FOODIE DELIGHTS ABOUND

Fort Lauderdale offers tons of tasty dining options to tease and tantalize. **Ya Mas! Taverna** is a charming Mykonos-style Mediterranean restaurant. Plop onto its plush outdoor seats and people-watch along Las Olas as you feast on a succulent lamb burger (its secret sauce is delicious).

Commemorating the classic automobile that was manufactured in Mexico, **El Camino** assembles *bueno* Mexican dishes inside its three-car-garage dining area. Its Brisket Nachos feed a tableful of hungry car buffs, while plenty of beer, wine, spirits and cocktails – including incredible margaritas and tasty coffee tequila drinks – also race off its production line.

At **Casa Sensei**, steak lovers drool while preparing their Interactive Wagyu Experience. Under strict supervision, diners at this Pan-Asian fusion hot spot can prepare a Wagyu steak (a Japanese delicacy) on their own table grill. Add a whiskey pairing, a slice of the creamy cheesecake, and a snap of the signature cotton candy...and book a room on cloud nine.

GO A BIT 'LOOP-Y'

Las Olas Oceanside Park (affectionately called 'the LOOP'), at the corner of A1A and Las Olas Blvd, is ground zero for family fun in Fort Lauderdale. After undergoing a major revitalization in 2019, the LOOP now welcomes visitors to special events, daily fitness classes, a splash pad and live music concerts.

Shop till you drop at the Saturday farmers and artisans' market (9am to 4pm), where you can score fresh fruit and veggies, smoothies, cheese, pastries, handcrafted clothes, gifts and jewelry.

Enjoy live music at **Friday Night Sound Waves** (March to July, 6:30pm to 9:30pm) or grab some popcorn to watch **Movies by Moonlight**.

Visit theloopflb.com for a full schedule of upcoming events.

GREAT BREAKFAST NOOKS IN FORT LAUDERDALE

Peter Pan Diner
Soda/shake counter, tiled floors, great prices and friendly staff. A throwback to simpler times. $

Egg & You Diner
Serving up home-cooked goodness since 1956 in generous proportions – with retro prices too. $

Lester's Diner
Vintage street sign, milelong counter, Texas-size cups, and sassy smiles. Corned beef omelets are superb. $

DRINKING WITH MERMAIDS

Fort Lauderdale's the only place in the US to catch a mermaid burlesque show, while enjoying espresso martinis and fresh-from-the-ocean seafood. The historic **Wreck Bar**, at **B Ocean Resort**, opened in the 1950s, when Frank Sinatra strutted its hallways. The bar's nautical theme, with chiseled wood bar and briny decor, suggests you're in a 1600s Spanish galleon.

But it's the aquarium portholes behind the bar that reveal some extraordinary sights. There, on Friday and Saturday nights, sexy mermaids and mermen appear, putting on a teasingly good show for 21+ barflies. Check the schedule for unique 'Aquamen Boylesque' shows, and some family-friendly performances too.

Broward Center for the Performing Arts

The world awaits at **Sistrunk Marketplace & Brewery**, the ultimate food and drink hall. Bench-style seats, high wooden tables, and live music add to its warm, rustic ambience. Choose from a dozen vendors, with culinary options ranging from tacos to pizza and crepes to sushi. Try the Shady Vodka and 12-Mile Rum, both distilled on-site. Ready for a new addiction? Ask the bartender for a specially concocted Coconut Coffee Rumtini. Don't say you weren't warned!

For a picture-perfect sunset, head over to **Coconuts**, overlooking the Intracoastal Waterway. Devour some Scoobies (crab bites marinated in a scrumptious olive oil and garlic butter sauce, with dipping bread), while watching passing yachts from the outdoor patio as the sky is set ablaze.

Art, Theater & Music

DISCOVER GALLERIES AND PERFORMING ART

Feed your eyes and stimulate your brain, with 7500 permanent artworks and wonderful rotating exhibits at the **NSU Art Museum**. It's Florida's largest collection of ethnographic

DON'T-MISS EVENTS IN FORT LAUDERDALE

Visit Lauderdale Food & Wine Festival
Week-long January event focusing on celebrated and upcoming chefs and local establishments.

Fourth of July Spectacular
Free event celebrates Independence Day with live music, family activities, beach games – and fireworks.

Fort Lauderdale International Boat Show
Massive October event showcasing new super yachts; plenty of family-friendly activities.

art, showcasing Indigenous American, West African, Cuban, pre-Columbian and Oceanic pieces. (Closed Mondays.)

No matter what type of art appeals, you won't want to miss the **Las Olas Annual Art Fair**, held each October along the famed boulevard. Ranked as one of the nation's top 100 art festivals, the fair features 200 artists gleefully chatting about their unique creations: paintings, photographs, sculptures, and blown and stained glass.

If it's theater that excites you, catch a Broadway play at the **Broward Center for the Performing Arts**, at the end of the city's Riverwalk. This popular venue also hosts ballets, operas and top-tier musical performances. Seats are plentiful but prepare to sniff your knees if you're over 5'7" in height. The parking garage is just as crammed; you'll need to summon all your patience when leaving.

Hard Rock Live at the Seminole Hard Rock Hotel & Casino in nearby Hollywood (you can't miss it, it's the fire-in-the-sky, guitar-shaped building you'll see from the plane as you're landing) is the place for headbanging concertgoers. Owned by the Seminole Tribe of Florida (one of the state's Indigenous peoples), it features A-list musicians, comedians...and those other headbangers, Mixed Martial Arts (MMA) fighters.

Get your groove on with local jazz greats during the **Sunday Jazz Brunch**, jamming the first Sunday of every month between 11am and 2pm at **Esplanade Park**.

Florida's LGBTIQ+ Capital

FORT LAUDERDALE'S THRIVING LGBTIQ+ COMMUNITY

Considered Florida's LGBTIQ+ capital, Fort Lauderdale has blossomed into one of the world's premier LGBTIQ+ holiday destinations. LGBTIQ+ retirees and remote workers flock to **Wilton Manors** (and its neighbor, **Victoria Park**), cementing its status as *the* hub for LGBTIQ+ nightclubs, bars, restaurants and social clubs. A flamboyant, rainbow-painted 'Love Wins' bridge welcomes visitors to Wilton Manors, where streetlamps shine with artistic wire sculptures. Its local community center, the **Pride Center**, distributes information on the area's highlights.

Wilton Drive ('The Drive') is abundant with restaurants, shops and watering holes. There's **Georgie's Alibi**, an LGBTIQ+ nightclub that's perpetually packed, and the **Manor**, a glamorous club featuring flashy chandeliers and more bars than you can shake a stick at. Its younger crowds often spill onto its second level. If leather's your thing, you'll enjoy the raunchy cowboy vibe at **Ramrod**, a popular hangout since 1994. Here, patrons rock to edgy tunes in a medieval dungeon-style setting.

LIPS: IT'S SUCH A DRAG

Brace yourself for high-energy drag dining at the glittery **Lips** club in Oakland Park, where nothing is as it seems. Catch its famous Sunday brunch with bottomless mimosas or keep an eye on the rotating weekly lineups: Diva Nights, Bitchy Bingo, Tilted Tuesdays or the, definitely-not-for-the-fainthearted, Taboo Show (Saturdays at midnight). Lips is especially popular with the younger bachelorette crowd, and you'll be smothered with lots of, er, attention, by 14 acrobatic performers if it happens to be your birthday or anniversary. Reserve early (they're not bluffing, baby).

GREAT EATING SPOTS IN WILTON MANORS

Voo la Voo Cafe
Tasty French omelets (try the pulled pork) and authentic savory crepes, in a garden setting. **$$**

Bubbles & Pearls
Romantic spot run by Bravo's *Top Chef* contestant, Josie Smith-Malave. Fresh oysters, juicy cauliflower steak. **$$**

Rosie's Bar & Grill
Stop in for some sassy service and award-winning burgers. **$$**

THE LEGEND OF PORKY'S HIDEAWAY

Fans of the *Porky's* cult classic movie series of the 1980s might be shocked to learn it wasn't all fiction. There really was a Porky's.

In the 1950s, Donald 'Porky' Baines founded a popular supper club, **Porky's Hideaway**, at 3900 N Federal Hwy in Oakland Park, attracting headliners Lawrence Welk, Flip Wilson and Guy Lombardo. In stark contrast, he operated a seedier den right next door: the **Birdcage**, where he'd reportedly sell $1.50 bottomless beers to college kids – and kept a pet lioness caged behind the bar. Porky's shuttered when Baines was arrested for tax evasion in 1968. His death in 1972 was ruled an apparent suicide.

MIKE KUHLMAN/SHUTTERSTOCK ©

Pride Fest, Wilton Manors

Eager to shop? **Out of the Closet**, a neighborhood thrift shop selling size 12 stilettos, offers free HIV testing while you browse. You'll find everything nostalgia at **To the Moon** – including candy from 1806!

The **Stonewall National Museum & Archives**, in Victoria Park, preserves an outstanding collection of LGBTIQ+ books and archival materials. With almost 30,000 books, it's one of the country's largest LGBTIQ+ libraries. Head next door to the **World AIDS Museum** for a journey that's heartbreaking and somber, yet inspiring and empowering.

LGBTIQ+ resorts abound in Fort Lauderdale, including **The Grand Resort & Spa**, Pineapple Point and **Royal Palms** (check gayftlauderdale.com). The city also hosts the popular **OUTshine LGBTIQ+ Film Festival** each October.

For up-to-date community listings, grab the latest copy of **South Florida Gay News** or visit sfgn.com.

GETTING AROUND

Avoid excessive parking fees and beach traffic by using public transit. Dodge the carts charging $20. Instead, use LauderGO! Community Shuttle buses. It runs five daytime transit routes, with stops by the beach, Las Olas and the downtown corridor.

Download the LauderGO! app to access maps and schedules. Micro Mover, a free electric rideshare program, supplements the shuttles (use Micro Mover by Circuit app). Rideshares are another great way to get around town.

Beyond Fort Lauderdale

- Pompano Beach
- Lauderdale-by-the-Sea
- **Fort Lauderdale**
- Dania Beach
- Hollywood

There's plenty of breathtaking scenery, fun activities and outdoor adventures awaiting visitors within a leisurely hour's drive from Fort Lauderdale.

South of Fort Lauderdale, toward Florida's grand metropolis of Miami, are the busy and energetic seaside communities of Dania Beach and Hollywood. Dazzling visitors since the 1920s, Hollywood's a classic Florida beach town that remains crazy popular with modern-day bohemians. These vibrant locales also offer an endless array of captivating activities and events.

Travel a bit north from Fort Lauderdale and, while there's still plenty to do, it's a much slower pace. It's generally an older demographic, who don't mind trading the party scene for laid-back serenity. Stringent building bylaws prohibit most hotels and condos from towering above the palms, ensuring a more neighborly atmosphere within these communities.

TOP TIP

While the ocean naturally steals the attention, be sure to enjoy the Intracoastal Waterway's beauty and charm as well.

Dania Beach (p182)

THE BEST PLACE TO STAY IN HOLLYWOOD... BAR NONE!

Rising triumphantly from the sands of Hollywood Beach, the 17-story **Margaritaville Beach Resort** embodies the area's tropical spirit and beach-village escapism like no other. All rooms, featuring mellow, tropical decor, overlook either the ocean or the Intracoastal – or both. But, more than just a cool place to stay, the Margaritaville is an entire experience, an entertainment community unto itself.

Jimmy Buffett, the brand's original co-owner, took a break from nibbling on sponge cake to launch the beachfront complex in 2015, entertaining Parrotheads at its Bandshell. Live music rocks the stage there every night, with crowds swaying in Hollywood's warm, salty ocean breezes. Grab a margarita from the **Lone Palm** tiki bar and join the party.

ANDRIY BLOKHIN/SHUTTERSTOCK ©

The Broadwalk

Walk or Bike the Broadwalk

WHITE SANDS, WIDE PROMENADE

Located just 11 miles south of Fort Lauderdale, no trip to Hollywood is complete without strolling its famous 2.5-mile, brick-paved thoroughfare, **The Broadwalk**. Just hop in your car (or grab a rideshare) and you'll be there in 15 to 20 minutes. As the star attraction of this classic Florida beach town, it's a magnet for joggers, bicyclists, rollerbladers, people-watchers and street performers. Mom-and-pop motels snuggle beside ginormous resorts, as tacky souvenir stores, taco stands and beach bars compete for your wallet. It's a vibrant, tacos-and-piña-coladas scene, paralleling the sparkling white beach and crystal-blue waters of the Atlantic, with coral reefs begging to be explored. Rent a bike, scooter or pedal buggy, learn to surf, or hire a beach chair and umbrella from **Margaritaville** and just flop! (Plenty of parking's available curbside, in surface lots and multilevel garages – including Margaritaville's.)

Just beyond the north end of the Broadwalk is **Keating Beach**, a quiet refuge from all the hustle and bustle further back. It's a great place to tie up a hammock, enjoy a little romance, or both. Just watch out for the jellyfish often spotted in its shallow waters.

WHERE TO EAT ALONG HOLLYWOOD'S BROADWALK

Taco Joint
Great beach vibe. Super lobster tacos and roasted corn. Strawberry daiquiris are killer too. **$**

Nick's Bar & Grill
Popular pub-style beach hangout. Order the blackened mahimahi sandwich with key lime pie and smile. **$$**

Grumpy Gary's Bar & Grill
Beach dining under palapas. Burgers, lobster mac and cheese, Italian beef eggrolls and key lime pie. **$$**

If you want an all-over tan, head south to **Haulover Beach**, where you can legally strip down to nothing in spots (look for lifeguard marker 14).

Explore Downtown Delights

ARTS, CRAFTS…AND CARS

Smack in the middle of a NASCAR-style roundabout (at US1 and Hollywood Blvd) is **ArtsPark at Young Circle**, an urban park seamlessly blending visual and performing arts with expansive greenery.

Wide pathways lead to an outdoor amphitheater, its 2500 lawn seats awaiting youths or retirees, depending upon the headliner. There's a covered playground, a splash pad, an art gallery and a visual arts pavilion. Catch a glassblowing demonstration by **Hollywood Hot Glass**…or join classes (if you've got 10 weeks to spare!). If there isn't a free bench, seek shade underneath one of five African baobab trees that host much of the park's wildlife. The park also shows free Friday night outdoor movies for the kiddies.

The **Downtown Hollywood ArtWalk** runs every third Saturday 6pm to 11pm, highlighting the best of the district's art, music, murals and markets as you visit local galleries, cafes and quaint shops. Bring comfortable walking shoes. If you miss it, consider a self-guided tour of the core 30+ murals; street maps guide your path.

Gearheads and muscle-car enthusiasts flock to the 1900 block of Hollywood Blvd the first Sunday of every month for the **Dream Car Classic**, held from 10am to 2pm. Dozens of hot rods, custom vehicles and classic cars compete to steal your attention.

Paddle Nature-Packed Mangroves

WADING BIRDS, CRABS AND ALLIGATORS

Saved from development by environmentalists in the 1970s, **West Lake Park** – just 16 miles and a short 15-minute drive from Fort Lauderdale, preserves over 1500 acres of the coast's original mangrove wetlands.

Rent a canoe or kayak ($15 per hour) from the marina and follow map trails, passing through marsh and lake. Keep an eye out for ospreys, crabs and shrimp (during low tide, listen for loud clicking and popping noises…that's the shrimp).

The **Anne Kolb Nature Center**, next door, offers boardwalk and nature trails (many are stroller and wheelchair accessible). A stretch of Intracoastal Waterway provides a great chance to spot manatees and dolphins. Cast a line

LEARN TO SURF

Ever yearned to grab a board, don a wetsuit and surf humongous waves, but lacked the courage? Well, now you can turn that fear into fun at Margaritaville Beach Resort's **FlowRider** wave machine, on Hollywood's famous Broadwalk. Novices are put at ease catching waves in the controlled and supervised environment. It's safe and fun – even for young kids. The passion of their expert, and patient, instructors transfers by osmosis. But be warned – it's not as easy as they make it look, and wipeouts are common…but hysterical! Open to the public, various packages cost about $1 per minute, with special promotions for hotel guests.

WHERE TO EAT AT DANIA BEACH

Grampa's Cafe
Opened in 1957. Grampa's hand-rolled water bagels and Carnegie corned beef sandwiches are legendary. **$$**

Tarks of Dania Beach
Unassuming local hangout, serving freshly shucked oysters, steamed crabs and signature curly fries since 1966. **$**

Oceans at Dania Beach
Delightful corner sandwich shop. Try the Dania Beach Reuben with a side of tropical slaw. **$$**

JAI ALAI RETURNS TO DANIA

Following a brief hiatus, during which the death of jai alai was widely predicted, players and fans are heralding the return of the world's fastest-moving ball sport to **The Casino @ Dania Beach**.

Originating in the Basque region of Spain, jai alai first came to Florida in 1924. Dania's fronton (court) opened in 1953, the second in the US.

During its 1970s and '80s heyday, thousands of fans packed arenas, but those numbers dwindled when professional hockey, baseball and basketball came to Florida soon afterwards.

Its current 500-seat capacity may be a far cry from yesteryear's 5600, but spectators now watch the harder-than-golf-ball pelotas whip around (up to 190mph) from less than five rows deep.

from the dock on the **Fishing Pier Trail**, or just watch the boats sailing by.

Tread quietly along their trails to encounter raccoons or iguanas. Bring hats or an umbrella for shade, though, and don't forget water, snacks...and bug repellent.

Before you leave, check out the panoramic view from the 68ft **lookout tower**, behind the Nature Center. Take an elevator or use the stairs.

Parking's plentiful, and it never costs more than $2. (Some naughty visitors park their cars here – and then walk or bike to Hollywood's nearby beaches.)

Take a Gamble

SLOTS AND CLASSIC TUNES

Drive 6 miles south of Fort Lauderdale and in less than 12 minutes you can be pulling slot handles at **The Casino @ Dania Beach**. What this small casino lacks in Vegas-style grandeur it delivers in charm and convenience. Following a $64 million renovation in 2016, this smoke-free venue's got over 750 slot machines and 20 poker tables. Although the famous buffets haven't returned post-COVID-19, **Luxe Restaurant** serves up hearty meals at reasonable prices. On weekends, catch free live music at **Sunrise Bar Stage**. But the best tunes are reserved for **Stage 954**, where big names and mind-blowing cover bands regularly rock the house (tickets are $30). If your timing's good, wager on a lightning-fast round of jai alai.

Canoe or Kayak Along Knee-Deep Channels

A SMUGGLER'S PARKLAND PARADISE

Paying tribute to two segregation-era civil rights activists, **Dr Von D. Mizell-Eula Johnson State Park** encompasses the former site of a 'colored beach,' just 7 miles south of Fort Lauderdale – a short 15-minute drive by car or rideshare. Previously, it had been a hideaway for Prohibition-era rumrunners. Antique bottles of whiskey and rum are occasionally still found tied to deep mangrove roots.

Today, the park is popular with locals, who'd prefer to keep its quiet beach a secret. There are trails to explore by foot or bike, and the **Whiskey Creek Hideout** provides kayak and canoe rentals ($20 per hour). A snack bar serves light meals, ice cream and alcohol. The water's only knee-deep in the channels during low tide – perfect for kayaking (that's why bootleggers loved it – larger enforcement vessels couldn't

GREAT EATS IN POMPANO BEACH

Brendan's Sports Pub
Some call it a dive bar. Others love the pool, darts, sublime cheesesteak and wings. $

Briny Irish Pub
Upscale pub serving superb fish and chips since 1945. Wash it down with a Guinness. $$

Rusty Hook Tavern
Romantic Intracoastal views; grilled snapper, lava cake and mango margaritas equal... divine dining delirium. $$

FENG CHENG/SHUTTERSTOCK ©

Dr Von D. Mizell-Eula Johnson State Park

navigate through). Crafty visitors avoid the park's $6 gate fee by beaching their boats instead.

Quiet Beach, Charming Town

RELAXING BEACH AND VILLAGE STROLL

Just a 15-minute drive north of Fort Lauderdale, coastal **Lauderdale-by-the-Sea** exudes small beach-town charm. It feels as though you've left a rowdy party to mellow on a quiet pier. The slower pace attracts those seeking peace; it's perfect for strolls, watching pelicans dive for mullets along the beach. Sadly, Anglin's Pier, popular with fishers, was permanently damaged by Hurricane Nicole in November 2022 and subsequently condemned. But the waters remain busy, with snorkelers plying the three-tiered coral reef just 100yd away (it's the offshore diving capital of the world, after all). There's also a busy farmers market on Saturdays, with ample free parking.

Take time to browse the hamlet's quaint and unusual stops – such as **Diamonds & Doggies**, selling souvenirs and…small dogs. Grab a 'Superman' ice-cream cone from **Kilwins**, then

A SPEAKEASY FOR POLITICIANS, CELEBRITIES & MOBSTERS

A throwback to the days of Prohibition, Captain Eugene 'Cap' Knight's 1928 speakeasy and gambling den, **Cap's Place**, still dispenses spirits from its original wood-framed buildings. The smell of yesteryear permeates this rustic restaurant, exuding the atmosphere of an old, decrepit fishing lodge. But that hasn't dissuaded a who's-who list of celebrities from visiting.

Among the mile-long roster are Johnny Carson, Walt Disney, Joe DiMaggio, Al Capone, Bugsy Siegel, Forrest Tucker, George Harrison and Colonel Sanders. Winston Churchill even dined here with President Roosevelt while discussing WWII strategy. Located on a peninsula at Lighthouse Point, the restaurant is accessed via ferry shuttle. The crab cakes are legendary.

Lucky Fish
Casual tiki restaurant affording great views of the beach and pier. Outstanding conch fritters. **$$**

Oceanic
Upscale oceanfront restaurant; try the Cashew Crunch Salmon and conch chowder. **$$$**

Beach House
Comfy terrace with postcard-perfect ocean views. Tasty grilled-fish sandwiches; and the bread pudding slays. **$$**

BEST BARS IN HOLLYWOOD

Sunset Club
Rooftop bar at Costa Hotel with spectacular views of the Intracoastal Waterway. Happy hour is from 6pm to 8pm.

LandShark Bar & Grill
Lively beachside bar with fish tacos, fried shrimp, and margaritas. Captivating views of the beach.

5 o'Clock Somewhere Bar & Grill
Chill dockside bar (on the Intracoastal) perfect for kicking back and enjoying some beer and wings.

CONNOR STRZELEWICZ/SHUTTERSTOCK ©

Butterfly World

feast at **Harat's by the Sea**. This former corner T-shirt shop, a minute's walk from the beach, has an amazing happy hour with 21 beers on tap. Don't miss its lobster mac and cheese.

Butterflies, Blimps & Horses

A WHIRLWIND TOUR OF POMPANO

Just a 15-minute drive from Fort Lauderdale, **Butterfly World** in Coconut Creek is the world's largest butterfly and bird park, swarming with hundreds of birds and 20,000 butterflies. Kids, and the young-at-heart, love exploring the misty cave and suspension bridge, and squirming at the live bug zoo. Macaws tickle your palm as they eat straight from your hand.

There's a horse stables right next door in **Tradewinds Park** (north side) with group and private trail rides on gentle and well-behaved horses. There's also a petting farm and pony rides for the young ones.

The ground base for the **Goodyear Blimp** is over at the **Pompano Beach Airpark**. See it in person from November to March (it spends the 'winter' here). It's free, open to the public and, if you time it just right, you might even catch it in flight.

GETTING AROUND

These destinations are just a short drive or rideshare from Fort Lauderdale. Broward County Transit also provides regular bus services to all these areas, costing $2 to $3, with commutes ranging from 15 to 40 minutes. Consider hopping aboard Fort Lauderdale's Water Taxi for a scenic cruise on its 'Hollywood Express.' It's one of 11 stops included with its $35 daily pass.

WEST PALM BEACH

Once home of the indigenous Jaega, this area of Florida was deemed 'a veritable paradise' by railroad tycoon Henry Morrison Flagler when he first visited in 1893. His plans envisioned the sparsely populated Palm Beach barrier island transformed into a luxury resort with hotels and opulent homes. To house his extensive workforce, he'd build a 'worker city' across the lagoon.

A year later, that blue-collar 'worker city' was incorporated as West Palm Beach. It quickly exploded into a booming frontier town, with industrious shops and saloons lining its rustic streets.

Nowadays, West Palm Beach is home to palm-lined boulevards commanding spectacular views of the Intracoastal waters. It's the county seat, welcoming visitors to its world-class shopping, dining and entertainment districts. Despite this, however, West Palm Beach still aspires to the grandeur and opulence of its wealthier neighbor, Palm Beach, right across the bridge.

TOP TIP

While there's plenty of big box stores, malls and outlet stores around the city, consider the smaller retail shops along Clematis St instead. Here you'll find lots of unique offerings in quaint, historic buildings. Hitting the buzzing flea market at GreenMarket on Saturday mornings is always an adventure too.

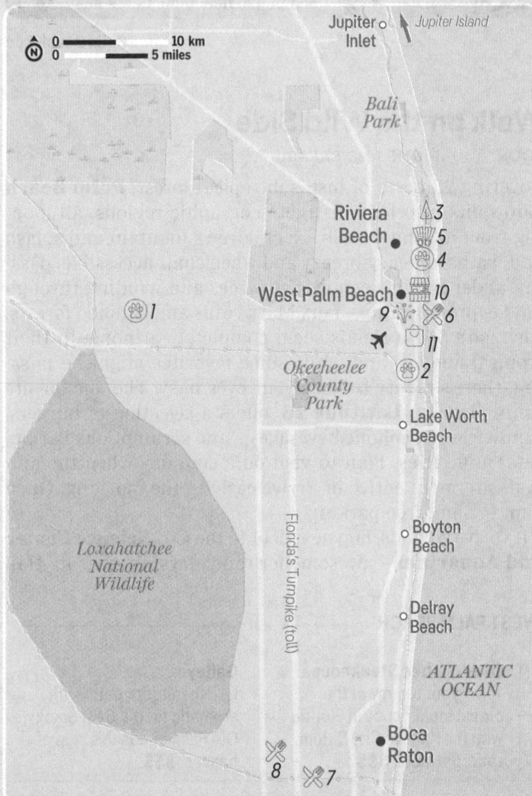

SIGHTS
1 Lion Country Safari
2 Palm Beach Zoo
3 Phil Foster Park

ACTIVITIES, COURSES & TOURS
see 2 Cox Science Center & Aquarium
4 Manatee Lagoon
5 Peanut Island

EATING
6 ER Bradley's
7 Sloan's Ice Cream
8 Sushi Yama Asian Bistro

ENTERTAINMENT
9 Clematis Street

SHOPPING
10 Greenmarket
11 The Square

GREAT PLACES TO STAY IN WEST PALM BEACH

Hilton West Palm Beach
Conveniently located across from the Square, 2 miles from the beach, this luxury property exudes style and grace. Its modern suites, resort-style pool, superb restaurants, full-service spa and complimentary valet parking ensure guests remain pampered. Free morning yoga classes ($10 for nonguests), complimentary bikes, and open-air, electric Moke carts available. $$$

The Ben
This luxury boutique hotel is part of the Marriott Autograph Collection. A block from Clematis St, many balconies overlook Palm Harbor Marina, with a panoramic view of the Intracoastal Waterway. Amenities include a saltwater pool with poolside cocktail service, elegant rooftop lounge, beach shuttle (with complimentary beach chairs and supplies), and a complimentary, to-your-door, book butler service. $$$

ALLMYROOTS/SHUTTERSTOCK ©

Palm Beach Zoo

Walk on the Wild Side

ZOOS, AQUARIUMS AND SAFARIS

Covering 23 acres of lush subtropical forest, **Palm Beach Zoo** splits into four distinct geographic regions, all looping from its central hub – a children's fountain and splash pad. Paths are easy-breezy and wheelchair accessible, passing under shady weeping ficus trees and winding through bald cypress swamps, faux Maya ruins and bamboo forests. The zoo's 550 animals seem completely at home in their tropical abodes, and while some favorites might be missing, there's plenty to keep your eyes busy. The one on-site dining option, **Latitude 26**, offers a selection of burgers, sandwiches, alcoholic beverages – and scrumptious Parmesan truffle fries. Plan to visit on a cool day when the animals are more active or arrive early in the morning. Open 9am to 5pm; free parking.

If you've got kids, hop next door to the **Cox Science Center and Aquarium** – awesome for rainy days. Wander its Hall

UPSCALE DINING IN WEST PALM BEACH

Spruzzo
WPB's only open-air rooftop bar and dining lounge. Try the Lamb Pappardelle. Fun, glamorous energy. **$$$**

Okeechobee Steakhouse
Tame your tummy at the oldest steakhouse in Florida with the Kansas City Sirloin. Unforgettable. **$$$**

Galley
Lavish outdoor patio with aromatic firepit. Best Smoky Old Fashioneds this side of... heaven. **$$$**

of Discovery, with over 100 hands-on exhibits covering the spectrum of science, space and technology. There's a 10,000-gallon saltwater aquarium, outdoor mini-golf, a splash pad, and cool planetarium shows.

Wanna go on safari? Grab your safari hat and head west to the self-guided **Lion Country Safari**. Over 900 exotic animals roam freely through open habitats. Enjoy amusement rides, a water park and camp at an on-site KOA campground.

Manatees & Mermaids

WARM SALTWATER FUN

After discovering the warm-water outflows from their Riviera Beach generating station attracted manatees during the winter, Florida Power & Light opened an eco-discovery center to honor these gentle giants. **Manatee Lagoon** provides educational exhibits and two levels of observation decks for visitors to view these docile sea cows (along with nurse sharks, sea turtles and other colorful marine life). Best viewing is November to March. Free admission and parking.

Manatees and mermaids are also found in the crystal-clear waters off pet-friendly **Phil Foster Park**, under the Blue Heron Bridge. These world-famous waters attract marine biologists and scuba divers for their unparalleled diversity of marine life. Octopuses, seahorses, starfish, rays, sea turtles, lobsters and boat wrecks are all encountered just a short swim from shore. The 2-acre **Snorkel Trail** leads novices along a 10ft-deep artificial reef, lined with limestone boulders and underwater shark sculptures. Families love the lifeguarded beach and fishing pier, as do the scores of boaters and kayakers who launch from here. Parking's free but remember to lock your car – theft is common here and many unsavory-looking characters loiter around.

Become Island Castaways

PEANUT ISLAND IN A NUTSHELL

Although it's artificially made, **Peanut Island** is still an endearing, if small-scale, tropical paradise. This 79-acre island was formed in 1918 from sand dredged completing the Lake Worth Inlet. Originally named Inlet Island, its name changed to reflect its intended purpose as a peanut-oil shipping operation; plans were later abandoned in the 1940s. As tensions with Castro's Cuban government escalated prior to the Cuban missile crisis, the US Navy built a nuclear bunker for President Kennedy here in December 1960. (It's still here, but under renovation until 2024.)

BECOME A MERMAID

Visit **Blue Heron Bridge** and you might question your own eyes. Are those real mermaids? Well, yes and no.

Kayleigh 'Keke' McBride, a PADI-certified mermaid instructor, offers a four-level course (plus instructor-level classes) in becoming a sea goddess. She and her partner, Farrell Tiller, run **Live Free Diving** (livefreediving.com), and the mermaid course grew organically from their popular scuba, snorkeling and free-diving programs. Available in many bright colors, realistic-looking tails are sculpted from silicon and covered with waterproof material with scale-like designs. Slink yourself into one and if you've dreamed about being Ariel since you were a young fry, here's your chance!

Proper Grit
Cozy, intimate. Try the Hanging Bacon appetizer. There's tasty wild salmon too, if you're still hungry. **$$$**

Blind Monk
A classy, romantically lit tapas and wine bar. Silent movies add to its retro-chic ambience. **$$**

Pistache French Bistro
Parisian-style bistro with linen-covered tables, decadent pastries and all-you-can-eat mussels on Mondays. **$$$**

I LIVE HERE: FAVORITE WEST PALM BEACH CAFES

Kaleigh McBride, diving and mermaid instructor at Live Free Diving, offers her picks for where to enjoy a post-dive cup of coffee.

Salento Coffee Shop On Clematis St, for killer coffee! It's run by a Colombian couple who use cloth filters instead of paper (ask them to explain the important difference). Order Pandebono buns to dip into your coffee – it's not as gross as it sounds.

Subculture Coffee It's decorated with splash art, painted skateboards and graphic tees. But bring earplugs, because they blast their tunes!

Pumphouse Coffee Roasters It's da bomb! Nestled in the Grandview Public Market, it's got a huge patio great for people-watching. Try their draft latte and everything croissant.

No bridges connect to the island, so visitors must arrive by boat, paddle or shuttle boats ($16 return, kids $8, pets free; departing regularly from Riviera Beach Marina).

With its shallow, crystal-clear waters, the island's a snorkeler's heaven. Even from the dock, visitors marvel at the exotic, real-life aquarium below. An easy-to-walk, ADA-accessible, 1.25-mile paved path loops around the island, passing mangroves, guarded swimming beaches (watch for jellyfish!), picnic areas and observation decks. Many boaters anchor their vessels offshore, crank some tunes and sunbathe in the Caribbean-style vibe of the secluded island (it's only 60 miles from the Bahamas, after all).

There's overnight camping and bathrooms, but no stores (and no alcohol allowed), so be sure to pack water and snacks. Last shuttle leaves the island at 5pm.

A Foodie's & Bargain-Hunter's Dream

SHOPPING AND DINING DELIGHTS

Once infamous for just its nightlife, West Palm Beach now features a smorgasbord of downtown shopping and dining options. Hit up **The Square**, a 72-acre shopping and entertainment district in the downtown core. Make all your purchases, then grab chairs and catch free classic rock and country concerts at the central fountain, Fridays and Saturdays from 6pm to 10pm. Lounging's encouraged around the fountain – a central meeting and gathering hub for shoppers, and loiterers, of all ages.

Stroll over to **Clematis Street**, a vibrant entertainment strip dripping with history (Flagler, the founder of West Palm Beach, was florally obsessed, naming downtown streets after plants and flowers). Trendy dining options have exploded, stealing attention from their flashy nightclub neighbors. **Clematis By Night**, a free live concert series, takes the stage here Thursday evenings from 6pm to 9pm.

Don't miss **Sushi Yama Asian Bistro** for yummy food at bargain prices: happy hour runs every day from 3:30pm to 6:30pm – with $4 appetizers, $6 sushi roll plates, and $4 wine and beer.

If Willy Wonka owned an ice-cream shop, it'd look like **Sloan's**. A child's technicolor dream brought to life, this colorful parlor uses all-natural ingredients, and only fresh, in-season fruits (such as coconut and mango). Don't miss it.

ER Bradley's is a classic beach restaurant that operated as an illegal gambling joint for over 50 years (it must pay to know the right people). Now family friendly (and legal) it serves legendary fish tacos, with mahimahi fresh from the ocean.

SWEET-TOOTH DESTINATIONS

Le Macaron French Pastries Delicious macarons, scrumptious red velvet cakes, and indulgent eclairs – feels like Paris in here. **$$**

Hive Bakery & Cafe A foodie's delight: coconut cream pie, key lime tarts, pumpkin cheesecake...need we say more? **$$**

Ganache Bakery Cakes and cupcakes that are out of this world. Also offers baking classes. **$**

The Square

Right behind the restaurant, a mammoth, 110-vendor farmers market, **GreenMarket**, takes over the streets on Saturday mornings (October to April). Sixty flea market vendors extend further up Clematis, hawking things you may never have seen or tasted before. Reserve a day to sample as much as you can. Like the crave-inducing GMO- and gluten-free pineapple jam from **Pascale's**, the apple cider mini doughnuts or a hundred other belt-busting sweets.

ADA ACCESSIBILITY

The Americans with Disabilities Act (ADA) outlines requirements for public businesses to provide full, unrestricted access to those with hearing, visual, mobility or cognitive impairment, detailing standards for accessible design (including ramps and other accommodations) necessary to remove barriers. See p420 for more on Accessible Travel.

BEST PLACES TO ENJOY CRAFT COCKTAILS

Proper Grit
Chic, speakeasy-style bar offers extended happy hours and live music. Recommended cocktail: Blueberry Old Fashioned.

Kapow Noodle Bar
Popular Asian fusion restaurant with anime-manga theme. Recommended cocktail: Blueberry Lavender Mojito.

Honor Bar (Palm Beach)
Snuggle in this cozy bar's dark wood ambience. Recommended cocktail: Churchill Martini.

Treehouse
Casual rooftop bar with mesmerizing views and equally impressive drinks. Recommended cocktail: Spicy Watermelon Margarita.

Spruzzo
Lively rooftop bar with a 360-degree panoramic view, ideal for sunsets. Recommended cocktail: Fumo Mule.

GETTING AROUND

Traffic can get busy, and parking expensive, so hop aboard either Downtown West Palm Beach Trolleys or Circuit West Palm Beach – both offer free rides around the city corridor.

Bikes and electric vehicles are often available for rent at local hotels. Rideshares are also popular options.

Beyond West Palm Beach

Coastal mansions, museums, beaches and trails are all within an easy half-hour drive of West Palm Beach.

Sparkling seaside jewels beckon visitors toward the northern stretch of Florida's Gold Coast. Take Jupiter, for example. Come and see why legendary actor Burt Reynolds called it 'the best place in the world.' This affluent picturesque town, its skyline dominated by an 1860s-era lighthouse, projects a comfortable, humble attitude. Palm Beach, on the other hand, exudes decadence and opulent pretentiousness – without trying to hide the fact that it doesn't even give a damn. But it's fun rubbing shoulders with the rich and famous while window-shopping and exploring its equally rich history, regardless. And you'll never get bored in Delray Beach, a social party town with loads of entertainment.

TOP TIP

Don't miss Lake Worth Beach. Considered by many to be South Florida's finest beach, it attracts surfers, loafers and bohemian types.

Jupiter Inlet Lighthouse (p194)

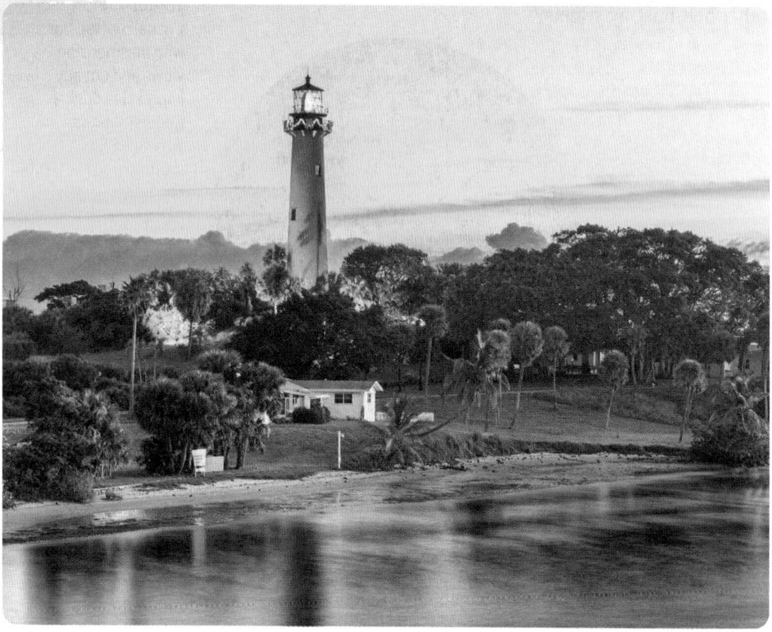

SEAN PAVONE/SHUTTERSTOCK ©

Flagler Museum

Palaces, Mansions & Churches

EXPLORING HISTORICAL BUILDINGS AND SITES

Take a short drive across the bridge to Palm Beach, and within minutes you'll feel as though you've been time-warped to another era. At a cost of $5 million in 1901, railroad, oil and real estate tycoon Henry Flagler commissioned the 75-room Whitehall as a wedding gift for his wife, Mary Lily Kenan. Designed by the architectural firm responsible for the NY Public Library and US Senate buildings, this monumental, beaux-arts mansion is now known as the **Flagler Museum**. Standing as a testament to Flagler's ambitious visions for Florida, its story is almost as grandiose as the Gilded Age home itself.

The home's exquisite design reflects the powerhouse of Flagler's empire. From its pink aluminum wallpaper (pricier than gold in the day) to its marble floors and Baccarat crystal chandeliers, everything screams decadence. Italian Renaissance decor blends effortlessly with other period styles, including Louis XIV, XV, XVI and Francis I, each room conveying a distinctively masculine or feminine appeal. Step back in time, wandering through Flagler's private Railcar No 91 – or enjoy a cup of tea in Mary's coconut-grove garden.

RIDING ON PALM BEACH CHARIOTS

Soon after homesteading in Palm Beach, Henry Flagler became entranced with an innovative form of transportation he felt was uniquely suited to the island. Developed by Palm Beach native John Thomas (JT) Havens, the 'wicker-wheel chair' was quickly adopted by Flagler as the island's only accepted mode of transportation. Consisting of a two-person, white-wicker easy chair set on two large wheels, the carriage-like device was powered from behind by a uniformed bicycle 'pilot.' Affluent hotel guests, particularly women, took a fancy – whether riding to the beach or to a glamorous ball.

These rickshaw-inspired buggies became affectionately known as Palm Beach Chariots. Although retired in the 1960s, two originals remain on exhibit at the Flagler Museum.

PALM BEACH'S NEARBY FESTIVALS & EVENTS

Oktoberfest
Annual event featuring bands and folk dancing, plenty of schnitzels and schnapps in Lake Worth.

Lake Worth Beach Street Painting Festival
In February, talented artists chalk sidewalk masterpieces – with food and music too.

Palm Beach Pride
Popular event, promoting equality and respect for the LGBTIQ+ community, jam-packs Bryant Park every March.

WHERE TO EAT IN PALM BEACH

Green's Pharmacy
Classic soda fountain. Serves breakfast, lunch and milkshakes. Many Kennedys lunched here after attending church nearby. $

Pizza al Fresco
Hidden spot off Worth Ave. Serves the best wood-fired pizza in town. Garden courtyard dining. $$$

Buccan Sandwich Shop
Best sandwiches in Palm Beach, with service to match. The Buffalo Chicken is divine. $$

Ta-boo
Cozy, Worth Ave bistro offers spectacular people-watching. The Bloody Mary was purportedly invented here. $$

Palm Beach Grill
Prime rib, kosher hot dog, cabbage with goat cheese...it's all great. Can get busy. $$$

Palm Beach Lake Trail

In 1904, Flagler followed up with a world-class hotel on the nearby shores of the Atlantic. Today, the **Breakers** is home to 538 rooms, two 18-hole golf courses, and maintains a staff of thousands. It's a short stroll from Whitehall; enter its gates to check out the scenic, mile-long stretch of beach before indulging in a crazily indulgent but unforgettable brunch or grabbing a quick drink in the gardens, where there are superb photo opportunities. Tours are occasionally offered through the Flagler Museum.

Love him or hate him, Donald Trump has his majestic **Mar-a-Lago** estate here, to which curious visitors are drawn (even the FBI). Although closed to the public, there's a limited view from a parking area to the west of the property, overlooking the lagoon. If you're lucky, and the gate opens for deliveries, you might even spy the executive mansion itself. (Trump is just one of 32 billionaires living in Palm Beach.)

Admire the stunning Gothic Revival architecture of **Church of Bethesda-by-the-Sea**, where Trump married Melania, back in 2005 (basketball star Michael Jordan also tied the knot here). Built in 1925, the Middle Ages design of this Episcopal

WHERE TO SATISFY SWEET CRAVINGS IN PALM BEACH

Piccolo Gelato
Sample a few before selecting from a broad, rotating selection of freshly made Italian gelato. **$$$**

Blue Provence
Take a pseudo break to Paris, for exquisite French pastries. Scrumptious tarts, cookies and doughnuts. **$$**

Mary Lily's
Inside lavish Breakers Hotel, this tiny shop scoops heavenly ice cream, frozen custards, and gelato. **$$$**

church seems completely weird in coastal Florida. Wander around its tranquil cloister using their map to identify the 10 varieties of palms growing around the gardens.

Palm Beach Trails, Beaches & Shops

NATURAL BEAUTY AND RETAIL EXCESSES

Despite all of Palm Beach's opulence, there's still something to do for free. (Although parking might cost a king's ransom.)

The paved **Palm Beach Lake Trail** – great for walking or biking – stretches 5 miles along the Intracoastal, from Indian Rd at the north to Worth Ave at the south. It's a short five-minute drive, or bike ride, across the bridge from West Palm Beach. Bikes and e-bikes can be rented from **Palm Beach Bicycle Trail Shop** on Cocoanut Row – be sure to ask for their trail map. The trail's easy to navigate, and ADA-accessible and originally designed by Flagler to flaunt the area's beauty to his guests. Many of his visitors would enjoy chauffeured two-seated wicker-wheel chair rides while traveling the royal palm-canopied trail along Palm Beach's scenic Waterway.

There's no shortage of places to spend money in Southeast Florida, such as flamboyant Worth Ave at the south end of the trail. A bevy of high-end stores and eating establishments here have sky-high prices to match. Welcomed by twin pillars at South Ocean Blvd, the extravagance extends four blocks to Lake Worth. Window shop for a $500 T-shirt, passing Mediterranean architecture and fashionable shops, such as Gucci, Chanel, Brioni and Tiffany's. Parking's available along Worth Ave, Peruvian Ave and South Ocean Blvd – at $6 per hour.

Once you've had enough, take a short jaunt outside the gate and dip your feet into the blue water at **Palm Beach Municipal Beach**. This see-and-be-seen beach is popular with a young and fit crowd. If you don't plan on being long, free two-hour parking is available on Barton Ave, near South County Rd.

A Mountain, a Lighthouse, Blowing Rocks

NATURAL AND ARTIFICIAL WONDERS

Driving north from West Palm Beach to Jupiter, you'll undoubtedly notice along the half-hour route that Florida's so flat that an anthill or sand dune qualifies as a mountain. In fact, **Hobe Mountain Observation Tower** at **Jonathan Dickinson State Park**, the highest natural point in all South Florida, is nothing more than a sand dune rising 86ft above sea level. Yet the panoramic view from the top still renders

HUNT FOR PREHISTORIC SHARK TEETH

Fossilized shark teeth routinely wash ashore along the sandy beaches of Palm Beach Island, Jupiter and Boca Raton, making them prime trolling grounds for collectors.

Having grown 30,000 to 50,000 teeth during their lives, with a skeleton composed of cartilage (not bone), shark carcasses disintegrate rapidly, leaving only razor-sharp teeth behind. Most of the teeth found on Florida shores are over 10,000 years old – some even prehistoric.

Head to where the tide hits the shore and search for dark triangular shapes mixed among broken shells and seaweed. Use a sifter to speed things up. Most are 0.5 to 2in in length. If you discover one longer than 4in, congrats, you've likely found a megalodon tooth!

GREAT JUPITER CAFES

I Need Coffee
Cozy plaza hideaway playing reggae and jazz. Try the butter coffee and coffee-infused apple cider.

Pumphouse Coffee Roasters
Outdoor seating only, with coffees from around the world. Small cups, but quality java. Pet-friendly.

Lokomotive
Eclectic decor; you'd swear film director Tim Burton had designed this nouveau-rustic cafe. Great coffee!

TRAPPER NELSON OF THE LOXAHATCHEE

In 1931, 23-year-old New Jersey native Vince Natulkiewicz, a skilled trapper and hunter bitten by wanderlust, settled amid the rugged beauty of Florida's remote Loxahatchee – anointing himself **'Trapper Nelson.'**

Self-sufficient, he survived off the proceeds of his trappings. Rumors of a Tarzan-like recluse in the jungle circulated through high society. Curious stalkers paid to watch him wrangle boas and wrestle alligators, so he cashed in by constructing a zoo. Demand for his pelts catapulted. Stockpiling money, he bought land like candy.

In 1968, on the cusp of a million-dollar government land deal, Trapper was found dead of a shotgun blast – ruled a suicide, though suspicions remain. Tour his rustic **homestead** at Jonathan Dickinson State Park.

visitors breathless. A gradually sloping (although not ADA-accessible) boardwalk provides an easy ascent to the 120 stairs awaiting at its base.

Once the site of a top-secret WWII radar training school, the park covers an astounding 10,500 acres and offers two family campgrounds (with cabin rentals). Twenty miles of nature trails and 9 miles of mountain-biking trails lead visitors through diverse ecosystems. The imperiled coastal sand pine scrub, home to many endangered animals – including the gopher frog, Florida scrub jay and Florida mouse – covers 20% of the park.

Hop aboard the *Loxahatchee Queen II* pontoon for a two-hour cruise through towering cypresses to the site of legendary Trapper Nelson's rustic homestead. Or rent a canoe, a kayak or a bike from the River Store to go exploring on your own.

For an even more awe-inspiring view of the Loxahatchee River and Jupiter Inlet, climb the 105 steps to the top of **Jupiter Inlet Lighthouse**. Built in 1860, its tower stretches 108ft skyward. The lamps of the lighthouse, one of the oldest remaining along the Atlantic seaboard, still beam today, protecting ships from nearby reefs and shoals. While you're here, be sure to visit the pioneer homestead, keeper's workshop and a Seminole *chickee* (wooden platform above the waterline) – built in 2009 to pay homage to the tribe's local history. Don't miss great photo ops from the observation pier overlooking the Loxahatchee River. (The adjacent museum was closed at the time of writing, due to nearby bridge repairs.)

A short drive along South Beach Blvd is the **Blowing Rocks Preserve**, where you'll discover an intriguing outcrop of limestone rocks along the beach. Perforated like Swiss cheese, the rocks are particularly impressive during high tide, when crashing ocean waves erupt fiercely, like a geyser, through its holes. It's along a serene, overlooked stretch of beach, perfect for a picnic lunch.

All beaches in Jupiter and Jupiter Island, including **Coral Cove Park**, **Carlin Park** and **Jupiter Beach Park**, provide free and plentiful parking. Carlin Park's a great place to watch avid surfers ride monstrous waves empowered by one of the best breaks along the coast.

Jupiter Island's Natural & Luxurious Beauty

JUPITER ISLAND AND INLET COLONY

Take a 35-minute drive north of West Palm Beach to enjoy the tranquil atmosphere of **Jupiter Island**. Although only 817 people live here, it's got a lion's share of celebrity homeowners.

UNFORGETTABLE PLACES TO EAT IN JUPITER

Dune Dog Cafe
Retro landmark serving huge, tasty portions at almost vintage prices. Great hot dogs, of course. **$**

Twisted Tuna
Quintessential Florida: a local favorite for fresh fish and sushi. Great mojitos – and spicy calamari. **$$**

Beacon
Owned by football legend and local, Joe Namath, Beacon bestows astounding waterfront lighthouse views. **$$$**

They've included Tiger Woods, Tammy Wynette, Alan Jackson and Celine Dion. Despite that glamorous roster, it's pleasingly unpretentious – although many residents christen their homes with cutesy names, like captains do their boats. Unlike other ritzy neighborhoods, many gates sit open, inviting gawkers to spy on the stately homes hiding beyond.

While many Jupiter locals encourage riding a bike down Beach Rd's scenic 10-mile stretch, this two-lane roadway isn't particularly bike-friendly. There's no bike lane, and its narrowness makes riding a tad precarious – especially if you're easily distracted by ritzy mansions! Luckily, traffic is minimal. Parking? Well, good luck with that. You're best to leave your car parked at Hobe Sound Beach (free), at the north end of the island, and walk or bike from there.

Hobe Sound Beach is probably the region's best-kept secret. Popular with locals, they'd prefer to keep it that way. Lifeguards monitor this pet-friendly beach, and those with mobility issues will appreciate the ADA-accessible picnic tables. Be sure to bring footwear, though, as the beach's gray sand often gets scorching hot. The beach at **Nathaniel P Reed Hobe Sound National Wildlife Refuge**, 3 miles north, is another local secret. Both beaches are spotless, peaceful, and great for shelling – with no high-rises in sight. You might just see more turtles than people. Dogs are only permitted on specific trails and must remain leashed. Parking is $5, but bikes enter free.

The tiny, ungated community of **Jupiter Inlet Colony**, at the south end of the island, is also great for stargazing. Perry Como lived here until his death in 2001, and Olivia Newton-John called it home until 2013. Kid Rock still lives here – and is reportedly seen perusing the local Home Depot on occasion. Community residents even have the on-duty police officer's cell phone number – just in case their cat's stuck in a tree or other alarming situations.

A BANDIT'S PARADISE

A sex symbol during the 1970s and '80s, **Burt Reynolds**, star of such hits as *Smokey and the Bandit* and *The Cannonball Run*, was America's top box-office draw from 1978 to 1982. But, despite Reynolds' Hollywood success, his heart remained in southeast Florida, where he spent his formative years.

Reynolds filmed scenes from *Smokey and the Bandit* at his 153-acre ranch at 16133 Jupiter Farms Rd in Jupiter.

But, after hitting tough times, Reynolds filed for bankruptcy in 1996. The property, Reynolds Ranch, eventually became a gated community of high-end homes with horse-riding trails. Properties there, on streets like Bandit Run, now sell for about $3 million.

Find Your Zen

MEDITATE IN A JAPANESE GARDEN

Take a pleasant half-hour drive from West Palm Beach and seemingly visit another continent. Maybe they're not secret, but the **Morikami Japanese Gardens** work wonders for dispelling negative energy and focusing on the power of positive thinking. This 200-acre labor of love was donated by Sukeji 'George' Morikami (1886–1976), a Japanese pineapple farmer and one of 140 original members of the area's Yamato Colony.

Meandering these manicured gardens, visitors escape and decompress from Southeast Florida's bountiful – and seemingly

UNIQUE SHOPS IN DELRAY BEACH

Scoopy Doo's
This ice-cream and bakery shop is for the dogs – literally. Doggie birthday cakes too!

Just Hearts
This romantic store, celebrating 35 years, sells only heart-themed items: clothing, dishes, jewelry, art, you-name-it.

Murder on the Beach Mystery Bookstore
The Holy Grail for mystery lovers, this bookstore stocks a mother lode of who-done-its.

endless – energy... and whatever else troubles them. Pack a lunch and a book and take your time strolling the rustic and scenic trails that cross koi-filled ponds on wooden bridges, spider-web through bamboo groves and pine-canopied rock gardens, and pass Samurai-inspired gates built from Japanese cypress. Find your serenity in a romantic garden, surrounded by lush, tropical flora that's native to both Japan and Florida, or retreat to a secluded, elevated Contemplation Pavilion to meditate with your thoughts. Check out the extensive collection of artistically contoured bonsai trees, on display at Yamato Island, then pop into the **Cornell Cafe** to enjoy some authentic Japanese cuisine. Tasty miso soup, coconut shrimp and sesame balls complement hot and cold green teas and Japanese beer.

BUSCH WILDLIFE SANCTUARY

If you love animals, the Busch Wildlife Sanctuary could bring tears of sorrow and happiness to your eyes. This caring sanctuary rescues over 6000 sick, injured and orphaned animals each year, nursing them back to health at its wildlife hospital.

Regrettably, almost 90% of those treated here suffer conditions caused by human abuse or negligence. Most are successfully returned to the wild, but those with injuries deemed too severe, continue to receive care here, housed in natural habitats. Many of those ambassadors can be seen touring the 11-acre site – including bobcats, alligators, bears and tortoises. There's no cost for admission, but donations are respectfully encouraged. Closed Sundays.

Travel Through Time

RETRO ARCADE GAMES

Take a 35-minute drive south of West Palm Beach to **Delray Beach**, and travel back in time to the pinball arcades of the 1970s and 1980s.

Possibly the coolest bar ever (they call themselves a 'museum,' but that's not exactly true), the two-storey **Silverball Retro Arcade** serves up bodacious booze, food and a ton of vintage fun. (Happy hour's half-priced drinks runs Monday to Friday from noon to 7pm.) The decor pays tribute to everything retro, including bands, TV shows and pop culture of the '70s and '80s. Surprisingly, at this flower-power saloon, millennials seem to outnumber Gen-Xers. But ages run the full gamut, and, unlike the trendy nightclub scene, nobody seems to care.

The entertainment roster includes 88 pinball games and 24 arcade games, with such classics as Playboy, Happy Days, Charlie's Angels, Indiana Jones, Pac-Man, Galaga and Donkey Kong. So grab your denim jacket, nimble up those fingers, and carpool in the Camaro. (Aim to hit it up between 10pm and 2am for unlimited play for only $10!)

Just For the Kids

CHILD-FRIENDLY ECOLOGICAL CENTER

Also located in Delray Beach, a 35-minute drive south of WPB – and just steps from the beach – the **Sandoway Discovery Center**, housed in an historic 1936 beachfront home, showcases Florida's natural coastal environments.

GETTING AROUND

While cars, rideshares or buses are necessary to reach these destinations, Delray Beach and Palm Beach offer free shuttle services around town. Circuit provides free rides in Palm Beach, while Freebee provides ecofriendly electric-car rides around central Delray Beach. Keep in mind that late-night service is usually unavailable. Palm Tran, a local bus service, connects Palm Beach and Jupiter for $1.50, no Sunday service. Rideshares are widely used throughout these areas.

VERO BEACH

Vacationers will surely hit the jackpot along Florida's Treasure Coast. From fishing to beachcombing, sunbathing to paddleboarding, antiquing to enjoying fine arts and culture, it's all right here at your fingertips.

Take some time to enjoy Vero Beach's uncrowded, windswept beaches and small-town charm. 'Sunrises, not high-rises' is the name of the game here. Its laid-back attitude enchants and de-stresses. Eighties songstress Gloria Estefan chose Vero Beach to build a home and resort because it reminded her of the slower-paced Miami of her youth. But this coastal community extends far beyond the sand, embracing nifty pubs, quaint cafes, fine dining, famous orange groves and botanical wonders. It may not appeal to the younger nightclub crowd, but plenty of places further south will take care of those needs. And the residents of Vero Beach seem quite content with that.

TOP TIP

Spend time exploring historic downtown neighborhoods. Stop into American Icon Brewery, housed in a 1926 heritage diesel plant, and cool your temperature with a cold Power Plant Lager. An antique generator serves as the decorative centerpiece of this captivating microbrewery, located in the heart of Vero's Art District.

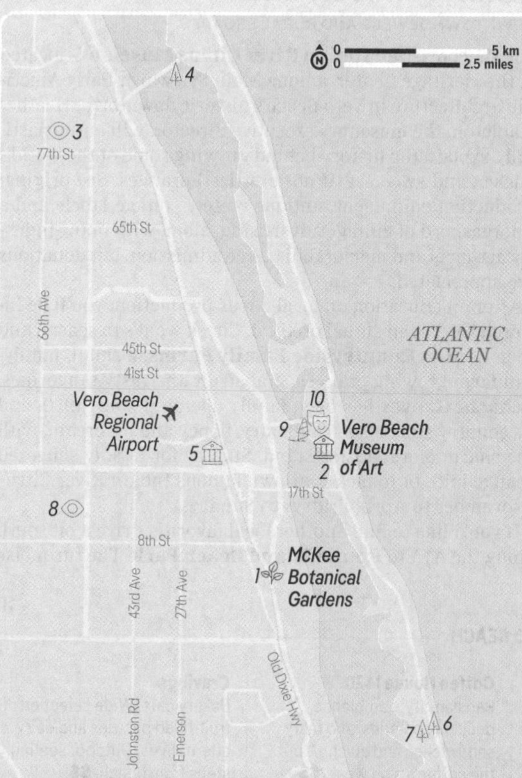

HIGHLIGHTS
1 McKee Botanical Gardens
2 Vero Beach Museum of Art

SIGHTS
3 Countryside Family Farms
4 Environmental Learning Center
5 Indian River Citrus Museum
6 Round Island Beach Park
7 Round Island Riverside Park
8 Schacht Groves

ACTIVITIES, COURSES & TOURS
9 Paddles by the Sea

ENTERTAINMENT
10 Riverside Theatre

GREAT PLACES TO STAY

Costa d'Este Beach Resort Gloria Estefan's beachfront resort. Live the rock-star life: complimentary sunrise yoga, poolside cocktails, valet parking. $$$

Driftwood Resort Built in the 1920s using locally sourced driftwood, a fun, unique and nostalgic beachfront hotel. $$

Holiday Inn Oceanside Lower-cost, no-frills option that's rough around the edges, but it's right on the beach. $

Disney's Vero Beach Resort Family-friendly resort with mammoth-sized pool and water park with a lovely sandy beach. $$$

NORM LANE/SHUTTERSTOCK ©

Round Island Riverside Park

Citrus, Farms & Parks

DOWNTOWN JEWELS AND RURAL ESCAPES

The shoebox-sized **Indian River Citrus Museum** is located in the Heritage Center, among Main St's warm Early American architecture in Vero Beach's historic downtown. Heather Stapleton, the museum's executive director, will enthusiastically explain the history behind growing some of the world's juiciest and sweetest (if not prettiest) oranges. See original production equipment, antique crates, vintage labels and a smorgasbord of vintage advertising, along with many industry artifacts and memorabilia. Free admission, but donations are appreciated.

After an education on local citrus production, you'll be inspired to visit an actual orchard. Check what's in season and then head to **Countryside Family Farms**, a small, family-run farm growing oranges, grapefruit and tasty tangerines. **Schacht Groves** has been family operated since 1950, and its country store sells fruit, dairy, honey and ice cream, with the charm of a roadside stand. Stop by for freshly squeezed orange juice or to pick your own famous Indian River Citrus (November to April, Fridays to Sundays).

If you'd like to find another local favorite, drive a bit south along the A1A to **Round Island Beach Park**. The turquoise

GREAT CAFES IN VERO BEACH

Rio Coco A comfy, ecofriendly, free-trade coffee house. Rich-tasting, locally roasted coffee at the lowest prices around. $

Coffee House 1420 Parisian-style ambience, delicious pastries, and tasty sandwiches and quiche – but the coffee's a bit weak. $$

Cravings Bakery cafe. Wide selection of fruit-filled pastries and dairy alternatives. Outdoor seating, steps from beach. $$

waters of this off-the-beaten-path, secluded stretch of beach are the perfect place to take a peaceful walk along the shore.

Across the road, on the other side of A1A, is **Round Island Riverside Park**. There's plentiful parking, and chances are good you'll have the park to yourself. Take a walk along its extensive network of shoreline boardwalk platforms and piers to spot manatees, dolphins, sea turtles and jumping mullets in this protected environment.

Theater & Art

EXPLORE LOCAL CULTURE

Looking for drama to spice up a rainy day? Check out Vero's **Riverside Theatre**. Celebrating its 50th anniversary in 2022, it's a great spot to catch Broadway plays, fun comedy acts and an eclectic mix of concerts. From April to December, park a lawn chair underneath the soaring oaks and enjoy live music from 5:30pm to 9pm while feasting on burgers, chicken and ice cream. Afterwards, shuffle inside and get ready for the humor at Comedy Zone's 9pm stand-up show.

If visual art's more your thing, check out the **Vero Beach Museum of Art**. Its permanent collection is small, but it does host engaging rotating exhibits of paintings, photographic images and sculptures. Closed Mondays.

Discover Natural & Botanical Wonders

ENCHANTING PARKS AND GARDENS

In 1932, visionary land developers Arthur McKee and Waldo Sexton opened a forested playland, McKee Jungle Gardens, on 80 acres of tropical hammock they'd purchased a decade before. They'd collected thousands of exotic plants – including orchids and bromeliads – from around the world to blend with native coastal hammock flora to create a lush jungle environment. Designed to attract curious travelers passing on US 1, this beta theme park lured adventurous *Tarzan* fans using monkeys, chimps and alligators to pique their interest. It was a resounding success until 1976, when a perfect storm arrived. A new interstate highway stole the traffic, a gas shortage hit and Disney opened mega parks in nearby Orlando.

Abandoned for 25 years, most of the acreage fell victim to condo and golf-course developers. Thankfully, 18 acres, considered 'the heart of the Jungle Gardens,' were saved by passionate locals. Now open to the public as **McKee Botanical**

THE FLORIDA HIGHWAYMEN

In 1950s Fort Pierce, an eclectic group of 26 African American men rebelled against cultural norms to follow their dreams of becoming artists. Now world renowned, these professional landscape artists became known as the **Florida Highwaymen**. Stroll down an alleyway in Theatre Plaza (a vintage Vero Beach theater converted into retail stores) to encounter one of these skillful masters: Roy McLendon.

Now in his 90s, Roy toils daily in his cubbyhole studio (Unit 14), still creating masterful works of art (for more, see p430). Ray McLendon, Roy's son, an accomplished landscape artist himself, runs **Florida Highwaymen Landscape Art Gallery**, just down 14th St, where he displays and sells several Highwaymen paintings.

SENSATIONAL BARS IN VERO BEACH

American Icon Brewery
Wide selection of on-site-brewed craft beers in a red-brick historic diesel power-plant building.

Kilted Mermaid
Lively spot with a rustic, yet whimsical, charm. Extensive selection of craft beers and cider.

Boiler
Beachside hole-in-the-wall bar where crazy-talented mixologists blend up incredible cocktails (try the whiskey sours).

Gardens, there's ponds, streams, waterfalls, a stone bridge, and over 2000 species of native and exotic plants to see. Don't miss the Polynesian-inspired Hall of Giants, built in 1941 to accommodate the world's largest one-piece mahogany table. The **Children's Garden** playland, complete with a pirate ship, is straight out of a child's whimsical imagination; all that's missing is Peter Pan. Budget for two hours – or all day, if you have children.

If the visit to McKee inspired your inner botanist, head to the **Environmental Learning Center (ELC)** to continue your education. Its 64-acre property, teeming with sabal palms and strangler figs, is a bona fide classroom to learn about Florida's diverse ecosystems. Guided hikes (by foot, kayak and canoe) inform visitors about native flora, edible plants and steps to becoming an active environmental steward. Indian River pontoons tour the most biodiverse estuary in North America. Aquariums and touch tanks are always a hit with the kids; and canoes, kayaks and paddleboards can also be rented.

DON'T-MISS DINING IN VERO BEACH

Waldo's
Rustic, casual oceanfront restaurant, serving superb seafood. Its coconut shrimp and conch fritters are must-haves. $$

El Sid Taqueria
Delicious tacos made fresh-to-order – with GOAT (great on any taco) sauce. Amazing margaritas too. $

Lemon Tree
Cozy diner across from the beach, serving homestyle meals with small-town charm. Complimentary post-meal mini muffins. $

Casey's Place
Popular 1970s-style outdoor diner; flips the best burgers in Vero Beach – with a requisite secret sauce. $

Riverside Café
Family-friendly waterfront dining. Secret-recipe tuna nachos – so tasty that Bahamian fishers dine here. $$

Fun on the Water

PADDLEBOARD, KAYAK AND CRUISE

Ever wanted to try paddleboarding but were too afraid of embarrassing yourself? Seize the opportunity to learn with a seasoned, patient and encouraging pro who'll make you chuckle while you practice. Feel at ease while learning (oftentimes awkward) balancing tricks.

Spend a day navigating Indian River with Chris Woodruff, owner of **Paddles by the Sea/Vero Beach Tackle & Watersports**. Self-guided rentals are available if you don't require his expert guidance. Chris and his staff also offer scenic catamaran tours and charter fishing trips, departing from the docks near Riverside Café.

GETTING AROUND

Driving offers the most flexibility to explore, but rideshares and buses are also readily available. GoLine, a free, convenient, wheelchair-accessible bus service, operates 15 routes throughout Indian River County.

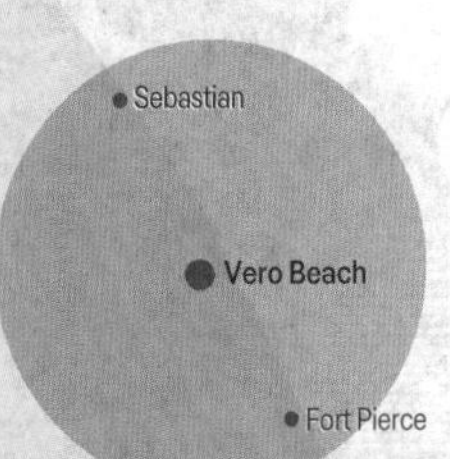

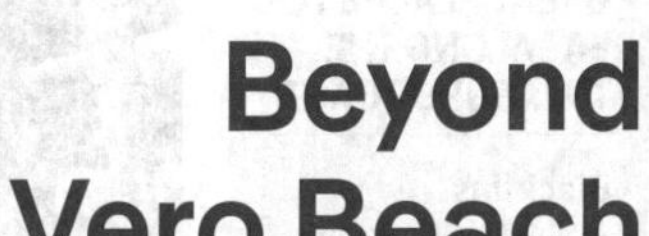

Beyond Vero Beach

A stone's throw away from Vero Beach, charming fishing and diving communities along Florida's Treasure Coast welcome travelers with open arms.

Plenty of fun and adventure awaits within an hour's drive of Vero Beach. Head south to Fort Pierce, site of the first US Navy SEALs training academy, now a museum honoring these heroes. It's a salty fishing town, ruled by all things oceanic, so it's a great place to go boating or embark on a deep-sea fishing adventure. Stuart, further south, is known as the 'Sailfish Capital of the World.' It's got an historic, pedestrian-friendly downtown shopping district, as well as an active fishing and water-sports scene. North of Vero Beach you'll find Sebastian. Famous for its shipwrecks and salvage diving, this small fishing town inspires the treasure hunter in all of us.

TOP TIP

Cycle or walk for miles along Sebastian's Historic Jungle Trail, a dirt road leading through hammocks of palms and nature-packed wetlands.

Kayaking, Blue Cypress Lake (p203)

GREAT PLACES TO EAT ALONG THE TREASURE COAST

Blackfins
At Captain Hiram's Resort, Sebastian. Delish chowders and breaded shrimp. Great seaside view. $$

Earl's Hideaway
Near Mel Fisher's in Sebastian, friendly biker bar serves cheap beer and New York-style pizza. $

Marsh Landing
Down-home cooking, this place in Fellsmere serves gator bites and frog legs. $$

Mrs Peters Smoke House
Queues at Jensen Beach for the tastiest fish dip this side of Atlantis. Excellent prices. $$

Roasted Record Coffee & Vinyl
Cool urban vibes. Cappuccinos, quiche, cupcakes...and records in Stuart. $$

McLarty Treasure Museum

Embark on a Treasure Hunt

BEACHCOMBING ALONG FLORIDA'S TREASURE COAST

Ever lifted an authentic gold bar? You'll get the chance at **Mel Fisher's Treasure Museum**, where, just a 20-minute drive north of Vero Beach along the US-1 (slightly longer via the much more scenic A1A), you can dive into **Sebastian**'s rich treasure-salvaging history. View 50 years of treasures gathered from the ocean floor and meet the family members who continue Mel's legacy (soon to embark on a quest for the lost city of Atlantis). This spectacular collection includes artifacts from Spanish galleons dating back to the 1600s. Some are even for sale! (Watch Mel Fisher, Jr, grandson of the late Mel Fisher, on the hit History Channel documentary series, *Beyond Oak Island*.)

Rent a metal detector from the gift shop ($30 per day) to search for your own bounty along the Treasure Coast, which extends south through St Lucie and Martin Counties. Gold, silver and jewels washed ashore from shipwrecks are occasionally found by lucky beachcombers. The quiet **Treasure Shores Beach** is a great place to start, but those in Fort Pierce (to the south) are popular too. (Chances are best after high tide has receded.)

BEACHES TO SCOUR FOR WASHED-UP TREASURE

Treasure Shores Beach
This quiet unguarded beach features lovely dunes, stunning views and lots of parking.

Sebastian Inlet State Park Beach
The tides are promising, with many wrecks offshore, including a Spanish fleet from 1715.

Ambersand Beach
You never know what you'll find along this stretch of protected beach, including nesting turtles.

More treasures await at the **McLarty Treasure Museum** at **Sebastian Inlet State Park**. After a massive hurricane sank several Spanish galleons off the coast in 1715, 1500 survivors struggled ashore and pitched camp right here. Weapons, gear and treasure salvaged from the ships are displayed in the museum, along with an informative video describing salvaging efforts.

Pelicans & Sunrises

DISCOVER NATURE'S BEAUTY

Established in 1903 to protect pelicans from feather hunters, **Pelican Island National Wildlife Refuge**, located just a 20-minute drive north of Vero Beach, encompasses 5445 acres of protected waters and land. With more than 218 species of birds, the area's a huge hit with avid bird-watchers. Almost 8 miles of nature trails lead hikers through multiple, wildlife-packed habitats. The **Centennial Trail** is ADA-accessible, ending at an observation tower. (Be careful – branching side trails confuse some hikers, sending them on an unintended, hours-long wild-goose chase.) Entry, parking and use of trails is free.

If photography's your game, head to nearby **Blue Cypress Lake** to discover another of Florida's hidden gems. Popular with sunrise-obsessed travel photographers, its clean water covers 6555 acres, with an average depth of 8ft. For winning shots, find **Middleton's Fish Camp**, then follow the footpath to the water's edge. (Be sure to bring bug spray.)

THE 'SHRIMP LADY'

Consider yourself lucky if you're visiting Fort Pierce on a Saturday. That's when a friendly local named Kelly (endearingly nicknamed the **'Shrimp Lady'**) sells (you guessed it) shrimp from the roadside, on the mainland side of the causeway. After her veteran husband passed away several years ago, she diligently assumed his duties. Nobody seems to know where she gets the tasty shellfish, nor does anyone seem to care. Because they're the most delicious crustaceans around. Look for her big yellow sign 'SHRIMP,' and bring some cash to grab yourself a bag or two.

Manatees & Navy SEALs

PRESERVING NATURE, PROTECTING THE US

Over 400 sightings of manatees are reported yearly (most between November and March) from the observation deck at the **Manatee Observation and Education Center** in Fort Pierce, less than a half-hour's drive south of Vero Beach. (Flags indicate when there have been recent sightings.) A 17-minute subtitled video educates visitors on local efforts to protect these threatened mammals. There's a few fish and amphibian aquariums too.

Learn about America's elite Naval Special Warfare teams at the **National Navy SEAL Museum**. Celebrating their valiant history, the museum occupies the site of the original 1942 training school for amphibious commandos. Interactive displays reveal SEALs' grueling training and work conditions, and spotlight several of their heroic, and since declassified, missions. Before you leave, step into flippers for a dress-like-a-SEAL photo op.

GETTING AROUND

Although driving and rideshares remain the preferred means of transportation, GoLine, a free, wheelchair-accessible bus service, serves all communities within Indian River County.

ORLANDO & WALT DISNEY WORLD®

THEME-PARK CAPITAL OF THE WORLD

'That's the real trouble with the world. Too many people grow up.' – Walt Disney

Once upon a time, there was a quiet swamp smack-dab in the middle of the Sunshine State. Then along came Walter Elias Disney, a Chicago-born animator, producer and entrepreneur, perhaps best known as the unofficial father of Mickey Mouse. Disney secretly snapped up more than 13 sq miles of marshland at the bargain basement price of $107 an acre to build a grand theme park where his beloved character creations could jump off the silver screen and into the lives and memories of millions of visitors.

On October 1, 1971, Walt Disney World opened its gates, and today it encompasses 47 sq miles of land dotted with over 173 thrilling rides that can bring out the inner kid in everyone. It's the only place in the world where you can swim along with Ariel, soar into the night sky on Aladdin's magic carpet and dine with Cinderella in her fairy-tale castle.

Other theme parks have also transformed this corner of central Florida from swampland to the fantasy-filled, theme-park capital of the world, including Universal Orlando Resort, LEGOLAND and Gatorland, a park dedicated to Orlando's unofficial mascot.

Beyond the hustle and bustle of Orlando's theme parks, the so-called 'City Beautiful' boasts a diverse list of activities that will engage any nature lover, culture-vulture or gourmand, including pristine parks and lakes, vibrant museums and a hot dining scene.

THE MAIN AREAS

Left: Minnie and Mickey Mouse plushies; above: Lake Eola Park, Orlando (p262)

Find Your Way

Welcoming over 10 million visitors every year, Orlando has become a theme-park mecca. It was planned as a car-friendly city, and renting a car or using a rideshare service are the most convenient options for getting around.

CAR

Most of the iconic attractions and key areas are connected by I-4, including Walt Disney World, Universal Orlando Resort and downtown Orlando. Try to avoid the morning and evening rush-hour periods, when traffic can be especially heavy.

HOTEL & RESORT SHUTTLE SERVICE

Many hotels located near I-4 offer inexpensive shuttles to area theme parks. If you're staying in one of the many hotels on International Dr, consider purchasing an I-Ride Trolley pass, which stops at six smaller area theme parks, the Orlando Convention Center and Orlando International Premium Outlets.

PUBLIC TRANSPORTATION

LYNX, Orlando's public bus system, can get visitors to most areas in the city, but 15- to 60-minute wait times, depending on the route, make a car rental or rideshare less of a hassle. Check golynx.com for schedules and route maps.

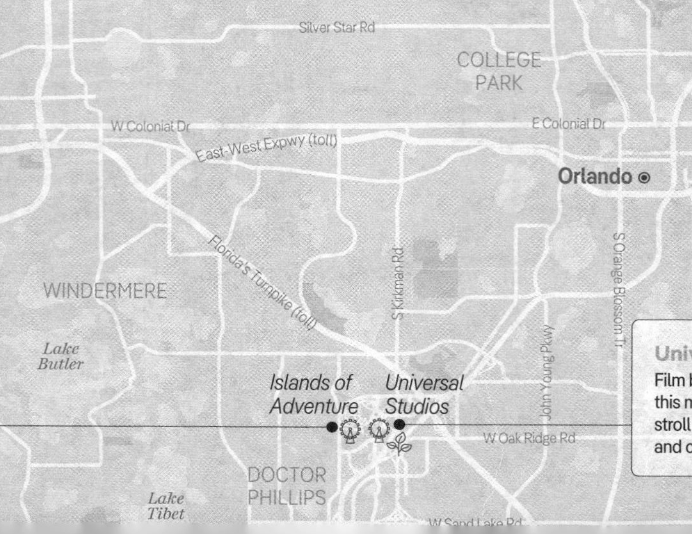

Islands of Adventure, p250

Mythical beasts, monsters, superheroes, wizards and wacky characters from the world of Dr Seuss unite at this theme park that guarantees epic adventures.

Universal Studios, p255

Film buffs will find themselves at home in this marvel-filled land where movie stars stroll the streets and blockbuster movies and classic TV shows are brought to life.

Magic Kingdom, p217
With Cinderella Castle at its center, the Magic Kingdom, Disney's most iconic theme park, bursts with enchanting attractions, festive fireworks and musical parades.

Disney's Animal Kingdom, p232
Encounter lions, tigers, gorillas and other exotic animals, and explore faraway lands featuring thrilling rides, at this theme park disguised as a tropical zoo.

Disney's Hollywood Studios, p226
Inspired by the glitz and glamour of the silver screen, Disney's Hollywood Studios transports guests back to the Golden Age of Hollywood and a galaxy far, far away.

Disney Springs, p243
Brand-name and Disney-themed boutiques, unique eateries, amphibious cars, bowling and even a hot-air-balloon experience round out the fun at Disney's walkable, lakeside entertainment hot spot.

Epcot, p237
Explore space, the deep sea, countries around the world, and the future that awaits at Walt Disney's Experimental Prototype Community of Tomorrow.

Magic Kingdom
Disney's Animal Kingdom
Disney's Hollywood Studios
Epcot
Disney Springs
Big Sand Lake
Dr Phillips Blvd
Beachline Expwy
Winter Garden Vineland Rd
Apopka Vineland Rd
Palm Pkwy
International Dr
World Dr
WILLIAMSBURG
LAKE BUENA VISTA
CELEBRATION
KISSIMMEE
Osceola Pkwy
Irlo Bronson Memorial Hwy
Irlo Bronson Memorial Hwy
Orange Blossom Tr
Central Florida Greeneway (toll)

FROM THE AIRPORT
Orlando International Airport is approximately 10 miles from Universal and 25 miles from Walt Disney World. Taxis and rideshares are available at Ground Transportation, Level 1 of Terminals A, B and C. Many local hotels also provide complimentary shuttle transportation to/from the airport.

Mears Destination Services, located in Terminal B, Level 1, provides ground transportation to many destinations in Orlando and beyond, including Walt Disney World Resort, via bus, sedan, limousine and shuttle van.

Universal's SuperStar Shuttle, located in Terminal A, Level 1, is the official shuttle service from the airport to all Universal Orlando Resort hotels.

N
0 10 km
0 5 miles

Plan Your Time

Orlando's theme parks offer year-round fun. But weather-wise, when is the best time to visit? And what other seasonal events are on Orlando's menu of fun?

WOODY WOODS/SHUTTERSTOCK ©

The Wheel at Icon Park, Orlando (p260)

If You Only Do One Thing

● **Walt Disney World®** (p210) is truly a world in and of itself, and this mega-scale park, with its thousands of acres of amusements, is a must-visit Orlando icon. Your best bet is to limit your day to one of its many theme parks. **Magic Kingdom** (p217), where you'll find Cinderella Castle and beloved vintage Disney rides as well as contemporary rides such as the recently inaugurated Tron, is a great pick for kids and adult kids at heart, thanks to the range of attractions, which also include toddler-friendly character meet-and-greets and top-speed roller coasters.

Seasonal Highlights

Visit Orlando when the weather is most pleasant, from March to May. Summertime's peak heat and humidity make it the worst season to travel here.

MARCH

Expect peak crowds due to sunshine and spring break. The **Epcot International Flower & Garden Festival** and **Orlando Whiskey Festival** are in March.

JUNE

Despite the humidity and heat, summer is one of Orlando's busiest times due to school vacation. **Gay Days** festivities welcome the LGBTIQ+ community.

JULY

Schools are out and theme-park crowds swell. Grand fireworks displays at theme parks light up the sky on July 4, **Independence Day**.

ANNA SCHEIBNER/SHUTTERSTOCK ©, JOSEPH SOHM/SHUTTERSTOCK ©, MELANIE BECHARD/EYEEM/GETTY IMAGES ©

Three Days to Travel Around

Reserve a morning or afternoon at the park where it all began, the **Magic Kingdom** (p217), then purchase a Park Hopper pass and ride the monorail or Skyliner to **Disney's Animal Kingdom** (p232), **Epcot** (p237) or **Disney's Hollywood Studios** (p226).

Opt for a one-day pass at Universal Studios Resort to check out its two theme parks, **Islands of Adventure** (p250) and **Universal Studios** (p255), home of **The Wizarding World of Harry Potter** (p258), where you can stroll Diagon Alley and soar aboard a hippogriff.

Venture beyond the colossal theme parks to smaller-scale **Gatorland** (p266), an alligator-friendly park that has been welcoming guests since 1949.

If You Have More Time

Outside of the theme-park frenzy, vibrant **Orlando** (p260) deserves a second look. Fuel up with coffee and stroll **Charles Hosmer Morse Museum of American Art** (p265) and the other art galleries of Winter Park, a charming suburb of Orlando.

Relax under the shade of two-century-old cypress trees at **Kraft Azalea Park** (p265), on the shores of Lake Maitland. Kayak along the emerald springs at **Wekiwa Springs State Park** (p268), located around 20 miles northwest of downtown Orlando, in Apopka, and see how many of the 190-plus species of birds recorded here you can spot.

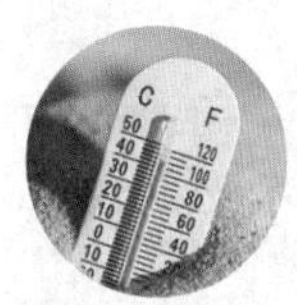

AUGUST

Sweltering temps and afternoon thunderstorms dampen the fun in August. **Megacon** celebrates comics, sci-fi, horror, anime and gaming.

SEPTEMBER

Less crowded than in summer. Theme parks begin Halloween events like **Mickey's Not-So-Scary Halloween Party** and **Halloween Horror Nights**.

OCTOBER

Ghosts, goblins and fall food-and-wine Halloween festivities bring the crowds back. The **Winter Park Autumn Art Festival** is held in Central Park.

NOVEMBER

Tourism spikes at **Thanksgiving**, when Christmas events usher in the holiday season. Hurricane season (beginning in June) runs through to November.

WALT DISNEY WORLD®

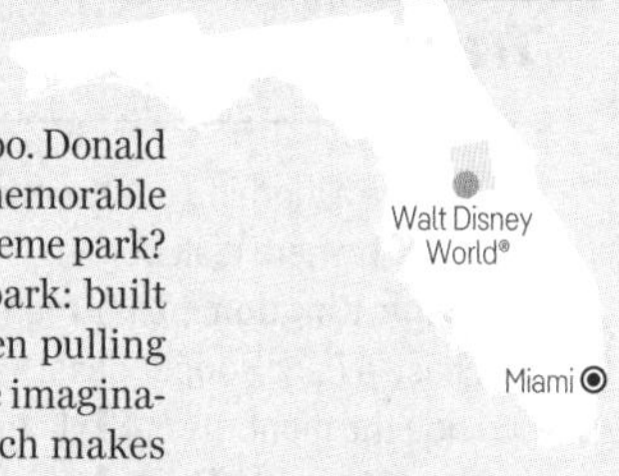

Cinderella. Mickey Mouse. Belle. Buzz Lightyear. Dumbo. Donald Duck. Darth Vader. Is it any surprise that the most memorable fictitious characters inhabit the world's most famous theme park?

Walt Disney World® is more than an amusement park: built around storytelling, since opening in 1971 it has been pulling out all the stops to create a magical destination where imagination reigns. From the use of forced perspective, which makes Cinderella Castle soar into the clouds, to Easter eggs and 'hidden Mickeys' concealed throughout the parks, Walt Disney World® continues to expand and improve its immersive experience that thrills millions of visitors every year.

While most of today's headlines focus on newer, high-tech rides, such as the out-of-this-world Star Wars: Rise of the Resistance and the Tron Lightcycle roller coaster, the classic rides like Peter Pan's Flight, the Pirates of the Caribbean and it's a small world will transport visitors down memory lane and straight into charming worlds inspired by timeless characters.

TOP TIP

Avoid the afternoon, which is the hottest and most crowded time of day to be at Walt Disney World. Instead, arrive at 'rope drop,' aka park opening time, and plan for pool time or a nap at around 3pm or 4pm.

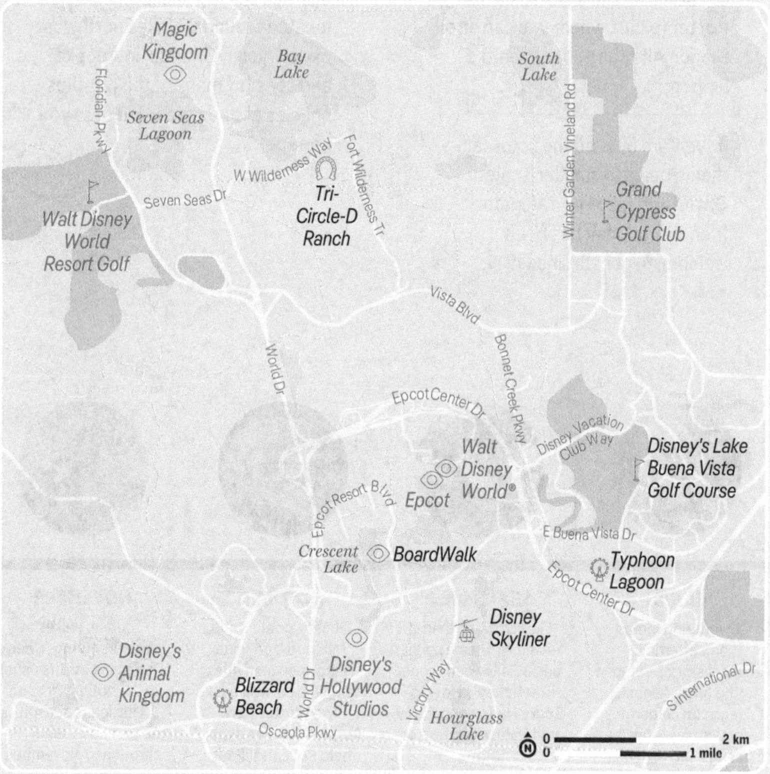

Magic Kingdom
Bay Lake
South Lake
Floridian Pkwy
Seven Seas Lagoon
W Wilderness Way
Fort Wilderness Tr
Winter Garden Vineland Rd
Seven Seas Dr
Tri-Circle-D Ranch
Grand Cypress Golf Club
Walt Disney World Resort Golf
Vista Blvd
Bonnet Creek Pkwy
World Dr
Epcot Center Dr
Disney Vacation Club Way
Walt Disney World®
Disney's Lake Buena Vista Golf Course
Epcot Resort Blvd
Epcot
E Buena Vista Dr
Crescent Lake
BoardWalk
Typhoon Lagoon
Epcot Center Dr
Disney Skyliner
Disney's Animal Kingdom
Blizzard Beach
World Dr
Disney's Hollywood Studios
Victory Way
Hourglass Lake
Osceola Pkwy
S International Dr
0 — 2 km
0 — 1 mile

Disney tour bus

First Things First: How to Get Around

TRANSPORTATION OPTIONS

You can get around Walt Disney World's 47 sq miles by land, sea or air. The following are the transportation options for getting around the various theme parks we've covered here.

Charmingly wrapped with Disney characters, **buses** run regularly between hotels and the parks, and are complimentary for guests. Schedules can be found on the My Disney Experience app.

The **Walt Disney World Monorail** (also free) has three lines for guests. The **Resort Monorail Line** serves the Transportation and Ticket Center (Magic Kingdom Parking), the Magic Kingdom Park, Disney's Polynesian Village Resort, Disney's Grand Floridian Resort & Spa and Disney's Contemporary Resort. The **Express Line** serves the Transportation and Ticket Center (Magic Kingdom Parking) and Magic Kingdom Park, while the **Epcot Line** serves the Transportation and Ticket Center.

Guests at some Disney Resorts Collection hotels can enjoy a **water taxi** to transport them to theme parks and even Disney Springs. Disney's Fort Wilderness Resort & Campgrounds,

GRAND 1 YACHT

By far the best way to cruise the Magic Kingdom's Seven Seas Lagoon is aboard *Grand 1*, a 52ft luxury yacht piloted by your very own captain and serviced by a butler, who stands at the ready with a bottle of chilled champagne. With three bedrooms, a bathroom and even a small kitchen, *Grand 1* holds all the comforts of home and can accommodate up to 18 guests.

Though you can choose to cruise any time of day, the best time to be aboard is during the Magic Kingdom fireworks spectacular, when the yacht's onboard speakers bring the show's synchronized music directly to your ears as you take in the most breathtaking view of the fireworks possible.

BUDGET-FRIENDLY DISNEY RESORTS

Disney's All-Star Movies Resort
Pays homage to film legends with whimsical decor. Sorcerer Mickey oversees the pool. **$$**

Disney's Art of Animation Resort
Larger-than-life statues inspired by hit Disney movies dot the grounds of this arty resort. **$$**

Disney's Pop Century Resort
A food court, affordable room rates, free Skyliner service and more make this resort popular with larger families. **$$**

HIDDEN MICKEYS

'Hidden Mickeys' are the silhouettes of the head and ears of the lovable rodent concealed in everyday spots throughout Walt Disney World. The history of 'hidden Mickeys' goes back to the design of Epcot in the early 1980s when Imagineers began sneaking in undercover Mickey Mouse profiles around the parks and resorts. 'Hidden Mickeys are especially fun for people who have visited the parks before,' said Steve Barrett, aka the 'Hidden Mickey Guy.' 'They offer an extra layer of appreciation for the care Disney puts in the details... and the detail is amazing. What makes it fun is that the Imagineers add new ones constantly, making finding them an evolving game.'

SHEA DANIELLE/SHUTTERSTOCK ©

Disney's Contemporary Resort

Disney's Wilderness Lodge Resort, Disney's Polynesian Village Resort and Disney's Grand Floridian Resort & Spa all offer **boat services** to Magic Kingdom Park. Guests at Disney's Board-Walk Inn, Disney's Yacht Club Resort and Disney's Beach Club Resort can take a water taxi (aboard Friendship Boats) to both Epcot and Disney's Hollywood Studios.

For quick, point-to-point drop-offs and pickups around Walt Disney World, take a polka-dotted **Minnie Van**. Download the Lyft app and select a Minnie Van vehicle to pick you up. Guests can also use the app to request an Accessible Minnie Van, and all Minnie Vans come equipped with two complimentary seats for tiny travelers.

Golf at Walt Disney World®

HAPPIEST GOLF COURSE ON EARTH

At **Disney's Lake Buena Vista Golf Course**, pros mingle with kids taking their first swings of the club. Host of the PGA Tour, the LPGA Tour and USGA events, these greens

BEST MODERATELY PRICED DISNEY RESORTS

Disney's Caribbean Beach Resort
Lush landscapes, zero-entry pool and water-play area – you'll think you're on the islands. **$$$**

Disney's Coronado Springs Resort
This resort has a spa, fitness center, business center and convention center. **$$$**

Cabins at Disney's Fort Wilderness Resort
Canoe, fish, ride horses and sing at the campfire with Chip 'n' Dale at this roomy resort. **$$$**

have seen the likes of Tiger Woods, but it's also a venue where anyone can learn the ropes of the game that originated in 15th-century Scotland.

Certified by Audubon International as a Cooperative Wildlife Sanctuary, the course winds through Florida pine and palmetto groves, past sparkling ponds and along a canal busy with boats, with a lighthouse that recalls the Florida of yesteryear. The 18-hole course was conceived by renowned golf-course architect Joe Lee. And, of course, no Disney golf course would be complete without a 'hidden Mickey'! See if you can spot his famous profile in bunker form just behind the 9th green. And be on the lookout for the Mickey Mouse roving refreshment cart.

Reservations are highly recommended, but walk-up golfers will be accommodated if possible – single or twosome walk-up players will have a better chance. However, it is best to reserve a tee time online, even if it's just a few hours before you plan to hit the links.

Giddy-up at the Tri-Circle-D Ranch

CINDERELLA'S PONIES

Walt Disney loved horses, and enjoyed buzzing around his Burbank studios at the reins of his stagecoach. Many of the most memorable Disney movie characters are horses: Samson, Prince Phillip's horse from *Sleeping Beauty,* Ichabod's horse in *The Adventures of Ichabod and Mr. Toad,* Maximus from *Tangled, Hercules'* flying Pegasus, Khan from *Mulan* and Merida's Shire horse Angus in *Brave.* So it's no surprise that Walt Disney World® has boasted its very own working ranch, Tri-Circle-D Ranch, since day one.

The barns are open during normal working hours, and guests are welcome to explore the public areas – no Magic Band required! – and learn more about the Appaloosas, Arabians, Belgians, Clydesdales, paint horses, Percherons, quarter horses and Shetlands that live here (these are the same horses that you'll see pulling trolleys and parading down Main Street). Knowledgeable cast members (ie Disney employees) can answer all your questions about the horses and their care. The six lovely little white ponies you'll meet take turns escorting Cinderella's Carriage during parades and wedding ceremonies.

You can also set off on a horseback ride through the surrounding woodlands teeming with deer, ducks, armadillos and rabbits. Small kids can ride into the sunset atop a hand-led pony.

FLAG RETREAT

All Walt Disney World parks have an American flag at their main entrance, and WDW Security raises and lowers the flags at the start and end of each day. At about 5pm every day, the Magic Kingdom holds a Flag Retreat ceremony to honor the nation and the brave men and women who protect it. Randomly selected children recite the Pledge of Allegiance, followed by a marching-band rendition of the national anthem, a chorus of 'God Bless America,' and then the flag retreat. A US veteran is also chosen randomly to participate in the ceremony, and is honored with a special pin and certificate.

BEST DELUXE DISNEY RESORTS

Disney's Contemporary Resort
The monorail runs through this resort, but it's also a short walk from the Magic Kingdom. **$$$**

Disney's Grand Floridian Resort & Spa
With its turn-of-the-century decor and a full-service spa, this resort exudes luxury. **$$$**

Disney's Polynesian Village Resort
Volcano-inspired pool and lush grounds. Two monorail stops from the Magic Kingdom. **$$$**

RESORT RUNNING TRAILS

Tonga Toast (849 calories), turkey legs (1136 calories), cheeseburger-stuffed spring rolls (1136 calories)... It's easy to overindulge while vacationing at Walt Disney World®. Thankfully over 16 miles of marked, paved running trails wind among the resorts. The most scenic of all is the 1-mile trail starting from Disney's Polynesian Village Resort's Moorea building, winding through the tropical gardens along the Seven Seas Lagoon and the manicured grounds of Disney's Grand Floridian Resort & Spa, then passing by the wedding chapel and ending at the Alice in Wonderland swimming pool.

This trail also brings runners close to the Magic Kingdom monorail, offering a great glimpse of the railway from below the elevated tracks.

runDisney

ADVENTURES IN FITNESS

Open to runners of all ages and levels, runDisney hosts multiple races per year, ranging from 5Ks (3.1 miles) and 10Ks (6.2 miles) to half-marathons and marathons, each themed after a character, attraction or movie. Lace up your running shoes and run with princesses, race under the sea or zip off faster than a rocket to a galaxy far, far away, before other non-running guests arrive – the races offer a chance to experience the parks at the crack of dawn.

Every January thousands of fitness-minded Disney fans line up at the start of the **Walt Disney World® Marathon**. Weekend events include a 5K, half-marathon and the marquee event, the 26.2-mile marathon winding through four parks. Go the extra mile with Goofy's Race and a Half Challenge, by completing both the half-marathon on Saturday and the full marathon on Sunday (for a combined 39.3 miles over two days), and you'll be awarded a coveted Goofy medal. Or take on the Dopey Challenge by completing all four weekend races, and you'll receive an extra-sweet medal featuring Snow White's pal.

Want to get fit before you pound the pavement at Walt Disney World®? Free, downloadable runDisney 13- to 29-week training programs promise to get you across the finish line with confidence (rundisney.com/running-training-programs).

The Skyliner

SMOOTHEST RIDE IN TOWN

In 2019, the Disney Skyliner soared up into the air over Walt Disney World®, adding an extra dash of pixie dust and an altogether new transportation option. From a central terminus at Disney's Caribbean Beach Resort, this 6-mile state-of-the-art gondola system travels at 11mph, connecting Disney's Hollywood Studios and the International Gateway at Epcot to Disney's Art of Animation Resort, Disney's Pop Century Resort and Disney's Riviera Resort. From above the treetops, it's perhaps the most relaxing way to ride around Walt Disney World.

The breathtaking views from 60ft up make the Skyliner feel more like an attraction and not simply an ultra-efficient transportation system. The gondolas pass by the Eiffel Tower (Epcot's World Showcase), the imposing Tower of Terror Hotel (Disney's Hollywood Studios), the beaches of the Riviera (Disney's Riviera Resort) and Spaceship Earth, which morphs from a dot in the distance to a massive sphere. Each

BEST RESORTS WITH LAKESIDE VISTAS AND BEACHES

Disney's Beach Club
Inspired by the elegance of the New England coast, this resort has its own beach and water park. **$$$**

Disney's Beach Club Villas
These homey villas sleep up to eight adults and are steps away from the resort's lakeside beach. **$$$**

Disney's Old Key West Resort
Surrounded by a golf course and four pools, this deluxe lakeside resort envelops guests in vacation vibes. **$$$**

VIAVAL TOURS/SHUTTERSTOCK ©

Walt Disney World Swan Resort

gondola can hold up to 10 guests, and they're wrapped with images of Disney characters, making it feel as if they're along for the ride too.

Blizzard Beach & Typhoon Lagoon

SPLASH, SLIDE AND SURF

Disney's two water parks offer high-speed slides, wave pools and perhaps best of all, a break from the Orlando heat. Themed as a former ski resort, **Blizzard Beach** is inhabited by Ice Gator, a ski bum of an alligator who resides in a cozy cabin on an island in Cross Country Creek, the park's lazy river. Blizzard Beach's 120ft-high Summit Plummet is the tallest and fastest free-fall waterslide in the country.

At the center of **Typhoon Lagoon** lies Mount Mayday, a 'dormant volcano' that unleashes a 50ft geyser every 30 minutes. The highlight of Typhoon Lagoon is the 2.75-million-gallon pool at its center: Disney engineers pioneered the implementation of mega-wave-makers, which crank out surf-worthy waves.

MANDARA SPA

Mandara Spa promises to take you on a sensory journey, far away from the frenetic energy of Walt Disney World® to the heart of Bali. Check your stress at the door as you enter this mystical 10,500-sq-ft sanctuary. A soft echo of chimes announces your arrival as you pass through the serene Meditation Garden, with its rock gardens and stone lanterns. A 25ft-tall replica of the Meru tower rises as a symbol of the most sacred realm of the ancient Balinese gods.

The spa's signature services include wraps, facials and massages, in particular the traditional Balinese massage. Sign up for sound wave therapy, which uses singing bowls to send you straight into a state of bliss.

BEST RESORTS WITHIN WALKING DISTANCE OF EPCOT

Walt Disney World Dolphin Resort
Deluxe retreat dotted with palm trees plus a 3-acre aquatic oasis. **$$$**

Walt Disney World Swan Resort
Enjoy Marriott Bonvoy perks, early theme-park entry and extended evening hours. **$$$**

Walt Disney World Swan Reserve Resort
This low-key place offers a tranquil escape from the theme-park crowds. **$$$**

PRESSED-PENNY MACHINES

For just 51¢ each, pressed pennies are one of the most inexpensive souvenirs in all of Walt Disney World®, with the added bonus that collectors can crank and press them into existence. The My Disney Experience app provides a location map of pressed-coin machines: there are over 130 of them in Disney's Hollywood Studios alone!

The machines take an ordinary penny and transform it into an oval-shaped, copper treasure embossed with a Disney character, attraction or unique logo. The available designs change constantly, making them highly collectible, but you'll find machines that roll out pennies with classic Disney characters, usually near their dedicated attraction. Most souvenir shops sell books and frames designed to showcase your shiny pressed pennies.

THE IMAGE PARTY/SHUTTERSTOCK ©

Pressed-penny machine

Disney's BoardWalk

RETRO FUN AND GAMES

A copycat of the famous boardwalks of yesteryear, like the promenades of Atlantic City and Coney Island, Disney's quarter-mile BoardWalk offers riverside views, live performances from local magicians, jugglers, buskers and plenty of opportunities for retro fun, making it one of the best stretches to stroll along in Walt Disney World®. It's easily accessible by foot via the International Gateway, and you don't even need park tickets or a Magic Band to enter. It's a budget-friendly place to enjoy an evening of entertainment.

Try your luck at one of the many retro, fairground-style games, including Lob-A-Lobster and Kewpie Doll Knock Down. Or set off on a two- or four-person Surrey bike and roll down the pier in style. The 1940s-themed **Atlantic Dance Hall** offers the perfect excuse to dance the night away.

BEST RESORTS FOR LUXURY

Four Seasons Resort Orlando
This resort is the pinnacle of luxury and one of the closest non-Disney hotels to the Magic Kingdom. **$$$**

Waldorf Astoria Orlando
Expect stylish sophistication with luxurious amenities and impeccable personalized service. **$$$**

Animal Kingdom Lodge
Book a Savanna View room here to wake up to giraffes and zebras outside your window. **$$$**

MAGIC KINGDOM

Disney mythology comes alive in the Magic Kingdom, starting with the grandest of 'Walt's Weenies' (visually magnetic architectural elements), Cinderella's castle, inspired by the 1950 animated film. Walkways extend from this main hub to the park's six themed 'lands': Main Street, USA, a replica, old-fashioned shopping district; jungle-like Adventureland, inspired by Walt's award-winning nature documentaries on Africa and Asia; wild, western Frontierland; Liberty Square, home of all things American history, including every (animatronic) US president; forward-thinking Tomorrowland; and Fantasyland, home to Walt Disney World®'s oldest and most beloved rides. Space Mountain's rooftop entices guests toward Tomorrowland, while the Splash Mountain ride, with its 52ft drop, and the reddish-brown Big Thunder Mountain, usher guests through Liberty Square and toward Frontierland, the furthest 'land' from the entrance.

Walt Disney himself oversaw the restoration of the vintage steam trains that loop around the park's 1.5-mile perimeter, making stops at Main Street, USA, Frontierland and Fantasyland.

TOP TIP

When nature calls, make a beeline for the Tangled Restrooms. Rapunzel's Tower, atop a rocky cliff with a waterfall, serves as a 'weenie,' or a beacon of sorts, so you can easily identify the location of these guest amenities below the tower. In addition to plentiful restrooms, there are charging stations disguised as tree trunks.

VIAVAL TOURS/SHUTTERSTOCK©

Entrance, Walt Disney World®

HIGHLIGHTS
1 Cinderella Castle

SIGHTS
2 Main Street, USA

ENTERTAINMENT
3 Carousel of Progress
4 Dumbo the Flying Elephant
5 Enchanted Tiki Room
6 Haunted Mansion
7 it's a small world
8 Pirates of the Caribbean

TRANSPORT
9 Walt Disney World® Railroad

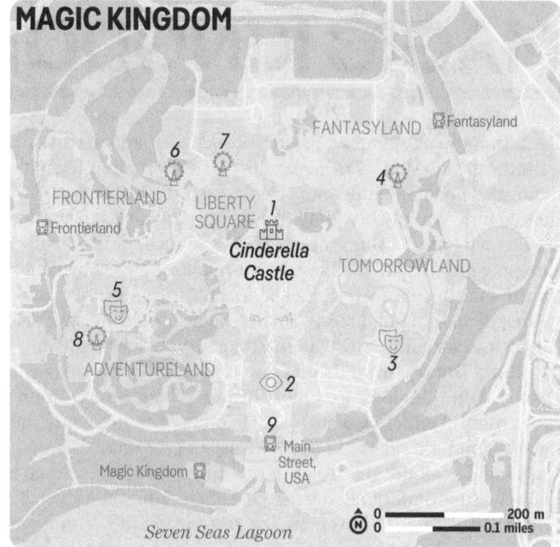

MAGIC KINGDOM EASTER EGGS

'Easter Eggs' are fun secrets, hidden in plain sight all around the Magic Kingdom. These include the following:

A giant peeking under the roof at Sir Mickey's gift shop, a reference to the 1947 short film *Mickey and the Beanstalk.*

The sidewalk by the exit of the Pirates of the Caribbean features the boot prints of a peg-legged pirate.

An engagement ring tossed by the Haunted Mansion's bride-to-be is hidden in the pavement of the area where visitors queue.

The axe of Paul Bunyan is on the walls of Pecos Bill Tall Tale Inn and Cafe.

Walt Disney World® Railroad

ALL ABOARD!

From the time he was a little boy, Walt Disney loved trains. Perhaps this passion grew via his father, who worked on a track-installation crew for the Union Pacific Railroad, or from his stint as a newspaper, candy and cigar salesman on the Missouri Pacific Railway. He loved trains so much that he built a railroad in his own backyard. The Carolwood Pacific Railroad was a 1/8-scale train pulled by the locomotive Lilly Belle.

So when it came to building a railroad that he could share with the world, Disney pulled out all the stops, meticulously restoring four vintage, narrow-gauge steam trains. Many visitors to the Magic Kingdom skip the Walt Disney World® Railroad, a relaxing 20-minute, 1.5-mile round-trip scenic tour, but it's worth hopping aboard at the Main Street, USA station and enjoying this nostalgic ride around the park.

The four Baldwin Locomotive Works locomotives, made between 1916 and 1928, were rescued from a railroad graveyard in Mérida, Mexico by Roger E Broggie, Disney's first Imagineer, at a cost of US$32,750. They were repaired, their

BEST SIT-DOWN RESTAURANTS IN THE MAGIC KINGDOM

Jungle Navigation Co LTD Skipper Canteen
Jungle Cruise skippers dig into Asian, South American and African dishes here. **$$$**

Tony's Restaurant
Share a plate of spaghetti and recreate the iconic scene beside a fountain depicting the canine couple. **$$$**

Be Our Guest
Immerses guests in the Disney classic *Beauty and the Beast*, with its prix-fixe, three-course, French-inspired menu. **$$$**

original wood burners converted to oil burners at the Tampa Ship Repair & Dry Dock Company, and then brought to Orlando, where they were named after Disney icons: Lilly Belle (Walt's wife), Roy Disney (Walt's brother), Roger E Broggie, the man who saved them, and Walter E Disney (the tallest at just under 12ft high).

Each of the four locomotives pulls a set of five passenger cars, with steam-driven generators at the rear of the tenders supplying electricity. The locomotives do not have any brakes, but thankfully, the passenger cars do!

it's a small world

PEACE IS POSSIBLE

Originally created for the 1964 New York World's Fair, it's a small world is one of the Magic Kingdom's most iconic rides. This delightful musical tour whisks guests off on a 10-minute cruise along the mythical Seven Seaways Waterway, through all seven continents, where 289 animatronic dolls represent dozens of nations. Though they're singing the earworm song in multiple languages, notice how they reach universal harmony as the journey reaches its grand finale, a joyful, multinational dance party.

The ride was personally overseen by Walt Disney to support the efforts of the United Nations Children's Fund (Unicef). Artist Mary Blair, who served as the art director on several Disney animated features, including *Cinderella* and *Alice In Wonderland,* created the attraction's whimsical backdrop, while artist Alice Davis designed over 300 traditional costumes for the dolls. The Sherman Brothers, Disney staff songwriters, delivered the ride's cheerful song of peace and brotherhood following the 1962 Cuban Missile Crisis, and it stands today as the single most performed piece of music on earth.

While this iconic ride is a must-do for the entire family, toddlers will especially enjoy the sounds and colors of the gentle cruise, and even babies can ride along on your lap.

Main Street, USA

TAKE A STROLL BACK IN TIME

Before mega-stores dominated the US retail scene, virtually every small town in the country had a cute main street that almost begged you to walk a little slower, smile at passersby and shop at local, family-owned shops and businesses. Main Street, USA was inspired by the main drag in Walt Disney's hometown, Marceline, Missouri, and other early-20th-century small towns across America.

CLASSIC MAGIC KINGDOM EXPERIENCES

Don't miss a ride on the attractions that have been delighting guests with Disney magic since opening day in 1971.

Fly over London and Neverland aboard **Peter Pan's Flight**.

Set sail on 'the happiest cruise on earth,' **it's a small world**.

Tour the world's most famous rivers on the **Jungle Cruise**.

Rocket to another galaxy on **Space Mountain**.

Explore the Swiss Family Robinson's treetop abode, the **Swiss Family Treehouse**.

Take a spin on Cinderella's pony on **Prince Charming Regal Carrousel**.

Pick up a hitchhiking ghost at the **Haunted Mansion**.

Race a gas-powered car that travels up to 7mph at **Tomorrowland Speedway**.

Twirl into a dizzy frenzy at the **Mad Tea Party**.

BEST FAST COUNTER-SERVICE RESTAURANTS IN THE MAGIC KINGDOM

Pinocchio Village Haus
Refuel with fast Italian fare such as subs, pizza and pasta. **$$**

The Friar's Nook
Tuck into bacon, egg and cheese breakfast sandwiches at the eatery inspired by the Disney film *Robin Hood.* **$$**

Pecos Bill Tall Tale Inn and Cafe
Quick serve Tex-Mex delights include tacos, fajitas and pork carnitas nachos. **$$**

Considered the 'opening credits' of the Magic Kingdom, this bustling main street is lined with shops and other businesses leading up to Cinderella Castle. Take a closer look at the second stories of the buildings: they're shorter than the first stories, while the third stories are even shorter, creating a visual effect that makes the buildings appear taller and bigger. Also note the business names on the windows, which honor the Imagineers who built the park.

City Hall, located at the start of the street, houses Guest Relations, where you can find guide maps and daily schedules, make dining reservations, access disability services and exchange foreign currency. The Main Street **Fire Station** shop, also known as Engine Co. 71, reveals a vintage fire wagon and showcases fire-station patches from across the US. **Harmony Barber Shop** is a real, working barber shop. Every plush Disney character under the sun sits on the display shelves of the **Emporium**, the largest gift and souvenir shop in the Magic Kingdom.

Cinderella Castle

WISH UPON A STAR

Cinderella Castle, inspired by the 1950 Disney animated feature film, reminds us all that sometimes, when you wish upon a star, your dreams just might come true. The castle serves as a 'weenie' that draws guests through Main Street, USA toward the central hub, from where all the other lands can be reached. A classic example of forced-perspective architecture, the castle appears to loom large over the Magic Kingdom but it's only 189ft tall. As your eyes make their way to the spires atop the castle, notice how the windows and other elements become progressively smaller in scale.

Five elaborate glass mosaic murals in the castle's breezeway tell the story of Cinderella. Designed by Imagineer Dorothea Redmond, the 15ft-by-10ft panels are made of over 300,000 multicolored tiles fashioned from Italian glass, silver and 14-karat gold.

A winding staircase leads back in time to the medieval era, where **Cinderella's Royal Table**, a restaurant located on the castle's 2nd floor, welcomes guests looking for a fairy-tale dining experience. Colorful stained-glass windows, woven tapestries and majestic flags add to the regal decor. Disney princesses dine here, too, and Cinderella is usually on hand for photo opps in the downstairs waiting area.

BEAT THE HEAT IN THE MAGIC KINGDOM

Cool off with air-conditioning and relax your tired feet by catching a longer, indoor show. **Country Bear Jamboree**, **Hall of Presidents** and **Carousel of Progress** are all over 15 minutes long and offer comfortable seating. You can also kick back and catch a breeze aboard the open-air **Tomorrowland Transit Authority PeopleMover**.

Located just near the entrance to the Jungle River Cruise, the so-called **Liki Tikis** are statues that spray cool mist from their mouths every so often, offering instant relief from the heat.

Plan for an afternoon dip in your resort's pool to recharge for the cooler post-sundown hours, when temperatures dip.

BEST FAST COUNTER-SERVICE RESTAURANTS IN THE MAGIC KINGDOM

Columbia Harbour House
Lobster rolls are the stars of the seafood-centric menu at this seaworthy New England-style restaurant. **$$**

Cosmic Ray's Starlight Cafe
Bite into a chili-cheese foot-long hot dog while watching a show by animatronic alien lounge singer Sonny Eclipse. **$$**

Sleepy Hollow Inn
It's breakfast all day at the inn that serves the iconic Mickey waffle topped with strawberries and whipped cream. **$$**

SIMON CRUMPTON/ALAMY STOCK PHOTO ©

Plaza Ice Cream Parlor

The Haunted Mansion

SCARED SILLY

Almost 1000 ghosts call the stately yet slightly eerie Haunted Mansion home, and there's always room for one more, as the dark ride's 'Ghost Host' likes to remind the foolish mortals that dare to step inside.

The Haunted Mansion is one of the Magic Kingdom's original opening-day attractions, and is perhaps one of the most beloved by Disney fans. Its Italianate exterior was modeled after an actual estate, the 1874 Harry Packer Mansion in Jim Thorpe, Pennsylvania, and the backstory behind the ride begins at the graveyard located adjacent to the queue, where six busts depict the Dread Family, a family that ended up killing one another via creative means for money: Bertie killed Jacob with snake poison, Florence shot Bertie, twins Wellington and Forsythia killed Florence after she killed their pet canary, Maude murdered the twins with her croquet mallet

PLAZA ICE CREAM PARLOR

The wondrous view of Cinderella Castle makes the Plaza Ice Cream Parlor one of the most treasured spots to sit and enjoy a sweet treat. Start a family tradition by settling in for a sundae to wind up the best day ever at the Magic Kingdom, with a cherry on top as the Happily Ever After fireworks light up the sky. Visitors have been enjoying the hand-scooped sundaes, floats and ice-cream cones at the same location since the park's opening day on October 1, 1971. Sugar-free and vegan options are also available. No reservations are required to gather at the old-fashioned, yellow-umbrella-topped tables that overlook the park's main hub.

BEST GRAB-AND-GO SNACK SPOTS IN THE MAGIC KINGDOM

Frontierland's Turkey Leg Cart
Sells world-famous, salt-cured jumbo turkey legs, recalling smoky ham on the bone. **$**

Aloha Isle
Serves the legendary Dole Whip – vanilla ice cream with a swirl of pineapple. Near the Enchanted Tiki Room's entrance. **$**

Casey's Corner
Grab a foot-long hot dog, which you can easily eat while strolling the park, from this baseball-themed eatery. **$**

THE BEST SOUVENIRS IN THE MAGIC KINGDOM

At the **Silhouette Artists' open-air studio** in Liberty Square, a talented Disney artist will cut card stock - completely freehand, making it an incredible process to watch - to match the shape of your profile.

Magic Kingdom popcorn buckets serve a dual purpose: popcorn is widely available to eat all day and you'll also have a collectible souvenir, as the buckets feature a variety of Disney characters.

Mickey ears are undoubtedly the most popular Magic Kingdom souvenir. Though they're available in dozens of varieties, nothing says 'Magic Kingdom' more than the traditional black hat and ears with embroidered letters on the back. **Curtain Call Collectibles** on Main Street, USA sells a variety of ears and offers on-the-spot embroidery.

MARK HARMEL FAP/ALAMY STOCK PHOTO ©

Visitor wearing Mickey Mouse ears

then accidentally set herself on fire after placing matches in her hair to hold up her bun! Despite this unsettling tale, the Haunted Mansion is less scary and more silly, with ghosts popping up around every corner and eventually gathering for a bonkers dance party in the ballroom. The grand finale lands riders in the mansion's crypt, where hitchhiking ghosts inevitably hop into the Doom Buggy with guests.

Carousel of Progress

TOMORROW IS JUST A DREAM AWAY

Disney World's Carousel of Progress was Walt's own idea from beginning to end. By all accounts it was his favorite attraction of all. Introduced at the World's Fair in New York City in 1964, the animatronic extravaganza showcasing the evolution of technology dazzled audiences and was one of the most visited pavilions at the fair. On January 15, 1975, the Carousel of Progress began swirling around once again, this time

BEST MAGIC KINGDOM RESORT RESTAURANTS

Ohana
Enjoy a bountiful breakfast at Disney's Polynesian Village Resort. Don't miss the banana-stuffed Tonga French toast. **$$**

Narcoossee's
Innovative, coastal cuisine and panoramic views await at the Grand Floridian's elegant in-house restaurant. **$$$**

California Grill
Ascend to the 15th floor of Disney's Contemporary Resort for Magic Kingdom views and inventive California cuisine. **$$$**

in the Magic Kingdom's Tomorrowland. The show has had more performances than any other stage show in the history of American theater.

Walt called on Imagineers Roger E Broggie and Bob Gurr to design the attraction's 'carousel theater,' a circle of theaters connected by divider walls that revolves clockwise around six fixed stages. Traces of the attraction's original sponsor, General Electric, can still be found in stage props, including the GE vacuum and GE refrigerator in the 1940s scene. You're bound to recognize some familiar voices among the animatronics. The Father is voiced by Jean Shepherd of *A Christmas Story* fame. Mel Blanc, known as the 'Man of a Thousand Voices' (including those of Bugs Bunny, Daffy Duck and Tweety Bird), voices the Parrot, the Radio Announcer and Uncle Orville.

The Sherman Brothers, the songwriting duo behind 'It's a Small World' and 'A Spoonful of Sugar,' encapsulated Walt's vision in the attraction's theme song, 'There's a Great Big Beautiful Tomorrow.'

Enchanted Tiki Room

ANIMATRONIC AVIARY

The Enchanted Tiki Room stars some of the most fascinating animatronics in the parks, thanks to its colorful cast of over 150 tropical birds. It's impossible to not tap your feet as the birds sing their signature song, 'The Tiki Tiki Tiki Room,' by the Sherman Brothers. Its oft-repeated chorus ('In the Tiki Tiki Tiki Tiki Tiki Room') is a guaranteed earworm for days.

When the attraction first opened in Disneyland in 1963, it was the first show ever to feature audio-animatronic technology. Harriet Burns, the first woman hired to work as a designer for Walt Disney Imagineering, once said that crafting the birds for the Enchanted Tiki Room was one of her most complex projects. During a meeting one day, Burns noticed how Walt's blue cashmere sweater moved with his arm when he bent his elbows. So she replaced the birds' feathery chest plates with fabric, and they began slowly breathing in and out, just like real birds.

The voice of Fritz, the macaw with the German accent, is Thurl Ravenscroft, whom you'll also hear as a singing bust in the Haunted Mansion, as several pirates on Pirates of the Caribbean and as the lead in the song 'You're a Mean One, Mr Grinch.' He also voiced the giant whale Monstro in the 1940 Disney classic *Pinocchio*.

HAPPIEST OF BIRTHDAYS!

Walt Disney World cast members love to celebrate birthday boys and girls of all ages. If it's your birthday, be sure to pick up a complimentary **'Celebratory Birthday Button'** at Guest Relations near the main Magic Kingdom entrance and wear it proudly on your lapel for a chorus of birthday greetings throughout your magical day. If you're staying at a Disney resort, tell the front desk it's your birthday, and you'll receive a special wake-up or goodnight birthday phone call from a Disney character. Every birthday celebration calls for a cake: preorder a Mickey Mouse–shaped birthday cake via the main reservations line, and it will arrive at your table at the Magic Kingdom table-service restaurant of your choice.

WHERE TO HAVE DESSERT OR A DRINK IN THE MAGIC KINGDOM

Gaston's Tavern
Indulge in glazed cinnamon buns and LeFou's Brew, its signature non-alcoholic, apple and marshmallow drink. **$**

Tomorrowland Terrace
Reserve a spot for the Fireworks Dessert Party: unparalleled views of the fireworks paired with sweet treats and drinks. **$**

Storybook Sweets
Step into a fairy tale of a sweet shop where ice-cream floats entice thirsty princes and princesses. **$**

I LIVE HERE: MAGIC KINGDOM SECRETS

Eric Wagner, Orlando resident and Disney mega-fan, shares his Magic Kingdom tips.

Look for the **old-school phone booths** in Tomorrowland under the PeopleMover or the Astro Orbiter, or in the Main Street candy shop. Pick up the receiver and you may hear a thing or two!

Hit up the **shops on Main Street** during the fireworks for mostly uncontested browsing. These stores stay open an hour after park closing for maximum merch time.

Every food and drink location with a soda fountain gives out **free cups of ice water**.

Hot and tired? Grab a **Dole Whip** from Aloha Isle and head into the Enchanted Tiki Room to consume your classic WDW treat alongside air-conditioning, ample seating and feathered friends.

Dumbo the Flying Elephant

SOAR OVER FANTASYLAND

As you enter Fantasyland's **Storybook Circus**, look down at the pavement and see if you can identify the footprints of the circus animals that stomped on the wet concrete. This colorful corner of the Magic Kingdom was created to highlight one of the park's most nostalgia-filled attractions. Based on the 1941 Disney animated classic, *Dumbo,* Dumbo the Flying Elephant has been spinning since opening day in 1971. Step into the big top, where an interactive queue makes the wait a little more delightful, before stepping aboard your very own Dumbo. You can adjust your altitude during the gentle elephant flight.

Post-flight, kids can cool off at **Casey Jr Splash 'N' Soak Station**, a water-play area where the circus animals spray visitors with water and the circus train blows off some refreshing 'steam.' Bring swimsuits or a change of clothes as you're guaranteed to get soaked. Minnie Magnifique (Minnie Mouse as a circus performer) and Madame Daisy Fortuna (Daisy Duck as a fortune teller) love to greet guests at **Pete's Silly Sideshow**.

The adjacent **Casey Jr RailRoad Mercantile** sells towels, sunscreen and clothing to replace wet duds. **Big Top Souvenirs** sells a wide selection of kid-focused merchandise, snacks and sweet treats, including housemade caramel corn, cotton candy and chocolate-dipped fruits.

Pirates of the Caribbean

DEAD MEN TELL NO TALES

At the far end of Adventureland lies an imposing golden Spanish fortress, where aspiring marauders can board a barge that travels back to the 17th century, when pirates raided and ruled the West Indies. Pirates of the Caribbean is fun for the entire family: despite inevitable encounters with the dastardly Blackbeard and Davy Jones, it's a gentle ride with just one quick plunge. More than 150,000 gallons of water are used to recreate the Caribbean Sea and over 125 lifelike animatronics set the stage for the rollicking adventure, which winds up in a fever pitch set to the tune of 'Yo Ho (A Pirate's Life for Me),' the ride's anthem and one of the Magic Kingdom's most celebrated songs.

The Disneyland version of Pirates of the Caribbean opened in 1967 and was the last ride that Walt Disney himself played a key role in designing. The Magic Kingdom version opened

BEST MAGIC KINGDOM RESORT COCKTAIL BARS

Trader Sam's
Sail for the South Seas with kitschy tiki cocktails at this immersive bar in Disney's Polynesian Village Resort.

Enchanted Rose
Unwind with French-inspired cocktails at this *Beauty and the Beast*-themed bar at Disney's Grand Floridian Resort.

Steakhouse 71 Lounge
Classic 1970ish cocktails are paired with steakhouse-style bites at the Contemporary Resort's comfy lounge.

Dole Whip

its gates to swashbucklers in 1973 and went on to become one of the park's signature rides, so popular that it inspired the *Pirates of the Caribbean* film franchise.

Be on the lookout for Captain Jack Sparrow, the main protagonist of the *Pirates of the Caribbean* films, who pops out unexpectedly from a barrel near the end of the ride.

UNOFFICIAL BIRD HABITAT

All around the Magic Kingdom, wild native birds mix and mingle with park visitors. Two of the most elegant bird species that have adapted to the theme-park lifestyle are the great egret and the ibis, who have claimed the area between Liberty Square and the Rivers of America as their habitat of choice.

The birds have learned that Disney-visiting humans are mostly harmless, so they tend to approach without fear as they search for snacks on the brick pavement. Though they might love a piece of jumbo turkey leg skin, it's best to keep your snacks to yourself so that they can maintain a healthy, natural diet.

WHERE TO STAY NEAR THE MAGIC KINGDOM

Disney's Contemporary Resort
Opened with Walt Disney World in 1971. Futuristic design; the monorail runs through it. **$$$**

Disney's Polynesian Village Resort
Pacific paradise with an active volcano (pool), lush landscaping and pristine beach. **$$$**

Disney's Grand Floridian Resort & Spa
Super luxe. Soak in the Victorian ambience and enjoy the grand piano in the lobby. **$$$**

DISNEY'S HOLLYWOOD STUDIOS

Disney's Hollywood Studios brings the magic of Hollywood to Walt Disney World. At the park's 1989 dedication, then Disney CEO Michael Eisner explained that it was not a place on a map, but a state of mind. It's divided into seven themed areas inspired by real-life LA film addresses or worlds that only exist on the silver screen, and the park's main 'weenie' is an exact replica of Hollywood's historic Grauman's Chinese Theatre and houses Mickey & Minnie's Runaway Railway, which whirls guests into the wacky world of a Mickey Mouse short.

The addition of Star Wars: Galaxy's Edge and Toy Story Land introduced exceptional, high-tech attractions. Many guests consider Star Wars: Rise of the Resistance the best ride in all of Walt Disney World®, while Toy Story Midway Mania!, which recreates the classic carnival midway experience, features the most technologically advanced animatronic, Mr Potato Head.

TOP TIP

Compete with other family members for the highest score on all the carnival games at Toy Story Midway Mania! From your carnival-inspired tram, use your spring-action shooter to blast hundreds of quick-moving targets. Aim for the long skinny balloons that pop out from the volcano at the Dino darts game – they're worth 500 points each.

BEST STAGE SHOWS AT DISNEY'S HOLLYWOOD STUDIOS

For the First Time in Forever: A Frozen Sing-Along Celebration
'Let It Go' with ice princess Elsa at this sing-along stage show.

Beauty & the Beast Live on Stage
Settle in for a tale as old as time at this timeless musical show.

Disney Movie Magic
This nightly spectacular lights up Grauman's Chinese Theatre with projections of classic movie moments – the perfect way to wrap up a cinematic day in the park.

Grauman's Chinese Theatre

HOLLYWOOD IN ORLANDO

Just like the original Hollywood Grauman's (now TCL) Chinese Theatre, this Disneyfied theater is home to a forecourt featuring the signatures and hand- and footprints of the biggest and brightest stars of all time. Disney's version of Grauman's Chinese Theatre is an exact replica, right down to the two giant lions, aka heavenly guard dogs, that stand at full attention at the entrance.

The theater holds **Mickey & Minnie's Runaway Railway**, a trackless dark ride inspired by the rodent duo's animated shorts. Prepare to step inside a cartoon world inhabited by Disney's earliest animated friends as you ride off on the train. It's also the first ride at any Disney park that stars Mickey Mouse.

At night the theater's iconic facade flickers with projected scenes of memorable Disney moments. The 10-minute journey through Disney movie history features both beloved characters and villains, and ends with a recording of Walt Disney reminding everyone, 'It was all started by a mouse.'

Walt Disney Presents

100 YEARS OF DISNEY

Born in Chicago in the 2nd-floor bedroom of a humble home built by his father, Walter Elias Disney would harness his talent for drawing to found his own studio in California, where he became a pioneer of the American animation industry.

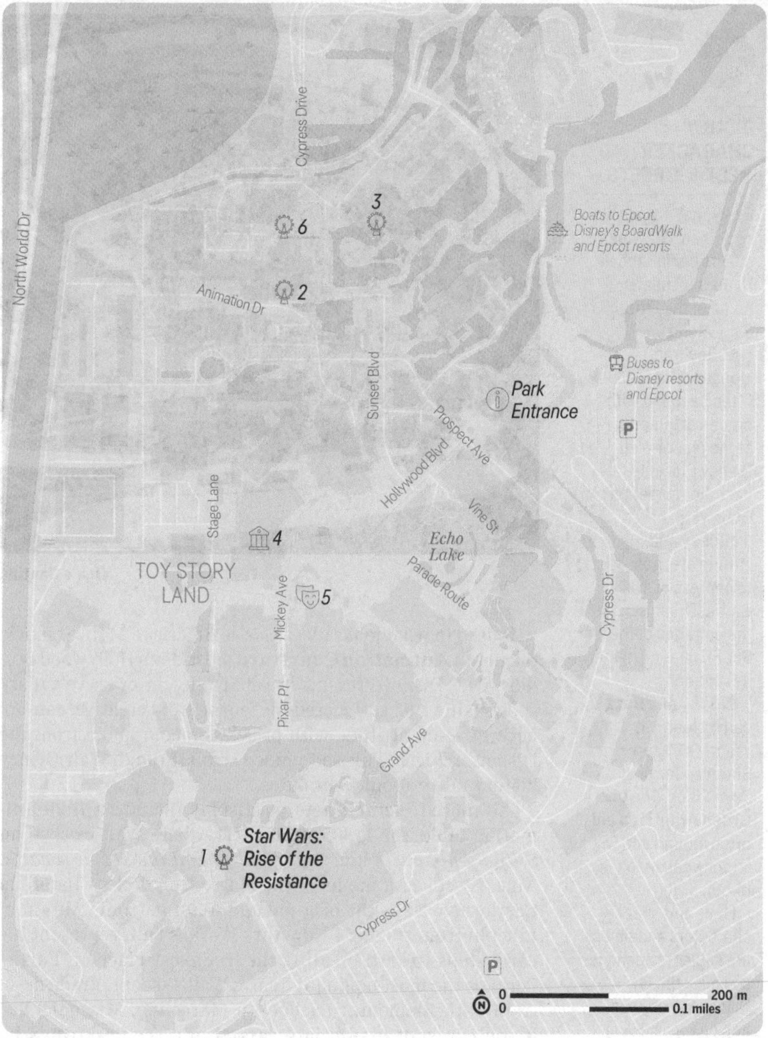

Cypress Drive
North World Dr
3
6
2
Boats to Epcot, Disney's BoardWalk and Epcot resorts
Animation Dr
Sunset Blvd
Buses to Disney resorts and Epcot
Park Entrance
P
Prospect Ave
Hollywood Blvd
Stage Lane
Vine St
4
Echo Lake
TOY STORY LAND
Parade Route
Mickey Ave
5
Cypress Dr
Pixar Pl
Grand Ave
1
Star Wars: Rise of the Resistance
Cypress Dr
P
0 200 m
0 0.1 miles

HIGHLIGHTS
1 Star Wars: Rise of the Resistance

SIGHTS
2 Rock 'n' Roller Coaster Starring Aerosmith
3 Tower of Terror
4 Walt Disney Presents
5 Grauman's Chinese Theatre
6 Lightning McQueen's Racing Academy

TABLE-SERVICE DINING AT DISNEY'S HOLLYWOOD STUDIOS

50s Prime Time Café
Time travel back to a 1950s kitchen and order comfort-food favorites (with a healthier, modern twist). **$$$**

Sci-Fi Dine-In Theater Restaurant
1950s-style drive-in theater with all-American cuisine. Diners sit in vintage cars. **$$$**

Brown Derby
Serves the same timeless dishes and cocktails that once graced the celeb-filled tables at the Hollywood original. **$$$**

DISNEY CHARACTER MEET-&-GREETS

Everyone's favorite snowman, **Olaf**, meets guests behind the Hyperion Theater, home of the Frozen Sing-Along.

Sulley from Monsters, Inc. can often be found with his can of laughter at the rear of Walt Disney Presents, near the Animation Courtyard.

Mickey and **Minnie** are dressed to impress at Red Carpet Dreams, near the entrance of the Sci-Fi Dine-in Theater Restaurant.

Woody and **Buzz** can be found at Woody's Picture Shootin' Corral at Pixar Place. The goofy **Green Army Men** are often around and will happily pause to take photos with you.

Meet-and-greet characters and times are subject to change, so check the My Disney Experience app or Times Guide on the day of your visit for the latest schedule.

GERARDO MORA/GETTY IMAGES ©

Oga's Cantina

Housed in what looks like a classic American Main St movie theater in **Animation Courtyard** at Disney's Hollywood Studios, Walt Disney Presents is a charming, interactive gallery showcasing Disney's incredible journey and creative, can-do, never-give-up attitude with priceless memorabilia from the Disney archives. This self-guided stroll through Walt Disney history takes about 15 minutes.

The incredible artifacts on display include a 1929 animation table, the 1930s studio desk where Walt worked on *Silly Symphonies* and *Snow White and the Seven Dwarfs*. An early concept model of the Magic Kingdom's Cinderella Castle, as well as the original audio-animatronic Abraham Lincoln from the 1964 New York World's Fair, represent his early steps toward creating the 'Happiest Place on Earth.' Perhaps the most poignant item is Walt's second-grade desk, from Park Elementary School in Marceline, Missouri. See if you can spot his initials, carved into the desk when he was a schoolboy.

The attraction also screens a 15-minute film of Walt Disney's life in the **Walt Disney Theater**. Display cases outside the theater showcase items from upcoming Disney films.

QUICK-SERVE EATERIES AT DISNEY'S HOLLYWOOD STUDIOS

Min & Bill's Dockside Diner
Food stand paying tribute to the 1930 Pre-Code MGM comedy-drama *Min and Bill* and its sequel *Tugboat Annie*. **$$**

Woody's Lunch Box
A walk-up window-style restaurant, housed in a retro lunch box. Gourmet takes on kiddie food favorites. **$$**

Catalina Eddie's
Located on Sunset Blvd, this modest eatery focuses on pizzas and Caesar salads. **$$**

Rock 'n' Roller Coaster

TAKE A RIDE WITH AEROSMITH

The **Rock 'n' Roller Coaster Starring Aerosmith** whisks passengers off to a concert via a super-stretch limousine. The highlight of this coaster is its high-speed launch: thanks to its linear motor electromagnetic technology, the coaster propels riders from 0 to 57mph in less than three seconds. Iconic Los Angeles radio DJ Bill St James greets listeners and riders, after which a traffic report notes unusually high traffic. A highway sign flashes 'Traffic bug you? Then STEP on it!' before launching the limo into a replicated highway tunnel and then through the crazy, simulated streets of LA. As you ride through three inversions, including a sea-serpent roll and a corkscrew, you'll feel the force of up to 5Gs.

Strobe lights and the specially recorded Aerosmith soundtrack give this thrilling ride a true live rock concert feel, as 'Love in an Elevator' morphs into 'Love on a roller coaster.' Each limousine coaster car holds a total of 120 speakers: two midrange speakers, two tweeters surrounding each individual rider and a powerful subwoofer placed under the seat. As each coaster features different Aerosmith songs, every ride offers fans an altogether new concert coasting experience. Limo license plate UGOBABE plays 'Love in an Elevator' and 2FAST4U plays 'Sweet Emotion.'

Lightning McQueen's Racing Academy

START YOUR ENGINES

Lightning McQueen is the star car who learns that there's more to life than winning the race in *Cars,* the hit Disney Pixar movie set in a world populated by anthropomorphic vehicles. Stranded in the remote Route 66–inspired town of Radiator Springs, McQueen meets a cast of car-centric characters that show him what it means to be a true champion.

The high-octane, high-jinks Lightning McQueen's Racing Academy puts you in the driver's seat in a state-of-the-art race-car simulator, with a wraparound screen that will make you feel like you're no longer in Orlando but instead cruising across America's Mother Road. Lightning McQueen, a full-size animatronic, kicks off the 10-minute show by demonstrating the tricks of the car-racing trade, with support from his bestie, Tow Mater. As a rookie racer you'll test your skills on the track, with race-car trainer Cruz Ramirez evaluating your skills along the way. While the attraction is geared toward young children (read: those who don't meet the height requirements

OGA'S CANTINA

Oga's Cantina, located in Star Wars: Galaxy's Edge, is earth's only smuggler-friendly cantina. Just like the cantina featured in the movie, this bar is loud and usually crowded with revelers, and though small bites are served, the emphasis is on cocktails. Playful cocktails like the grapefruit-infused Jedi Mind Trick and the yuzu-puree Bespin Fizz are refreshing, too, while the mocktails are perfect for anyone looking to sip the world of *Star Wars* minus the booze. Droid DJ R-3X, a former Starspeeder 3000 pilot, spins the otherworldly tunes from his DJ booth, and it's almost impossible not to feel the urge to get up and dance, or at least tap your feet along to the oddball beat.

GRAB-AND-GO SNACK SPOTS AT DISNEY'S HOLLYWOOD STUDIOS

Dinosaur Gertie's Ice Cream of Extinction
Ice-cream stand inspired by the silver-screen dinosaur that now bathes in Echo Lake. **$**

The Trolley Car Café
Grab your fave Starbucks drink and pastry or sandwich for a quick on-the-go breakfast. **$**

Epic Eats
This *Indiana Jones*–style dessert canteen serves funnel cakes, a favorite carnival treat. **$**

MAGIC SHOT PHOTOPASS OPPS

Disney PhotoPass photographers roam the parks to capture family memories on film. Some PhotoPass photo-opp sites offer an extra dose of pixie dust. Ask your photographer to transform your standard pic in front of an attraction into a 'Magic Shot,' and by the time it lands in your My Disney Experience account, you'll discover a little magic added to the frame: Tinker Bell in Magic Shots snapped along Hollywood Boulevard, or in Star Wars: Galaxy's Edge, a stellar backdrop of flying X-wings, or a porg posing on your shoulder. There's no extra charge for a Magic Shot. Minutes after your photo is snapped, your pictures are ready to view in your gallery - online or via the My Disney Experience app.

for many rides), the show will energize anyone who loves fast cars and fun.

Post-race, Lightning McQueen and Tow Mater regularly appear at the **Winner's Circle** (formerly Luigi's Garage) near the Streets of America for photo opps.

Tower of Terror

FALL INTO ANOTHER DIMENSION

Hop on the elevator and ascend, then descend...into the fifth dimension, in the Tower of Terror, a hotel that you can check into (and perhaps never leave). It's one of the most thrilling rides in Walt Disney World®, inspired by the TV series *The Twilight Zone* and a ramshackle hotel, recalling the Golden Age of Hollywood, with a wonky elevator.

Otis Elevator Company was used to building standard elevators when Disney tasked it with creating a vertical ride system. These elevator cars have cables that pull the cars down at speeds faster than a freefall. Powered by enormous motors located at the top of the tower hotel, the ride sees passengers drop multiple times at top speeds of 39mph, and may induce vertigo, especially when the wide elevator doors open in an instant, revealing a bird's-eye view of the park.

Disney Imagineers wanted Twilight Zone creator Rod Serling to be part of the intense attraction, so they pulled archival footage of him from the episode 'It's a Good Life' for the preshow scene.

A camera captures the wide-eyed fear of passengers as they freefall toward the hotel's basement. In the gift shop, the 'Lost & Found' desk of the hotel has been converted to display the ride photographs.

Star Wars: Rise of the Resistance

THE BATTLE BEGINS

Though it's located in sunny Orlando, **Star Wars: Galaxy's Edge** transports visitors to a remote frontier outpost on the planet Batuu populated by smugglers, stormtroopers, bounty hunters, and of course, fun-loving tourists.

The star of this faraway galaxy is the most technologically advanced theme-park attraction in existence today. Star Wars: Rise of the Resistance is a massive, trackless, 18-minute-long dark ride that immerses guests in a battle between the Resistance and the First Order.

As it's one of the most popular rides in the Disney theme parks, expect to wait in line; queue times can fluctuate from one to three hours, depending on the time of day.

WHERE TO DRINK AT DISNEY'S HOLLYWOOD STUDIOS

BaseLine Tap House
California craft ales, lagers and cider are paired with California-inspired snacks at this cheery pub.

Star Wars: Galaxy's Edge Milk Stand
Luke Skywalker drinks blue milk in *Star Wars: Episode IV – A New Hope*. Find the exotic drink here.

Tune-In Lounge
Sip mid-century-mod cocktails while watching TV classics at this retro bar.

Grauman's Chinese Theatre

The battle begins in the briefing room, where BB-8 and Rey escort you via turntable into the **Star Destroyer** where you board pod-like vehicles guided by R5 droids.

There are over 65 audio-animatronic figures so realistic you'll wonder if they're real, including towering AT-ATs (there are only two; the use of a mirror makes it look like there are four), plus stellar special effects like explosions, glowing lightsabers and blasters.

Celebrate victory by making a beeline post-ride to the covert **Savi's Workshop**, where you can create your very own customized lightsaber to take back to your home planet with help from the 'Gatherers.' Advance registration for this stellar shopping experience is recommended.

WHY I LOVE DISNEY'S HOLLYWOOD STUDIOS

Amy Bizzarri, writer

Disney's Hollywood Studios is the only theme park that manages to take me back in time to the Golden Age of Hollywood. In one afternoon, I can catch Mickey and Minnie on screen at Grauman's Chinese Theatre, dine on the classic Cobb salad at a replica of the eatery that invented it (the Brown Derby) and drop into the fifth dimension after checking in to the Tower of Terror. And as a lifelong *Star Wars* fan, climbing aboard a starspeeder and traveling to a galaxy far, far away makes me feel like a 10-year-old girl again. I like to think that I'm too cool for character meet-and-greets, but I'll never pass up a quick side hug with Chewbacca.

WHERE TO STAY AT DISNEY'S HOLLYWOOD STUDIOS

Disney's Coronado Beach Resort
A lakeside oasis with a swimming pool centered by a 50ft replica Mayan pyramid. **$$$**

Disney's Art of Animation Resort
Budget-friendly choice offering daily drawing classes in the Children's Playroom. **$$**

Disney's Pop Century Resort
Experience fads of the 1950s through to the 1990s at this resort connected to Hollywood Studios by the Skyliner. **$$**

DISNEY'S ANIMAL KINGDOM

Around 2000 animals representing 300 species of wildlife, including Sumatran tigers, western lowland gorillas and cotton-top tamarin monkeys, live here in Disney's Animal Kingdom, the wildest theme park of all. Half theme park and half zoo, it's also the greenest, and the calmest, of all the Disney theme parks.

The park's key attraction, Kilimanjaro Safaris, whisks guests away in an open-sided safari vehicle over savannas, rivers and rocky hills to spot African animals. Pandora – The World of Avatar brings James Cameron's 2009 film *Avatar* to life with its mystical, immense, yet intricate landscapes. The Expedition Everest train climbs up to the peak of the tallest (artificial) mountain in the world, Forbidden Mountain, where a frightening yeti lurks. The massive Tree of Life centers Animal Kingdom, reminding us that we all play a role in the mystical circle of life.

TOP TIP

As with all Walt Disney World® parks, the crowds here are at their lowest in the morning. The animals are most active in the mornings, too, and tend to seek shady spots for a nap during hot Orlando afternoons. Arrive at park opening to enjoy smaller crowds and see the animals out and about.

Entrance, Animal Kingdom

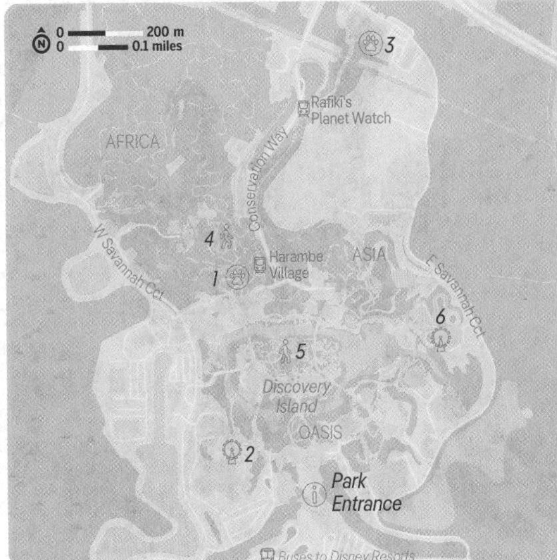

SIGHTS
1 Kilimanjaro Safaris
2 Pandora – The World of Avatar
3 Rafiki's Planet Watch

ACTIVITIES, COURSES & TOURS
4 Gorilla Falls Exploration Trail
5 Tree of Life

ENTERTAINMENT
6 Expedition Everest

The Tree of Life

EXPERIENCE THE CIRCLE OF LIFE

At 145ft tall, the massive Tree of Life is a marvel of modern engineering. It was built, leaf by leaf, over the course of 18 months, with 20 artists carving the 50ft-wide trunk with the shapes of over 300 animals. The trunk is steadied with a refitted oil platform, while 45 secondary branches lead up to the tree's crown of more than 103,000 leaves.

For a close-up view of the animal carvings, take a self-guided hike along the picturesque **Discovery Island Trails**, serene paths, wooden footbridges and cave-like tunnels below the great tree. The Disney story of the tree's origins begins with an ant that planted a seed and asked for a tree to provide shelter for all the animals, and a homage to the ant that inspired the tree can be found through a knothole in the tree's carvings – a sweet reminder of the interconnected nature of earth's creatures, from the tiny ant to the towering giraffe.

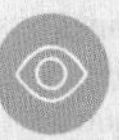

BEST ADVENTUROUS ATTRACTIONS

Step into the shoes of a paleontologist or a river navigator, or enter a bug's world at these three Animal Kingdom attractions.

Dinosaur's trackless ride vehicles
Travel back to prehistoric times, where dinos lurk in the darkness.

Kali River Rapids
Get soaked as you navigate a wild river with a 30ft drop as a finale.

It's Tough to be a Bug
This 4D movie attraction stars the tiny characters of the Pixar movie *A Bug's Life*. Watch out for the stink bug!

WHERE TO EAT AND DRINK IN DISNEY'S ANIMAL KINGDOM

Yak & Yeti Restaurant
At the base of Expedition Everest, serving dishes from various Asian regions. Vegetarian options abound. **$$**

Harambe Market
Savor African-inspired fare at this open-air spot. *Lion King* fans will want to save room for a Simba cupcake. **$$**

Boma
In the Animal Kingdom Lodge, with an all-you-can-eat buffet featuring dishes from over 50 African countries. **$$$**

GIRAFFE HABITATS

Standing up to 20ft in height, giraffes are the world's tallest land animal. They're also among the most fascinating, thanks to their long, stately necks and unique spotted patterns. Disney's Animal Kingdom is home to a herd of giraffes, who can usually be found browsing high in the treetops at their Kilimanjaro Safaris habitat.

See if you can spot the moats and fences, camouflaged with greenery, that keep them within their designated living space, or the giraffe feeders camouflaged as broken tree limbs.

The **Uzima Overlook**, located at Disney's Animal Kingdom Lodge's Jambo House, is home to yet another herd of giraffes. The concierge desk here offers the use of night-vision goggles for viewings between sundown and 9:30am.

Giraffe

Kilimanjaro Safaris

WILD AND FREE

Kilimanjaro Safaris simulates an East African safari adventure, with an open-sided safari vehicle taking guests through lush scenery. At 110 acres, the safari grounds are the largest attraction in any Disney theme park in the world – the Magic Kingdom could just about fit inside the safari space. Every expedition is a unique experience, as the animals sometimes nap out of sight or leap into view. You might spot a hippo bathing, a lion perched on a rock or a family of giraffes grazing.

Though the animals in the park seem to be roaming wild and free, with no animal barriers in sight, this is perhaps the safest safari on the planet. Disney revolutionized the world of animal habitats by creating large-scale spaces that used water features, moats and camouflaged fences to create barriers, with a carefully curated collection of fauna and flora, including millions of trees, grasses and shrubs from every continent except Antarctica. Here you have the chance to see some of the most powerful animals on the planet, including rhinos, hippos and crocodiles, up close and personal – minus the danger factor.

WHERE TO EAT AND DRINK IN DISNEY'S ANIMAL KINGDOM

Tusker House Restaurant
Meet your favorite costumed characters as you munch on warm cinnamon rolls and more at the breakfast buffet. **$$**

Tiffins Restaurant
Take a global culinary journey at this restaurant featuring inventive takes on classic dishes from three continents. **$$$**

Pongu Pongu Lounge
The Pandora has its own bar, where you can order a Night Blossom, a glowing, rainbow-colored limeade.

Pandora – The World of Avatar

THE WORLD OF AVATAR

While animals are the heart of Disney's Animal Kingdom, Pandora – The World of Avatar transports guests to mysterious landscapes where other curious creatures roam. Hop on the back of a winged banshee for an incredible airborne ride through Pandora aboard **Avatar Flight of Passage**, a 3D flying simulator considered one of the best rides in Walt Disney World. Fuel up after your aerial adventures at the **Satu'li Canteen**, a tranquil, fast-casual restaurant decorated with Na'vi art.

Expedition Everest

FORBIDDEN MOUNTAIN

Expedition Everest is a tea-company-run train that climbs up to the snow-capped peak of the tallest (artificial) mountain in the world, **Forbidden Mountain**. It took three years, 5000 tons of steel, 10,000 tons of concrete, 2000 gallons of paint and $100 million to build the 200ft-high mountain and its coaster, once listed in the *Guinness World Records* as the most expensive roller coaster in the world. The imposing mountain is surrounded by the mythical kingdom of Anandapur ('City of Happiness').

Near the mountain's base camp lies a jungle, located just past the entrance to Kali River Rapids. The self-guided **Maharajah Jungle Trek** introduces visitors to fascinating creatures, including acrobatic gibbons, a komodo dragon (the largest lizard in the world) and herbivorous tapirs. Mysterious Malayan flying foxes, among the largest known bats, also hang from vines, while tigers regally await passersby from their dedicated temple, and three water buffalo named Rose, Dorothy and Blanche (after *The Golden Girls*) graze gracefully.

The frightening **yeti** lurking at the mountain peak is the largest and most complex audio-animatronic figure ever built by Walt Disney Imagineering. At 25ft tall, he has also earned the nickname 'Disco Yeti' due to the strobe lights that flash on him, mimicking movement.

Rafiki's Planet Watch

CONSERVATION STATION

Board the Wildlife Express Train in fictional Harambe, Africa, for a peaceful seven-minute, 1.2-mile journey to reach the Conservation Station at Rafiki's Planet Watch, an area dedicated to the preservation and conservation of animals.

DISNEY WILDERNESS EXPLORERS

For a fun way to increase your animal knowledge, set out on a series of wild nature-themed challenges as you work toward becoming an official Disney Wilderness Explorer. Complete 25 animal-themed challenges at special stations around the park, and you'll earn the chance to take the Wilderness Explorer oath. The self-guided activities are free (and secretly educational) and range from taking notes on animal behavior to practicing important wilderness survival skills.

Begin the challenge by picking up a free *Wilderness Explorer* handbook from headquarters – located on the bridge between the Oasis and Discovery Island – or drop by Wilderness Explorer Troop Leader locations in Africa, Rafiki's Planet Watch, Asia, DinoLand USA or Pandora – The World of Avatar.

WHERE TO GET SNACKS IN DISNEY'S ANIMAL KINGDOM

Isle of Java
Start your day here with the perfect breakfast on the go: mini cinnamon buns with coffee-caramel sauce. **$**

Mr Kamal's
The seasoned fries here have four different types of sweet and savory dipping sauce. **$**

Yak & Yeti
Chicken fried rice in a convenient to-go container – the perfect snack to enjoy as you stroll the park. **$**

STAYING COOL IN DISNEY'S ANIMAL KINGDOM

Though it's immersed in lush greenery, Disney's Animal Kingdom is considered the hottest and most humid of all the Disney theme parks. To stay cool, aim for an early morning arrival, bring a portable fan (also available at most gift shops) or head into an air-con-chilled theater (eg It's Tough to be a Bug) during the hottest part of the day. Take a cue from the animals, who seek shade and nap in the afternoon heat, escaping back to your hotel for the afternoon, or enjoy the park after sunset. Stay hydrated by bringing a water bottle and refilling it at water stations around the park, and ride Kali River Rapids for a guaranteed big splash of cool water.

Alpacas, cows, deer, miniature donkeys, goats, llamas, pigs and sheep live here, and some of them can be seen playing with their soccer balls or monkeying around on the playground equipment. Tarantulas, millipedes, scorpions and snakes reside here, too, but they're safe and sound in glass habitats. Follow the outdoor walking trail to see the resident cotton-top tamarin monkeys.

Glimpse vets in action at the **Veterinary Treatment Room** or watch as experts prep animal-friendly meals at the **Nutrition Center**.

At the **Animation Experience** at the Conservation Station, guests can learn how to draw the beloved animal characters featured in popular Disney films and create a personalized piece featuring Simba, Nala, Jafar, Pumbaa or Timon from *The Lion King*. Each session is different so guests are encouraged to visit often in order to complete their collection. And be on the lookout for Rafiki himself, as he loves to pose for photos with visitors to his conservation-minded corner of the park.

Gorilla Falls Exploration Trail

GORILLAS IN THE MIST

A troop (family) of western lowland gorillas, the world's largest primates, calls Disney's Animal Kingdom home. Meet them on the Gorilla Falls Exploration Trail, a winding path, three-eighths of a mile in length, where you'll encounter animals at every turn.

Along the way, meerkats often mingle on their rocky perch and zebras can usually be found grazing on the savanna. Smaller animals live here, too, including the adorable Arabian spiny mouse, the naked mole-rat and the pancake tortoise.

Over 20 species of birds can be spotted flying overhead or nesting in the trees along the trail, including the African olive pigeon, the tambourine dove and the snowy-crowned robin-chat.

But the primates that graze on their lush, hilly home are perhaps the most awesome of all. During your self-guided tour, observation stations make it easy to spot the gorillas and learn more about Disney's global conservation efforts to protect their habitats. It's hard to miss **Gino**, the park's resident 400lb silverback. One of the first gorillas in the world to allow his caretakers to perform a cardiac ultrasound without anesthesia, Gino helped launch a new method to protect his fellow gorillas from cardiac issues. He's a father, too, and can often be spotted roughhousing with his juvenile sons.

WHERE TO GET SNACKS IN DISNEY'S ANIMAL KINGDOM

Satu'li Canteen
Try the cheeseburger pods: bao-style buns stuffed with ground beef, ketchup, mustard, pickle and cheddar cheese. **$**

Tamu Tamu Refreshments
Its Simba Sunset is a pineapple-spiked soft-serve ice cream served with a swirl of sweet watermelon syrup. **$**

Drinkwallah
Cool off with a frozen Coca-Cola from this kiosk. **$**

EPCOT

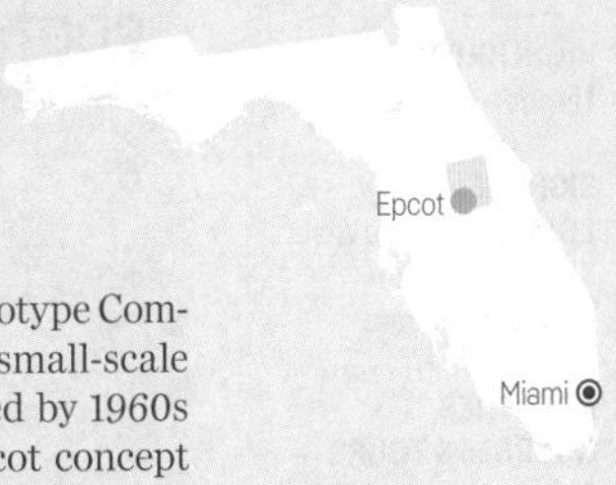

When Walt Disney envisioned the Experimental Prototype Community of Tomorrow (Epcot), he hoped to create a small-scale city to counter the inefficient infrastructure created by 1960s urban sprawl. But after his death in 1966, the Epcot concept was scrapped when it was realized it wouldn't be easy to run an actual city. So in 1982 Epcot opened as a theme park instead.

Spaceship Earth stands as the park's symbolic icon, and the park is divided into four 'neighborhoods.' World Showcase and World Celebration bring the world to Florida, with 11 pavilions representing various countries, including Norway, where Frozen Ever After guides guests on a boat through Elsa's snowy kingdom, and France, where you can hop inside Ratatouille and spin through a Parisian restaurant. World Nature and World Discovery have natural-world and STEM-focused rides and interactive exhibits. Don't miss Test Track, a high-octane simulated concept-car testing experience, and Mission: SPACE, a centrifugal motion simulator that recreates a NASA launch.

TOP TIP

Epcot is home to a world of culinary delights. If there's a full-service restaurant that you really want to try, don't forget to make a reservation up to 60 days in advance. Some places, such as Space 220 Restaurant, will have their advance reservations filled within minutes of making them available.

Entrance, Epcot

HIGHLIGHTS
1 Mission: SPACE

SIGHTS
2 Soarin' Around the World
3 Spaceship Earth
4 World Showcase

ACTIVITIES, COURSES & TOURS
5 Fantasia Gardens & Fairways

ENTERTAINMENT
6 Living with the Land

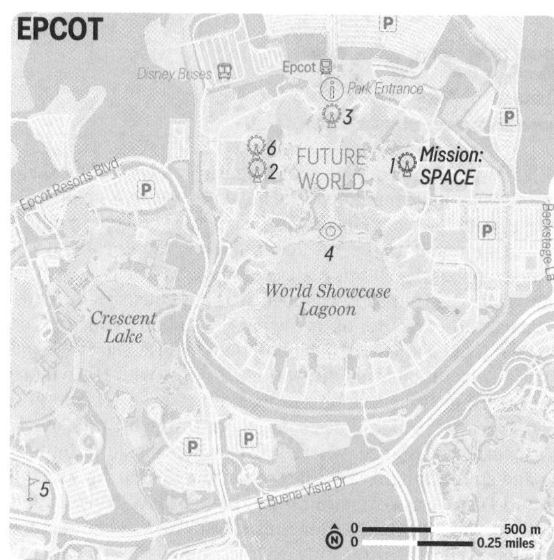

BEHIND THE SEEDS TOUR

The **Living with the Land Behind the Seeds Tour** whisks visitors behind the scenes for a tour of the fish farm and greenhouses that make up **The Land** pavilion. Learn more about the catfish and shrimp that make their way from the fish farm to restaurants around Walt Disney World®, discover new plant-growing techniques and learn about raising mega-sized, Disney-character-shaped fruits. You'll even get to sample one grown on-site! Make your reservation for the tour on the My Disney Experience app. You'll be on your feet for this tour, so wear comfortable shoes.

Spaceship Earth

EXPERIMENTAL PROTOTYPE COMMUNITY OF TOMORROW

It took almost two years to construct the 180ft-tall, 16-million-lb Spaceship Earth, the first large-scale geodesic sphere ever built. Spaceship Earth isn't just an architectural icon – it also houses an attraction of the same name, which takes guests on a 15-minute ride through time, in vehicles traveling along a track that spirals up to the top of the sphere.

Science fiction writer Ray Bradbury, author of *The Martian Chronicles,* helped write the original storyline for the ride. In a 1982 interview with *OMNI* magazine, Bradbury shared his thoughts on the park: 'What Disney is doing is showing the world that there are alternative ways to do things that can make us all happy. If we can borrow some of the concepts of Disneyland and Disney World and Epcot, then indeed the world can be a better place.'

Living with the Land

DISNEY-STYLE FARMING

Living with the Land, an innovative, educational attraction in Epcot, is not just a 12-minute boat ride through a fantastical

TABLE-SERVICE DINING IN EPCOT

Coral Reef Restaurant
Dine with marine creatures at the Seas with Nemo & Friends pavilion, overlooking the living coral reef. **$$$**

Via Napoli
In the Italy pavilion, serving traditional, Neapolitan-style pizzas in ovens named after notorious volcanoes. **$$$**

Yorkshire County Fish Shop
Enjoy batter-fried fish and chips and draft beer over views of the World Showcase Lagoon in the UK pavilion. **$$$**

garden – it's also a forward-thinking farm and research facility dedicated to experimental horticulture and hydroponics. The amazing fruit and veggies grown here (along with fish) are served at restaurants across Walt Disney World.

Your boat journey will carry you through a series of greenhouse labs to see futuristic growing techniques in action. One greenhouse holds a vertical garden, where Disney's 'tomato tree' grows along a special trellis. In 2006 it set the record for the largest and most productive tomato plant in the world, when it produced over 32,000 tomatoes in just 16 months! Yet another greenhouse highlights hydroponics, a method of growing plants using just water and nutrients, which researchers here use to produce over 27,000 heads of lettuce.

In the equally dirt-free **Aeroponics** greenhouse, plant roots dangle freely in the air and are periodically sprayed with a fine mist of nutrients. Epcot partnered with NASA to explore aeroponics as a potential food-producing technique for a long-term space mission. Veggie crops grow directly above the tanks of striped bass, tilapia, catfish and freshwater shrimp.

The most incredible produce on display here include Mickey-shaped pumpkins and cucumbers – they're grown in plastic molds – and lemons that can weigh upwards of 15lb!

Soarin' Around the World

TRAVEL THE WORLD IN FIVE MINUTES

Buckle up and get ready to lift off on a hang glider and soar over six of the seven continents and the world's most iconic landmarks. Fly over the snow-capped Alps, glide above the Great Pyramids of Egypt, wave hello to polar bears in Greenland, swoop past elephants marching toward Mt Kilimanjaro and ride over the Iguazu Falls' rapids. Soarin' Around the World, arguably the most inspiring ride in Epcot, brings the world to you. Though this flight promises zero turbulence, ask to be seated to the far right in the back row if you have a fear of heights.

Soarin' riders board their 'paraglider,' an 87-passenger vehicle that uses a cantilever system to lift you into the air, where you'll be surrounded by a 180-degree dome screen. As the vehicle sways gracefully toward the center of the dome, the ride simulates flight. Riders are seatbelted, but your dangling feet will add to the illusion that you're gliding over the world.

Pleasant scents synced to the visual scenes are added, including rose blossoms in the Taj Mahal scene, and a South Pacific ocean breeze as you sail above the islands of Fiji. See if you can spot the 'hidden Mickey' that forms when fireworks blast off above Spaceship Earth in the final, celebratory scene.

EPCOT'S INTERNATIONAL FLOWER & GARDEN FESTIVAL

Every spring, Epcot at Walt Disney World® bursts into bloom during its nearly three-month-long International Flower & Garden Festival. While the Epcot gardenscapes are always a delight, this cherished festival elevates the gardens of Epcot up a notch. The Disney-character-shaped topiaries that pop up across the park are true 'shrubs of art,' with new characters appearing on the green scene every year. A few favorite topiaries also return year after year, including Tinker Bell, who wears a dress made from reindeer moss.

Hundreds of butterflies flutter into the festival's **Goodness Garden Butterfly House**, where you just might see cocoons transforming into butterflies.

QUICK-SERVE EATERIES IN EPCOT

Katsura Grill
One of the healthiest quick-service places in Epcot, with options including sushi, ramen and vegetable udon. **$$**

Regal Eagle Smokehouse
The mouthwatering BBQ ribs, brisket and smoked chicken served here come with a thick slice of garlic Texas toast. **$$**

Kabuki Café
Cool off with *kakigōri* (shaved ice flavored with syrup and condensed milk) in the Japan pavilion. **$$**

WORLD SHOWCASE WINE WALK

Sip the world's top-rated wines in a single evening on the 1.2-mile World Showcase Wine Walk, which gives guests the chance to sip, savor and stroll across six continents from one evocative wine cellar to the next. Begin your wine journey, centered around the sparkling lagoon, in the Germany pavilion at the **Weinkeller**, a cozy wine bar lined with fine German wines.

Next stop: Italy, where the rustic **Tutto Gusto Wine Cellar** welcomes wine lovers with 200-plus dazzling vintages and a small-plates menu focused on Italian wine and cheese pairings. Mere steps away at **Les Vins des Chefs de France**, world-class sommeliers pour wine and the champagne flows.

Mission: SPACE

FEEL THE FORCE OF UP TO 2.5 GS

If you've ever wondered what it would feel like to be an astronaut rocketing toward deep space, head for Mission: SPACE, a ride that simulates a NASA-style mission to Mars.

Real-life astronauts were on hand to inaugurate the ride when it opened in 2003. Four separate spinning centrifuges recreate the sensation of blasting off into space. The ride is so intense – riders experience a force up to 2.5 Gs, more than twice the force of gravity – that Imagineers installed fans to prevent nausea, and motion-sickness bags were also added in case any astronauts in training feel a tad too much force.

Passengers can also choose from two missions. The orange mission is the most intense, and riders need to be 44in or taller to experience its simulated space launch and reentry. The green mission is the family-friendlier option, with a launch that has more laughter and no spinning at all, though passengers still need to be 40in or taller to ride.

Kids that don't meet the height requirement can still explore deep space at **Space Base**, a climbable play area located at the exit of Mission: SPACE. Try the astronaut ice cream available at the dedicated, space-themed gift shop, **Cargo Bay**, where a life-sized astronaut Mickey Mouse greets customers.

Fantasia Gardens & Fairways

THE FANTASTICAL WORLD OF MINI GOLF

Located across from the Swan and Dolphin Resorts in the Epcot resort area, Fantasia Gardens & Fairways has two 18-hole mini-golf courses, both themed after the movie *Fantasia* and offering a tranquil escape from the busy parks.

Putt-putt through five whimsical scenes featuring *Fantasia's* tutu-clad hippos and dancing mushrooms. Beware of the marching broomsticks – they love to surprise passersby with a splash. Good shots are rewarded with musical tones, and the Pastoral Symphony is represented by a 40ft-tall Mt Olympus, complete with waterfalls.

Voted the longest and most challenging mini-golf course in the world by *Golf Digest*, **Fantasia Fairways** is a traditional golf course built on a miniature scale and is great for families with mini-golf experience. Sand traps, bunkers, water hazards and sloping greens make this a course of skill over chance.

QUICK-SERVE EATERIES IN EPCOT

Les Halles Boulangerie & Patisserie
Say *'bonjour'* to soups, quiches and sandwiches made from freshly baked French breads. **$$**

Lotus Blossom Cafe
Chinese takeout meets Disney at this go-to spot for Mongolian beef, orange chicken and chicken fried rice. **$$**

Sunshine Seasons
Tacos, stir-fries, salads, veggie korma, pizza...there's something for everyone at this cafe in The Land pavilion. **$$**

Les Halles Boulangerie & Patisserie

World Showcase

TRAVEL THE GLOBE AT ONE LOCATION

At World Showcase, Epcot's 1.3-mile-long lakefront exhibit, country-themed pavilions celebrate unique cuisine, architecture and cultural traditions. Start your day with croissants at **Les Halles Boulangerie & Patisserie** in the France pavilion, then take a 4D whirl through a restaurant aboard your very own rat vehicle at **Remy's Ratatouille Adventure**. The Mexico pavilion's Mesoamerican pyramid towers over the **World Showcase Lagoon** and houses a restaurant with a twilight market backdrop and **The Three Caballeros**, a slow boat ride through Mexico led by Donald Duck. Meet Anna and Elsa at the **Royal Sommerhus** in the Norway pavilion and set off on a slow boat journey through Arendelle on **Frozen Ever After**. In the China pavilion, a replica of Beijing's Temple of Heaven offers an immersive **Circle-Vision 360°** visit to China. The Germany pavilion's **Biergarten Restaurant** recreates an open-air beer garden at twilight, complete with a live polka band, while the **Via Napoli Ristorante** in the

MITSUKOSHI – EPCOT'S EPIC DEPARTMENT STORE

Housed in a sprawling, two-story building reminiscent of an imperial ceremonial hall, the Japan pavilion's **Mitsukoshi Department Store** offers more than shopping till you drop. Separated into four key zones named Festivity, Silence, Harmony and Interest, this location is the only outpost of the department-store chain to be found outside Japan (its first location was founded in Tokyo in 1673!). It's filled to the brim with imported items rarely sold in the US, including the ever-elusive green-tea KitKat bars, traditional kimonos and every flavor of marble-capped Ramune soda under the sun. Disney characters share shelf space here with iconic anime characters such as Hello Kitty and Pokémon. Legendary Mikimoto pearls are also available for sale.

WHERE TO DRINK IN EPCOT

Choza de Margarita
The signature margaritas (on the rocks or frozen) feature unique flavors like blackberry and blood orange.

Champagne Kiosk
Toast the end of a beautiful day with bubbly at this belle-epoque-style stand at the France pavilion's waterfront.

Joy of Tea
Beyond specialty teas, this beverage cart serves Tsingtao beer and China-inspired cocktails.

THE TEMPLE OF HEAVEN

With its picturesque gardens dotted with lotus-filled ponds, festive footbridges and colorful, detailed architecture, Epcot's China pavilion is centered by a perfect, half-size replica of the **Hall of Prayer for Good Harvests**, part of the Temple of Heaven, the imperial complex of religious buildings founded in Beijing in the 15th century. This was where the Emperors of the Ming and Qing dynasties sent their prayers for a bountiful harvest directly up to heaven.

Step inside the temple, say your own wish aloud, and, if you're standing at exactly the precise spot, your voice will literally rise up toward the heavens. Because this special room is acoustically perfect, your voice will bounce off the dome and be directed straight back at you.

CLAUDIAH/SHUTTERSTOCK ©

Kakigōri

Italy pavilion serves wood-fired Neapolitan pizzas; look out for the authentic Venetian gondolas docked on the lakefront. Snack on edamame and *kakigōri* at the Japan Pavilon's **Kabuki Café**, or strike a pose with Aladdin and Jasmine and feast on baklava at the Morocco pavilion. Get lost in the hedge maze and take in afternoon tea at the UK pavilion, or try the best steaks in Walt Disney World® at the **Le Cellier Steakhouse** in the Canada pavilion, and stock up on maple syrup and NHL apparel at **Northwest Mercantile**.

WHERE TO STAY NEAR EPCOT

Disney's Beach Club Resort
New England coastal charm, a 3-acre water park overlooking Crescent Lake, and only two minutes' walk to Epcot. **$$$**

Disney's Yacht Club Resort
Also on Crescent Lake, with the feel of a swanky, nautical club. Shares amenities with the adjacent Beach Club. **$$$**

Walt Disney World Swan
This slightly more budget-friendly 750-plus-room Marriott-owned option is just a short boat ride or walk from Epcot. **$$$**

DISNEY SPRINGS

Shop till you drop at 100-plus stores and play all day at Disney Springs, a vast entertainment district stretching along a lake teeming with Amphicars – mid-20th-century automobiles that can travel on land and water. Beyond the unique shops, you'll also find a multiplex, Cirque du Soleil, a waterfront concert venue, a mini choo choo train, a retro bowling alley, a classic Venetian merry-go-round and a tethered, hot-air balloon experience. Disney Springs is also a dining destination, with over 60 bars and restaurants to choose from, plus an AMC dine-in theater with 24 screening rooms where food and drinks are delivered right to your seat. Savor sunset while having drinks along the waterfront at Dockside Margaritas, sample Pan-Asian fare while relaxing on Morimoto's open-air patio or indulge in out-of-the-ordinary ice-cream flavors at the family-run Salt & Straw... there's an eatery to fit every taste bud under the Florida sun.

TOP TIP

The Art of Disney shop is more a gallery than a souvenir boutique, displaying Disney limited-edition paintings, prints and more. The store also stocks original Disney animation cels. Short for 'celluloid,' cels are animation drawings traced (or machine-transferred for later films) on transparent plastic sheets. Renowned Disney artists make special appearances and sign their pieces.

Amphicars, Disney Springs (p244)

ACTIVITIES, COURSES & TOURS
1 Aerophile

EATING
2 Boathouse
3 The Edison

SHOPPING
4 Disney's Pin Traders

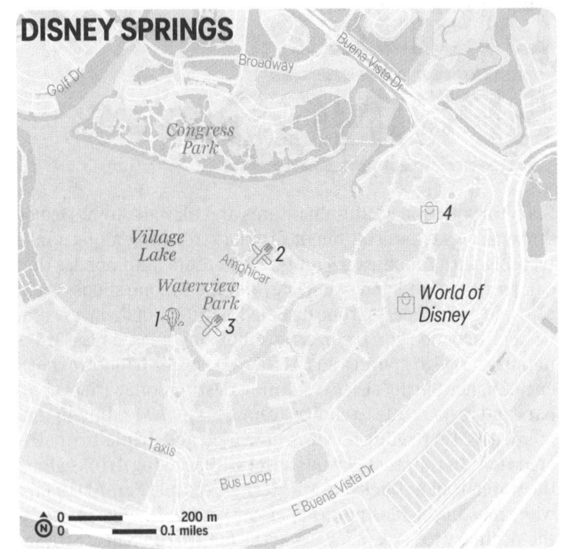

LIVE-MUSIC VENUES IN DISNEY SPRINGS

One of Disney Springs' most popular late-night hangouts, **Raglan Road** offers Irish pub fare plus live Celtic music and dancers.

Fuel up with 30-plus types of tequila, then get down on the always hoppin' dance floor at **Paradiso 37**, a restaurant/bar with an upbeat, live-music-driven atmosphere.

The legendary **House of Blues** pairs southern bites with the best blues musicians from across the US. Cabaret-style seating promises every guest a great view of the stage. It also hosts one of the best Sunday brunches in Orlando, with special guest singers.

Marketplace Stage hosts free live music throughout the year, with a beautiful Lake Buena Vista backdrop to boot.

Amphicars

BY LAND AND SEA

An incredible new vehicle made quite a splash when it was launched at the 1961 New York Auto Show: the Amphicar Model 770, an amphibious automobile that can travel on land and water. The West German manufacturer anticipated sales of 25,000 units, but the fad fizzled due to the car's poor performance and the fact that, after it operated in water, its rear seat needed to be removed to grease 13 points in the motor. By 1965, after fewer than 4000 Amphicars came off the assembly line, production had stopped. Only 400 exist worldwide today.

Disney Springs' **Boathouse** is the only place in the world where you can take a land and water tour in a vintage Amphicar. Restaurateur and car collector Steven Schussler is the creator of three other Disney Springs' restaurant concepts: **Rainforest Café**, **Yak & Yeti**, and **T-Rex**. He dreamed up the upscale waterfront restaurant, where vehicles serving as both retro dreamboats and slow-moving cars shuttle guests to and fro. Highly trained captains pick up patrons curbside and then plunge them into the water.

WHERE TO EAT IN DISNEY SPRINGS

Boathouse
Enjoy waterfront views, jumbo lump crab cakes, shrimp and andouille mac 'n' cheese, and other seafood delights. **$$$**

Morimoto Asia
The sushi at TV star and chef Masaharu Morimoto's restaurant is consistently voted among the best at Walt Disney World®. **$$$**

Sprinkles
Satisfy your sweet tooth here, where the Cupcake ATM dispenses treats even in the wee hours of the night. **$**

Traveling at 8mph on land and 7 knots in the water, the unique vehicles offer scenic 25-minute tours of Disney Springs landmarks, weather permitting. Walk-up reservations can be made at the **Boathouse BOATIQUE**.

Aerophile Balloon

BIRD'S-EYE VIEW OF WALT DISNEY WORLD®

At Disney Springs, a giant tethered balloon, among the biggest helium-filled balloons in the world, gives guests the chance to soar high above Orlando (like the characters in the movie *Up*), to a height of over 400ft, where views reaching up to 20 miles away also offer a bird's-eye glimpse of Walt Disney World®. The eight- to 10-minute experience on the Aerophile balloon is incredibly peaceful and gentle.

Built for Disney by the Paris-based company Aérophile, the **Aéro30** is the biggest balloon in town, one of only 60 mega-balloons operating around the world. The balloon, filled with 210,000 cu ft of helium, might not be able to carry you to the Amazon basin but will gently lift you far into the sky. The balloon's design highlights favorite Disney characters and changes every four years.

Pin Traders

SHOP, SWAP AND COLLECT

Disney pin trading – the buying and trading of collectible enamel pins featuring Disney characters, park attractions and special events – is a hobby officially supported and promoted by Walt Disney World®.

If you see a cast member wearing a pin lanyard, they'll be happy to trade with you. Their lanyards each have about a dozen unique pins. You may only trade two pins – genuine and in good shape – with the same cast member in one day.

Shops and kiosks throughout the parks and resorts each sell a unique inventory of pins. But the grand pooh-bah of pin-scoring spots is by far **Disney's Pin Traders**, a mega-store that sells almost every new pin under the sun. Thousands of them line the walls and kiosks of this colorful store. As the premier pin-trading destination, Disney's Pin Traders also hosts daily and monthly pin-trading events. Everything you need to showcase your pins is available here, including lanyards, vests, pin books, bags and hats.

Disney pins come with a Mickey-shaped rubber backing, but they can still fall off while you're having fun at the parks. So if you have some special pins you want to keep safe, purchase locking pin backs as an extra precaution.

BOWLING IN DISNEY SPRINGS

The mid-century-modern, 45,000-sq-ft **Splitsville Luxury Lanes** takes bowling to an entirely new (luxury) level. With 30 lanes spread over two floors, the venue also features billiards, bars, live entertainment and TVs screening sports. During the day, kids are welcome, but in the evening, it's popular among adults looking to dine, drink, dance and bowl. Hand-rolled sushi, wood-oven-fired pizzas, handcrafted cocktails and fine wines go well beyond your typical bowling fare. You can get everything from gourmet burgers to overloaded nachos also delivered directly to your bowling lane. Plus the desserts are over-the-top and shareable.

Book your lane in advance so you can bowl down memory lane minus a long wait.

WHERE TO STAY IN DISNEY SPRINGS

Disney's Port Orleans Resort – Riverside
Evoking rural Louisiana with rooms overlooking the woods or the Sassagoula River. **$$$**

Disney's Port Orleans Resort – French Quarter
Wrought-iron balconies, antique lamps and a Mardi Gras–themed pool area. **$$$**

Grand Villas at Disney's Saratoga Springs Resort
Inspired by 19th-century wellness retreats, these villas sleep up to 12 adults. **$$$**

BEST BOUTIQUES IN DISNEY SPRINGS

Basin
Get pampered with all-natural body and hair-care products here.

LEGO Store
Challenge your kids to create a brick masterpiece at this store.

Stance
At this socks-only boutique you can find all your fave characters in sock form.

Super Hero Headquarters
Here, at the only Marvel-themed store at Walt Disney World, you can stock up on Avengers gear.

Crystal Arts
Every princess needs a handcrafted tiara from this store.

VIAVAL/ALAMY STOCK PHOTO ©

The Edison

The Edison

DANCE THE NIGHT AWAY

The Edison is an industrial steampunk, Gothic-themed hot spot for classic American cuisine and inventive, signature craft cocktails. With its seven distinct dining and bar areas and lakefront balcony views, it's one of the best places to eat and drink in Disney Springs. Its steady lineup of unique acts – family-friendly by day and edgy by night – makes for an especially memorable Disney dining experience. The massive, split-level space was designed to resemble an abandoned 1920s power plant, transporting guests to the Great Gatsby era.

If you want to dance the night away, the dance floor here is almost always hoppin': **The Pearl Street Players** house band is on call most evenings, playing the blues, before the rest of the evening's entertainment begins, ranging from burlesque dancers plucked from the roaring 20s to vintage-costumed aerialists. Stilt walkers are known to roam the space, while sleight-of-hand magicians visit tables and can trick unsuspecting guests. Advance reservations are highly recommended.

WHERE TO STAY IN DISNEY SPRINGS

Hilton Orlando Buena Vista Palace
Lakeside hotel with a pedestrian bridge leading to Disney Springs and Magic Kingdom shuttles. **$**

Wyndham Garden Lake Buena Vista
After a day at the parks take a dip in one of this hotel's two sparkling swimming pools. **$**

B Resort & Spa
This convenient hotel offers affordable, chic comfort and contemporary guest rooms, plus a full-service spa. **$**

UNIVERSAL ORLANDO RESORT

Universal Orlando Resort

Miami

Embrace your inner teenager with fast rides inspired by the biggest characters from movies, TV and pop culture at Universal Orlando Resort, the second-largest resort in Orlando after Walt Disney World®. Two incredible theme parks, including Volcano Bay (a water theme park), and a walkable shopping and dining district, CityWalk, offer endless opportunities for fun. Founded in 1990, Universal is the only resort in Orlando where you can choose your own roller-coaster soundtrack before reaching a maximum speed of 65mph, battle 120 animatronic aliens, step aboard the famed Hogwarts Express and enter the world of classic Marvel comic books. Though older kids will want to take on the thrilling roller coasters, six play areas, including Woody Woodpecker's KidZone, will delight younger ones, from toddlers to preschoolers. The eight hotels located within the resort complex are the most convenient options and offer choices at every budget level.

TOP TIP

Buy a pair of good walking shoes and put some miles on them before your trip. Unlike Walt Disney World®, there's really no transportation inside the Universal Orlando theme parks (apart from Hogwarts Express). Be prepared to walk, and also expect plenty of standing in line if you don't have an Express Pass.

TERRY KELLY/SHUTTERSTOCK ©

Entrance, Universal Orlando Resort

BEST PLACES TO EAT & DRINK IN CITYWALK

The Cowfish Sushi Burger Bar
Offers a new spin on surf and turf, with burgers and sandwiches made with sushi, and sushi created with burger ingredients. $$

Vivo Italian Kitchen
Watch chefs prep pizzas, pasta and other classic Italian mains. $$

Toothsome Chocolate Emporium & Savory Feast Kitchen
Serves everything from steaks to seafood, but is best known for its over-the-top milkshakes and sundaes. $$

Pat O'Brien's
Family-friendly by day, but by night locals and out-of-towners sip hurricanes at the restaurant's lively bar.

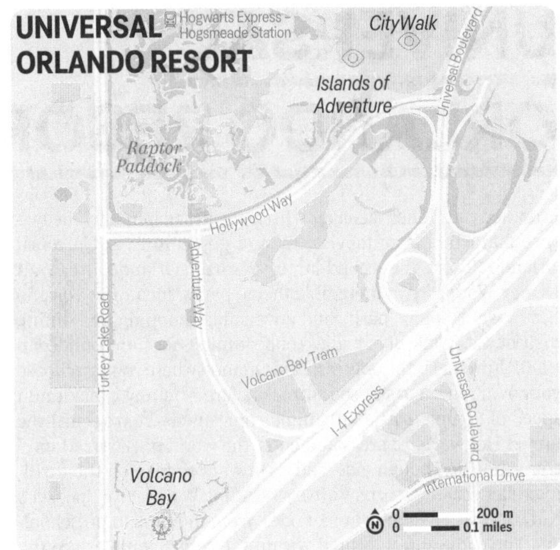

Volcano Bay

THE HEART OF AN ACTIVE VOLCANO

Make a splash at Universal's Volcano Bay. This half water park, half theme park is divided into four distinct areas, each inspired by the islands of Polynesia, with a 200ft volcano at its center. The volcano isn't flowing with lava but rather humans: it houses the **Ko'okiri Body Plunge**, the tallest body slide in America at 125ft, with a near-vertical (70-degree) drop, and the **Kala & Tai Nui Serpentine Body Slides**, the tallest drop-capsule slides in the world (125ft). The **Krakatau Aqua Coaster** is a water coaster that zips through the heart of the Krakatau volcano before plunging through a waterfall.

Families with little ones will enjoy **River Village**. Float on the lazy Kopiko Wai Winding River, or ride down Honu's two slides aboard multipassenger rafts. Toddlers to preschoolers can ride the (mini) slides and splash among the spray features at **Tot Tiki Reef** and **Runamukka Reef**.

Rainforest Village has the most high-thrill slides, including the multipassenger slide Maku, which shoots riders up

WHERE TO STAY IN UNIVERSAL ORLANDO RESORT

Loews Portofino Bay Hotel at Universal Orlando
Guests staying at this Italian-themed deluxe hotel can enjoy later stays at the parks. $$

Hard Rock Hotel at Universal Orlando
Orlando's most musical hotel: even the swimming pool streams underwater tunes. $$$

Loews Royal Pacific Resort at Universal Orlando
Settle into an elegant, island-style suite and enjoy exclusive theme-park benefits. $$$

high banks, while the Puihi whisks riders through multiple tunnels, two funnels and a final spellbinding drop. TeAwa, the 'Fearless River,' simulates white-water rafting.

Wave Village is home to Waturi Beach, the park's main, surf-worthy wave pool, and The Reef, a calm pool with relaxing, subtle waves.

CityWalk

'EPICENTER OF AWESOME'

Between Universal Studios and Islands of Adventure is CityWalk, an energetic hub featuring restaurants, shops and live entertainment. Start your day with a coffin full of colorful doughnuts from **Voodoo Doughnuts**. You can get tatted at **Hart & Huntington Tattoo Company**, one of Orlando's top-rated tattoo parlors, founded by motocross legend Carey Hart. Shop at the **Universal Studios Store**, the largest souvenir shop in Universal Orlando, then rock out with music-themed apparel and souvenirs at **The Rock Shop**, a rock-and-roll-themed boutique filled with instruments once played by famous musicians. Catch the latest flick at **Universal Cinemark**, where state-of-the-art projection and sound systems and oversized luxury recliners welcome film buffs, or play 18-hole mini golf with a 1950s sci-fi-movie backdrop at **Hollywood Drive-In Golf**.

Part museum, part restaurant, **Bob Marley – A Tribute to Freedom** recreates the legendary singer's Kingston home. Artifacts and photos surround diners, and the menu features Caribbean-influenced appetizers, mains and desserts. The iconic **Hard Rock Live Orlando** hosts touring musicians and stand-up comedians. Meanwhile, at CityWalk's **Rising Star**, a rockin' bar and karaoke club, catch a rising star or take the stage to belt out top hits with a live backup band. Drink, dine and watch a game on the high-definition screens at **NBC Sports Grill & Brew**, or head south of the border and try made-from-scratch Mexican street fare with a side of live mariachi music at **Antojitos Authentic Mexican Food**.

End your evening with a round of cocktails and live music at the restaurant that's always on island time, **Jimmy Buffett's Margaritaville**.

BEST PLACES TO EAT & DRINK AT VOLCANO BAY

Kohola Reef Restaurant & Social Club
At the base of the majestic Krakatau volcano, Kohola Reef Restaurant & Social Club serves island favorites, including mango barbecue pulled-pork sandwiches and coconut-crusted fried chicken. $$$

The Feasting Frog
Dine on poke bowls, chicken tacos and loaded nachos on the patio surrounding this tropical frog-shaped place. $$

Dancing Dragons Boat Bar
Unwind with tropical cocktails at this outrigger-canoe-shaped full-service bar.

Goo Goo Dolls, Hard Rock Live Orlando

Loews Sapphire Falls Resort at Universal Orlando
This deluxe on-site hotel has 1000 rooms, plus a grand pool surrounded by waterfalls. **$$$**

Universal's Cabana Bay Beach Resort
Steps from Volcano Bay, with retro-style rooms and suites that are chic and affordable. **$$**

Universal's Aventura Hotel
Enjoy a hoppin' rooftop bar, modern, affordable rooms and free park shuttles at this simple yet stylish hotel. **$$**

ISLANDS OF ADVENTURE

Islands of Adventure
Miami

Fight off villains and mythical beasts on an island adventure in a colorful comic-book world inhabited by a cast of characters beyond belief: Betty Boop, the Grinch, Wolverine, Popeye, She-Ra, Dr Doom and the Cat in the Hat can all be found here, strolling their eight-island nation. This is a theme park where you're tasked with saving the day: at Marvel Super Hero Island you might be called to fly alongside Spiderman to protect the Statue of Liberty, while at Jurassic Park, you'll be fighting off velociraptors as you zoom through four inversions at a maximum speed of 70mph. Take a break from battling villains at playful Seuss Landing, where Dr Seuss–themed attractions are geared toward smaller children. The eighth island here is home to The Wizarding World of Harry Potter – Hogsmeade, where three thrilling rides will send you straight into the pages of the iconic book series.

TOP TIP

If you have a limited amount of time to spend at the parks or are traveling during peak season, consider purchasing the Universal Orlando Express Pass, an add-on to your regular admission ticket that gives you access to a separate, shorter line on most rides.

VIAVAL TOURS/SHUTTERSTOCK ©

Marvel Super Hero Island

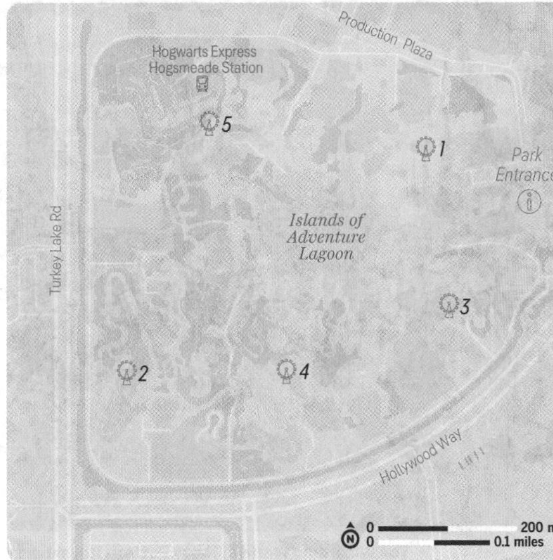

SIGHTS
1 Seuss Landing

ENTERTAINMENT
2 Jurassic Park
3 Marvel Super Hero Island
4 Toon Lagoon
5 Wizarding World of Harry Potter - Hogsmeade

Marvel Super Hero Island

MINGLE WITH HEROES AND VILLAINS

At Marvel Super Hero Island you just might take on the hue of the beloved green beast as you launch at speeds of over 60mph through seven inversions aboard **The Incredible Hulk Coaster**. Defeat the evil Magneto as you spin your ride vehicle through a storm, generating lightning-bolt energy on Storm Force Accelatron. Take part in a mad experiment that seeks to suck the fear out of unsuspecting riders as you drop 185ft at 40mph on **Doctor Doom's Fearfall**. Encounter the Marvel Universe's most dastardly villains as you attempt to foil a sinister plan to kidnap the Statue of Liberty on the indoor 3D simulator **The Amazing Adventures of Spider-Man**. Visitors are invited to strike a pose with Spider-Man at his dedicated meet-and-greet station, but expect encounters with other heroes and villains wandering the island, including Captain America, Storm, Wolverine and Green Goblin.

On select nights inside **Cafe 4**, the Marvel Character Dinner is the perfect opportunity to mingle with Marvel's finest over an all-you-can-eat Italian-inspired feast. Meanwhile, even villains enjoy choosing a good read at the **Comic Book Shop**, where the shelves are brimming with books, graphic novels, posters and Marvel comics and collectibles.

SKULL ISLAND: REIGN OF KONG

One of the first monsters to hit the silver screen (in 1933), King Kong is synonymous with Universal Pictures, so it's no surprise that he has his very own island here at Universal Orlando. Set off on a multidimensional expedition on his ride, Skull Island: Reign of Kong. You'll board a 72-seat, trackless expedition vehicle and head into the interior of the island, where you'll encounter giant bugs and dinosaurs (thanks to the 3D technology that Universal excels at), before coming face to face with King Kong himself, one of the most stunning animatronic creatures in Orlando. Though it's not a roller coaster, this ride may not be suitable for kids due to the scary elements, including countless skulls.

WHERE TO EAT IN ISLANDS OF ADVENTURE

Cafe 4
At the Fantastic Four's HQ, serving Italian-American classics like meatball subs and chicken Caesar salads. **$$**

Fire Eater's Grill
This place is best known for its grilled gyros plates and salads. **$$**

Doc Sugrue's Desert Kebab House
Healthy Mediterranean bites like chicken, beef and vegetarian kabobs or a Greek salad. **$$**

MYSTIC FOUNTAIN & MYTHOS RESTAURANT

Mystic Fountain is more than a bubbling spring. Beware when its glowing eyes come alive, as this feisty fountain is ruled by a mischievous water spirit who plays music, jokes around with and even splashes unsuspecting visitors.

Steps away from the fountain, Mythos Restaurant goes beyond your standard theme-park fare with full-service fine dining and a Mediterranean menu featuring grilled octopus, lamb burgers and brick-oven-roasted chicken, as well as vegetarian options like the signature Greek salad and spinach and garlic ravioli. Cool off with a mango lassi (yogurt blended with mango nectar), and take a moment to explore the rock formations and pathways overlooking the lagoon at the rear of the restaurant.

KAMIRA/SHUTTERSTOCK ©

The Wizarding World of Harry Potter – Hogsmeade

Toon Lagoon

STEP INTO THE COMICS OF YESTERYEAR

Take a dip into nostalgia and chill with Popeye and friends at Toon Lagoon, a water-park area themed on the classic Sunday morning newspaper comics of King Features Syndicate. While little ones might not get all the visual gags or be acquainted with all the featured characters, it's the perfect time to teach them a thing or two about pre-internet entertainment and the power of eating all your spinach.

The Rocky and Bullwinkle–inspired log flume ride whisks riders down a steep plummet where they're bound to be drenched: for a dollar you can even blast riders with the water cannons on the bridge overlooking the falls. **Popeye & Bluto's Bilge-Rat Barges** are 12-person rafts commandeered by Bluto down treacherous river rapids in an attempt to kidnap Olive Oyl. **Me Ship, The Olive** is suitable for kids aged 10 and under looking to stay cool. Climb the stairs and ladders into this three-level play ship, slip down a waterslide or shoot the water cannons. A separate play zone, **Sweet Pea's Playpen**, gives toddlers a chance to make a splash, too. Powerful People Dryers are available to dry yourself off for a $5 fee, then you can share a platter of the cheeseburgers made famous by Popeye's best buddy Wimpy.

WHERE TO EAT IN ISLANDS OF ADVENTURE

Blondie's
The Blondie's menu includes hearty deli sandwiches and subs. **$$**

Confisco Grille
Try the ahi-tuna nachos, pork-belly banh mi and other global bites at Confisco Grille. **$$**

Circus McGurkus Cafe Stoo-pendous
Enjoy fried chicken, pizza and burgers under the big top at this Seuss-inspired place. **$$**

Jurassic Park

MEET THE DINOSAURS

In the iconic eponymous movie, Jurassic Park, located on the island of Isla Nublar, just off the coast of Costa Rica, is a wildlife park where de-extinct dinosaurs wreak havoc on visitors. Try your best to avoid being eaten as a snack by velociraptors as you zoom through a habitat infested by the flying creatures aboard the **VelociCoaster**, the tallest and fastest launch coaster in Orlando. Ride the rapids of **Jurassic Park River Adventure** and beware of the dinosaurs that lurk among the flora at the river's edge.

The **Pteranodon Flyers** invites kids to gently swing beneath the 10ft wings of the largest known flying reptiles, while at **Camp Jurassic**, a giant playground, smaller kids can blow off steam as they fight imaginary dinos lurking in secret pathways along rope bridges and in lost caves.

Watch out for the sharp teeth of Blue the Velociraptor, a friendly, lifelike dino who loves flashing his sharp teeth in photos with visitors to the **Raptor Meet and Greet**. Observe as dino eggs hatch or pet a baby triceratops at the **Jurassic Park Discovery Center**, where scientists work to bring dinosaurs back from extinction.

A busy afternoon fending off dinosaurs calls for a nonalcoholic Raptor Refresher – Jurassic blue punch with yogurt boba – available at the park's very own tiki bar, **Isla Nu-Bar**.

THE NIGHTTIME LIGHTS AT HOGWARTS CASTLE

The four houses of Hogwarts are celebrated on select evenings with this stunning light-and-sound show projected onto the majestic castle. Check the calendar of events for the latest details and show times. Typically, the show begins at dusk, at around 7:15pm (though sometimes it begins as early as 6:45pm depending on daylight savings time), and is repeated every 20 minutes until the theme park closes.

The projections are more pronounced during the later shows, when the sky is darker. The grand fireworks finale is a wonderful way to mark the end of the day at Universal's Islands of Adventure. For the best views, nab a spot on the bridge that leads from Hogsmeade to Jurassic Park.

The Wizarding World of Harry Potter – Hogsmeade

SPEND TIME WITH HARRY AND HERMIONE

Nestled at the foot of Hogwarts Castle, The Wizarding World of Harry Potter – Hogsmeade is a snow-blanketed village home to enchanting shops, a magical tavern and a forbidden forest. **Harry Potter and the Forbidden Journey** is a high-tech flight simulator that tricks riders into believing they're touring Hogwarts by pairing 3D special effects with immersive screen backdrops. The immersion in Hogwarts begins in the queue, which snakes through the castle and is filled with props from the Potter series, before riders are loaded onto a 'magical bench.'

Encounters with dementors, giant spiders and the Hungarian horntail dragon might scare little ones, but the entire family can enjoy a flight deep into the Forbidden Forest at a top speed of 50mph on **Hagrid's Magical Creatures Motorbike Adventure**, a thrilling yet kid-friendly roller coaster. And though the **Flight of the Hippogriff** is considered a

GRAB-AND-GO SNACKS IN ISLANDS OF ADVENTURE

Moose Juice, Goose Juice
Pop into the whimsical Moose Juice, Goose Juice for fresh fruit cups and churros. $

Chill Ice Cream
Scoop up a sundae served in a freshly made waffle cone. $

Cinnabon
Follow the warm, fresh-from-the-oven aroma over to Cinnabon for scrumptious, mega-cinnamon buns. $

ALL THE BOOKS YOU CAN READ

'The more that you read, the more things you will know. The more that you learn, the more places you'll go.' Dr Seuss encouraged a love of reading in his beloved book, *I Can Read With My Eyes Shut!* Encourage a love of reading with a visit to All The Books You Can Read, a charming, cozy bookstore located in Seuss Landing, a rare educational outpost in the middle of a theme park. Among the shelves you'll find all the colorful Dr Seuss classics to add to your home library, as well as book-focused apparel and toys. Comfy chairs and tables plus books galore make this a great destination if you're looking for a little downtime with your little one.

KAMIRA/SHUTTERSTOCK ©

Seuss Landing

kiddie coaster, it's worth a ride for its breathtaking views of the castle and village alone.

Fill up a souvenir jar with all the sweets beloved by Harry and his friends – chocolate frogs, Fizzing Whizzbees and Bertie Bott's Every Flavour Beans – at **Honeydukes**, the flagship candy shop at The Wizarding World of Harry Potter.

Seuss Landing

CELEBRATE DR SEUSS' MOST BELOVED BOOKS

Seuss Landing sends kids straight into the pages of Dr Seuss' stories. Since Dr Seuss rarely drew straight lines, everything in this far-out land is wonderfully wonky. All the rides here are made for the under 48in-tall bunch. Swerve through the pages of the classic tale on **The Cat in the Hat** and watch as the crew tries to clean up a mega-mess before mom gets home. Climb inside a Dr Seuss flying fish and use the controls to maneuver up and down past an array of fountains that squirt water to the beat of a musical rhyme on **One Fish, Two Fish, Red Fish, Blue Fish**. **The High in the Sky Seuss Trolley Train Ride!** is a slow-moving train with spectacular views of the entire theme park, while the **Caro-Seuss-el** merry-go-round features creatures you animate by pulling on the reins or pushing the lever on their necks.

You can also feast on the dish made famous by Dr Seuss, green eggs and ham (green eggs, diced ham and white cheese sauce in a bowl of crispy Tater Tots). The Cat in the Hat, Sam I Am and the Grinch often stroll the park when they aren't posing for photos with kids at their dedicated meet-and-greet area near the Caro-Seuss-el.

WHERE TO DRINK IN ISLANDS OF ADVENTURE

Watering Hole
Kick back under an umbrella and relax with frozen cocktails and appetizers.

Hog's Head
British pub fare and butterbeer are always on tap here, along with imported beers and cocktails.

Backwater Bar
Relax with a beer on the outdoor patio of this tropical watering hole, or catch a game on TV.

UNIVERSAL STUDIOS

Universal Studios
Miami

Universal Studios offers visitors a behind-the-scenes glimpse into blockbuster film and TV production. In this theme park, you'll step into the starring role, where you can cast spells with a wand just like Harry Potter, transform into a lovable Minion and fight aliens with the Men in Black. The nine themed areas here, all situated around a large lagoon, recreate the excitement of popular film locations, starting with Hollywood, where you can dine at Schwab's Pharmacy and Mel's Drive-In, recreations of actual historic Hollywood sites. Discover New York City aboard Race Through New York Starring Jimmy Fallon, dive into the world of *The Simpsons* in Springfield, USA and stroll Diagon Alley in The Wizarding World of Harry Potter. Don't miss a photo opp with the eclectic cast of costumed characters that inhabit this vibrant theme park: Frankenstein, Optimus Prime, Shrek, Puss in Boots, Scooby-Doo and Shaggy are always happy to snap selfies with visitors.

TOP TIP

Get a head start in the morning and plan to arrive at the park at least half an hour before the gates open. Try to stay on resort property, too, as Universal Orlando hotel guests receive early park admission in addition to being steps away from the fun.

CHANSAK JOE/SHUTTERSTOCK ©

Entrance, Universal Studios

HIGHLIGHTS
1 The Wizarding World of Harry Potter – Diagon Alley

ENTERTAINMENT
2 Production Central
3 San Francisco
4 Springfield, USA
5 The Bourne Stuntacular

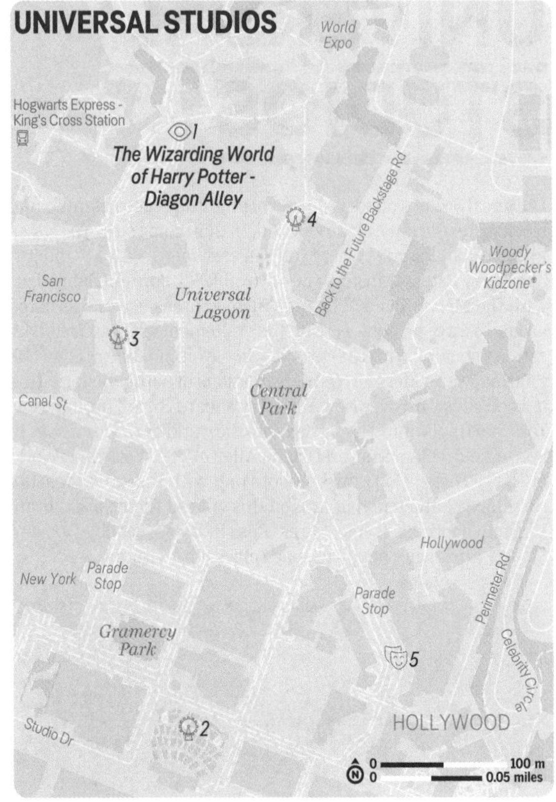

UNIVERSAL ORLANDO'S HORROR MAKE-UP SHOW

Universal Pictures is widely considered a pioneer of horror as a film genre, and its main monster creations, such as the Wolf Man, the Mummy, and the Bride of Frankenstein still scare audiences.

Housed within a recreation of Hollywood's historic Pantages Theatre, the fascinating live Universal Orlando's Horror Make-Up Show delves into the secrets behind the make-up and special effects that artists use to craft some of the creepiest characters ever seen on film. You'll even learn the recipe for movie-quality fake blood. Arrive early so you can check out the lobby's collection of authentic props from legendary Universal Pictures horror movies.

Production Central

TRANSFORMERS, MINIONS AND MUMMIES

Located beyond the main entrance, Production Central is a bustling backlot that sets the stage for the park's movie-making theme. Everything you need to start your cinematic day of fun can be found here, including Guest Services, reservations kiosks and the main hub for **My Universal Photos**, a program that enables guests to view and share photographs taken by park photographers and to also create custom souvenirs.

Movie characters jump off the screen and into the attractions here, starting with the banana-loving Minions that recruit

WHERE TO EAT IN UNIVERSAL STUDIOS

Mel's Drive-In
Recreates the LA original with vintage cars, burgers and root-beer floats. **$$**

Schwab's Pharmacy
This retro soda and ice-cream shop was inspired by the original Sunset Blvd hangout. **$$**

Bumblebee Man's Taco Truck
This taco truck serves up a variety of Mexican street food. **$**

guests to join their cause on **Despicable Me Minion Mayhem**, an animated, motion-simulator theater ride that transforms riders into Minions. Meanwhile, the Autobots need your help to save the AllSpark aboard **Transformers: The Ride**, a 3D simulated dark ride. Hop into Evac, your personal Transformer vehicle, and fight alongside Optimus Prime.

From **Studio 6-B**'s backstage, hover over the Flatiron Building, the Hudson River, the Statue of Liberty and other iconic NYC sites with the *Tonight Show* host on the 3D simulator **Race Through New York Starring Jimmy Fallon**. **Revenge of the Mummy** is an indoor coaster based on *The Mummy* film franchise established in 1932 with cinematic icon Boris Karloff in the bandage-wrapped leading role. It rockets riders from a standstill to a maximum speed of 45mph in mere seconds, sending them straight into a cursed, scarab-infested Egyptian tomb. Meanwhile, on the steel coaster **Hollywood Rip Ride Rockit** aspiring rock stars are launched at 65mph through hair-raising corkscrews timed to the beat of some of rock's biggest hits.

San Francisco

FAST AND FURIOUS FUN

Ushering guests into San Francisco are the Beat Builders, four construction workers who halt progress on Universal's latest improvement project to put on a percussion show utilizing buckets, wrenches, hammers and other tools. The most coveted attraction here is **Fast & Furious – Supercharged**, a 360-degree immersive ride that recreates the *Fast* universe with actual movie props and supercharged vehicles direct from the big screen. The entire family can ride along with Dom, Letty, Hobbs and Roman on a 120mph street chase set in the high-octane world of the blockbuster films.

Post- or pre-ride, gas up with sweet or savory breakfast grab-and-go panini at **San Francisco Pastry Company**, or take a break from the theme-park chaos and treat yourself to luscious layer cakes, iced éclairs or character-themed cupcakes from the dockside dining tables. Also on the waterfront, the park's signature restaurant, **Lombard's Seafood Grille**, recreates San Fran's dockside restaurants and serves fresh seafood favorites, including tuna poke and lobster rolls. At the adult-friendly watering hole **Chez Alcatraz** you can have your own cocktail hour with cold beer, mixed drinks and hearty appetizers. Be sure to snap a photo inside the mouth of the killer great white shark from the 1975 film *Jaws* that hangs next door.

HOLLYWOOD CHARACTER ZONE

You can always count on spotting a celebrity at Universal's dedicated Hollywood Character Zone. Bonus: these stars are no snobs and love to sign autographs and pose for photos. The characters change daily, but the familiar faces you might find here include Marilyn Monroe, Scooby-Doo, Woody Woodpecker, Betty Boop and Bart Simpson. When you enter the park, you'll be greeted by a photographer who will offer to take your party's picture and hand you a My Universal Photos card with a QR code.

Photographers will also be on hand to capture your best moments at the park, including meet-and-greet photos with your favorite characters, which you'll be able to digitally download later.

Lisa's Teahouse of Horror
Offers healthier options such as salads, veggie wraps and fruit plates. **$**

Krusty Burger
Best known for its burgers, but it's worth trying the foot-long hot dog topped with homemade chili. **$**

Louie's Italian Restaurant
Dine on a pizza, a meatball sub or a salad on the patio here. **$**

INTERACTIVE MAGIC WANDS

Casting 'spells' is easy in Diagon Alley, where wizards and witches lurk around every corner. Of course, you'll need a magic wand to make the magic happen: you can find collective, interactive wands in dozens of styles at **Ollivanders Wand Shop**, makers of fine wands since 382 BCE. (These wands don't come cheap but can be reused every time you return to the park.) Wave your wand at one of the many spell locations (look out for the bronze medallion markers) hidden throughout the park, and you can light up lanterns, flush a suspicious toilet, make rain fall from beneath an umbrella, silence shrunken heads and more, surprising your non-wizard companions.

The Wizarding World of Harry Potter – Diagon Alley

STROLL THE WORLD OF HARRY POTTER

The Wizarding World of Harry Potter – Diagon Alley is a charming streetscape lined with shops carrying skulls, stuffed owls, Quidditch competitive gear, wands, broomsticks and even Bertie Bott's Every Flavour Beans. The magic-filled alleyway leads to the dragon-protected Gringotts Bank, home to one of the park's most popular attractions, the multisensory **Harry Potter and the Escape from Gringotts**, a steel coaster that whisks riders through underground vaults, where villains Voldemort and Bellatrix lurk around every bend.

Trade your US currency for Gringotts bank notes in $10 or $20 denominations at **Gringotts Money Exchange** and use the colorful currency for purchases within Diagon Alley. Build your wizarding wardrobe at the cheerfully curated **Madam Malkin's Robes for All Occasions**, then gather your dark-art wares at **Borgin and Burkes**. If it croaks, creeps or slithers, you'll find it in plush toy form at **Magical Menagerie**, while **Scribbulus** sells wizard-worthy writing supplies, including ink, inkwells and feather quills. **Wiseacre's Wizarding Equipment** showcases spellbinding items such as crystal balls, telescopes and hourglasses.

British pub fare is on the menu at the **Leaky Cauldron**, best known for its bangers and mash, fisherman's pie, toad-in-the-hole, ploughman's platter, and its kids' menu offering fish and chips and cottage mini-pie. The **Fountain of Fair Fortune** pours unique brews you can only find in the world of Harry Potter: pumpkin juice, pumpkin fizz and, of course, butterbeer.

Springfield, USA

HOME OF THE SIMPSONS

Bright, cheerful and larger than life, Springfield, USA is the theme-park home of Homer, Marge, Bart, Lisa and Maggie, members of the fictitious family depicted in the longest-running animated TV series in history. The park's landmark attraction, **The Simpsons Ride**, sends visitors off on a virtual-reality roller-coaster ride through yet another theme park, the low-budget **Krustyland**, which comes to life on a gigantic 80ft-diameter domed surface. **Kang & Kodos' Twirl 'n' Hurl** is an aerial carousel that puts passengers in the saucers of the titular, dastardly aliens, where they need to activate targets bearing the faces of Springfield citizens.

Fast Food Boulevard is lined with several Simpsons-themed fast-food outlets, including Krusty Burger, Cletus' Chicken Shack,

WHERE TO EAT IN UNIVERSAL STUDIOS

Cletus' Chicken Shack
Bite into a chicken and waffle sandwich in Springfield. $

KidZone Pizza Company
Super kid-friendly fare like pizzas, fries and funnel cakes are always on the menu here. $

Cafe La Bamba
Grab a burrito to go or settle into the patio with tacos and a salsa flight. $

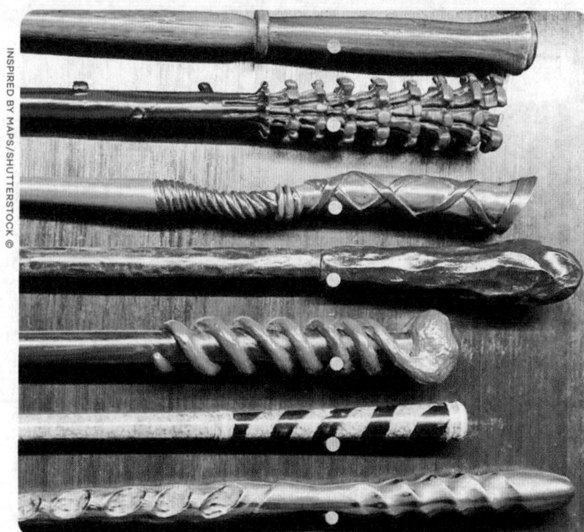

Wands, The Wizarding World of Harry Potter – Diagon Alley

The Frying Dutchman and Moe's Tavern, covering the four major Simpsons food groups: burgers, chicken, battered and fried seafood, and alcohol. Towering over the town is Lard Lad, purveyor of everyone's favorite fried circular treats, including the massive pink-iced doughnut covered in rainbow sprinkles. Modeled after Springfield's go-to convenience store, the Kwik-E-Mart here sells Simpsons merch, with Bart Simpson's best friend Milhouse Van Houten overseeing the main entrance. Cool off with an icy glass of Homer's favorite suds and watch your favorite Simpsons clips in the open-air **Duff Brewery** beer garden.

The Bourne Stuntacular

THE SECRETS OF HOLLYWOOD STUNTS

If you've ever wondered how Jason Bourne managed to dangle from a helicopter, make an escape across rooftops in Tangier or jump multiple cars with a motorcycle, all without breaking a sweat, check out The Bourne Stuntacular, a stunt show that unveils the science and stagecraft behind Hollywood's riskiest stunts. Based on the Bourne film franchise starring Matt Damon, the live show follows the ex-spy as he outruns evil lurking around every corner. Expect fistfights, shoot-outs and high-octane thrills that seem as real as can be until the secrets to their success are revealed – you'll never look at an action movie the same way again.

QUEUING TIPS

When the queue seems never-ending, skip to the head of the line as a single rider. Since most people ride in groups of two or more, attendants will move single riders aged 10 or above to the front of the line and pair them with another single rider. Another queue-busting option is the 'child swap' program, which allows families traveling with little ones to wait in the queue together: one parent stays off the ride and waits in the designated 'child swap area' with the child who isn't tall enough to ride, while the rest of the family hops on the ride. The parent who initially stayed back can then simply walk to the front of the line for their opportunity to ride.

WHERE TO DRINK IN UNIVERSAL STUDIOS

Chez Alcatraz
Create your own cocktail hour and snap a pic of Jaws' toothy grin.

Duff Brewery
Delight in an icy-cold glass of beer or a frozen margarita in this shaded beer garden.

Eternelle's Elixir of Refreshment
Mysterious potions are mixed into colorful beverages before your eyes.

ORLANDO

Orlando
Miami

Most visitors to Orlando rarely venture past the fabricated worlds of Walt Disney World® and Universal Orlando, yet beyond the theme-park thrills, the city of Orlando is home to several fantastic gardens and nature preserves, plus a delightfully slower pace. Prior to 1965, when Walt Disney announced plans to build Walt Disney World®, Orlando had been a sleepy city. Its historic core, 'Old Orlando,' is located along Church St between Orange and Garland Aves. Orlando is mostly wetlands, its landscape dotted with lakes, the largest of which is Lake Apopka. Though the rainy season lasts from May until late October, northern sunseekers flock to Orlando for its delightful warm and dry season, which lasts from November through April. While the average visitor to Orlando spends their vacation indulging in theme-park food, locals know that just a few miles outside of these tourist attractions are some outstanding restaurants and bars.

TOP TIP

Prepare for Orlando's heat and humidity, which is especially intense in summer. Daily thunderstorms can also be expected. Dress is typically casual in this theme-park capital of the world, so pack clothing made with lightweight, breathable materials, comfortable shoes, a rain poncho and a wide-brimmed hat to keep the sun off your face.

BEST PLACES TO EAT IN ORLANDO

Artisan's Table
This locavore favorite offers breakfast bowls of eggs and grits and organic smoothies. $$

Slate
Serves wood-fired pizzas and meats as well as seafood and light bites. $$

White Wolf Cafe & Bar
Indulge in breakfasts and Bloody Marys at this gourmet bistro. $$

Domu
This popular ramen spot makes its own noodles. $$

Black Rooster Taqueria
Start with guacamole and chips and then order a plate of tacos at this counter-service restaurant. $

African American Heritage at Wells' Built Museum

BLACK HISTORY AND CULTURE

Located in the center of Orlando's historic Parramore district, the small Wells' Built Museum is dedicated to Orlando's African American history and culture. It's housed in the former Wells' Built Hotel, opened in 1926 by Dr William Monroe Wells to host African American performers forbidden from staying in the city's strictly segregated accommodations. Count Basie, Cab Calloway, Billie Holiday, Ella Fitzgerald and Duke Ellington all spent a night under its roof. On the top floor you'll find a hotel room frozen in time, complete with furniture and decor that would have greeted guests in the 1930s.

Board the Wheel at ICON Park

TAKE A SPIN ABOVE ORLANDO

The Wheel at ICON Park rises 400ft above Orlando, where spectacular views of the surrounding city and theme parks await. The massive Ferris wheel's rotation takes about 20 minutes. Connect to the free, in-capsule Bluetooth, open any music player on your device, and press play for an insightful narrative on the history of central Florida.

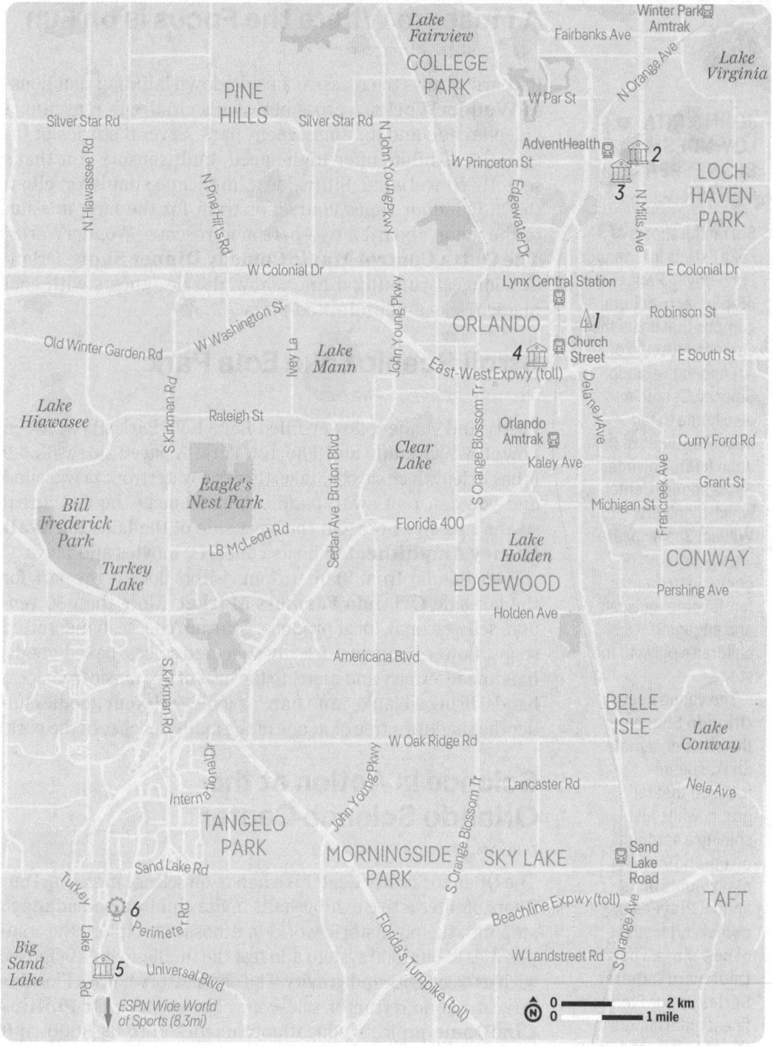

SIGHTS
1 Lake Eola Park
2 Orlando Museum of Art
3 Orlando Science Center
4 Wells' Built Museum
5 WonderWorks

ENTERTAINMENT
6 The Wheel at Icon Park

WHERE TO STAY IN ORLANDO

EO Inn & Spa
Understated elegance and value, tucked in a shady enclave of downtown Orlando near Lake Eola's northeastern shore. **$$**

Grand Bohemian Hotel
Downtown Orlando's most luxurious option, with a small rooftop pool echoing a 1950s Miami beach. **$$$**

Aloft Orlando Downtown
Features minimalist, modern rooms. Meet friends at the WXYZ bar, or grab a snack at the 24/7 pantry. **$$**

JOHN & RITA LOWNDES SHAKESPEARE CENTER

Set on the shores of Lake Estelle in Orlando Loch Haven Park, the 45-plus-acre cultural campus that hosts the Orlando Museum of Art and the Orlando Science Center is also home to the intimate stages of the John & Rita Lowndes Shakespeare Center, which highlights William Shakespeare's legacy by bringing compelling dramas, fan-favorite musicals and engaging children's plays to the stage.

The venue houses **Orlando Shakes**, the city's ensemble Shakespeare-focused theater group, while also shining a spotlight on up-and-coming playwrights at its annual **PlayFest**, a weekend festival of new plays. The **Courtyard Cabaret Series** brings Florida's finest entertainers to the open-air courtyard stage. See details of upcoming shows and purchase tickets at orlandoshakes.org.

A Museum Where the Focus is on Fun

THAT'S 'EDU-TAINMENT'

It's hard to miss the massive, upside-down building that houses **WonderWorks**, a cross between a children's museum, a video arcade and an amusement park. Several stories of interactive exhibits offer high-speed, multisensory fun that's secretly educational. Sit inside a hurricane simulator, climb the 36ft indoor ropes course, or train for the next mission to the moon aboard a two-person gyroscope. WonderWorks' **The Outta Control Magic Comedy Dinner Show**, Orlando's longest-running dinner show, dazzles guests with cool magic tricks and unlimited pizza.

Stroll Scenic Lake Eola Park

PICTURE-PERFECT PARK

Pretty and shaded, flower-filled Lake Eola Park sits between downtown Orlando and Thorton Park. A paved sidewalk 0.9 miles in length circles the lake, there's a waterfront playground and you can rent swan paddleboats to meet the many real swans that live here. On the west side of the lake, the **Walt Disney Amphitheater** hosts concerts, movies and plays.

Every Sunday from 10am to 3pm visitors flock to the park for the lakeside **Orlando Farmers Market**. More than 50 vendors sell seasonal, local produce, gourmet cheese, handcrafted soaps, flower bouquets, freshly squeezed juices, baked goods, handmade jewelry and more, to the beat of live music from local bands. Bring a blanket and have a picnic with your goodies under the shade of a tree or at one of the many benches in the park.

Science in Action at the Orlando Science Center

FUN AND EDUCATIONAL

The Orlando Science Center is a hands-on science museum. Four floors of interactive exhibit halls invite children and adults to step into the prehistoric world of dinosaurs, explore the complexities of our food system and test the fundamentals of forces, such as electricity and gravity. The observatory houses Florida's largest public refractor telescope. The center's **Dr Phillips CineDome** projects educational movies onto its 8000-sq-ft screen, while kids will enjoy designing, building and testing tiny race cars at the **Hot Wheels: Race to Win** exhibit. You can also catch a Science Live! show in the **Digital Adventure Theater** to learn more about the science behind the exhibits.

WHERE TO DRINK IN ORLANDO

Icebar
Sit on an ice seat and sip icy drinks at this gimmicky yet out-of-the-ordinary place.

Pharmacy
Speakeasy-style joint (look for the unmarked elevator door) with reasonably priced cocktails and farm-to-table cuisine.

Stubborn Mule
Gastropub serving handcrafted cocktails with flair (yes, including Moscow mules) and contemporary American food.

Make a Date with World-Class Art

ART AND CULTURE COMMUNITY HUB

Founded in 1924 by local art enthusiasts, the **Orlando Museum of Art (OMA)** showcases over 2400 objects, including contemporary art, African art, American art from the 18th century to 1945, and art of the ancient Americas. The museum also hosts adult and family-friendly art events and classes, including yoga classes in the galleries and stroller tours for art-loving little ones (and their parents). The popular First Thursday initiative celebrates local artists with regional work, live music and food from Orlando restaurants on the first Thursday evening of the month.

Catch a Game at the ESPN Wide World of Sports

LIVE SPORTS GALORE

Disney delved deep into the world of sports when it opened its $100-million, 220-acre multisports complex in 1997. Welcoming amateur and pro athletes from around the world, the nine venues at the ESPN Wide World of Sports host more than 100 annual athletic events and over 70 different sports. Check what's on the schedule when you're in town: you might catch the National Jump Rope Championship, the Pop Warner Super Bowl, the AAU Girls' Junior National Volleyball Championships or the Varsity Summit All-Star Cheerleading Championship. It's also the spring-training location for the Atlanta Braves baseball team. At the **ESPN Wide World of Sports Grill** countless TVs broadcast every game of the season for just about every professional sport.

SAK COMEDY LAB

Voted Orlando's Best Comedy Club by the city's main newspaper, the *Orlando Weekly*, the SAK Comedy Lab hosts shows guaranteed to make you laugh almost every day of the week. Many of the writers and actors for hit shows like *Saturday Night Live* and *Mad TV* got their start onstage here. The hilarious ensemble of improv actors asks the audience for input and then makes up characters, songs and skits on the spot. Though the venue hosts occasional kid-friendly shows, most performances are on the edgy side of humor and thus suitable for adults and mature teens (though some of the gags might fly over the heads of younger audience members).

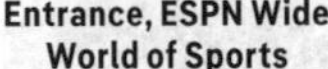

Entrance, ESPN Wide World of Sports

GETTING AROUND

Many hotels near I-Drive and other popular attractions offer free or inexpensive shuttles. LYMMO is the free downtown Orlando circulator bus, providing public transportation in the downtown business, entertainment and shopping districts. The I-Ride Trolleys serve the International Drive resort area year-round, seven days a week, from 8am to 10:30 pm, with scheduled stops every 20 minutes.

With hundreds of dockless bikes across Orlando, HOPR Bike Share is the most fun form of transit in the Orlando area. Download the HOPR Transit app, scan the QR code on the bike or scooter, and ride around town to your heart's content. To end your ride, lock the wheel and let the app know you've reached your destination.

Central Florida Zoo & Botanical Gardens
Wekiwa Springs State Park
Winter Park
Lake Louisa State Park
Orlando
Orlando Wetlands Park
Kissimmee
LEGOLAND
Bok Tower Gardens Bird Sanctuary

Beyond Orlando

Go beyond Orlando's bustling, skyscraper-dotted downtown and surrounding theme-park madness and enjoy a more tranquil taste of central Florida.

Greater Orlando's lovely state parks, lush botanical gardens and smaller-scale attractions offer a delightful escape from the tourist-filled theme-park capital of the world. Nature plays a starring role here, and flower-filled parks and pristine lakes dot the entire region. State parks welcome adventurers looking to hike, kayak, canoe or simply enjoy a picnic, while central Florida is one of the top bird-watching spots in the US, so keep your eyes peeled for bald eagles, belted kingfishers, black vultures and bobolinks. Less hectic theme parks welcome families looking for a more relaxing vacation, with the chance to encounter alligators or jump into a world made of LEGO bricks.

TOP TIP

The best way to explore Greater Orlando is by car. It pays to shop around for a rental as competition here is fierce.

Bald eagle, Orlando

ROMEO GUZMAN PHOTOGRAPHY/SHUTTERSTOCK ©

JEFF HOLCOMBE/SHUTTERSTOCK ©

Lake Tohopekaliga

See the Treasures of Tiffany

LOUIS COMFORT TIFFANY'S ART

Noted for its outstanding art nouveau collection, the **Charles Hosmer Morse Museum of American Art** in **Winter Park** houses the world's most comprehensive collection of masterpieces by American artist and designer Louis Comfort Tiffany, including a reconstruction of the brilliant Tiffany Chapel, originally created for the World's Columbian Exposition of 1893.

Download the free smartphone audio tour; remember to bring headphones or earbuds. The museum's gift shop offers jewelry, art glass and ceramics inspired by the work of Louis Comfort Tiffany. On the first Thursday of December each year, the museum kicks off the holiday season in Winter Park when it lights up its Tiffany windows in Central Park, and hosts a concert featuring the Bach Festival Choir and Brass Ensemble.

Picnic in the Shade at Kraft Azalea Park

RELAX UNDER CYPRESSES

Open year-round from 8am until dusk, the 5-acre Kraft Azalea Park is situated on the shores of picture-perfect Lake Maitland in Winter Park, just north of Orlando.

Towering cypress trees that are over 200 years old provide shade from the Florida sun, and benches scattered throughout

FISHING ON LAKE TOHOPEKALIGA

Plentiful sunshine and numerous lakes make central Florida a year-round prime fishing destination for both experienced anglers or novices hoping to catch their first fish. The temperate climate brings the best-known and most popular game fish in the world – the largemouth bass (Florida's state freshwater fish) – to the region's many lakes. Head to a local bait and tackle shop to rent gear.

Orlando Fishing Charters offers two- to five-hour guided freshwater fishing excursions to Kissimmee's **Lake Tohopekaliga**, the largest lake in Osceola County. Fishing poles, bait, tackle and Florida fishing licenses are included in the charter fees. Expect to reel in bluegill, crappie, bream, tilapia, chain pickerel, sunfish and catfish in the lake locals call Lake Toho.

WHERE TO STAY BEYOND ORLANDO

LEGOLAND Hotel
Located 130 steps from the park entrance, with a separate kids' sleeping area in every room and free breakfast buffets. **$$**

Reunion Resort & Golf Club
Stay in a one- to three-bedroom villa or a three- to 13-bedroom private vacation home. **$$**

Star Island Resort and Club
Offers affordable, luxurious, all-suite accommodations and an on-site full-service spa. **$$**

PEPPA PIG THEME PARK

Join Peppa Pig and her pals at the world's first Peppa Pig Theme Park, situated steps away from LEGOLAND. Toddlers and preschoolers will appreciate the themed playscapes, water-play areas, character meet-and-greets and tame rides (with not-so-scary queues to boot). Take a ride in Daddy Pig's Roller Coaster, the perfect first roller coaster, set sail in search of hidden treasure aboard the kid-sized boats on Grandad Dog's Pirate Boat Ride, or ride a rocking dinosaur past a smoking volcano on Grampy Rabbit' s Dinosaur Adventure.

A menu of healthy, kid-friendly delights like PB&J, mac 'n' cheese and mini-pizzas (plus salads and sandwiches for adults) awaits at the sit-down, quick-service Miss Rabbit's Diner.

ROB HAINER/SHUTTERSTOCK ©

Entrance, LEGOLAND

the park are perfect for relaxing, reading and picnicking. The park is also home to a great egret rookery and one of the tallest banyan trees in the US.

A Colorful World Built With the Iconic Bricks

A MORE RELAXED THEME-PARK EXPERIENCE

Manageable crowds and lines, interactive and educational exhibits, plus a colorful, fun backdrop and a water park make **LEGOLAND** a fantastic destination for families looking for a more stress-free vacation. Located in Winter Haven, about 50 miles southwest of downtown Orlando, LEGOLAND has attractions geared toward children aged two to 12. At **Ford Driving School**, kids can drive cars through a pretend town, while Miniland is a grand LEGO-made model of iconic American landmarks and cities. And don't miss the **Imagination Zone**, an interactive learning center where skilled LEGO builders are on hand to help children of all ages build their next block masterpiece.

A Swampy Adventure at Gatorland

MINGLE WITH ALLIGATORS

Gatorland in **Kissimmee** is home to over 2000 alligators, including two 'swamp ghosts' – rare white leucistic alligators with bright blue eyes. Though there are no coasters in this

WHERE TO STAY BEYOND ORLANDO

Holiday Inn Winter Haven
Located at the halfway point between Orlando and Tampa, with a fitness center, swimming pool and in-hotel cafe. **$**

Hampton Inn & Suites Lake Mary At Colonial Townpark
A stay at this clean, convenient place just off I-4 includes a complimentary hot breakfast. **$**

Artisan Downtown
In the heart of vibrant downtown DeLand, the historic Artisan Downtown offers a relaxed boutique-hotel experience. **$$**

reptile-focused theme park, there is a free-flight aviary, a petting zoo and a host of fun (and covertly educational) reptile shows.

Soar 350ft above an alligator breeding marsh, where 100-plus giant alligators lurk, on the **Screamin' Gator Zip Line**. Or set off on a swampy adventure aboard a 12ft-high custom-made off-road vehicle and meet the biggest gators in Gatorland, Bonecrusher and Cannibal Jake.

If you've ever dreamed of feeding and wrangling an alligator, the Gatorland **Trainer-for-a-Day** experience gives visitors aged 12 and up a glimpse into what it takes to work with some of the largest living reptiles on the planet (they can grow up to 20ft long!). Your behind-the-scenes day begins by taking care of recent hatchlings, the smallest members of the Gatorland family, and you'll have the chance to cuddle with a baby alligator. Then you'll help the trainer tend to the full-sized gators and other creatures. You'll need to reserve your spot in advance for this experience, which begins at 8am and lasts two hours.

However, please keep in mind that interaction with humans can be stressful for animals and Lonely Planet does not condone the practice of cuddling baby alligators.

Hike or Paddle Lake Louisa State Park

ESCAPE TO NATURE

Lake Louisa State Park is located just 20 minutes west of Walt Disney World in Clermont. Cycle the park's 7 miles of paved road or hike through woods and orange groves along 25-plus miles of trails and see if you can spot some of the critters that call this corner of central Florida home, including deer, bobcat, bald eagles, osprey and tortoises. Rent a canoe, kayak or paddleboard on-site and paddle the park's three lakes, Louisa, Hammond and Dixie. There are 20 budget-friendly cabins offering lake views.

Amazing Animal Education

MEET CREATURES IN THEIR LUSH ENVIRONMENT

Come face to face with an endangered Indian rhino or wander a butterfly haven at the **Central Florida Zoo & Botanical Gardens**, the lakeside home of more than 350 animals representing over 100 species from around the world.

Beyond meeting some of the most amazing animals on earth, kids can cool off at the **Wharton-Smith Tropical Splash Ground** and navigate through treetops via rope bridges or the on-site zipline. Learn more cool facts about the creatures at the expert-led animal encounters and demonstrations offered throughout the day.

AIRBOATING THE EVERGLADES

The Everglades is a subtropical wetland ecosystem that spans more than 3000 sq miles across central and South Florida. Zipping through these wetlands aboard an airboat – a flat-bottomed boat powered by an aircraft engine – is an iconic Florida experience. Keep your eyes peeled for gators, but also otters, water snakes and the rarer crocodiles that live here too.

Boggy Creek Airboat Adventures in Kissimmee provides several excursion options, including day, sunset, night and private tours, all of which offer a front-seat view of authentic Florida from the safety of an airboat piloted by a US Coast Guard–certified captain. Fuel up for your adventure with Florida-style BBQ and all the fixins' at lakeside **Boggy Bottom BBQ**, the on-site restaurant.

WHERE TO EAT BEYOND ORLANDO

Donut Man
Order a box of old-fashioned doughnuts to go at this classic bakery 5 miles from LEGOLAND. **$**

Prato
Romantic Winter Park place serving Italian classics in its rustic interior and on its dog-friendly, year-round patio. **$$**

Luke's Kitchen
The raw bar's always hopping at Luke's Kitchen in Maitland, while the open fire grills all-American steaks and burgers. **$$**

LAZY H RANCH

Ride off into the sunset at Kissimmee's Lazy H Ranch. Owned and operated by sixth-generation Floridians, it offers scenic horseback trail rides through century-old oak hammocks and along Lake Tohopekaliga.

On the way, your guide will share tales of Florida's horse heritage and you'll learn all about the Florida Cracker, an American breed of cattle that originated in colonial-era Florida.

Book a private sunset trail ride for a wildly romantic view of authentic Florida. The minimum age for riders is 10 years old, the maximum weight limit is 225lb and close-toed shoes are required for riding. As for most outdoor activities in central Florida, wear a hat and bring sunscreen and bug repellent. Reservations are required.

Wander a Pristine Ecosystem

EXPLORE THE EVERGLADES

The 18-sq-mile **Disney Wilderness Preserve** in Kissimmee is a living tribute to Walt Disney's love of nature and an essential part of the Everglades ecosystem. Welcome Center staff are happy to give you a trail-map guide, so you can easily follow the half-mile White Harden Trail, the 2.5-mile Red Wilderness Trail or the 3.6-mile Yellow Trail through the wetlands. The Red and Yellow trails combined are a 6-mile hike. Bring a picnic – the preserve's picnic area is situated along the shores of **Lake Russell**, one of the few lakes in the Orlando area without people populating its waterfront.

Make a Feathered Friend

A REHAB CENTER FOR BIRDS

Maitland near Winter Park is the historic Florida home of self-trained artist, naturalist and ornithologist John James Audubon. The **Audubon Center for Birds of Prey** is a small lakeside rehabilitation center for hawks, screech owls and other talon-toed winged creatures, where you can see the birds up close or just hanging out on caregivers' arms. Look out for Trouble, the bald eagle, splashing and playing in his bathtub. The center is located on 3 acres along the southern shore of Lake Sybelia.

Kayak the Wekiwa Springs State Park

TAKE A DIP IN SPRINGS

Cool off in the emerald springs at Wekiwa Springs State Park, located in Apopka, about 20 miles northwest of downtown Orlando. Hike the miles of trails that meander through the woods, swamplands and along the banks of the Wekiva River, or rent a kayak or canoe from **Wekiwa Springs State Park Nature Adventures**, an outfitter located within the park, and paddle the scenic, still waters. Over 190 species of birds have been recorded at the park, which is part of the Great Florida Birding & Wildlife Trail. Campsites are available, but you'll need to reserve in advance.

Walk the Birding Loop at Orlando Wetlands Park

HIKE THE SWAMP

The artificial Orlando Wetlands Park located in Christmas, about 30 miles east of downtown Orlando, was designed to provide advanced treatment for reclaimed water. Its Education Center

WHERE TO EAT BEYOND ORLANDO

The Ravenous Pig
This seasonal gastropub in Winter Park pairs handcrafted cocktails with house-made charcuterie. **$$**

Woodsby's Countryside Cafe
Specializes in big, American-style breakfasts. Try the fried-catfish breakfast basket with a side of stick-to-your-ribs grits. **$**

Soseki Modern Omakase
Offers an intimate (10-seat) multicourse sushi dining experience. Located in Winter Park. **$$**

Harry P Leu Gardens

houses seasonal exhibits that include live animals and interactive displays. From here, set off on the 2-mile **Birding Loop**, one of many trails that wind through the park. Not all trails are open to cyclists, but many are accessible for horseback riders. Be cautious of alligators on the trails – they're especially attracted to the sun-warmed, lime-rock surfaces that line many trails.

Hiking at the Bok Tower Gardens Bird Sanctuary

BIRD-WATCHERS' PARADISE

Hike the trails that lead through four diverse native Florida ecologies: a pine savanna, oak hammock, wetland prairie and bog, home to 126 species of birds, at the Bok Tower Gardens Bird Sanctuary. Designed by famed landscape architect Frederick Law Olmsted Jr, the gardens here have azaleas, camellias and magnolias that burst into bloom in the springtime. Twice a day the 23 bronze bells of the gardens' centerpiece, a 205ft-tall carillon, ring with a melody that reverberates among the magnificent flora. Pick up picnic provisions at the on-site **Blue Palmetto Café**, located next to the visitor center. The Bok Tower Gardens are located in Lake Wales, about an hour south of Orlando, near LEGOLAND.

HARRY P LEU GARDENS

Stroll the 50-acre Harry P Leu Gardens, an impressive botanical oasis located minutes from downtown Orlando. The plant collection includes cycads (primitive plants that have existed for nearly 200 million years), bright red hibiscus and almost 400 species of palm trees. The citrus grove's 50 different kinds of citrus trees highlight Florida's agricultural bounty, while the Native Wetland Garden invites wading birds and other wildlife.

Tours of the 18th-century Leu House run every 30 minutes: former owner Mary Jane Leu loved roses, and her collection of old garden roses (those existing before 1867) forms the most extensive formal rose garden in Florida. Bring provisions for a lakeside picnic.

GETTING AROUND

Rent a car to explore Greater Orlando. It's the largest car-rental market in the world, and you'll find all the major rental companies at many locations around the city and at Orlando International Airport, where pickup and drop-off is quick and convenient and prices are reasonable.

Above: Rocket launch, Cape Canaveral (p286); right: Kennedy Space Center (p277)

THE SPACE COAST

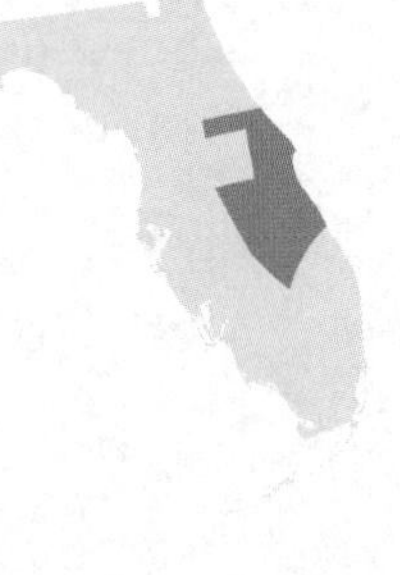

ROCKETS, SURF AND WILD NATURE

Rocket launches, lagoons teeming with wildlife, surfers and science: a combination bound to delight.

Stretching for more than 70 miles along Florida's Atlantic coast, just east of Orlando, the Space Coast got its name in the 1980s at the height of NASA's space-shuttle era. Today, the area is the global epicenter of cutting-edge commercial space exploration, with big names SpaceX and Blue Origin in the mix, and regular rocket launches making the Space Coast moniker more apt than ever. And while most visitors to Florida have hopes of seeing a rocket launch into outer space or visiting Kennedy Space Center Visitor Complex, those who linger longer and go deeper along the Space Coast are treated to some of the area's incredible nature, too.

The Indian River Lagoon, a 156-mile-long estuary home to rare and protected species that runs parallel to the Atlantic Ocean, stretches along the entire Space Coast, with ecotours on its glistening waters to see manatees, dolphins, countless bird species and perhaps even bioluminescence, a summertime special.

These golden shores are also storied among surfers, with a break for every board rider, from Jetty Park in Cape Canaveral and the historic Cocoa Beach Pier to Sebastian Inlet State Park, down south.

Detours inland bring you to atmospheric historic districts, such as Cocoa Village and downtown Melbourne. Most visitors use Cocoa Beach or Titusville as a base for exploring, but you can really start from anywhere here.

THE MAIN AREAS

MERRITT ISLAND & TITUSVILLE
Rockets and nature. p276

COCOA BEACH & COCOA VILLAGE
Surf style and beachy bars. p281

PORT CANAVERAL & CAPE CANAVERAL
Cruise ships and seafood. p286

MELBOURNE & THE BEACHES
Quintessential beach-town vibes. p291

Find Your Way

The Space Coast stretches for 72 miles along Florida's east coast, from Titusville in the north to Melbourne and the beaches down south, with detours inland well worth making, too.

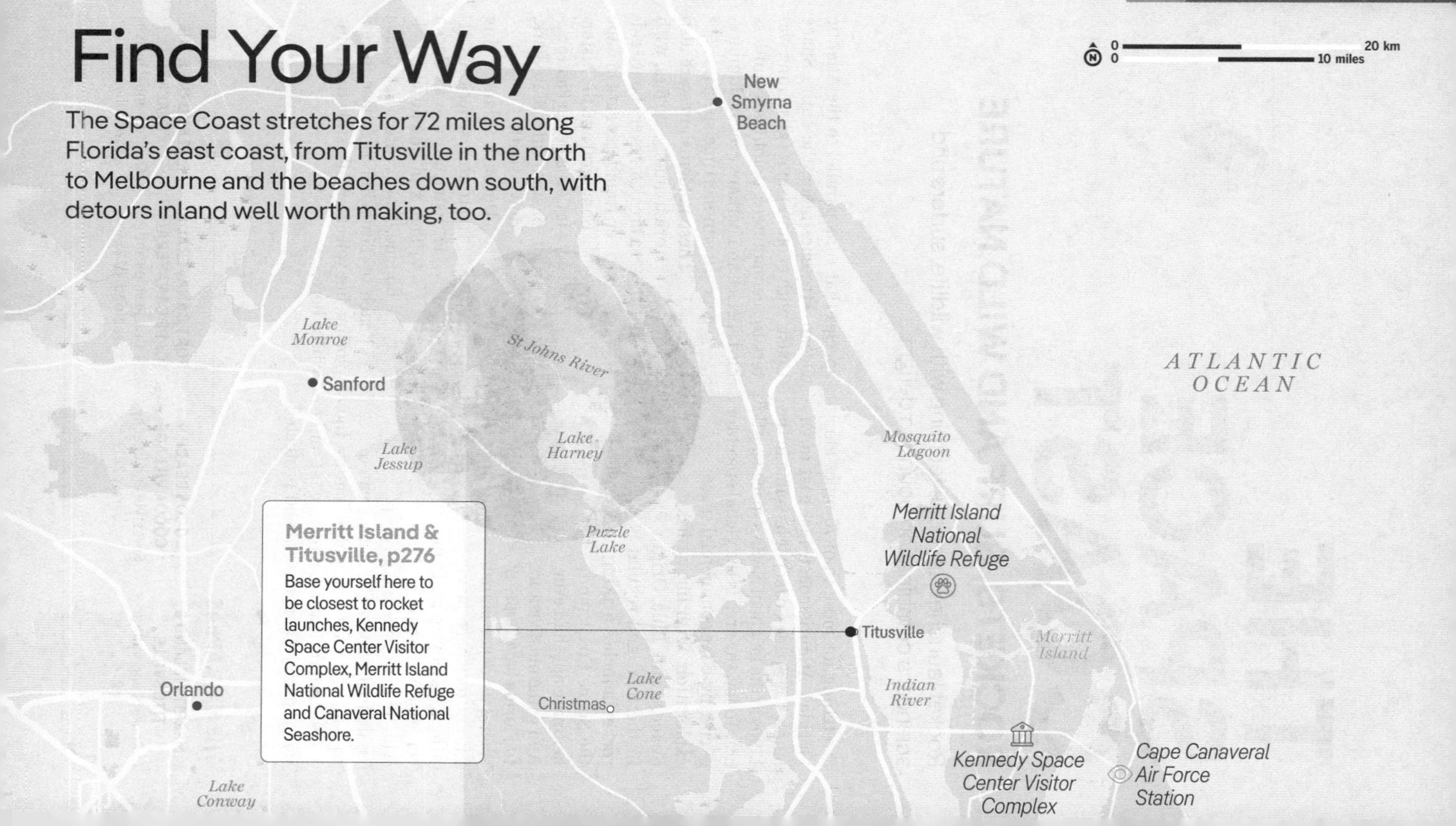

Merritt Island & Titusville, p276

Base yourself here to be closest to rocket launches, Kennedy Space Center Visitor Complex, Merritt Island National Wildlife Refuge and Canaveral National Seashore.

PETER TITMUSS/SHUTTERSTOCK ©, L PAUL MAN/SHUTTERSTOCK ©

CAR

Having your own car is far and away the best option for maximizing your time exploring the area. This way, you can stop off at all the different beach parks, towns and sights on your own schedule throughout a day trip, weekend away or longer.

BUS

If you don't have a car, Space Coast Area Transit (SCAT) connects most of the cities and beach towns within Brevard County and the Space Coast, with 23 routes, set schedules and wheelchair lifts, bike racks and space for surfboards inside.

TROLLEY

The Cocoa Beach Trolley (a favorite ride for local kitesurfers doing downwinders) runs seven days a week between Port Canaveral in the northern reaches of the Space Coast and 13th St in Cocoa Beach.

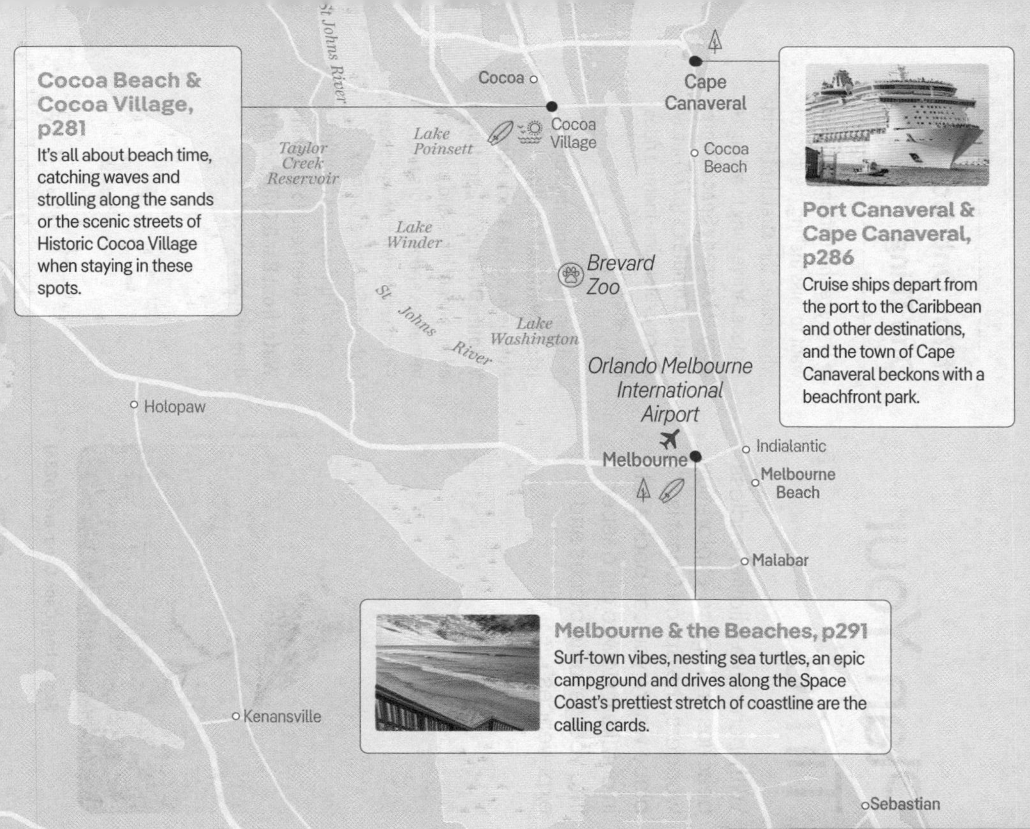

Cocoa Beach & Cocoa Village, p281

It's all about beach time, catching waves and strolling along the sands or the scenic streets of Historic Cocoa Village when staying in these spots.

Port Canaveral & Cape Canaveral, p286

Cruise ships depart from the port to the Caribbean and other destinations, and the town of Cape Canaveral beckons with a beachfront park.

Melbourne & the Beaches, p291

Surf-town vibes, nesting sea turtles, an epic campground and drives along the Space Coast's prettiest stretch of coastline are the calling cards.

Plan Your Time

With incredible wildlife, endless beaches and space-exploration wonders, the Space Coast is a place where you can pack a lot in or take it slow to dig deeper into your favorite places and experiences.

TRUE WILLIAMS/SHUTTERSTOCK ©

Sanderling, Cape Canaveral (p286)

If You Only Do One Thing

- If you're short on time, you don't want to miss making the most of what makes this stretch of Florida famous. Arrive early to maximize a day at **Kennedy Space Center Visitor Complex's** (p277) many space exploration-themed rides, films and exhibits.

- Then head to nearby **Merritt Island National Wildlife Refuge** to do the **Black Point Wildlife Drive** (p280), spotting all manner of birds and perhaps manatees and alligators too. Finish with a swim along Canaveral National Seashore to enjoy some of Florida's most pristine beaches, then head to **Dolphins Waterfront Bar & Grill** (p288) to dine with canal views.

Seasonal Highlights

Summers can be sweltering, but the beach breezes always beckon. November through April sees milder temperatures, lots of sunshine and drier climes.

JANUARY

Melbourne's Wickham Park sets the scene for the **Brevard Renaissance Fair**, one of the best in the state.

MARCH

The busy **spring break** enters full swing, as water temperatures in the ocean warm up too.

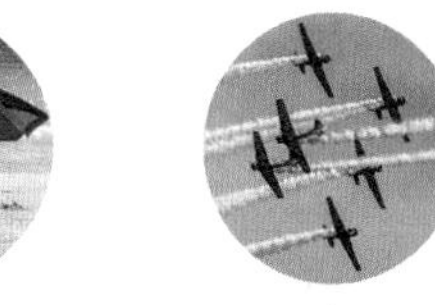

APRIL/MAY

Eyes skywards for aerial acrobatics during the **Cocoa Beach Air Show** and **Space Coast Air Show**, held in alternating years.

BOB POOL/SHUTTERSTOCK ©, CHARLES T. BENNETT/SHUTTERSTOCK ©, MICROFILE.ORG/SHUTTERSTOCK ©

Three Days to Explore

- Follow the previous itinerary then head south to Cocoa Beach for an oceanfront stay. Sign up for surf lessons at **School of Surf** (p283), or rent a board from **Ron Jon Surf Shop** (p285) and paddle out near the **Westgate Cocoa Beach Pier** (p283).

- Spend your third day enjoying an ecotour – head out with **Cocoa Beach Dolphin Tours** (p285) into the Banana River or, if visiting during the warmer months, paddle in search of bioluminescence in the Indian River Lagoon with **A Day Away Kayak Tours** (p279). Don't miss dinner and drinks at oceanfront hangout **Coconuts on the Beach** (p289).

If You Have More Time

- The Space Coast definitely warrants lingering longer to fill an entire week's vacation. With more time, you can tack onto the previous highlights, exploring further south along the Space Coast, taking in cute inland towns, such as **Historic Cocoa Village** (p283) and **Melbourne** (p292), and tracing the coast all the way south to **Sebastian Inlet State Park** (p293).

- Consider spending a few nights around **Titusville** (p276) and **Cape Canaveral** (p286), especially if there's a rocket launch happening. Then road trip south to focus on the beautiful beaches near the Space Coast's southern border, where it meets Florida's Treasure Coast and Vero Beach.

JUNE

Kicking off this month (and running through July): **sea-turtle night walks** to see nesting mothers lumber ashore to deposit their eggs.

AUGUST

See the Indian River Lagoon's **bioluminescence** at its brightest during late summer and early fall.

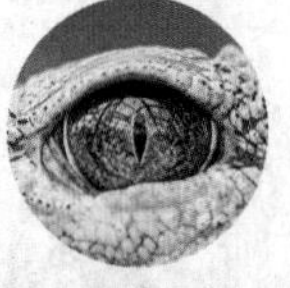

OCTOBER

Celebrate Halloween all month long during weekend **Boo at the Zoo** events at the Brevard Zoo.

DECEMBER

On December 24 Santa-costume-clad surfers paddle out by the hundreds to catch waves at Cocoa Beach's annual **Surfing Santas** event.

IRINAK/SHUTTERSTOCK ©, RUGLIG/SHUTTERSTOCK ©, JOLANDA AALBERS/SHUTTERSTOCK©, LORI BARBELY/SHUTTERSTOCK ©

MERRITT ISLAND & TITUSVILLE

If you've come to the Space Coast to check out its eponymous space exploration highlights, the area around Merritt Island and neighboring Titusville (just west across the Indian River) is where you'll be spending time. In 1958, in the aftermath of WWII, the US government selected the east coast of Florida as the base for its newly formed National Aeronautics and Space Administration (NASA). From here new-age captains would launch rockets, telescopes and shuttles into the orbiting circle of the earth to discover new worlds and galaxies. Thousands of acres of scrubland were commandeered at the northern end of Merritt Island; a third of it was cleared to form the new NASA base, while the remainder was given over to the US Fish and Wildlife Service to operate as the Merritt Island National Wildlife Refuge and the Canaveral National Seashore. Nature and technology live in harmony here, surrounded by valuable waterways and beach for maximum recreation pleasure.

TOP TIP

For a hotel stay with the best views of rocket launches on Cape Canaveral, it's hard to top the Courtyard by Marriott Titusville Kennedy Space Center's riverfront location on the Indian River Lagoon, across from Kennedy Space Center. Head up to the hotel's Space Bar rooftop deck at launch time.

JESSE KUNERTH/SHUTTERSTOCK ©

Titusville

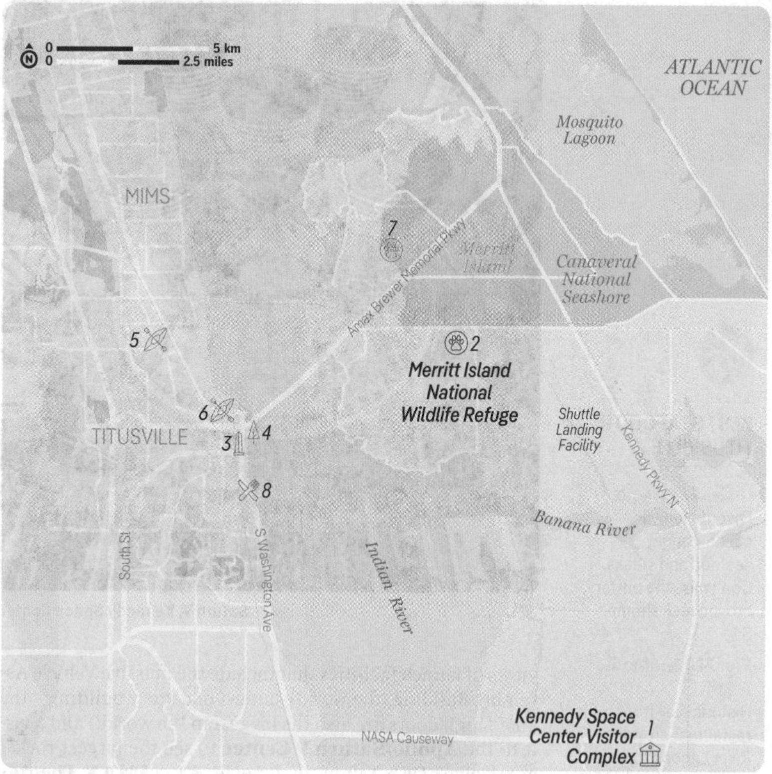

HIGHLIGHTS
1 Kennedy Space Center Visitor Complex
2 Merritt Island National Wildlife Refuge

SIGHTS
3 American Space Museum & Space Walk of Fame
4 Space View Park

ACTIVITIES, COURSES & TOURS
5 A Day Away Kayak Tours
6 BK Adventures
7 Black Point Wildlife Drive

EATING
8 Moonlight Drive-In

Be Wowed by Kennedy Space Center

SPACE EXPLORATION COMES ALIVE

No visit to the Space Coast is complete without several hours, if not an entire day, spent at ground zero for the past, present and future of US space travel. **Kennedy Space Center Visitor Complex** can truly offer something for every visitor. Will you head out on the 90-minute bus tour for close-as-you-can-get

WHERE TO STAY IN TITUSVILLE

Courtyard by Marriott Titusville Kennedy Space Center
Riverfront hotel with an outdoor pool and rooftop deck with launchpad views. **$$$**

Hyatt Place Titusville/ Kennedy Space Center
Three-star hotel with a free daily breakfast buffet and outdoor pool. **$$**

Casa Coquina Del Mar Bed & Breakfast
Historic, family-run B&B with river views and a 2nd-floor deck for scoping rocket launches. **$$**

BEST SEAFOOD IN TITUSVILLE

Dixie Crossroads
Favorite for wild ocean-caught seafood and steaks. Don't miss the buttery, broiled rock shrimp. $$

Pier 220 Seafood & Grill
Historic pier-front restaurant on Indian River Lagoon for grouper tacos and peel-and-eat shrimp. $$

Orleans Bistro & Bar
Shrimp and crawfish get the Cajun treatment at this New Orleans-style spot. Try the Nola Boil. $$

ROBERT HOETINK/SHUTTERSTOCK ©

Saturn V, Kennedy Space Center

views of launch facilities that include the massive Vehicle Assembly Building (the world's largest one-story building – the 465ft-high doors are also the biggest in the world!) and a visit to the **Apollo/Saturn V Center** to see the largest rocket ever flown? Or is taking in a movie at the **IMAX Theater** and catching some thrills aboard immersive rides at **Gateway: The Deep Space Launch Complex** – new in 2022 and starring the awesome Red Planet ride that takes you to Mars – more your speed?

This is the kind of attraction that can be as deeply cerebral and full of reflection (note the **US Astronaut Hall of Fame's** films and multimedia exhibits) or brimming with thrills and wonder as you like. And that's what makes a visit here so fulfilling for the more than 1.7 million visitors that descend on the complex each year. You can even meet real NASA astronauts at KSC and hear all about their training and experiences in space during the daily scheduled **Astronaut Encounters** – just be sure to check the center's event calendar in advance of your visit if you have your heart set on meeting a certain someone.

WHERE TO FIND A BREWERY ON THE SPACE COAST

BeachFly Brewing Company
For beach-inspired brews. Try Space Kölsch (a light German ale) and Turtle Trax (citrusy wheat ale).

Hell 'n Blazes Brewing Company
Ten-barrel brewery in historic downtown Melbourne with craft beers and tasty barbecue.

Carib Brewery
Low-key Cape Canaveral taproom with tropical hard cider, Caribbean lager and American pale ale.

Bioluminescent Kayaking Tour

PADDLE THROUGH WATERS THAT GLOW

During the sultry summer months along the Space Coast, something truly magical happens in the shallow waters of the Indian River Lagoon, where you can paddle through bioluminescent waters that sparkle with a greenish-blue glow. As the water temperatures warm up during the summer months, the phenomenon of bioluminescence, caused by the presence of single-celled organisms called dinoflagellates, becomes more prevalent in the lagoon's nutrient-rich waters. And that's when you'll find Titusville-based tour operators **A Day Away Kayak Tours** and **BK Adventures**, among other local outfits, offering guided excursions to various spots within the Indian River Lagoon and Banana River to see the glow where it's strongest on any given evening. For the best chance at seeing the brightest display, choose to paddle out on a tour on a moonless summer night (tours are generally scheduled for June through early October). But even when the moonlight is shining, you can still get good bioluminescence here, too.

Tours start with a briefing on dry land about what to expect (and a strong application of bug spray) before you push off in your choice of clear or regular kayaks, glow sticks affixed to your life jacket, and paddle out into the lagoon. When the bioluminescence is really doing its thing, you'll see mullet and other fish shooting through the shallows like rockets – bright sparkles flying behind them. Be sure to dip your hand into the water to watch its glow drip off your fingers.

Space Out

MUSEUMS AND A RETRO DINER

While Kennedy Space Center Visitor Complex is far and away the top calling card in the Titusville/Merritt Island area when it comes to out-of-this-world space attractions, there are a few other worthy museums and experiences to set your sights on here, too.

Fascinating donated artifacts from astronauts and other space workers make up the collection at the **American Space Museum & Space Walk of Fame**, a neat little museum in downtown Titusville where you can see training suits used in *Apollo* and shuttle missions, marvel at the retro-technology of consoles from the shuttle firing room used to launch *Columbia,* and learn about lesser known space-exploration-related heroes (including janitors and cafeteria staff) who helped make the space program into what it was. Also right in downtown Titusville and a popular place to view rockets

CLOTHING-OPTIONAL BEACH

Golden sands are a thing along this stretch of Florida's coastline. But if you're hoping to glow a little extra on the beach, the Space Coast is also home to one of Florida's most beautiful and best known clothing-optional beaches. Located along the pristine and undeveloped 24-mile stretch of shoreline (the longest on Florida's east coast) that belongs to Canaveral National Seashore, **Playalinda** is one of Florida's top nude beaches. And you'll be in the minority here if you're not textile free. Follow the coastal road north to parking lots 12 and 13 and just step out on the sand for sunbathing in your birthday suit. Needless to say, slap on the sunscreen.

Playalinda Brewing Company
Craft microbrewery housed within an atmospheric century-old hardware store in downtown Titusville.

Bugnutty Brewing Company
Flights, pints and ciders served with giant pretzels and beer cheese in Cocoa Village.

Intracoastal Brewing Company
Handcrafted sours, stouts and IPAs are on tap in Melbourne's Eau Gallie Arts District.

I LIVE HERE: WHERE TO WATCH A LAUNCH

Chris Eckles, who works in the commercial space industry on Cape Canaveral, shares locations he loves for catching a launch.

Westgate Cocoa Beach Pier
It's hard to beat a perch over the ocean at the tiki bar at the end of the pier, something frosty in hand, for scoping the horizon.

Port St John Boat Ramp
Right on the Indian River in Port St John, the boat ramp at the end of Fay Blvd has great views across to the launchpads.

Harbor Heights Beach
Grab a spot on the sand at this Cape Canaveral beach or head out for a surf and look north to see the streak in the sky at launch time.

launching across the river on Cape Canaveral, **Space View Park** is worth strolling even when it's not a launch day, to see moving monuments to the *Mercury, Gemini, Apollo* and shuttle missions and the astronauts behind them.

If you've worked up an appetite, there's no place for a retro space-related fix like **Moonlight Drive-In**, a diner that dates back to 1964 and was named to honor the *Apollo* missions. You never know when this place will be open (it keeps odd hours), but when it is, slide into a parking spot, place your order, and wait for the carhop to deliver comfort fare like fried shrimp platters, thick milkshakes and chili dogs.

The Delights of Black Point Wildlife Drive

SCOUT FOR ALLIGATORS AND MANATEES

A very Florida self-drive safari awaits when you arrive by car to **Merritt Island National Wildlife Refuge**, a 140,000-acre refuge buffered by the Indian River Lagoon and Atlantic Ocean, home to innumerable bird, mammal and marine species. There's no better way to get a taste of this special environment than by taking your time to slowly drive along the paved 7-mile loop through the refuge that makes up the **Black Point Wildlife Drive**. Roll the windows down to hear the sounds of birdlife, insects buzzing and water lapping all around you and take it slow to make the most of a truly unique experience in some of Florida's most profound nature.

The one-way loop takes you through a surprisingly diverse range of ecosystems, including shallow saltwater marshes and mudflats, pine-filled flatwoods, coastal dunes and scrub environments. The refuge sits right along the Atlantic Flyway, a major bird migration corridor, so it's easy to do some bird-watching – spotting everything from herons, egrets, ibis and waterfowl to brilliantly colored roseate spoonbills – right from your car. There are several spots along the drive where you can get out to stretch your legs and enjoy scenic viewpoints overlooking the river. And among the many creatures you might see along the way are alligators, manatees, otters and perhaps even a bobcat. For the best shot at seeing the most wildlife and bird species, visit between October and March and try to arrive at the refuge as close to daybreak as possible, when animals tend to be at their most active.

GETTING AROUND

Distances are large between the space attractions and surrounding wildlife refuge and national seashore, and you'll definitely want your own car to explore. If you're just coming over from Orlando for the day, Gray Line Orlando offers round-trip sightseeing excursions from Disney, Kissimmee and Orlando to Kennedy Space Center Visitor Complex aboard comfortable buses.

COCOA BEACH & COCOA VILLAGE

Cocoa Beach & Cocoa Village
Miami

As America raced to the moon in the wake of WWII, Cocoa Beach hustled to keep up with growth, building dozens of motels and gaining a reputation as a party town. That vibe has remained intact, and the area seems perennially populated with beer-wielding, scantily clad youth, often visiting on day trips from inland Orlando. The further south you go in Cocoa Beach, away from the pier, the more chilled out the vibe gets.

Cocoa Beach's other claim to fame is surfing. Eleven-time surfing world champion Kelly Slater, born and raised here, learned to ride waves in Cocoa Beach and put it on the global wave-obsessed radar as one of Florida's best surf towns.

From the beach, head due west across the Banana River and Indian River to reach Historic Cocoa Village, which draws a more sophisticated and somewhat older crowd to its park-like downtown, lined with cute cafes, boutiques and antique shops.

TOP TIP

The further south you toss out your beach towel in Cocoa Beach, the prettier and lonelier the sands get. The dunes are particularly gorgeous along the stretch of sand heading south of 13th St South in Cocoa Beach to Patrick Space Force Base.

Cocoa Beach

COCOA BEACH & COCOA VILLAGE

See Cocoa Village Enlargement

HIGHLIGHTS
1 Carolyn Seiler & Friends Gallery
2 Westgate Cocoa Beach Pier
3 Cocoa Riverfront Park
4 Cocoa Village
5 Ramp Road Park
6 Thousand Islands Conservation Area

ACTIVITIES, COURSES & TOURS
7 Adventure Kayak of Cocoa Beach
8 Cocoa Beach Dolphin Tours
9 Cocoa Beach Surf Company
10 Ron Jon Surf School
11 School of Surf

EATING
12 Milpa Tacos y Tortillas
13 Village Bier Garten

DRINKING & NIGHTLIFE
14 Wine Lady

SHOPPING
15 Alley
16 Antiques & Collectibles Too
17 Ron Jon Surf Shop

Dive into Surf Culture

CATCH A WAVE

If you've always wondered what it felt like to catch a wave and perhaps even ride one all the way to the shore, that's a dream you can easily make a reality during a beach vacation

ROMANTIC RESTAURANTS IN COCOA BEACH & COCOA VILLAGE

Fat Snook
Gourmet seafood restaurant in a mall in south Cocoa Beach; perfect for a date night. **$$$**

Café Margaux
Snag a patio table at this Cocoa Village cafe; French food and fab wine pairings. **$$**

Pompano Grill
Sweet hideaway for steak, seafood and crème brûlée in Cocoa Beach. Family-run, welcoming hospitality. **$$**

in **Cocoa Beach**. The mellow waves and sandy bottom here make it an ideal place for beginners to learn.

But before you attempt to paddle out on your own, it's a good idea to take a lesson to master the basics of lying on a board, pushing yourself up into the standing position and riding a wave down the line. And it never hurts to take some inspiration by spending time watching local wave riders do their thing too.

A good place to see local surfers bobbing in the ocean waiting for approaching sets to break into something rideable is the **Westgate Cocoa Beach Pier**, a historic spot where you can stroll out 800ft over the Atlantic Ocean and watch surfers on both sides of the tiki bar at the pier's tip paddling into the surf below. Lifeguards stationed year-round on the beach here make the pier a popular place for families to spend a day on the sand and in the surf too. And it's a fun place just to snack on a frozen chocolate banana or sip a Bloody Mary at the bar.

Several surf shops and local surfers offer group and private surf lessons in Cocoa Beach too, including **School of Surf**, owned by former local professional surfer Todd Holland, in addition to larger-scale operators **Ron Jon Surf School** and **Cocoa Beach Surf Company**.

I LIVE HERE: SURF SPOTS FOR ALL WAVE RIDERS

Calvin Holland, who gives surf lessons at School of Surf in downtown Cocoa Beach, shares his favorite local places to catch a wave.

Cocoa Beach
A fantastic place for people starting out with surfing, with chest-high waves available almost daily and a soft-sand bottom. The paddle out to the break is on the easier side too.

Sebastian Inlet
Florida's only world-class wave and one of your best options for getting a good barrel in the Sunshine State.

Satellite Beach
A coquina reef on the inside really helps the waves push through with some power. This spot really handles a large swell well.

Explore Historic Cocoa Village

ANTIQUING AND CAFE HOPPING

Lest you think the Space Coast is all rockets, surfers and wildlife, you can also find one of Florida's most atmospheric downtowns for cafe hopping, boutique shopping and antiquing here. Drive roughly 8 miles inland (west) from Cocoa Beach – crossing the sparkling waters of the Banana River and Indian River Lagoon – to reach downtown **Cocoa Village**, a former riverfront trading post turned eclectic, artsy town.

A leafy urban oasis by the lagoon's edge, it's lined with historic buildings housing independent restaurants and cafes, wine bars and shops. Start your explorations at **Cocoa Riverfront Park**, where an amphitheater overlooking the Indian River often hosts concerts and festivals. The surrounding park is a nice area to sit for a spell atop benches that are painted with images of flamingos and octopuses by local artists and watch boats plying past. Then venture the few blocks inland from there to explore the village's cute retail outlets.

Carolyn Seiler & Friends Gallery is a wonderful artist co-op housed inside a colorful cottage where you can shop for things like glass jewelry, coasters, wind chimes and paintings created by more than 30 local makers. **Antiques & Collectibles Too** has a warren of rooms filled with things like estate jewelry, decades-old Disney snow globes, rare chess sets and

WHERE TO STAY IN COCOA BEACH

Beach Place Guesthouses
Oceanfront property; suites with full kitchens; hammocks and firepits just back from the dunes. **$$$**

Beachside Hotel & Suites
Retro surf vibes, balconies with ocean views and lazy river pool for water-park fun. **$$**

Hilton Garden Inn Cocoa Beach Oceanfront
Three-star hotel featuring an oceanfront pool with a pool bar. **$$$**

WHY I LOVE COCOA BEACH

Terry Ward, writer

Florida brims with atmospheric beach towns. But Cocoa Beach is one I've grown to love more with every visit. An ex-boyfriend, a surfer who loved this town, always said it was like Huntington Beach, California, back in the day. I've come to grasp what he meant. Cocoa Beach is a place with zero pretensions, beach bars where you can truly come as you are, and dune-backed stretches of golden sand that are my far-and-away favorite in the state. Wake before sunrise to stroll the beach somewhere south of 13th St, where the dunes are particularly beautiful, and you can be all alone with sandpipers, terns and the odd surfer on dawn patrol.

Ron Jon Surf Shop

vintage NASA mission patches. And **Alley** is a great little gift shop selling crystal jewelry and chic women's apparel.

Favorite spots for a drink or meal include the German-style **Village Bier Garten**, **Milpa Tacos y Tortillas** for Oaxacan and Baja-style fare, and boutique wine store and tasting bar, the **Wine Lady**.

Exploring the Thousand Islands Conservation Area

GORGEOUS ISLANDS IN THE STREAM

Part of the Indian River Lagoon System, the **Banana River Lagoon** buffers Cocoa Beach to the west. Within the shallow brackish waters here you'll find the Thousand Islands Conservation Area, a verdant labyrinth of mangrove islands that weave a maze and are a paradise for paddlers to explore calm waters where dolphins and manatees frolic.

If you have your own kayak, SUP or canoe, the public boat ramp at Ramp Rd is the place to put in and paddle out on a solo mission. But heading out on a guided ecotour is a better option if you're unfamiliar with the lay of the land.

WHERE TO ENJOY LIVE MUSIC IN COCOA BEACH

Heidi's Jazz Club & Restaurant
Cocoa Beach mainstay for local and international jazz acts in intimate surroundings.

Lou's Blues Bar & Grill
Strong cocktails, cool ocean views and live bands most nights at this Indialantic bar.

Grills Seafood Deck & Tiki Bar
Port Canaveral hangout, where live rock and country bands jam alongside waterfront views.

Adventure Kayak of Cocoa Beach runs 2½-hour-long guided ecotours that lead from **Ramp Road Park** to explore mangrove trails and tunnels. Your guide can point out eagles and pelicans and help you to spot the telltale sign on the water of an imminently surfacing manatee.

Fancy something involving less work on your part? **Cocoa Beach Dolphin Tours** runs two-hour tours into the Thousand Islands Conservation Area aboard a comfortable and shaded 50ft pontoon boat, with onboard beverages, bathrooms and a naturalist guide to help you spot wildlife from a drier vantage point. The captains are masters at finding the Indian River Lagoon's resident Atlantic bottlenose dolphins too; always a thrill to see up close.

HOMETOWN SURFING LEGEND

Look for a statue of the Space Coast's most famous surfer on the median strip as you approach downtown Cocoa Beach on A1A from the north. It pays homage to Kelly Slater, who was born in Cocoa Beach and surfed the area's local beach breaks from the age of five. In fact, Slater's prowess is often attributed to the area's consistent if not-the-best-shaped waves, since it's harder to master riding imperfect waves than perfect ones. The record-holding 11-time World Surfing League champion still occasionally visits the Space Coast, so you never know when or where you might spot him on a casual paddle out (especially if the surf is up at Sebastian Inlet).

Surf-style Shopping at Ron Jon

A STORE AND AN EXPERIENCE

It's impossible to talk about Cocoa Beach without mentioning its most famous surfing and shopping emporium. **Ron Jon Surf Shop** has grown into so much more than a place to buy surfboards and bars of surf wax since it first opened its doors in Cocoa Beach in 1963. Glowing like a gaudy art deco palace and sporting a towering statue of hometown surfing hero Kelly Slater riding a wave out front, the sprawling complex with a massive interior waterfall and glass elevator can't be missed as you drive along A1A. And whether you're looking to sign up for surf lessons, shop for waterproof speakers to bring for a day at the beach, find the perfect unicorn pool floatie for the hotel pool or snag a Ron Jon's logo-emblazoned cup decorated with a surfing astronaut, you're going to find it here.

With locations across Florida as well as in New Jersey (the original), Alabama, South Carolina and Maryland, Ron Jon's Cocoa Beach outpost is the largest surf shop in the world and sprawls across two stories and 52,000 sq ft. Across the street, adjacent buildings rent everything from surfboards and beach cruisers to wetsuits, beach wagons and kiteboards. While Ron Jon's used to be open 24 hours a day, since the COVID-19 pandemic that's no longer the case. Whenever you come, just don't expect to get in and out in a hurry, as there's always something tempting to be found down the next store aisle.

GETTING AROUND

Three causeways – Hwy 528, Hwy 520 and Hwy 404 – cross Indian River Lagoon, Merritt Island and the Banana River to connect Cocoa Beach to the mainland. At Ron Jon's, Hwy 528 (also known as Minutemen Causeway) cuts south and becomes Hwy A1A (also Atlantic Ave), a north–south strip with chain hotels and restaurants, tourist shops and condos. Hwy A1A divides into two one-way roads (southbound Orlando Ave and northbound Atlantic Ave) for a couple of miles, reconnects and continues south along the barrier-island coast 53 miles to Vero Beach and beyond.

Having your own car is the best option for getting around, but Cocoa Beach is also served by SCAT buses. Rte 9 connects Cocoa Beach with Cape Canaveral, and Rte 26 connects it with beaches to the south all the way to Indialantic.

PORT CANAVERAL & CAPE CANAVERAL

In 1951 the US Army Corps of Engineers carved out an inlet to facilitate the shipping of goods to the Space Center. In the process, it laid the foundations for Port Canaveral, the second-busiest cruise port in the US and a home port for such big-name cruise lines as Disney Cruise Line, Royal Caribbean International and Carnival Cruise Line, among others.

To the north of the port, Cape Canaveral Space Force Station remains the primary launch head of the nation's Eastern Range. To the south, Cape Canaveral has evolved into a quiet, residential community for space workers and their families, though several chain hotels and restaurants here cater to cruise-ship passengers and space tourists. Everywhere you go in Port Canaveral and Cape Canaveral, you'll find links to the shipping, cruising and commercial space industries – through the people who live and work here, and at themed cafes and shops.

TOP TIP

If you want to join the crowds lining Port Canaveral and Jetty Park to wave off behemoth cruise ships leaving port, that happens Thursday through Monday, so plan your visit accordingly. Some people even bring giant foam hands to wave at passengers as the ships cruise past, adding to the fun spectacle.

Jetty Park, Port Canaveral

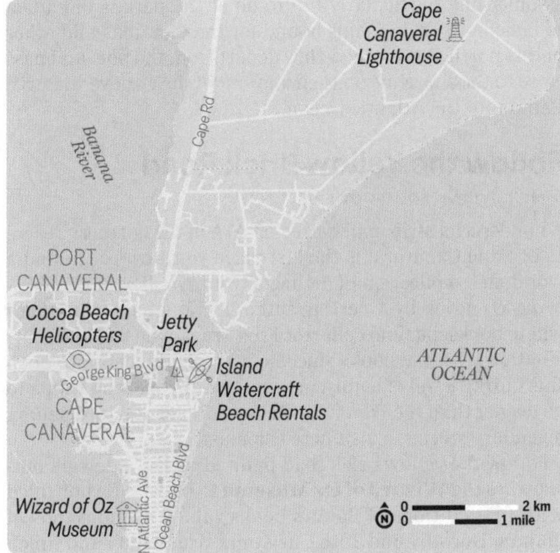

A Perfect Beach Day in Jetty Park

GREAT SURF AND PRISTINE SANDS

When is a park more than a park? When it's fabulous Jetty Park, a 35-acre oasis located right in the port at the northern tip of the town of Cape Canaveral, where it's tempting to settle in for a beautiful beach day or spend a star-filled night or longer camping in a tent or RV (recreational vehicle) at the excellent on-site campground.

When there's a rocket launch scheduled just north on Cape Canaveral – which happens regularly these days – the park's golden strip of beach and 1200ft-long fishing pier are as good of a lookout-point as it gets for watching a liftoff over the ocean.

The sloping sandbar just offshore makes Jetty Park a popular surf break for consistent wave action, and you'll usually find a gaggle of surfers scanning the horizon, waiting for something to roll in. If you're feeling tempted to paddle out, you can rent boards from **Island Watercraft Beach Rentals**, which also has umbrellas, beach chairs, kayaks and other beach-day essentials for rent.

When the fishing pier isn't closed due to hurricane damage and refurbishments, anglers line it, hoping to hook red fish, jack, Spanish mackerel and more.

BEST SPACE COAST CAMPGROUNDS

Long Point Park Campground
Just north of Sebastian Inlet, campsites with full hookups. Popular with surfers, anglers and kayakers.

Manatee Hammock Campground
Titusville campground with towering pines and palm trees. Great location to see a rocket launch.

Wickham Park Campground
Melbourne campground; 7 miles of hiking/mountain-biking trails, eight fishing lakes, playground and disc golf course.

BEST HOTELS FOR PRE- OR POST-CRUISE

Homewood Suites by Hilton Cape Canaveral-Cocoa Beach
Just a mile from the port, three-star hotel with tiki bar and hot breakfast included. **$$$**

Holiday Inn Club Vacations Cape Canaveral Beach Resort
Right near Jetty Park. Families love the lazy river, waterslide and easy beach access. **$$$**

SpringHill Suites by Marriott Cape Canaveral Cocoa Beach
Open since 2020, this hotel near the port has a pool, firepits and complimentary breakfast. **$$$**

Something particularly fun to do at the park is bid adieu to behemoth cruise ships bound for the Bahamas and other points north and south as they depart from the port and pass close to the shoreline on their way out of the Canaveral Barge Canal into the Atlantic Ocean.

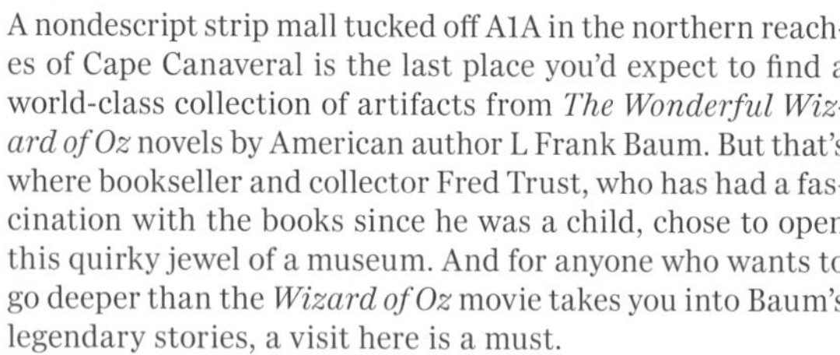

Follow the Yellow Brick Road

IMMERSIVE WIZARD OF OZ MUSEUM

A nondescript strip mall tucked off A1A in the northern reaches of Cape Canaveral is the last place you'd expect to find a world-class collection of artifacts from *The Wonderful Wizard of Oz* novels by American author L Frank Baum. But that's where bookseller and collector Fred Trust, who has had a fascination with the books since he was a child, chose to open this quirky jewel of a museum. And for anyone who wants to go deeper than the *Wizard of Oz* movie takes you into Baum's legendary stories, a visit here is a must.

Follow the yellow brick road painted on the sidewalk outside into the **Wizard of Oz Museum** to find a gift shop filled with first editions of Baum's books valued at thousands of dollars, Dorothy and Toto Christmas ornaments and lunch boxes, ruby slipper replicas and the like. Then proceed into the museum itself, where over 2000 artifacts amassed by Trust date as far back as 1850 and include Baum's old family journals, original props and costumes, dolls and more. QR codes on display cases pair with signage to lead you on a self-guided tour. The museum's highlight is an immersive experience within a 2000-sq-ft room in the back, where 30 projectors bring to life scenes from the books and you can skip down the moving yellow brick road and peer into the witch's castle. The show also includes an immersive Vincent Van Gogh experience and, for a Space Coast twist, incredible deep-space images from the James Webb Space Telescope.

BEST SEAFOOD RESTAURANTS IN PORT CANAVERAL

Seafood Atlantic
Local seafood delivered right from the fishing fleets gets grilled to perfection at this mainstay. $$

Rusty's Seafood & Oyster Bar
Platters of oysters, steamed shrimp, and fish dip smoked in-house at this long-standing waterfront favorite. $

Rising Tide Tap & Table
Near Canaveral Barge Canal; try the mahimahi and shrimp tacos. Abundant Florida craft beers. $

Explore Cape Canaveral's Historic Lighthouse

TOUR A HIDDEN LIGHTHOUSE

Even for some people living along the Space Coast, the fact that you can tour **Cape Canaveral Lighthouse** – a historic lighthouse still used as an active navigation aid that's located within a stone's throw of launchpads and facilities on Cape Canaveral Space Force Station – might come as a surprise.

Since the lighthouse is situated on an active military base, you'll need to provide your driver's license to be able to gain

WHERE TO FIND A TIKI BAR ON THE SPACE COAST

Rikki Tiki Tavern
Tropical cocktails above the rolling surf at the end of the Westgate Cocoa Beach Pier.

Dolphins Waterfront Bar & Grill
Beautiful Merritt Island option overlooking the Canaveral Barge Canal.

Ellie Mae's Tiki Bar
Friendly neighborhood place in Cape Canaveral with tiki cocktail specials and smoked fish dip.

Cape Canaveral Lighthouse

access to the free tours, which are currently open to US citizens only, due to Department of Defense restrictions on military installations worldwide. After all, this is the only lighthouse owned by the US Space Force.

But it's worth arranging things ahead of time (72 hours is usually enough for base access to be granted) for the chance to tour this unique cast-iron lighthouse lined with bricks that date to 1848. It was moved to its current inland location in 1893.

Be sure to wear closed-toed shoes with a strap on the back (no flip-flops) to climb 48 steps to the 151ft-tall lighthouse's 5th floor, as high as the tours go. It's worth visiting the little museum nearby to learn how Fresnel lenses work and see a scale of the lighthouse and how it compares in height to the *Space Shuttle* and *Saturn V* rocket. With a maximum of 10 people, the guided bus tours also get you access to Hangar C to see restored ballistic missiles and early rockets, and Launch Complex 26 – the control room for early satellite launches.

SPACE COAST STATE PARKS & REFUGES

Sebastian Inlet State Park
Pristine beaches, great waves, one of Florida's best fishing piers and a secluded snorkeling cove.

Archie Carr National Wildlife Refuge
Stretching more than 20 miles along the coast, important habitat for nesting loggerhead sea turtles.

Merritt Island National Wildlife Refuge
Originally acquired for NASA's Space Program, 140,000 acres of hiking trails and a self-guided wildlife drive.

Coconuts on the Beach
Classic oceanfront tiki bar, steps from the sand in Cocoa Beach. Killer piña coladas, too.

Beach Shack
Right next door to Coconuts on the Beach, with an even mellower tiki scene.

Fishlips Waterfront Bar & Grill
Rooftop tiki bar serving frosty drinks as you overlook passing cruise ships in Port Canaveral.

Aerial view, Cocoa Beach

Take Flight on a Helicopter

LIFTOFF FROM THE PORT

Astronauts and commercial space travelers aren't the only humans lucky enough to get a bird's-eye view of the Space Coast's staggering beauty below. For one of the area's most fun and thrilling tours that doesn't require you to be a rocket scientist or a billionaire, book a seat with **Cocoa Beach Helicopters**.

The company's bright-yellow Robinson R-44 helicopter, dubbed 'Goldie,' has room for three passengers along with the pilot, and makes for an incredibly smooth ride as you lift up from the landing pad in Port Canaveral and hover like a bumblebee over behemoth cruise ships lining the second-busiest cruise port in the world. Your pilot will likely point out barges used to recover rockets by the commercial space industry and be quick to show you any wildlife passing below, too, with dolphins and manatees often seen frolicking right there in the Canaveral Barge Canal.

There are several different tours to choose from, ranging from quick five-minute adventures up to see the NASA launchpads and Canaveral Locks to Port-to-Pier adventures that fly south over the surfers (and sometimes sharks!) that frequent the Cocoa Beach Pier. It's worth splurging on the **Classic Tour of Cocoa Beach and the Thousand Islands** for an incredible view of the uninhabited mangrove islands dotting the Banana River that look like a mini Everglades below.

BEST SPACE COAST COUNTY BEACH PARKS

Lori Wilson Park
Cocoa Beach park with shaded pavilions, barbecue grills and a boardwalk leading through the dunes.

Canova Beach Park
Surfers and families flock to this beachfront park in Indialantic. Leashed dogs allowed; outdoor showers.

Spessard Holland South Beach Park
Gorgeous swath of Melbourne Beach with 100ft-long boardwalk through the dunes. Anglers come for surf fishing.

GETTING AROUND

There are two ways to arrive in Cape Canaveral: traveling north on A1A from Cocoa Beach, or west on A1A across the Banana River via Merritt Island. Having your own car is best, but Cape Canaveral is also served by SCAT buses. Rte 9 connects it with Cocoa Beach and Rte 4 connects it with Cocoa Village.

If you're coming from the airport in Orlando, Go Port runs shared shuttles from there to Port Canaveral from US$29.99 per person.

MELBOURNE & THE BEACHES

Historic Melbourne was established in the 1870s by freed slaves and pineapple farmers who built homesteads on a peninsula between the Indian River Lagoon and Crane Creek. A fire destroyed the burgeoning town in 1919, but the newly reconstructed downtown along New Haven Ave remains much as it was in the 1920s, offering a small-town feel with several good restaurants, coffee shops and a thriving weekend nightlife. Across the lagoon, Melbourne Beach and surrounding beaches Satellite, Indian Harbour and Indialantic, have a mellow vibe and a variety of beachfront accommodations. Downtown Melbourne bursts to life on weekend evenings, drawing crowds of the young and energetic to stroll its shaded streets and hop from pub to live music venue to rooftop bar. The beach scene is all about casual outdoor restaurants, oceanfront parks and surfers at every ocean approach, scoping the waves and deciding where to paddle out.

TOP TIP

June and July are the months to be here to head out on guided night tours along beaches that are among the most important in the world for nesting loggerhead and green sea turtles. Be sure to book in advance (and bring plenty of insect repellent), as places fill quickly.

DOUG FRAZIER/SHUTTERSTOCK ©

Melbourne Beach

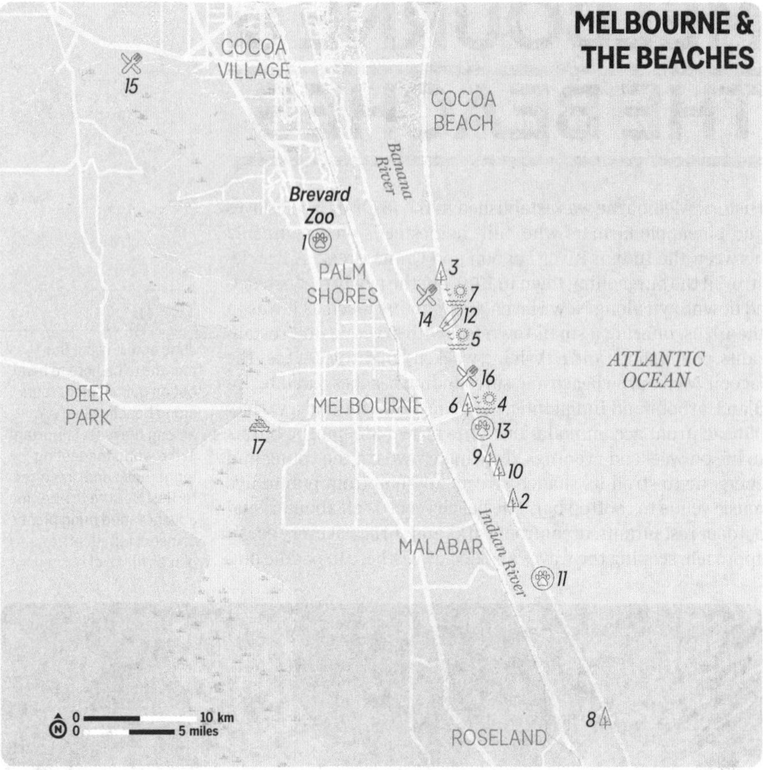

MELBOURNE & THE BEACHES

HIGHLIGHTS
1 Brevard Zoo

SIGHTS
2 Coconut Point Park
3 Hightower Beach Park
4 Indialantic Beach
5 Indian Harbour Beach
6 James H Nance Park
7 Satellite Beach
8 Sebastian Inlet State Park
9 Spessard Holland North Beach Park
10 Spessard Holland South Beach Park

ACTIVITIES, COURSES & TOURS
11 Archie Carr National Wildlife Refuge
12 Balsa Bill
13 Sea Turtle Preservation Society

EATING
14 Da Kine Diego's Insane Burritos
15 Lone Cabbage Fish Camp
16 Long Doggers

TRANSPORT
17 Camp Holly Airboat Rides

Melbourne's Chilled-Out Beach Towns

SUN, SURF, SAND AND STYLE

The entire Space Coast is lined with fun enclaves, where life revolves around whether or not the surf is pumping and when the

WHERE TO EAT IN MELBOURNE

Chart House
Upscale place for surf and turf dishes with Indian River views. $$$

El Ambia Cubano
Casual Cuban restaurant with a breezy deck and classic dishes *ropa vieja* and chicken fricassée. $$

Crush XI
Craft cocktails, charcuterie platters and catch of the day in a stylish downtown Melbourne setting. $$

next swell is coming. But there's a pleasant, laid-back residential feel to things when you get south of Cocoa Beach and Patrick Space Force Base to the cool little beach communities around Melbourne Beach and south to Sebastian Inlet State Park.

Satellite Beach has long stretches of golden sand and beautiful oceanfront parks backed with dunes, including **Hightower Beach Park**, with its scenic boardwalk leading through the dunes. RC's is the go-to local surf break for catching mellow waves. Shop for a new pair of board shorts or a surfboard at **Balsa Bill**, a cool little surf shop, or pick up a burrito to bring to the beach from **Da Kine Diego's Insane Burritos**, a Hawaiian-theme surf shack where you order at the counter.

Indian Harbour and **Indialantic Beaches** are up next, with **Long Doggers** – a beachy beer and burger joint – a must-stop, along with **James H Nance Park**, a gorgeous oceanfront park with an excellent adaptive playground.

Melbourne Beach has more great oceanfront beach parks, including **Spessard Holland North** and **South Beach Parks** and **Coconut Point Park**.

You'll want to make it all the way south of here, too, to the Space Coast's southernmost reaches and **Sebastian Inlet State Park**, where two of Florida's best surf breaks (Monster Hole and First Peak), a fishing pier, mountain-biking trails and an incredibly beautiful stretch of sand to plop atop await.

SPACE COAST MUSEUMS

Valiant Air Command Warbird Air Museum
Roughly 50 historic aircraft in three hangars, including pre- and post-WWII planes, and a *M*A*S*H*-style helicopter.

American Police Hall of Fame & Museum
Dedicated to American law enforcement officers who lost their lives in the line of duty.

Brevard Museum of History & Natural Science
Ice age to the space age, dive deep into Florida history at this Cocoa museum.

A Day at the Brevard Zoo

KAYAK ALONGSIDE GIRAFFES, TO START

There's so much incredible Florida wildlife to be seen along the Space Coast in its many parks, preserves and waterways, not to mention right on the beaches tracked by nesting sea turtles, that you might wonder if hitting a zoo is really necessary in these parts. But the Brevard Zoo is no ordinary zoo. And for any animal lover visiting this part of Florida, a visit here is an inland detour in Melbourne well worth making.

With open-air habitats home to more than 900 animals from around the world, the community-built zoo offers a particularly immersive experience to visitors. Walk along winding boardwalks that weave through typical Florida hardwood hammocks to visit the zoo's distinct geographical zones, featuring Florida wildlife as well as animals from South America, Africa and Australia. You can see everything from rescued Florida bobcats and bears to spider monkeys, Komodo dragons, rhinos and sloths here.

Enclosures are built to seamlessly integrate with the surrounding nature. And free-flight aviaries you can stroll through add to the absorbing feel.

WHERE TO STAY IN MELBOURNE

Hotel Melby
Art-filled boutique hotel within stumbling distance of downtown Melbourne; has best rooftop bar around. $$$

Port d'Hiver Bed & Breakfast
Romantic luxury inn fronting the ocean in Melbourne Beach, with heated pool and hot tub. $$$

Seashell Suites Resort
All-suite property fronting a private beach near the Archie Carr National Wildlife Refuge. $$$

EAU GALLIE ARTS DISTRICT SIGHTS & GALLERIES

Eau Gallery
Fine-art gallery in Melbourne's Eau Gallie Art District (EGAD), with original works by local artists.

Pineapple Park
Pretty, palm-lined park fronting the Indian River, with picnic benches, a gazebo and fishing pier.

Fifth Avenue Art Gallery
Member-owned and operated gallery, where you can browse handcrafted jewelry, fine crafts and paintings.

Anaya Coffee
Artisan-roasted beans and handcrafted espresso drinks within an artsy space right on Highland Ave.

Rehab Vintage Market
Boutique selling vintage furniture, linens, jewelry and more.

JOSE ANTONIO PEREZ/SHUTTERSTOCK ©

Archie Carr National Wildlife Refuge

For one of the zoo's most unique experiences, visitors age five and over can sign up for guided kayaking tours along the zoo's Nyami Nyami River in **'Expedition Africa'** to float past giraffes, lemurs, rhinos and more, offering a truly unique vantage point on the zoo's wildlife.

See Nesting Sea Turtles

MAGICAL MOMENTS ON THE SAND

Nighttime walks on Melbourne's beaches, to see nesting sea turtles lay their eggs, kick sand around to cover the eggs up and lumber their magnificent-if-unwieldy-on-land bodies back into the surf, have to be among Florida's best wildlife experiences.

Established in 1991, Melbourne's **Archie Carr National Wildlife Refuge** covers more than 20 miles of beach and shoreline in Brevard and Indian Counties and protects the most important habitat in the world for nesting loggerhead sea turtles (the season runs from April to September). These protected beaches are also among North America's most vital

WHERE TO FIND ROOFTOP BARS ON THE SPACE COAST

Space Bar
Prime location fronting the Indian River Lagoon in Titusville for scoping rocket launches.

Landing Rooftop
DJs spin and craft cocktails flow at downtown Melbourne's 'sceniest' nightlife spot.

Pineapples
Rooftop hangout in Melbourne's Eau Gallie Arts District for live music and prickly pear margaritas.

for nesting green sea turtles, which nest in Florida between June and late September.

While you could get lucky during the aforementioned period to be out on the beach at night and see a mother sea turtle come ashore, heading out on a guided tour into the refuge during June and July is your best chance at making it happen.

The **Sea Turtle Preservation Society** in Indialantic has the required permits to guide groups at different locations in South Brevard County. The evening starts out with a presentation about sea turtles, explaining why they're under duress, while scouts scour the shoreline for nesting mothers. Once the moment is right, you'll be led to the nesting site to watch a loggerhead mother try her best to keep the species going. **Friends of the Carr Refuge** is another reputable group offering guided sea-turtle walks several nights a week in June and July.

Take an Airboat Ride

GLIDE LIKE A WATER BUG

Airboat rides are often associated with the Everglades (p112). But you can embark on some epic ones along the Space Coast, too, where you're likely to see all manner of wading birds and waterfowl, turtles and tons of alligators in the area's interior waterways.

Never been aboard an airboat before? It's serious fun. The flat-bottomed watercraft are propelled by a gigantic fan on the stern that makes a real ruckus, for which you'll be provided ear protection to use when you're in motion. The best captains not only spin you out in motions that make you feel like you're levitating for a second, but they also stop to share commentary about Florida's wildlife and important freshwater sources (they also make entertaining quips like 'Drowning is not not an option, the gators will eat you before you drown.').

Among the best of the best operators are **Camp Holly Airboat Rides** in Melbourne, with a happening on-site bar and a shop selling gator meat as well as airboats that take you out onto the St Johns River for 35-minute rides. And don't miss twister airboat rides from **Lone Cabbage Fish Camp** into the grassy marshes of the St Johns River and Lake Poinsett. Refuel with a meal of gator tail, turtle and catfish afterwards with the biker-heavy crowd that frequents the fish camp.

BEST SPACE COAST BREAKFAST PLACES

Juice 'N Java Cafe
Enjoy breakfast sandwiches, smoothies and strong coffee at this art-filled cafe in Cocoa Beach. $

Backwater
Make your own pancakes at the fun griddle tables at this popular downtown Melbourne joint. $$

Water's Edge Cafe
Near Port Canaveral's Jetty Park, sip mimosas, eat shrimp and grits or country-fried steak. $

GETTING AROUND

Driving to and from Melbourne is the most sensible option, although several SCAT bus routes do connect Melbourne to most neighboring destinations and loop through several areas of the city.

The Melbourne Orlando International Airport is located to the northeast of the city and works with a limited number of commercial airlines.

NORTHEAST FLORIDA

OLD FLORIDA & NEW EXPERIENCES

Unspoiled beaches, centuries of history and wild secluded spaces mingle with metro areas and world-class entertainment.

Northeast Florida is an interconnected web of shoreline towns, rural enclaves, state parks and miles of beaches surrounding lively metro areas. The people here live at a slower pace than in iconic Florida areas further south, like Miami, Fort Lauderdale, Orlando and Tampa. However, there's plenty to do and see, with world-class entertainment such as NFL games, Nascar and Bike Week. With only 1.6 million people (compared to the Miami metro area's six million), it's the fourth most populous area in the state. But you can still observe and experience what locals call Old Florida.

By this, they mean a friendly, Southern, slow-paced attitude quartered in a semi-tropical environment. Old Florida means hundreds of miles of water – from the gray and rippled St Johns River to clear natural springs – flowing beneath endless old-growth oaks draped with Spanish moss. Old Florida also means beaches, which you can have mostly to yourself if you go at the right time to the right beaches.

Old Florida is the Florida that existed here after people began moving South, but before they started packing into areas around larger cities by the millions. And it lives throughout Northeast Florida, which includes seven counties, two metropolitan areas (Jacksonville and Daytona Beach), St Augustine (the nation's oldest city) and well over 100 miles of beaches.

CARMEN ZISS/SHUTTERSTOCK ©

THE MAIN AREAS

ST AUGUSTINE
History and beaches. p302

JACKSONVILLE
NFL, entertainment and shopping. p315

AMELIA ISLAND
Historic districts and lush shoreline. p323

DAYTONA BEACH
Motorsports and beaches. p327

MARGARET.WIKTOR/SHUTTERSTOCK ©

Right: Jacksonville (p315); above: Skimboarder, Daytona Beach (p327)

CAR

It's easy to navigate Northeast Florida because all roads lead directly or indirectly to I-95 North or South. For a beautiful and scenic (albeit slower) drive that takes you along the coast and through multiple beachside hamlets, take A1A Coastal Hwy North or South.

UBER, LYFT & TAXI

If you choose not to rent a car, you can call an Uber, Lyft or local taxi. You may have to wait much longer in smaller cities or during busy times, so try to reserve a ride as far ahead as possible.

LOCAL TRANSPORT

The metro areas have dependable bus services, and some of the smaller towns offer limited bus services. Amelia Island and St Augustine offer trolley or shuttle services in historic districts or during special events. Amtrak runs a limited train service from Jacksonville to Daytona Beach.

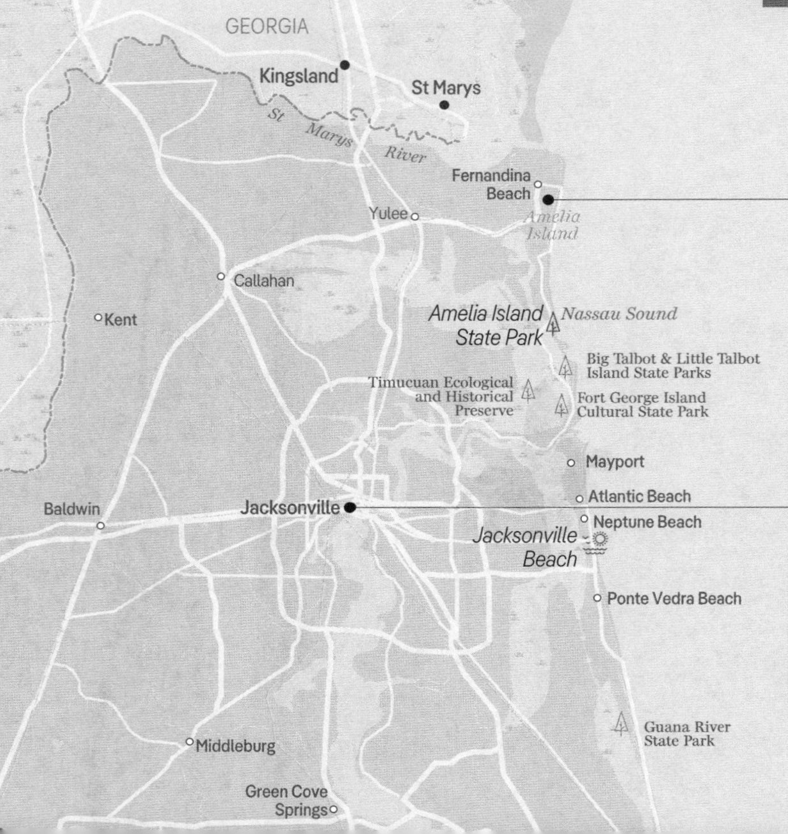

GEORGIA
Kingsland
St Marys
St Marys River
Fernandina Beach
Amelia Island
Yulee
Callahan
Kent
Amelia Island State Park
Nassau Sound
Big Talbot & Little Talbot Island State Parks
Timucuan Ecological and Historical Preserve
Fort George Island Cultural State Park
Mayport
Atlantic Beach
Baldwin
Jacksonville
Neptune Beach
Jacksonville Beach
Ponte Vedra Beach
Guana River State Park
Middleburg
Green Cove Springs
ATLANTIC OCEAN

Amelia Island, p323

This pristine barrier island is known for its golf and luxury resorts, historic downtown areas, and pristine beaches and a state park that evoke Old Florida.

Jacksonville, p315

The largest city by landmass in the country, Jacksonville is home to an NFL team, major entertainment events and miles of busy beaches.

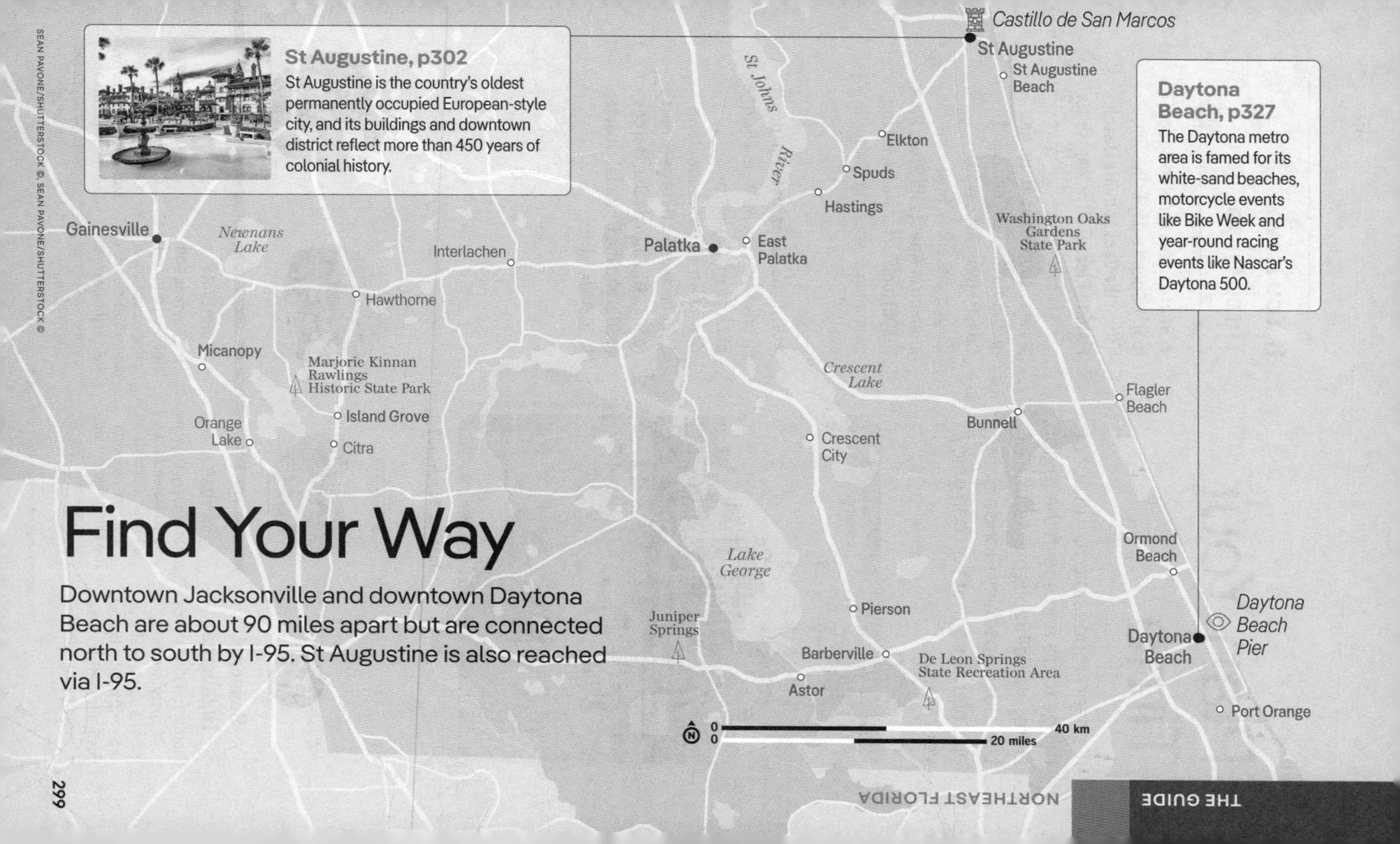

Find Your Way

Downtown Jacksonville and downtown Daytona Beach are about 90 miles apart but are connected north to south by I-95. St Augustine is also reached via I-95.

St Augustine, p302

St Augustine is the country's oldest permanently occupied European-style city, and its buildings and downtown district reflect more than 450 years of colonial history.

Daytona Beach, p327

The Daytona metro area is famed for its white-sand beaches, motorcycle events like Bike Week and year-round racing events like Nascar's Daytona 500.

Plan Your Time

It's near-impossible to run out of things to do and see in the region. Here, we've highlighted some of the must-not-miss Florida doings and sights so that you can enjoy your visit.

SEAN PAVONE/SHUTTERSTOCK ©

Daytona Beach (p327)

If You Have Three Days

- Start at **Jacksonville Beach** (p317). Spend a day in the sun, fish on the **Jacksonville Beach Fishing Pier** (p317) or learn to surf.
- Head south to **St Augustine** (p302) via the A1A Scenic and Coastal Byway and enjoy gorgeous scenery. Spend the morning at **Anastasia State Park** (p305) looking for shells, fishing, swimming or spotting sea-turtle nests.
- Visit the **Alligator Farm** (p307) or drive over the 1920s-era **Bridge of Lions** (p308) into historic downtown. Head for downtown St Augustine: **St George Street** (p303), **Castillo de San Marcos** (p305) and the **Colonial Quarter** (p304) are musts.

Seasonal Highlights

Northeast Florida loves its sporting events, plus its blues, seafood, jazz and holiday lights festivals. And of course motorcycle rallies!

JANUARY

In late January, Daytona hosts **Rolex 24**, a 24-hour sports-car endurance race with live entertainment and a carnival.

FEBRUARY

The **Daytona 500** (p328) is the most prestigious Nascar race, a 500-mile dash held at the Daytona International Speedway each February.

MARCH

Bike Week (p329) motors into Daytona Beach. St Augustine's **Lions Seafood Festival** offers food trucks, contests and some axe throwing.

JEAN PIERRE KATHOEFER/SHUTTERSTOCK ©, GRINDSTONE MEDIA GROUP/SHUTTERSTOCK ©, PERRIS TUMBAO/SHUTTERSTOCK ©

If You Have Five Days

- Celebrate in the sun at **Jacksonville Beach** (p317). Drive toward St Augustine and head to **Anastasia State Park** (p305). Take in **historic downtown** (p303) St Augustine, including St George St, Castillo de San Marcos and the Colonial Quarter.

- Head south to **Daytona Beach** (p327) for its beach, shopping and dining options with live entertainment. Visit the **Daytona International Speedway** (p330), the city's famous racetrack. Catch a race, shop, eat or reserve a ride-along.

- On the way to Daytona, explore the formal gardens at **Washington Oaks Gardens State Park** (p313) or kayak among dolphins in the **River to Sea Preserve** (p312).

A Week or More

- From **Jacksonville Beach** (p317) drive south to **Anastasia State Park** (p305) in St Augustine. Take in **historic downtown** (p303) St Augustine. Tour **Flagler College** (p309), then check out **Castillo de San Marcos** (p305) and galleries nearby.

- Head south to **Marineland** (p311), hike and kayak in the **River to Sea Preserve** (p312), and explore formal gardens at **Washington Oaks Gardens State Park** (p313).

- Continue south to Daytona Beach for **beach** (p330) time before visiting **Daytona International Speedway** (p330). Enjoy family-friendly **Ponce Inlet** (p331) and climb up its lighthouse at the **Ponce de León Inlet Lighthouse & Museum** (p331). Kids love the **Marine Science Center** (p331).

MARCH, APRIL & MAY

Springing the Blues offers free concerts in downtown Jax Beach, and the **Jacksonville Jazz Festival** features jazz's most famous names.

AUGUST

The **Jacksonville Jaguars** kick off the preseason (before the regular NFL season in September) with games at TIAA Bank Field.

OCTOBER

Biketoberfest is a four-day motorcycle congregation in Daytona Beach. The **Florida-Georgia college football game** is the year's big showdown.

NOVEMBER

Over three million white holiday lights outline St Augustine during **Nights of Lights**. Jacksonville's historic Springfield neighborhood fills with music over **PorchFest**.

St Augustine

ST AUGUSTINE

Founded in 1565, St Augustine is the oldest city of European origin in the United States. Its narrow, cobblestone streets, wooden balconies, tabby walls and aged cemeteries breathe its European past.

The historic downtown is the heart of the area, especially Plaza de la Constitución (built 1573). The landmark Cathedral Basilica borders it to the north, St George St and the Government House to the west, and the Bridge of Lions to the east. The Colonial Quarter is located across from the bayfront, near St George St, with its many shops and colonial-themed restaurants. The Castillo de San Marcos, aka 'the fort,' is a few blocks northeast.

The super-walkable city draws millions of people annually, and many end up at the shore: St Augustine has 42 miles of beaches, and state parks, including Anastasia State Park, offer coastal forests and uncrowded beaches that truly give you a feel for Old Florida.

TOP TIP

Parking is the most-bemoaned aspect of visiting downtown. Save yourself lots of hassle and park in the Historic Downtown Parking Facility, 1 Cordova St. It's next to the Visitor Information Center and within walking distance of everything downtown.

Bridge of Lions (p308)

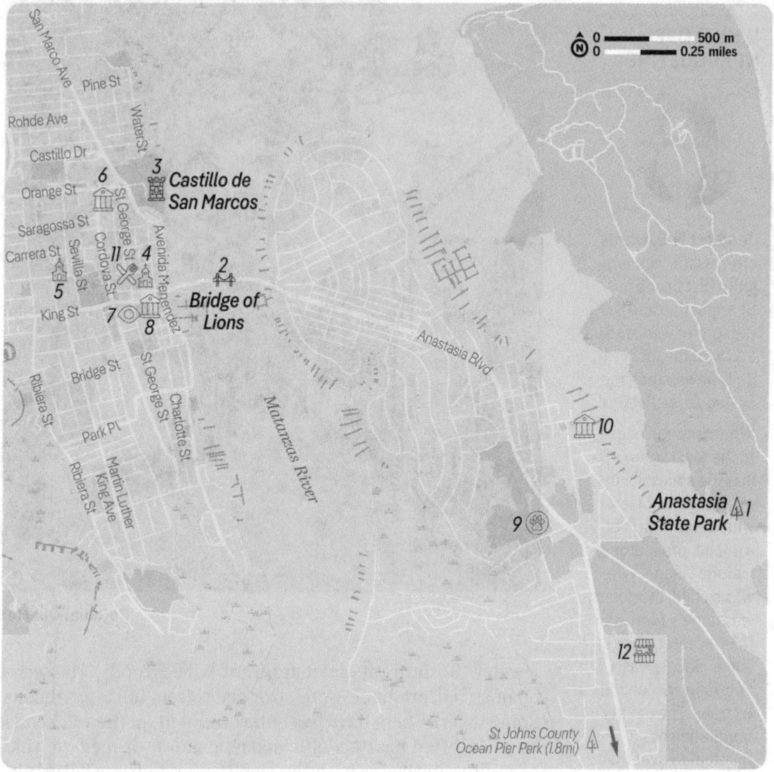

HIGHLIGHTS
1 Anastasia State Park
2 Bridge of Lions
3 Castillo de San Marcos

SIGHTS
4 Cathedral Basilica of St Augustine
5 Memorial Presbyterian Church
6 Oldest Wooden School House Museum & Gardens
7 Plaza de la Constitución
8 Slave Market
9 St Augustine Alligator Farm Zoological Park
10 St Augustine Lighthouse & Maritime Museum

EATING
11 Kilwin's

SHOPPING
12 Amp Farmers Market

Strolling St George Street

SHOPPING FOR A SENSE OF PLACE

The first place locals take visitors to is St George St, the town's de facto (if not geographical) heart.

Shops housed in restored Colonial buildings sell handmade sweets, funky clothing, blown-glass confections and artisanal

WHERE TO STAY IN ST AUGUSTINE & THE BEACH

Bayfront Westcott House Bed and Breakfast
This Victorian-style, two-story B&B is within walking distance of the historic downtown. **$$$**

Hilton St Augustine Historic Bayfront
A hotel with a commanding view of the bayfront and the Bridge of Lions. **$$$**

Doubletree by Hilton St Augustine Historic District
North of the historic district. Offers room service and reasonable prices. **$$**

WHY I LOVE ST AUGUSTINE

Jennifer M Edwards is an award-winning journalist based in St Augustine and the former weekend editor of the local daily newspaper, the *St Augustine Record*.

What drew me back to the town I grew up in is the accessibility of nature combined with the comforts of a quaint, prosperous, historic village. When I was a child, the county was largely rural, and US-1, now six lanes in some places, was a two-lane ensconced by trees. The county's population has quintupled over the past decades, but the area has held onto large pockets of serene, natural beauty. Downtown has kept its characteristic one-way cobblestone streets, but city officials, residents and businesspeople have lovingly polished its buildings, roads and public spaces.

LAZYLLAMA/SHUTTERSTOCK ©

Colonial Quarter

jewelry. Restaurants offer fragrant baked goods, glasses of Spanish red, aromatic espresso or plates from full tapas menus. Some taverns here have live entertainment on the weekends, so you'll often hear a violin, acoustic guitar or melodic voices mixing in the air with the smell of fudge from **Kilwin's**.

The **Oldest Wooden School House Museum & Gardens** is on St George St, and the **Colonial Quarter** is behind it (although you'll have to get to it from the bayfront side). The street is closed to all but pedestrian traffic. However, cabs and trolleys stop at either end – the city gates to the north and the street light at the south, adjacent to the historic and sumptuous **Cathedral Basilica of St Augustine**, built in 1797 and then rebuilt after a fire and reopened in 1887.

You can walk from the southern end to **Plaza de la Constitución**, with its giant old oaks and diminutive open-air covered market, called the **Slave Market**, for its short-lived but significant use centuries ago. You can also choose from more restaurants and several galleries around the plaza.

All the traffic-light intersections are pedestrian-friendly with crosswalks and buttons to cross, and you can stroll across

WHERE TO STAY IN ST AUGUSTINE & THE BEACH

Embassy Suites by Hilton St Augustine Beach
This oceanfront resort has an on-site restaurant. Next to St Augustine Beach. **$$$**

Guy Harvey Resort
This laid-back resort has a tiki bar, clothing shop, restaurant and private beach entrance. **$$**

Casa Monica Hotel
Beautiful Spanish Revival hotel on the plaza. Valet parking, gorgeous rooms, ground-floor restaurant and Starbucks. **$$$**

the **Bridge of Lions**, built in 1927 and restored in 2010. The other side of the bridge affords a fantastic view of downtown with its red Spanish tile roofs and B&Bs along the bayfront.

History at Castillo de San Marcos

THE FORT THAT NEVER FELL

St Augustine has been through its fair share of pirate attacks, military onslaughts, pillaging, raiding, looting and burning. In fact, the British invaded the Spanish outpost in 1702 and torched every building to the ground, except the formidable **Castillo de San Marcos** (known just as 'the fort' to locals). The town was rebuilt after the fires per the original Spanish governor's plan, but the fort is much as it was, including the deep slopes that once contained moats to keep out invaders.

Built in the late 1600s, the fort's also the only 17th-century military construction still standing in the US. It's made of a rare material called coquina, which is common in and around the town but scarce elsewhere. Fort Matanzas National Monument (p313), a few miles south of St Augustine, is the only other fort made of the material. It is a porous rock of fossilized shells from tiny native coquina clams that were once white, pink, yellow or lavender before the persistent Florida sun bleached them gray and white. While the fort has changed hands a few times, it has never fallen, even while housing as many as 1500 people during the English siege. It still bears the scars, though: cannonballs embedded in its walls.

Spain eventually bequeathed the fort to England in 1763 under the Treaty of Paris, and the British signed it back to Spain under another treaty before the Americans bought it in 1821. Today, it's a national monument abuzz with live, timed cannon blasts, fully costumed reenactors, tour guides and plenty of visitors to the **museum** on the ground floor.

The Castillo is located in the heart of historic downtown, along the Matanzas River bayfront, and is accessible by foot, trolley or horse-drawn carriage. It's also one of those rare places with nearly adequate parking. The lot has digital parking meters, so bring a card.

Exploring Anastasia State Park

SEA TURTLE NESTS AND UNSPOILED BEACHES

About 1600 acres of unspoiled beaches, dun-colored dunes and coastal hammocks comprise Anastasia State Park, located east of downtown St Augustine and right along the Atlantic Ocean. **Salt Run** crosses directly through the park, between a spit of land and the Atlantic Ocean to the east. Salt Run is one of the

DUCK SEASON? NO, TURTLE TIME

The local beaches aren't just popular with residents and visitors; every year, mariners of a more leathery variety come ashore.

Sea-turtle nesting season technically begins on April 15 statewide. But this far north in Florida, it begins May 1 and runs through to October 31. Sea-turtle-patrol volunteers scour the sands and mark off the nests with stakes to protect the burrows, which often appear in the morning because turtles nest at night.

Be sure not to disturb the nests; the odds are already against the hatchlings, as only one in 100 usually survives. The eggs typically hatch at night, releasing loggerheads, greens, leatherbacks and, once in a while, a Kemp's ridley sea turtle.

WHERE TO EAT LIKE A LOCAL IN ST AUGUSTINE & THE BEACH

Columbia
A long-standing Spanish-Cuban restaurant. Offers sangria, tapas, and unique cocktails and entrees. **$$$**

A1A Ale Works Restaurant & Taproom
Try the beer cheese soup or local craft beer at this bayfront spot with 2nd-floor views. **$$**

Athena
Located on Plaza de la Constitución. Serves authentic Greek items like saganaki, souvlaki and retsina. **$$**

BEST PLACES TO GET ICE CREAM

Coneheads
This St Augustine Beach shop is a local favorite with rich ice cream, outdoor seating and many options. $

Kilwin's
You can't walk St George St without smelling Kilwin's cooking pralines and fudge. Its ice cream tastes as rich as the sweet shop smells. $

Mayday
This local favorite and relative newcomer to downtown offers flavors like Icebox Lemon and Coffee+Donuts. $

Cold Cow
It's off the beaten track but worth it for its enormous variety and velvety textures. $

best places to boat or kayak to view the famously striped St Augustine Lighthouse & Maritime Museum and share the ripples with dolphins, stingrays and an array of native and migratory birds. An assortment of sea turtles also likes to nest here.

The park is Old Florida at its finest, with a touch of human history; when the Spaniards built the Castillo de San Marcos and Fort Matanzas in the late 1600s, they quarried the coquina rock for the fortifications here. That said, the park has a lot of modern amenities, including a place to rent canoes, kayaks and sailboats. There are also boat launches, restrooms, showers, picnic areas, a playground and a boardwalk to the beach. If you're swimming, pick your spot carefully because the currents here can be dangerous.

The park is a beautiful place to camp. Seasoned campers usually book their spots as many as 11 months out (max allowed) if they plan to come during popular times like weekends and holidays. At $28, camping is less expensive than a hotel room and offers a more intimate view of the scenery. Sites are available for tents or RVs.

Coastal Fun at St Johns County Ocean Pier Park

SWIMMING, SURFING, FISHING AND COMMUNITY

The St Johns County Ocean Pier Park is right on the Atlantic Ocean within the tiny **City of St Augustine Beach**. The town is only about 2.5 sq miles, and the park is just four beachfront acres, but it plays an outsized role in the community.

There's direct access to a beach popular with surfers, a pavilion that hosts free live concerts throughout the summer and holidays, and a **farmers market** that pops up in the parking lot every Wednesday from 8am to noon. You can chat with locals at the market and find everything from handmade soap to authentic African food and organic produce. Then there's the splash park, playground, volleyball courts and the namesake pier.

The **pier** extends 800ft, and for $6 (less for veterans and kids), you can spend all day fishing for sheepshead, black drum, whiting (or sometimes sharks), watching cannonball jellies float under the bridge, and checking out the surfers and swimmers below. If the beach is more your thing, head down the stairs leading from the park's seawall and spread a blanket over the sand. There are restrooms and a little gift shop to pick up some simple, kid-friendly food and souvenirs.

There's also a lot of parking, and an assortment of hotels are nearby, as are some of the best-known beach restaurants, like **Sunset Grille** and **Panama Hattie's**.

WHERE TO EAT LIKE A LOCAL IN ST AUGUSTINE & THE BEACH

Sunset Grille
St Augustine Beach hangout that serves fresh seafood, award-winning chowder and full bar options. **$$**

Panama Hatties
Restaurant-bar with live music, outdoor seating and great 2nd-story views. **$$$**

Osteen's Restaurant
Seafood restaurant beloved among locals. It offers no frills, just daily specials and fresh seafood. **$$**

St Augustine Lighthouse

Haunting St Augustine Lighthouse & Maritime Museum

SPECTACULAR VIEWS AND GHOSTLY TALES

Venture onto Anastasia Island, the small barrier island across the Bridge of Lions from historic downtown St Augustine. You'll see the black-and-white barber-pole stripes of the St Augustine Lighthouse & Maritime Museum. At night, the fully functional lighthouse slowly spins its light, although ships no longer need it to navigate the Atlantic Ocean and Intracoastal Waterway.

Besides the lighthouse, built in 1874, the museum has a playground, exhibits and nature trails. You can also climb up the 165ft lighthouse for the best view in Northeast Florida. That includes the heavy gray-green tree canopy of **St Augustine Alligator Farm Zoological Park** close by. The birds roost above the alligator and crocodile habitats, and you can spy the pink feathers of roseate spoonbills and the stark white plumes of snowy egrets. You have to be 44in tall to climb, though.

TRAIN OR TROLLEY?

Hands down, the easiest, most enjoyable way to navigate the nation's oldest city is via a conveyance that most people here call the trolley. They are long, open-sided trains with rows of seats that take passengers through downtown on regular routes. The drivers regale riders with stories about the historic buildings passing by. They throw in entertaining snippets of local lore.

The **Old Town Trolley** has 22 stops and offers regular, seasonal and ghost tours. You can get on or off the trolleys at the stops. **Ripley's Red Train Tours** are an hour long and motor through the city, but you can't get on and off during the tours. The trains run hourly.

WHERE TO HAVE A DRINK IN ST AUGUSTINE & THE BEACH

San Sebastian Winery
Blends made from native muscadine grapes, free tours and tastings, and a music bar upstairs.

El Taberno del Caballo
A Colonial Quarter tavern with a covered patio, Spanish wines and a small-bites menu.

Ice Plant
This stylish bar and restaurant is in a 1927 building that was once (you guessed it!) an ice-packing plant.

THE BRIDGE OF LIONS

Built in 1927, this two-lane drawbridge stands out among the many beautiful structures of downtown, even though it sometimes frustrates locals by opening for several minutes to let sailboats on the Matanzas River skim underneath. Closed in 2006 for restoration, it reopened in 2010 with historically accurate street lamps, which outline the graceful arch at night. A bridge tender keeps watch around the clock, alert to boat traffic. During the holiday season, it's ribboned with white lights to match the rest of the historic downtown.

The bridge is the entryway to Anastasia Island, a barrier island with beach access, Anastasia State Park, popular restaurants and the tiny City of St Augustine Beach.

SHARKSHOCK/SHUTTERSTOCK ©

Memorial Presbyterian Church

Like many buildings and streets of historic downtown, the lighthouse also has stories of hauntings, and they seem to have multiplied since **Ghost Hunters International** filmed a 2019 episode at the lighthouse. The lighthouse tour guides often entertain with stories of ghostly touches, phantom smells and objects moving on their own. If you fancy a brush with the paranormal, stay alert as you ascend the 219 steps to the observation deck, perhaps for a spectacular sunrise or sunset tour. Some tours end with a few glasses of vino.

Browsing Amp Farmers Market

EAT, DRINK AND SHOP LOCAL

The **St Augustine Amphitheatre** (aka 'the Amp') is an open-air theater on Anastasia Island that hosts an outsize number of events and attracts major national artists whose music carries for miles on the mild sea breezes. Still, every Saturday morning from 8:30am to 12:30pm, the venue transforms into a more humble hub of shopping activity with a farmers market.

The **Amp Farmers Market** draws locals and people from all over Northeast Florida with fair trade coffee, handmade

WHERE TO HAVE A DRINK IN ST AUGUSTINE & THE BEACH

Milltop Tavern & Listening Room
A full bar, pub food and live music in a cozy, comfortable atmosphere.

Trade Winds Tropical Lounge
Friendly atmosphere, local music and good drink prices (especially for downtown).

Ancient City Brewing Taproom
Sip local brews at this craft-beer tasting room with flights and wine offerings.

jewelry, imported baskets, locally carved wood crafts and artists selling their handiwork. But perhaps its main draw is a wide variety of fresh, local and organic food.

There are organic-produce tents from farms in Hastings and outside Gainesville, including **Frog Song Organics**, which offers organics and unusual fare like native Seminole pumpkins, lion's mane mushrooms, elderberries, locally blended teas, jellies and fermented salsa. At other tents, you'll also find microgreens and small-batch kombucha. **Olive My Pickle**, a Jacksonville company, offers wooden barrels full of probiotic, fermented foods like pickles, sauerkraut and (of course) olives. You'll also find bread from Jacksonville bakeries, Indian sauces and food made with buffalo milk, and more food trucks than you can shake a spork at.

The publisher of *Edible Northeast Florida,* a regional foodie mag, is also usually in attendance with free copies. Area bluegrass musicians also fiddle for tips, and there's a public donation-based yoga class twice a month.

Admiring Architecture at Memorial Presbyterian Church

TOUCHING TRIBUTE TO A LOST DAUGHTER

You won't stay long in St Augustine without hearing about Henry Morrison Flagler, the wealthy industrialist who died in 1913 after transforming old St Augustine into a tourist destination with a railroad and several businesses and hotels. His idea was to turn Florida's east coast into the 'American Riviera,' and he made a fortune by following his vision. Some of his more notable buildings are now home to **Flagler College** and the **Lightner Museum**. But one of his most beautiful legacies is **Memorial Presbyterian Church**, which he commissioned in memory of his daughter, Jenny Louise Benedict, who died due to complications of childbirth.

The church, with its blue-gray walls and cross-topped dome, was dedicated in 1890 in her memory. It's an example of Second Renaissance architecture, and its crafters modeled it after St Mark's Basilica in Venice, but with a St Augustine twist: they constructed the walls of concrete blended with native coquina stone. Benedict, Flagler, Flagler's wife, Mary, and his granddaughter, Marjorie, are buried here in the family mausoleum.

FLAGLER COLLEGE

The first resort Flagler built was the Hotel Ponce de León on King St, now home to Flagler College.

The Spanish Revival building, with its red-tile roof, was the first significant poured-in-place concrete building in the US. When the hotel was new, it was one of the first buildings in the country to feature electric lighting, and Louis Comfort Tiffany himself designed the building's stained glass and mosaics.

Guides will show you a 68ft-tall domed ceiling supported by caryatids and take you to a dining room full of Tiffany stained-glass windows and hand-painted murals. You'll also visit the **Women's Grand Parlor**, with its Austrian crystal and displays from Flagler's family. Tour reservations recommended.

GETTING AROUND

Downtown St Augustine is best navigated by foot because it was founded when most walked, which also means parking is a nightmare. Save yourself frustration and park in the Historic Downtown Parking Facility right by the historic district.

You can take guided rides by train, trolley, pedicab or horse-drawn carriage. There's limited bus service, and you may need a car to get to the beaches and other places. Uber, Lyft and taxis are here but not always available.

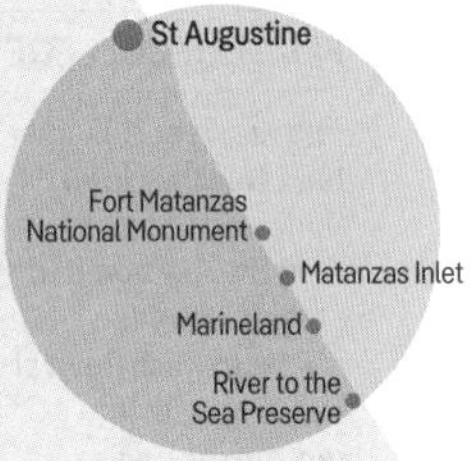

St Augustine
Fort Matanzas National Monument
Matanzas Inlet
Marineland
River to the Sea Preserve

Beyond St Augustine

Marineland is a small stretch of coast along State Rd A1A. It's often overlooked – which is exactly why you should stop.

If you head to the coast and take the striking State Rd A1A south, you'll eventually hit the tiny town of Marineland. With only a dozen or so residents, it's more of an outpost than a residential district. Still, it claims beautiful uncrowded terrain, a cinnamon-dusted beach that's part of the River to Sea Preserve, a sea-turtle hospital and Marineland Dolphin Adventure. The oceanarium is synonymous with the town's name (locals call both 'Marineland') and was built on the site of a former movie studio from 1938. Now it's home to dolphins, sea turtles and other aquatic wildlife you can view and learn about. The town also has a kayak and boat launch into the Matanzas River, home to dolphins, sea turtles, sharks and the occasional manatee.

TOP TIP

State Rd A1A changes names as it traverses cities, although it's still the same road. In Marineland, it's also called Ocean Shore Blvd and A1A Scenic and Historic Coastal Byway.

River to Sea Preserve (p312)

PAUL BRENNAN/SHUTTERSTOCK ©

Marineland Dolphin Adventure

Sea Creatures at Marineland Dolphin Adventure

AQUARIUM FROM THE GOLDEN AGE OF HOLLYWOOD

What's now known as Marineland Dolphin Adventure is the latest transformation of a storied aquarium made to film underwater movie scenes in an era before scuba diving and waterproof cameras. Marine Studios, a three-story, nearly 1-million-gallon 'oceanarium,' was built in 1938 just off State Rd A1A. It was featured in several movies and TV shows, including *The Creature from the Black Lagoon, The Flamingo Rising* and *Bernie the Dolphin*. The first dolphin born in captivity, Spray, was welcomed here in 1947, and so was Nellie, the world's longest-lived dolphin, who died in 2014 at age 61. Later, it became a family-friendly destination with a colorful kids' area, enormous shark jaws at the entrance and regular shows with trained dolphins.

Saltwater, hurricane damage, aging and shifting societal awareness about the harm done to animals kept in captivity for entertainment closed the site. It reopened in 2006 after extensive reconstruction and without the dolphin shows. The Georgia Aquarium now owns Marineland Dolphin Adventure, which offers visitors many opportunities to learn about

WHITNEY LABORATORY SEA TURTLE HOSPITAL

While visitors are befriending dolphins at Marineland Dolphin Adventure, staff across the road are helping other sick and injured sea creatures rest and mend.

The **Whitney Laboratory for Marine Bioscience**, on the west side of Ocean Shore Blvd (State Rd A1A), is a center for research and learning and home to the only sea-turtle hospital in Northeast Florida. It's one of the few places where sea turtles can be treated for fibropapilloma, a common and life-threatening disease that causes tumors.

Kids enjoy touring the hospital, where you can view the turtles – most often loggerheads and greens – and marvel at their colossal size. Tours are paid, and you make a reservation at turtletours@whitney.ufl.edu.

WHERE TO STAY BEYOND ST AUGUSTINE

Beacher's Lodge
Nice oceanfront hotel with a pool on the beach a few miles north of Marineland. **$$$**

Devil's Elbow Fishing Resort
Popular boat launch, bait shop, and boat and ocean-view cottage rentals north of Marineland. **$$$**

Four Winds Condominiums
The condo complex offers a variety of rooms in the Crescent Beach area. **$$**

BEST PLACES FOR LUNCH

Ragga Surf Cafe
Food truck by the beach with excellent coffee, filo-dough 'pop tarts,' sandwiches and outdoor tables. $

Captain's BBQ
Acclaimed barbecue place at Bing's Landing. Has water views and outdoor seating. $

JT's Seafood Shack
Casual American with vegetarian options and indoor and outdoor seating. $$

Bronx House Pizza & Brew Hammock
Pies, calzones, heroes, salads, and unusual appetizers like lasagna balls and fries with gravy and mozzarella. $

JOANNE DALE/SHUTTERSTOCK ©

Kayaking, Matanzas River

and view common bottlenose dolphins, red-footed tortoises, stingrays and other sea creatures.

While all of Marineland's dolphins were born in captivity, research indicates that keeping animals in captivity is harmful and stressful. Somewhat controversially, the site allows visitors to swim with, pet or feed dolphins, but remember that human interaction can be stressful for aquatic creatures.

Kayak the Matanzas River

KEEP PACE WITH WILD DOLPHINS

A major draw to the town is its access to the Matanzas River, one of the purest and most serene waterways in North Florida, via the **River to Sea Preserve**.

The preserve is 90 acres on both sides of State Rd A1A/Ocean Shore Blvd. You can access the beach on the eastern side and hike through coastal scrub, maritime hammock and narrow bands of hardwood trees on the western side. It also has a picnic pavilion, primitive campsites and an overlook of the river.

The west is also where you can launch a canoe, kayak or motorboat onto the Matanzas, part of the Atlantic Intracoastal waterway, which extends 1100 miles from Key West to Norfolk, VA. Playful Atlantic bottlenose dolphins like to pace your boat, and it's not uncommon to see the heads of curious sea turtles poke above the gray waves. Depending on the time of year, you might spy a West Indian manatee.

WHERE TO STAY BEYOND ST AUGUSTINE

Safari by the Sea
Gorgeous tropical villa in the hammock area off State Rd A1A near Washington Oaks Gardens State Park. $$$

Sand Dollar Condominium Rentals by Coastal Realty
Get a selection of home-rental options through this agency. $$$

Summerhouse Beach & Racquet Club
Condos and townhomes with four climate-controlled pools and gated beach access. $$

The Matanzas is also part of a research reserve that extends along the coast and is home to 48 protected animals and eight protected plants.

Some fish that call the Matanzas home are the southern puffer fish, flounder, red drum, Florida pompano and a variety of sharks. The park is pet-friendly and has restrooms, and you can bring your boat or kayak, or book a tour with **Ripple Effects**, which partners with Marineland Dolphin Adventures and Whitney Laboratory. The eco-focused company offers educational canoe and kayak tours and trips aboard motorboats fueled by used vegetable oil.

Lay a Blanket at Marineland Beach

A DIFFERENT KIND OF BEACH

Marineland's beach is part of the **River to Sea Preserve**, located on the east side of State Rd A1A/Ocean Shore Blvd. There's a wooden walkway, restrooms and a food truck nearby in the morning and early afternoon.

Jagged gray rocks line the beach here, and low tide often confines fish and other sea creatures to their crevices. The water has picked the dark rocks into twisted shapes that contrast with the pale sand and transform the shore into a slightly surreal scene. Storms can leave the sand reddish and littered with shells, driftwood and sometimes little jellyfish. It is a great place to enjoy solitude.

The area has a lonesome, rugged natural beauty that contrasts with typical Florida postcards of white sand and packed sunbathers, but it's uncrowded and a great place to lay a blanket. You can swim here, but keep in mind that there are no lifeguards.

The Bloody History of Fort Matanzas National Monument

STRUGGLE FOR THE NEW WORLD

The east coast of Florida has its first European roots in the 1500s when Spain claimed this land and established St Augustine in 1565. The same year, the French established their own military encampment at Fort Caroline, on land Spain considered its own. To make matters worse, the Frenchman Jean Ribault set sail with soldiers to attack St Augustine but was blown off course by a hurricane.

In the meantime, Spain's General Pedro Menéndez de Aviles attacked Fort Caroline and killed most of the men. He later learned of French shipwreck survivors who had come ashore south of St Augustine, and he and his men attacked and killed them, too. Two weeks later, more French shipwreck survivors,

FORMAL GARDENS, INFORMAL BEACH AT WASHINGTON OAKS

Just a couple of miles south of Marineland's singular beaches is an equally distinct state park known for its manicured formal gardens, riverfront dock and wild, pristine beach. **Washington Oaks Gardens State Park** is famous first and foremost for its 20-acre botanical gardens, which incorporate native and regional plants, and for its location on both the Matanzas River and the Atlantic Ocean. The beach side features ancient coquina rock formations that evoke Mars, especially at sunrise.

You can fish on either side and hike or bike through the centuries-old oaks and gardens. There are often themed events here, like native plant sales, garden and history walks, Earth Day events and other goings-on.

WHERE TO EAT BEYOND ST AUGUSTINE

Commander's Shellfish Camp
Much-loved seafood restaurant; if you like oysters or low country boils, try them here. **$$**

386 A Fusion of Fine Eating
Great prime rib and a large, friendly bar area. It's in the hammock area of State Rd A1A. **$$$**

Viola's Pizza, Pasta & Seafood
A lovely, smaller Italian restaurant a few miles north in the Crescent Beach Area. Good espresso. **$$**

including Ribault, arrived at a nearby inlet only to die at Menéndez' hand. The inlet became known as Matanzas, Spanish for 'slaughters.'

Almost two centuries later, the Spanish built the Fort Matanzas out of local coquina. By the time it was completed in 1742, the fort served more as a watchtower than a fort. Today, it is a testament to centuries of Spanish power in the new world.

The National Park Service (NPS) offers a limited ferry service to the dock from the visitor center (8635 A1A South), or you can get there by boat. Fort Matanzas is surrounded by a rich, natural estuary that makes for excellent fishing and wildlife viewing on the way. You might see manatees, dolphins, sea turtles or river otters if you're lucky.

GONE FISHING IN MARINELAND

Although the town of Marineland only spans about half a mile, it's near a variety of fishing spots. You can fish from the Atlantic shore, rent a boat to head further out into the salt or book a deep-sea-fishing charter.

Or fish from your boat in the brackish Matanzas River on the west side of Ocean Shore Blvd (Scenic A1A). The area around Fort Matanzas is especially popular for both boat fishing and spotting manatees, sea turtles and dolphins. You also have the option to fish from the bridge over Matanzas Inlet nearby or from the shore beneath it. Locals swear that high tide and low tide are the best times.

On the Water at Matanzas Inlet

FROM BATTLEGROUND TO PEACEFUL HAVEN

About 2.5 miles north of Marineland on State Rd A1A is Matanzas Inlet, which links the Atlantic Ocean to the Matanzas River. With its fishing, beaches and historic Fort Matanzas, the inlet is worth a day trip by itself.

While the bridge that spans it is nondescript and has just two lanes, it usually bristles with the fishing poles of locals hooking flounder, whiting, blue fish and an occasional sea turtle. Matanzas Inlet flows at high volume underneath the bridge during the tides, making for excellent fishing from above and exciting opportunities to see sea turtles, Atlantic bottlenose dolphins and cannonball jellyfish drift in from the ocean.

Beneath the bridge, high tide makes for dangerous swimming, but low tide is an excellent time for families to walk and explore tidepools, find seashells and gather driftwood along a long, hook-shaped strip of shore that runs from the Atlantic Ocean to the east, under the bridge and into the Intracoastal on the west. Because the west side of the bridge is sheltered from the waves and removed from the road, it gives a feeling of seclusion and security.

On the western side, you can spread a blanket in the golden sand and watch dolphins race with kayaks, see luxury boats zip by or hop aboard a free ferry that takes you from the dock to **Fort Matanzas National Monument**. You can access both sides of the beach by parking at lots on the east and west sides of State Rd A1A. Hurricane Nicole damaged parts of the walkovers, so check with the NPS to see if they're open before you go.

GETTING AROUND

There isn't much to Marineland, really. The town and its main attractions and businesses are along one main road, State Rd A1A/Ocean Shore Blvd. There isn't public transportation, but there's plenty of parking in the beach lots. Once you're here, you can pretty much walk to everything.

Jacksonville
Miami

JACKSONVILLE

Even with its skyscrapers, historic districts, international airport, rush-hour congestion, architecturally unique bridges, NFL team and nearly a million residents, Jacksonville still feels like a small country town dressed in big-city clothes.

People here are friendlier than in other big Florida cities and spend much time outdoors fishing, surfing and watching sports events. They love football and love to hate on their Jaguars (although nobody else better talk bad about them). During football season, tailgating takes on as much (or more) importance than church, and the Florida-Georgia game at TIAA Bank Field is hands down the most anticipated event of the year.

Head east to the beaches for an attitude change. Jax Beach is number one for nightlife, Neptune Beach is small and surfing-oriented, and Atlantic Beach is great for nature, shopping and art. All are laid-back, and flip-flops are tolerated here.

TOP TIP

Stay off the Interstates and major roads during rush hour (7am to 9am, 4pm to 6pm weekdays). Accidents happen, traffic gets backed up and sometimes trips take three times as long. Trouble spots include I-95 downtown; east-to-west thoroughfares like Butler, Southside and Blanding Blvds; and the Main St, Buckman and Acosta bridges.

JUDY KENNAMER/SHUTTERSTOCK ©

Riverfront, Downtown Jacksonville

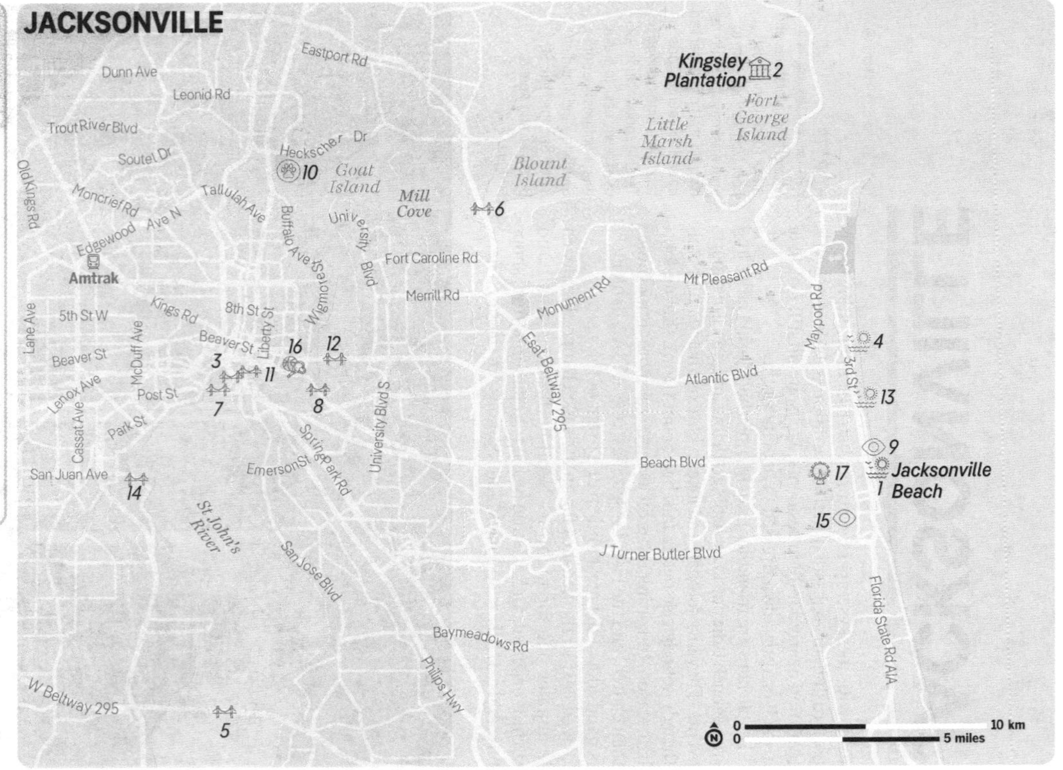

HIGHLIGHTS
1 Jacksonville Beach
2 Kingsley Plantation

SIGHTS
3 Acosta Bridge
4 Atlantic Beach
5 Buckman Bridge
6 Dames Point Bridge
see 3 FEC Strauss Trunnion Bascule Bridge
7 Fuller Warren Bridge
8 Isaiah D Hart Bridge
9 Jacksonville Beach Fishing Pier
10 Jacksonville Zoo & Gardens
11 Main Street Bridge
12 Matthews Bridge
13 Neptune Beach
14 Ortega Bridge
15 Sunshine Playground
16 TIAA Bank Field

ENTERTAINMENT
17 Adventure Landing Jacksonville Beach

Beach Hopping

PICK YOUR BEACH EXPERIENCE

Jacksonville has a lot of entertainment, dining and shopping opportunities in the city, but when its residents want to relax, they hit its beaches, 20 miles outside of downtown. The white, sandy shore is punctuated by distinct towns that each have their own feel and offer different experiences. North of the beaches is **Mayport**, home to Naval Station Mayport and famous for the fresh, plump shrimp harvested here and sold throughout the region.

Jacksonville Beach is the most active spot and a favorite with people in their 20s and 30s who come here to dance, hit a bar or listen to live entertainment. Then there's the beautiful Atlantic Coast, with its blue-gray waves dotted with colorful surfboards, pelicans, boats and trawlers. You can reach it east from I-295 on Beach Blvd to the coast.

Located off Atlantic Blvd, **Neptune Beach** is the next beach town north of Jacksonville Beach. It's a quiet, residential town that began in the 1930s as a community of vacation rental cottages. Neptune Beach shares the **Beaches Town Center** with Atlantic Beach. The town center offers an assortment of tiny boutiques, a wine and cigar bar, a surf shop hawking boards and gear, restaurants with open-air seating, and a place to park your car and walk to the beach.

Atlantic Beach is the northernmost of Jacksonville's beaches. **Kathryn Abbey Hanna Park** (known to the locals as just 'Hanna Park') is located here and is considered one of the best places to surf. It has a plaza, bike and walking trails, a splash park and picnic areas. Atlantic Beach is located off Atlantic Blvd.

Footprints in the Sand at Jacksonville Beach

LIVELY, FAMILY-FRIENDLY BEACH TOWN

Jacksonville Beach is one of the most popular weekend spots for Jacksonvillians and their families because of its wide range of indoor and outdoor activities.

First St offers a boardwalk, and you can fish from the 1300ft **Jacksonville Beach Fishing Pier** here. Anglers catch a variety of saltwater fish, from black drum to flounder and the occasional stingray or shark. The pier has bait-cutting and cleaning stations, a bait shop and a beautiful ocean view.

The surrounding beach is perfect for sunbathing and swimming, and there's surfing, too. You can enjoy a leisurely bike ride or stroll along the boardwalk, and there are plenty

MUSIC FESTIVALS

Springing the Blues
At Jacksonville Beach, this event draws up to 125,000 over three days of free concerts in March and April. The artists play by the beach at the Seawalk Pavilion in downtown Jacksonville Beach.

The Jacksonville Jazz Festival
In May, see some of jazz's most famous names during a free weekend of concerts and events in downtown Jacksonville. It begins with a jazz piano competition and continues with a long lineup of recognizable names.

Jacksonville PorchFest
This is a free music festival that takes place in May on the porches of historic Springfield homes and Sesquicentennial Park on North Main St. It features local artists, vendors and lots of food trucks.

WHERE TO STAY IN JACKSONVILLE

Hampton Inn Jacksonville-Downtown-I-96
Clean, comfy Southbank hotel with free breakfast. Its location downtown is the main draw. **$$**

Hyatt Regency Jacksonville Riverfront
Excellent river and skyline views, a steak and seafood restaurant, and a pool. **$$**

Southbank Hotel Jacksonville Riverwalk
This hotel is in a great location near downtown and the historic San Marco neighborhood. **$$**

FINE ART & GREENERY

The **Cummer Museum of Art & Gardens** blends fine art and beautiful landscaping for a relaxing experience on the river. Housed in Ninah Cummer's spacious riverfront home on Riverside Ave, the Cummer has more than 5000 works of art. But people come here as much for the gardens as they do for the exhibits. Acres of oak trees frame reflecting pools, sculptures, arbors, and English and Italian gardens. The museum also offers lectures, children's programs, concerts and sometimes tai chi or storytelling.

It also has a cafe and gift shop. Corporate sponsorships allow you to visit the Cummer for free on some days, so check the website for dates.

SEAN PAVONE/SHUTTERSTOCK ©

Jacksonvlile Pier

of restaurants, a beach-trolley shuttle service and a free beach-buggy service in the summer.

Kids like **Adventure Landing Jacksonville Beach** on Beach Blvd. It has Shipwreck Island water park, gokarts, miniature golfing and an arcade. And the newly renovated **Sunshine Playground** at South Beach Park offers new playground equipment, shade and pavilions with fans, while the park has a skate park, walking trails, grills, volleyball courts and a seasonal splash pad.

Jacksonville's Historic Neighborhoods

EXPLORING HISTORIC RIVERSIDE AND AVONDALE

Jacksonville, aka 'The River City,' existed as a settlement, river crossing and Native American enclave for centuries before officially being recognized as a town in 1822. But growth, expansion, humidity, hurricanes and the ravages of time have erased many buildings that testify to its history. (And the Great Fire of 1901 didn't help, either; it razed 146 city blocks, changed 2368 buildings to ash, and left nearly 9000 people homeless.)

But two of Jacksonville's oldest neighborhoods, Riverside and Avondale, have fought to hold onto their architectural

WHERE TO STAY AT THE BEACHES

Casa Marina Hotel and Restaurant
European-style boutique hotel with a 3rd-floor rooftop bar and restaurant and ocean views. **$$**

Margaritaville Beach Hotel
This beachside hotel has a resort feel, with bar, restaurant, coffee shop and gift shop. **$**

One Ocean Resort & Spa
Atlantic Beach resort with oceanfront spa, swimming pool, fitness center, pool bar and restaurant. **$$$**

history. The neighborhoods have a community organization called Riverside Avondale Preservation (RAP), whose primary mission is to protect and promote that history. Thanks to RAP's efforts, there are still structures and homes dating back to the 1800s and early 1900s.

Located off Riverside Dr, **Riverside** is in the National Registry of Historic Places. It's home to a younger population, and you'll find historic buildings, upscale apartment complexes, waterfront homes, and a relaxed, chill vibe. The Cummer Museum of Art & Gardens is here, and so is the **Five Points** neighborhood, which offers funky, local-run boutiques, vintage clothing stores and restaurants. The walkable historic district is also home to **Riverside Park** and the popular **Riverside Arts Market**, held every Saturday morning beneath the Fuller Warren Bridge. You can also take a self-guided tour of the historic homes of Riverside here (visitjacksonville.com/blog/historic-homes-of-riverside-tour).

The **Avondale** neighborhood is a wealthy, upscale neighborhood located on and around St Johns Ave and is filled with multimillion-dollar and historic homes. **Boone Park** has a playground and acres of green space, and there's shopping, dining and sometimes entertainment at the **Shoppes of Avondale**.

Go Gators! The Florida-Georgia Game

GATORS, BULLDOGS, RIVALRY, OH MY!

There's arguably no more significant event in Jacksonville than the annual October showdown between the University of Georgia Bulldogs and the University of Florida Gators. Football is huge here, and so are the festivities surrounding it. But when you throw cross-state rivalry into the mix, the energy hits a higher level. That's because, while Jacksonville is firmly in Florida, it's only 33 miles south of the Georgia line. People in the area share a culture, a community, and some of the same workplaces and stomping grounds. (One of the area's most popular groups is country-music duo Florida Georgia Line, after all.)

The Bulldogs and Gators have played each other here every year since 1933, except for 1994 and 1995, when the current stadium, **TIAA Bank Field**, was under construction. Fans usually celebrate the game with a week of events in the days leading up to it, including concerts, luncheons, events and massive tailgating gatherings that include beer, food and live entertainment enjoyed in their parked vehicles or under tents.

The game is big enough that parking gets sold out, the Jacksonville Transportation Authority runs shuttle buses, and fans

TIAA BANK FIELD

TIAA Bank Field on the St Johns River is where people from all over the far-flung metro area come to enjoy concerts, watch the Jacksonville Jaguars play, or attend a food, fitness or music festival.

The field contains the Jaguars' home stadium, finished in 1995 on the site of the historic Gator Bowl. There's also a 5500-seat amphitheater called **Daily's Place**, attracting top-level artists like Nick Cannon, Kenny Chesney and Matchbox Twenty. But the biggest draws to the site are the Jags games, the TaxSlayer Gator Bowl, the Florida-Georgia game and Monster Jam.

Tip: get here early if you're coming to a big game and want to see the kick-off.

WHERE TO EAT IN JACKSONVILLE

Bellwether
The menu takes notes from several ethnic cuisines. Try poutine, char siu or vegan entree. **$$**

Restaurant Orsay
Local favorite offers what it calls Parisian bistro classics infused with Southern influence. **$$$**

Biscotti's
Avondale restaurant offering tasty, bistro-style lunch, dinner and weekend brunch. **$$**

arrive super-early to make it through parking, crowds and security before the kickoff. There is usually a significant police presence, with uniformed and undercover officers. Up to 80,000 fans can pack the stadium to the rafters.

Tip: while you'll see the showdown sometimes billed as the 'Georgia-Florida' game on the TIAA website, locals know it's *really* the Florida-Georgia game, even if the name technically flip-flops each year to make it even. Go Gators!

BLACK ROCK BEACH

Black Rock Beach at **Big Talbot Island State Park** is a prime example of Old Florida, *really* old Florida. Ancient, even. The beach is radically different from the hard-packed, golden-sand beaches. Black Rock formed at the end of the last ice age 10,000 years ago, and it looks like it. Live oak and cedar tree skeletons carved by wind and water line the shore, which is made of geological soil formations that look primordial. It's not so much a beach to sunbathe on as a place to connect with the prehistoric landscape, before humans came along and transformed it. It's 20 minutes from downtown Jacksonville off State Rd A1A North.

Crossing Jacksonville's Seven Bridges

ADDING COLOR, CONNECTING THE CITY

Some people you don't want to cross, but some bridges you do. If you spend time in Jacksonville, you'll probably pass over at least one of the city's seven bridges spanning the St Johns River. Here's a little about each, plus which to avoid and two honorable mentions.

The walkable 1645ft-long concrete **Acosta Bridge** on the Acosta Expwy is near the excitement of downtown, but slow-moving traffic can clog it during rush hour. It's lit in neon at night.

The concrete and steel **Buckman Bridge** has tandem spans for eastbound and westbound traffic on the west I-295 beltway. It's one of the worst rush-hour traffic spots.

Twenty-one miles of cable secured into a harp design stabilizes **Dames Point Bridge**, one of the coolest-looking bridges on this list. At 174ft high, the span gives you a spectacular aerial view.

Eight lanes of I-95 traffic head north and south over the downtown concrete **Fuller Warren Bridge**. It's colorfully lit at night, but avoid it during rush hour.

The **Isaiah D Hart Bridge** is a green, 1960s-era truss bridge that carries fans to and from TIAA Bank Field via Alt-1 and hosts the annual Gate River Run 15K each year.

A walkable blue bridge that's part of the city's skyline, the **Main Street Bridge** takes you downtown via Main St and glows bright blue at night.

Built in the 1950s, the maroon **Matthews Bridge** takes southbound traffic into downtown and toward TIAA Bank Field.

The two honorable mentions are the **FEC Strauss Trunnion Bascule Bridge**, a 1925 railroad truss bridge that runs beneath the Acosta Bridge and has a drawbridge that stays open except when a train thunders across. And at 1143ft, the **Ortega Bridge** is the shortest bridge and mainly serves the affluent and historic Ortega neighborhood.

WHERE TO EAT IN JACKSONVILLE

Ruth's Chris
This riverfront steakhouse is located in the Riverplace Boulevard Crown Plaza Hotel. **$$$**

V Pizza and Sidecar
A popular spot serving brick-oven pizza, pasta and other Italian fare. The pizza's the star, but the wings are tasty, too. **$$**

Terra Gaucha Brazilian Steak House
Locals love this *churrascaria* for its classically prepared meats and salad bar. **$$$**

Jacksonville Zoo

A Day at Jacksonville Zoo & Gardens

LEARN ABOUT ANIMALS AND PLANTS

There are 2500 animals at the Jacksonville Zoo and Gardens. Some are the critters you'd expect to see, like rhinos, zebras and a smattering of warthogs. Others are more exotic, like vampire bats, giant anteaters and Magellanic penguins. (The latter come from coastal South America and not Antarctica, and it's fun to watch them toddle around their watery habitat.) There are also 1000 different kinds of plants.

This is a different zoo than it used to be. Years ago, the habitats were less numerous and colder, and fewer animals lived here. But the zoo continues to grow and add new research, learning and educational opportunities. It has a 4D movie theater, a carousel for kids under 12, and a manatee critical care center, one of just a handful in the state. About one million people a year visit the zoo, located about 8 miles north of downtown Jacksonville.

The zoo spans more than 100 acres. That can be a lot to walk, especially for kids, but you can buy a ticket for a train that brings you to different parts of the park. The zoo is dedicated to being interactive and offers lots of special events throughout the year, such as a holiday lights festival and a dress-up Halloween event.

MOSH

The small, colorful, kid-friendly **Museum of Science and History** (MOSH) has been located on the Southbank Riverwalk for over 50 years. Visiting has been a family tradition for generations of residents, who first came as kids, spent the night on scouting field trips and returned years later with their children. It has fixed and rotating exhibits covering everything from severe weather (tornado machine) to dinosaurs (full-scale animatronics) or the human body. There's also a planetarium that immerses you in the night sky.

The museum is expected to move to a $100 million site in the Jacksonville north bank's Shipyards area sometime around 2026 or 2027. For now, visit the multi-level 74,000-sq-ft building at 1025 Museum Circle.

WHERE TO EAT AT THE BEACHES

Cantina Louie
Atlantic Beach's Day-of-the-Dead-themed Cantina Louie styles itself as Mexican street food. **$$**

Dockside Seafood Restaurant
Views of boaters and the marsh. Plenty of seafood, but also Po' Boy tacos and a kids' menu. **$**

Seafood Kitchen
Atlantic Beach favorite. Great for seafood and comfort food in a laid-back atmosphere. **$$**

SKYDIVING INTO JACKSONVILLE

Want to get Jacksonville's big picture real quick?

Try ascending 10,000ft in a plane and looking down over its vast expanse of sparkling skyscrapers, hardened industrial districts and the long, smooth muscle of the St Johns River – just before jumping out. You can try skydiving at **World Skydiving Center** or **Skydive the Beach Jacksonville**. (Note: If you haven't done it before, you'll likely stay hooked to an instructor at all times while traveling outside the airplane.)

If you're looking for a rush with less chance of mishap, **iFly Indoor Skydiving**, located off the I-295 beltway, iFly allows kids and adults to feel weightless without the risk. It's an excellent fallback for stormy weather.

NICK FOX/SHUTTERSTOCK ©

Kingsley Plantation

Learn About the Past at Kingsley Plantation

LEARNING LESSONS FROM THE PAST

In 1814 Zephania Kinglsey brought his formerly enslaved wife and their three children to Fort George Island to what today is known as Kingsley Plantation. Seven years later, the United States bought Florida from Spain, ending the territory's liberal policies, such as freedom for escaped enslaved people. The couple ran Kingsley Plantation for decades, growing Sea Island cotton, citrus, sugar cane and corn. Many enslaved people lived here in homes made of a material called tabby, made with oyster shells. In 1898 plantation owner John McQueen built the main plantation house, kitchen and smaller saltbox house here by the Fort George River.

Today, visitors come to Kingsley Plantation to see the house, the oldest plantation house in the state, and the immaculate grounds. The grounds also hold the remnants of several dozen tabby slave cabins, and the NPS tells beautiful stories of the strength and ingenuity of some of the enslaved people. Abraham Hanahan served Kingsley with courage and intelligence and eventually secured his freedom, great wealth and his own slaves. Another, Carpenter Bill (renamed William Kingsley), worked his entire life to buy the freedom of most of his family.

It's free to visit Kingsley Plantation, located in the **Timucuan Ecological & Historic Preserve** among Spanish moss-draped oaks. It's at 11676 Palmetto Ave, off State Rd A1A. Check the park website for hours and dates.

GETTING AROUND

You'll need a car to visit many of Jacksonville's sites, attractions and beaches. There's a reliable bus service, but it doesn't go to all areas. You can rent a car or get a taxi, Uber or Lyft. There's a free elevated monorail downtown with a few stops, and the St Johns River Taxi takes you to some riverfront parks, docks, hotels and TIAA Bank Field. Historic neighborhoods like Riverside and Avondale are great places to park and walk.

Miami

AMELIA ISLAND

Amelia Island is located a hair south of Georgia and offers island vibes, pristine parks and uncrowded beaches with a dash of history. There's a pronounced arts culture here in the island's three communities: Fernandina Beach, American Beach and American City. Here's where you'll find film festivals, chamber-music festivals and the enormously popular Isle of Eight Flags Shrimp Festival, which attracts 150,000 people to the area in May. A bit less than 40,000 people live on the island year-round, and it tends to be more affluent than other areas in Northeast Florida.

There are striking state parks, including Fort Clinch and Amelia Island State Park, and great weather year-round means there's plenty of opportunity to golf, hike, boat, kayak, canoe, fish or swim. The area is also known for the horses you'll occasionally see on the beaches, where horseback riding isn't just allowed but encouraged.

TOP TIP

Spring and summer are the peak times here. Try fall and winter if you want the beaches, state parks and popular venues more to yourself.

Fernandina Beach, Amelia Island (p324)

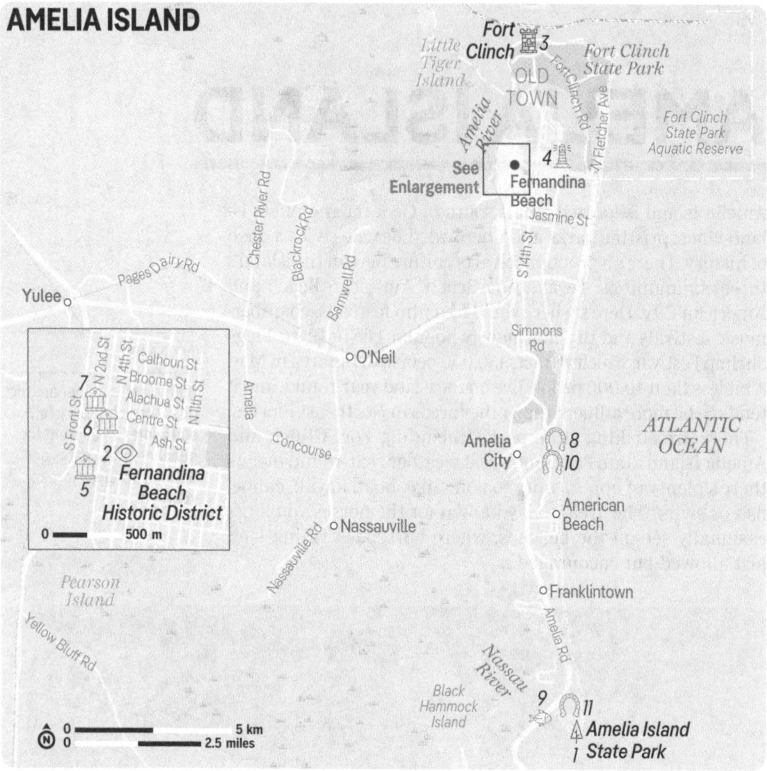

AMELIA ISLAND

HIGHLIGHTS
1 Amelia Island State Park
2 Fernandina Beach Historic District
3 Fort Clinch

SIGHTS
4 Amelia Island Lighthouse
5 Amelia Island Museum of History
6 Florida House Inn
7 Palace Saloon

ACTIVITIES, COURSES & TOURS
8 Amelia Island Horseback Riding
9 George Crady Bridge Fishing Pier State Park
10 Happy Trails Walking Horses
11 Kelly Seahorse Ranch

The Historic District

VICTORIAN-ERA TRAPPINGS, ECLECTIC SHOPPING

The downtown historic district is one of the big draws to **Fernandina Beach**. The walkable, shoppable Victorian-era section reaches 50 blocks and is part of the National Registry of Historic Places. It contains the state's oldest continually operated bar, the **Palace Saloon** (established 1903), the

WHERE TO STAY ON AMELIA ISLAND

Amelia Schoolhouse Inn
This unique boutique hotel is the first school built on Amelia Island in 1886, right in the heart of Fernandina Beach. **$$**

Beachside Motel
A no-frills value hotel right on the beach. **$**

Hoyt House Bed & Breakfast
Fernandina Beach Victorian-style B&B with beautiful interior and wrap-around porch, pool and hot tub. **$$$**

oldest hotel in Florida, the **Florida House Inn** (built 1857), and lots of charming period B&Bs.

There's plenty of shopping to do, too. There are local artists, bookstores, candle makers, surf shops and even a store dedicated to needlepoint.

But don't confuse the downtown historic district with **Old Town**. While the latter is on the National Registry of Historic Places, it's a primarily residential neighborhood just north of the historic district. Towngate St, Bosque Bello Cemetery, Nassau Marine St and Ladies St define it. The neighborhood sits on what was once the original Fernandina Beach.

BEST CAFES ON AMELIA ISLAND

Amelia Island Coffee
Laid-back cafe that serves locally roasted coffee, espresso, and breakfast and brunch in the heart of downtown Fernandina Beach. $

Hola Cuban Coffee
Cuban coffee and fare are served in a relaxing atmosphere with an outdoor patio. $

Nana Teresa's Bake Shop
Bright and cheerful, with appealing baked goods, coffee, espresso and an old-timey soda fountain. $

Mocama Coffee
The shop sells French press, brewed coffee, espresso, a monthly coffee special and various teas. $

Record Attempts at Amelia Island State Park

SERENE BEACHES AND AMAZING FISHING

Amelia Island State Park is a beautiful, popular place to be outside – so popular that the park closes after 600 people come in. The park's 200 acres are located off State Rd A1A North at the southern tip of Amelia Island. The park is just a few miles south of Fernandina Beach and past a famous fishing spot, the **George Crady Bridge Fishing Pier State Park**.

The pier is a mile-long dock over Nassau Sound where anglers come to catch tarpon, redfish, speckled sea trout, whiting and redfish (sometimes with shrimp and mullet they caught at the park in a cast net). Someone who fished here now holds the record for biggest flounder, but note that you'll already need to have a fishing license to try beating the record because the park doesn't sell licenses.

It's the only state park that lets you ride a horse on the beach (and offers you the chance via visitor service provider Kelly Seahorse Ranch), through the pale dunes and maritime hammock. The pet-friendly park is a favorite site for birders following the **Great Birding and Wildlife Trail** and for shellers and shark-tooth hunters. There are showers and restrooms on-site, and you can drive on the beach, but you'll need a 4WD.

Horseback Riding on the Beach

SAND, STIRRUPS AND SADDLES

There are a few horseback riding operators, but the one that's been around the longest is **Amelia Island Horseback Riding**. You can choose from among several options, including hour-long sunset, sunrise, proposal and day rides. All the rides take place on the beach. **Kelly Seahorse Ranch** is a family-run ranch based on the beach and endorsed by

Riding on the beach

Ritz-Carlton Amelia Island
Resort with its own golf course, full-service spa with massage packages and one of the island's best restaurants, Salt. **$$$**

Omni Amelia Island Resort
Every room at the Omni has an ocean view, and the full resort has a spa, resort pools and its own golf courses. **$$$**

Seaside Amelia Inn
One of the few hotels right on the beach in Fernandina, it has a pool, rooftop sundeck and fresh cookies at the desk. **$$**

SHRIMP FESTIVAL

Fernandina Beach has about 13,000 full-time residents, but that number can swell to as many as 150,000 during the **Isle of Eight Flags Shrimp Festival**, a huge bash that lasts over three days in early May. That's when merrymakers swarm the city to enjoy a long list of events like fireworks, a food festival, antiques shows, the Miss Shrimp pageant and a race called the Shrimp Run.

Pirates usually invade at some point during the festival, and community organizations hold a parade a few days before the festival to warm up visitors and residents.

the State of Florida for rides in Amelia Island State Park. It also offers hour-long rides. **Happy Trails Walking Horses** organizes rides on Tennessee Walker horses, a special breed of plantation horse. Guides can take you on a sunset or sunrise ride or a two-hour, 13-mile trail ride. Expect to spend between $125 to $175 per hour for a ride.

All tours begin at **Peters Point Beachfront Park** in Fernandina Beach.

Going North to Fernandina Beach

BEACHES, BUILDINGS AND A SHRIMP FESTIVAL

Fernandina Beach is the northernmost city on Florida's east coast, the Nassau County seat, and the largest community on Amelia Island. Fernandina is the place most people think of when they're mulling a trip to the island. The city has a downtown historic district with buildings dating from the 1800s and early 1900s, copious restaurants and shopping, plenty of beaches, and Fort Clinch State Park, not to mention a hugely popular shrimp festival. It's also the site of the municipal airport, beachfront hotels and the **Amelia Island Museum of History**.

While you're here, also consider checking out the **Amelia Island Lighthouse**. Built in 1838 and maintained by the City of Fernandina Beach and the Coast Guard, it's the oldest in Florida.

Re-enacting the Civil War at Fort Clinch

NATURAL BEAUTY AND LIVING HISTORY

Fort Clinch State Park offers an Old Florida combination of natural beauty and living history. It's located at the northern tip of Amelia Island, just across the St Mary's River from Georgia's Cumberland Island, but it feels remote in both place and time. A drive through old oaks sets the tone as you head to the fort to find several buildings colonizing well-maintained grounds.

Built in 1847 and restored in the 1930s, the Fort Clinch complex has brick walls and tunnels, a staged kitchen area and a museum. One weekend a month, re-enactors dress as Union soldiers and fire the cannons. (During the Civil War, the fort belonged to the Confederates, but General Robert E Lee ordered troops to withdraw and the Union seized it in 1862.) Re-enactors are here year-round, though, demonstrating forgotten skills and answering questions.

As striking as the fort experience is, many people who come here skip it and go right to the beach instead. And who can blame them? It's a lush, beautiful, mostly uncrowded place to sun, swim or find conch shells, sand dollars, sharks' teeth and other sea treasures.

GETTING AROUND

It's easiest to get around the island by car, but Nassau County does offer an inexpensive Saturday bus service called the Island Hopper. There are plenty of shuttle services to and from the airport, and you can rent a car or a bike at a few places on the island.

DAYTONA BEACH

Daytona Beach
Miami

As the name implies, Daytona Beach is known first for its beaches – 23 miles of blue waves washing up on hardpacked white sand. The beaches are especially popular during spring break when high school and college students from all over the state descend to sunbathe and club. In fact, area leaders dubbed the beautiful, iconic shore 'The World's Most Famous Beach' in the 1920s, and the title stuck.

Then there are the other biggies Daytona Beach is known for: Nascar, the Daytona 500, motorsports and Bike Week. The blend of residents, tourists, motorsports fans and bikers makes for an eclectic and high-energy mix. There are about 72,000 full-time residents in the city. But with Daytona's high-rise oceanfront hotels and apartment buildings and its packed beaches and venues, it seems like a much bigger, busier city at certain times. Area promoters have dubbed Daytona Beach part of 'The Fun Coast,' and it fits.

TOP TIP

Nor'easters, tropical storms, hurricanes and weird weather sometimes plague Daytona Beach. Heck, a random 18ft rogue wave even battered the beach out of nowhere one night in 1992, damaging 100 parked cars. If there's been a storm recently, check the Volusia County website to ensure your beach destination is still open and accessible.

Daytona Beach

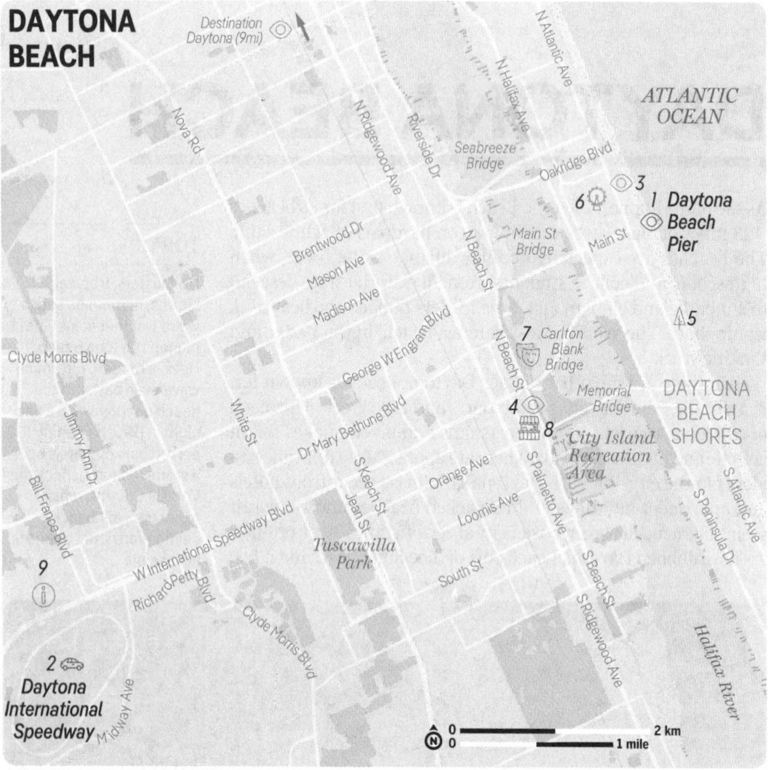

DAYTONA BEACH

HIGHLIGHTS
1 Daytona Beach Pier
2 Daytona International Speedway

SIGHTS
3 Daytona Beach Bandshell
4 Downtown Historic District
5 Sun Splash Park

ENTERTAINMENT
6 Daytona Lagoon
7 News-Journal Center

SHOPPING
8 Downtown Daytona Beach Farmers Market

INFORMATION
9 Bike Week Welcome Center

Going Fast at the Daytona 500

A LEGACY OF BEACH RACING

The Daytona Beach auto-racing story begins with two men, two 1903 cars, an argument over whose horseless carriage was faster and a subsequent race on Daytona Beach. While there's no word who won, legend holds that their sandy grudge

WHERE TO STAY IN DAYTONA BEACH

Club Wyndham Ocean Walk
This high-rise beachside resort features a lazy river, pool and kids' play areas. **$$**

Hilton Daytona Beach Oceanfront Resort
Spacious resort with great views of the ocean and Daytona Beach Pier and excellent amenities. **$$**

River Lily Inn Bed & Breakfast
A five-story, late-1800s B&B with a widow's walk, a swimming pool and verandas overlooking the Halifax River. **$$$**

match was the beginning of the city's tradition of motor racing, mostly on the beach until the area got too populated. In 1947, Bill France Sr went on to help organize racing as a sport by creating the National Association for Stock Car Auto Racing, or Nascar. The next year, Nascar had its first official race in Daytona, again on the beach.

Years later, on February 22, 1959, the city saw the first Daytona 500, with 59 cars and 41,000 spectators, at the Daytona International Speedway. These days, sell-out crowds of more than 100,000 fans attend the annual event in February. The Daytona 500 is named after the 500 miles in total cars must speed (via 200 2.5-mile-long laps around the track), and it's celebrated with a week of races and special events at the speedway. On race day, there's usually entertainment by major headliners, like Trace Adkins, Luke Combs and Better than Ezra, and a red-carpet walk.

Revved up for Bike Week

10 DAYS OF BIKER CULTURE

The closer it gets to spring, the closer it gets to Bike Week, the city's other defining event besides the Daytona 500.

Bike Week has been a thing since the first Daytona 200 motorcycle race in 1937, and it's continued to grow ever since. Tourism officials estimate around 400,000 people come here to attend events throughout Volusia County, and it's now 10 days instead of just a week.

There's an official **Bike Week Welcome Center** at One Daytona, a mall across from the Daytona International Speedway. There are swap meets, organized rides and even a Burning Bike event (the bike is 75ft and wooden) with stilt walkers, high-wire acts, fire dancers and food and beverage vendors. Main St and State Rd A1A are popular cruising spots. **Destination Daytona**, a 150-acre complex featuring a motorcycle museum and Harley-Davidson dealership, is a popular stop.

BIKETOBERFEST

You might consider the fun autumn event Biketoberfest to be Bike Week lite. At four days long, it's shorter, has about a quarter of the attendance, and tends to draw younger people. It also has the advantage of cooler weather, fewer crowds, less expensive hotel rates and more vacancies than during Bike Week.

Biketoberfest highlights include the Rat's Hole Custom Bike and Chopper Show, the Main St drag and live music events. Enthusiasts can get the fill of custom bike builds. Main St is a popular place to watch motorcycles cruise by and enjoy festival-like scenery and events at local businesses.

Daytona Beach Boardwalk & Pier

RIDES, GAMES BY THE OCEAN

Drive over the Main St Bridge toward the ocean, and it will be hard to miss the Daytona Beach Boardwalk & Pier, one of the most popular places for families because of its combination of shopping, rides, pizza, ice cream and an arcade. It's also home to the **Daytona Beach Bandshell**, which offers free concerts every Friday from May through December. Fireworks explode every Saturday during the summer. The end of the 1000ft pier is also open for fishing, with no license required.

Daytona Beach Pier

WHERE TO EAT IN DAYTONA BEACH

Caribbean Jack's
A popular local hangout with a fun, lively atmosphere, live music, great food and marina views. **$$**

Sakana Japanese Steakhouse and Sushi Bar
The standout feature is the sushi boats that float by, letting you choose your premade sushi. **$$**

Sloppy Joe's Daytona Beach
Beach-themed Sloppy Joe's is next to the Bandshell, giving diners an excellent seat for the concerts there. **$$**

DAYTONA INTERNATIONAL SPEEDWAY

The Daytona 500 is the best-known race held here, but the speedway hosts plenty more races and events throughout the year, including the Daytona supercross indoor dirt bike race and the Daytona 200 motorcycle road race, which happen during Bike Week in March. The Tickets and Tours building houses the Motorsports Hall of Fame. It showcases all kinds of motorsports, from racecars to motorcycles to powerboats and more, as well as sculptures of hall-of-fame inductees. Daily speedway tours are $25 and include admission to the hall of fame.

You can drive a Nascar racecar by yourself or take a Nascar ride-along on certain dates. Expect to pay between $176 and $352.

But it's the rides near the boardwalk that you'll notice first. There's the V-shaped 'Slingshot,' which launches you close to 37 stories into the air; the Vomitron (dubbed 'the ride the astronauts feared') that spins you around at 70mph, creating 5G force; and the bar down below that features jello shots, presumably to help you recover. That might be a little much for younger kids, but they can try **Daytona Lagoon**, a couple of blocks north, with its waterslides, lazy river, arcade, bumper cars, ziplines and miniature golf. The park was set for an update in 2023; the owners plan on adding laser tag, arcade games, an ice-cream shop and new landscaping.

Beachcombing on the Sand

DISCOVER WHAT DAYTONA'S FAMOUS FOR

Daytona Beach is best known for its beaches; after all, it's in the name. It also draws thousands upon thousands of high school and college students and families with young children here for spring break. The beach is also where auto racing, one of the city's other claims to fame, began.

There are 23 miles of beaches in Volusia County and 15 publicly maintained coastal parks. They are Argosy, Cardinal Dr, Dahlia Ave, Edwin W Peck Sr, Frank Rendon, Hiles Blvd, Lighthouse Point, Mary McLeod Bethune, Al Weeks Sr North Shore, Tom Renick, Sun Splash, Smyrna Dunes, Toronita Ave, University Blvd and Winterhaven beach parks. Each coastal park offers a unique experience, and the Volusia County government website has an entry for each.

That said, the beach around the **Daytona Beach Pier** is a favorite spot (although it can get crowded). **Sun Splash Park** is an excellent option for kids because it has a splash park and is about five minutes away from downtown on Atlantic Ave.

A unique feature of beaches here is that you can drive on them as long as you stay in designated areas and get a pass, which costs $20 per day and includes re-entry. There's plenty of surfing here, too, as long as you stay in designated areas, away from personal watercraft zones, and further than 300ft of a pier.

You can also make a bonfire if you bring your own pit or get a free one from the city. Don't make them during turtle-nesting season because it can interrupt nesting and hatching.

Riverfront Shops of Daytona

HISTORIC DISTRICT SHOPPING AND DINING

Part of Daytona's **downtown historic district** stretches along Beach St, a beautiful promenade along the Halifax River. You can spend the day strolling here among the breeze and palm

WHERE TO EAT IN DAYTONA BEACH

Aunt Catfish's on the River
A Port Orange local favorite serving Southern-style food, seafood, its namesake dish and fried Cajun shark. **$$**

Chart House
A high-end restaurant with excellent food and outside waterfront seating. **$$$**

The Garlic
Popular New Smyrna Beach restaurant that offers classic Italian food and outside seating. **$$**

PISAPHOTOGRAPHY/SHUTTERSTOCK ©

Traffic signs, Daytona Beach

trees, taking in some architecture from the early 1900s and choosing from about 60 merchants. The retail district is located along Beach St between Bay St and Orange Ave. The corridor has an Old Florida feel that simultaneously manages to feel current.

Part of what makes shopping here a worthwhile experience is the history, combined with the view and the diversity of offerings. There are art galleries, book and records stores, and yoga and dance studios. You can also find American and foreign repair shops and restaurants with everything from hot dogs to Venezuelan and vegan food. There are also wine bars and taverns (and a coffee shop and health-food store that may come in handy the morning after indulging).

The **Downtown Daytona Beach Farmers Market** adds to the choices every Saturday morning when it opens around the corner on Magnolia Ave between Beach St and Palmetto Ave. It's a smaller market with an emphasis on produce. Bring cash if you go.

The north block of Beach St is also home to the **News-Journal Center** at Daytona State College, which has an art gallery and performing-arts events.

PONCE INLET

A quiet residential area, Ponce Inlet allows you to spend a restful day amid history and nature. You can climb the 175ft red **Ponce de León Inlet Lighthouse** built in 1887, or tour the museum below. The **Ponce Inlet Historical Museum** is nearby and showcases two historic Florida Cracker-style houses, one built in 1880, and a 100-year-old cemetery.

Kids love the **Marine Science Center**, where they can learn about native aquatic life and see examples in the many tanks and aquariums. There's also a sea-turtle hospital, turtle talks and daily presentations with raptors.

GETTING AROUND

You'll need a car to get to all that Daytona Beach has to offer. That said, Volusia County runs a fairly extensive bus service called Votran that can get you to most of the major places of interest. Uber and Lyft are here, too, but make sure to book ahead, especially during peak times. Amtrak will also take you to and from Jacksonville by train, but the trip is almost four hours.

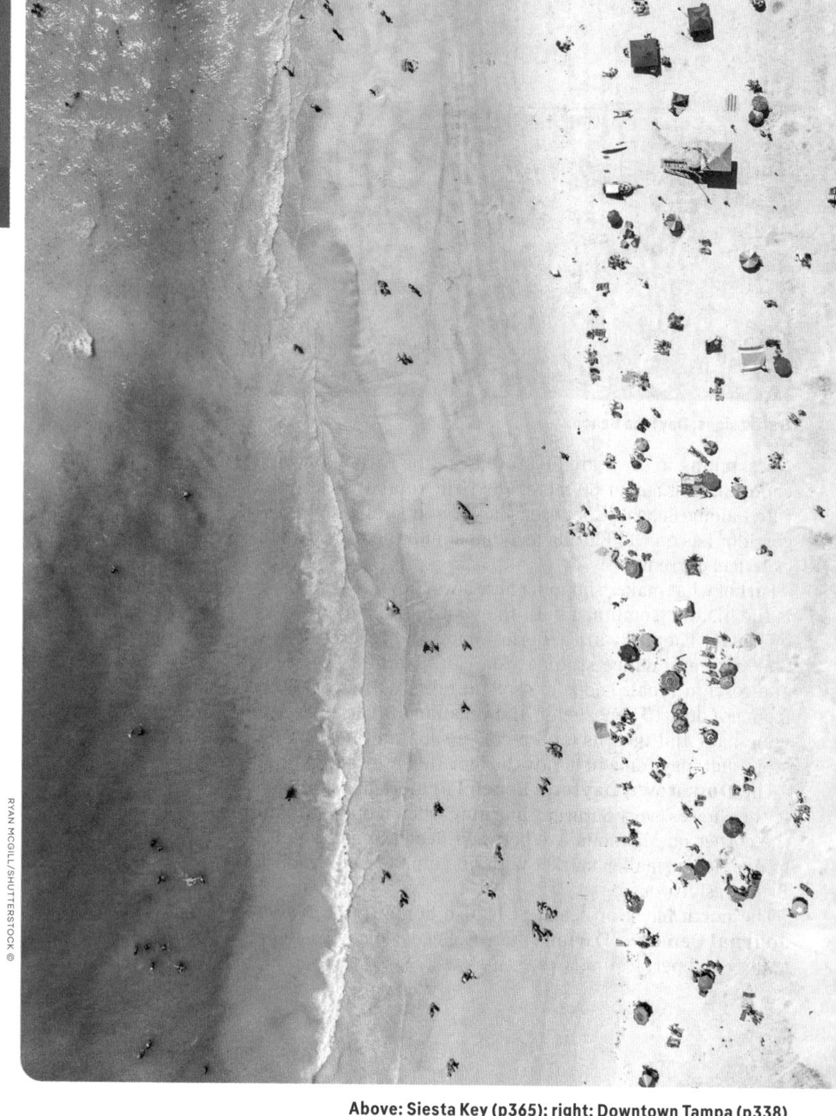

RYAN MCGILL/SHUTTERSTOCK ©

Above: Siesta Key (p365); right: Downtown Tampa (p338)

THE MAIN AREAS

TAMPA
Riverside paths, history, museums. **p338**

ST PETERSBURG
Art-loving city on the bay. **p348**

SARASOTA
Gateway to beach-lined keys. **p359**

TAMPA BAY & THE SOUTHWEST

ISLANDS, OUTDOOR ACTIVITIES AND CITY LIFE

Southwest Florida has long captivated visitors with its picturesque islands, art-fueled cities and jungle-clad parks full of wildlife.

In 1885 Thomas Edison came to Florida looking for a winter escape from the frigid northern temperatures. It was love at first sight when he stepped onto the waterfront along the Caloosahatchee River in Fort Myers. There he built a garden-lined estate to which he returned frequently until the end of his life. Edison is but one of many people, from circus magnate John Ringling to novelist Stephen King, who have fallen under the spell of Southwest Florida.

While some things have changed since Edison first sailed onto the scene, this vast swath of island-fringed coastline has lost none of its allure. The region boasts white quartz sand beaches, crystal-clear spring-fed rivers where manatees graze, and forested pockets brimming with diverse plant and animal life.

Given its natural beauty, it's not surprising that humans have such a long presence in the region. The Calusa fiercely protected their land from the first Spanish incursions in the 16th century. Before them, little known tribes had established coastal settlements dating back millennia, and archaeologists are still uncovering finds related to the peninsula's earliest inhabitants.

More recently, the rise of vibrant cities has redefined life in Southwest Florida. Tampa's iconic riverside and the burgeoning art scene of St Petersburg feature among the region's many attractions. You'll also find a dynamic food scene, magnificent botanical gardens and countless historical sights bringing the past to life, plus some of the world's best sunsets awaiting at day's end.

FORT MYERS
Picturesque downtown. **p369**

NAPLES
Gardens, beaches, restaurants. **p372**

CAR

Unless you're sticking to the main cities, you'll want a vehicle in order to explore the small towns, beaches and scenic keys here. There are several toll roads in the area, most of which are electronic, cashless systems.

BUS

Greyhound runs buses up and down the coast through Tampa, St Petersburg, Sarasota, Fort Myers and Naples. Local transport connects some towns with nearby beach areas: SCAT runs to Siesta Key from Sarasota, while the Suncoast Beach Trolley runs along the barrier islands near St Petersburg.

BOAT

Boat service is limited in the region, though if you're visiting on a weekend, you can take advantage of the Cross Bay Ferry that links St Petersburg with Tampa. Ferries also provide service to Caladesi Island, Egmont Key and Shell Key.

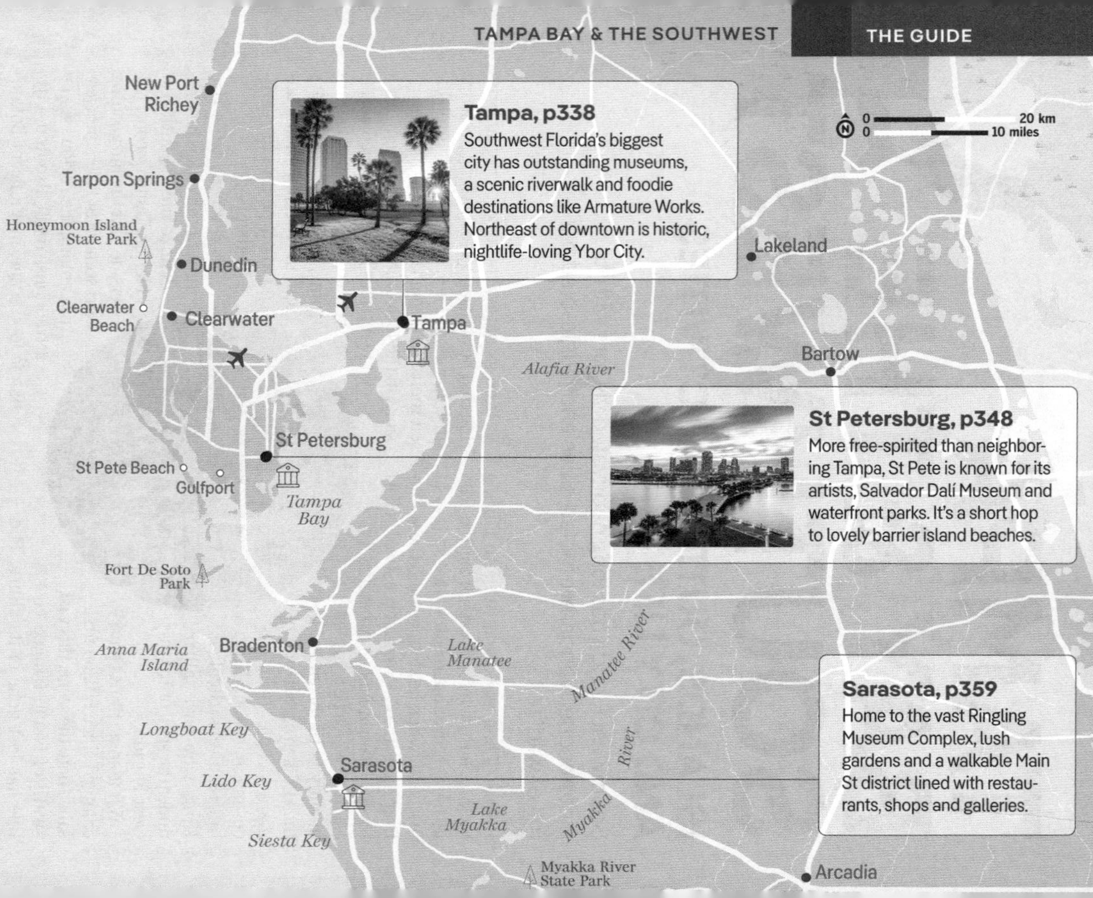

Tampa, p338

Southwest Florida's biggest city has outstanding museums, a scenic riverwalk and foodie destinations like Armature Works. Northeast of downtown is historic, nightlife-loving Ybor City.

St Petersburg, p348

More free-spirited than neighboring Tampa, St Pete is known for its artists, Salvador Dalí Museum and waterfront parks. It's a short hop to lovely barrier island beaches.

Sarasota, p359

Home to the vast Ringling Museum Complex, lush gardens and a walkable Main St district lined with restaurants, shops and galleries.

New Port Richey
Tarpon Springs
Honeymoon Island State Park
Dunedin
Clearwater Beach
Clearwater
Tampa
Lakeland
Bartow
Alafia River
St Petersburg
St Pete Beach
Gulfport
Tampa Bay
Fort De Soto Park
Anna Maria Island
Bradenton
Lake Manatee
Manatee River
Longboat Key
Sarasota
Lido Key
Siesta Key
Lake Myakka
Myakka River
Myakka River State Park
Arcadia
0 20 km
0 10 miles

Find Your Way

Stretching along the Gulf Coast, this long swath of Florida runs for over 200 miles from the clear streams of Crystal River to the sandy beaches of Naples. Tampa is the key gateway to the region.

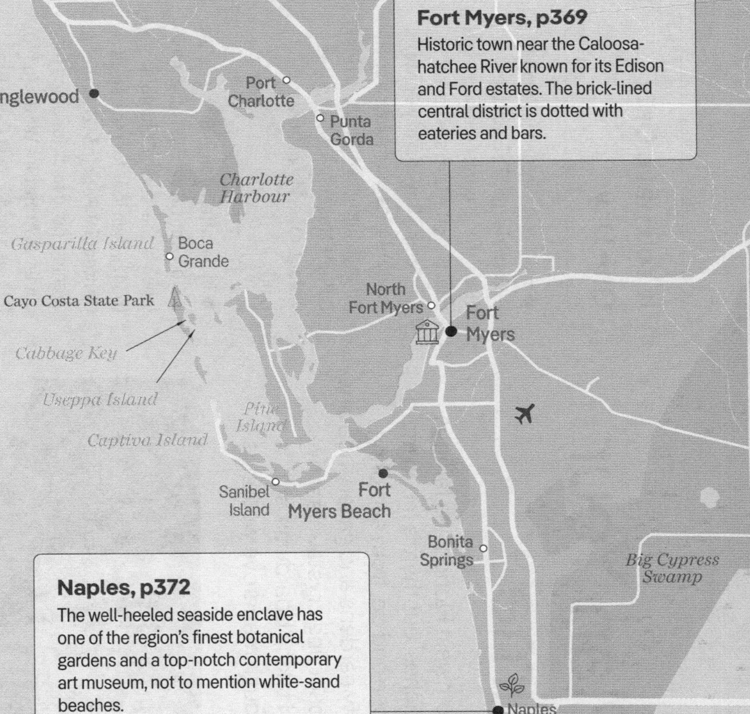

Fort Myers, p369
Historic town near the Caloosahatchee River known for its Edison and Ford estates. The brick-lined central district is dotted with eateries and bars.

Naples, p372
The well-heeled seaside enclave has one of the region's finest botanical gardens and a top-notch contemporary art museum, not to mention white-sand beaches.

Plan Your Time

Southwest Florida has famous beaches, but there's much more to see and do, from exploring leafy gardens and gallery hopping to paddling crystal-clear rivers and taking boardwalk strolls through mangrove wetlands.

GABRIELE MALTINTI/SHUTTERSTOCK ©

Tampa Riverwalk (p339)

If You Have Only One Day

- Start your day on the **Tampa Riverwalk** (p339). Enjoy the morning views over the river, then peel back the layers of time at the **Tampa Bay History Center** (p340). Cross the river for a stroll through the minaret-topped **Henry B Plant Museum** (p341), with its vintage rooms from the early 1900s.

- In the afternoon, ride the trolley up to **Ybor City** (p342) for a late lunch at the iconic **Columbia** (p342), then look for roosters in **Centennial Park** (p342). In the evening, head back to Tampa for dinner at **Armature Works** (p340), followed by drinks at **CW's Gin Joint** (p341).

Seasonal Highlights

Winter is ideal for outdoor activities, spring and fall for beach weather. In summer, stay near water for cool swims.

JANUARY

Tampa kicks off the new year with a bang during the carnivalesque **Gasparilla Pirate Fest** held in late January.

FEBRUARY

Cool (occasionally chilly) nights and pleasant days make Fort Myers the place to be for the **Edison Festival of Light**.

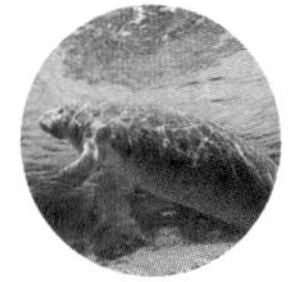

MARCH

On inland waterways like Crystal River, March is prime season for **spotting manatees**, with December to March the best months.

JERI BLAND/SHUTTERSTOCK ©, RUSLAN_127/SHUTTERSTOCK ©, THIERRY EIDENWEIL/SHUTTERSTOCK ©

A Three-Day Weekend

● On your next morning, cross the bay to **St Petersburg** (p348) and spend the day taking in artwork at the **Salvador Dalí Museum** (p348), enjoying breezy views from a lunch spot at the **St Pete Pier** (p350), and browsing the shops and galleries along Central Ave. In the evening, have drinks at one of St Pete's buzzing **craft breweries** (p350).

● Cap your weekend with some time at the beach. At **Honeymoon Island State Park** (p354), you can relax on a lovely shoreline. You can also catch a ferry to **Caladesi Island** (p354), which has forested paths and mangrove-lined shores that you can explore by kayak.

If You Have More Time

● Rise early for the one-hour drive up to **Weeki Wachee Springs State Park** (p344), where you can go for a memorable paddle on a spring-fed river and catch a kitschy mermaid show that has been delighting visitors since the 1940s. North of there, you can take in native Florida wildlife at **Ellie Schiller Homosassa Springs Wildlife State Park** (p345).

● South of Tampa, you can spend some time in scenic **Sarasota** (p359) before heading off to the powdery beaches of **Siesta Key** (p365) and **Anna Maria Island** (p366). Delve into the past at **Historic Spanish Point** (p367), with its archaeological exhibits and early pioneer cottages. Lastly, take a journey around the globe at the **Naples Botanical Garden** (p372) and indulge in the city's celebrated restaurant scene.

APRIL

The days are hot but bearable, making it a fine time to hit St Petersburg's **Mainsail Art Festival** or Sarasota's **Sailor Circus** (p359).

JUNE

As the heat and humidity soar, tourists disappear (hence the **good hotel deals**). June marks the start of hurricane season, which runs through November.

OCTOBER

Fall barely appears in steamy Southwest Florida, which embraces the sunny days during events like the **Shine** mural festival in St Petersburg.

DECEMBER

Snowbirds (wintertime Florida residents) arrive to escape the cold and join in **holiday events**, including Christmas markets, concerts and boat parades.

FELIX MIZIOZNIKOV/SHUTTERSTOCK ©, HAYDEN DUNSEL/SHUTTERSTOCK ©, DOMCRITELLI/SHUTTERSTOCK©, MINGMING JIANG/SHUTTERSTOCK ©

TAMPA

Florida's second-biggest metropolitan area revolves around Tampa, a city of just under 400,000 on the north shore of its eponymous bay. Little is known about the region's first inhabitants, though the indigenous people repelled early efforts by the Spanish to establish a colony here in the 16th century. Only a few pioneers and seasonal fishers passed through over the next few centuries, and settlement began slowly – even after the US established Fort Brooke in present-day downtown in 1824.

Tampa's boom began in earnest in the late 19th century. The discovery and mining of phosphates coincided with the arrival of the railroad and a cigar manufacturing boom in the suburb of Ybor City. Explore the past at the city's fine history collections.

These days Tampa's finest features are linked to its waterfront. The pedestrian- and bike-friendly Riverwalk boasts some of the city's best museums, performing arts halls and sporting arenas.

TOP TIP

Tampa has an excellent restaurant scene, though precious little is downtown. Ybor City is jam-packed with restaurants, while the Seminole Heights neighborhood (along Florida Ave) is a hipster hangout. Gentrified Hyde Park Village, south of downtown, also has a dense concentration of attractive eating and drinking spots.

Henry B Plant Museum (p341)

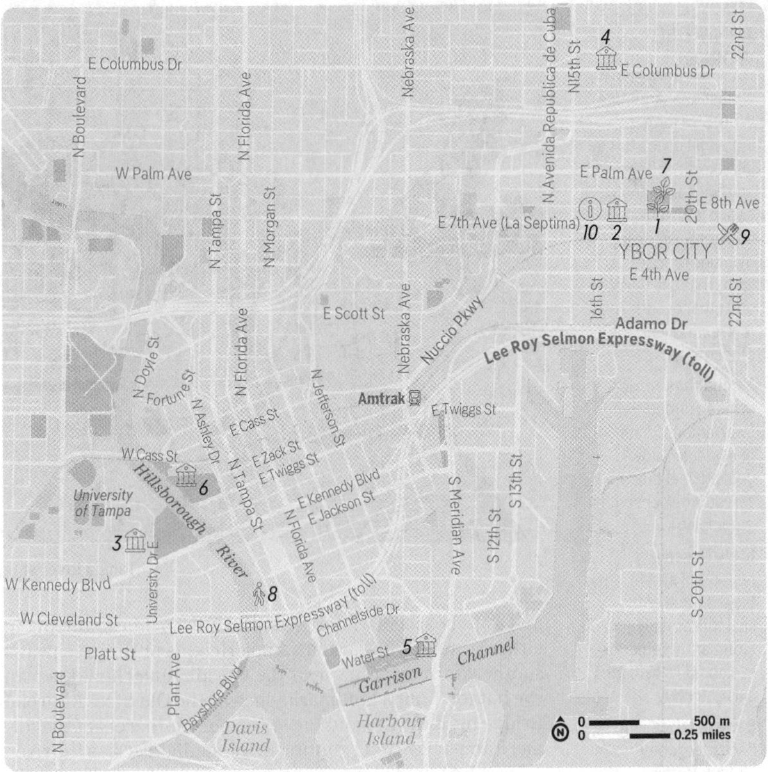

SIGHTS
1 Centennial Park
2 Florida Museum of Photographic Arts
3 Tampa Bay Hotel & Henry B Plant Museum
4 JC Newman
5 Tampa Bay History Center
6 Tampa Museum of Art
7 Ybor City Museum State Park

ACTIVITIES, COURSES & TOURS
8 Tampa Riverwalk

EATING
9 Columbia

INFORMATION
10 Ybor City Visitor Center

Strolling the Tampa Riverwalk

PARKS, VIEWS AND LANDMARKS

Stretching along the Hillsborough River, Tampa's best-loved green space takes you past a mix of palm-fringed parks and shimmering skyscrapers, always within view of the waterway. For the full experience, you can join the runners, cyclists

BEST SPOTS FOR KIDS IN TAMPA

Florida Aquarium
Unique habitats, such as coral reefs and the Florida wetlands with alligators, river otters and roseate spoonbills.

Glazer Children's Museum
Interactive museum with creative play spaces for kids under 10, from an engineer's workshop to a vet clinic.

ZooTampa at Lowry Park
Get an up-close look at native Florida wildlife like black bears and panthers. There are also Africa safari rides.

ARMATURE WORKS

A must-see, Armature Works is a former industrial space turned into the city's best food hall, with abundant eating and drinking spots. The adjoining riverside outdoor space has live music and other events. A few recommended places to hit:

Muchachas Mexican-inspired street fare, famous for its *quesatacos* (slow-cooked beef tacos served with consommé for dipping).

Ulele Upscale restaurant and brewery that showcases native Floridian ingredients in dishes like okra fries and gator tail.

Bake'n Babes Perfectly gooey chocolate chip cookies, plus thick rich shakes.

VIAVAL TOURS/SHUTTERSTOCK ©

Tampa Riverwalk

and skateboarders who traverse the full 2.5 miles, starting in either Waterworks Park in Tampa Heights or the greenway's southeastern terminus near the Florida Aquarium. Keep an eye out for Tampa landmarks such as the Old Steel Railroad Bridge built in 1915 and the silver-hued minarets of the former Tampa Bay Hotel glinting in the sunlight across the river.

Apart from providing a scenic backdrop to a bit of exercise, the Riverwalk is also a great way to travel between key attractions, with major museums (like the Tampa Museum of Art and the Tampa Bay History Center) perched just steps from the vehicle-free path. The Riverwalk is also a gateway to adventures along the Hillsborough. You can hire stand-up paddleboards and kayaks at two key places along the river: from **Urban Kai** near Armature Works and from **Tampa Riverwalk Rentals** near the Sail Plaza. For less strenuous aquatic activity, you can hire electric boats from the Riverwalk Boating Company (also handily located near the Sail Plaza).

Nighttime provides an entirely different perspective of the city, with colorfully illuminated pathways and underpasses, and the lights of waterfront buildings flickering on the river like fireflies.

ART GAZING

Across the bay, the **Salvador Dalí Museum** (p348) is a must for art lovers. In addition to works by the famous Spanish surrealist, the gallery stages some of Florida's best temporary exhibitions, all held in one architecturally striking building.

WHERE TO STAY IN TAMPA

Hotel Haya
Boutique hotel with art-filled rooms, pool and a great restaurant and cafe in Ybor City. **$$$**

Floridian Palace
In a central downtown location, this landmark 1920s hotel has spacious rooms, some with sweeping city views. **$$**

Gram's Place
A small, welcoming hostel in Seminole Heights for travelers who prefer personality over perfect linens. **$**

Art & History

TAMPA'S QUINTESSENTIAL MUSEUMS

The Tampa experience is about many things, from delving into the region's indigenous heritage to exploring cutting-edge art.

One of the best places to learn about the past is at the **Tampa Bay History Center**. Three floors of interactive exhibits give insight into the native peoples who were here when the Spanish arrived, Seminole arts and culture, and the emergence of Cigar City in the 1880s. Don't miss the two films that illustrate the clash of Europeans with Native Americans, and the devastation of the Seminole Wars. There's also a floor devoted to Tampa Bay in the 20th century, and a gallery focused on conquistadors, pirates and shipwrecks. There's a good restaurant on the ground floor overlooking the water.

Architect Stanley Saitowitz' cantilevered **Tampa Museum of Art** appears to float above Curtis Hixon Park overlooking the Hillsborough River. Inside its sculptural shell, six galleries house a permanent collection of Greek and Roman antiquities beside contemporary exhibitions of photography and new media. Visit Thursday night for free admission (4pm to 8pm).

The aptly named five-story Cube building with its soaring atrium houses the **Florida Museum of Photographic Arts**. Thought-provoking temporary exhibitions explore topics like war and conflict, life on the reservation (tying into the acclaimed TV series *Reservation Dogs*) and the intriguing realm of human-animal interactions.

A Gilded Age Confection

A VINTAGE HOTEL TURNED MUSEUM

The silver minarets of Henry B Plant's 1891 **Tampa Bay Hotel** rise majestically above the Hillsborough River. The structure is testimony to the ambitions of its creator, who brought the railroad to the city – and then extended it so guests could disembark straight into the lobby of his 511-room hotel. Never-before-seen-luxuries such as private baths, telephones and electricity became the talk of the town, as did the hotel's decor of Venetian mirrors, French porcelain and exotic furnishings.

At the **Henry B Plant Museum**, it's easy to feel like you've stepped into the past while peering inside the well-preserved rooms – all with period furnishings – including many pieces occupying the same chambers of decades past. Gaze across a dining room elegantly set for a meal (with mismatched porcelain as was the fashion in Victorian times), the breakfast menu advertising honeycomb tripe, fried mush and pigs feet. In the Writing and Reading Room, you can see where captains

I LIVE HERE: WHERE TO EAT IN TAMPA

Stephanie Swanz, the founder of the Armature Works food stalls Empamamas and Muchachas, shares her favorite restaurants.

Sparkman Wharf
Similar to Armature Works but smaller and on the opposite side of the Riverwalk, Sparkman Wharf is an outdoor food hall made of shipping containers.

Olivia
Serves upscale Italian food. Everything on the menu is incredible, especially the arancini.

Wicked Oak Barbeque
A small hole-in-the-wall place that makes the best barbecue in Tampa.

West Tampa Sandwich Shop
Anything is good at the best Cuban place in town: *picadillo, ropa vieja,* the Cuban sandwich, and the fried *palomilla* steak sandwich which is what I always get.

WHERE TO DRINK IN TAMPA

CW's Gin Joint
A beautiful, vintage-inspired drinking den with bespoke cocktails made by nattily attired barkeeps.

Stones Throw
Enjoy drinks and snacks while taking in the breezy views over the riverside.

Magnanimous Brewing
An essential and unpretentious stop for beer lovers with knowledgable staff who pour quality brews.

BEST BARS OF YBOR CITY

Prana
The long-running five-story nightclub has a 4th-floor dance club and a rooftop bar with views over town.

BarrieHaus
Sip a well-balanced lager or IPA on the terrace at this community-centered microbrewery located a few blocks south of the mayhem of East 7th Ave.

Gaspar's Grotto
Paying homage to the region's pirate past, Gaspar's has nautical knickknacks, ample outdoor space and live music or DJs most nights.

of industry gathered to smoke cigars, read the newspapers and send correspondence (via the inkwells on each table).

Today the former hotel is part of the University of Tampa, and upstairs quarters have been converted into classrooms. You can freely wander through other parts of the building. Opposite the entrance to the museum, a long corridor leads down to the Fletcher Lounge, which was the elegant dining room for the hotel.

The museum hosts regular events throughout the year, including a Victorian Christmas Stroll, a Great Gatsby party, afternoons of live music and Upstairs/Downstairs at the Tampa Bay Hotel, where a historic character from the hotel's gilded days brings the past to life (Sundays at 2pm).

Exploring Cigar City

HISTORY, ROOSTERS AND NIGHTLIFE

Ybor (ee-bore) City is a short car or trolley ride northeast of downtown. Like the illicit love child of Key West and Miami's Little Havana, this 19th-century district is a multiethnic neighborhood that hosts the Tampa Bay area's liveliest party scene. It also preserves a strong Cuban, Spanish and Italian heritage from its days as the epicenter of Tampa's cigar industry. You'll quickly find out why the rooster is Ybor's symbol: the birds are wild and proudly strutting everywhere.

A good place to begin your visit is at the **Ybor City Museum State Park** (open Wednesday to Sunday). Set in a former bakery, this small history museum preserves a bygone era, with exhibitions full of striking photos and audio narratives from prominent members of the community. You can also explore the quaint Mediterranean-style gardens and three cigar-worker houses *(casitas)* that were built in 1895.

Opposite the museum is leafy **Centennial Park**, the epicenter of avian action in town. You'll see plenty of chickens, roosters and possibly little chicks, living wild and free as direct descendants of the hens kept by Ybor City's working-class residents over a century ago.

Cigar making is mostly a thing of the past, though **JC Newman** keeps the old traditions alive at its recently restored El Reloj building. You can peruse the museum or book a guided factory tour and see the art of hand-rolling cigars in action.

Ybor City

End your day with a meal at the **Columbia**, a striking Spanish-Cuban restaurant that's been going strong since 1905. The Cuban sandwich is legendary.

Pick up a map at the **Ybor City Visitor Center** located in the heart of the historic district.

GETTING AROUND

Old-fashioned TECO Line Streetcars connect downtown attractions, and also run to Ybor City, running every 20 to 30 minutes.

HART (Hillsborough Area Regional Transit) runs buses around the area. Downtown's Marion Transit Center is a hub for services to the zoo, Busch Gardens and the Henry Plant Museum.

Beyond Tampa

Beyond the metropolis, you can paddle on meandering rivers, look for wildlife and get your heart racing on death-defying roller coasters.

Over three million people live in the greater Tampa Bay area, but pockets of wilderness still lie within relatively easy reach of the city.

At Hillsborough River State Park, you can walk trails amid Spanish-mossed-draped bald cypresses while belted kingfishers dart along the water. Further north, exchange hiking shoes for kayaks as you glide across spring-fed waterways where manatees gather in the winter months, or check out a whimsical mermaid show that has been going strong for nearly 80 years.

Closer to Tampa, you can get your fill of adrenaline-fueled rides, without the hassle of going to Orlando, at Busch Gardens, which has some of America's most exciting roller coasters.

TOP TIP

Before hitting the road, be sure to pick up picnic supplies. Dining options are sparse in this area.

Hillsborough River State Park (p346)

NATURE IMMERSION

A 10-minute drive west of Weeki Wachee Springs, 135-acre **Linda Pedersen State Park** makes a great spot for an unstructured activity. You can go fishing, climb a 40ft tower for views over the salt marshes or walk a nature trail in search of wildlife (there's also a playground and shaded spots for a picnic). The winter is the best time to see manatees.

Northeast of Linda Pedersen State Park (a 10-minute drive), you can continue on to **Bayport Park**. Though small in size, this green space is worth a visit to the scenic dock where you can sometimes spot manatees. It's also a great place to catch the sunset.

EXPLORING AND LIVING/SHUTTERSTOCK ©

Weeki Wachee Springs State Park

Mermaids & River Kayaking

FUN, KITSCHY STATE PARK

Travelers have been lured by the siren song of **Weeki Wachee Springs State Park** since 1947 and it remains one of Florida's original roadside attractions. Even Elvis Presley sat in the glass-paneled underwater theater and watched as pink-tailed mermaids performed pirouettes while turtles and fish swam past. The half-hour shows remain gleeful celebrations of nostalgic kitsch, particularly the mainstay, *The Little Mermaid*. Performances happen two to three times a day; check the schedule before visiting.

While there's no mystery to the trick – the mermaids hold air hoses as they swim and gulp air as needed – there's an undeniable theatrical magic to their effortless performances. The park also offers a sedate riverboat cruise, ranger talks about wildlife and a swimming area with a beach on the springs (plus waterslides and inner tubing in the summer).

Even more impressive than the mermaids is the kayaking trip along the spring-fed river. Very little paddling is required as you glide smoothly

SPRING-FED WONDERS

Florida is famous for its fresh water sources, with hundreds of springs found across the state. Some of these, including Weeki Wachee, are categorized as first magnitude, meaning they discharge at least 100 cubic feet of water per second. Learn more about **Florida's springs** on p433.

THEME PARK REFRESHMENT BEYOND TAMPA

Hang Ten Tiki Bar
In Adventure Island, cool off with a frozen tropical cocktail, empanadas, smoked fish dip and other light fare.

Zambia Smokehouse
Tuck into brisket, barbecue ribs and pulled pork sandwiches at this fast, casual spot in the Stanleyville section.

Serengeti Overlook
Linger over craft beers at Giraffe Bar or refuel at Oasis Pizza while enjoying panoramic views over the Serengeti Plain.

along the swiftly flowing, crystal-clear waterway. You'll see fish swimming past, turtles sunning themselves on logs and twittering birds amid the dense canopy along the banks. Keep an eye out for belted kingfishers, pileated woodpeckers and great blue herons. In the winter, you may also see manatees. Near the park entrance, **Weeki Fresh Water Adventures** rents kayaks for the two-hour trip, with return shuttle provided. Reserve well ahead.

Wildlife, Roller Coasters & Waterslides

THEME PARK ADVENTURES

Orlando doesn't hold a monopoly on Florida theme parks. Tampa presents two enormous thrill-seeker destinations 10 miles north of downtown. If you'll be visiting both, get combo tickets.

Home to some of the best roller coasters in the country, the Africa-themed **Busch Gardens** has a dozen different sections that flow together without much fuss. The entire park is walkable. Admission includes three types of fun: epic roller coasters and rides, animal encounters and various shows, performances and entertainment. All are spread throughout the park, so successful days require some planning: check show schedules before arriving and plan what rides and animals to visit around the shows. Coaster lines only get longer as the day goes on.

Highlights include a ride aboard the **Serengeti Railway**, where you can see free-roaming herds of African animals like zebras and giraffes. For something more extreme, head to the **Iron Gwazi**, North America's tallest (206ft), fastest (76mph) and steepest (91 degree drops) hybrid roller coaster.

Nearby, **Adventure Island** has everything a modern, top-flight water park requires: a long lazy river, a huge wave pool, bucket-dumping splash zones, a swimming pool with jumping platforms, sandy lounge areas and enough twisting, plunging, adrenaline-fueled waterslides to keep teens lining up till closing. Adventure Island also features outdoor cafes, picnic and sunbathing areas, a gift shop and a championship sand volleyball complex for hours of fun in the sun.

BEST ANIMAL ENCOUNTERS

Edge of Africa
Take a walking safari with sightings of hippopotamuses, lions, lemurs, meerkats and crocodiles in an African-style fishing village.

Animal Care Center
Educational behind-the-scenes tours of vets at work with some of the park's 200 species of animals.

Animal Connections
In the Nairobi section, you can see sloths and other animals up close.

Serengeti Safari Tour
For $40 extra, you'll get some amazing photo opportunities of giraffes and other wildlife while joining a naturalist on a ride in an open-topped vehicle.

Manatees, Gators & Bears

VISITING NATURE RESERVES

Around 70 miles north of Tampa, the small fishing community of Homosassa is home to **Ellie Schiller Homosassa Springs Wildlife State Park**. This is essentially an old-school outdoor

WHERE TO EAT NEAR WEEKI WACHEE SPRINGS

My Nanny's
Get an early start to the day with pancakes, grits or breakfast bagels at this small locally owned diner. **$**

LaurieCue
Seek out this food truck for tender brisket sandwiches, creamy mac and cheese, and satisfying collard greens. **$**

Masa Asian Bistro & Bar
Never mind the strip mall setting, Masa serves mouthwatering seafood and creative Asian fusion. **$$**

MEETING MANATEES

Dozens of operators in Crystal River offer kayak rentals and boat tours, as well as the chance to swim with wild manatees – the only place in Florida where it's legal to do so. Recommended outfits follow strict protocols: no loud noises, touching the manatees or getting too close.

Crystal River Kayak Company has a sterling reputation for its sustainable approach, and it rents out kayaks, runs manatee swimming encounters and leads scuba-diving tours.

Note that although manatees live in Kings Bay year-round, the population dwindles to a few dozen between April and September or October.

Florida animal encounter that features Florida's wealth of headliner species: American alligators, black bears, whooping cranes, Florida panthers, tiny Key deer and – especially – manatees.

Homosassa's highlight is an underwater observatory directly over the springs, where through glass windows you can eyeball enormous schools of some 10,000 fish and ponderous manatees nibbling lettuce. Various animal presentations happen daily, but time your visit for the manatee program (11am and 1pm).

It's worth paying a little extra to take the boat ride to the park from the visitor center (you can also take a tram or walk along a birding trail). This 20-minute narrated journey gives a bit of history of the park while following a jungle-lined waterway with opportunities to spy kingfishers and alligators along the way.

Start the day early and you can also tack on a visit to the **Crystal River National Wildlife Refuge** 7 miles further north. This reserve protects much of Kings Bay and draws hundreds of manatees from mid-November through March.

Getting out on the water is the best way to see these gentle giants, though you can also see them from land at **Three Sisters Springs**. The 57-acre refuge has boardwalk trails that wind past underwater vents, sand boils and manatee-filled crystal-clear spring water that feeds Kings Bay, the headwaters of the Crystal River.

Woodland Escape

HIKING AND KAYAKING

Just 12 miles northeast of Tampa, you can trade the concrete jungle for a verdant oasis at the 3400-acre **Hillsborough River State Park**. After passing through the gatepost (and paying a modest entrance fee), you can explore the sites along a one-way road that loops around the park.

At the first stop, you can take in a bit of history at the small interpretive center. Display cases show remnants from Seminole peoples (beads, arrowheads) as well as weaponry from the US soldiers (musket balls, bayonets) sent to drive them off their land. You can also peek in the log cabin built in 1933 by the Civilian Conservation Corps (CCC), President Roosevelt's ambitious work program created during the Great Depression.

In fact, much of the park was developed by the CCC, and you can still see other original rustic architecture, particularly along the 1.2-mile **River Rapids Trail** (stop 3 on the road). Here you can walk among dense woodlands skirting the edge

WHERE TO STAY IN CRYSTAL RIVER

Retreat at Crystal Manatee
Upscale motel with colorful, contemporary guest rooms and a leafy location near several waterside parks. **$$**

Port Hotel & Marina
Budget-friendly option with clean but dated rooms with balconies and large grounds overlooking the water. **$**

Plantation on Crystal River
Well-located resort with modern rooms, restaurants and bars, spa, 18-hole golf course and tour operator. **$$**

DENNIS MACDONALD/ALAMY STOCK PHOTO ©

Fort Foster State Historic Site

of the scenic Hillsborough River. Near the start of the trail, you'll see a few small rapids, just upriver from a thicket of bald cypress trees and live oaks stippled with epiphytes. Past the tiny verdant river islands, you can cross over the photogenic suspension bridge made of huge logs.

At stop 3, an outpost rents out one-speed **cruiser bikes** as well as **canoes** and **kayaks** for trips along the serene river. Whether walking or paddling, keep an eye out for wildlife, including alligators, deer, foxes, wading birds, raptors and the odd bobcat.

The park opens from 8am to sunset, but if you have the gear, you can pitch a tent in the campground. The sites are amply shaded, but don't offer much privacy.

FORT FOSTER STATE HISTORIC SITE

Less than a mile up the road from the turnoff to Hillsborough River State Park, **Fort Foster** is a reproduction of a wooden bastion built in 1836 during the Second Seminole War. US troops were tasked with building a supply bridge across the river, and constructing a fort to protect the bridge. Even before its completion, Seminoles attempted to set fire to the whole enterprise, though their attack was ultimately repelled. Afterwards, troops used the fort for only short periods before it was abandoned for good in 1855.

GETTING AROUND

You can reach Busch Gardens on the number 5 bus from Tampa, but to reach all of the other destinations covered here, you'll need a car.

ST PETERSBURG

St Petersburg
Miami

An uncanny element of chance played a crucial role in the fortunes of this city. In the mid-19th century, the area was populated by only a handful of homesteaders. Seeing promise in the landscape, Peter Demens opened a rail line to the area in 1888. The only problem: the place had no name. So Demens, a Russian-born aristocrat, named it after the city of his birth.

Some years later, when two avid collectors from Cleveland were looking for a place to donate their trove of surrealist artwork, St Petersburg stole the thunder from bigger cities like NYC and LA, winning the works of Dalí and paving the way for the city's cultural renaissance. Today St Petersburg is known for its dynamic arts district, with galleries sprinkled amid creative restaurants, buzzing cafes and craft breweries. Locals are just as fond of their waterfront parks, including the sustainably designed St Pete Pier.

TOP TIP

Time your visit for a Saturday, when the Al Lang Field parking lot hosts one of Florida's best open-air markets (9am to 2pm). Over 130 vendors sell foods from around the globe, drinks, crafts, housewares and clothing, and there's also live music. From June to September it's held in shadier Williams Park.

WHY I LOVE ST PETERSBURG

Regis St Louis, writer

The Dalí Museum first drew me here years ago, and since then I've learned how fitting it is that St Petersburg contains the greatest collection of works by the surrealist painter outside of Spain. The city has long been a magnet for artists, and its gallery scene continues to evolve. There's also St Pete's aesthetic virtues, from its waterfront to the beaches west of town. Although Dalí never visited St Pete, he drew inspiration from Catalonia's coastline, and I imagine he'd be delighted to find his work living on in a creative city fringed by alluring seaside.

Surrealist Wonderland

CUTTING-EDGE ART AND ARCHITECTURE

The theatrical exterior of the extraordinary **Salvador Dalí Museum** speaks of great things: out of a wound in the towering white shoe box oozes a 75ft geodesic glass atrium. Even better, what unfolds inside is everything a modern art museum devoted to the life, art and impact of Salvador Dalí should be. Even those with no time for his dripping clocks and curlicue mustache will be awed by the museum and its grand works, such as the *Hallucinogenic Toreador*.

The Salvador Dalí Museum's 20,000 sq ft of gallery space was designed to display all 96 oil paintings in the collection, along with key works of each era and medium: drawings, prints, sculptures, photos, manuscripts, movies and even a virtual reality exhibit in which guests enter a fantastical Dalí painting. Everything is arranged chronologically and explained in context. The garden out back is also a delight, with a melting clock bench, a giant steel mustache sculpture and sparkling views of the bay.

Excellent, free docent tours occur throughout the day; these are highly recommended to help crack open the rich symbolism in Dalí's monumental works. With a smartphone you can also download the Salvador Dalí Museum app, which has a self-guided tour of the collection and unique ways to experience paintings like *Augmented Reality,* which transforms static pieces into kinetic, dreamlike installations that also reveal hidden facets of the works.

There's a Catalan-inspired cafe and a first-rate gift store. Up to 5000 people have been known to visit in a day, so purchase a timed ticket in advance to avoid disappointment.

Vinoy Park
North Yacht Basin
Pier Plaza
Pier
Tampa Bay
South Yacht Basin
St Petersburg Municipal Marina
Salvador Dalí Museum
Williams Park
Mirror Lake
Looper Trolley
Beach Dr NE
Bayshore Dr NE
Bayshore Dr
Dalí Blvd
5th Ave NE
2nd Ave NE
5th Ave N
4th Ave N
3rd Ave N
2nd Ave N
1st Ave N
Central Ave
1st Ave S
2nd Ave S
3rd Ave S
4th Ave S
5th Ave S
1st St N
3rd St N
4th St N
1st St S
2nd St S
3rd St S
4th St S
5th St S
6th St S
8th St S
500 m
0.25 miles

HIGHLIGHTS
1 Salvador Dalí Museum

SIGHTS
2 Chihuly Collection
3 Morean Arts Center
4 Discovery Center
5 Glazer Family Playground
6 Myth (Pelican)
7 St Pete Pier

EATING
8 Teak

DRINKING & NIGHTLIFE
9 Bending Arc
10 Morean Glass Studio
see 8 Teaki

SHOPPING
11 Florida CraftArt
12 Marketplace

WHERE TO EAT IN ST PETERSBURG

Pardeco Coffee Roasters
Start the day with avocado toast and foamy lattes at this lively art deco cafe and coffee roaster. **$**

Bodega
Latin-inspired spot with slow-roasted pork (or grilled tempeh) sandwiches best enjoyed on the back patio. **$**

The Mill
In a barnyard-chic interior, The Mill has a famously wide-ranging menu, plus St Pete's best brunch. **$$$**

BEST MUSEUMS & GARDENS

St Petersburg Museum of History
Oddball collection with a 3000-year-old mummy and a two-headed calf, plus exhibits on Tampa Bay's ecology and the evolving waterfront.

Museum of Fine Arts St Petersburg
Spans 5000 years of human history, from the world's antiquities to the present, following art's progression through nearly every era.

Florida Holocaust Museum
One of the country's largest Holocaust museums presents mid-20th-century events with moving directness.

Sunken Gardens
Small but verdant oasis with resident flamingos, koi ponds and unique tropical flora from around the world.

SUNSHOWER SHOTS/SHUTTERSTOCK ©

St Pete Pier

Strolling St Pete Pier

WATERFRONT EXPLORING

One of St Pete's best-loved free attractions is the 26-acre park that juts out into Tampa Bay. Green spaces, public artwork, picnic areas and waterfront restaurants draw a wide cross-section of visitors both day and night.

The $93 million design was 14 years in the making and after opening in 2020, it earned rave reviews from visitors and critics alike. Among other accolades, the pier was one of six worldwide winners for the 2022 Global Awards for Excellence conferred by the Urban Land Institute.

Near the pier's entry opposite 2nd Ave NE, you'll stroll past Nathan Mabry's red origami-like sculpture **Myth (Pelican)**, which pays homage to the city's official bird. Nearby, local vendors sell clothing, sun hats, jewelry, artwork and other wares at the open-air **Marketplace**.

Further along, you can walk beneath **Bending Arc**, a net sculpture created by Tampa Bay artist Janet Echelman. The 428ft-wide work references Martin Luther King's words: 'The arc of the moral universe is long, but it bends toward justice.'

WHERE TO GO FOR A NIGHT OUT IN ST PETERSBURG

Floridian Social Club
The striking beaux-arts setting is a favorite weekend spot for cocktails and dancing, with concerts and cabaret.

Green Bench
Craft brewery with a beer garden and a regular lineup of live music, sports screenings and movie nights.

Intermezzo
Coffee by day, cocktails by night, stylish Intermezzo lies on a buzzing stretch of Central Ave.

Several key attractions draw families here, including the colorfully painted **Glazer Family Playground** and a splash pad, where kids cool off beneath the spurting fountains of **Pier Plaza**. There's also Spa Beach, where you can dig your toes in the sand, and a hands-on aquatic themed **Discovery Center** (adult/child $5/3). The easternmost end of the pier has a solid three-story structure with several eating and drinking spots, including the seafood-centric bistro **Teak** with its floor-to-ceiling windows overlooking the water and the rooftop **Teaki**, a bar with fine tropical drinks, breezy views and Floridian snacks (grouper sandwiches, fish tacos).

The Pier hosts a range of events, including free outdoor concerts, film screenings and sunset yoga classes.

The Vibrant Central Arts District

EPICENTER OF THE ART SCENE

Galleries, studios and indie boutiques line Central Ave of St Pete's key arts district, an area roughly anchored by 4th and 8th Sts. One of the best places to begin the journey is at **Florida CraftArt**, a nonprofit gallery that displays (and sells) the works of over 200 Florida artists. You'll find one-of-a-kind pieces featuring ceramics, fiber, metal, wood and mixed media, with details on the artists behind the pieces.

Up the road, you can delve into the work of one of America's best-known glass artists at the **Chihuly Collection**. Dale Chihuly's glass works are displayed at the Metropolitan Museum of Art in New York, the Louvre in Paris and countless other places, but major works reside here in St Petersburg. Small in size, the museum houses large-scale installations like the site-specific *Ruby Red Icicle Chandelier* as well as otherworldly pieces like *Tumbleweeds* and the sinuous forms of *Persians*.

Tickets for the gallery include a glass-blowing demonstration nearby at the **Morean Glass Studio** (closed Monday and Tuesday). These happen hourly from 1pm to 4pm on Wednesday to Sunday. For an even more immersive experience, reserve ahead for a one-on-one 'personal glass experience' ($90) and take home your own creation. The neighboring **Morean Arts Center** (closed Sundays) hosts thoughtful rotating exhibits in all media.

ART IN NAPLES

Another pillar of the contemporary art scene is the **Baker Museum** (p372) in Naples. Here you can discover groundbreaking works by painters, sculptors and video artists from around the globe.

I LIVE HERE: ST PETERSBURG ART SCENE

An anchor of the Warehouse Arts District, acclaimed glass artist and gallery owner **Duncan McClellan** shares his recommendations on the St Petersburg art scene.

Florida CraftArt
It's a great overview from all Florida artists. Katie Diets is the director and we're so lucky to have her.

The James Museum
Some people are surprised to find western art here in St Petersburg. Founders Tom and Mary only buy from live artists, and they're real supporters of Native American art.

Warehouse Arts District
The ArtsXchange, with 28 artists, and Soft Water Gallery, with 14 artists, are must-sees. At Soft Water, Carrie Jadus is one of the best painters in St Pete.

GETTING AROUND

The Downtown Looper is an old-fashioned trolley bus that runs a useful downtown circuit every 15 to 20 minutes. The free SunRunner bus is a great way to explore sights along Central Ave. It runs west on 1st Ave N and east on 1st Ave S.

Beyond St Petersburg

Whether you hope to relax on the beach or kayak through mangrove trails in a state park, don't miss the stunning shorelines near St Petersburg.

Palm-fringed keys and sandy barrier islands line the coastline outside of St Petersburg, and for many visitors this is Florida at its sun-drenched best. Powdery beaches and scenic inland waterways form the front and back of this long seaside, with some sections full of restaurants, resorts and holiday bustle, and other areas blissfully free of development.

Several state parks in the area have vestiges of old Florida. At Fort De Soto, you can bask on wild beaches, fish to your heart's content or camp out under the stars. Honeymoon Island and Caladesi Island are other spots to enjoy the peaceful seaside. The region also has its share of surprises, including the bohemian enclave of Gulfport, the famous bottlenose residents of Mote Aquarium, and a jungle-clad park with a pre-Columbian past.

TOP TIP

Make a plan to be somewhere along the shore in late afternoon so you don't miss the often impressive sunsets.

Caladesi Island and Honeymoon Island State Park (p354)

MARIAKRAY/SHUTTERSTOCK ©

St Pete Beach

SEASIDE SEABIRD SANCTUARY

Apart from beaches, the barrier island chain is home to the largest wild-bird hospital in North America, which is also part of a sanctuary that's home to over 100 sea and land birds for public viewing. You'll see a resident population of permanently injured pelicans, owls, gulls and birds of prey, including a bald eagle. There are also several resident parrots with saucy personalities. Several thousand birds are treated and released back to the wild annually. For a fine view over the beach, climb up the observation tower nestled in the back of the property.

Beachside Escapes

MAGNIFICENT BEACH GETAWAYS

The closest oceanfront to the city is **St Pete Beach**, a mere 15-minute drive (on a good day) from bustling Central Ave in St Petersburg. The shoreline's key landmark is the towering Moorish Mediterranean **Don CeSar Hotel**, a historic confection built in 1928 that's sometimes dubbed the 'pink palace.'

The extra-wide beach itself ranks high for its natural beauty, and draws plenty of sun seekers who come for lounging by the waterside, long walks by the crashing waves and fiery sunsets. Proximity to the city has made St Pete the most developed of the barrier-island beaches, with resorts, motels and restaurants just a few steps from the dune-backed sands.

Heading down from St Pete, **Pass-a-Grille** anchors the southern end of Long Key. Here you'll find the most idyllic barrier-island beach, a narrow stretch of sand backed only by beach houses and metered public parking. You can watch boats coming through Pass-a-Grille Channel, hop aboard the **Shell Key Shuttle** (departures at 10am, noon and 2pm) to unspoiled **Shell Key**, and retire for food and ice cream in the laid-back village center (essentially 8th Ave).

WHERE TO EAT IN ST PETE & THE BARRIER ISLANDS

Paradise Grille
Casual walk-up spot with tasty seafood, cold drinks and picnic tables overlooking the beach. $

Spinners
A high-end rotating restaurant with 360-degree views from its 12-story perch. $$$

Salt Rock Grill
Classy dinnertime spot (plus lunch on weekends) renowned for its seafood and steaks. $$$

YESTERYEAR I LIVED IN PARADISE

Myrtle Scharrer Betz was 87 years old when she decided to write about her years growing up in a pioneer homestead. She was born in 1895 on Caladesi Island, and her father raised her to be fully self-sufficient. When she was nine, she rowed herself every day across St Joseph Sound to attend a one-room schoolhouse in Dunedin. In the 1920s and '30s, she worked as a commercial fisher alongside her husband. Later she ensured her beloved island would be preserved as a park. Read more about her in the memoir *Yesteryear I Lived in Paradise.*

ANASTASIIA SHADRINA/SHUTTERSTOCK ©

Gulfport

Slender barrier islands continue north of St Pete, harboring a handful of communities, from the tourist traps of **John's Pass Village** to the quieter, family-oriented **Indian Rocks Beach**. This is where you'll find the **Indian Rocks Beach Nature Preserve**, which has a short boardwalk trail winding through mangroves out to a viewpoint of Boca Ciega Bay.

Pristine Islands

PRISTINE ISLAND STATE PARKS

Two of the best beaches in the US are just north of Clearwater: **Honeymoon Island**, which you can drive to, and the ferry-only **Caladesi Island**. In fact, the two islands were once part of a single barrier island, split in half during the hurricane of 1921, a reminder of the forces of nature that sometimes batter the state. Together, they offer nearly a thousand acres of coastal wilderness not much changed since Spanish explorers first surveyed this coast in the mid-1500s.

The undeveloped shores of **Honeymoon Island State Park** offer plenty of space to find an idyllic slice of the subtropics. The **Cafe Honeymoon** has snack fare and also rents bikes for rides along the vehicle-free lanes (4.5 miles) inside the park.

WHERE TO EAT NEAR THE ISLANDS

Dunedin Downtown Market
Pick up baked goods, cheeses, fruits and other picnic fare from this Friday and Saturday morning markct. $

Dunedin Brewery
Toast the day's adventures over IPAs and fish tacos while sitting on the terrace outside Florida's craft brewery. $

High & Dry Grill
A thatch-roof beachfront spot serving wraps, bratwurst and snacks on the causeway to Honeymoon Island. $

Near the cafe you can hire kayaks and stand-up paddleboards for a glide along the shore. The island has a handful of hiking trails, including the aptly named **Osprey Trail**, a 2.2-mile loop where you can often see ospreys (and their nests) perched along the bare trunks above the ancient coastal forest.

Just past the entrance to Honeymoon Island you can catch the 20-minute ferry to **Caladesi** (half-hourly from 10am, last boat back at 4pm). Less visited than Honeymoon, Caladesi feels like a forgotten slice of old Florida. Here you can walk a memorable 2.7-mile trail through the forest, passing ancient live oaks, virgin strands of slash pines and curious formations like the 'harp tree' – a double-trunk pine that has been around since at least the 1800s. You can also hire kayaks for a well-marked 1.5-mile aquatic trail through mangroves.

The Bayside Town of Gulfport

CREATIVE WATERFRONT VILLAGE

Little known outside St Pete, **Gulfport** is a charming, bohemian waterfront town that's not on the barrier island beaches. Nestled at peninsula's end within Boca Ciega Bay, this LGBTIQ+-friendly artist community exudes that elusive, easy-going, fun-loving attitude that Florida made famous. The hard-to-resist spell is in full effect on sultry evenings when the trees along Beach Blvd glow with lights and the outdoor restaurants burble with laughter.

On the edge of Chase Park, the tiny **Gulfport History Museum** (10am to 2pm Tuesday through Friday) gives insight into the town's past with old photos and memorabilia from its heyday in the early 20th century.

From there, you can take a stroll down Beach Blvd past the heart of town with its cafes, craft shops and restaurants to the waterfront. You can stop for coffee at **Sumitra**, where you'll find well-made drinks and a strong community vibe, or refresh over microbrews at the **North End Taphouse**, which has an inviting courtyard tucked just off the main street. The best restaurant in town is **Pia's Trattoria**, known for its mouthwatering Italian-American fare, including a buttery shrimp scampi. Eat alfresco and hear live music at **Pia's Veranda** next door.

Nearby, you can get a dose of nature at the **Clam Bayou Nature Park**, a small preserve with short upland trails and boardwalks that skirt the mangroves to overlooks along the water.

It doesn't compare to the barrier islands, of course, but Gulfport does have a beach with a playground and a shady picnic area. If you're around at sunset, join locals out on **Bert and Walter Williams Pier** for a fiery conclusion to the day.

OVERNIGHT IN GULFPORT

If you're tempted to spend the night in Gulfport, the **Historic Peninsula Inn** is an atmospheric choice. The cheery yellow guesthouse, which first opened its doors back in 1905, has played many roles over the years, from a fishing lodge in the early 1900s to a hospital for injured vets after WWII, and later a nursing home. By the 1980s it was boarded up and nearly demolished but was saved from oblivion by a pair of entrepreneurs who restored the building into a 12-room hostelry in the early 2000s.

These days, the inn is helmed by a woman with serious travel credentials. Veronica Champion has managed properties in the Caribbean, Djibouti and South Sudan, and invested in eco-friendly renovations after purchasing the inn in 2016.

WHERE TO EAT & DRINK ON THE WATERFRONT

O'Maddy's
This classic American bar and grill is best known for its sandwiches, like the decadent lobster BLT. **$$**

Caddy's
Caddy's has a welcoming vibe with outdoor tables, tropical cocktails and live music Thursday through Saturday. **$$**

Neptune Grill
Grab a table on the patio and indulge in some of Gulfport's best seafood as well as classic Greek fare. **$$**

I LIVE HERE: TOP HISTORIC SITES OUTSIDE ST PETERSBURG

David Anderson, historian and founder of Discover Florida Tours, shares his recommendations for connecting with Native American history.

Egmont Key
Reachable by boat from Fort De Soto, Egmont Key is a great combination of beaches, natural beauty and historic sites. It's a place that the Seminole tribe considers to be their Alcatraz because they were taken here before being moved out of South Florida.

Weedon Island
The largest Native American canoe ever found in Florida (45ft long) was found here. It's shining new light on the people that used to live here during the Tocobaga days and on how far they traveled – possibly to the Caribbean or Mexico. The canoe is on display at Weedon Island's natural history center.

Pre-Hispanic Days in Jungle Prada

DISCOVERING INDIGENOUS HISTORY

On the western reaches of St Petersburg (around 8 miles from downtown), the leafy neighborhood of Jungle Prada hides an important pre-Columbian site that's little known to most Floridians. Tucked along the shore of Boca Ciega Bay, the forested site was a settlement of the Tocobaga people for some six centuries (roughly 1000 to 1600 CE). An estimated 14,000 people lived in the area. They built large earthwork mounds, one of which still stands in the area.

On a small-group guided tour, you'll pass resident peacocks while learning a bit about the Tocobaga. The native group harvested plants like the coontie, which has edible but toxic roots that become safe to eat only after soaking. They also made a tea from the leaves (dried and roasted) of the yaupon holly. Called 'the black drink,' the caffeinated beverage was used in purification ceremonies as an emetic – the excessive vomiting followed by a clear-headedness that would lead to keen insight.

You'll ascend to the top of 'the plaza,' a raised area some 24ft above sea level, and get insight into the shell-based tools, jewelry and utensils used by the Tocobaga.

The site was also the likely landing spot of Pánfilo de Narvaez, the Spanish conquistador who arrived in Florida in 1528 in search of gold. You'll hear how his expedition went horribly wrong, with only four survivors of the 300 soldiers that undertook the expedition.

Visit the site by reserving a spot with **Discover Florida Tours**, a small outfit run by David Anderson, who grew up in a home on the Jungle Prada site. Anderson's parents operate Sacred Lands, which hosts live music events as well as periodic meditation workshops and drum circles.

Exploring Fort De Soto Park

BEACHES, FISHING AND HISTORY

Spread across five keys southwest of St Petersburg, Fort De Soto Park encompasses 1136 acres of unspoiled wilderness. The big draw is the sparkling shoreline, with 7 miles of waterfront including white-sand beaches facing the Gulf of Mexico. The park's namesake is a 19th-century fort that still has vestiges from its role in coastal defense.

Beachgoers have plenty of options when it comes to finding their own subtropical slice of paradise, especially along **North Beach**, a protected lagoon that's popular with families for its calm, shallow waters and ease of access. The beach has

WHERE TO EAT ON NEARBY TREASURE ISLAND

Crabby's on the Pass
Look for dolphins while munching on coconut shrimp, conch fritters and blackened grouper. **$$**

Caddy's Treasure Island
This casual beachfront restaurant and bar is the place to be at sunset. **$$**

Shake Shop
Beat the heat by heading to this small, locally owned spot for milkshakes and soft-serve ice cream. **$**

BRIAN LASENBY/SHUTTERSTOCK ©

Fishing pier, Fort De Soto Park

earned many accolades over the years, appearing regularly on top 10 lists of Florida's best beaches. **East Beach**, meanwhile, is smaller and coarser, and consequently less crowded.

In between the beaches are two long **fishing piers**, and you can buy bait, fishing tackle and other essentials from shops at the pier entrance. Before setting your sights on mackerel, pompano and redfish, make sure you have a fishing license (purchase it online at myfwc.com).

In the southwest corner of Mullet Key, across from the 1000ft Gulf Pier, you can explore the **fort**, which dates from the 1898 Spanish-American War. You can wander the cool, empty rooms that were once part of the base, peer down the 40-caliber guns or climb to a lookout above the waterfront. Nearby, the reconstructed **Quartermaster Storehouse** has exhibits on the human presence on the keys.

Reach the park via the Pinellas Bayway (a toll road). It's about a 20-minute drive from downtown St Petersburg. If you plan to extend your stay, book early to get a waterfront site at the **Fort De Soto Campground**.

EGMONT KEY

Southwest of Fort De Soto Park, Egmont Key has white-sand beaches, clear seas and no development in sight – apart from a lighthouse and the ruins of Fort Dade, a 19th-century military garrison. Roughly half of the 280-acre island is an off-limits nature reserve, which protects loggerhead sea turtles that nest on the shores and over 100 species of resident and migratory birds.

Spend the day basking on the beach, snorkeling in the water or looking for shells and wildlife, including gopher tortoises. The one-hour boat journey from Fort De Soto Park is a rewarding part of the experience; you might see dolphins along the way. Book tickets ahead through **Hubbards Marina**.

ARCHAEOLOGICAL TREASURES

Historic Spanish Point (p367) gives even more insight into the ancient cultures that thrived on the Gulf Coast before Europeans arrived. There's even an impressively well-preserved shell mound that you can see from the inside.

FORT DE SOTO ACTIVITIES

Paddling
Hire a kayak or SUP from Topwater Kayak and paddle along a calm mangrove-lined estuary.

Biking
Parallel to the road, the park has 7 miles of paved multi-use trails. Topwater Kayak also rents bikes.

Hiking
Near North Beach, you can walk the 1.5-mile Arrowhead Nature Trail, a loop through coastal forest.

CLEARWATER MARINE AQUARIUM

Some 8 miles north of the Florida Botanical Gardens (a 20-minute drive), the Clearwater Marine Aquarium rescues and rehabilitates injured sea animals, such as dolphins, sea otters, fish, rays, loggerhead turtles and Kemp's ridley sea turtles. Many of the animals are resident due to injuries that prevent their return to the wild. The aquarium also runs boat tours around Clearwater Bay. Sadly, the aquarium's star resident, Winter – whose rescue story was featured in the 2011 film *Dolphin Tale* – died in 2021. Be on the lookout for Hope, Winter's costar in the sequel *Dolphin Tale 2*.

DREW HORNE/SHUTTERSTOCK ©

Heritage Village

Botanical Beauties

FLORA, FAUNA AND HISTORIC ARCHITECTURE

A 30-minute (20-mile) drive north of St Petersburg, the **Florida Botanical Gardens** stretch across more than 100 acres, with some 1500 different species of plants from six continents. Unlike similar gardens in the state (and elsewhere), a visit here won't cost you anything.

There are numerous different sections to explore connected by 2.5 miles of pathways. You can look for winged beauties in the butterfly gardens, where some 75 different species have been spotted. The Wetlands Walkway and Wildlife has boardwalks that meander past lily-covered ponds, while the palm garden showcases dozens of palm species from the aptly named bottle palm (native to the Mascarene Islands) to the New Caledonian flamethrower palm.

Wildlife is also part of the garden's allure, and you might hear the squawk of monk parakeets as they fly over the treetops, watch a gopher tortoise munching along the trail or spy an alligator basking by the waterside. Come early in the morning for the best chance to see wildlife. The gardens open daily from 7am to 5pm.

Adjoining the gardens is the **Heritage Village**, with its collection of restored and replica buildings that date back to the 19th century. You can peek into a colonial revival one-room schoolhouse, see a 1905 church that survived two hurricanes and imagine life for the frontier settlers who once lived in the property's oldest building – the 1852 McMullen log cabin, which once stood near Clearwater. The village opens 10am to 4pm Wednesday to Saturday and 1pm to 4pm Sunday; it's also admission free.

GETTING AROUND

You can reach St Pete Beach from downtown St Petersburg on the free SunRunner bus. Out on the shoreline, the Sun Coast Beach Trolley (SCBT) hugs the waterfront between St Pete Beach and Clearwater.

SARASOTA

Like many other parts of Southwest Florida, Sarasota was once home to the Seminole, a Native American tribe that flourished in the area in the 1700s. Their rule came to an end in the decades after Spain sold Florida to the US in 1819. Federal troops drove the Seminole off their lands to open up the region's settlement to those of European descent.

In 1910 only a few homesteaders were living in the bayside settlement when several of the Ringling brothers – future circus magnates – built estates in the area. The time of the Ringlings coincided with the roaring 1920s, when Sarasota saw its earliest boom days. Today Sarasota feels like an upscale waterfront town with a walkable downtown full of restaurants and galleries, botanical gardens and a photogenic marina. The town also has outstanding museums and a full calendar of events – part of the legacy left behind by the arts-loving Ringling family.

TOP TIP

Sarasota has a vibrant theater scene, and it's worth seeing what's on when you're in town. The Westcoast Black Theatre Troupe produces high-quality musicals and thought-provoking dramas. The Asolo Repertory Theatre stages acclaimed works, while the smaller Players Theatre is a highly regarded nonprofit community theater.

A Dazzling Circus Estate

CIRCUS LORE AND WORLD-CLASS ART

The 66-acre winter retreat of railroad, real-estate and circus baron John Ringling and his wife, Mable, is one of the Gulf Coast's premier attractions. You could easily spend a half day exploring this complex with its various museums planted amid lush bayside gardens.

After getting oriented at the **McKay Visitors Pavilion**, head to the **Circus Museum**, which spreads across two buildings. The first features the astonishing miniaturized world entitled *Howard Bros Circus Model,* a 1:16 scale of the entire Ringling Bros and Barnum & Bailey Circus in action. Among the 40,000 pieces, you'll see elephants balancing on balls, performers putting on makeup and crowds lining up for ice cream. The intricately detailed work is the 60-year labor of love of one man, Howard Tibbals.

Other parts of the Circus Museum showcase famous acts over the years, from the tiny boots of 27in-tall Tom Thumb

ACROBATIC YOUNGSTERS

One of the most inspiring circuses in Sarasota is performed by kids. The **Sailor Circus** is a unique extracurricular activity for Sarasota County students, who gear up for multiple shows in late December and in March or April. They call it 'The Greatest Little Show on Earth,' but there's nothing little about it. It includes acrobatics, high wire and trapeze. Purchase tickets via the **Circus Arts Conservatory**.

WHERE TO SEE ART IN SARASOTA

Sarasota Art Museum
Has a winning formula with knowledgeable docents and thoughtfully curated contemporary exhibitions.

Marietta Museum of Art & Whimsy
This bright pink museum and sculpture garden showcases works by local artists.

Art Center Sarasota
Discover new works by innovative painters, sculptors and mixed-media artists at this nonprofit gallery.

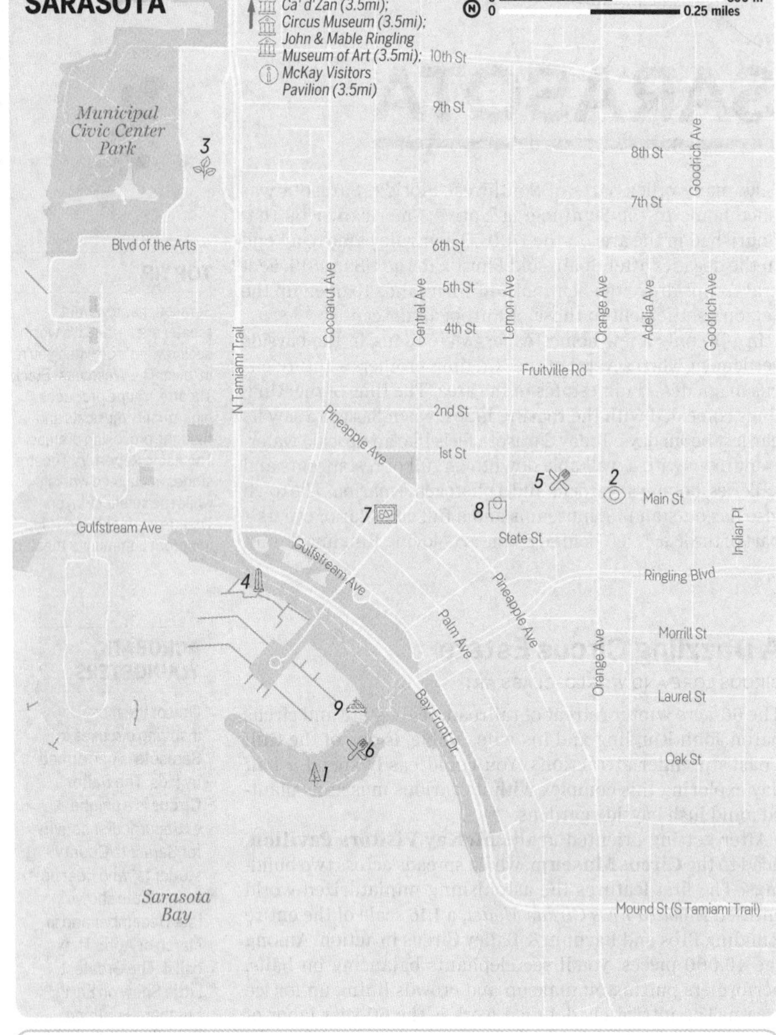

SIGHTS
1 Bayfront Park
2 Main Street
3 The Bay
4 Unconditional Surrender

EATING
5 C'est La Vie
6 O'Leary's Tiki Bar & Grill

SHOPPING
7 Art Uptown
8 A Parker's Books

TRANSPORT
9 LeBarge Tropical Cruises

to the Flying Wallendas, a daredevil seven-person high-wire act that performed without safety nets (and suffered multiple tragedies). The history galleries display eye-catching circus posters, an 8-ton bandwagon and the elaborate private railcar the Ringlings traveled in around the country.

Head toward the waterfront to reach **Ca' d'Zan** (House of John in the Venetian dialect). Built in the 1920s, the Ringlings' winter home is a daring confection of Mediterranean Revival style, with Italian, Spanish, Moorish and Venetian elements. Download the free audio guide as you tour the house. Highlights include the painted dancers from global cultures adorning the ballroom ceiling, and the palatial Great Hall with its tapestries and dramatic glimpse of the waterfront through stained-glass windows. Even better views await on the terrace, where you can take in the ornate architecture (16th-century Spanish tiles once covered the roof) as well as the panorama across Sarasota Bay.

Exiting the house, take a meandering stroll through the **Bayfront Gardens**, stopping for a look at the towering banyan trees, the live oaks dripping with Spanish moss and the rose gardens founded by Mable Ringling back in 1913.

The largest complex on the estate is the **John & Mable Ringling Museum of Art**. The Ringlings aspired to become serious art connoisseurs and they amassed an impressive collection of work dating from the late Middle Ages to the 20th century. Housed in a grand Mediterranean-style palazzo, the museum covers 21 galleries showcasing many works by European masters, including Velázquez, Tintoretto and Veronese. The gallery opens with Rubens' *Triumph of the Eucharist,* five massive canvases painted for the Spanish princess Isabella Clara Eugenia.

Some of the rooms are also works of art. The Late Gothic gallery with its gilded doorways and wainscoting is modeled on a chamber from the Villa Palmieri, where Boccaccio allegedly wrote and set *The Decameron*. Outside, the Italian Renaissance-style **courtyard** with its colonnades and symmetrical parterres is watched over by a full-sized bronze replica of Michelangelo's *David*.

The **Searing Wing** presents some rotating exhibits and one permanent collection of contemporary art, along with *Joseph's Coat,* a stunning 3000-sq-ft James Turrell–designed 'Skyspace.' The newest wing contains historical and contemporary Asian art. The art museum and grounds are free on Mondays (but you'll have to pay full price to see the Circus Museum and Ca' d'Zan).

SPECIAL EVENTS AT THE RINGLING

Historic Asolo Theater
You can catch periodic concerts, plays, dance performances, puppetry shows and film screenings in the Historic Asolo Theater (a 1798 Italianate hall that was acquired by the museum in 1949). Check the season's schedule on Art of Performance.

Ca' d'Zan
The terrace of Ca' d'Zan becomes an open-air setting for yoga classes, meditation workshops and even sound baths – acoustic journeys designed to calm the mind.

Bayfront Gardens
At noon Saturday to Monday, you can book a guided walking tour of the gardens. From late November to mid-May, Ringling by the Bay is an outdoor concert series with bands playing rock, funk, soul and blues.

WHERE TO EAT IN SARASOTA

Owen's Fish Camp
Outstanding seafood and a convivial atmosphere. No reservations, so go early. **$$**

Boca Sarasota
The wide-ranging global menu showcases seasonal fare, with good sharing plates and creative cocktails. **$$**

Indigenous
Chef Steve Phelps whips up sustainably sourced new American creations in this Old Florida bungalow. **$$$**

I LIVE HERE: SARASOTA NATURE ESCAPES

Frances Bermudez, Activation Program Manager at The Bay Park Conservancy, shares her favorite nature escapes.

Marie Selby Botanical Gardens
The gardens are an incredible place that everyone loves, and you can also learn so much here. They have an incredible orchid collection and some visionary plans for the future.

Celery Fields
The highest vantage point in Sarasota County is adjacent to the Big Cat Habitat so when you're up on these walking trails you might hear lions roar.

John Ringling Causeway
Walking this bridge gives a beautiful view over Sarasota, especially around sunrise or sunset.

An Innovative Green Space

ACTIVITY-FILLED WATERFRONT PARK

Unveiled in 2022, **The Bay** is Sarasota's best new sustainably designed outdoor space, which spreads across the waterfront near downtown and attracts a wide cross-section of residents and out-of-towners. You'll find a short mangrove walking trail, an eye-catching playground built around giant ibises, a mini-beach dotted with Adirondack chairs, and a lawn fronting a stage where open-air concerts take place.

The Bay hosts an array of events, with all programming free of charge. You can come for yoga, Zumba and tai chi classes, enjoy guided stargazing during astronomy nights, join a nature walk and catch live music throughout the year. Family movie nights and weekend screenings of pro games (the Rays, the Buccaneers) are also part of the lineup.

Keep an eye out for manatees along the waterfront. For a closer look at wildlife along the shore, you can hire kayaks and paddleboards from **Ride & Paddle**, which offers daily rentals (and occasional guided tours) from an ADA-accessible launch in the mangrove bayou.

You can pick up park information from the blue-tiled **Welcome Center** just off the Tamiami Trail (Hwy 41). More development is on the way, with added shoreline improvements underway just north of The Bay during phase 2 of the project. The entire 53 acres (estimated to cost around $300 million) is slated for completion in 2026.

The Heart of Sarasota

SHOPPING AND DINING

The heart of downtown Sarasota is **Main Street**, in particular a stretch that runs for about a dozen blocks from Osprey Ave to Marina Plaza near the waterfront. This is a good place to explore from mid-morning till evening, with galleries and shops, interspersed with cafes, restaurants and bars.

A promising way to start the day is over brunch fare or pastries (probably Sarasota's best) at **C'est La Vie**, a casual French-owned bistro and bakery with shaded outdoor tables on the sidewalk. Up the road, you can browse the well-curated selection of used and antiquarian titles inside **A Parker's Books**, hallowed ground for book lovers. At **Art Uptown**, you can browse works in a variety of mediums created by over two dozen regional artists.

When you need a break from city streets, head toward the bay and take a stroll along the marina. You'll pass by the towering statue of **Unconditional Surrender**, depicting WWII's

WHERE TO GO FOR A NIGHT OUT IN SARASOTA

Pangea Alchemy Lab
Sarasota's best cocktails are stirred up at this low-lit speakeasy reached via an alley behind Main St.

Mandeville Beer Garden
A kid- and dog-friendly beer garden with over 30 brews on tap plus good pub fare.

The Mable
Chandeliers, oil paintings and a horse's head adorn the walls of this laid-back bar and grill north of downtown.

SUNCOAST AERIALS/SHUTTERSTOCK ©

Bayfront Park

most famous kiss. The small palm-dotted grassy green space known as **Bayfront Park** affords fine views over the water, and there are several well-located eating and drinking spots nearby, including the festive **O'Leary's Tiki Bar & Grill**.

A great way to cap the day is on a sunset boat ride with **LeBarge Tropical Cruises**. The outfit also offers daytime nature cruises and easygoing bay excursions accompanied by live music – steel drums, which adds the tropical flavor to LeBarge's outings.

LEGACY TRAIL

When you need a break from city life, go for a spin on the **Legacy Trail** (p368), a picturesque greenway that runs all the way to Venice. Pick up the trail off Fruitville Rd, about 1 mile east of Main St.

DOWNTOWN HAPPENINGS

First Fridays, Fresh Fridays
The liveliest time downtown is First Friday Sip & Shop, when stores bust open the bubbly and live music spills out over Main St (5pm to 8pm October to May). The action continues (7pm to 10pm) at Fresh Fridays, a free outdoor dance party with food vendors.

Sarasota Farmers Market
Every Saturday (7am to 1pm) near the intersection of Main St and Lemon Ave, you can browse some of the freshest produce in town. Apart from seasonal fruits and vegetables, you'll find vendors selling artisanal breads, cheeses, smoothies, coffee drinks, crepes and pizzas. Non-edible temptations range from clothing and jewelry to sea sponges and vegetabowls – earthenware bowls slip-cast from real fruit and vegetable molds.

GETTING AROUND

Bus 99 run by SCAT (Sarasota County Area Transit) provides handy service between downtown and Bradenton with a stop near the Ringling museum.

Beyond Sarasota

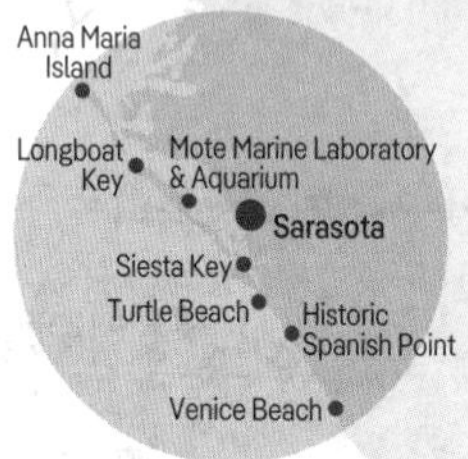

Whether you make an afternoon visit or plot a multiday road trip along the keys, don't miss the sublime coastline near Sarasota.

Powdery white-sand beaches, wildlife-rich bays and fiery sunsets: it's easy to fall for the dramatic coastline just outside the city. Just ask the American master of horror Stephen King, one of many famous residents of Sarasota County.

Siesta Key is perhaps the best-known of the barrier islands along this stretch of the Gulf Coast, but you could easily spend a few days exploring this area. This is the place for morning strolls on vast empty beaches, afternoon paddles through mangroves where manatees gather and sunset cocktails at well-positioned bars overlooking the water.

Further south, you can delve into the region's pre-Columbian past at Historic Spanish Point and bike along a former rail line turned greenway that connects Sarasota with Venice.

TOP TIP

On Sunday nights, don't miss the Siesta Key Drum Circle. It kicks off near 948 Beach Rd about one hour before sunset.

KDOTAYLOR/SHUTTERSTOCK ©

Lifeguard hut, Siesta Key

SARAH SHUMWAY/SHUTTERSTOCK ©

Turtle Beach

Enchanting Islands

BREATHTAKING BEACHES AND AQUATIC ADVENTURES

Sarasota's backyard consists of a long stretch of barrier islands linked by bridges to the mainland. From downtown, it's less than a 20-minute drive to **Siesta Key**, home to one of Florida's most dazzling shorelines. The beach here stretches for 8 miles and consists of pure quartz sand so fine it's like confectioners' sugar. The enormous free parking lot (at the corner of Beach Rd and Beach Way) has an information booth dispensing info on all types of activities and water sports in the area. There are also ample changing facilities, a snack bar and covered eating areas. A smooth 450ft-long mat gives easy access for wheelchairs and strollers to reach the shore.

Further south, you can escape the crowds on more secluded **Turtle Beach**. The sun and teal waters are the same, but the beach is narrower with ash-gray sand, so few prefer it. Not so the sea turtles, who nest here from May through October. Just inland from Turtle Beach, you can rent kayaks through **Kayaking SRQ**, and head off on a paddling adventure past the mangrove islands and hidden beaches of the **Jim Neville Marine Preserve**. Keep an eye out for manatees, ospreys and other wildlife along the way.

ST ARMANDS CIRCLE

Conceived by John Ringling in the 1920s, St Armands Circle is an upscale outdoor mall that functions as an extension of Sarasota's center, where everyone strolls in the early evening, window shopping while enjoying a Kilwin's waffle cone. Numerous restaurants, from diners to fine dining, serve all day. The circle is also an unavoidable traffic choke point; mid-morning and late-afternoon beach commutes are the worst. Don't forget to pay for parking, which is strictly enforced.

WHERE TO STAY IN THE SARASOTA KEYS

Anna Maria Island Inn
Seven different locations across Anna Maria, from budget-friendly Haleys to the upscale Seaside. **$$**

Capri at Siesta
Charming guesthouse within walking distance of Crescent Beach and restaurants on Midnight Pass Rd. **$$**

Turtle Beach Resort & Inn
Has a secluded, tropical vibe with suites and cottages overlooking a lagoon near Siesta Key's south end. **$$$**

PINE AVENUE

One street not to miss on Anna Maria is Pine Ave, a charming slice of Old Florida that runs between beach and bay near the island's north end. Here you can stroll past colorfully painted cottages that house galleries, shops and restaurants, and get a dose of island history at the **Anna Maria Island Historical Society**. The museum is partially set in a 1920s home that was rescued from the bay, and the tiny jail once housed rabble-rousers. The avenue ends near City Pier, where you can stroll to the end of the dock and admire the views of the **Sunshine Skyway Bridge**. You can grab a bite or a drink (or bait for your fishing needs) at the end of the pier.

SUNCOAST AERIALS/SHUTTERSTOCK ©

Anna Maria Island

Several keys lie even closer to downtown Sarasota, reachable by the John Ringling Causeway. After maneuvering through the traffic surrounding St Armands Circle, make your way up to the **Mote Marine Laboratory and Aquarium**. Exhibits include otherworldly jellyfish, a large shark tank and a preserved giant squid (37ft long when caught). In a separate building, the aquarium organizes encounters with rescued sea turtles as well as manatees, otters and alligators.

Continue north across the New Pass Bridge onto **Longboat Key**. Once a quiet fishing village, the 12 long miles of Longboat Key are now lined with upscale resorts and condos. A few tiny public parking lots don't offer much access for day-trippers. **Beer Can Island** at the northern tip of Longboat is one of the area's prettiest beaches.

The star of Sarasota's coastline is **Anna Maria Island**, connected to the north end of Longboat Key by a drawbridge over the pass. The perfect antidote to party-loving Siesta Key, Anna Maria

TRAVEL BY BOAT

Historic Spanish Point is run by the Selby Gardens in Sarasota. On Saturdays, they run full-day campus-to-campus boat tours, which include historical narration along the way, admission to both sites and lunch.

WHERE TO EAT IN THE SARASOTA KEYS

Ginny's & Jane E's
An old village grocery in the north of Anna Maria now a much-loved cafe, restaurant and curio shop. **$**

Sandbar
This favorite Anna Maria haunt has casual beachfront dining with Gulf seafood and plenty of tropical cocktails. **$$**

Miguel's
Tuck into perfectly cooked scallops, French onion soup or filet mignon at this old-school French bistro on Siesta Key. **$$**

Island lies marooned in a 1950s time warp, with sun-faded clapboard houses, teenagers hanging outside ice-cream stores and a clutch of good seafood restaurants. The island has three beach towns: at the southern end is **Bradenton Beach**, mid-island is **Holmes Beach**, considered the hub, and at the northern tip is **Anna Maria village**.

Anna Maria's southernmost jewel is **Coquina Beach**, a peaceful stretch of soft white sand backed by Australian pines. Across the road, you can look for wildlife along the boardwalk trails of the small nature preserve of **Coquina Baywalk** at **Leffis Key**.

Beautiful beachfront also adorns the northern reaches of Anna Maria. Here you'll find low dunes overlooking the waterfront at **Bean Point Beach**, and fewer crowds than you'll find near the center of the island at Manatee Public Beach.

Echoes of the Past in Historic Spanish Point

ANCIENT PEOPLES AND PIONEERS

Around 10 miles south of Sarasota, you can explore layers of history on a 30-acre peninsula jutting out into Little Sarasota Bay. Shell middens, small pioneer cottages and gardens provide a fascinating window into those who lived here over the years. A 1-mile **trail** loops around the property, taking you past the leafy grounds surrounding well-preserved sites.

Over 4000 years ago, indigenous people settled near a freshwater spring and harvested clams, oysters, scallops and whelks from the sea. They built a mound from the shells, which later formed an elevated base for the settlements (20ft above sea level). Subsequent groups came after them, building new mounds that ultimately gave the peninsula its shape.

The first non-native settlers came in 1867. Looking for land, the pioneering Webb family heard about the location from Spanish fishers, and built a homestead there. When Webb discovered human remains while plowing his garden, he invited the Smithsonian Institution to come take a look. So began archaeological research into the area, which continued into the early 1960s.

Among the finds are some of the oldest known Native American pottery. You can see this and other unique finds by entering a partially excavated shell midden. This is the only such site in Florida where you can see the layers of shell deposits and prehistoric paraphernalia from the inside.

Wandering the trail (tours via electric cart are also available) around the site, you can see the wooden packing house, Mary's Chapel, the Webb-family cemetery and Frank Guptill's beautiful wooden homestead, which he built in 1901.

THE GUPTILL HOME

A boat builder from Maine, Frank Guptill befriended the Webbs in the 1870s and ended up marrying into the family. Frank married Ginnie in 1877, but after her tragic death the following year, he married her sister Lizzie. They lived on a boat for a time until Guptill constructed the house atop a small hill (now known to contain a shell midden). It remains remarkably well preserved thanks to Guptill's foresight to use Florida yellow pine, which is resistant to termites and strong enough to survive hurricanes.

Inside, you can check out Frank's fiddle and Lizzie's piano, which the pair played to entertain guests at the Webb winter resort. Docents are on hand to share more knowledge about the site.

NATURE VIEWS AT HISTORIC SPANISH POINT

Sunken Gardens
Grab lunch from the on-site food truck nearby and admire views through the bougainvillea-draped pergola.

Cock's Footbridge
Spy living creatures amid the mangroves and buttonwoods, then look for wading birds out in the bay.

Butterfly House
See giant swallowtails, zebra longwings (the Florida state butterfly) and other winged beauties flittering past.

CYCLING THE LEGACY TRAIL

One of the best-kept secrets in Sarasota County is a former rail line turned greenway that runs for 18.5 miles between Venice and Sarasota's Fruitville Rd (just east of downtown Sarasota). The scenic **Legacy Trail** runs past leafy parks, suburban backyards and across several trestle bridges over the Intracoastal Waterway. In town, the trail starts at the historic 1927 Venice train depot. From there it's another 5 miles to Oscar Scherer State Park, another trail highlight. Near the start, you can rent bicycles from Real Bikes or e-bikes from Big Bam.

Caspersen Beach

Beach-Hopping & Shark-Tooth Hunting in Venice

YOGA, CONCERTS, FISHING AND FOSSIL-HUNTING

Venice doesn't bear much resemblance to its Italian namesake, but the island city's lovely beaches make for a rewarding, low-key getaway, and there's free parking by the shore.

Venice Beach lies at the end of West Venice Ave and has a wide stretch of sandy coastline stretching north and south. Sea turtles nest here and shorebird watching is excellent. You can start or end the day here with **free yoga** (8am and 9am daily, and 5pm Monday to Thursday). There's also live music nightly from about 6pm.

About 2 miles south of there (reachable by a long walk or short drive), the 700ft **Venice Pier** is a favorite spot for sunset. It's also a choice fishing spot, with a bait and snack shop and fine views across the water. Around dusk, **Sharky's** draws a garrulous crowd who come for drinks and seafood.

Keep heading south (another 1.5 miles from the pier) to reach **Caspersen Beach**, an area famous for the sharks' teeth that wash ashore – including fossilized prehistoric teeth. You can join the seaside scavengers by renting a sifting basket (aka a 'Florida snow shovel') from **Papa's Bait Shop** on Venice Pier.

North of Venice on Casey Key, **Nokomis** is yet another attractive, palmetto-backed beach. An hour before sundown on Wednesday and Saturday nights things get groovy: the **Nokomis Beach Drum Circle** gathers and its rhythm draws upward of several hundred folks.

GETTING AROUND

The free Bay Runner trolley runs from downtown Sarasota to St Armands Circle and Lido Key. It is more complicated to reach Siesta Key by bus (you'll need to transfer between buses), though once there you can ride the free Siesta Key Breeze trolley to get around. Anna Maria Island also runs a free trolley service.

FORT MYERS

The Calusa weren't the first inhabitants in this part of Southwest Florida, but they were the ones the Spanish encountered in the 16th century. They lived in stilted huts roofed with palmetto leaves and subsisted on a diet of fish and shellfish – some of the great mounds of their discarded mollusk shells and fish bones survive today. Present-day Fort Myers lies along the Caloosahatchee ('river of the Calusa').

The city itself was named after a US military fort built during the Seminole Wars (mid-19th century). Only a few cattle ranchers lived in the area up until 1885, when the inventor Thomas Edison fell in love with the area. He and his wife jump-started development, planting royal palms along the avenue and helping to bring electrification to the town. Fort Myers has a well-preserved historic quarter – today lined with restaurants, shops and cafes – that provides a fascinating window into the past.

TOP TIP

If you're contemplating a trip to Key West, but don't want the hassle of driving, book a trip with Key West Express. The catamaran makes the journey from San Carlos Island near Fort Myers Beach to Key West in just under four hours. It departs daily at 8am and returns at 5pm.

SADIE MANTELL/SHUTTERSTOCK ©

Edison Theatre (p370)

HIGHLIGHT
1 Edison & Ford Winter Estates

SIGHTS
2 Edison Theatre
3 Sidney & Berne Davis Art Center

ENTERTAINMENT
4 Arcade Theatre

SHOPPING
5 Franklin Shops

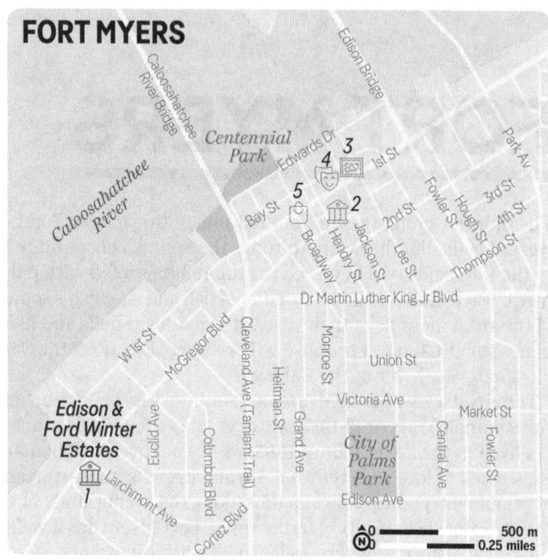

HURRICANE IAN

In late September, 2022, a category 4 hurricane roared ashore near Fort Myers Beach, causing catastrophic damages across Southwest Florida. Over 140 people died, making Hurricane Ian the deadliest storm to hit the state since 1935. The scale of devastation was hard to comprehend: hundreds of homes were destroyed, large fishing vessels were tossed ashore like toy boats, and bridges were swept away, including the only road to Sanibel Island. In all, the state suffered an estimated $50 billion in damages, and some worried that hard-hit communities would never be the same.

The Soul of Fort Myers

SOUTHWEST FLORIDA'S MOST PHOTOGENIC DOWNTOWN

The **River District** has brick streets lined with eye-catching buildings that house a growing array of shops, cafes and restaurants. It's an easygoing place for a stroll, particularly during the **Art Walk** (first Friday of the month) when artists and artisans sell their creations along the sidewalks. During the **Music Walk** (third Friday of the month) bands and soloists perform on the city streets.

Though it no longer functions as a performing venue, the **Edison Theatre** is an art deco beauty built in the 1920s that's well worth a look. Up the street, you can browse for gift ideas inside the **Franklin Shops**. Set in a 1937 building with a Vitrolite glass facade, this two-story emporium sells unique items, like locally harvested sea sponges, bracelets featuring Fort Myers Beach sand, raw honey and paintings by South Florida artists. There's even peach-infused Fort Myers wine.

Further along First St, the **Arcade Theatre** is yet another grand dame – this one built in 1915 as a Vaudeville House.

WHERE TO FIND NIGHTLIFE IN FORT MYERS

Social House
An indoor-outdoor space with craft cocktails and creative snacks, plus mellow live music.

86 Room
Off the Patio de Leon (courtyard), the 86 Room has a vintage 1920s vibe and classic drinks.

Beacon Social Drinkery
Up on the 12th floor of the Luminary Hotel, you can enjoy Tampa's best views over the river.

Today, you can catch musicals and plays performed by the **Florida Repertory Theatre**.

One block east, the **Sidney and Berne Davis Art Center** is one of Fort Myers' grandest addresses. Constructed in 1933 out of coral rock from the Florida Keys, the neoclassical Revival building served as a post office and later a federal courthouse before its transformation into an arts center in recent days. Today you can catch art exhibitions, concerts, plays, dance parties and DJ sessions on the roof.

Touring Edison & Ford Winter Estates

HISTORIC ESTATE OF AMERICAN INNOVATORS

Thomas Edison built his winter home in 1885 and lived in Florida seasonally until his death in 1931. Edison's friend Henry Ford built his adjacent bungalow in 1916. Together, and sometimes side by side in Edison's lab, these two inventors, businessmen and neighbors changed our world. The **museum** does an excellent job of presenting the overwhelming scope of their achievements. Download the free Edison Ford app for a self-guided tour, or join one of the knowledgable historians on a guided tour of the estate, held throughout the day.

Edison, Ford and Harvey Firestone were dedicated 'tin-can tourists' who enjoyed driving and camping across America together, and exhibits chronicle their journeys and how these fed their refinements of the automobile. Indeed, the main purpose of Edison's Fort Myers lab was to develop a domestic source of rubber (primarily using goldenrod plants) for auto manufacturing, although he then went on to file 1093 patents for things like the light bulb, the phonograph, waffle irons and sprocketed celluloid film.

The rich **botanical gardens** and **genteel homes** very nearly glow, and are decked out with period furniture and a few original pieces – like the piano of Mina, Edison's wife, and their original green wicker furniture on the porch. You can't miss the massive banyan tree. Planted as a single sapling back in 1927, it's now the largest of its species in the continental US, with its canopy covering 1 acre.

SANIBEL ISLAND

Sanibel, which suffered heavy damages during Hurricane Ian, is not like other Florida beach communities. It prides itself on its egalitarian spirit, and riches are rarely flaunted. Development here has been carefully managed: the island's northern half is almost entirely protected within the **JN 'Ding' Darling National Wildlife Refuge**, a 6300-acre reserve full of wildlife.

The island's lovely beaches are famed for the quality of their shells. Dedicated hunters are identified by their hunchbacked 'Sanibel stoop.' Recovery from Hurricane Ian will likely continue years into the future; visitors can help out by supporting local businesses on the island.

GETTING AROUND

Fort Myers has a good transport network, including two free trolley buses that run seasonally (December through April). Take the blue line to reach the Edison & Ford Winter Estates.

NAPLES

Naples has long been one of Florida's most coveted retirement destinations, with the average age of its residents hovering around 66. Lovely beaches, year-round sunshine and handsomely manicured streets are all part of the appeal, along with museums, botanical gardens and abundant recreational possibilities. Even those who aren't in their golden years tend to give high marks to Naples. In their 2021 roundup of the best beach towns to live in, *Travel + Leisure* ranked the city number one.

Named after the captivating southern Italian city, Naples was founded in 1886, and from the beginning marketed itself as a tourism destination. The early boosters of the town (which had a population of less than 100) opened the first hotel in 1889 as well as an ambitious 600ft pier jutting into the Gulf that would provide steamship access. Though damaged by Hurricane Ian in 2022, the Naples Pier remains a symbol of the city today.

TOP TIP

Naples has two primary retail corridors: the main one is 5th Ave between 9th St and 3rd St. Another retail district runs along 3rd St S between Broad Ave S and 14th St S. This area, called Third Street South, forms the heart of Old Naples and features regular events, including a Saturday-morning farmers market.

EPICENTER OF THE ARTS

One of Southwest Florida's most important cultural institutions, **Artis–Naples** is a showcase for both the performing and the visual arts. At the **Baker Museum**, you can peruse works by 20th- and 21st-century artists. Past exhibitions have featured Ran Hwang, Magritte, Mauricio Lasansky and Helen Frankenthaler.

Next door to the Baker are Artis–Naples' two performing arts venues. **Hayes Hall** stages Broadway shows, ballets and concerts by the Naples Philharmonic. The 283-seat **Daniels Pavilion** hosts jazz, comedy and chamber music.

Naples in Bloom

LUSH GARDENS AND WILD SPACES

The **Naples Botanical Garden**, one of the finest gardens in the state, encompasses both manicured spaces as well as wilder areas that showcase Southwest Florida's natural ecosystems.

The **Brazilian Garden** bristles with bromeliads, palms and other species from the tropics, including a silk floss tree with its spiky, medieval-looking trunk and the jurema, whose limbs resemble a flexing bodybuilder. Beneath a mural by the Brazilian landscape architect Roberto Burle Marx, a waterfall flows into a pond full of Victoria amazonica. Dragonflies alight on these gargantuan water lilies that can grow up to 9ft wide.

Afterwards, stroll into the **Caribbean Garden**, and breathe in the richness of tropical fruit species. Cross the small River of Grass, then enjoy the breezes in the **Florida Garden**, the highest point in the property. Pathways meander past wildflower-fringed cascades, oolite rocks and legacy tree species like date palms and lemon ficus.

Nearby, you can enjoy the meditative calm of the **Asian Garden**. Take a seat in a Balinese-style pavilion and listen to the sound of water moving through lotus ponds as guardian statues keep watch. Naturally, the stone Buddha sits beneath a fig tree – of a similar species as the sacred Bodhi tree.

Asian Garden, Naples Botanical Garden

JILLIAN CAIN PHOTOGRAPHY/SHUTTERSTOCK ©

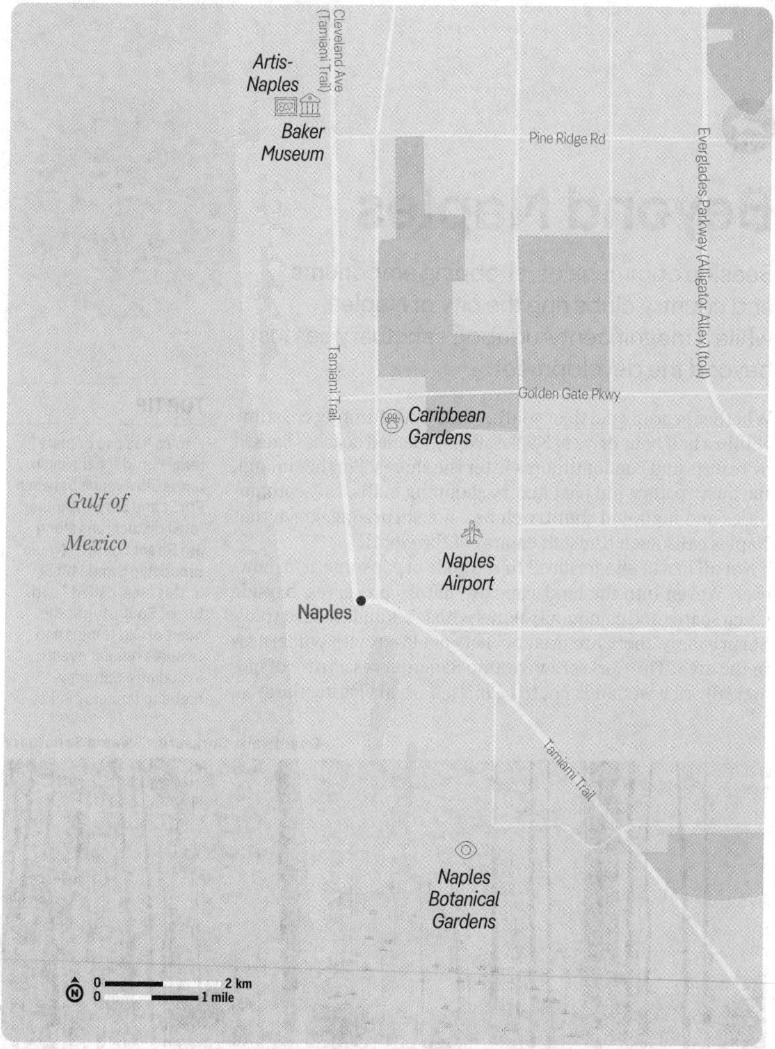

Cleveland Ave (Tamiami Trail)
Artis-Naples
Baker Museum
Pine Ridge Rd
Everglades Parkway (Alligator Alley) (toll)
Tamiami Trail
Golden Gate Pkwy
Caribbean Gardens
Gulf of Mexico
Naples Airport
Naples
Tamiami Trail
Naples Botanical Gardens
0 2 km
0 1 mile

Once you've explored the gardens, see the wilder side of things in the **Preserve**, with its slash pine forest, marshes and mangroves. Here you can look for wildlife on a boardwalk trail through a freshwater swamp and see an osprey nest while circling the lake. There's also a birding tower.

GETTING AROUND

Naples runs a numbered, color-coded bus system. Several lines loop through downtown, including 13 and 14, both of which continue on to the Naples Botanical Garden.

Beyond Naples

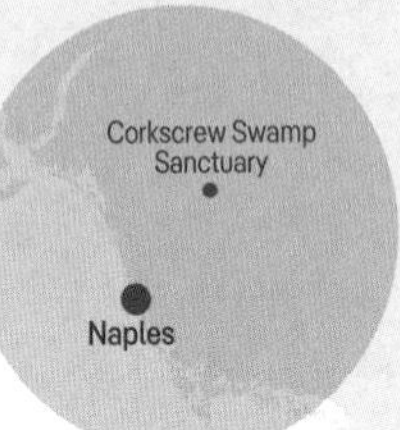

Seaside communities, shopping emporiums and country clubs ring the city of Naples, while a magnificent Audubon sanctuary lies just beyond the development.

Whether heading north or south, you'll find stunning coastline within a half hour drive of Naples. Well-groomed beaches backed by resorts and condominiums litter the shores. Further inland, the busy roads wind past luxury shopping malls, tiny communities and high-end country clubs – not surprising, given that Naples calls itself 'the golf capital of the world.'

Not all has been sacrificed to the gods of consumerism, however. Woven into the landscape are nature preserves, bayside green spaces and community parks with lakes and wooded trails. Surprisingly, there are even pockets of old-growth wilderness in the area. The Corkscrew Swamp Sanctuary is a trove of biologically rich wetlands not to be missed when visiting the area.

TOP TIP

Naples has two primary retail corridors: the main one is 5th Avenue between 9th St and 3rd St. Another retail district runs along 3rd Street South between Broad Ave S and 14th St S. This area, called Third Street South, forms the heart of Old Naples and features regular events, including a Saturday-morning farmers market.

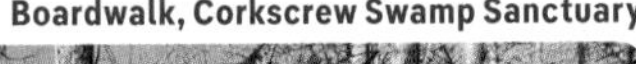

Boardwalk, Corkscrew Swamp Sanctuary

Walking the Corkscrew Swamp Sanctuary

SPECTACULAR OLD-GROWTH FOREST

The crown jewel in the National Audubon Society's nature preserves, the Corkscrew Swamp Sanctuary provides an intimate exploration of six pristine native habitats along a shady and stunning 2.25-mile boardwalk trail. The centerpiece is the largest old-growth bald cypress forest on earth, with majestic specimens more than 600 years old and towering above 100ft tall.

As you set out on the path, you'll pass through pine flatwoods before skirting the edge of a sawgrass pond. Ferns lie at the bases of slender bald cypress trees, with epiphytes sprouting from their trunks and branches. Further along, a short detour leads to the Plume Hunters Camp, where vast numbers of birds were slaughtered for their feathers before Audubon Wardens began guarding the site in 1910.

You'll find breezy views across the wet prairie (aka marsh), where grasses and sedges grow above the saturated soil. From here, the forest grows taller and darker as you enter the realm of virgin bald cypress trees. As you leave the younger forest behind, **Sentry** marks the boundary – it is one of more than a dozen trees of such great age and size that they have names.

Take things slowly as you travel through this forest, listening for the rat-a-tat-tatting of woodpeckers, looking for warblers flitting through the treetops and keeping watch for movement across the inky waters. Rare plants, including the famed ghost orchid, lie hidden among the branches of some cypresses. You might also spot anhingas drying their wings in the sun, alligators basking on small islands, trees full of ibis and otters swimming near the boardwalk.

GUARDIANS OF THE PLUME

In the late 19th century, the height of women's fashion was wearing a hat featuring the long feathers of wading birds. With an ounce of egret feathers worth more than an ounce of gold, hunters slaughtered birds by the millions, driving some species to near extinction. Concerned citizens raised the alarm, forming the Florida Audubon Society in 1900. They fought hard to save the birds, eventually inspiring the legislature to pass laws protecting them. Enforcement was lacking, however, so Audubon hired wardens, including Rhett Green who risked his life defending rookeries. One bald cypress in the forest bears his name and aptly attracts flocks of migratory birds.

SOUTH FLORIDA NATURE ENCOUNTERS

You can find even more birds, alligators and orchids amid the wilderness preserves farther south. It's a little over an hour's drive to **Big Cypress National Preserve** (p115), with boardwalk views across wildlife-filled wetlands.

GETTING AROUND

Unfortunately, there's no public transportation that runs to the Corkscrew Swamp Sanctuary, so you will need your own set of wheels to get there.

THE PANHANDLE

EXPLORE BEACH, OCEAN AND SPRING WILDERNESSES

Immerse yourself in more than 100 miles of undeveloped beaches, an underwater shipwreck trail and natural springs.

The Florida Panhandle holds 13 counties clustered like cockles along the clear green waters of the Gulf of Mexico. The largest city here is Tallahassee, at about 200,000 people, followed by Pensacola (54,000) and Navarre (about 40,000). White sand called 'sugar' carpets the Gulf beaches and forests, and spring-laced wilderness surrounds the small cities.

The Panhandle is primarily rural. Because of that, this area feels more like the Deep South than the rest of coastal Florida. The pace is slow, laid-back and dreamy, and the smallest towns feel like sets from old black-and-white TV shows. Interstate and coastal highways connect more than 100 miles of beaches. You'll also find flea markets and roadside stands with hot-boiled peanuts, seasonal vegetables and Georgia peaches as you travel them.

It's hard to get tired of the gorgeous white-sand beaches that edge the coastal town, but if you do, you could escape inland to canoe or float along chilly natural springs that still look much like they did when the Native Americans roamed here thousands of years ago.

Pensacola, on the border with Alabama, marks the Panhandle's western extremity, and Tallahassee is the largest city at its eastern extremity. To the south is the Gulf, and the state of Georgia is a few miles to the north.

BRENT BARNES/SHUTTERSTOCK ©

THE MAIN AREAS

PENSACOLA
Emerald beaches with seafood galore. **p382**

DESTIN
Constant entertainment and pristine beaches. **p389**

PANAMA CITY
White-sand beaches and family fun. **p397**

JOSHUA WHITCOMB/SHUTTERSTOCK ©

Left: Diving, Panama City (p397); above: Pensacola Beach (p382)

APALACHICOLA
Historic fishing village, Old Florida landscape. **p401**

TALLAHASSEE
Capitol views and lush springs. **p404**

Find Your Way

The Panhandle stretches from the Alabama border along the Gulf and south to the coastal curve called Big Bend. US 98 connects the cities and towns along the shore. I-10 links Mobile, Tallahassee and Jacksonville.

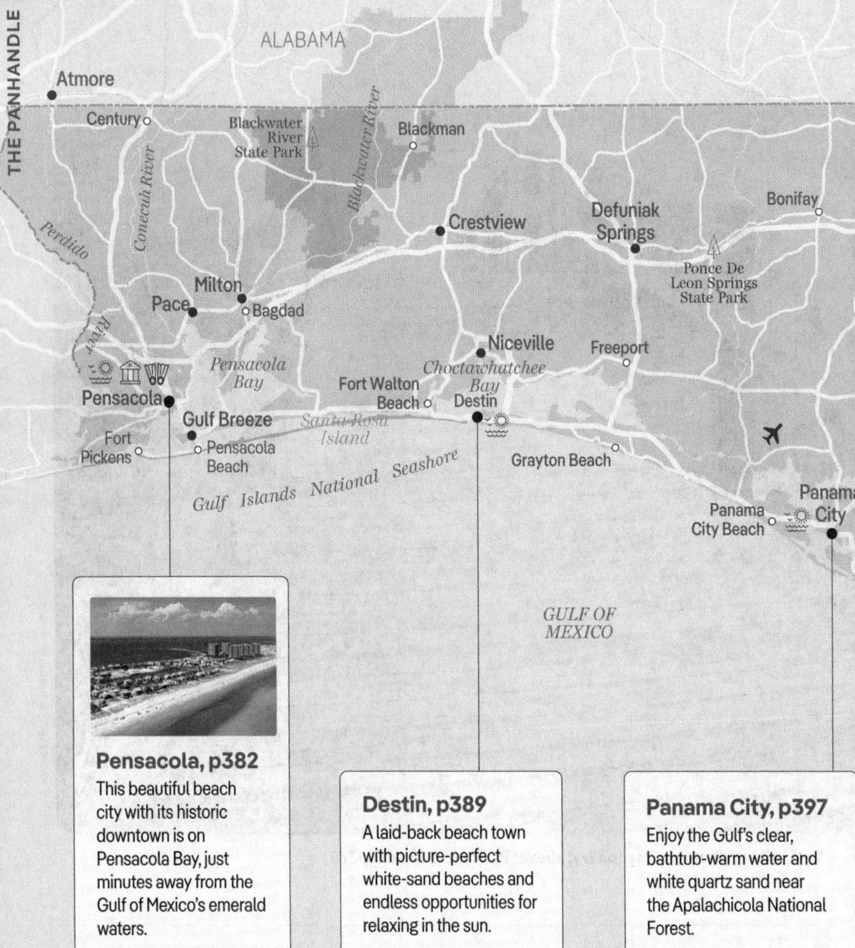

Pensacola, p382
This beautiful beach city with its historic downtown is on Pensacola Bay, just minutes away from the Gulf of Mexico's emerald waters.

Destin, p389
A laid-back beach town with picture-perfect white-sand beaches and endless opportunities for relaxing in the sun.

Panama City, p397
Enjoy the Gulf's clear, bathtub-warm water and white quartz sand near the Apalachicola National Forest.

CAR

You can easily navigate in and among Panhandle towns by car. US 98 traces the coastline. I-10 is a direct route from Pensacola to Jacksonville and passes through Tallahassee without veering to the coast. Lyft, Uber and taxis are in the larger towns.

PLANE

The question isn't whether you can fly between Panhandle towns. It's whether you'd want to. Flights are available via the numerous regional airports, but they take longer than driving between locations. Still, they're there if you need them.

BUS

The larger cities have extensive bus services. Pensacola has ECAT and a free seasonal beach trolley. EC Rider goes to Destin, Miramar Beach (where Sandestin is) and Fort Walton Beach. Panama City has the Bay Town Trolley (actually the bus) and Tallahassee has StarMetro.

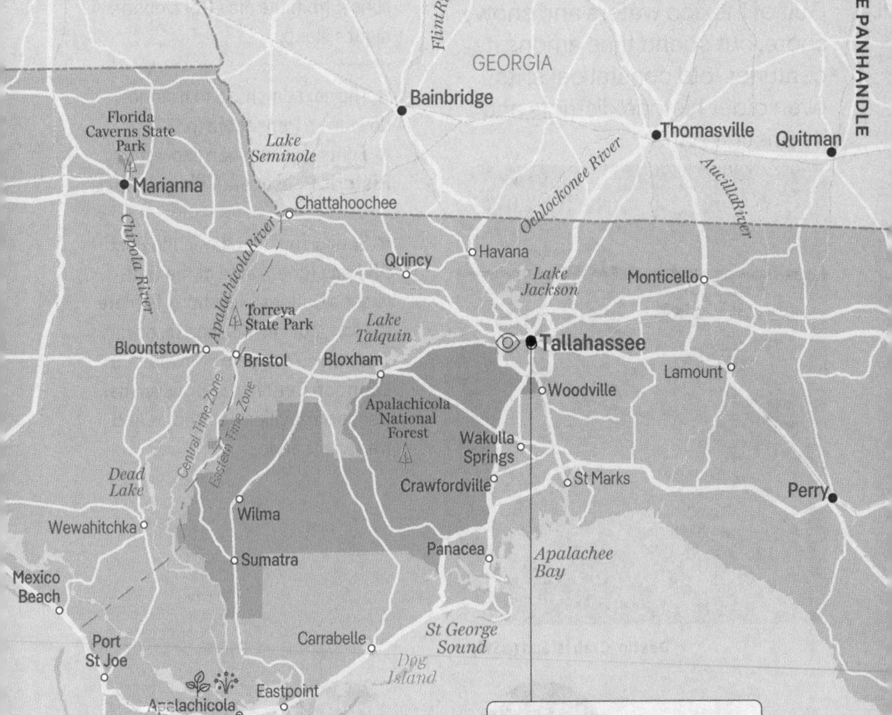

Tallahassee, p404

Tour the historic Capitol Complex and enjoy untouched natural springs and relaxing state parks.

Apalachicola, p401

A tiny, historic fishing village that offers glimpses into unspoiled Old Florida rivers, beaches and coastal forest.

Plan Your Time

The Florida Panhandle is famous for its glass-clear, aquamarine Gulf of Mexico waters and snowy shore, but spend time among its centuries-old coastal oaks, its even older historic districts and its pristine parks.

ROTORHEAD 30A PRODUCTIONS/SHUTTERSTOCK ©

Destin, Crab Island (p391)

Three Days to Travel Around

● Spend your first day relaxing at **Casino Beach** (p386), where you can sunbathe, swim, snorkel or fish from the pier nearby. Enjoy a casual lunch nearby and take in the sunset from the pier. Get a good night's sleep.

● The next day, head to historic downtown **Pensacola** (p382) to sightsee, dine, shop and visit **Historic Pensacola Village** (p387).

● Spend your last day in the **Fort Pickens** (p388) area of the Gulf Islands National Seashore. Explore the fort, built in 1861, and discovery center. You can also swim at **Langdon Beach** (p388), which has a shaded pavilion, restrooms and free tram service.

Seasonal Highlights

The Panhandle knows how to party; it's worth visiting during a festival. Mardi Gras, holidays and food and wine festivals are big here.

FEBRUARY

Experience the **PCB Mardi Gras & Music Festival** and the Krewe of Dominique Youx's great **Mardi Gras at the Beach** parade.

APRIL–MAY

Wine and food celebrities host the **South Walton Beaches Wine and Food Festival** in Grand Boulevard at Sandestin.

JULY

July 4 fireworks bloom in the Panhandle cities, with the **Pensacola Beach Airshow** (p385) the next week.

CHERYL CASEY/SHUTTERSTOCK ©, CARLO PREARO/SHUTTERSTOCK ©, CHERYL CASEY/SHUTTERSTOCK ©

Five Days to Travel Around

- Head about 48 miles east to **Destin** (p389), taking US Hwy 98. It will take about an hour, depending on the traffic. Spend your fourth day in Destin's exquisite **Henderson Beach State Park** (p390), enjoying a rare glimpse of Old Florida at its most beautiful and undeveloped. Head out on the town for excellent, fresh-caught local seafood.

- On your fifth day, head out to **Destin Harbor** (p391). There's a high-energy, carnival-like atmosphere at the boardwalk during events and lots of shopping opportunities. You can ride a charter cruise, board a pirate ship or turn your prow toward **HarborWalk Village** (p391), with its abundance of shopping and kid-friendly activities.

Six Days or More

- Head still further east to **Panama City** (p397). It's located another 47 miles away on Hwy 98.

- Spend day six enjoying quartz-white beaches and clear water at **Panama City Beach** (p398) and sightseeing on the **Russell-Fields Pier** (p398). Later, dine and shop at **Pier Park** (p398), a popular outdoor complex. On day seven, have an up-close-and-personal encounter with the wet Florida wild at **St Andrews State Park** (p298) or spend the day at **ZooWorld Zoological Park** (p399).

- If you have longer, consider a side trip to **Tallahassee** (p404) to see the **State Capitol** (p406) or a foray into **Apalachicola** (p401) for outdoor activities and the freshest seafood you've likely ever eaten.

SEPTEMBER
Panama City Beach's **Gulf Coast Jam** celebrates three days of country and **SandJam** features alternative.

OCTOBER
The **Destin Seafood Festival** on Destin Harbor attracts around 70,000 with live music, local seafood and scores of vendors.

NOVEMBER
Apalachicola's **Florida Seafood Festival** (p402) brings fresh local seafood, foot races and oyster eating and shucking contests to downtown.

DECEMBER
Panama City Beach has an annual tree lighting, a parade, and the New Year's Eve **Beach Ball Drop** event.

Pensacola

Miami

PENSACOLA

Pensacola is the westernmost city in Florida, built around Pensacola Bay and sheltered by Santa Rosa Island. It's famous for beaches with snow-white sand and cut-glass water, seasonal festivals and parades, and plenty of water sports like sailing, diving, snorkeling, swimming and fishing – not to mention its fantastic seafood. It's not large (about 54,000 people), but it's the Escambia County seat and part of the 500,000-plus Pensacola Metropolitan Area.

In 1559 Spain's Don Tristan de Luna founded a short-lived outpost here, but a hurricane foiled a permanent settlement until 1698. You can see the city's colonial heritage in downtown's period architecture, which mingles with luxury condos. Palafox St runs through the center of the historic district, a 40-block area that's home to galleries, boutiques, restaurants, parks and historic buildings.

TOP TIP

The Pensacola Bay Bridge (aka Three-Mile Bridge) from downtown to Gulf Breeze can back up pretty easily, due to heavy traffic or accidents, so gas up and have patience if driving its span. Also, don't speed in Gulf Breeze

The coast at Pensacola

SIGHTS
1 African American Heritage Society
2 Children's Museum
3 Fort Barrancas
4 Fort Pickens
5 Fort Pickens Area of Gulf Islands National Seashore
6 Historic Pensacola Village
7 Langdon Beach
8 NAS Pensacola
9 National Naval Aviation Museum
10 Pensacola Beach Gulf Pier
11 Pensacola Lighthouse & Maritime Museum
12 Pensacola Museum of Art
13 Pensacola Museum of History
14 Santa Rosa Island

EATING
15 Casino Beach Bar & Grille

SHOPPING
16 Palafox Market
17 Pensacola Beach Boardwalk on Quietwater Beach

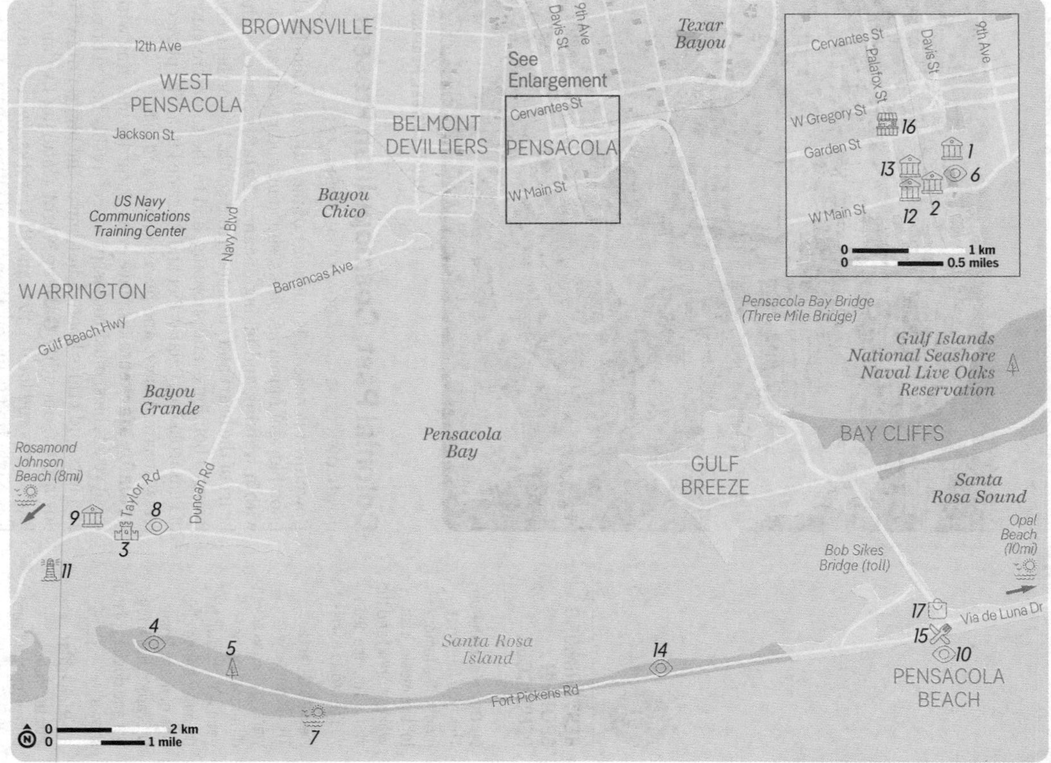

BOWN MEDIA/SHUTTERSTOCK ©

Palafox Street, Pensacola

Colonial Past, Cosmopolitan Present

DOWNTOWN PENSACOLA BOASTS SHOPPING, ARTS

Downtown Pensacola is the heart of the city and offers block upon block of museums, parks, shopping and restaurants, all within walking and biking distance. **Palafox Street** is the heart of the heart and runs north and south. Its northern end features boutiques and shopping, and to the south are views of Pensacola Bay, Palafox Pier and Plaza de Luna. The plaza offers waterfront views and places to bike and fish.

Palafox Market takes place every Saturday morning with fresh vegetables, mushrooms, produce, freshly baked bread, and arts and crafts booths. But one of the biggest draws is downtown's monthly **Gallery Night** featuring live music, food trucks and local artists and their works. Even when Gallery Night isn't going on, there are plenty of museums to explore, like the **Pensacola Children's Museum** on Zaragoza St, the **African American Heritage Society** on Church St, the **Pensacola Museum of Art** and the **Pensacola Museum of History**, both on South Jefferson St.

BEST DRINKING SPOTS IN PENSACOLA

McGuire's Irish Pub
This, you must not moose. It's famous for live music, Irish Wake (a drink) and the stuffed moose head you're urged to kiss.

Seville Quarter
This former warehouse has seven different 'rooms,' each with its own bar, theme or dance club. One of them, Rosie O'Grady's, has a full bar and dueling piano shows.

Sir Richard's Public House
British-themed pub with unique drinks, pub food, darts, pool tables and a cozy atmosphere.

WHERE TO EAT IN PENSACOLA

Leisure Club
This popular casual brunch spot also offers breakfast, lunch, vegan options and a coffee bar. $

Misu Food Truck
A funky food truck in the heart of downtown offers Mexican-American street food and some of the best burgers in town. $

Grand Marlin of Pensacola Beach
Beautiful views and a popular namesake drink, a mix of fruit juice and rums. $$$

The **Belmont-DeVilliers** neighborhood was historically Black when the Jim Crow laws enforced segregation in the city where jazz and blues greats like Billie Holiday and Etta James once performed. Now, it's an excellent place for the comfort of authentic Southern cooking.

Colonial architecture recalling the French Quarter of New Orleans, sleek modern condos and higher-end storefronts provide beautiful backdrops for shopping and a full schedule of festivals, parades and holiday events throughout the year.

The Navy Takes to the Blue

BLUE ANGELS INSPIRE DURING AIRSHOWS

Pensacola has a robust military presence. Naval Air Station (NAS) Pensacola employs 16,000 military members and 7400 civilians in nearby Warrington. Several Navy training centers and offices serve throughout Pensacola, not to mention the 350,000-sq-ft **National Naval Aviation Museum** here.

Twice a year, visitors take note of another of the city's claims to naval fame: the **US Navy Blue Angels**, a flight demonstration squadron that performs about 62 shows all over the country but calls NAS Pensacola home.

Two Blue Angels annual airshows also help residents and visitors feel a part of the naval mission. July's **Pensacola Beach Airshow** draws tens of thousands to the beach to watch the two-day show and the full rehearsals preceding it. But November's **Pensacola Blue Angels Homecoming Airshow** is a far larger event, drawing between 150,000 and 180,000 people over two days with its static aircraft displays and a long list of aerial performers. The event is held along Sherman Field at NAS Pensacola and is free, but bring your own chairs.

Pompano & Circumstance

ANGLING FOR FISH, AND VIEWS

The **Pensacola Beach Gulf Pier**, 41 Fort Pickens Rd, stands out for its fishing and strolling opportunities, even in a city surrounded by miles of crystalline water and plenty of access.

You have to pay $2.25 to step onto the 1471ft-long pier off Casino Beach, but you're rewarded with the chance to spot dolphins, stingrays and jellyfish below, and planes flying above, not to mention views of the shore. You may reel in flounder, whiting, sailfish or pompano if you fish. (It's $7.50 to fish, and you don't need a license.)

It's hard to find a better spot to watch the sunset in the Panhandle. It's also a very popular place to watch a Blue Angels airshow, and there's usually plenty of parking nearby.

FIRST PLACE

You've probably heard St Augustine call itself the nation's oldest (European) city, but the truth is that this title belongs to Pensacola. Well, technically.

While Spanish explorer Pedro Menéndez waited until 1565 to found St Augustine, Spanish settlers led by Don Tristan de Luna, a conquistador, arrived in Florida in 1559. The settlers established a small encampment, but thanks to a hurricane and lack of supplies, it only lasted a year before the settlers abandoned it. The Spanish crown later removed Luna due to his poor leadership, and the Spanish didn't return for another 138 years.

WHERE TO STAY IN PENSACOLA

Margaritaville Beach Hotel
The resort locals send their friends to, with access to the most popular beaches and a poolside bar. **$$$**

Oyster Bay Boutique Hotel
This specialty hotel is housed in a 19th-century building in historic downtown Pensacola. **$$$**

Paradise Inn
A mid-century-modern hotel on Santa Rosa Sound, close to shopping, dining and entertainment. **$$**

Best Bet Beach

CASINO BEACH'S RELAXING VIBE

While there's no casino now, **Casino Beach** got its name from an activity center built in 1931 called the Pensacola Casino. It featured bathhouses, shopping, a restaurant and regular boxing matches until its demolition in 1972. Casino Beach has the benefit of lifeguards, volleyball nets, a shaded pavilion, many restaurants, and live music at the **Casino Beach Bar & Grille**. It's also next to the **Pensacola Beach Gulf Pier**. The beach on either side of the pier is a popular spot to lay a blanket, bask in the sun and people-watch.

Casino Beach is part of Pensacola Beach and is located on **Santa Rosa Island**, a barrier island that stretches like a ribbonfish along the coast. (Santa Rosa Island also includes **Gulf National Seashore** and the **Pensacola Beach Boardwalk on Quietwater Beach**, a boardwalk with shops and restaurants near Casino Beach.)

THE SINKING OF THE SAN PABLO

Unlike some wrecks along the Florida Panhandle Shipwreck Trail, the *San Pablo* was sunk deliberately. Twice.

Once called 'The Russian Freighter,' it was actually Irish and hailed from Belfast. In 1915 the vessel ferried bananas between Central America and the US before a U-boat sunk it off Costa Rica early in WWII. The US military refloated the boat shortly before testing its new weapons system in 1944. Three thousand pounds of aimed explosives later, Pensacola had a new artificial reef.

If you dive it, expect to see more entrails than boat. Think boilers, refrigerator coils and lots of twisted metal.

Lighting the Way

SHEDDING LIGHT ON HISTORY

The **Pensacola Lighthouse & Maritime Museum** is a picturesque black-and-white landmark from 1859. Climb its 177 steps for an unsurpassed view of the Gulf and surrounding area. You'll also have a chance to tour the museum in the keeper's quarters, which houses exhibits that celebrate the area's history, including its natural history.

It's also a rare chance for civilians to enter **NAS Pensacola**, an active military base, although you'll have to book your visit in advance. If you're not a military member with a Department of Defense ID, you must take the lighthouse shuttle bus to the lighthouse. Check the website for a list of events, like the Blue Angels practice flights or the Sunset & Full Moon climbs, that allow civilians.

A World Beneath the Sea

TRACE AN UNDERWATER SHIPWRECK TRAIL

Diving is a massive pursuit in the Panhandle thanks to the clear water, natural and artificial reefs, sand flats, underwater geological formations and diverse underwater wildlife. There's also the **Florida Panhandle Shipwreck Trail**, a string of 20 shipwrecks off Pensacola, Destin, Panama City and Port St Joe.

The shipwrecks include oilfield supply vessels, a WWII minesweeper, and a tugboat named *Miss Louise*. While some sank unintentionally, others were deliberately scuttled and plunged

WHERE TO STAY IN PENSACOLA

Pensacola Beach RV Resort
This smaller RV park is excellent for RV enthusiasts and has a tiki bar and private beach. **$**

Surf and Sand
Slightly kitschy hotel with a mid-century-modern theme. Right by the water with a private beach and paddleboards. **$$**

Holiday Inn Resort Pensacola Beach Gulf Front
Great price for lots of amenities, including a lazy river and a fantastic location. **$$**

JAMES KIRKIKIS/SHUTTERSTOCK ©

Historic Pensacola Village

to the ocean floor to become a habitat for wildlife and an attraction for divers. One of them is the USS *Oriskany,* aka the 'Great Carrier Reef,' and 'the Mighty O,' which was deliberately sunk in 2006 after service in the Korean and Vietnam Wars. It's now the largest artificial reef in the world.

Historic Village Life

A WINDOW ONTO THE PAST

You can easily spend a day in **Historic Pensacola Village** wandering among lovingly restored period buildings from the 1800s and 1900s and engaging with the costumed re-enactors populating them.

Historic Pensacola Village is about 8.5 acres between Plaza Ferdinand VII and Seville Sq, with 28 properties, including museums, historic churches and restored homes and cottages. The architecture runs the gamut from Victorian to classical revival. Some offer guided tours, while others provide self-guided ones. Either way, you can buy a unified ticket that admits you to the village and the **Pensacola Museum of**

HEADY BREW

Bodacious Brew
This espresso bar and cafe on Palafox St downtown offers a long list of coffee drinks and several brewing methods. $

The Drowsy Poet Coffee Company
A cute, comfy coffee shop that roasts its own beans every day and offers standard coffee, frozen 'poetchinos,' bakery items, salads and sandwiches. $

Coffee Guy Cafe
The cafe offers a long list of coffee, smoothie, tea and other beverages like the 'Pensacolada.' $

Quality Inn & Suites Bayview
This budget hotel has quick access to I-10 and has a pool, restaurant and weekend bar. $

Red Roof Inn Pensacola Fairgrounds
A hotel located near I-10 and 15 minutes from downtown. It offers good rates and a pool. $

Hilton Garden Inn Pensacola Airport-Medical Center
A bright, clean Hilton with a bar, restaurant, pool and free area shuttle service. **$$**

History, the **Pensacola Children's Museum** and the **Pensacola Museum of Art**.

Tip: if you're going during a busy time (such as around the holidays or summer), consider booking a tour and buying your tickets online.

HOLD THE FORT

The Gulf Islands National Seashore also has three historic forts: Fort Pickens, Fort Barrancas and Advanced Redoubt. Only **Fort Pickens**, a Civil War fortification, is open to the public. Built in the early 1800s by enslaved people, it also became a stop along the path to freedom as part of the Underground Railroad. There's a discovery center with exhibits, ranger-led walks, a bookstore and a museum celebrating its long history, including in the Civil War and the Apache Wars.

Nearby **Fort Barrancas**, built in 1844, and **Advanced Redoubt**, finished in 1870 after 25 years of construction, are at NAS Pensacola. Active duty military and veterans with proper ID can visit.

Solitude by the Seashore

FEDERALLY PROTECTED STRANDS OFFER ADVENTURE

The **Gulf Islands National Seashore** is a national park that includes barrier islands along the Gulf of Mexico. The park's Perdido Key in Pensacola and Santa Rosa Island in Fort Walton Beach stretch alongside the mainland like an ornamental rail.

Because of the park's protected status, long stretches of snow-white, sandy beaches remain undeveloped and uncrowded. As such, they're an excellent place to enjoy solitude and the natural beauty of the ocean, sea and sky.

Not all areas of the shore are swimmable. The most popular swimming places are **Rosamond Johnson Beach** on Perdido Key, **Langdon Beach** at Fort Pickens (which also has a fishing pier), **Opal Beach** at Santa Rosa, and **Okaloosa**. Langdon Beach is a favorite spot for locals because it's serene, less crowded and has a seasonal lifeguard, bathrooms, a shaded pavilion and outdoor showers. The Florida National Scenic Trail connects the campground to the historic district and Langdon Beach.

You can also hike self-guided trails and enjoy visitor centers at Fort Barrancas, Fort Pickens and Naval Live Oaks. Perdido Key also has a hiking trail.

Tracing African American Heritage

WALKING THROUGH HISTORY

Pensacola has historically contained a mix of cultures and people, from Spanish and English colonists to Native Americans and African Americans. The **African American Heritage Society** commemorates Black life in the city with a museum in the historic **Coulson House** (built in 1865). Its staff encourages visitors to follow the city's **African American Heritage Trail**, a list of 19 culturally significant sites. They include historic African American churches, museums, markers and historic homes throughout downtown Pensacola and the **Belmont-DeVilliers** neighborhood, a historically Black district. The society has posted the complete list on its website.

GETTING AROUND

Pensacola is directly off I-10, although most of the attractions, including the beach and downtown, are south of the Interstate. Take I-110 south from I-10 into the heart of downtown, and cross the Three-Mile Bridge to get to Gulf Breeze and the beaches.

DESTIN

Destin is happily situated in Okaloosa County on a thin peninsula dividing Choctawhatchee Bay from the Gulf of Mexico. About 14,000 people call Destin home. The small city is known for its beautiful, white-sand Gulf beaches, its pristine state parks and easy access to all things water-related. People come to Destin from around the world to scuba dive, snorkel, fish, parasail, waterski and surf. It's also a great place to bring kids because of the abundance of outdoor activities and family-friendly restaurants and businesses. It's just 8 miles from Sandestin, but it isn't to be confused with it! Destin is the town, while Sandestin is a trendy development a few miles east of Destin in Miramar Beach.

Destin is midway between Pensacola to the east and Panama City to the west and is connected to the mainland by State Rd 293 and the Mid-Bay Toll Bridge.

TOP TIP

Paper, plastic, glass...oyster shells? Yep, you can recycle those, too. At least a dozen area restaurants are helping build oyster reef habitats by recycling the shells from your Oysters Rockefeller. The habitats are needed in the nearby Choctawhatchee Bay, where oyster populations have declined.

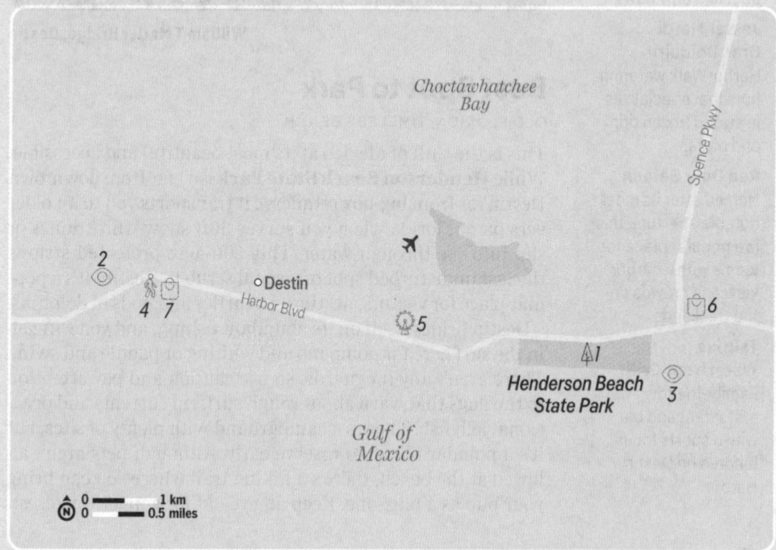

HIGHLIGHTS
1 Henderson Beach State Park

SIGHTS
2 Crab Island
3 Crystal Beach

ACTIVITIES, COURSES & TOURS
4 Destin Harbor Boardwalk

ENTERTAINMENT
5 Big Kahuna's Water Park

SHOPPING
6 Destin Commons
7 HarborWalk Village

BEST SPOTS TO HAVE A DRINK

Lucky's Rotten Apple Unassuming and relaxed, it's a great place to watch a game, play cheap pool and unwind.

Jester Mardi Gras Daiquiri HarborWalk watering hole that specializes in strong frozen drinks and pizza.

Red Door Saloon Named after its most notable aperture, this is a popular place for locals with a harbor view and crowds on the weekends.

Tailfins Waterfront Grill Family-friendly restaurant and bar with a sports focus, located on Destin Harbor.

MICHAEL FITZSIMMONS/SHUTTERSTOCK ©

William T Marler Bridge, Destin

Best Spot to Park

OLD FLORIDA, TIMELESS BEACH

This is the Gulf of Mexico at its most beautiful and accessible. While **Henderson Beach State Park** isn't far from downtown Destin (or from big-box retailers), it transports you to an older version of Florida when you survey 30ft snow-white dunes or slip into see-through water. This 200-acre protected strip is the last undisturbed spot of coastal scrub in Destin. It's a popular place for visitors, nesting sea turtles and pods of dolphins.

Destin prides itself on its abundant fishing, and you can fish in the surf here for pompano and whiting or paddle and swim. There aren't any lifeguards, so use caution and pay attention to the flags that warn about rough surf, rip currents and occasional jellyfish. There's a campground with plenty of sites, but it's a popular place, so reserve early. Although pets aren't allowed at the beach, there's a hiking trail where you can bring your pup as a plus-one. Keep an eye out for gopher tortoises!

WHERE TO EAT IN DESTIN

Edge Seafood Restaurant & SkyBar A dog-friendly restaurant with excellent views and a fish-food dispenser downstairs. **$$**

East Pass Seafood and Oyster House The restaurant is in HarborWalk Village and specializes in local seafood and oysters. **$$**

Beach Walk Cafe at Henderson Park Inn Romantic and elegant dining (no young kids) with beautiful beach views. **$$$**

Crystal Clear

SHARE THE SOFT WHITE SANDS

Located next door to Henderson Beach State Park, **Crystal Beach** is another stunning example of what Gulf beaches can and should be. Green-blue transparent waves push onto the soft white sand, where you'll see weddings, happy couples and families. It's not as secluded as some beaches because vacation rentals and condos of all heights and varieties edge the shore – though they also add visual variety to miles of sand, sea and sky.

The beach has a shaded pavilion, restrooms and showers, but parking is limited, so get here early. Bonus: the beach is a mile south of **Destin Commons**, a super-popular eating, dining and shopping area.

Getting Crabby

EXPERIENCE FLORIDA'S MOST POPULAR SANDBAR

The beaches on the Gulf side of the island may temporarily steal the show, but make sure you don't miss **Crab Island** on the north of the island, in Choctawhatchee Bay.

It's one of the most popular destinations in Destin, but its name is slightly inaccurate because time and tide have ground it down into more of a sandbar. But it's a fun sandbar within view of the William T Marler Bridge and five minutes by boat from Destin Harbor. The only way to get here is by boat or water taxi.

The sandbar glows turquoise or emerald green, depending on the tide. The currents around it can get dangerous, but the shallow water on the sandbar is a great place to splash with kids and break out the frisbees and water toys.

While new regulations have banished the inflatables and vendors that used to populate Crab Island, it's still a popular place to moor a boat and have a watery tailgate party complete with BYOB cocktails.

It Takes a Village

MAKE MEMORIES IN HARBORWALK VILLAGE

To give your skin a break from the brilliant Florida sunshine or take refuge from afternoon showers, head down to Destin Harbor and explore **HarborWalk Village**. The village is located by the Harbor Boardwalk and on the harbor, which has chartered water excursions and the Destin Fishing Fleet. The fleet claims to be the largest charter fishing fleet in the US.

BEST PLACES TO FISH

Given Destin's nickname, 'The World's Luckiest Fishing Village,' you can expect lots of angling opportunities.

Okaloosa Island Pier
A day pass allows you to fish from the pier and watch a beautiful sunset.

The Jetties and East Pass
Catch pompano, flounder and redfish at the jetties east of Destin Harbor. Watch your footing on the slippery, artificial rocks.

Destin Bridge
Catch beautiful views, tarpon, snapper, cobia and other fish.

Norriego Point
Fish from the shore for flounder and redfish and take a quick swim.

Camille's at Crystal Beach
A cafe serving breakfast and lunch, and a restaurant featuring live music Thursday, dinner, sushi and kids' menus. **$$**

Boshamps Seafood and Oyster House
Waterfront spot with excellent Southern-themed food, two full bars and live music. **$$**

Merlin's Pizza
This perennial local favorite offers salads, wings, and classic and creative pizzas. **$**

This retail destination is perpetually busy, with a carnival-like atmosphere. There's a lot to choose from based on your interests. There are clubs and bars, colorful shops, and plenty of places to occupy kids and teenagers. There are bounce houses, a four-story rock-climbing wall and the **HarborWalk Adventures Zip Line**, which whizzes you past 1000ft of harbor views. There's also a seasonal kids' train parked by Harry T's.

There are plenty of live events, too, including music on the Main Stage, themed holiday parties and weekly fireworks.

BEST SPOTS FOR COFFEE

Bad Ass Coffee of Hawaii
As you might surmise, this cheerful coffee shop specializes in Hawaiian coffee (but also offers smoothies and teas).

Capriccio Coffee
Small local coffee shop with good brew and popular crepes with ingredients like Nutella, mascarpone and prosciutto.

Birds Cafe+Coffee
This local 'coffee forward' breakfast/brunch place also offers craft beer, wine and fried PB&Js.

East Past Coffee Co
A small, soothing space off US 98/Harbor Blvd specializing in coffee, acai bowls and smoothies.

Held at Bay

BORED WALK? NOT LIKELY

The **Destin Harbor Boardwalk** is only a quarter-mile long, but it's a perfect place for attending a festival or parade or watching a fleet of charter boats cut through the harbor. Restaurants line the boardwalk's length; many offer a cook-your-catch option if you've been lucky enough to hook a great catch in 'The World's Luckiest Fishing Village.' There are also plenty of opportunities for kids to play, with ziplines, rock walls and a free-fall ride nearby at HarborWalk Village. Or, hop on a pirate ship, chartered dolphin tour or a fishing foray.

The boardwalk runs east from HarborWalk Village to the Destin Yacht Club. Note: it gets busy on afternoons, and you can expect to pay for parking.

Big Kahuna

A DIFFERENT WATER EXPERIENCE

It can be fun to change it up after a blissful few days of lolling on pale beaches. **Big Kahuna's Water Park** lets you play in Florida's favorite element, but adds a few high-speed thrills.

It has all your standard Florida water-park features: a lazy river, a wave pool, artificial waterfalls and views of slick skyscrapers. There are also lockers and beach chairs by the water features, so parents can work on preserving their take-home tans. There's also a nice assortment of colorful waterslides – from the tall and twisty to the short and twisty – and tamer splash parks. You can race other parkgoers on the five-story Kowabunga speed slide or stick around for a round of miniature golf on the 54-hole course.

WHERE TO STAY IN DESTIN

Henderson Beach Resort
Between the beach and miles of nature preserve, this gorgeous resort offers five eateries, rooftop bar and spa. **$$$**

Hampton Inn & Suites Destin
The hotel offers a pool and fitness center near Henderson Beach State Park. **$$$**

Inn at Crystal Beach
Beautiful condominium complex offering two- to seven-bedroom condos on the water. **$$**

KRISTI BLOKHIN/SHUTTERSTOCK ©

Destin Harabor Boardwalk

BEST PLACES FOR ICE CREAM

Shake's Frozen Custard
Fresh, creamy frozen custard (aka super-premium ice cream) that's made fresh daily.

Wave Ice Cream & Boba Tea
Get caffeinated and sugar-sedated in the same spot at this colorful, multi-purpose shop that also sells coffee drinks.

Moo La La
Cute little ice-cream place with malts, shakes, soda floats and a couple-of-dozen flavors.

Bruster's Real Ice Cream
Local favorite with thick shakes, an old-timey feel and plenty of outdoor seating.

Charter Member

GETTING OUT ON THE WATER

One of Destin's greatest strengths is the number of chartered water experiences here, from diving to deep-sea fishing, snorkeling and shelling.

HarborWalk Charters has well over a dozen boats offering group and private fishing trips. Depending on the season, you could hook anything from vermillion snapper to Spanish mackerel to tuna (although you've got a chance at sharks year-round). Snorkeling outfits like **Destin Snorkel** and **Flippers Snorkel Adventure** offer excursions, and you can dive along the coast among shipwrecks with any of several companies. Some places also offer dolphin and sunset cruises and high-speed boat rides.

GETTING AROUND

It is super-easy to get to and around this narrow barrier island. Just follow Hwy 98 east over the William T Marler Bridge (Destin Bridge) from Fort Walton Beach or follow it west from Panama City. The road is the main drag across Destin.

Beyond Destin

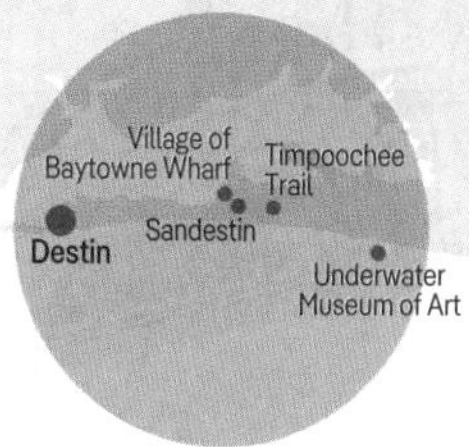

Sandestin is the bustling resort area that makes up the greater part of Miramar Beach. It's known for copious entertainment and shopping.

Sandestin Golf and Beach Resort (Sandestin to the locals) is often confused with Destin by people who aren't from here. It's a huge resort area about 11 miles east of Destin, comprising much of Miramar Beach. It touches Choctawhatchee Bay to the north and the Gulf of Mexico to the south. Sandestin's claims to fame include live entertainment, festivals, shopping, dining and nightlife framed by aquamarine water. There are also 30 'neighborhoods,' or distinct sections, 19 swimming pools, 15 tennis courts and four championship golf courses.

The Village of Baytown Wharf, north of Hwy 98, is the leading entertainment and shopping area, and locals love it for its long list of concerts.

TOP TIP

If you're going to a festival, think about staying in the Village of Baytowne Wharf area for easy access.

RUTH PETERKIN/SHUTTERSTOCK ©

Sandestin Golf and Beach Resort

PISAPHOTOGRAPHY/SHUTTERSTOCK ©

Village of Baytowne Wharf

Wharf Rats

CHOOSE YOUR OWN ADVENTURE

There's a lot to see in the **Village of Baytowne Wharf**, arguably the first place people think of when they consider a trip to Sandestin. Although it's part of Sandestin Golf and Beach Resort, you don't have to stay (or live) here to come to this dining and entertainment venue.

Many things draw people here, including views of the Choctawhatchee Bay and seasonal events and festivals. Among the many to consider are the Mardi Gras parade and street party, St Paddy's Day celebration, the Sandestin gumbo and wine festivals, and Monday movies on the event lawn. Local and regional artists give free concerts here on certain days, and live music is a part of the culture.

There are also some top-notch restaurants, lots of shops, and the **Baytowne Farmers Market** from 10am to 2pm every Saturday and the second and fourth Sunday.

BEST PLACES TO EAT IN SANDESTIN

Seagar's Prime Steaks & Seafood
Watch servers prepare your meal tableside at this well-known steakhouse in the Hilton Sandestin Beach Golf Resort & Spa. $$$

Donut Hole
This bakery on Hwy 98 offers fantastic doughnuts, pastries, brunch, and a complete and tasty breakfast menu. $

Rum Runners
The restaurant is island-themed and kid-friendly, and stands out for its dueling-pianos performances. $$

WHERE TO STAY IN SANDESTIN

Hilton Sandestin Beach Golf Resort & Spa
Several restaurants, an upscale spa, a fitness center and rooms with bunkbeds for kids. **$$$**

Sleep Inn near Sandestin Beach
Good budget-friendly choice in a nice location. Breakfast in the morning. **$**

Sandestin Golf and Beach Resort
The 2400-acre beachside resort has a variety of rooms and condos across the area. **$$$**

BEST PLACES FOR LIVE MUSIC

Marina Bar and Grill
Live music Fridays are a thing at this Sandestin dockside bar/restaurant with sunset views.

Lulu's Destin
Jimmy Buffett's sister, Lucy, owns this bright, high-energy venue with waterfront views and regular entertainment.

Graffiti & the Funky Blues Shack
This quirky, family-friendly restaurant with two bars is a local pick for live music, from alternative to zydeco.

Club LA
A local favorite for concerts, touring and tribute bands, dancing and drinks.

Boardwalk of Directors

ADVENTURES ON THE WATERFRONT

If you're bringing kids to the Village of Baytowne Wharf, they'll probably be the first to spot a few of the many places that cater to them on the Village Boardwalk. There's a playground, an old-timey carousel, an adventure venue and an arcade and laser-tag maze.

The **Baytowne Adventure Zone** offers tower climbs, ropes courses and a zipline. In the Golf Challenge, you can also chip birdie balls onto a platform in the water. Not far away, the **Blast Arcade & Laser Maze** offers its namesake pursuits, including 40 arcade games from classic to current.

Walls of Water

ART BECOMES LIFE

If you love art, museums or diving, the area offers a novelty that's probably nothing like you're used to.

The **Underwater Museum of Art**, located less than a mile off the coast from Grayton Beach State Park, is the country's first permanent underwater sculpture garden. The sculptures are beautiful pieces of art and functional too. The pieces include 34 sculptures, abstract designs, an octopus, a tree and a skull (with more to come in 2023).

Over time, the sculptures become habitats for marine life, such as fish, corals, dolphins and sea turtles, on what would otherwise be a barren sand flat. You can only get here by boat. **Dive30A** makes regular trips from Grayton Beach, while **Emerald Coasts Scuba** makes trips from Destin. (Don't forget your scuba gear.)

Follow the Trail

PART OF A VIRTUOUS CYCLE

Biking enthusiasts like to gush about the **Timpoochee Trail**, an 18.5-mile bike path that runs in tandem with Scenic Hwy 30A. The trail weaves in and out of parks, sand dunes, lakes, forests and 16 beach communities. It begins in Dune Allen, close to the entrance of **Topsail Hill Preserve State Park** and its secluded beaches. It then runs through various neighborhoods and architectural styles before ending in Inlet Beach. On the way, you'll pass plenty of restaurants and beautiful spots where you can sightsee, picnic or take a breather.

GETTING AROUND

You can get to Sandestin from the north on Hwy 331 and from the east and west on Hwy 98. Hwy 98 is also the main drag and the rest of the area is set out in a fairly straightforward grid.

PANAMA CITY

Panama City is the largest city between Pensacola and Tallahassee and is immensely popular with college students who flock here during spring break. It's a year-round tourist destination with an airport and a bus and train service. There's a military presence here, too, because it's close to Tyndall Airforce Base and home to the Naval Support Activity Panama City.

Like other Panhandle cities, it has stunningly beautiful beaches with white quartz sand. In Panama City, they're along St Andrews Bay. In Panama City Beach, across the Hathaway Bridge, there are 27 miles of beaches on the bay and the Gulf of Mexico. This is an excellent spot for snorkeling along the coast and diving among dozens of artificial reefs and shipwrecks offshore.

The Panama City area has some of the region's best beaches and coastal state park areas. The fresh, local seafood here is nothing to sneeze at, either.

TOP TIP

This is a popular tourist and college-student destination. Try to avoid peak times, such as spring break, to avoid dealing with the heaviest traffic and highest rates.

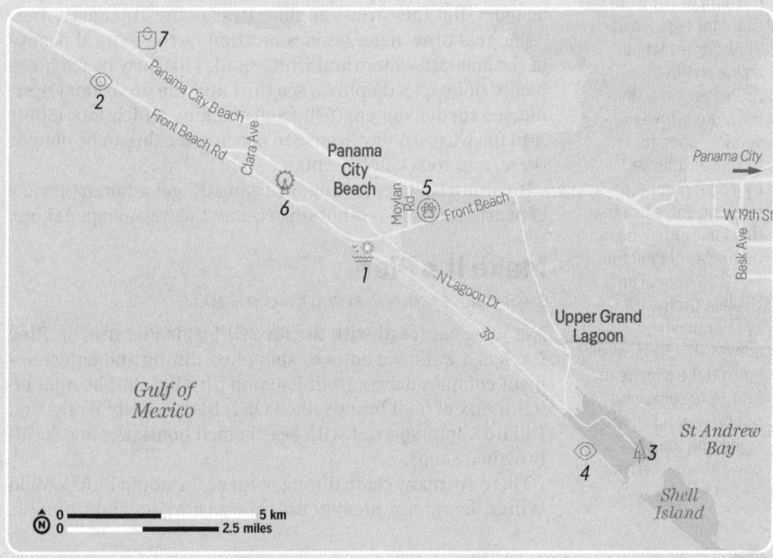

SIGHTS
1 Panama City Beach
2 Russell-Fields Pier
3 St Andrews State Park
4 St Andrews State Park Pier

ACTIVITIES, COURSES & TOURS
5 ZooWorld Zoological Park

ENTERTAINMENT
6 Shipwreck Island Waterpark

SHOPPING
7 Pier Park

Watersports Galore

FORMER MILITARY INSTALLATION TURNED WILD

A former military installation, **St Andrews State Park** is a present-day 1200-acre outdoor nirvana. With St Andrews Bay on one side and the Gulf of Mexico on the other, if ever there was a spot to take part in just about every outdoor water sport, this is it.

You can fish from the jetties or snorkel along them, hike into the flatwood pine forest, take scuba-diving lessons, and canoe or kayak. People like to windsurf here, and others like to watch them – or the birds. This is a popular birdwatching spot along bird and butterfly migratory routes. There's also a fishing **pier** on the Gulf, 1.5 miles of mainland sugar-sand beach to bask on and a ferry to the undeveloped (no restrooms!) **Shell Island**. (Note: storm damage closed the pier in April 2022, and park management has not set a completion date for repairs.)

SOCKS AFIRE

Residents and visitors get to bless the fleet, burn their socks and enjoy a good fish fry all at once every May. That's when the annual, day-long **Blessing of the Fleet, Fish Fry & Burning of the Socks** event takes place at St Andrews Marina on West 10th St. Festivities begin in the morning, when vendors open for business, followed by a boat parade, a blessing and a fish fry that lasts either most of the day or until the fish is all gone. The Ukulele Orchestra of St Andrews sometimes plays, and you get the chance to burn your socks and put on your flip-flops, signifying the start of warm weather and beach season.

Pier One

FISHING, BASKING AND SHOPPING

Two of the most popular destinations in the area are **Panama City Beach** and its **Russell-Fields Pier** because they're easily accessible and near plenty of restaurants and Pier Park, a popular outdoor shopping venue. There are other, quieter beaches, but they aren't as close to as many other activities.

The real draw here, besides location, is the natural beauty of the emerald waters and white sand. This busy beach hosts plenty of people, dolphins, seagulls and the occasional nesting sea turtle. You can fish from the pier, which juts 1500ft into the waves. A day license to fish and tackle can be bought there, and rods can be rented.

If fishing isn't your thing, you can still get a fantastic view of pearly sunrises, red-hot sunsets and the wave-lapped shore.

Make It a Pier

SHOPPING, EATING AND WALKING THE MALL

Not to be confused with the Russell-Fields Pier nearby, **Pier Park** is a walkable outdoor shopping, dining and entertainment complex across from Panama City Beach. The mall offers a mix of mall brands like LOFT, Bath & Body Works and Dillards, interspersed with sea-themed boutiques and locally owned shops.

There are many chain dining options, including Buffalo Wild Wings, Longhorn Steakhouse, Margaritaville and Chipotle.

WHERE TO EAT IN PANAMA CITY

Bayou Joe's Marina and Grill
Comfortable and casual, Bayou Joe's is an Old Florida–style restaurant on the Massalina Bayou. **$**

Firefly
This restaurant offers a fine-dining experience with fresh Gulf seafood under an oak tree lit with white lights. **$$$**

Dave's Sno-Balls
New Orleans–themed eatery serving po'boys, muffuletta, beignets and its namesake crushed-ice dessert. **$**

PUGALENTHI INIABARATHI/SHUTTERSTOCK ©

St Andrews State Park

Kids and teens might enjoy **Dave and Buster's** arcade, a mirror maze, laser tag or the **Grand Imax Pier Park 16 Theatre**. There's **Tootsie's Orchid Lounge** for people who like live country music and dancing, but it's 21 and up after 8pm.

It's a Zoo

CONSERVATION, EDUCATION AND LEMURS

Count on a whole day if you're planning to go to **ZooWorld Zoological Park** in Panama City Beach. The conservation-focused park offers educational opportunities, daily shows and more than 200 animal species. You can see giraffes, lemurs, goats, kangaroos, tapirs, capybaras and many other species here.

One of the zoo's selling points is specially booked animal interactions led by zoo staff. 'Check it off your bucket list and pet a sloth!' urges the zoo website. (If you don't think stroking a sloth is on anyone's bucket list, try asking your kids.) The zoo also encourages you to 'defy common sense' and pick up

BEST PLACES TO SLEEP IN PANAMA CITY

Holiday Inn Resort Panama City Beach
This upscale beachside Holiday Inn has a pool, a lazy river and a cocktail lounge. $$

Bluegreen's Bayside Resort
Bluegreen's is in a nature preserve on St Andrews Bay, with restaurants, pools and diner cruises aboard the resort yacht. $$

Radisson Panama City Beach – Oceanfront
The beachfront Radisson has an outdoor heated pool. $$$

Pearl Hotel
The Pearl has luxury boutique accommodations in nearby Rosemary Beach. $$$

Schooner's
A laid-back restaurant offering excellent seafood, live music and drinks while you wait. **$$**

Hunt's Oyster Bar and Seafood Restaurant
This family-owned and operated local favorite serves local oysters and seafood. **$$**

Nick's Slice of Heaven Pizzeria and Bar
A popular place for New York-style pizza, strombolis, hot sandwiches and beer. **$**

FEELING LUXE

One of Panama City's newest additions to a full list of events is its **Flluxe Arts Festival**, conducted in the spring. It's a fun, colorful and accessible festival that pulls together local, regional and out-of-area artists and the public for two days of creation in the downtown arts district. Festivalgoers are encouraged to fashion sidewalk chalk art, watch graffiti and other art demonstrations, listen to live music, and enjoy food trucks, vendors and face painting. The event is free and the website has tips on where to park. (PS: It's pronounced, 'Florida Luxe Arts Festival.')

TONY CAMPBELL/SHUTTERSTOCK ©

Young alligator

a (baby) alligator. That said, if you're considering booking, you might keep in mind that interacting with humans can be stressful for animals.

Shipwrecked

FUN AT THE WATERPARK

Shipwreck Island is a fun, clean and well-maintained waterpark and a generational favorite with Panama City Beach locals and visitors.

Its 15 acres have all the best Florida waterpark basics: lazy river, wave pool, bucket-soaker area, flume ride, steep plunge and other assorted slides. It is a little smaller than some parks but also less expensive. The park is open from the last Saturday in April through Labor Day.

GETTING AROUND

It's pretty easy to navigate the area; just follow Hwy 98, the main artery, along the coast. Hathaway Bridge connects Panama City Beach with Panama City, and Hwy 98 leads you east and out of the city.

APALACHICOLA

Apalachicola is a tiny town on Apalachicola Bay and the mouth of the Apalachicola River. It is home to more than 2000 people and many more oysters. Established in 1831, it's one of Florida's oldest port towns. It's most famous for the popular bivalve and its seafood in general – so renowned, in fact, that the Florida Seafood Festival draws tens of thousands of people here annually to enjoy a day of fresh fare harvested from local waters.

The warm, friendly town is along Florida's Forgotten Coast, branded as the last stretch of pristine, undeveloped Gulf coast. The downtown area has many quaint shops and restaurants in restored historic buildings.

TOP TIP

St George Island, across Apalachicola Bay, is a favorite local spot to fish and crab.

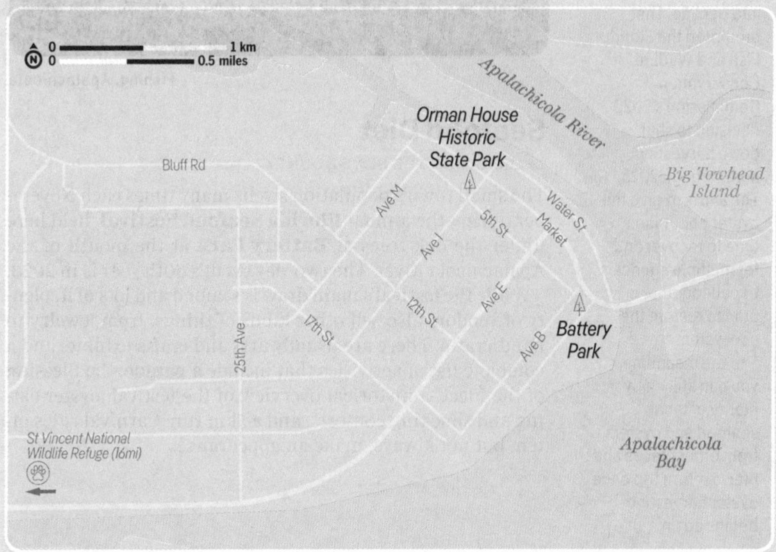

IN ITS SHELL

While Apalachicola Bay once yielded 90% of the state's wild oysters and 10% of the country's, the oyster industry here took a blow when problems like pollution, salt-level changes, hurricanes, intense storms and other factors sent the oyster population into decline. That prompted the Florida Fish and Wildlife Conservation Commission's 2020 decision to shut down harvesting here through 2025. The aim is to give the oyster population time to recover and for multiple agencies to pull together a plan to restore the ecosystem.

In the meantime, you can still enjoy plenty of local seafood and oysters from other places and plan a return trip once oyster harvesting begins again.

Fishing, Apalachicola

Seafood Diet

CELEBRATING THE SEA'S BOUNTY

The small town's population swells many times each November during the annual **Florida Seafood Festival**, held here under the oak trees at **Battery Park** at the mouth of the Apalachicola River. The two-day event's 60th year is in 2023.

While the festival's main draw is seafood and lots of it, plenty of vendors also sell other kinds of things, from jewelry to handicrafts. There are usually arts and crafts exhibits and a complete list of activities that include a parade, the Blessing of the Fleet, a historical overview of the festival, oyster eating and shucking contests, and a 5km run. Carnival rides often, but not always, make an appearance.

WHERE TO STAY IN APALACHICOLA

Apalachicola Bay Inn
The inn is budget-friendly, low on frills and about a mile from the historic district. **$**

Coombs House Inn & Suites
A historic Victorian Inn (1905) that features a Southern-style porch with rocking chairs and several suites. **$$**

Gibson Inn
This 45-room boutique hotel set in a historic 1907 building houses the popular Franklin Café and Parlor Bar. **$$$**

Visiting the Saint

ON YOUR OWN IN THE WILDERNESS

The two barrier islands at **St Vincent National Wildlife Refuge** contain more than 12,000 acres that have remained genuinely wild. You can reach the refuge only by boat (your own or a local service). The short trip across St Vincent Sound or Apalachicola Bay is worth it for the unparalleled opportunities to fish, boat, bicycle, nature watch or photograph.

It's an important site for migratory birds, a breeding pair of endangered red wolves and other wildlife. You'll have to bring your equipment. There are no restrooms, drinking water or developed campsites. With only rough, sand roads and no signs or trail markers, you're on your own once you're here.

You can fish here year-round, perhaps spotting loggerhead sea turtles in the process, but the refuge is closed to the public three times a year during lottery-based, big-game public hunts from November through January. Overnight camping is only allowed for hunters, who go after white-tailed deer, wild hogs, raccoons and Sambar deer that can weigh up to 700lb.

GRAND HOUSE & GARDENS

The mansion and gardens at the **Orman House Historic State Park** recall the past. The park name is a bit of a misnomer: its defining feature isn't a house, but a mansion that predates the Civil War. Thomas Orman built it in 1838 after making a fortune in cotton, and his ancestors lived in it for 165 years. His home overlooks the docks of the small town he turned into a bustling port with his cotton business. You can tour the home or the nearby **Chapman Botanical Gardens**.

Orman House

GETTING AROUND

Apalachicola is about 60 miles east of Panama City on Hwy 98 and about 75 miles southwest of Tallahassee via Hwys 319 and 98. Hwy 98 is also the main drag in town, and you can follow it over the John Gorrie Memorial Bridge to East Point and then take State Rd 300 South over the Bryant Patton Bridge to St George Island.

TALLAHASSEE

Tallahassee is known for government goings-on, college football and history. The city is home to many layers of local and state government. As the state capital, it's home to the state capitol building, the Florida legislature, the governor's mansion and 20-plus state agency offices. The Florida Supreme Court convenes here, too, and the city is also the Leon County seat.

Florida State University (FSU), with its 45,000-plus students, has some pull. You'll find its influence in the scores of trendy coffee shops, novel restaurants and funky boutiques.

Still, Tallahassee is nestled in the old South with its live oak trees covered in Spanish moss and centuries of polite tradition. Those factors, plus New Orleans–like humidity, create a molasses-soft, slow-paced atmosphere. While it's inland with no coast access, Tallahassee is surrounded by miles of thick forests, wildlife management areas and stunning nature opportunities.

TOP TIP

Visit in spring when gardens and state parks are abloom and the hottest, stickiest days are yet to come. The March/April highs are mid-70s to low 80s degrees Fahrenheit (mid to high 20s Celsius) and it's not as rainy. To avoid crowds and high rates, don't book during spring break.

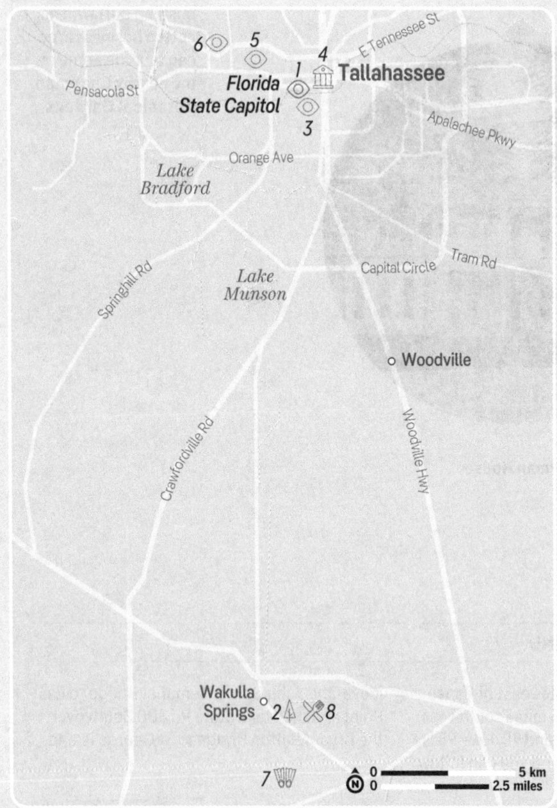

TOP SIGHTS
1 Florida State Capitol

SIGHTS
see 5 Doak S Campbell Stadium
2 Edward Ball Wakulla Springs State Park
3 Florida Agricultural and Mechanical University (FAMU)
4 Florida Historic Capitol Museum
5 Florida State University
6 Mission San Luis

ACTIVITIES, COURSES & TOURS
7 Cherokee Sink

EATING
8 Edward Ball Dining Room

Florida State University

State Spirit

FSU FOOTBALL, HISTORIC CAMPUS

The sprawling 485-acre **Florida State University** complex is a couple of miles west of the state capitol building. It's an active research university filled with the energy of more than 45,000 undergrad and graduate students. The university was founded as a seminary in 1851, before the Civil War, and became the Florida State College for Women in 1905, a school for white women only. After WWII, it became coed under its current name. It was integrated in 1963.

You can see the university's history in its Collegiate Gothic-style architecture, much of which dates back to the early 1900s. The university offers guided tours, self-guided tours and virtual tours. You have to make arrangements ahead of time for the tours, which fill up.

The FSU football team, the Seminoles, play on the Bobby Bowden field at **Doak S Campbell Stadium**. The stadium, with its 57ft-high video screen, is located at Pensacola St and Stadium Dr. More than 84,000 fans attend some of the biggest games, which in the past have included games against dedicated rivals, the University of Florida Gators.

KEEPING THEM RATTLED

About a mile south of FSU is **Florida Agricultural and Mechanical University (FAMU)**, the only public historically Black college in the state. FAMU was founded in 1887 with just 15 students and two teachers as the State Normal College for Colored Students. Now there are about 10,000.

The university's nationally designated historic district contains 370 acres of campus and 14 buildings, mostly red-brick Georgian Revival built between 1924 and 1940. The entire 420-acre campus includes 132 buildings. FAMU offers virtual and in-person tours.

As you drive through Tallahassee, you'll see plenty of cars and people sporting FAMU's green-and-orange colors and supporting its sports teams, the Rattlers.

WHERE TO STAY IN TALLAHASSEE

Hyatt House Tallahassee Capitol – University
Modern hotel in the Railroad Square Art District, within walking distance of FSU. **$$$**

Hotel Indigo Tallahassee – Collegetown
Near FSU and Doak Campbell Stadium. Offers upgrades and sports-complex views. **$$$**

Doubletree by Hilton Tallahassee
A 17th-floor rooftop lounge with great city views. Close to the Capitol. **$$**

BEST PLACES TO SHOP

Sure, there's the Governor's Square mall, but for something different try the bohemian stores of the Railroad Square Art District. It has live music, food trucks and merrymaking on the first Friday of each month.

Other Side of Vintage
Thirty-five booth spaces offer vintage and retro men's and women's clothing, home furnishings and vinyl.

Wonsaponatime Vintage
Railroad Square venue with 'consciously curated' pieces from the '50s to the '90s

Curio
Curio has vintage wares and modern goods designed by artists, craftswomen and independent brands.

SEAN PAVONE/SHUTTERSTOCK ©

Florida Historic Capitol Museum

A Capitol Idea

EXPLORE THE CAPITOL BUILDINGS

The **Florida State Capitol** building is many things: 'The Tower on the Hill,' the tallest building in town and the tower of power.

But popular, it ain't. Residents have been grumbling since 1977 that the 'new' Capitol complex – a 22-story straight-up-and-down tower in the middle of two squat, symmetrical office buildings topped by cupolas – looks spare.

Whether you're a fan of the architecture or not, it's hard to ignore the importance of the Capitol complex. It's home to Florida's Executive and Legislative branches (in the Capitol Building), House of Representatives and the Senate (in those smaller buildings). On weekdays from 8am to 5pm, you can **tour** the complex on Apalachee Pkwy and Monroe St.

The **Florida Historic Capitol Museum** is housed in the center of the complex in the original, restored Capitol Building, with its stained-glass dome. There are temporary and long-term exhibits, grounds to explore and in-person and virtual tours.

WHERE TO EAT IN TALLAHASSEE

Momo's
Great pizza and huge slices. There are two near FSU and one in the Market District. **$**

Bird's Aphrodisiac oyster shack by FSU
A local favorite: fun, artsy, homey atmosphere and great food. Near FSU. **$$**

Crum Box Gastgarden
Servers dish up classic sandwiches and hoagies from a red caboose in the Railroad Square Art District. **$**

On a Mission from God

COMBINING TWO WORLDS

Mission San Luis, in what is now Tallahassee, was once the western capital of Spanish Florida in the late 17th and early 18th centuries. In 1703, Spanish colonists and as many as 1500 descendants of the Native Apalachee displaced or killed by conquistador Hernando de Soto lived together in a blend of cultures. They intermarried, raising new generations that mingled Spanish and Native American ideas, customs, ways and foods.

Today this Apalachee-Spanish living-history museum reconstructs that mingled legacy with costumed re-enactors and replicas of thatched mission buildings. Volunteers display traditional crafts like blacksmithing, soldiering (Spanish) or traditional pottery (Apalachee). There are maize, beans and squash gardens, representing the original Apalachee field crop gardens. There are also Spanish gardens with medicinal herbs like comfrey, mint and yarrow, and culinary herbs like cilantro, tarragon and bay. It's the only reconstructed Spanish mission in the state. There's a gift shop and a gallery with centuries-old artifacts and Spanish Colonial artwork.

The museum offers historical cooking and basket-making workshops and cannon and flintlock rifle safety training.

At the Ball

EXPLORE THE DEEPEST FRESHWATER SPRING

Sixteen miles south of downtown Tallahassee is **Edward Ball Wakulla Springs State Park**. It's the world's largest and deepest freshwater spring, a torrent of deep blue water bubbling up in the shade of ancient cypress swamps.

The springs stay a refreshing – or nippy, depending on your point of view – 70°F (21°C) year-round. You can swim, snorkel, scuba dive, or take a plunge off the park's 22ft diving platform. Riverboat tours let you spy on turtles, manatees, white-tail deer or alligators (of course). There are 9 miles of nature trails, including picnic tables, places to horseback ride and scuba diving at **Cherokee Sink**.

You can also stay the night in a restored 1930s Spanish-style lodge converted into a full-service hotel, or have lunch or dinner at the lodge's **Edward Ball Dining Room**. If you're here in spring or fall, consider hanging around until twilight when the chimney swifts come home to dive and swoop into the lodge's chimneys.

WHY I LOVE ALFRED B MACLAY GARDENS

Jennifer Edwards, writer

Wealthy financier and vacationer Alfred B Maclay planted the gardens in 1923 in Tallahassee's **Killearn Plantation Archeological and Historic District** (just 'Killearn' to locals). It's a magical place that blends the area's different periods and moods. There are classic manicured gardens with reflecting pools and cobbled walkways. But there's also nearby **Lake Hall**, with its smooth glassy waters and sandy lake beach; it's Old Florida before development. If you drag your kayak in for a quick paddle, you'll sometimes be the only one around. When you leave, you'll walk under old-growth Florida oaks that have been here since before you were born and likely will be here long after you leave.

GETTING AROUND

I-10 takes you to Tallahassee, but US 90 takes you into it. Hwy 90 becomes Tennessee St inside the city, from which you can navigate east to west and access FSU. Monroe St, or US 27, runs north to south and brings you to the Governor's Mansion and the Capitol.

TOOLKIT

The chapters in this section cover the most important topics you'll need to know about in Florida. They're full of nuts-and-bolts information and valuable insights to help you understand and navigate Florida and get the most out of your trip.

Nine Mile Pond (p124)

Arriving

Despite having two dozen international airports, Florida is accessed by most vacationers through one of its four primary hubs: Miami, Orlando, Tampa or Fort Lauderdale–Hollywood. All these airports offer modern amenities, including free wi-fi and a wide selection of eating establishments. Free shuttle buses are provided to off-site car-rental agencies when they are not located within the terminal buildings.

Visas

Canadian citizens need a passport but can visit the US without a visa for up to six months. The Visa Waiver Program permits travelers from 40 additional countries to visit for business or tourism for up to 90 days (longer stays require a visa). A chip-encoded, electronic passport is required for this program. If traveling from a country not in the Waiver Program (consult the US Department of State's website at travel.state.gov), you'll need a nonimmigrant visa.

Traveling with Children

If you're traveling internationally, alone with your child(ren), be sure to carry a notarized letter of consent from the other parent or guardian, granting permission to travel with the child(ren) outside the country (be sure to specify dates and destinations). Customs may deny you entry if you cannot produce one.

Public Transportation from Airports to City Centre

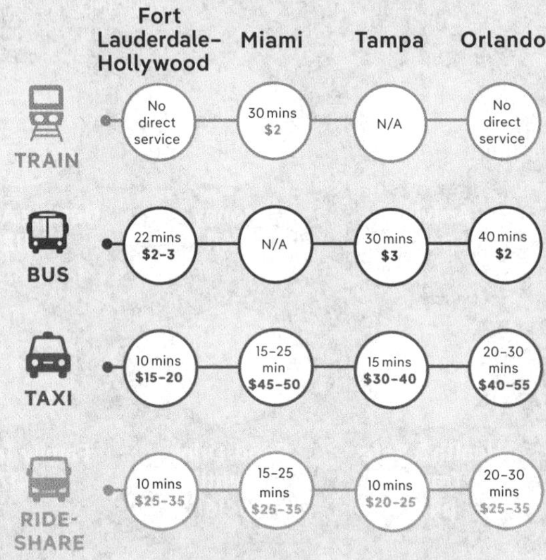

	Fort Lauderdale–Hollywood	Miami	Tampa	Orlando
TRAIN	No direct service	30 mins $2	N/A	No direct service
BUS	22 mins **$2–3**	N/A	30 mins **$3**	40 mins **$2**
TAXI	10 mins **$15–20**	15–25 min **$45–50**	15 mins **$30–40**	20–30 mins **$40–55**
RIDE-SHARE	10 mins $25–35	15–25 mins $25–35	10 mins $20–25	20–30 mins $25–35

AIRPORT PROS & CONS

Fort Lauderdale–Hollywood (FLL)
Pro: Cheapest flights in Florida. **Con:** Poorly laid out, frustrating to navigate by car, frequent construction.

Orlando (MCO)
Pro: Efficient, with plenty of carrier options. **Con:** Often extremely busy and time-consuming.

Tampa (TPA)
Pro: Economical flights, easy to navigate, fewer crowds. **Con:** Some travelers have complained of inefficient service.

Miami (MIA)
Pro: Centrally located, so an easy commute. **Con:** Congested, with long lines and frequent delays. Some reports of poor service and baggage control.

Money

CURRENCY: **US DOLLAR ($)**

Credit Cards

Credit cards are widely accepted throughout Florida. However, if it's not a US card, check whether foreign transaction fees apply. Many creditors charge 2.5%.

Debit Cards

Most international visitors are able to use their debit cards in Florida, but be wary of extraneous fees charged by banks for out-of-country transactions.

Sales Tax

Florida's sales tax rate is currently 6% (2023). Municipalities can charge an additional sales tax of up to 1.5%. Therefore, sales taxes could reach as high as 7.5% on purchases. Unlike the VAT in other countries, the US government doesn't refund sales tax to international visitors.

Tipping

Be wary: many restaurants and bars in Florida automatically add 18% gratuity to each bill – often without drawing the customer's attention to it. You can, of course, request to have the tip adjusted, but many unaccustomed visitors make the unfortunate mistake of 'double tipping.'

HOW MUCH FOR A...

Parking space at the beach
$3–6/hr

State park entrance fee
$6

Valet parking tip
$3–5 upon pickup

Beach chair rental
$25–45/day

HOW TO... Live Like a Local & Save

It's no secret: wherever tourists go, prices rise. Sometimes to the stratosphere. Better prices, reserved for locals, are often just a few streets away. So, here's a pro tip: using this guide, target off-the-beaten-path restaurants, bars and cafes popular with residents. Get chatting, and pick their brains. Locals know how to avoid tourist traps and they're often glad to share these golden nuggets with budget-minded travelers.

SENIOR DISCOUNTS

Many Florida retailers offer perks (often a 5–25% discount) to those who've earned the privilege – though minimum qualifying ages range from 50 to 65. Check with retailers if you qualify.

SAVING MONEY ON CURRENCY EXCHANGE

You'll often enjoy a better rate of exchange through your credit-card company than what's offered by local banks and currency-exchange kiosks (especially at airports and hotels). Bank debits made through local ATMs can offer similarly better rates, but avoid making multiple withdrawals to avoid repetitive transaction fees. If you're transferring large sums of money (for extended travel, real estate or other significant purchases), consider using the services of a professional currency exchange firm, such as Canada's Firma Foreign Exchange. When exchanging large amounts, the savings can be significant.

Getting Around

Convenient transport options exist throughout the state, including modern road infrastructure, passenger train systems and public and private airport services.

TRAVEL COSTS

Rental
From $38/day

Gasoline
Approx. $3.40/gallon

EV charging
Often free; if not approx. 43 cents/kWh

Bicycle rentals
From $35/day

Major Highways

Florida's infrastructure includes four primary interstate highways. The I-75 runs north from Miami along Florida's western coast to Michigan. The I-95 follows the eastern seaboard from Miami to Georgia. I-4 extends from Tampa on the west to Daytona on the east, while the I-10 travels west from Jacksonville to Alabama.

Renting a Car

Car-rental agencies are abundant, and many offer an option to return vehicles to a different location. Cars generally include unlimited mileage, with full insurance options available if your own policy doesn't extend to rentals. Renters must be 21 or older (those 25 and under may be subject to a surcharge).

TIP

Many credit cards with 'travel rewards' include insurance for rental cars. Check with your issuer to confirm coverage and limitations.

HIGHWAY TOLLS

Toll highways in Florida are quickly converting to an electronic, cashless system. Thanks to license-plate-recognition software, you'll receive a bill in the mail. Frequent users can save about 25% with a SunPass transponder (Florida's prepaid toll program), sold at many retail outlets (installation and activation required). Most car-rental agencies push SunPass transponders for an additional fee, so do some advance route planning to judge if you'll really need one.

DRIVING ESSENTIALS

It's **illegal to use your phone** (except for GPS directions) while your vehicle's in motion.

55

Speed limit is 55mph on highways, 30mph in municipal areas, if not posted. Some interstates allow up to 70mph.

.08

Blood alcohol limit is 0.08%.

Buses

Although automobiles are the most recommended way to get around Florida, Greyhound Lines provides intercity coaches between 40 Florida cities. They might move at the pace of a sea turtle, but they're also ecofriendlier and more economical. Check greyhound.com for route details. Megabus (megabus.com) also serves Miami, Orlando and Jacksonville.

Trains

Amtrak provides only limited service within Florida, but other rail services pick up the slack. Tri-Rail (Tri-Rail.com) connects cities in the south, while SunRail (SunRail.com) serves 16 stops in central Florida. Brightline (gobrightline.com) offers economical high-speed service connecting Miami and West Palm Beach (extending to Orlando in 2023).

Planes

Florida has an abundance of international and regional airports, so there's always a fast way to get around. Southwest Airlines (southwest.com) is a popular go-to if you need to quickly hop from one city to another. Otherwise, save the airport hassle and drive or use commuter rail service instead.

ROAD DISTANCE CHART (MILES)

FLORIDA

	Tampa	Fort Lauderdale	Fort Myers	Jacksonville	Key West	Miami	Orlando	Pensacola	St Augustine
Fort Lauderdale	265								
Fort Myers	125	140							
Jacksonville	200	325	315						
Key West	415	190	300	505					
Miami	280	30	155	345	160				
Orlando	85	215	155	140	390	235			
Pensacola	465	650	590	360	830	675	450		
St Augustine	190	290	260	40	465	310	105	395	
Tallahassee	275	455	390	165	640	480	260	195	205

Accommodations

Houseboats

Ever wanted to live on a houseboat? Well, Florida's a great place for a test-run. Several companies statewide provide short-term houseboat rentals. Boats range in size from tiny tugboats to uber-luxurious yachts. Prices vary accordingly. For smaller, four-passenger houseboats, rates start around $130 per night (for two or more nights). Special arrangements are often offered for people with disabilities. Renters must be aged over 25, and complete a free boater's safety course.

Glamping

This high-end form of camping is booming in Florida. Furnished tent structures feature queen beds, linens, electricity and coffeemakers. Some even have air-conditioning. Glamping is currently available at six state parks (some near Orlando and Tampa) and numerous private campgrounds across Florida. Nineteen state parks also offer furnished cabins with similar amenities. These options require your own wheels, as most parks and campgrounds are in remote areas.

Vacation Rental Sites

These are ideal if you're looking to rent entire condos, houses, campers or houseboats. Listings are searchable by budget, property type and/or location. Many snowbirds rent out well-kept Florida homes to cover expenses while they're away. Renters can save a bundle by cooking at home and packing lunches. Check Airbnb.com, VRBO.com and VacationRentals.com for great long- and short-term deals.

HOW MUCH FOR A NIGHT IN...

A hotel room
$80

A glamping tent
$130–200

A furnished cabin
$125–200

Green Lodging

Launched in 2004, the Florida Green Lodging Program, administered through the Florida Department of Environment Protection (DEP), recognizes and promotes properties that have voluntarily pledged their ongoing commitment to conserve and protect the state's valuable natural resources. These properties aim to reduce waste, conserve water, and improve energy efficiency and the quality of indoor air. Search property listings atfloridadep.gov/osi/green-lodging.

Hotels & Motels

These run the gamut from cheaper, dingy motels to five-star hedonistic resorts. But beware, if a hotel's amenities and entertainment qualify as a resort, you'll accrue additional 'resort fees' (often arriving as a surprise at checkout). If flying by the seat of your pants gives you a rush, try scoring some great last-minute deals on hotwire.com or HotelTonight.com.

COST VS CONVENIENCE

Common with most coastal communities, the further you travel from the beach in Florida, the cheaper the accommodations becomes. The allure of beachfront abodes is undeniable. Shower off the sand steps from the beach, then drift off to the rhythm of crashing waves. And sacrificing the convenience of closer proximity to the beach, along with the added costs for fuel and beachfront parking (unless you enjoy hauling your bulky gear back and forth), might make you regret those penny-pinching efforts. Saving a few coins often costs more in the long run.

Health & Safe Travel

INSURANCE

Florida doesn't require foreign travelers to carry insurance, but with the US high cost of health care, and the nominal costs for such coverage, it's a no-brainer. It's best to pay a bit extra to secure coverage that offers protection against lost luggage and costs associated with trip cancellation or interruption.

Hurricanes

It's no secret that Florida and hurricanes go together like chili and cornbread. Hurricanes visit frequently, with most occurring between the months of June and October (peaking in August and September). Heavy rain, powerful winds and ocean surges can cause property damage, personal injury and even death, so it's imperative to follow official directives during any storm emergency.

Jellyfish & Sea Urchins

These common saltwater creatures are often seen close to shore or washed up along Florida's beaches (particularly after heavy storms). Encounters can be painful, but rarely fatal. If you're stung by a jellyfish or step on an urchin, remove any embedded tentacles or needles with tweezers and immerse the skin in hot water. Seek medical attention.

TAP WATER

Although far from pure, Florida's tap water is considered safe to drink. All federal guidelines on water quality are strictly observed.

FLORIDA BEACH WARNING SIGNS

Green flag
Low hazard. Calm conditions, exercise caution

Yellow flag
Medium hazard. Moderate surf and/or currents

Red flag
High hazard. High surf and/or strong currents

Red flag + Red no swimming flag
Water CLOSED to the public

Purple flag
Stinging marine life present

Cannabis Laws

Although widely used, cannabis products are illegal in Florida when used as a recreational drug. Only those who hold a valid Medical Marijuana Use Authorization may legally purchase and use these products. Possession of up to 20 grams is a misdemeanor offense, carrying a penalty of up to one year imprisonment and a maximum fine of $1000.

PERSONAL SAFETY PRECAUTIONS

In Florida, neighborhoods and situations can change drastically within a short walk, so always use street sense and better judgment to stay safe. Distressed neighborhoods are commonly found near bus depots and train stations. Aggressive driving is a problem in larger cities – ignoring traffic signs and signals, speeding and rushing turns. Pedestrians should always remain vigilant.

Food, Drink & Nightlife

HOW MUCH FOR A...

Regular coffee
$2.50–3.50

Specialty coffee
$5–6

Large meat pizza
$10–15

Scoop of ice cream
$4–5

Bottle of beer
$7–8

Glass of wine
$10–12

Types of Eating Establishments

Florida's culinary scene is a mishmash of all manner of restaurants and watering holes. From Michelin-starred fine dining to food trucks, mom-and-pop diners, pie and seafood stands, and the smorgasbord offerings of multi-kiosk food halls, there's something to suit everyone's palate. Drinking establishments are just as varied, ranging from sports pubs, piano bars, and jazz and blues clubs to the throbbing lights of vibrant nightclubs catering to every demographic, musical taste and fetish imaginable. If you enjoy eating and drinking, you've certainly come to the right place.

Happy Hours in Florida

Times for 'happy hours' range widely between establishments. Although normally restricted to weekdays, most commonly you'll find they run between 4pm and 7pm (but sometimes they'll begin as early as noon). In addition to cheaper drinks, yummy appetizers are often deeply discounted as well. Take advantage of these promotions to save up to 50% off your bar tab at participating bars and restaurants.

Florida's Drinking Laws

Although you can bartend in Florida at the age of 18, you can't legally consume alcohol until you're 21 (the national standard). Consuming alcohol in public is prohibited – so no drinking on the street, in parking lots or on the beach. Many stores – including supermarkets and gas stations – sell beer and wine, but if you want spirits, you'll need to find a dedicated liquor/package store (opening and closing times vary by municipality – in Miami-Dade they're 24/7). A few 'dry' counties remain in Florida, where alcohol sales are prohibited, with most in the Panhandle area. If you try to use fake ID here, you'll be facing five years in the slammer and a $5000 fine! And don't dare climb behind the wheel of a car or boat if your blood-alcohol reading is 0.08% or higher.

FLORIDA'S DESSERT WARS

Key lime became the state's official pie in 2006. But, in 2022, the famous dessert was forced to share the limelight with strawberry shortcake, when the state legislature crowned it Florida's official dessert. The intention was to boost Florida's billion-dollar strawberry industry, responsible for 75% of the country's winter crop. The key lime lobby was flabbergasted, circulating petitions that call for the mayors of Plant City and Key West to duel it out, using their respective desserts as weapons. (Florida does have a peculiar way of dealing with things, after all.)

Five of Florida's Most Popular Cocktails

- Mojito
- Miami vice
- Piña colada
- Key lime daiquiri
- Rum runner margarita

Family Travel

There's possibly no place in the world as inviting to families as Florida. Catering to childhood fantasies in all of us, it attracts the young, and the young-at-heart, like Pooh Bears to honey. From its great climate to its 825 miles of sandy beaches, exciting theme parks, endless water sports and outdoor safari parks, Florida's got it covered.

Fun Beyond the Theme Parks

Theme parks might be top of your list, but there's plenty more to keep families entertained. Search for washed-up treasure or prehistoric shark teeth along Florida's shell-carpeted beaches. Go snorkeling and explore the undersea world. Build giant sandcastles. Marvel at sea turtles nesting on the beach, or zip around on an airboat searching for alligators in the Everglades. The opportunities here are endless.

Child Discounts

At many Orlando theme parks, children under the age of three are free. Kids aged three to nine pay reduced rates, while those 10 and older pay as an adult. Ages are accepted on an honor system and (at the time of writing) no ID is required to prove a child's vintage. Outside Orlando, children usually qualify for discounted rates, but age restrictions will vary.

Family-Friendly Facilities

Stroller rentals are available at most major attractions. Many also offer locker facilities (for storing heavy or bulky baby supplies until needed), and diaper-changing stations in men's, women's and family restrooms. Some larger parks also offer feeding areas.

Car Seat Laws

Under Florida law, children zero to three years require federally approved car seats (rear-facing until one year or 20lb). Children four to five years need booster seats (until 4ft 9in, or 80lb). Children under 13 must travel in the back seat.

KID-FRIENDLY PICKS

Orlando Theme Parks (p210)
Disney, Universal, LEGOLAND... all fail-safe hits with the kids.

Kennedy Space Center (p277)
Tour launch pads, ride simulators, maybe meet a real astronaut.

Everglades Airboat Tours (p267)
Spot alligators and turtles in the wetlands.

Mel Fisher's Treasure Museum (p202)
See salvaged treasures, then rent a metal detector and scavenge the beach.

Daytona International Speedway (p330)
Tour the grounds and museum, or catch an live Nascar race for fast-paced excitement.

MONEY-SAVING TIPS FOR A FAMILY VACATION

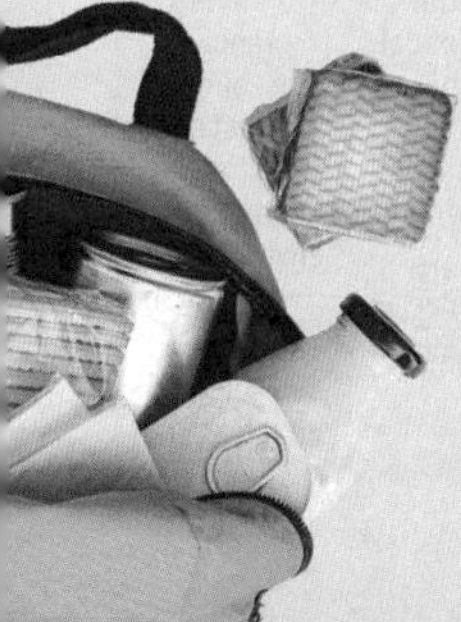

Road tripping saves the costs of an airfare, airport parking and a destination car rental. Avoid peak travel times as best you can (prices skyrocket during spring break, summer and holidays – with longer queues). Shop for discounted attraction tickets online, and pack your own snacks and cold drinks (it's acceptable to bring refreshments into big attractions and theme parks, with the exception of glass or food requiring heating). For lodgings, grab a rental with a kitchen, or a hotel that offers free breakfast and theme-park shuttle rides. Finally, if traveling with kids, be sure to discuss a daily budget – ahead of time.

OPPOSITE: NADIR KEKLIK/SHUTTERSTOCK ©, LEFT: PIXEL-SHOT/SHUTTERSTOCK ©

Responsible Travel

Climate Change & Travel

It's impossible to ignore the impact we have when traveling, and the importance of making changes where we can. Lonely Planet urges all travelers to engage with their travel carbon footprint. There are many carbon calculators online that allow travelers to estimate the carbon emissions generated by their journey; try resurgence.org/resources/carbon-calculator.html. Many airlines and booking sites offer travelers the option of offsetting the impact of greenhouse gas emissions by contributing to climate-friendly initiatives around the world. We continue to offset the carbon footprint of all Lonely Planet staff travel, while recognizing this is a mitigation more than a solution.

Volunteer

If you have some time to invest, consider volunteering with one of many organizations in Florida dedicated to protecting its natural environment and resources. Opportunities include:

The Nature Conservancy
This organization aims to protect Florida's lands and water and promote food and water sustainability. Visit nature.org for more details.

Keep Florida Beautiful
Volunteer to transform communities and help improve the environment through various pollution control measures. Visit keepfloridabeautiful.org.

Various wildlife sanctuaries
Many such organizations exist throughout the state, such as **Busch Wildlife Sanctuary** in Jupiter (p196), whose mission is to rescue and rehabilitate injured and sick animals, quite often including sea turtles. Once rehabilitated, most of the animals are released back to the wild.

Spend Time in Nature

Visit botanical gardens and arboretums to learn more about sustainable resources and ecofriendly gardening. Visit nature centers and national wildlife refuges to learn more about conservation efforts and how you can help. Donations are always appreciated.

Respecting the Turtles

Sea turtles are fun to watch as they nest on the beach from May to October. But getting too close, shining lights or using flash photography can scare or disorient the turtles – and it's illegal.

Leave a Positive Footprint

Use ecofriendly transportation whenever possible. Consider biking (rentals are abundant) or walking whenever traveling short distances. Most areas in Florida are very bike friendly. Canoes and kayaks are also widely available for rent and have little effect upon the environment.

Clean Beaches

Baskets are often found at beach access points for visitors to thoughtfully dispose of trash.

Camp at one of Florida's many state or national parks, state forests or one of the myriads of private camping and RV parks across the state.

Support local farmers markets and buy locally produced organic food products. Find one at farmersmarket.net.

RESOURCES

Wearefcc.org
The Florida Conservation Coalition.

Eco-usa.net/orgs/fl.shtml
Alphabetical list of Florida's environmental organizations.

Centralfloridasierra.org
Florida's branch of the country's oldest and largest grassroots environmental organization.

LGBTIQ+ Travelers

Despite the state government's well-publicized 'Don't Say Gay' agenda, Florida remains one of the world's most popular LGBTIQ+ destinations. Many inclusive municipalities, including Fort Lauderdale, Palm Beach, Orlando, Miami and Key West, continue to roll out the rainbow carpet, offering millions of those within the LGBTIQ+ community a warm and welcome embrace each and every year.

Fabulous Rainbow Festivals

Pridefest hits Key West in June: a week of sunset cruises and a lively street festival. Five-day **Fantasy Fest** in October mixes colorful costumes with a massive parade. The country's oldest and biggest HIV/AIDS fundraiser, **White Party Week**, pervades Miami in November. **Pride Fort Lauderdale** is a week-long February event with live music and partying. For **Gay Days** (Orlando in June), don a red shirt and join the throngs around theme parks. Sarasota holds its annual **Pride Fest** in October. Don't miss **Sunshine Stampede Gay Rodeo** in Davie each April.

ENJOY A LGBTIQ+ TOUR

Join Miami's 90-minute **Gay & Lesbian Walking Tour** and learn of the community's many important historical contributions to the city, stopping at contemporary hot spots. Tours begin at the **Art Deco Welcome Center**, 1001 Ocean Dr, at 11am, the second Saturday of every month.

SAME-SEX MARRIAGE TOURISM IN FLORIDA

After same-sex marriage became legalized here in 2015, Florida experienced a boom in gay wedding tourism, sparking a predictable economic benefit. Couples from across the country converged to marry on Florida's beaches – even if the marriage wasn't recognized in their own home state. Check out EnGaygedWeddings.com/florida-gay-wedding.html for a comprehensive list of LGBTIQ-friendly wedding vendors.

The Best 'Gayborhoods'

Fort Lauderdale
Wilton Manors is ground zero for LGBTIQ+ bars, restaurants and nightclubs.

Key West
Head to Duval St to hit up the district's famous bars, clubs and endless stores. Check out 801 Bourbon Bar for entertaining drag shows.

Tampa
Don't miss the GaYbor District, a 12-block stretch of pride at the west end of the historic Ybor City neighborhood.

Glorious LGBTIQ+-Friendly Beaches

Fort Lauderdale
Sebastian Street Beach is always packed with fun and friendly sun-worshippers.

Miami
The 12th Street Beach is Miami's best-known, and sometimes rowdy, LGBTIQ+ beach.

Sarasota
More secluded than the two above, North Lido Beach is still considered one of the best LGBTIQ+ beaches in Florida.

RESOURCES

South Florida Gay News: sfgn.com

Visit Lauderdale LGBTQ+ info: sunny.org/lgbt

Fort Lauderdale travel, entertainment and general information: gayftlauderdale.com

Key West LGBTQ+ info: gaykeywestfl.com

Florida Gay Nightlife: hotspotsmagazine.com

Miami's Gay Scene: miamiandbeaches.com/travel-interests/lgbtq-miami/

Accessible Travel

Florida has made major gains toward accommodating visitors with accessibility issues since 2018. Visit Florida's 2021 campaign, 'Limitless Florida,' showcased their efforts to make the state the world's foremost accessible destination.

ADA-Friendly Beaches

Many of Florida's most popular beaches are wheelchair-accessible, with ramp access to boardwalks. Several offer complimentary beach wheelchairs and Mobi-mats (interlocking pads create a solid path over the sand).

Airport

Florida airports provide barrier-free paths and accessible services throughout their terminals, including guided mobility assistance at designated locations. If a wheelchair is required upon arrival, be sure to request it in advance through your airline.

Accommodations

Compliance with the Americans with Disabilities Act (ADA) may be less consistent in smaller lodgings; verify their status in advance. Most higher-end hotels and resorts offer fully ADA-accessible facilities. State parks and many campgrounds also have fully accessible services.

Visually Impaired Visitors

Braille guides and signs are becoming common at tourist attractions. State law requires all public facilities to permit trained service dogs, a requirement embraced by Florida's many pet-friendly business owners.

Mobile on the High Seas

Mobility challenges needn't restrict fun on the water. Accessible catamarans and adaptive sailing and boating experiences are widely available throughout the Sunshine State, with providers such as Shake-A-Leg in Miami making excursions easy and enjoyable.

HIGHLY ACCESSIBLE ATTRACTIONS

Disney Parks These parks rank highly for wheelchair accessibility. Enjoy rides without leaving your chair.

Kennedy Space Center Services for those with mobility, hearing and visual restrictions. Wheelchair, scooter and stroller rentals available.

ZooTampa Wheelchairs and electric scooters available for rent.

The Ringling Sarasota museum celebrating the life of circus tycoon John Ringling. It's wheelchair accessible, with audio recordings and ALDs for those with visual or hearing challenges.

RESOURCES

Visit Florida (visitflorida.com/things-to-do/accessible-travel) provides an extensive list of accessible sights and attractions in Florida, as well as website resources for wheelchair and scooter rentals, childcare services, oxygen supplies and other relevant topics.

Bright Feats (brightfeats.com) helps families and loved ones of children with special needs find resources to plan successful vacations in many areas around Florida.

SERVICES FOR HEARING IMPAIRED VISITORS

Many attractions endeavor to provide sign language service; advance bookings of up to two weeks may be required. Printed guides are frequently available for museum/gallery tours. Some locations provide Assistive Listening Systems (ALDs) that improve sound clarity to hearing aids and cochlear implants.

Nuts & Bolts

SHOPPING HOURS

Hours of service vary, depending upon the area and type of store. Most retailers close at 9pm on weekdays and 5pm or 6pm on weekends, although some big box stores (ie Walmart) stay open later, as do some outlet malls.

Smoking

Florida law prohibits smoking in most public and private businesses – including restaurants (and their patios). Counties and municipalities have authority to ban smoking at their beaches and parks, so check local ordinances.

GOOD TO KNOW

Time Zone
EST

Country Code
+1

Emergency Number
911

Population
21.78 million

PUBLIC HOLIDAYS

Eight public holidays are recognized throughout the year in Florida. On these dates, government offices and most businesses (other than essential services) will remain closed.

New Year's Day
January 1

Martin Luther King Jr Birthday
Third Monday of January

Memorial Day
Final Monday of May

Independence Day
July 4

Labor Day
First Monday of September

Veterans Day
November 11

Thanksgiving
Fourth Thursday of November

Christmas
December 25 (when Christmas falls on a Sunday, the next day is also a recognized holiday)

Weights & Measures

US customary units of measurement: inches, feet, miles, gallons and pounds. Temperatures in degrees Fahrenheit.

Wi-Fi

Free wi-fi is widely available at restaurants, cafes, parks, bus stations, airports and train stations.

Electricity 120V/60Hz

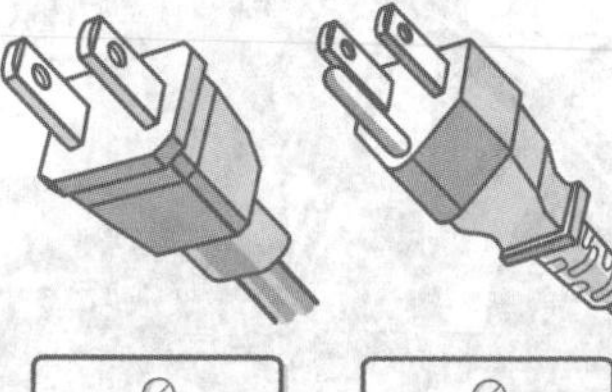

Type A
120V/60Hz

Type B
120V/60Hz

STORYBOOK

Our writers delve deep into different aspects of Floridian life

Surfer, Miami (p50)

A HISTORY OF FLORIDA IN 15 PLACES

The land of hurricanes, primeval swamps and hostile climate (at least in the days before air-conditioning) has certainly had its share of dramas over the centuries, from Spanish explorers in search of gold to industrial titans envisioning equally epic fortunes as they laid railroad tracks across the sea.

IN 1896, ARCHAEOLOGISTS on Key Marco unearthed one of the oldest preserved artifacts in North America: a small, beautifully carved figurine, half-man, half-cat, that was likely created over 1000 years ago. Though today it hangs in the Smithsonian in Washington, DC, the work alludes to the astonishing historical secrets lurking in America's southeasternmost peninsula.

Florida has always followed a different path than other parts of the US. The oldest European settlement in North America remained under Spanish possession for its first two centuries, then passed to the English, back to the Spanish, into US protection (where it became the 27th state in 1845) and into the hands of the confederates, before its readmission to the union following the end of the Civil War in 1865. Parts of Florida even saw French rule for several years during the 18th century.

Florida is the proud home of the only unconquered indigenous tribe in the US. It was also the setting for some of the 20th century's most ambitious projects, from paradigm-shifting architecture to a launchpad into outer space. In some ways, Florida is a place of ceaseless reinvention, with a steady influx of immigrants (both foreign and domestic) alongside the constant rebuilding following devastating storms. Yet, the past remains very much alive in many parts of Florida.

1. Historic Spanish Point

THE ANCIENT PEOPLE OF FLORIDA

All across Florida, pre-Columbian cultures left behind a great many middens – mounds full of mollusk shells, fish bones, pottery shards, old bits of rope, discarded jewelry and other detritus. While most was destroyed by later inhabitants, the middens on Spanish Point lay untouched for centuries and provided a wealth of information on ancient cultures to the archaeologists who excavated the site in the 19th and 20th centuries. Among other things, they learned that humans first occupied the site over 4000 years ago, making it one of the oldest settlements in Florida.

For more on Historic Spanish Point, see p367.

2. Castillo de San Marcos

FORTRESS IN AMERICA'S OLDEST CITY

St Augustine had been around for more than a century when the stolid fort of Castillo de San Marcos was completed in 1695. It's entirely fitting that the oldest city in America contains its oldest masonry fort, built as a bulwark against pirate attacks like the devastating raid by Robert Searle in 1668.

Visit on weekends to hear the cannons roar, and imagine being on the firing line during the Siege of 1702 when English troops attacked (and failed to breach) the fortress, but nevertheless burned St Augustine to the ground during their retreat.

For more on Castillo de San Marcos, see p305.

3. Dry Tortugas

REMOTE ISLAND WITH A HIDDEN PAST

A few months after explorer Ponce de León first came ashore near present-day St Augustine, he passed through a small archipelago located off Florida's southern coast. He and his crew caught over 150 sea turtles (*tortugas*), though they found no water on the islands, which later earned the region its Spanglish sobriquet. History lies both above and below the waves on this isolated outpost (which is now a national park), with shipwrecks dating back to the 17th century and a well-preserved fort (pictured) that was built in the mid-19th century.

For more on the Dry Tortugas, see p157.

CHRIS LABASCO/SHUTTERSTOCK ©

4. Ah-Tah-Thi-Ki

LAND OF THE UNCONQUERED

Located in the northern reaches of the Everglades on the Big Cypress Indian Reservation, Ah-Tah-Thi-Ki delves into the history and culture of the Seminole people. The museum showcases artifacts such as dugout canoes, clothing and crafts, while the boardwalk out back takes you past the plants and trees that have played a pivotal role in the wellbeing of the tribe. Seminoles trace their roots in the area back to the 1700s and having survived wars and betrayal by the US government, they proudly call themselves 'the unconquered people.'

For more on Ah-Tah-Thi-Ki, see p119.

5. Kingsley Plantation

GRAPPLING WITH SLAVERY

Northeast of Jacksonville, you can explore one of America's darkest periods at Florida's oldest surviving plantation. Built in the 1790s, the well-preserved central house is ringed by the remains of 23 cabins where some of the enslaved workers once resided. For over a century, hundreds lived in forced servitude on this once sprawling estate. Some of their stories have been preserved through oral histories, which you can discover on a guided visit to this site run by the National Park Service.

For more on the Kingsley Plantation, see p322.

6. Tampa Bay Hotel

LUXURY OF ANOTHER ERA

Walk the lush grounds beneath the silver minarets of the former Tampa Bay Hotel and it's easy to forget that you're standing amid one of Florida's largest cities. An eclectic blend of Moorish and Turkish architecture, the building housed one of America's finest hotels when it opened in 1891. One wing (the Henry B Plant Museum) gives insight into how high society spent their time here, relaxing in splendid quarters, gossiping in the reading room and enjoying nightly entertainment. The hotel was also the staging post for US soldiers during the Spanish-American War, with Teddy Roosevelt and other commanders making plans while seated in rocking chairs on the terrace.

For more on the Tampa Bay Hotel, see p341.

7. Historic Cocoa Village

ENDURING HISTORIC STOREFRONT

In the 1880s much of Florida was a roadless frontier and the statewide population was around 300,000. Based on a merchant boat in the village of Cocoa, Samuel Franklin Travis made deliveries by waterway, selling merchandise up and down the Indian River. As his business grew, he purchased a store in 1902 and became a mainstay of the community, selling everything from groceries to furniture. Supplies sold here helped build Cocoa Village, the Kennedy Space Center and the Banana River Naval Air Station. Still owned by the same family, the SF Travis Company store is the city's oldest brick building and one of the oldest hardware stores in Florida.

For more on historic Cocoa Village, see p283.

8. Pigeon Key

LAYING RAILROAD TRACKS ACROSS THE SEA

Back in the early 1900s, Key West was Florida's biggest city (population 20,000-plus), and yet the only way to reach the island was by boat. Eager to expand trade with Latin America, the Gilded Age industrialist Henry Flagler sought to link the city to the mainland via an ambitious Overseas Railroad. The project was a mammoth undertaking, with 4000 workers laboring over seven years (through three hurricanes) before its completion in 1912. Pigeon Key served as a base camp for the men, and some of its buildings survive. Touring the old structures gives insight into the hardships the workers faced completing what was once dubbed 'the eighth wonder of the world.'

For more on Pigeon Key, see p154.

9. Art Deco Historic District & the Colony Hotel

AN ARCHITECTURAL ICON

In 1926 Miami Beach was hit by a devastating hurricane. As rebuilding began, developers looked to bring new design forms to the city. Prolific Miami-based architect Henry Hohauser played a pivotal role in creating the art deco style that would soon become ubiquitous. He designed many eye-catching works, including the Colony Hotel, one of Miami's first art deco buildings when it opened in 1935. The bold but playful geometric design has windows shaded by horizontal 'eyebrow' overhangs, rounded corners and a neon sign that lent a touch of electric allure by night. Since then it has become an iconic symbol of South Beach architecture and one of its most photographed buildings.

For more on the Art Deco Historic District, see p56.

10. Ybor City Museum State Park

TOBACCO-FUELED BOOM DAYS

From the late 19th century to the 1920s, Ybor City was one of Florida's most vibrant towns thanks to its burgeoning cigar industry. Set in a former bakery from that era, a small history museum sheds light on the lives of the workers and their social clubs. After checking out the exhibits and peering inside a few restored *casitas* (small homes), visit the park across the street, which is full of free-roaming hens and roosters – they are descendants of chickens that were once raised by the families of the cigar makers.

For more on Ybor City Museum State Park, see p342.

11. Vizcaya

OLD-WORLD EUROPE IN MIAMI

Named after the Basque-speaking province in northern Spain, Vizcaya is a grand slice of Europe plunked down on the edge of Coconut Grove in Miami. In 1910 businessman James Deering purchased the land upon which he would build his estate, a Mediterranean Revival work complete with Renaissance-style gardens full of sculptures. After the purchase, Deering embarked on a series of trips around Europe, accruing the artwork, tapestries and furnishings that would fill his quasi palace. Today the house museum contains many of the original antiques and furniture, and provides a remarkable window into Deering's life.

For more on Vizcaya, see p93.

12. Salvador Dalí Museum

A TRANSFORMATIVE COLLECTION

As for the Spanish city of Bilbao (home to a Frank Gehry–designed Guggenheim), a museum changed everything in

St Petersburg. Designed by local architect Yann Weymouth, the Salvador Dalí Museum (pictured) opened in its fantastical new space in 2011 and helped transform the city into an arts mecca. The collection, the largest of its kind outside of Spain, ended up here thanks to city officials who agreed to provide a waterfront gallery space to the Morses, avid Dalí collectors from Cleveland. The original 1982 building proved insufficient, so in 2008 new ground was broken on Weymouth's avant-garde design, and its construction heralded a new era for St Petersburg.

For more on the Salvador Dalí Museum, see p348.

13. Wells' Built Museum

ORLANDO'S AFRICAN AMERICAN HISTORY

When the African American physician Dr William Monroe Wells moved to Orlando in 1917, there were no hotels or entertainment venues catering to black visitors. So in 1926 he opened the Wells' Built Hotel and a casino and performing-arts venue next door. Some of the top singers of the day stayed here and played next door, including Ella Fitzgerald, Ray Charles and BB King. Other luminaries like Thurgood Marshall and Jackie Robinson also lodged here. Although the casino has been torn down, you can still explore the original building that helped shape Orlando's cultural life and provided a vital lifeline for African American travelers during the dangerous days of segregation.

For more on Wells' Built Museum, see p260.

14. Walt Disney World® & Prince Charming Regal Carrousel

RIDE A PIECE OF DISNEY HISTORY

When Florida's most famous theme park opened in 1971, one of its attractions had already been around for nearly half a century. Walt Disney World®'s oldest ride, the Prince Charming Regal Carrousel, features 90 elaborate wooden horses, which were carved by the Philadelphia Toboggan Company back in 1917. It once delighted young visitors in Detroit's Belle Isle Park before its arrival in warmer climes. Take a spin on the carousel while admiring the views of nearby Cinderella Castle, and you can't help but feel the same sense of joy that has brought a smile to spinning riders for over 100 years.

For more on rides in Walt Disney World®, see p210.

15. Kennedy Space Center

ROCKETING INTO THE FUTURE

With the race to the future underway after the 1958 creation of NASA, aerospace engineers looked for the ideal location to build a rocket launchpad. They found the perfect place in Merritt Island, on Florida's east coast, whose closer proximity to the equator than many other US sites allows rockets to take optimum advantage of the earth's rotational speed. In the early 1960s crews set to work building facilities for an ambitious goal: to one day launch humans into outer space. Dozens of missions have since fired into the sky from Kennedy Space Center, some of which have changed our very idea of what lies beyond our tiny planet.

For more on the Kennedy Space Center, see p277.

MEET THE FLORIDIANS

Floridians are a mash-up of people from all backgrounds and cultures, drawn here for as many reasons as there are sunny days in the year. TERRY WARD introduces her people.

CONDUCT A RANDOM survey about what comes to mind when people imagine a Floridian, and there's a good chance it'll default to a Florida Man internet meme – a joke even Floridians love to laugh at. If the Sunshine State is the punchline in many a geographical joke in the US, then Florida Man (p439) is usually the perpetrator – a general term conveying the real-life, headline-grabbing and often absolutely crazy things people do on our sun-drunk stage.

But the reality of who most Floridians actually are for those of us living here is, thankfully, far more nuanced. Floridians are Brits who've married Floridians and swapped gray skies for something entirely sunnier. They're Floridians, born here, who left to make it big in cities up north and out west and swore they'd never come back – then missed never having to force boots over their toddler's feet in winter snow.

They're retired Haitian-Americans who flew south after decades in New Jersey to warm up and chill out, and military veterans from Michigan who fell in love while stationed abroad and followed their heart's trail south.

They're Cubans who arrived on rafts decades ago or at the US border just last year after a long and treacherous journey north (and nothing will make you more grateful for this state than chatting with them and hearing why).

They're scuba divers and marine biologists, rocket scientists and treasure wreck divers, airplane pilots and pilot boat captains who all found this state the perfect place to follow their dreams and make a living doing what they love.

They're Afghanis who fled from Kabul when it fell to the Taliban, and Colombian musicians who wouldn't miss a Sunday playing guitar at their church.

They're born-and-raised-under-the-Florida-sun types who know all the state's faults but still wouldn't live anyplace else for that promise that's never undelivered of a perfectly mild winter with balmy temperatures and nonstop sunshine the rest of the country craves, and an admittedly hot and humid summer worth weathering it for.

They're the military heroes who traveled the world but decided to settle near that base at the beach that they always loved best.

They're New Yorkers who found a real-estate deal they couldn't resist someplace under the sun, Canadians who just want to warm the heck up, and South Americans who made a permanent move to where they can go outlet shopping every day.

They're Moroccans and Mexicans who worked at EPCOT when they were younger, and fourth-generation Florida Keys fishing guides who still know the secret spots to hook a tarpon.

They're also just people who never want to shovel snow another day of their lives. They're all of the above and so much more too.

A TRUE MELTING POT

Variety is the spice of life in Florida, home to more than 22 million people. Over 25% of the population is Latino, with more than 20% of Floridians born in a foreign country.

FLORIDA, FOUND

I came to Florida as a 20-year-old college student who couldn't escape my snowy Pennsylvania university quickly enough. I got a brand-new lease on life that first time I road-tripped with new friends to the Florida Keys to snorkel in waters as crystalline as in the Caribbean and teeming with fish in every color of the rainbow. I couldn't believe such a tropical place existed in my own country, and that you could just hop in a car and drive there.

When I look at the friends I've made over 20 years of calling the Sunshine State home, I feel it's a fair and diverse representation of who you might meet on vacation too – whether in line for a Cuban sandwich in Miami, while scoping a rocket launch on the Space Coast, or at any beautiful beach and cute town in between. To enjoy Florida to the max, it's all about diving in headfirst and enjoying the ride.

The late James Gibson, one of the original Florida Highwaymen

DON BARTLETTI/LOS ANGELES TIMES/GETTY IMAGES ©

THE INSPIRING STORY OF THE FLORIDA HIGHWAYMEN

Dreams of struggling citrus-and-cotton-field workers gave rise to an impassioned art movement in 1950s Florida. By David Gibb.

DURING THE 1950S, Florida boomed in America's postwar economy. Its population surged as people flocked to the southern state, lured by its rising affluence and sunny climate. Tourism rocketed to all-time highs, with hundreds of thousands making yearly pilgrimages to brand-new theme parks like Cypress Gardens and Marineland. But despite Florida's geographic charms and financial prowess, socially, at least, it was a tumultuous mess.

Racial Tension

Racial segregation remained deeply entrenched around Fort Pierce. Everything from buses to beaches had separate areas for 'whites' and 'coloreds.' Civil rights movements and protests were gaining traction, but despite being considered at the forefront of the movement, Florida continued to drag its feet. African Americans endured powerful discrimination, including pressures over which types of jobs to hold.

African Americans were expected to toil laboriously in citrus groves and factories, never as professionals, business people… or artists. But a small group of loosely knit African Americans from Fort Pierce dared challenge the status quo, rebelling against the senseless stereotypes. Trading machetes for palettes, they chose to express themselves through art. Eventually, there would be 26 of them, from disparate backgrounds, their only common threads being the color of their skin and their shared passion for painting.

Roadside Art Entrepreneurs

Harold Newton, a 20-year-old self-taught artist, born in Florida but raised in Georgia, found himself at the cusp of this artistic movement. After years laboring in tobacco and cotton fields and hawking handcrafted black velvet religious paintings for extra cash, Newton returned to his birthplace. There, after being captivated by the paintings of preeminent landscape artist, AE 'Beanie' Backus, he became his protégé. Backus persuaded Newton to switch from religious paintings to landscapes, a change he readily embraced. Newton worked using only a palette knife to spread the colorful paints, a common technique at the time.

Since art shows refused to display works by African Americans, he'd hit US 1 (Florida's

main thoroughfare at the time), selling paintings for $25 from his trunk – a mode later adopted by all Highwaymen.

Living a stone's throw away from Newton, RA 'Roy' McLendon became inspired watching him paint outside his house, and quickly jumped on the bandwagon. Embracing the techniques of capturing sunset-emblazoned skies, moonlit beaches and breezy palms on cheap Upson board, and painting discarded crown molding to design frames, he too became an overnight sensation.

McLendon's landscapes reflect his great skill at capturing subtle changes in light reflecting off various surfaces. But over the years, his versatile works extended beyond landscapes, embracing still life, portraits and wildlife – the broadest range of all Highwaymen.

A humble man, Roy never expected his paintings to find their way into a gallery or museum. In recent years, however, they've been exhibited at the AE Backus Museum in Fort Pierce, Fort Lauderdale Museum of Art (now the NSU Art Museum Fort Lauderdale), Orlando Museum of Art, Vero Beach Museum of Art and the Tampa Museum of Art, among others. His sons Ray and Roy Jr are also accomplished painters, as are his grandchildren, Mish and Cee, whose work appears stunningly similar to his.

At the ripe age of 90, the eldest of seven surviving Highwaymen, Roy continues to paint masterpieces at his cozy alleyway studio in Vero Beach, Florida.

Doretha's Story

It was 1959 when 16-year-old Doretha Smith stepped off a Greyhound bus into the blazing sun of Fort Pierce, Florida. A few months after arriving, she was approached by a curious young man at a drive-in. He made a peculiar first impression, she recalls.

'Do negroes and whites go to different schools in West Virginia?' he asked. (They didn't.) But that one simple question, perhaps the most unique pick-up line ever used, launched an enduring romance between Doretha and Alfred Hair, a future Highwayman.

Doretha got a job at the bus station, just a few blocks from Beanie Backus' art studio. Alfred Hair was taking vocational art classes there, and she'd sneak away at break times to visit.

Alfred blazoned a path of his own, making an art form of speeding up the process of painting, producing more in less time. His assembly-line style of 'fast painting' later became a Highwayman benchmark.

Alfred and Doretha soon married and started a family. Later, after opening a home-based studio, Alfred encouraged Doretha's own dreams by teaching her to paint. After years of working as an elementary schoolteacher, she resigned in 1969 to follow her passions and paint full-time in her husband's studio.

But it wasn't long until tragedy struck. Alfred was killed in 1970 at the age of 29 outside a local bar. Widowed at just 27, Doretha returned to teaching, and eventually reinvented herself again, this time in New Jersey. She returned to Fort Pierce in 2010, after hearing that the home she shared with Alfred was virtually condemned and heading for tax sale. She rescued it and with strong support from the City of Fort Pierce, she's also planning to open a museum in the summer of 2023 to commemorate the Highwaymen. The two-story museum will ensure that the Highwaymen's legacy, both their artistic style and their tenacious fight for equal rights, will endure for future generations.

Today's Highwaymen

The term 'Florida Highwaymen' wasn't coined until 1994, when art historian Jim Fitch suggested the name based upon the artists' early marketing methods. Today, only seven of the original 26 members remain – most of whom are still actively plying their trade. They range in age from their seventies to nineties, their nimble fingers and ample imaginations refusing to retire. Al Black and Curtis Arnett often hold painting classes at Paint the Town Citrus in Tampa. Al also donates a lot of his artwork to raise money for children with autism. Roy McLendon continues to paint at his Vero Beach studio. Their art has become world renowned and universally acclaimed, with collectors as diverse as Steven Spielberg, Michelle Obama and Jeb Bush. Paintings that once sold from trunks for $25 now fetch upwards of several thousand dollars at art shows, and they're showcased at the White House and Smithsonian Institution. In 2004, the group was inducted into the Florida Artists Hall of Fame.

FLORIDIAN LANDSCAPES

Crystal-clear springs, wilderness wetlands and ancient reefs are all quintessential elements of the subtropical peninsula.

ONE OF THE USA's most easily identified states on a map, Florida stretches off from the mainland's southeastern edge like an extended paw plunging into the sea. With its highest point just south of the Alabama border at Britton Hill (345ft), Florida is also the flattest state in the nation, with elevation that rarely exceeds 25ft above sea level.

Yet, despite its pancake-like topography, Florida's ecology is remarkably diverse, home to dozens of different ecoregions: from mixed hardwood and pine forests in the Panhandle's Western Highlands to coastal ridges and dry prairie marshes near Miami. In between stretch areas of Miocene-age limestone deposits, vast cypress swamps and ancient dunes – not to mention over 7000 lakes.

Water, Water Everywhere

It's fitting that the apocryphal story of Ponce de León searching for the Fountain of Youth was set in Florida, home to one of the plain's largest concentrations of freshwater springs. With over 700 across the state, they range in size from trickles pushing out a pint per minute to behemoth flows forming the headwaters of fast-flowing rivers, with a daily discharge of over 500 million gallons. In

Clockwise from top left: Everglades National Park (p112); Captiva Island and Sanibel Island (p371); mangrove swamp, Florida Keys (p134); Grayton Beach (p396)

all, some 8 billion gallons flow from Florida's springs every day. Some support entire ecosystems of plants and wildlife, including wintering manatees drawn to the warmer water in places like Three Sisters Springs.

Lake Okeechobee is sometimes referred to as Florida's inland sea. With an average depth of 9ft, it's so shallow at points you could almost wade across...though that's probably a bad idea, given the 30,000 alligators that live in its waters. The lake is vital to the ecology of southern Florida. Until the 1900s, waters from the Kissimmee River flowed freely into Lake Okeechobee, and south into the lands comprising America's greatest subtropical wilderness area.

Today known as the Everglades, this shallow sheet of water once covered nearly 11,000 sq miles, creating a patchwork of sawgrass marshes, freshwater sloughs, cypress domes and forested uplands. Humans have transformed the landscape since then, draining the swamps for farmland and urban development and building canals and levees to manage the flow of water. Only about 50% of the original wetlands now remain, though a multi-decade, $10 billion restoration project has been underway since 2000.

Multifaceted Mangroves

Historically, water from Lake Okeechobee took about 16 months to journey through the Everglades and into Florida Bay. Where fresh- and saltwater mingle, mangrove forests flourish. Three different species are found across Florida. The more widespread red mangroves have stilt-like prop roots, while black mangroves tend to grow at slightly higher elevations and are identifiable by numerous finger-like projections (pneumatophores) that extend from the soil near the tree's trunk. White mangroves have no visible root structure and tend to grow further inland, though in the Everglades you can sometimes find all three species in close proximity. The national park protects the largest contiguous stand of protected mangrove forest in the western hemisphere.

Once thoughtlessly destroyed to make way for human development, mangroves are vital to protecting coastlines from storms by reducing wind and wave action, plus prevent erosion by helping bind and build soils. They also form a key habitat for fish, crabs and bivalves, as well as aquatic birds who nest in the branches and feed off organisms nourished by the trees. Without mangroves, the productive coastal ecosystem collapses.

History Written in Stone (and Sand)

Anchoring the eastern edge of Florida Bay is a series of islands made up of exposed ancient coral reefs and sandbars: the Florida Keys, a crescent-shaped archipelago of over 800 islands stretching from just south of Miami through Key West and out to the uninhabited Dry Tortugas. Around 130,000 years ago, during the last interglacial period in North America, sea levels were 20ft to 30ft higher, and these exposed islands existed as coral reefs. As sea levels dropped, the exposed reefs fossilized over time, forming the rock that makes up these islands today.

Sea levels rose following the last Ice Age some 10,000 years ago, forming the Florida Reef, the USA's only living coral barrier reef. Though most visitors associate it with the Keys, the reef stretches for more than 350 miles – from Dry Tortugas to the St Lucie inlet, north of Jupiter on the Atlantic Coast – making it the world's third-largest coral barrier reef system. One of the world's biodiversity hot spots, the Florida Reef is home to more than 6000 species of marine life and is, along with seagrass beds, mangrove-fringed islands and countless shipwrecks, part of the Florida Keys National Marine Sanctuary. It faces significant threats from climate change, with mass coral-bleaching events resulting from higher temperatures and ocean acidification (caused by seawater absorbing excess carbon dioxide from the atmosphere).

Florida's beaches contain their own hidden histories, which are far older than the rocky keys of the southeast. Many beaches here consist of 99% pure quartz, resulting in a soft, flour-like texture. The sand of the sparkling white-sand beaches along the Gulf were once part of the Appalachian Mountains. Eons ago, this ancient mountain range (which towered over the Rockies) eroded, and over millions of years, crumbling stones were carried by rivers southward, grinding down into tiny grains before their arrival on the Gulf and south along the Florida coast. So strolling those squeaky, powdery beaches (like the Panhandle's Grayton Beach) is like walking on mountaintops – albeit ones that have long since succumbed to the good life by the seaside.

FANTASTICAL BEASTS

Florida's wildlife stirred early explorers' imagination. The species of its wetlands, waterways and beaches are even stranger than fiction.

CENTURIES AGO, SAILORS believed mysterious creatures lived in uncharted seas. Early explorers only fueled the fantasy, as they returned sharing tales of giants, boat-crushing serpents and sirens that would lure men to their deaths with songs. There were also alleged sightings of mermaids, including a report from Christopher Columbus, who wrote in his ship's log in 1493 of the appearance of three mermaids off the coast of the present-day Dominican Republic who were 'not half as beautiful as they are painted.'

With dark doe-like eyes, round faces and wide tails, these creatures – perhaps seen under a foggy night – were almost certainly manatees. Florida residents for over 45 million years, these massive herbivores generally stay close to the surface as they munch on seagrasses, consuming up to 100lb per day. Given their great girth (the largest can grow 13ft long and weigh over 1300lb), you might assume they'd have plenty of blubber. But in fact they have very little body fat and can't survive in prolonged water temperatures below 68°F (20°C). During the summer Florida manatees, a subspecies of West Indian manatees, range as far west as Texas and up the Atlantic Coast to Massachusetts. But in

Clockwise from top left: Manatee, alligator, baby loggerhead sea turtle, roseate spoonbill

winter, much like humans seeking to escape the frozen cities of the northeast, they migrate to the warmer climes of Florida. The manatees gather, sometimes by the hundreds, in natural springs where the temperature remains constant throughout the year.

Sadly, seagrass in some waterways in Florida is disappearing due to pollution, and manatees are literally starving to death. In 2021 a record 1100 manatees died because of starvation – an estimated 10% of the Florida population. State wildlife officials have resorted to extreme solutions to keep them alive. In an experimental program launched in 2022, the calorically deprived sea cows were fed 55 tons of lettuce. Rescue teams have also cared for dozens of abandoned calves at facilities in Florida. These stop-gap measures have helped, though conservationists have called for long-term solutions to revitalize the depleted ecosystems. Florida legislature has allowed $8 million for several seagrass restoration projects around the state, though much more is needed to stop pollution from flowing into coastal waters.

In the 16th century, sea monsters lurked off the coast of Florida – at least according to a map created by cartographer Jacques Le Moyne de Morgues, who in 1564 was part of an ill-fated French expedition to northern Florida. Though Le Moyne never drew any detailed close-ups of the toothy sea dwellers, he did go on to show encounters with other fearsome beasts, including indigenous battles with an ancient reptile that was around during the Cretaceous period – a time when velociraptors and T. rexes roamed. The Spanish called it *'el lagarto'* ('the lizard'), a description eventually bastardized into its present name: the alligator. Growing up to 15ft long and weighing as much as 1000lb, the alligator has a deep connection to Florida and has long served as a symbol of the state's untamed wilderness.

Alligators also play a pivotal role in the health of the Everglades' ecosystem. In fact, without this keystone species, nearly all aquatic life would be detrimentally impacted. Among other things, alligators create depressions (alligator holes) in the wetlands that retain water during the dry season when other water sources disappear. These small ponds support various wildlife including insects, fish, turtles and wading birds. After mating season, females build their nests above water level to reduce the chance of flooding (which would kill the eggs). The old nests are later used by turtles to incubate their eggs. They also provide elevated areas for the growth of plants less tolerant to flooding. Alligators – the females at least – are heavily invested in raising their young, a rarity among reptiles. During the incubation period, the mother stays near her clutch of around 30 eggs to keep away predators. Once they hatch, mama gator carries them in her mouth in groups of 10 or so down to the water, where she gently shakes her head, encouraging them to swim. The juveniles stick together, remaining close to their mother for a year or more, helping ensure they have the best chance of survival at their most vulnerable stage.

Nature's spectacles often happen unobserved by humans. Several billion birds fly over the US during the annual migration. Vast swarms fill the sky, sometimes stretching over 80 miles wide. These flights happen during the night, however, and at elevations upwards of 5000ft, meaning the astonishing event mostly goes unnoticed.

On the shoreline, far below, another nocturnal event unfolds. By day Florida's beaches pack with ocean goers, but after sunset, the empty sands become the backdrop to another fantastical event from the animal kingdom. Out of the foaming waves, a massive sea turtle lumbers ashore. In Florida, this is likely a loggerhead, a green sea turtle or, rarer still, a leatherback. She crosses the beach and picks out her spot. Using her hind flippers, she digs a nest in the sand about 2ft deep and lays her future progeny (in a clutch of about 100 eggs). This process, which lasts around 30 to 60 minutes, happens along both the Atlantic and Gulf Coasts, with over 130,000 sea turtles depositing their eggs on Florida's beaches each year.

After incubating for two months, hatchlings emerge and make a dash for the ocean. There, the lucky few (less than one in 1000 will make it to adulthood) will spend most or even the rest of their lives in the sea. Upon reaching sexual maturity, which may not happen until the age of 40 for a green sea turtle, the female will mate and begin the journey back to the same beach where she was born decades earlier. There she will continue the complicated and perilous cycle of one of Florida's most endangered residents.

SKYLER SARGENT/SHUTTERSTOCK ©

FIGHTING FOR RIGHTS IN THE SUNSHINE STATE

The struggle for equity has not just defined Florida's history, but continues to shape its modern political landscape.

THE AMERICAN CIVIL RIGHTS movement is often memorialized as a series of iconic moments: Dr Martin Luther King Jr's 'I Have A Dream' speech; the Freedom March from Montgomery to Selma; the integration of Little Rock's public schools. These events all took place in the American South, a geographic unit that includes Florida, but this state is often unjustly overlooked in the greater historical narrative.

But Florida has always played a part in the fight against oppression: during colonial and territorial days, enslaved black people from Georgia frequently escaped into the Florida swamps to take refuge with the indigenous Seminoles, who themselves engaged in one of the earliest successful guerrilla wars for their own homelands. Ultimately, the relatively small space Florida occupies in the popular memory of mid-20th-century civil rights history comes down to the fact that many of the more dramatic moments played out in the so-called Deep South, namely Alabama, Georgia, Louisiana and Mississippi.

South of the South

Yes, Florida *is* in the South – it's impossible to get any further south in the contiguous 48 states, but in this case it's as much a cultural as a geographic signifier. A paradox: in Florida, the further north you go, the more 'Southern' the state becomes. Conventional wisdom holds that the South of boiled peanuts and magnolias does not reside in South

Black Lives Matter protest, Tampa (p338)

Florida – widely held to be more steeped in the Caribbean than the Confederacy – but instead is found in the sawgrass of the Panhandle and the lakes and springs around Ocala and Jacksonville. Amelia Island is closer to Georgia's ritzy-yet-rural sea-island resorts than to anywhere in the Florida Keys.

And yet Florida was the third Confederate state to secede from the Union. Militias were raised from the Panhandle to Key West to defend secession and slavery, but as Florida was the least-populated rebel state, the skirmishes fought here between 1860 and 1865 (mainly around Jacksonville, Tampa and Gainesville) were relatively minor. But as the Civil War laid the seeds of the Jim Crow segregation laws that necessitated the civil rights movement, it also strengthened many white Floridians' fierce commitment to white supremacy under the guise of 'states' rights.' Florida's Confederate governor shot himself at the end of the war, after writing that Northerners had 'developed a character so odious that death would be preferable to reunion with them.'

Florida in the Civil Rights Era

As a result of this legacy, Florida became a battleground in the fight over legal segregation and racial justice. In 1904, activist and educator Mary McLeod Bethune opened the Daytona Literacy and Industrial Training School for Negro Girls in Daytona Beach, a school that has grown from one small house rented for $11 a month into Bethune-Cookman University, a major, private institution and HCBU (historically black college or university). Yet Florida remained segregated. Following WWII, more transplants moved here, but their presence did not dislodge old power structures. On December 24, 1950, educators and civil rights activists Harry T and Harriette Moore, a couple who together developed the Brevard County chapter of the National Association for the Advancement of Colored People (NAACP), were murdered by members of the Ku Klux Klan.

Five years later, the Montgomery bus boycotts threw legalized segregation under a harsh public spotlight; soon after, students at another HBCU, Florida A&M University, replicated that boycott in Tallahassee. In 1964, Florida's most famous civil rights showdown occurred in St Augustine at the segregated Monson Motor Lodge, where Dr Martin Luther King Jr led a sit-in protest. King was arrested, and appealed to his friend Rabbi Israel Dresner to organize a Jewish protest in solidarity; a week later, a group of 17 rabbis from around the US joined protesters in a march from the city's former slave market, culminating in a multiracial 'swim-in' at the Monson's pool, plus more arrests. As captured in a series of now-infamous photos, the hotel's owner poured hydrochloric acid into the pool to drive off the protestors. The next day, the Civil Rights Act was passed at the federal level, dismantling segregation. The Monson Motor Lodge was demolished in 2003 and replaced by another hotel; a plaque at the entrance commemorates the historic events.

A Modern Political Battleground

But even hard-won rights can be subsequently lost, and battles for social justice are still being fought, especially in Florida. Contemporary culture wars over abortion rights, civil rights for transgender people, safety for the LGBTIQ+ community and the Black Lives Matter movement are at the heart of many a Floridian political debate, especially as policymakers here have shifted further and further to the conservative right. Ron DeSantis, elected governor in 2019, likes to say that 'Florida is where "woke" goes to die' – and to this end has enacted legislation banning: abortion after 15 weeks; the teaching of historical racism or human sexuality in public schools; gender-affirming medical care for minors; and transgender girls from participation in school sports. When Trayvon Martin's killer was found not guilty of murder in 2013, a new generation of activists was inspired to create the Black Lives Matter movement; similarly galvanizing was the 2016 shooting at Orlando's Pulse Nightclub that killed 49 patrons, the deadliest attack against LGBTIQ+ people in US history.

Though Republican-leaning in recent years, Florida has long been considered a swing state; voters here recently approved referendums to restore voting rights to convicted felons and increase the minimum wage, and local activists continue to fight Governor DeSantis' legislative agenda. While Florida doesn't always feature in discussions of the historical civil rights movement, it sits front and center in many of the political struggles for freedom today.

THE MANY MISADVENTURES OF FLORIDA MAN

Famous for beautiful beaches, laid-back lifestyles and exotic wildlife, Florida is also renowned for another endemic resource: weird news.

ABOUT 22 MILLION people live in Florida, and a tiny percentage is...how can we say it politely? They're odd, bless their hearts. And some of these strange Floridians regularly appear in the national news for the seemingly-unique-to-Florida things they do. Call it an impulse control problem, a tendency toward recklessness or maybe one too many trips to Tipsy Town...but the phenomenon is better known simply as 'Florida Man.'

Defining 'Florida Man'

'Florida Man' (as the headlines inevitably call it) has become shorthand for a news story about a Florida resident committing sometimes illegal, often absurd and usually just plain hilarious acts. (While it began as a meme lambasting low-income white men doing dumb things and getting arrested, the term grew to include outlandish acts from Floridians of all genders, races and socioeconomic classes.) A typical example is the headline 'Drunken Florida Man on Segway Charged with DUI' (WFTV, 2019), which appeared after a 43-year-old man was spotted swerving through traffic on the two-wheeled device near a sheriff's office in Davenport.

Various sources trace the beginning of the phenomenon to the early 2000s, but the term really took off in 2013 when a *GQ Magazine* editor created a Twitter account (@_FloridaMan) to repost choice Florida Man headlines, eventually gaining over 340,000 followers. Other social media sites soon picked up the meme, leading to a bona-fide cultural trend with a never-ending supply of new headlines.

Florida Man Meets Florida Alligator

Many of the headlines read something like a fever dream and – perhaps unsurprisingly – alligators figure prominently. A select few:

Florida Man Takes 5-Foot Alligator on Beer Run, Chaos Ensues (*Thrillist,* 2018)
A man brought a 5ft alligator into a Jacksonville convenience store on a beer run, chasing other people with the creature. He then took the gator outside, where another man grabbed it by the neck and yelled, 'Florida State, baby! Florida State, baby! Florida State, baby!' (Florida State University's football team, the Seminoles, are rivals to the University of Florida's Gators.) The alligator-toting man later admitted that he'd been drinking.

Florida Man Charged with Throwing Alligator into Wendy's (*Washington Post,* 2015)
A 23-year-old man drove up to a fast-food window in Loxahatchee; after collecting his drink from an employee, he tossed in an alligator – an encounter that *Esquire* termed, 'one of the most "Florida Man" feats ever attempted at a Wendy's drive-thru.' After being arrested and charged with assault with a deadly weapon, he threw himself on the mercy of the court and received one year of probation. (This wasn't the last time Wendy's would have problems with local reptiles. In May, 2021, a massive alligator chased customers through a Wendy's parking lot in Lehigh Acres.)

Florida Man Bitten in Face by Alligator while Playing Disc Golf (*New York Post,* 2020)
A 40-year-old man was bitten on the face while trying to reclaim a Frisbee golf disc from an alligator's home pond in a park in Largo. (Two years later, an alligator would kill another man doing the same thing in the same pond.)

Non-Reptile-Related (But Still Outlandish) Headlines

Not every Florida Man headline contains alligators, but nearly all of them include some oddity.

'Bad Idea, Brad': Florida Man Tries to Steal from Walmart Filled with Deputies (*Fox News,* 2022)
The Osceola County Sheriff's Office reported arresting a man, first name Brad, who rather unwisely tried to shoplift items from a Walmart during a 'Shop with a Cop' community event. Nearly 40 deputies were on-site at the time, as well as teams from forensics and community services – and Sheriff Marcos R Lopez himself. Brad was arrested and charged with stealing items such as perfume and gloves. 'Bad idea, Brad,' the department noted in a post on its Facebook page.

Florida Man Finds WWII-era Grenade, Brings it to Taco Bell, Forcing Evacuation (*ABC7,* 2019)
A man magnet-fishing for salvage in Ocklawaha took his haul to a local Taco Bell and called the police about one particular item...which they confirmed to be a WWII-era hand grenade. The fast-food restaurant was evacuated and the bomb squad called in. No one was hurt, and employees reopened the restaurant later that day.

Allegedly Drunken Woman on Motorized Scooter Leads Officer on Chase through Florida Airport (*Fox KTVU,* 2021)
A bike-riding cop gave chase and arrested a woman who, after being barred from her flight due to appearing intoxicated, tried to make a getaway from the Orlando International Airport while sitting atop her motorized suitcase and using it as a micromobility vehicle.

Other News of Note

- In 2020, a man impersonating a police officer was arrested in Casselberry after trying to pull over a genuine (but off-duty) cop driving his own car.
- Also in 2020, an Orlando man tried to elude police officers by wriggling out of an officer's grasp – and then cartwheeling away.
- In 2018, a Florida man driving a car filled with trash bags of stolen mail crashed into a trailer of alpacas while fleeing police across the Florida–Georgia line.
- Also in 2018, two men – one of them dressed in a bull onesie – robbed a former lover's home in DeLand, then tried to burn the house down with boiling spaghetti sauce and a rag near the burner.

Yet all those headlines are not even a drop in the sea of meme-worthy Florida Man headlines constantly generated by the state's residents. There are so many that you can even input your birthday at floridamanbirthday.org to find a raft of Florida Man articles published on your natal day.

Why So Many 'Florida Men'?

People who spend any amount of time reading Florida Man headlines inevitably ask: Why are Floridians so weird? But reporters working the crime beat in other states will tell you that weird news happens everywhere – it just gets reported much more in Florida. So the real question is, why do we hear more of it from the Sunshine State?

It's thanks to the so-called Sunshine Laws, which give media outlets here unprecedented access to public records. Any Florida resident is entitled to view police files, arrest records, court reports and most documents (with a few exceptions) generated or held by publicly funded institutions, such as governments and law enforcement agencies. In short, if you request it, they have to fork it over (though authorities can redact sensitive information like social security numbers and the names of victims), which is unheard of in many other states.

In general, many Florida governmental and law enforcement agencies also operate

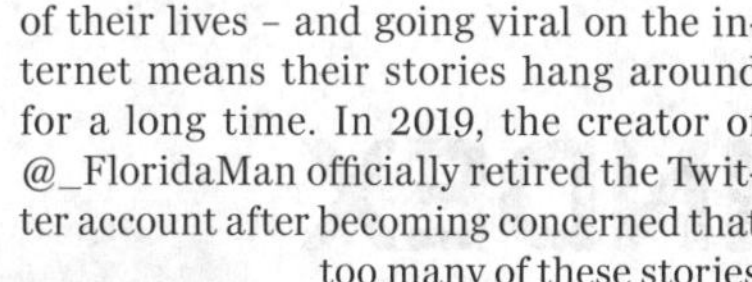

transparently, and in many cases aren't waiting for the media to twist their arms to hand over the goods: often they email reporters arrest records and daily booking logs from the local jail. Many agencies even post their most entertaining arrests on their websites and social media accounts – hence the 'Bad idea, Brad' Facebook post by the Osceola County Sheriff's Office.

So the sheer abundance of easily accessed police files means just about anyone can report the funniest, weirdest crimes in Florida, from private bloggers to online gossip sites and television outlets. And some crimes are so bizarre they make it to news outlets outside the state, or even the country.

The Other Side of Florida Man

But while Florida Man news stories can be tremendously entertaining, they can also be messy, offensive and downright cruel, and some people have raised ethical concerns around the exploitation of private citizens for entertainment purposes. Many of the 'Florida Men' have debilitating medical issues, such as mental illness or alcohol and drug addictions; some have no housing and are living on the streets, and many are victims of domestic abuse or other crimes. They've been exposed to national media attention after one of the worst days (or decisions) of their lives – and going viral on the internet means their stories hang around for a long time. In 2019, the creator of @_FloridaMan officially retired the Twitter account after becoming concerned that too many of these stories were cruelly thrusting people into the humiliating glare of national (and even international) infamy.

LANE PITTMAN PARLAYED HIS NEWFOUND FAME INTO MINOR CELEBRITY, GARNERING A FOLLOWING FOR POSTING VIDEOS OF HIMSELF SHIRTLESS AND HEAD-BANGING TO HEAVY METAL IN THE MIDDLE OF CATEGORY-5 HURRICANES.

If you are going to enjoy these stories, we suggest choosing ones in which we laugh with Florida Man, not at him – like that of 'Lane Pittman, aka Jacksonville Man Shreds National Anthem so Hard, Cops are Forced to Arrest Him' (*Orlando Weekly,* 2015). Feeling patriotic one July 4, Pittman played the 'Star-Spangled Banner' on his electric guitar outside a friend's house, drawing a crowd of around 200 people; police claimed he was obstructing traffic and arrested him on the misdemeanor charge of 'breach of peace.' He parlayed his newfound fame into minor social-media celebrity, garnering a following for posting videos of himself shirtless and head-banging to a heavy metal soundtrack in the middle of various category-5 hurricanes (pictured).

So when you peruse Florida Man stories, you'll have plenty of headlines to choose from – and perhaps unlike Florida Man, you'll be able to choose wisely.

RANDALL HILL/ALAMY STOCK PHOTO ©

INDEX

A

B

Map Pages **000**

Map Pages **000**

"There is no wilderness in the world quite like the Everglades (p107). Called the 'River of Grass', it's not just a wetland, lake, river or grassland."

REGIS ST LOUIS

"Key West (p156) is the far frontier: edgier and more eccentric than the other Keys, and also more captivating. At its heart, this 7-sq-mile island feels like a tropical oasis."

ADAM KARLIN

LEFT: FLORIDASTOCK/SHUTTERSTOCK ©, RIGHT: LUNAMARINA/SHUTTERSTOCK ©

THIS BOOK

Design Development Marc Backwell

Content Development Mark Jones, Sandie Kestell, Anne Mason, Joana Taborda

Cartography Development Katerina Pavkova

Production Development Sandie Kestell, Fergal Condon

Series Development Leadership Darren O'Connell, Piers Pickard, Chris Zeiher

Destination Editor Sandie Kestell

Production Editors Sofie Andersen, Clare Healy

Book Designer Nicolas D'Hoedt

Cartographers Mark Griffiths, Rachel Imeson, Chris Lee-Ack, Bohumil Ptáček

Assisting Editors Nigel Chin, Soo Hamilton, Ali Lemer, Anne Mulvaney, Karyn Noble, Charlotte Orr, Simon Williamson

Cover Researcher Norma Brewer

Thanks Ronan Abayawickrema, Jessica Boland, Karen Henderson, Alison Killilea, Ania Lenihan, Katerina Pavkova, Caroline Trefler

Paper in this book is certified against the Forest Stewardship Council™ standards. FSC™ promotes environmentally responsible, socially beneficial and economically viable management of the world's forests.

Published by Lonely Planet Global Limited
CRN 554153
10th edition – August 2023
ISBN 978 1 83869 778 5

10 9 8 7 6 5 4 3 2 1
Printed in Malaysia